Dictionary
of the
Holocaust

DICTIONARY OF THE HOLOCAUST

Biography, Geography, and Terminology

Eric Joseph Epstein
and
Philip Rosen

Foreword by Henry R. Huttenbach

GREENWOOD PRESS
Westport, Connecticut • London

Library of Congress Cataloging-in-Publication Data

Epstein, Eric Joseph, 1959–
　　Dictionary of the Holocaust : biography, geography, and terminology /
　　Eric Joseph Epstein and Philip Rosen; foreword by Henry R.
　　Huttenbach.
　　　　p.　cm.
　　Includes bibliographical references and index.
　　ISBN 0–313–30355–X (alk. paper)
　　1. Holocaust, Jewish (1939–1945)—Dictionaries.　I. Rosen,
　　Philip, 1928– .　II. Title.
　　D804.25.E67　1997
　　940.53'18'03—dc21　　　97–8779

British Library Cataloguing in Publication Data is available.

Library of Congress Catalog Card Number: 97–8779
ISBN: 0–313–30355–X

First published in 1997

Greenwood Press, 88 Post Road West, Westport, CT 06881
An imprint of Greenwood Publishing Group, Inc.

Printed in the United States of America

The paper used in this book complies with the
Permanent Paper Standard issued by the National
Information Standards Organization (Z39.48–1984).

10 9 8 7 6 5 4 3 2

In loving memory of our parents
Helen and Robert Rosen
and
Sheldon Epstein

CONTENTS

FOREWORD

As the Holocaust recedes into history, human memory of it fades. What was once known graphically and directly by the first generation will become acquired knowledge for the next. True, word-of-mouth recollections will be passed on anecdotally by a few survivors to their children, but, for the most part, this transmission of memory and its details will be exceptional. Future generations will need all the help possible to learn about a complex event increasingly moving into the distant past. That is precisely why this *Dictionary of the Holocaust* is such a timely publication.

The *Dictionary* is an essential teaching aid at the moment when the average person's knowledge of Holocaust events becomes increasingly general, lacking precision, and factual content. An almost predictable repertoire of fifty or so words make up the sum total of the Holocaust vocabulary the typical college-educated graduate will carry through life: names such as Hitler, Goering, and Goebbels; places such as Auschwitz and Warsaw Ghetto; and terms such as Einsatzgruppen, SS, and Gestapo. Clearly these are insufficient for an intelligible grasp of the Final Solution and the issues it embodies. What is needed is a handy reference book to supplement introductory readings about the Holocaust, most of which suffer from insufficient detail to flesh out various aspects of the Holocaust reality.

Thanks to the yeoman's task rendered by Eric Joseph Epstein and Philip Rosen, the *Dictionary* compilers, this wealth of basic detail has now been made accessible in compact form. Their alphabetically arranged, itemized text consists of three categories of Holocaust information: biographic, geographic, and terminological.

Thanks to condensed, information-packed sketches, central players in the Holocaust drama spring to life; place names allow the student/reader to pinpoint key Holocaust locations; and a set of 200–300 obligatory Holocaust terms supply the reader with accurate definitions. Most important, each item is cross-listed so that the *Dictionary* can be read for its own sake, from item to cross-referenced item. No high school library should be without this handy reference tool; this goes for Holocaust research centers with educational activities, as well as for high school teachers and college instructors.

What is especially commendable about the *Dictionary* is its disciplined focus: all details point to the Holocaust; very little is extraneous. Even though the purpose of the book is to provide fundamental information about the Holocaust itself, it does more; it spares the reader from being engulfed by too much detail. The temptation to provide an overabundance of historical background to the point of confusion is carefully avoided by the compilers' devotion to conciseness and precision. The *Dictionary* lies midway between the multivolume *Encyclopedia of the Holocaust* and the far too-short glossaries appended to some monographs. It is an ideal tool for high school students as they prepare for a Holocaust ''unit.'' Most important, the *Dictionary* should remain a major learning tool for the upcoming postsurvivor stage of Holocaust Studies. It is a pleasure to recommend the *Dictionary* without major caveats.

Henry R. Huttenbach
The City College of New York

ACKNOWLEDGMENTS

First, we need to thank our wives, Lillian Schachter Rosen and Veronica Rodriguez-Epstein, for their moral support and for putting up with long absences. Gabriela Rodriguez-Epstein, now four, was patient, well-behaved, and rarely complained during research sessions.

A special thanks to Dr. Henry R. Huttenbach for his invaluable advice and suggestions.

We are especially grateful and indebted to our editors, Cynthia Harris and Arlene Belzer.

The following individuals and institutions have lent support and suggestions over this six year odyssey: Lillian Schachter Rosen, Robert Manstein, and Hayim Sheynin of Gratz College Tuttelman Library; Nina Apfelbaum; Schoen Books; Cherie Fieser; Rachel Gibbs; Dr. Louise Hoffman; Dr. Simon Bronner; Professor Ambrose Klein; West Chester University Green Library; Pennsylvania State University at Harrisburg; The Pennsylvania State Library; Tri County OIC; the United States Holocaust Memorial Museum; and students too numerous to list.

INTRODUCTION

The worst crimes were dared by a few, willed by more, and tolerated by all.

—Tacitus

Students, teachers and the general readers' understanding of the Holocaust is limited by the inaccessibility to a single research text. Often people, places, and terms are alluded to without enough explanation. The *Dictionary of the Holocaust* bridges that gap. While there are glossaries in the back of books, they have a very limited number of entries, and they do not always connect how each entry affected the Jewish people. The purpose of this work is to provide the reader with a concise, but not pithy, bibliographic, place, and terminology reference work that will not overwhelm the reader, yet will provide him/her with background on basic facts crucial to the Jewish catastrophe.

The *Dictionary* is different than cognate references. It contains the most up-to-date information, data revealed as late as 1997. This new information, such as the exposé in the November 1996 *New York Times* of the British code breaking intercepts of the German High Command (Ultra), revealing killing squad reports by German Order Police in Byelorussia, June-September 1941, gives scholars a better perspective on Allied indifference and protestations of ignorance about the Holocaust.

Each entry is tied to the Holocaust or Nazi war crimes. The *Dictionary*'s scope is broad. It tells more than other works about the role of women in the period (1933–1945) and more about the complicity of doctors in the German euthanasia and concentration camp practices. Entries deal with the collaboration of non-German peoples in the Final Solution and the entanglement of industrial firms and their leaders. The entries go beyond 1945, describing the fate of survivors as displaced persons and the attempt at restitution and reparations, including the recent Swiss banks' scandal. Many entries deal with war crimes and the search for war criminals. While the *Dictionary* focuses on the fate of Jews, the reader learns about Nazi crimes against other peoples—Soviet prisoners of war, homosexuals, foreign forced and slave laborers, Poles, Jehovah's Witnesses, Roma (Gypsies), and people in conquered lands.

This volume tries to achieve balance. Entries include resisters, collaborators, rescuers, and bystanders, both Jewish and Gentile. The reader learns the "why" of the Jewish genocide, for entries discuss anti-Semitic forerunners of the Nazis as well as the world-view of the murderers. The reader learns that the Jewish genocide was a harvest of hate.

History is a very controversial subject. The writers have spent thousands of hours researching, referencing, and cross-referencing this book. Some scholars or readers may object to the omission or content of some definitions. The writers attempted to distill the most important and commonly used terms and present the descriptions based on the most recent scholarship. History is a fluid record in the sense that new data and information comes forward on a daily basis. We hope to update the *Dictionary* periodically. We recognize that some nationalities, organizations, institutions, and persons may disagree with how some entries are presented. This cannot be avoided without making serious compromises with the truth. However, references after entries and the bibliography try to suggest other points of view.

Entries can be classified as biographies, places, and terms. Biographical descriptions record the person's birth or death dates. Where this has not been found, the account gives the time of the person's most relevant activity. The figure's connection to the Holocaust is emphasized, and the entry concludes with the person's fate.

Geographical places such as cities, towns, regions, and countries that the writers believe are important to know are identified immediately by reference to large well-known locations. The number of Jewish inhabitants before and after liberation is recorded, as is the date of liberation. When a place is known by two names, a common occurrence in Europe because of annexations and conquests, both names are cited. The first place cited is the one known during the war years (1939–1945). For example, the entry of Gdansk, Poland, was known at the outbreak of war in 1939 as Danzig. Romania is an exception; the current spelling rather than the old spelling, Rumania or Roumania, is used.

The writers have provided a great deal of statistics—exact dates, mortality, and population figures. Great reliance has been placed on Martin Gilbert's *Atlas of the Holocaust*, the volumes of *Encyclopedia Judaica*, editor Judah Gribetz's *The Timetables of Jewish History*, and the seven-volume United States Holocaust Memorial Museum's *Fifty Years Ago, Days of Remembrance (1939 thru 1945)*. Where there was a conflict of statistics, the writers used a specialized reference. For example, the number of Jews murdered at Iasi (Jassy) was taken from I. C. Butnaru's work, *Waiting for Jerusalem: Surviving the Holocaust in Romania*. Both writers have traveled recently to historical sites, museums and Holocaust centers in Europe and Israel. Data found there was given preference.

Concentration camps receive the longest descriptions. Each one is identified geographically and by class. The reader learns of their great variety and numbers. Each entry records when the camp opened, when it closed or was liberated and by whom, nationalities incarcerated and the extent of numbers murdered and gross violations of human rights that occurred at the site. Of course, not all camps receive attention. As with all entries, the writers have chosen ones most relevant to the general reader. The commandants of these camps are placed in biographical entries and are cross-referenced in the camp accounts.

There are a number of foreign terms described because they are important in understanding the period. Most are German expressions, while the second most are Yiddish/Hebrew, since the bulk of Holocaust victims were familiar with them. Foreign terms are identified immediately by this code:

Cr	Croatian	La	Latvian
Cz	Czech	Latin	Spelled out
Du	Dutch	P	Polish
Fr	French	Ro	Romanian
G	German	Ru	Russian
H	Hebrew	Sl	Slovakian
Hu	Hungarian	U	Ukrainian
It	Italian	Y	Yiddish
L	Lithuanian	Yu	Yugoslavian

The reader will note H/Y since many words in Yiddish are also Hebrew. There is no attempt to place all the diacritical marks in the foreign language, however; the German umlaut is indicated by adding an "e" to the word right after the letter that would carry the umlaut. If the English equivalent is more well known, the English term goes first and the foreign term next. Each foreign term is literally translated, however, often the word "Reich" meaning empire, nation, or state may not be.

The *Dictionary of the Holocaust* is a research tool for serious students of the Holocaust and the war against Nazi Germany. (One must have some knowledge of the latter to understand the former.) There are numerous cross-references both within the descriptions of the entries and at the end of most entries; all are in boldface type. The reader may use the index to locate the entry and any person, place, or term found in any description. If a reader cannot find a term, he/she would do well to consult the index. A reader who looks up the entry "Romania" could find much more information by noting the many cross-references—Bukovina, Czernowitz, Iasi, Antonescu, Bessarabia, Iron Guard, Axis, and so on.

At the conclusion of most entries about people, places, and terms are suggested readings, books in English, so the reader may pursue the topic. These have been carefully selected as to availability, relevance, and recency. Many are copyrighted after 1990. Some high interest accounts, or entries that may evoke controversy, have two or more suggested readings giving contrasting points of view. These references, which may also include a magazine article or newspaper account, are cited again in the bibliography with complete data—author's full name, full title, publisher, publication date, etc. There was an attempt to cite works that back up the content of the entry.

This dictionary was prompted by many years of teaching experience. The authors have found students lacking in general information relating to the Holocaust and the historical background that explains the plight of Jews and others during the Nazi era and World War II. With nearly 2,000 entries, many, many cross-references, books and articles cited, a bibliography and index, the authors have striven to provide the most current, accurate, and easy-to-use Holocaust reference book available.

Dictionary
of the
Holocaust

A

Abegg, Elisabeth (1882–1957). German resister and **Righteous Gentile**. Abegg created a Quaker rescue network using her home in **Berlin** as a temporary shelter and assembly point for Jews planning escape. She exhausted her personal resources in these efforts. (See also **American Friends Service Committee.**)

SUGGESTED READINGS: Paldiel, *The Path of the Righteous*; Marrus, "Coming to Terms With Vichy."

Abetz, Otto (1903–1958). German ambassador to **Vichy**. He met with **Hitler** and **Himmler** on September 16, 1941, to encourage the **deportation** of French Jews to the East. Abetz gained the support of both men and was personally involved in the deportation of French and foreign Jews in southern **France**. (See also **Theodor Dannecker** and **Dr. Carltheo Zeitschel.**)

SUGGESTED READING: Browning, *The Final Solution and The German Foreign Office.*

Aboulker, Jose (b. 1921). Algerian Jewish **resistance** fighter. He was a member of the family of Aboulker who was allied with the French Algerian resistance. Of the 377 resistance members who seized control of Algiers during the night of November 7–8, 1942, 315 were Jews. The fighters were ill-equipped, yet secured most of the strategic points before the Americans arrived. They also captured **Admiral Francois Darlan** in November 1942 and aided in the negotiations for a cease-fire between **Vichy** French troops and the Americans. (See also **Casablanca Conference**).

SUGGESTED READING: Steinberg, *The Jews Against Hitler.*

Abwehr (G., self-defense). German Intelligence Agency. Formed in 1933, it was attached to the **Wehrmacht** High Command's foreign and counterintelligence department. Its head, **Admiral Wilhelm Canaris**, was an opponent of the Nazi regime. After 1938, Abwehr became the center of a conspiracy against the **Hitler** government. On February 18, 1944, the Abwehr was dissolved into the **RuSHA**. (See also **Dietrich Bonhoeffer, General Reinhard Gehlen, Bandi Grosz** and **Oskar Schindler**.)

SUGGESTED READINGS: Manvell and Fraenkel, *The Canaris Conspiracy*; Prittie, *Germans Against Hitler.*

Action Francaise. French, **fascistic anti-Semitic** movement active from 1899–1945. Founded by Charles Maurras, its newspaper, *Action Francaise* advocated extreme right-wing monarchism. Banned in 1936, the movement was revived under **Vichy** and **collaborated** with German occupational forces.

SUGGESTED READING: Nolte, *Three Faces of Fascism.*

Adamowicz, Irena (1910–1963). **Righteous Gentile**. A devout Polish Catholic, and one of the leaders of the Polish Scout Movement, Adamowicz became a member of the **Jewish Fighting Organization**. In 1943, she informed the various fighting organizations of developments of Jewish underground groups in other **ghettos**. She was also a conduit to the **Armia Krajowa**.

SUGGESTED READING: Bartoszewski and Lewin, *Righteous Among Nations.*

Adenauer, Konrad (1876–1967). German statesman. Adenauer was dismissed from his post as mayor of Cologne, arrested and imprisoned for his opposition to Nazism. After the war, he co-founded the Christian Democratic Union party. Adenauer was elected chancellor of the German Federal Republic in 1945 and reelected in 1953, 1957 and 1961. He admitted German guilt for the **Holocaust** and favored **reparations** to Jews. After negotiations with **Nahum Goldmann** of the **World Jewish Congress**, West Germany began $845 million in payments to Israel. The Bundestag (German Parliament) also passed a **restitution** law on October 1, 1953, authorizing payment to individual survivors to compensate them for their suffering. (See also **Dr. Hans Globke**.)

SUGGESTED READINGS: Goldmann, *The Jewish Paradox*; Sachar, *The Redemption of the Unwanted.*

AEG. (See **Allgemeine Elektriztaets-Gesellschaft**.)

Aeltestenrat (G., **Council of Elders**). Analogous to a **Judenrat**. Established in **Terezin, Kovno** and other areas in **Poland**, the Baltics and Eastern Europe, these councils **collaborated** with the Nazis. (See also **Liepaja**.)

AFL (American Federation of Labor). Umbrella labor organization of major unions. Along with the **CIO**, the AFL opposed increased immigration during the Depression, fearing their membership would lose jobs. However, as Nazi persecution of Jews increased, both the AFL and CIO favored emergency **visas**

to admit **refugees** in 1938 and 1940. In 1943, when the **Holocaust** became publicized, the AFL and CIO joined with Jewish organizations demanding rescue and relief. The Federation supported the **Bergson** rescue resolution in Congress in the fall of 1943. (See also **Jewish Labor Committee**.)

SUGGESTED READING: Wyman, *The Abandonment of the Jews: America and the Holocaust 1941–1945.*

AFSC. (See **American Friends Service Committee**.)

Agudat Israel (H., Union of **Israel**). Worldwide, **Orthodox Jewish** movement. Founded in 1912, it became a political party in **Poland**. Agudat had an anti-**Zionist** bias before the establishment of the State of **Israel**, viewing Zionists as antireligious. The organization joined **Va'ad ha-Hatzala** and sent packages to Jews in Polish **ghettos** until the time of America's entry into the war in December 1941. This action was strongly opposed by the U.S. Boycott Council as "aiding the enemy." (See also **Joint Boycott Council** and **Aleksander Lados**.)

SUGGESTED READINGS: Kranzler, *Thy Brother's Blood*; Wein, *Triumph of Survival.*

Ahlwardt, Hermann (1846–1914). German **anti-Semitic** politician. In 1890, Ahlwardt published *The Aryan Peoples Battle of Despair Against Jewry*. As a member of the **Reichstag** (1895), he urged Germans to "exterminate these beasts [Jews] of prey." Ahlwardt asserted that Jews were dangerous, not because of their religion, but because of their racial qualities. His contention influenced **Hitler's** anti-Semitic and racial theories.

SUGGESTED READING: Katz, *From Prejudice to Destruction: 1700–1933.*

Ahnenerbe (G., ancestral heritage). Name given to the Society for Research into the Spiritual Roots of Germany's Ancestral Heritage. Founded in **Berlin**, on July 1, 1935, by **Heinrich Himmler**, this pseudoscientific organization was politically motivated and rife with chicanery. The Society sponsored archeological research into early German history and forums on Himmler's vision of **Aryan** origins. During the war, Ahnenerbe was involved in unethical "medical experiments" on altitude, freezing and skull collections. **Dr. Sigmund Rascher** and **Dr. August Hirt** were practitioners at Ahnenerbe's Institute of Military-Scientific Applied Research. (See also **Dr. Wolfram Sievers**.)

SUGGESTED READINGS: Levenda, *Unholy Alliance: The History of Nazi Involvement With the Occult*; Lumsden, *The Black Corps.*

AK. (See **Armia Krajowa**.)

Aktion(en) (G., "operation"). Terroristic murderous campaign undertaken for political, racial, or eugenic ends. Often referred to the rounding up of Jews for **deportation** or execution, a practice most viciously employed in the **Eastern Territories**. Aktionen were executed by the **SS** with the help of Latvian, Lithuanian, Ukrainian, and White Russian auxiliary police forces. Aktionen were later deployed in **France, Greece, Italy, Slovakia**, and the **Netherlands**, also with the aid of local **collaborators**. (See also **Aktion 1005, Aktion Kugel [Erlass], Aktion Reinhard, "Judenaktion,"** and **Razzia**.)

Aktion Kugelerlass (G., Bullet Operation Decree). Two decrees issued by **Ernst Kaltenbrunner** late in 1944 promoted operations with escaped inmates. The first order focused on foreign civilian workers and the second order included officers who were prisoners of war. Victims were taken to **Mauthausen** and executed by a bullet to the back of the neck. Summary execution of **Soviet POWs** was also sanctioned by this decree. (See also **Block 20**.)
   SUGGESTED READING: Persico, *Nuremberg: Infamy on Trial.*

Aktion 1005 (also referred to as **Sonderkommando 1005**). An attempt to cover up Nazi mass murder by using **slave laborers** (335 Jews and **Soviet POWs**) to exhume corpses from pits and burn the remains in pyres. This means of disposal was developed by **Paul Blobel** in the summer of 1942. (See also **Janowska [Road], Kovno**, and **Semlin**.)
   SUGGESTED READING: Hilberg, *The Destruction of European Jews.*

Aktion Reinhard (G., **Operation Heydrich**). Plan named for **Reinhard Heydrich** soon after his assassination in 1942. It called for the mass murder of Jews, expediting the implementation of the "**resettlement**" program in the **Generalgouvernement** and the plundering of Jewish property. Nazi administrative headquarters was located in **Lublin**, and looted materials were shipped to **Majdanek concentration camp. Death camps Sobibor, Belzec** and **Treblinka**, were established exclusively to facilitate the mass murder of Jews.
   SUGGESTED READING: Arad, *Belzec, Sobibor, Treblinka.*

AL. (See **Armia Ludowa**.)

Alaskan Development Bill. Immigration legislation proposed by Secretary of the Interior **Harold L. Ickes** in 1940. The bill, initially designed for Jewish **refugees**, proposed to settle 10,000 people annually in Alaska. Under this legislation, the Europeans would have to live in Alaska for five years before being eligible to enter the United States and to apply for citizenship. The bill never got out of committee due to isolationist anti-immigrant feelings. The plan was opposed by mainstream Jewish organizations. (See also **American Jewish Committee** and **American Jewish Congress**.)
   SUGGESTED READING: Wyman, *Paper Walls.*

Albania. Balkan nation with a Jewish population of several hundred. **Italy** invaded Albania in April 1939, and it came under German control in the spring

of 1941. Although a signatory to the **Tripartite Pact** and supportive of **Operation Barbarossa**, Albania served as a haven for Jews fleeing persecution in other Balkan states. Several Albanian Jews were **deported** to **Bergen-Belsen**.
  SUGGESTED READING: Silver, *The Book of the Just.*

Alexander, Leo (1899–1985). Chief Medical Advisor to **Doctors' Trial**. Born to German Jewish parents, Alexander was the first medical officer to review and analyze reports of the **Dachau** hypothermia experiments. He reviewed the inhumane "medical experiments" of German physicians. Alexander's "Memorandum on the Ethical and Non-Ethical Experimentation" sent to **General Telford Taylor** became a major document governing the formation of the **Nuremberg Code**. (See also **Dr. Sigmund Rascher.**)
  SUGGESTED READING: Annas and Grodin, *The Nazi Doctors and the Nuremberg Code.*

Alex Zink Factory. Factory in **Nuremberg** that recycled hair from gassed victims.

Algeria. North African colony of France. Anti-Jewish legislation was extended to about 120,000 Algerian Jews under **Vichy**. Some Jews were interned at **concentration camps**, most notably, Badu. Anti-Jewish laws remained in effect well after the American **liberation** in November 1942. Little changed until late 1944. (See also **Jose Aboulker, Casablanca Conference, General Charles de Gaulle, Statut des Juifs** and **Trans-Sahara Railway.**)
  SUGGESTED READING: Abitol, *The Jews of North Africa During the Second World War.*

Aliya (H., going up or immigration). The movement to immigrate to the **Yishuv** in **Palestine**. (See also **Joseph J. Schwartz.**)

Aliya Bet (H., "B" immigration). Organized "illegal" Jewish immigration by **Haganah** and **Irgun** to **Palestine** during the **British Mandate**. Active in the 1930s to 1946, Aliya Bet operations grew in scale from 1946–1948. The immigration was considered "illegal," however, because the British betrayed the **League of Nations** mandate establishing a national homeland for Jews by drastically curtailing Jewish immigration. (See also **Yitzhak Arad, Bricha**, Enzo Sereni, Dr. David Wdowinski and **White Paper.**)
  SUGGESTED READING: Offer, *Escaping the Holocaust.*

Allgemeine Elektriztaets-Gesellschaft (German Industrial Electric Corporation). German electrical company that utilized **concentration camp** labor. A total of 2,223 claims against the company by former **slave laborers** was vali-

dated by the **Conference on Jewish Material Claims**. Each claimant was awarded $500. (See also **Kaiserwald**.)
SUGGESTED READING: Ferencz, *Less Than Slaves.*

Allied Control Council Law Number 10. The legal basis for the prosecution of Nazis within the **occupied zones**. It was modeled on the **London Charter Conference** and established in December 1945 by the **Allies**. Twelve **Subsequent Nuremberg Trials** took place in the **American Zone of Occupation** from October 1946 to April 1949. (See also **Doctors' Trial, Einsatzkommando Trial, I. G. Farben, Frankfurt Trial, International Military Tribunal** and **Nuremberg Trials**.)
SUGGESTED READING: Harris, *Tyranny on Trial.*

Allies (also called United Nations). Comprised of the major powers, the United States, Great Britain, the **Soviet Union** and governments-in-exile that joined in the war against the **Axis**. All told, twenty-six nations that signed onto the alliance were indifferent to the fate of European Jews. After World War II, the Allies applied this name, United Nations, to the new international organization replacing the **League of Nations**. While they were aware of the **Holocaust**, they were reticent and evasive in calling attention to the mass murder. There were virtually no serious attempts at rescue until near the end of the war.

Over 1,397,000 Jewish soldiers served in Allied armies: the United States had 550,000, the **USSR** 500,000; **Poland** 140,000; Great Britain 62,000 plus 36,000 **Palestinian** Jews in the British army, **France** 46,000. (See also **Allied Control Council Law Number 10** and **War Refugee Board**.)
SUGGESTED READINGS: Finger, *American Jewry During the Holocaust*; Gribetz, Greenstein, and Stein, *The Timetables of Jewish History.*

Alter Kaempfer (G., ''old fighter''). Nazi who joined the party prior to **Hitler's** ascent to power in January 1933.

Altreich (G., ''old empire''). Nazi term for Germany before 1938, prior to the annexation of **Austria** and the **Sudetenland**.

''Amcho'' (H., ''one of our people''). Code word created during the war for Jews to identify one another in the **Warsaw Ghetto** and other occupied areas.

American Army's Counter Intelligence Corps. Originally established to detect possible sabotage, espionage and German military infiltration, it enlisted the support of Nazis after the war to combat the Soviets during the cold war. (See also **Ratline**.)
SUGGESTED READING: Bird, *The Chairman: John J. McCloy, The Making of the American Establishment.*

American Federation of Labor. (See **AFL**.)

American Friends Service Committee (**AFSC**). International arm of the Quakers that engaged in relief work. It began to aid Jews after **Kristallnacht**, particularly **refugees** who made their way to **France**. In addition to feeding Jews in France, they were actively involved in **Kindertransport**. Also, they provided relief in neutral **Portugal** and **Spain**. The Friends cooperated fully with such Jewish organizations as the **Joint Distribution Committee** and lobbied for a liberal American immigration policy to admit oppressed refugees. (See also **Elisabeth Abegg, Varian Fry**, and **Roswell McClelland**.)
  SUGGESTED READING: Wyman, *Paper Walls*.

American Jewish Committee. Non-**Zionist**, Jewish defense organization. It favored quiet diplomacy, believing that open, massive protests would engender **anti-Semitism**. The Committee urged the **Roosevelt** administration to protest Nazi policies against Jews and supported the **American Jewish Congress'** anti-Nazi rally in March 1933. Thereafter, the Committee refused to support similar rallies. They were unsupportive of liberalizing America's immigration laws. The American Jewish Committee was one of eight organizations that formed the **Joint Emergency Committee for European Jewish Affairs** and submitted a twelve-point rescue proposal to the **Bermuda Conference**. After this unproductive conference, the Committee turned its attention to postwar Jewish concerns, convinced rescue was not feasible.
  SUGGESTED READINGS: Cohen, *Not Free to Desist*; Medoff, *The Deafening Silence: American Jewish Leaders and the Holocaust*.

American Jewish Conference. Jewish umbrella organization of mainstream Jewish institutions that was established in 1943. The Conference downplayed the issue of rescue of European Jews and instead passed a pro-Jewish commonwealth in **Palestine** resolution. The **American Jewish Committee** and the **Jewish Labor Committee** were angered by this stance. **Orthodox** elements were disappointed by the lack of emphasis on rescue. The Conference failed to unite American Jewry or influence the U.S. government on Palestine policy. On January 10, 1945, this organization, along with the **World Jewish Congress**, asked the **Allies** to rescue 550,000 Jews stranded in Nazi-occupied areas and to provide aid to some 650,000 others who had been **liberated**. (See also **Dr. Isaac Lewin**.)
  SUGGESTED READINGS: Finger, *American Jewry During the Holocaust*; Lookstein, *Were We Our Brothers' Keepers?*

American Jewish Congress (**AJC**). A stridently **Zionist** Jewish defense organization. It was created before World War I to protest the elitism of the **American Jewish Committee**, under the leadership of **Rabbi Stephen S. Wise**. The Congress organized a number of anti-Nazi boycott movements. After **Kristallnacht**, it decided against open and public anti-Nazi demonstrations. The AJC did not favor legislation that would change American immigration restrictions, thereby allowing a greater influx of Jewish **refugees**. Affiliated with the **World Jewish Congress**, the AJC was a prime sponsor of the **American Jewish Conference** in the summer of 1943. (See also **Alaskan Development Bill, Jewish Labor Committee** and **Joint Boycott Council**.)

SUGGESTED READINGS: Urofsky, *A Voice That Spoke for Justice*; Wyman, *The Abandonment of the Jews: America and the Holocaust 1941–1945*.

American Joint Distribution Committee ("**Joint**"). An American Jewish relief agency. It sent funds to the **Jewish Self-Help Society** (later called the Jewish Organization for Social Care) and was the most aggressive agency in its mission to save European Jewry, channeling aid to many Jewish areas and **ghettos**. The "Joint" has been criticized for not recognizing the extent of **anti-Semitism** in postwar Eastern Europe and for encouraging surviving Jews to return to their native lands, including the **Soviet Union**. American Jewish army chaplains took the lead in relief for survivors until the "Joint" took over and gave aid to **displaced persons**. This organization also worked with the United Nations collecting information on Jewish orphans. The "Joint" spent more money on humanitarian aid to European Jews than all of the **Allies** combined. (See also **Armee juive, Dominican Republic, HICEM, Bernard Loesener, Josef Loewenherz**, *Saint Louis*, **Shanghai**, and **War Refugee Board**.)

SUGGESTED READINGS: Bauer, *American Jewry and the Holocaust*; Finger, *American Jewry During the Holocaust*.

American Zone of Occupation. After the defeat of **Germany** in May 1945, Germany-**Austria** was divided into four zones of occupation. Each major power (Great Britain, **France**, the United States and the **Soviet Union**) was given jurisdiction over an area of Germany. Word reached the survivors that treatment of **displaced persons** was far better in the American Zone, so many DPs sought to leave the other zones to be under U.S. rule. Also, the British were hostile to Jewish DPs for they feared that the stateless Jews would go to **Palestine**. (See also **General George S. Patton**.)

SUGGESTED READING: Sachar, *The Redemption of the Unwanted*.

Anders, General Wladyslaw (1892–1970). Polish military commander. He was captured by the **Red Army** when it invaded **Poland** in September 1939. Anders was released under pressure exerted by Britain and America and permitted to recruit an army from Polish POWs and civilians incarcerated within the **Soviet Union**. This army, rife with **anti-Semitism**, was sent to the Middle East where **Menachem Begin** left the unit and took control of the **Irgun**. (See also **Wladyslaw Sikorski**.)

SUGGESTED READINGS: Garlinski, *Poland in the Second World War*; Lukas, *Forgotten Holocaust: The Poles Under German Occupation, 1939–1944*; Wheal, Pope, and Taylor, *Encyclopedia of the Second World War*.

"**Angel of Belsen.**" (See **Luba Tryszynska**.)

"**Angel of Curaco.**" (See **Jan Zwartendijk**.)

"**Angel of Death.**" (See **Dr. Josef Mengele**.)

Der Angriff (G., *The Attack*). Nazi newspaper published by **Dr. Paul Joseph Goebbels** from 1927–1945. The paper spread **anti-Semitism** and incited the population against **Berlin's** so-called Jewish press. The readership tended to be more sophisticated than subscribers to **Julius Streicher's Der Stuermer**.

Anielewicz, Mordecai (1919–1943). **Warsaw Ghetto** fighter. He was the **Socialist Zionist** commander of **Ha-Shomer ha-Tzair** (The Young Guardians), an underground youth movement. A full-time activist by 1940, Anielewicz commanded the **ZOB**. He gave the signal to begin the **Warsaw Ghetto Uprising**. This event led to his death in a **bunker** on **Mila 18** Street in May 1943.
    SUGGESTED READINGS: Ainsztein, *The Warsaw Ghetto Revolt*; Gutman, *Resistance: The Warsaw Ghetto Uprising*.

Ani Maamin (H., "I believe"). Credo and chant. It is based on Maimonides' thirteen confessions of faith and was chanted by many Jewish **concentration camp** inmates on their way to the **gas chambers**. The hymn reaffirmed faith in God and in His justice.

Anschluss (G., union or linkage). Term for the German annexation of **Austria** on March 13, 1938. This union was accompanied without Austrian **resistance**. Racial laws were implemented immediately for Austria's 185,000 Jews. Soon after the Anschluss, the Jews were compelled, under brutal conditions, to clean up anti-Nazi slogans. In November, they suffered **Kristallnacht**, incarceration and expropriation of property. (See also **Reparations and Restitution, Artur Seyss-Inquart** and **William Shirer**.)
    SUGGESTED READINGS: Berkley, *Vienna and Its Jews*; Shirer, *The Rise and Fall of the Third Reich: A History of Nazi Germany*

Anthoni, Arno. Leader of Finnish State Police during World War II. Involved in Jewish **deportations** to **Estonia**, he was tried for **war crimes** after the war in **Finland**. (See also **Valpo**.)
    SUGGESTED READING: Cohen and Svensson, "Finland and the Holocaust."

Anti-Comintern Pact. Treaty signed in **Berlin** on November 25, 1936, by **Germany** and Japan joined by **Italy, Bulgaria, Hungary, Romania** and **Spain** in 1937. (**Finland** later agreed to adhere to the Pact.) Signatories pledged to fight the Soviet-led Communist international, that is, Comintern. The Nazis viewed communism as a form of international Jewish conspiracy and saw themselves as defenders against Bolshevism.

SUGGESTED READING: Bullock, *Hitler and Stalin.*

Anti-Jewish Boycott. Coordinated by **Julius Streicher** and announced by **Dr. Joseph Goebbels** on April 1, 1933. The boycott lasted for one of five scheduled days due to adverse international response. Goebbels justified the boycott as a reprisal against world Jewry's anti-Nazi propaganda. It was the first official salvo against German Jews. The **SA** was responsible for enforcing the boycott; they harassed, and not only intimidated Jewish retailers, lawyers and doctors, but also maintained a presence outside of Jewish shops. (See also **Boycott** and *Juedische Rundschau.*)

SUGGESTED READING: Schleunes, *The Twisted Road to Auschwitz.*

Anti-Semitism. Hatred against Jews based on supposed racial characteristics rather than religion. In the latter part of the nineteenth century the concept of a war between the **Aryans** and the Semites (meaning Jews) was fully developed. The term "race" was applied to the Jewish people. They were accused of fomenting the social ills of European nations. Prior to this time, antipathy was based largely on religious grounds. The switch to racial explanations, according to the anti-Semites, meant that the negative aspects of the Jews could not be changed. **Hitler** and the Nazis based their **genocidal** policies on this belief. After 1949, overt anti-Semitism was made illegal in the Federal Republic of **Germany**. (See also **Hermann Ahlwardt, Judeophobia, Wilhelm Marr**, *Protocols of the Learned Elders of Zion*, and **Voelkerchaos.**)

SUGGESTED READING: Goldhagen, *Hitler's Willing Executioners*; Nicholls, *Christian Anti-Semitism: A History of Hate.*

Antonescu, Ion (1882–1946). Pro-Nazi Romanian general and dictator. He ruled **Romania** from 1940–1944 and was known as the **Conducatur** and the "Red Dog." Romania joined the Nazi cause in June 1941 and was rewarded with **Bessarabia, Bukovina**, and **Transnistria**. The Antonescu policy toward the Jews was fluid and based on the course of war and the desire not to be occupied by the **USSR**. Initially, he adopted a hard line of "Land Cleansing" for the destruction of Romanian Jews. Between 1941–1942, this policy was pursued aggressively. Antonescu prepared for the extermination of the Jews in Transylvania, Bessarabia, and Bukovina by **deporting** them to killing centers in Transnistria in 1941. Under his rule, over 250,000 Jews and 20,000 **Roma** were murdered. The dictator was tried, convicted and executed in 1946 as a **war criminal**. (See also **Czernowitz, Dr. Wilhelm Filderman, Iron Guard, Radu Lecca, Traian Popovici**, and **Horia Sima.**)

SUGGESTED READING: Butnaru, *Waiting for Jerusalem: Surviving the Holocaust in Romania*; Butnaru, *The Silent Holocaust.*

Appeasement. Foreign policy of acquiescence by England and **France** toward **Nazi** Germany. The strategy adopted by Western leaders, particularly British Prime Minister **Neville Chamberlain**, who caved in to **Hitler's** demands for the **Sudetenland, Czechoslovakia**, in 1938 in order to avoid war. When applied to **Palestine**, this policy led to a drastic curtailment of Jewish immigration, a betrayal of the **British Mandate**. (See also **Munich Pact** and **White Paper**.)
   SUGGESTED READING: Cohen, *Churchill and the Jews.*

Appell/Appellplatz (Zhlapell) (G., formation/formation area). Roll call at **concentration camps** and **forced labor** sites. Inmates had to bring dead bodies to the staging area in as much as every prisoner had to be strictly accounted for. Appell was held in the morning and evening regardless of weather, time, or labor demands. It was not uncommon for inmates to die during the excessive length and rigors of roll call. (See also **Rapportfuehrer**.)

Arad, Yitzhak (b. 1926) **Vilna partisan**. He fought in the **ghetto** and later in the **Rudninkai Forest**. Later he became a Soviet partisan. Arad was active in **Bricha** and **Aliya Bet**. He became the Chairman of the Directorate of **Yad Vashem** and wrote *Vilna Jews in the Holocaust, Family Camps in the Forest*, and *Extermination of Lithuanian Jewry.*
   SUGGESTED READING: Arad, *Ghetto in Flames.*

Arajis, Viktor. Latvian mass murderer. Head of the Latvian police force known as the Arajan Commandos. They participated in mass murder in **Latvia** and north Russia, working with the **Einsatzgruppen** and **SD** from 1941–1943. The Commandos were involved in the murder of approximately 30,000 Jews. (See also **Latvian SS Legion, Heinrich Lohse, Perkonkrust**, and **Franz Walter Stahlecker**.)
   SUGGESTED READING: Ezergailis, *The Holocaust in Latvia, 1941–1944.*

Arazi, Yehuda (1907–1959). Palestinian Jewish activist. He was a **kibbutz**-born agent for **Haganah**, who engaged in **Aliya Bet**. He smuggled arms from **Poland**, Britain, and other sources. This Jewish agent headed **Bricha** activities in Italy. Arazi organized a hunger strike against the British there in 1946 to bring attention to the **Holocaust** survivors and their desire to go to **Palestine**.
   SUGGESTED READING: Sachor, *The Redemption of the Unwanted.*

Arbeit Macht Frei (G., Work Makes Free). Part of the **Nazi** deception policy. These words were forged at the entrance of **Auschwitz, Dachau, Theresienstadt, Buchenwald**, and several other sites. All Jews and other inmates had indeterminate sentences with no chance of freedom. (See also **Theodor Eicke** and "**Jedem Das Seine**.")

Arbeitsdienst (G., work service). German men from 18–25 years of age who were conscripted to labor on public works projects for six months to a year from 1935–1939.

SUGGESTED READING: Burleigh and Wipperman, *The Racial State: Germany 1933–1945.*

Arbeitsdienstfuehrer (G., work service leader). **SS** officer responsible for labor service at **concentration camps**.

Arbeitseinsatz (G., work task). Labor at **concentration camps**.

Arbeitsjuden (G., work Jews). Jews who had skills or who were picked to labor for the **Reich**. There was a conflict among high-level Nazis who wished to kill Jews immediately (**Heinrich Himmler**) and those who wished to use their labor (**Albert Speer.**) Often the **Wehrmacht** wished the latter.

Arbeitskarten/Arbeitsschein (G., work card). Temporarily exempted holder from **selection** or **deportation**. When the Nazis were determined to carry out an **Aktion**, they often ignored the card. (See also **Ausweis** and **Schein.**)

Arbeitskommando (G., work detail). (See **Aussenkommando.**)

Arbeitslager (G., work camp). **Labor camps** where conditions were so wretched that the vast majority of **slave laborers** died of malnutrition, disease, exhaustion, and brutality. These camps often were satellites of large **concentration camps** or **ghettos**.

Archbishop of Canterbury (William Temple, 1881–1944). Chief prelate of the Anglican Church from 1942–1944. He protested the widespread murder of European Jews in the House of Lords on March 23, 1943. The Archbishop urged the government to give temporary refuge to those Jews in the most danger—a motion that passed in the House of Lords, but was ignored by the House of Commons. (See also **Bishop George Bell** and **Channel Islands**.)

SUGGESTED READING: Finger, *American Jewry During the Holocaust.*

Ardeantine Caves. Caves outside **Rome** where 335 Italian **hostages**, including 75 Jews, were murdered on March 24, 1944, upon the orders of **Gestapo** Lt. Colonel **Herbert Kappler**. The murder of innocent hostages carried out in retaliation against **partisan** activity is a **war crime**. **Eric Priebke**, a former **SS** captain, was **extradited** from Argentina to **Italy** and put on trial in 1996. He was retried and convicted in July 1997. (See also **Collective Responsibility** and **Erich Priebke**.)

SUGGESTED READING: Katz, *Death in Rome.*

Arendt, Hannah (1906–1975). German Jewish philosopher. She was a political scientist whose work, *The Origins of Totalitarianism*, is a classic study of Nazi **Germany** and **Stalin's Soviet Union**. She studied philosophy under **Martin Heidigger** who later severed his relationship with her and joined the **Nazi Party**. Arendt's thesis in the controversial book, *Eichmann in Jerusalem*, that **Adolf Eichmann** was the product of a totalitarian society and a banal bureaucrat who did his job, stimulated serious debate. She saw Eichmann's participation in the **Holocaust** as being normal within a social structure that condoned mass murder. He was then an example of the "banality of evil." Arendt also postulated that **Judenraete** not only served their own interests by sacrificing others, but also gave the Germans valuable statistical data, thereby aiding the Nazis in the administration of the **Final Solution**. Arendt reasoned that Jewish communities would have been better off leaderless in the face of Nazi oppression. (See also **Emergency Rescue Committee** and **Varian Fry**.)
   SUGGESTED READING: Arendt, *Eichmann in Jerusalem*; Hughes, *The Sea Change*.

Armee Juive (F., Jewish Army). French, **Zionist resistance** movement. It was founded in 1942 by **Abraham Polonski** and **Lucien Lublin** and continued armed **resistance** under a Jewish flag until **liberation**. Armee juive organized escape routes across the Pyrenees to **Spain**, smuggling 300 Jews from 1943–1944 and distributing millions of dollars from the **American Joint Distribution Committee** to relief organizations and fighting units within **France**.
   SUGGESTED READINGS: Cohen, *The Burden of Conscience*; Steinberg, *Jews Against Hitler*.

Armia Krajowa (AK) (P., Home Army). Polish underground and **resistance** movement. Its 400,000 **partisans** fought for a non-Communist, conservative Catholic **Poland** and was aligned with the **Polish Government-in-Exile** in London. Some elements of the Armia Krajowa refused to aid Jewish resistance. **ZOX**, the military wing of the AK, assisted Jews during the **Sonderkommando** revolt in **Birkenau** and maintained ties with **Beitar** through the **ZZW**. (See also **Tadeusz Bor-Komorowski, Jan Karski, NSZ**, and **SWIT**.)
   SUGGESTED READINGS: Ainsztein, *The Warsaw Ghetto Revolt*; Bartoszewski and Lewin, *Righteous Among Nations*; Gutman and Krakowski, *Unequal Victims: Poles and Jews During World War II*.

Armia Ludowa (AL) (P., Peoples' Army). This organization was the military wing of the Polish Communist Party. It operated separately from the larger **Armia Krajowa** and was sympathetic to Jews. The Armia Ludowa supported **Stalin**, opposed the **NSZ**, and fought the Nazis for a communist **Poland** from 1943–1945.
   SUGGESTED READINGS: Ainsztein, *The Warsaw Ghetto Revolt*; Garlinski, *Poland in the Second World War*.

Armstrong, Hamilton Fish (1893–1973). Editor of *Foreign Affairs* and member of President **Franklin Delano Roosevelt's** Advisory Committee on Political Refugees. He suggested that the United States offer sanctuary to leading intellectual **refugees** caught in **France** in 1940–1941. Armstrong wrote a list of prominent people to be saved. The *Jewish Labor Committee* and the **AFL** took his list and added their own to obtain special emergency visitors' **visas** from **Breckinridge Long** in the State Department. (See also **Emergency Rescue Committee** and **Varian Fry**.)

SUGGESTED READING: Wyman, *Paper Walls.*

"Arrange"/"Arrangement." To bribe, manipulate, or **"organize."** An accepted and respected way of doing business in the **concentration camps**.

Arrow Cross (Hu., **Nyilas Part**). Hungarian, **anti-Semitic** political party created by **Ferenc Szalasi** in 1937. It advocated a pro-German policy, persecuted Jews, and aided the **SS** in **deportations**. The Arrow Cross assumed power in October 1944 under Nazi supervision and was directly responsible for a **death march** of about 80,000 Jews to the Austrian border beginning on November 8, 1944. The Arrow Cross was driven out of power by the **Red Army** when it arrived in Budapest in January 1945. (See also **Budapest March of Death, Zsido Tanacs**, and **Raoul Wallenberg**.)

SUGGESTED READING: Braham, *The Destruction of Hungarian Jewry.*

Artukovic, Andrija (1899–1986). Croatian Interior Minister. He was complicit in the slaughter of Jews, **Roma**, Serbs, and Communists in his homeland. Artukovic signed **anti-Semitic** laws, established twenty **concentration camps**, and along with **Anton Pavelic**, was responsible for the slaughter of 300,000 Serbs, Jews, Roma, and Communists. In 1941, the Croats and the **Ustashi** murdered 180,000 people. Artukovic announced: ''If you can't kill Serbs or Jews, you are an enemy of the state.'' The **war criminal** found safe haven in the United States via the **Ratline** before being **extradited** to **Yugoslavia** in 1986. He was sentenced to death for his crimes, but died before the sentence was carried out.

SUGGESTED READING: Blum, *Wanted! The Search for Nazi War Criminals.*

Aryan. People speaking an Indo-European dialect and a term perverted by the Nazis to mean a so-called master race (**Herrenvolk**) of pure-blooded Teutons. The Nazis considered Aryans superior to all other races. The Germans were the prime example of Aryan stock according to Nazi theory. **Dutch**, Flemish, and Scandinavians were also considered Aryan. The idealized Aryan was blond, blue-eyed, tall, and muscular. The term was also used to indicate non-Jewish Europeans, that is Aryan Warsaw, however, Nazis viewed these people as having less worth than Nordics. (See also **Hermann Ahlwardt, Houston Stewart Chamberlain, Lance von Liebenfels**, and **Guido von List**.)

Aryanization. Nazi expropriation of Jewish property and businesses in **Germany** and occupied Europe. There was little or no compensation; it was outright plundering and stealing. For the most part, this illegal transfer of Jewish assets was not overturned after the war. (See also **Einsatzstab Rosenberg, Friedrich Flick, August Frank, Walther Funk, Heimeinkaufvertrag, "Inventorization," Dr. Alfred Rosenberg, Statut des Juifs, Switzerland, Dr. Joseph Tiso,** and **Werterfassung**.)

  SUGGESTED READING: Nicholas, *The Rape of Europa.*

Aryan Paragraph. Passed in April 1933, it was required by the Nazi regime to bar Jews from political parties, economic establishments, and volunteer organizations. This decree excluded non-**Aryans** and their spouses from the clergy or church offices. Non-Aryans occupying church positions were dismissed (1933–1935.) The German Protestant Church capitulated to the policy while the Catholic and **Confessional Churches resisted**. The paragraph became moot with the passage of the **Nuremberg Laws** in September 1935.

  SUGGESTED READING: Schleunes, *The Twisted Road to Auschwitz.*

Aryan Status. First developed under the Civil Service Law (1933). A German was deemed to be **Aryan** if all four of his/her grandparents were non-Jewish Germans. Churches routinely supplied the required baptismal records.

Ash Brigade. Jewish inmates assigned to help **Sonderkommandos** clean up the ashes of corpses burned in pits.

Ashkenazim/Ashkenazi (H. and Y., German). Jews from Europe whose customs and roots can be traced to medieval German Judaism. They usually spoke a hybrid form of German called **Yiddish**.

Askari (G., slang). **Soviet POWs** who **collaborated** with the Nazis as guards in **labor** and **concentration camps**.

Asocials. Catch-all group whom the Nazis deemed socially unfit or unable to abide by social norms of the "national community." Affected groups included habitual criminals, juvenile delinquents, **homosexuals**, prostitutes, vagrants, "work shy people," drug addicts, and **Roma**. The Nazis believed deviance was biologically determined and asocial behavior was an innate degeneracy rooted in **miscegenation**. In the **concentration camps** these inmates were identified by a **black triangle** on their clothing with the exception of homosexuals who wore a **pink triangle** and Roma who wore a brown triangle. (See also **Lichtenburg** and **"Productive Annihilation."**)

  SUGGESTED READING: Burleigh and Wipperman, *The Racial State: Germany 1933–1945.*

Assisi. Town 100 miles north of **Rome**. In September 1943, Father Rufino Niccacci was head of the seminary there. He hid 300 Jews in twenty monasteries and convents. Two schools were set up for Jewish children.

SUGGESTED READING: Ramati, *The Assisi Underground.*

Association of Jews of Belgium (AJB). The **Jewish Council** was submissive to the Germans, but less active in the **deportation** of Jews than other **Judenraete**, for example, Amsterdam. It was established on November 25, 1941. The AJB's orders were often ignored by the Jewish community. The Jewish underground often burned lists of Jews to be deported, thereby undermining the AJB's authority. This body did provide educational and social activities during the winter of 1941 through the fall of 1944. Almost 35,000 of Belgium's Jewish population of 66,000 were deported to **labor** and **concentration camps** and at least 30,000 perished in the **Holocaust**. Only 10 percent of the Jews living in Belgium were citizens. (See also **Breendonck, Comite de Defense des Juifs, Leon Degrelle, Drancy**, and **Mechelen**.)

SUGGESTED READING: Steinberg, "The Trap of Legality: The Association of the Jews of Belgium."

Athens. Greek capital where Jews, especially **refugees** from **Salonika**, sought relief. Greek gentiles hid Jews, while **Italy** (which occupied portions of **Greece**) attempted to thwart German persecution. Archbishop Damaskinos urged protection for Jews. The Nazis **deported** 1,800 Jews to **death camps**. After **liberation**, 5,000 Jews emerged from hiding. (See also **Rhodes, General Jurgen Stroop**, and **Dieter Wiscliceny**.)

SUGGESTED READING: Gaon and Serels, *Sephardim and the Holocaust.*

Athlit. British **internment camp** located south of Haifa, **Palestine**, set up in 1939 to house so-called **illegal** immigrants. British policy established by the **White Paper** made absorption into the **Yishuv** illegal. **Refugees** desperate to reach safety were detained at Athlit. (See also **Aliya Bet**.)

SUGGESTED READING: Wasserstein, *Britain and the Jews of Europe, 1939–1945.*

Atlas, Dr. Yeheskiel (1910–1942). Physician and Jewish **partisan** commander in the Dereczyn district in White Russia. Atlas was well known for his military exploits and for sheltering Jewish **refugees**. He attacked German garrisons and derailed trains. The partisan was killed in combat on November 21, 1942.

SUGGESTED READING: Eckman and Lazar, *The Jewish Resistance.*

Auerswald, Heinz. Nazi officer in Warsaw. A former **Berlin** attorney and as Commissar of the **Warsaw Ghetto**, Auerswald befriended and deceived **Adam Czerniakow** on the real motives of the ghetto. Auerswald forced the **Jewish Police** to execute Jews who violated Nazi decrees from 1942–1943. (See also **"Blue Police"** and **Joseph Szerynski**.)

SUGGESTED READING: Trunk, *Judenrat.*

Aufbau (G., reconstruction). German Jewish weekly newspaper. It was published in New York from 1934 to the present. Popular among **refugees** and **Holocaust** survivors, its circulation peaked at 30,000 in 1946.

Aufbaukommando (G., construction detail). Early labor squad at **Auschwitz** that helped to build the complex.

Aufseherin (G., matron). **SS** female overseer. Technically women were not true SS, but merely employees. The highest female rank was Chef Oberaufseherin—chief senior overseer. (See also **Irma Grese** and **Maria Mandel**.)

Auschwitz (G.), **Oswiecim** (P.). The largest, most notorious, and murderous **concentration, death**, and **labor camp** complex located outside the city of **Oswiecim** in southwest **Poland**. It contained three major camps and thirty-six subcamps. The original and main camp, Auschwitz I, prior to its use as a concentration camp, served as a military barracks and warehouse for tobacco. It served as a concentration camp for Polish political prisoners from 1939–1942. The first inmates, 700 Polish Catholics, arrived in June 1940. **Birkenau** (P., **Brzezinka**,) or Auschwitz II (located two miles from Auschwitz I), was opened in October 1941, particularly for Jews and **Roma**, and was the site of four **gas chambers**. Most of the 1.6 million people (including 40,000 children) murdered at Auschwitz were gassed at Birkenau; 1.3 million were Jews and 300,000 were **Soviet POWs**, Polish Catholics, and **Roma**. One hundred thousand Hungarian Jews were murdered at Birkenau from May 16–24, 1944. **Monowice** was set aside as a labor camp in 1942 for the chemical giant **I. G. Farben** to produce **buna** (synthetic rubber).

On October 7, 1944, inmates staged a revolt at Birkenau in which three **SS** were killed. Jewish women shipped from **Bergen-Belsen** assisted in the first recorded revolt at Birkenau on October 23, 1943. **Heinrich Himmler** ordered the gas chambers and **crematoria** dismantled on November 25, 1944.

The **death march** from Auschwitz began on January 17, 1945 with 50,000 prisoners. Auschwitz I, II, and III were occupied by the **Red Army** on January 27, 1945. Approximately 7,600 sick inmates were **liberated**. (See also **Lothar Hartjenstein, Rudolf Hoess, J. A. Topf und Soehne, Hans Kammler, Roza Robota, Dr. Horst Schumann, Heinrich Schwarz, Yarnton Declaration**, and **Mala Zimetbaum**.) (See **Block 10** for information on medical experiments.)

SUGGESTED READINGS: Czech, *Auschwitz Chronicle, 1939–1945*; Gutman and Berenbaum, *Anatomy of the Auschwitz Death Camp*; United States Holocaust Memorial Museum, *Darkness Before Dawn*; United States Holocaust Memorial Museum, *1945: The Year of Liberation*.

Auschwitz-Birkenau "Family Camp." A separate site was established in Birkenau for 5,000 Jewish adults and children shipped from **Theresienstadt** in September through December 1943. These Jews were allowed to wear civilian clothing, receive parcels, send letters, and keep their hair. They were identified with a red X on the back of their outer garments. Approximately 3,800 Czech Jews were murdered on March 8, 1944. (See also **Freddy Hirsch**.)

SUGGESTED READING: Czech, *Auschwitz Chronicle, 1939–1945.*

Auschwitz Protocols (Vrba-Wetzler Report). Document detailing activities at Auschwitz I and II. It included maps of the **gas chambers** and rail hubs en route to the **death camp**. The Protocols were publicly released after the successful escape from Auschwitz by Walter Rosenberg (Rudolf Vrba) and Alfred Wetzler, on April 7, 1944. Vrba and Wetzler managed to reach Bratislava, **Czechoslovakia**, and contact Jewish leaders. Their detailed report on Auschwitz was passed on to **Rabbi Michael Dov Weissmandel** and the **Working Group** in Bratislava. The report, which was smuggled out to the West through **Switzerland**, exhorted the **Allies** to bomb the extermination camp complex and the rail lines leading to Auschwitz. The plea was ignored. (See also **Karl Barth, Emil Brunner, George Mandel Mantello, Roswell McClelland, John McCloy, Dr. Heinrich Rothmund**, and **War Refugee Board**.)

SUGGESTED READINGS: Finger, *American Jewry During the Holocaust*; Kranzler, *Thy Brother's Blood*; Vrba, *I Cannot Forgive*.

Auschwitz Trial. (See **Frankfurt Trail**.)

Ausgemerzt; Ausgerottet; Ausmerzung; Ausschaltung (G., exterminate, annihilate, or evacuate).

Ausrottung (G., terminate; eliminate).

Aussenkommando (G., outside detail). Work brigade that labored outside the confines of a large **concentration camp**. Those inmates had the opportunity to smuggle goods and information into the camp. Normally, the **camp orchestra** would perform music as the inmates departed for and returned from work.

Aussenpolitisches-amt (G., Foreign Policy Bureau). Foreign affairs body that put pressure on German allies to carry out the **Final Solution**. For example, its diplomats exhorted **Benito Mussolini**, unsuccessfully, to **deport** Jews under Italian jurisdiction.

"Aussiedlung" (G., **"resettlement"**). A population transfer that often was a euphemism for **deportation** to death.

Austria. Landlocked country in central Europe, bounded in the north by **Germany** and **Czechoslovakia**, and in the south by **Italy** and **Yugoslavia**. The German-speaking, culturally German state was once part of the large Austro-Hungarian Empire. Its vast holdings in **Galicia** were given to form **Po-**

land, the **Sudetenland, Bohemia-Moravia**, and **Slovakia** became part of the new state of Czechoslovakia. Northern **Bukovina** was given to **Romania**, and **Hungary** was detached and became a separate state. This was all part of the peace settlement after its defeat in World War I.

Austria experienced chronic strife from its inception in November 1918 to its annexation by Germany in March 1938. At the time of the **Anschluss**, 185,000 Jews lived in the Republic, 170,000 in **Vienna**, its capital. The Austrian population was 7 million. **Artur Seyss-Inquart**, former interior minister, and the one who invited the Germans into Austria, became governor of a new province of Germany, **Ostmark**. In the first hours of the Anschluss, wholesale arrests of Jews occurred. Two weeks later **deportations** to **Dachau** commenced. All the negative decrees levied upon the Jews of Germany now fell on Austrian Jews. In 1938, the Central Agency for Jewish Emigration (**Zentralstelle fuer Juedische Auswanderung**) was set up under **SS** Lt. Colonel **Adolf Eichmann**. The Jewish population was 66,600 by the end of 1939. All Jews of Austria had to concentrate in Vienna and come under the jurisdiction of the **Gestapo**-controlled Israelitische Kulturgemeinde (a **Judenrat**). The Austrian Jews suffered the fate of German Jews including **Aryanization** and deportation. Austria was **liberated** in 1945 by the American armies moving west to east and the **Red Army** from east to west. Like Germany, it was occupied by the four great powers: Great Britain, **France**, the United States, and the **USSR**. The estimated Austrian Jewish death toll was a low of 58,000 to a high of 65,000. (See also **American Zone of Occupation, Alois Brunner, Anton Brunner Odilo Globocnik, Greater Reich, Ernst Kaltenbrunner, Wilhelm Kube, Josef Loewenherz, Baldur von Schirach, Versailles Treaty**, and **Kurt Waldheim**.)

Ausweis (G., work certificate). Card issued to conquered peoples and Jews. Failure to possess this document usually resulted in **deportation** to a **concentration camp**. The Germans often changed its color to prevent falsification. Individuals caught with documents printed in the wrong color were immediately deported. (See also **Arbeitskarten**.)

Auto-Union. German automobile company that exploited **concentration camp** labor.

Avengers. Jewish **partisans** who were determined to continue the war against the Nazis in revenge for the murder of the 6 million. A major organization was called DIN, a Hebrew word meaning justice. **Abba Kovner**, a leader in the fighting organization of **Vilna**, played a central role. The groups infiltrated POW camps posing as German soldiers to detect murderers of Jews. They summarily executed them. Plan A in late 1945 was to poison the German water supply. The poison was detected by the British. Plan B, in 1946, had some success; bread in **Dachau's** prison camp, then in the British Zone of Occupation was poisoned by Avengers, causing 1,900 deaths. Kovner, **Shaul Avigur**, and Vitka

Kempner, the major leaders, decided that the creation of Israel had a greater priority. They became very involved in the **Bricha** movement and then in Israel defending the land against the Arabs.

SUGGESTED READINGS: Ben-Zohar, *The Avengers*; Elkins, *Forged in Fury*.

Avigur, Shaul (b. 1899–1978). Jewish **Palestinian** underground activist. The military commander, conspirator, and spymaster served in the 1920s and the 1940s as a **Haganah** fighter. In 1939, he headed the **Mossad le Aliya Bet**. He also purchased weapons for the Haganah and gathered intelligence. After World War II, operating from Paris, Avigur transported many surviving Jews to the **Yishuv**. (See also **Avengers** and **Bricha**.)

SUGGESTED READING: Szule, *The Secret Alliance: The Extraordinary Story of the Rescue of the Jews Since World War II*.

Axis. Term coined by **Benito Mussolini** in May 1939. The Italian dictator believed world events passed through **Rome** and **Berlin**. The political, military, and ideological alliance of **Nazi** Germany was augmented by Japan in September 1940. It later included **Finland, Hungary, Slovakia, Romania**, and **Bulgaria**. (See also **Allies**.)

SUGGESTED READING: Bullock, *Hitler and Stalin*.

B

Babi Yar (Ru., Grandmother's Ravine). Ravine outside of **Kiev**. At this site, approximately 33,800 Jews were murdered by machine guns between September 29–30, 1941. Babi Yar is also the location of the large-scale murder of **Roma, Ukranian Nationalists** (10,000), and **Soviet POWs**. Over 135,000 people were murdered here by the end of 1941, an undertaking spearheaded by **Einsatzgruppe** C. (See also **Partisan Order, Emil Rasch**, and **Dimitri Shostakovich**.)

    SUGGESTED READING: Seiden, *The Survivor of Babi Yar.*

Bach-Zelewski, Erich von dem (1899–1972). **SS** general. He headed anti**partisan** forces and commanded **Einsatzgruppe** B and **Order Police**, which engaged in the mass murder of Jews in **Belorussia**. In October 1942, **Heinrich Himmler** appointed Bach-Zelewski Plenipotentiary of ''Bandenkampf'' (war against bandits) to coordinate the antipartisan forces. The general crushed the **Warsaw Polish Uprising** in 1944 in which thousands of Polish Catholics were killed and 90 percent of the city was destroyed. However, he treated rebel Poles as POWs. The general testified at the **Nuremberg Trials** and Einsatzgruppe Trials for the **Allies**. In 1951 and 1961 he was indicted in West German courts, but served less than ten years in prison.

    SUGGESTED READINGS: Harris, *Tyranny on Trial*; Reitlinger, *The SS: Alibi of a Nation.*

Backa. District in **Yugoslavia** with a prewar Jewish population of 16,000. Five thousand Jews were murdered in Backa by the Hungarians in 1942. In 1944, the Hungarian **Gendarmerie deported** 2,500 Jews to **Auschwitz**. The surviving Jews joined **Tito's partisans**, and a number died fighting the **Ustashi** and **SS** in **Croatia**.

Baeck, Leo (1873–1956). Chief Rabbi of **Berlin** (Reform). The rabbi headed the **Reichsvertretung (Reich Association of German Jews)**. He refused to emigrate while the Nazis were in power to preserve the internal unity of German Jewry. In 1943, Baeck was **deported** to **Theresienstadt** where he became a member of the **Jewish Council**. The religious leader survived the **Holocaust** and died in London. An institute was named in his honor. (See also **Martin Buber.**)

SUGGESTED READING: Baker, *Days of Sorrow and Pain: Leo Baeck and the Berlin Jews.*

Baer, Richard (1911–1963). Member of guard company in **Dachau**, he was transferred to the **Totenkopfverbaende** formation where he was injured in 1942. Baer served as aide de camp at **Neuengamme**. He became head of the Political Division of **Concentration Camp** Inspectorate. In 1944, Baer became a commandant at **Auschwitz** and then commandant at **Dora-Nordhausen**. Baer headed the Political Department of the **WVHA Hauptamt**. He died in a Frankfurt prison before he could be brought to trial.

SUGGESTED READING: Smolen et al., *KL Auschwitz Seen by the SS.*

Baky, Laszlo (1889–1946). Hungarian diplomat. Undersecretary of State in the Ministry of Interior of the **Arrow Cross** government who coordinated the **deportation** of Jews from **Hungary** in the fall of 1944. He was executed as a war criminal in Hungary.

SUGGESTED READING: Lacko, *Arrow Cross Men, National Socialists, 1933–1944.*

Balfour Declaration. Statement favoring the establishment of a Jewish national homeland in **Palestine** on November 2, 1917. It was composed by Lord Arthur James Balfour, British foreign secretary, in personal correspondence to Lionel Walter Rothschild, head of the English Jewish community. Balfour was advised in the matter by **Chaim Weizmann**, and the Declaration was also was prompted by the desire of the British War Cabinet to urge world Jewry to side with the **Allies** against the Central Powers. The British cabinet falsely believed American and Russian Jews could greatly influence their respective governments. The Declaration was formally incorporated into the **League of Nations** mandate. (See also **Appeasement, Josiah Clement Wedgwood**, and **White Paper.**)

SUGGESTED READING: Gilbert, *Exile and Return.*

"Ballastexistenzen" (G., "useless lives"). The mentally and physically ill whom the Nazis considered grist for the **euthanasia** program. Term coined by **Karl Binding** and Alfred Hoche. (See also **"Lebensunwertes Leben."**)

Bandera, Stefan (1909–1959). Leader of a faction of **Ukranian Nationalist Organization** (Bandera-**OUN**). He despised Jews, Soviets, and Poles and fought for an independent **Ukraine** in the 1940s. Many of his followers were arrested

by the **Gestapo** and sent to **concentration camps**. These units fought both the Nazis and the Soviets and were eventually defeated by **Stalin** in the 1950s.
  SUGGESTED READING: Sabin, *Alliance for Murder.*

Baranowski, Hermann (1884–1940). Deputy kommandant of **Dachau** and Kommandant of **Sachsenhausen-Oranienburg** when it was the largest camp in the Nazi complex (1938–1940).
  SUGGESTED READING: Segev, *Soldiers of Evil: The Commandants of the Nazi Concentration Camps.*

Barbarossa. (See **Operation Barbarossa**.)

Barbie, Klaus (1905–1987). **Gestapo** official in **France**. Known as the "**Butcher of Lyon**," Barbie was responsible for the **deportation** of many Jewish children from Lyons to **Auschwitz**. He murdered the French **Resistance** leader Jean Moulin. After the war, Barbie escaped France through the **Ratline** and worked as a counterintelligence agent for the U.S. government before immigrating to Bolivia in 1951. The **war criminal** was exposed in 1972 by **Serge** and **Beate Klarsfeld**. In 1987, he was **extradited** and then convicted by the French for his activities against Jews and for the torture of resistance fighters during the war. Barbie died in prison.
  SUGGESTED READINGS: Linklater, Hilton, and Ascherson, *The Nazi Legacy: Klaus Barbie and the International Fascist Connection*; Morgan, *An Uncertain Hour.*

Barrack 11. Living quarters at **Birkenau** for male twins **selected** for **Dr. Josef Mengele's** experiments. Out of 3,000 sets of twins, 100 survived **Auschwitz**. (See also **"Twins' Father."**)

Barth, Karl (1886–1968). Swiss Protestant theologian who led the German **Confessing Church** from 1933–1935. Barth opposed paganized, Nazified German Protestant Churches, and for this, he was expelled from Germany to Basel in 1939. The cleric authored the Barman Declaration, which condemned the idolatry of Nazism but did not deal with **anti-Semitism**. Barth's writings affirmed the commonality between Christians and Jews as heirs to biblical revelation. In 1944, the theologian wrote a prologue to the **Auschwitz Protocols**. (See also **Emil Brunner** and **Switzerland**.)
  SUGGESTED READINGS: Kranzler, *Thy Brother's Blood*; Lovin, *Christian Faith and Public Choice.*

Bartoszewski, Wladyslau (b. 1922). Pro-Jewish, Polish anti-Nazi. He aided Jews during the **Holocaust** and helped to establish the committee that became the **Zegota**. After his release from **Auschwitz**, Bartoszewski was with the **Armia Krajowa** and helped to transmit information on the **Final Solution** to the **Polish Government-in-Exile**. He also represented Rebirth of Poland, a Catholic civic organization. In addition to serving as Poland's foreign minister, Bartoszewski was designated a **Righteous Gentile** and became an honorary Israeli citizen in 1991.

SUGGESTED READING: Bartoszewski, *The Warsaw Ghetto.*

Bastard Jews (BJ). Designation in the **Netherlands** for those Jews whose mothers were not Jewish. These individuals were not considered full Jews and were less severely persecuted. (See also **Sperre**.)

Bath Certificate. Document that certified an individual had been deloused. (Lice were carriers of **typhus**.) Certificates could be purchased on the black market.

Bauarbeiter (G., construction worker). **Concentration camp** construction worker.

Bauleitung SS (G., construction management). **SS** unit that coordinated **concentration camp** construction including the installation of **gas chambers** and **crematoria** at **Auschwitz**.

Baum Gruppe. Underground anti-Nazi movement. It was composed of Jews who joined the Communist Party during the **Hitler** regime and founded in **Berlin** by Herbert and Marianne Baum (1914–1942). Between 1937–1942, the Baum Gruppe distributed **Zionist** and communist brochures and organized a number of cultural events, and in 1942, set fire to an anti-Bolshevik art exhibit. In 1942–1943, most of the members were caught and executed, including the Baums. The **Reichsvereingung der Juden in Deutschland** (Reich Association of Jews in Germany) was dissolved, its members **deported** under the pretext of retaliation for Baum **resistance**. The street leading to the Berlin Jewish Cemetery has been renamed Herbert Baum Strasse.

SUGGESTED READINGS: Merson, *Communist Resistance in Nazi Germany*; Steinberg, *The Jews Against Hitler.*

Bauminger, Heshek ("Zvi") (1919–1943). Jewish **partisan** leader. He served in the Polish and **Red Army** and was captured by Germans, but escaped to **Krakow**. Bauminger became the leader of the unified **ZOB** and engaged in hit-and-run actions against the German military. When he was captured by the Germans in 1943, the partisan took his own life.

SUGGESTED READING: Krakowski, *The War of the Doomed: Jewish Armed Resistance in Poland.*

Bayer. Subsidiary of **I. G. Farben**. The chemical firm tested new drugs, for example, sulfa compounds, on **concentration camp** inmates in **Auschwitz** and **Mauthausen**. Helge Wehmeier, head of Bayer, apologized to **Eli Wiesel** in 1995 for deaths caused by I. G. Farben. (See also **Dr. Helmut Vetter** and **Dr. Eduard Wirths**.)

SUGGESTED READINGS: Mann and Plummer, *The Aspirin Wars: Money, Medicine, and 100 Years of Rampant Competition.*

Becher, Kurt (b. 1919). **SS** officer. He served with **Einsatzgruppe** in 1941 and on the Russian Front. Becher negotiated with **Dr. Rezso Kastzner** and represented **Heinrich Himmler** in meetings with **Saly Mayer**. Becher confiscated the **Weiss-Manfred** factory in **Hungary** and was involved with Kastzner in the transfer of **Bergen-Belsen** from German to British control. The officer was arrested by the **Allies** but released upon the recommendation of Kastzner. Becher currently lives in Germany. (See also **Budapest Rescue Committee** and **Irme Finta**.)

SUGGESTED READINGS: Arendt, *Eichmann in Jerusalem*; Bauer, *American Jewry and the Holocaust.*

Bedzin. City in south **Poland**. In July 1940, a **ghetto** was formed comprising 27,000 Jews. A huge **Aktion** occurred on August 12, 1941, when 5,000 Jews were **deported** to **Auschwitz** and murdered. The ghetto was liquidated on August 11, 1943, after a major uprising. **Mordechai Tenenbaum** emerged as **ZOB** leader. Two notable female resisters took part: Frumka Plotnicka (1914–1943), who was killed in action and Chaika Klinker (1917–1958), who escaped and survived the **Holocaust**.

SUGGESTED READING: Trunk, *Judenrat.*

Befehl ist Befehl (G., Orders are orders). Frequent defense utilized by Nazis to evade responsibility at **war crimes** trials. The **International Military Tribunal** rejected this excuse.

Begin, Menachem (1913–1992). **Zionist Revisionist**. He was the leader of the **Beitar** in **Poland** (1939) and the **Irgun** in **Palestine** (1943). Begin was **Ze'ev Jabotinsky's** successor. Arrested by the Soviets in 1940 and sent to **Siberia**, the activist was released to fight for **General Wladyslaw Anders'** Polish Army. In Palestine, he became leader of the Irgun succeeding **David Raziel**. Begin attacked the British in Palestine in January 1944 for their complicity in the **Holocaust**. The Irgunist became the first Likkud Prime Minister of Israel.

SUGGESTED READINGS: Begin, *The Revolt*; Bell, *Terror Out of Zion.*

Beigelboeck, Dr. Wilhelm. Professor at the Medical Faculty of **Vienna**. He, along with **Dr. Hans Eppinger**, conducted seawater experiments on **Dachau** inmates. The doctor was sentenced to fifteen years in prison during the **Doctors' Trial** in **Nuremberg** (1947).

SUGGESTED READING: U.S. Government Printing Office, *Trials of War Criminals Before the Nuremberg Military Tribunals Under Control Law No. 10, Volume 1, ''The Medical Case.''*

Beitar Revisionists. Nonsocialist, right-wing **Zionist** youth group, which adhered to the principles of **Ze'ev Jabotinsky**. In Warsaw, they formed their own military organization **Zydowski Zwiazek Wojskowy (ZZW)**, which maintained close ties with the **Armia Krajowa** and fought independently during the **Warsaw Ghetto Uprising**. (See also **Menachem Begin**, **Josef Glazman**, and **Dr. David Wdowinski**.)

   SUGGESTED READING: Katz, *Lone Wolf.*

Bekanntmachungem (G., posted decree). Affixed in captured areas by German authorities. Removal could result in the death of the person.

Bekenntniskirche. (See **Confessional or Confessing Church**.)

Belgium. A constitutional monarchy in northwestern Europe having a common boundary with the **Netherlands** (north), **Germany** (east), **France** (south), and an eastern coastline on the North Sea. It was a highly industrialized country, densely populated with two major ethnic groups: the Flemish, a Germanic people largely in Flanders in the north, and Walloon, French-speaking people in the south. In World War II, Belgium was invaded and conquered by Germany in May 1940. In September 1944, **Allied** armies began **liberation**, but **Hitler's** last offensive delayed that until early spring of 1945.

   Belgium's Jews numbered 90,000 in 1940 in a general population of 9 million. However, that melted away to 52,000 as many Jews fled to France or elsewhere. Fifty thousand Jews resided in Antwerp, many working in the diamond industry. Another 30,000 Jews lived in Brussels, the capital. Thirty thousand Jews sought refuge in Belgium during the 1930s. Only a small percentage of Belgian Jews held citizenship papers. They were not as assimilated as **Dutch** Jews. A **Judenrat** was established, but most did not pay attention to its decrees. The Belgian **resistance** movement broke into the Jewish Council's (**Association of Jews of Belgium**) offices and destroyed the lists of Jews. The Royal Family warned that expropriation of Jewish property was a crime with penalties after the war. The Catholic Church, under Cardinal von Roez, protested all anti-Jewish measures. Most Belgians opposed the German occupation and translated this into aiding the Jews. This meant ignoring decrees, hiding Jews, and providing them with false papers. Even the military governor was reluctant to deport Jews. General Alexander von Falkenhausen was tried by his superiors for insubordination.

   Belgian Jews did more to help their own people than most other trapped Jews. However, they did have the advantage of a local sympathetic population. A Jewish group (**Comite de Defense des Juifs**), formed by Gerts and Yvonne Jospa, did much to aid fellow Jews, including the rescue of 3,000 Jewish children by finding "safe" houses.

   There were local Nazi supporters. **Leon Degrelle** formed a native National Socialist Party—the **Rex**—basically a Walloon organization. Belgian fascists produced 40,000 volunteers for the **Waffen-SS**. The VNB, a Flemish party, aided the German police forces and the **Wehrmacht** in their endeavors.

About 26,000 Jews were **deported** mainly from (Malines) **Mechelen**, a **transit camp** in Belgium, to **Auschwitz**. Only 1,800 deportees returned after the war. (See also **Breendonck, Collaborators**, and **Drancy**.)

Bell, Bishop George. Resister. Prelate from Chichester, England. He rescued German Jews from **internment camps** on the **Isle of Man** in the summer of 1940. (See also **Archbishop of Canterbury**.)
SUGGESTED READING: Gill, *An Honorable Defeat.*

Belorussia (Byelorussia) (Belarus). Area in Northeastern Europe bounded by **Latvia, Lithuania**, and **Russia**. Its territory was divided between Russia and **Poland** between the two world wars. The Jewish population in the western zone was 670,000. Auxiliary units from this region aided the **Einsatzgruppen** in mass murder. In the eastern sector, the Jewish population of 405,000 was subject to raging **pogroms**, especially in **Minsk, Mir, Mogilev-Podolski**, and **Vitebsk**. (See also **Lida, Novogrudok, "Sonderwagon," Franz Walter Stahlecker, LT. General Andrei Vlasov, Zamosc**, and **Zhitomir**.)

Belzec. Death camp in eastern **Poland**. It operated from March 17, 1942, until November–December 1942. This camp was staffed by **euthanasia** veterans and Ukrainian guards. Jews from **Lublinland, Lvov (Janowska), Krakow**, and **Galician** districts were among the camp's victims. During the first month of the camp's operation, 80,000 Jews were murdered. Later 600,000 Jews and 1,500 non-Jews were killed there. This extermination camp was razed by the Nazis in the fall of 1943. Mass graves were exhumed and corpses burned through the spring of 1943. Only one person is known to have successfully escaped. (See also **Aktion 1005, Aktion Reinhard, Kurt Gerstein, Odilo Globocnik, Jan Karski, Roma**, and **Stanislaw**.)
SUGGESTED READING: Feig, *Hitler's Death Camps.*

Benes, Eduard (1884–1948). Czech statesman. He was a diplomat, premier (1935–1938), and head of the Czechoslovakian Government-in-Exile (London) from 1939–1945. A liberal democrat, Benes fought **anti-Semitism**, protected Jews, supported **Zionist** aspirations, and later worked with **Jan Masaryk** to expose the **Final Solution**. He stepped down as premier after the **Munich Pact** in 1938. (See also **Emil Hacha**.)
SUGGESTED READING: MacDonald, *The Killing of SS-Obergruppenfuehrer Reinhard Heydrich.*

Ben-Gurion, David (1886–1973). Jewish statesman. A central figure in **Yishuv** leadership, he proposed a number of plans to the **Allies** to save Jews, including bombing German cities to avenge the destruction of European Jews. Yet he has been criticized for not being vigorous enough in attempting rescue. As head of the **Jewish Agency** in 1945, he visited **Displaced Persons** camps in **Germany** and arranged for **Zionist** indoctrination. Ben-Gurion became prime minister of the new State of Israel in 1948 and under his leadership, between 1948–1951, over 700,000 immigrants, mostly **Holocaust** survivors, settled in Israel.

SUGGESTED READINGS: Segev, *The Seventh Million*; Teveth, *Ben Gurian and the Holocaust*.

Benoit, Abbe Marie (b. 1895) ("Father of the Jews"). **Righteous Gentile**. A French Capuchin priest based in Marseilles and later in the Italian zone of occupation in southern **France**, Benoit smuggled 4,000 Jews to safety. He ran a smuggling operation out of the Capuchin monastery in rue Croix de Regnier in Marseilles until the Nazis occupied the south of France in November 1942. Benoit moved his operation to the Italian zone; known for its tolerant attitude toward Jews. He headed **DELASEM** there and moved that committee to the College of Capuchin. However, the Italian surrender in September 1943 made the Jews in this zone vulnerable to the Nazis. Nevertheless, he produced 3,000 forged documents through 1945.

SUGGESTED READINGS: Friedman, *Their Brothers' Keepers*; Leboucher, *Incredible Mission*.

Bergen-Belsen. **Concentration camp** located in a rural area outside of Hanover, **Germany**. The camp opened on August 2, 1943. Belsen never had an official designation, but **Heinrich Himmler** envisioned the facility to be a model **transit camp** and also a camp for the sick. The camp was divided in two: Camp I was for **Soviet POWs**, but later encompassed a **Frauenlager** for women, which also included children. Camp II, or the **Star Camp**, was for Jews. The conditions were among the worst of any of the concentration camps. Before **liberation** on April 15, 1945, this site had deteriorated to the point that inmates transferred from **Auschwitz** were shocked by the camp's poor conditions. The Germans approached the British and negotiated the takeover of the camp on April 12, 1945. The site was occupied by British and Canadian units on April 15. Approximately 60,000 inmates, mostly Jewish (40,000–45,000), were **liberated**. A **typhus** epidemic claimed 30,000 lives. Two hundred children under 12 survived. Bergen-Belsen served as a British **DP camp** for five years after the war. (See also **"Angel of Belsen," Kurt Becher, Anne Frank, Dr. Rezso Kastzner, Josef Kramer, Saly Mayer, Dr. Siegfried Seidl**, and **Luba Tryszynaska**.)

SUGGESTED READINGS: United States Holocaust Memorial Museum, *Darkness Before Dawn*; United States Holocaust Memorial Museum, *1945, The Year of Liberation*.

Berger, General Gottlob (1895–1975). **Waffen-SS** general and recruitment chief. He headed the policy division for **Eastern Territories** and was the author of *The Subhuman* in 1941. Berger suppressed the **Slovakian National Revolt**

and became inspector general for POW camps (1945). The general was sentenced to twenty-five years at **Nuremberg** in April 1949 for the murder of Jews. He was released in 1951 as part of the clemency program of **John McCloy**.
SUGGESTED READING: Krausnick et al., *Anatomy of the SS State.*

Berggrav, Bishop Eivind. Norwegian prelate. He wrote a pastoral letter in February 1941 against the persecution of the Jews and the brutalities of the Norwegian "**stormtroopers**." The bishop resigned and soon, along with six other bishops, was arrested. (See also **Norway**.)
SUGGESTED READING: Abrahamsen, *Norway's Response to the Holocaust.*

Bergson, Peter (Hillel Kook) (b. 1914). **Zionist Revisionist** member of **Irgun** and leader of the **Bergson Group**. The Irgunist came to the United States in 1940 to raise funds for a Jewish **Palestinian** Army. Bergson learned of the Nazi extermination policy from **Rabbi Stephen S. Wise's** press conference on November 20, 1942. His group turned their attention to the rescue of European Jewry. Bergson created the **Emergency Committee to Save the Jewish People of Europe** to make Americans aware of the destruction of European Jewry. The campaign included demonstrations in five major cities, which drew over 100,000 people. The Emergency Committee's March on Washington was supported by leading Orthodox rabbis. Legislation drafted by Bergson's group in the U.S. Congress was a major factor in inducing **Franklin Delano Roosevelt** to establish the **War Refugee Board**. The Bergson Group operated outside of the Jewish establishment and was detested by mainstream Jewish leaders such as Rabbi Wise. (See also **Ben Hecht, Samuel Merlin**, and **Union of Orthodox Rabbis of America**.)
SUGGESTED READINGS: Ben-Ami, *Years of Wrath, Days of Glory*; Morrison, *Heroes, Anti-Heroes and the Holocaust.*

Bergson Group/Bergson Boys. (See **Peter Bergson**.)

Berle, Adolf (1895–1971). Assistant U.S. secretary of state. He tightened **visa** procedures in March 1941, making it difficult for **refugees** to enter the United States. The ruling was prompted by the fear that the refugees might be spies. Some historians have interpreted this ruling as covert hostility to Jews. (See also **Breckinridge Long**.)
SUGGESTED READING: Wyman, *Paper Walls.*

Berlin. Germany's largest city and its capital during the war. Before 1933, it had a Jewish population of 160,564 out of a total German Jewish population of 503,000. Like the rest of German Jews, there was an intermarriage rate of 60 percent. The **Fuehrer Chancellery**, and later his bunker, were located in Berlin. On April 30, 1945, the Fuehrer committed suicide as the **Red Army** closed in.

On May 2, 1945, the **Soviets** were in complete control; they found 162 Jews in hiding, 800 half-Jews in the former Jewish hospital, 4,790 Jews married to non-Jews, and 992 mixed parentage Jews who declared themselves Jewish by religion. (See also **Axis, Leo Baeck, Baum Gruppe**, and **Rudolf Hess**.)

SUGGESTED READINGS: Gross, *The Last Jews in Berlin*; Ruerup, *Topography of Terror*.

Berman, Adolf Abraham (1906–1978). Underground agent. He was the **Warsaw Ghetto's** representative to the Polish underground and also the Jewish secretary to the **Zegota**. Berman worked in tandem with **Leon Feiner, Bundist** representative to Zegota. (See also **Central Agency for Care of Orphans**.)

SUGGESTED READING: Tomaszewski, *Zegota*.

Bermuda Conference. Meeting between the British and Americans (April 19–28, 1943) to discuss solutions to the Jewish **refugee** problem. No Jewish representatives were invited. The American delegation was instructed by the State Department not to adjust immigration barriers. The British refused to open **Palestine** to Jewish refugees. The Conference was a meaningless political gesture because Britain and America agreed that Jews could not be aided until the war was won. The **Warsaw Ghetto Uprising** took place while the Conference was in session. Mainstream Jewish organizations were convinced that rescue was not possible by this discouraging conference. (See also **Evian Conference, Joint Emergency Committee for European Jewish Affairs, Breckinridge Long, Robert Borden Reams**, and **White Paper**.)

SUGGESTED READINGS: Morse, *While Six Million Died*; Wyman, *The Abandonment of the Jews*.

Bernadotte, Count Folke (1895–1948). Vice-president of the Swedish **Red Cross**. He was an intermediary for negotiations of **concentration camp** inmates late in the war, and in March 1944, met directly with **Heinrich Himmler**. The Count is associated with the "White Buses" that rescued thousands of Scandinavian and Jewish inmates from German concentration camps; particularly **Ravensbrueck**. Bernadotte lobbied **Sweden** to take 60,000 concentration camp survivors for treatment and rehabilitation. The statesman was assassinated by the **Lohamei Herut Israel** underground in 1948. The motive was Bernadotte's proposal in the UN for a rump-sized Jewish **Palestine**. The Jewish National Fund planted a forest in his honor.

SUGGESTED READING: Schwarz, *Walking With the Damned*.

Bernardini, Monsignor Filippo. Rescuer, papal **nuncio** in **Switzerland**. He used his office to aid **Rita and Isaac Sternbuch** and provided couriers to **Rabbi Michael Dov Weissmandel**. He shamed Swiss officials into keeping French Jewish children, orphans, and escapees contrary to the Swiss policy of **refoulement**.

SUGGESTED READINGS: Kranzler, *Thy Brother's Blood*; Kranzler, *Heroine of Rescue*.

Bernays, Murray C. (b. 1894). Jewish lawyer and American Lieutenant Colonel in Army Civil Affairs Division. He was a force behind the concept of an **International Military Tribunal** to convict **war criminals**. Bernays postulated four charges, that were later to be the basis of the **Nuremberg Trial**, which covered all the atrocities committed by the **Third Reich**. Bernays' overarching view was that before and during the war, the **Nazi Party** was part of a criminal conspiracy based on racism and territorial expansionism. Also, he formulated the idea that the **Reich's** repressive agencies, that is, **SS, Gestapo**, and so forth, were criminal organizations and membership constituted *prima facia* evidence of criminality. The lawyer was heartbroken when General **Telford Taylor** was given the job as assistant prosecutor. (See also **Rafael Lemkin**.)

SUGGESTED READING: Taylor, *The Anatomy of the Nuremberg Trials: A Personal Memoir.*

Bernheim Petition. The 1922 German Polish **Silesian Convention** guaranteed minority rights. Franz Bernheim, a resident in Upper Silesia, suffered under the 1933 anti-Jewish laws. His petition to the **League of Nations** was honored and the League insisted on German observance. The Germans complied and nullified the anti-Jewish legislation until the German Polish Convention (treaty) expired in May. (See also **Minorities Treaties**.)

SUGGESTED READINGS: Johnson, *Modern Times*; Yahil, *The Holocaust: The Fate of European Jewry, 1932–1945.*

Bessarabia. Large province located between the **USSR** and **Romania** which bandied back and forth between the two countries. It was ceded by the latter in June 1940 to the **Soviet Union**, and it became the Soviet Moldavian Republic. **Kishinev**, a city of 41,405 Jews, was the focal point of Jewish religious and cultural life. Under Soviet rule, Moldavian Jewish institutions were closed and ''wealthy'' Jews were exiled to **Siberia**. The Bessarabian Jews (207,000) met the same **deportation** fate as the Bukovinian Jews (93,000). Bessarabia and **Bukovina** residents were not protected by the Romanian government. Those born under Czarist or Austro-Hungarian administrations (especially after World War I) were not considered Romanian citizens. On August 30, 1941, an agreement between **Germany** and the Romanians was signed in Tighina, Bessarabia, giving the area between the Bug and Dniester Rivers (coined **Transnistria**) to Romanian authorities. At the **Wannsee Conference**, 340,000 Jews were to be murdered in Romania and Bessarabia. (See also **Iasi**.)

SUGGESTED READING: Butnaru, *The Silent Holocaust: Romania and Its Jews.*

Best, Dr. Werner (1903–1988). German diplomat. As one of **Reinhard Heydrich's** deputies, he played a key role in the **deportation** of French Jews. Paradoxically, it was during his administration of occupied **Denmark** that 95 percent of Danish Jewry escaped to freedom. Best was sentenced to death by a Danish court in 1949, but was released two years later for there was a suspicion that he warned the Dutch about the **Final Solution**. (See also **Georg Duckwitz**.)

SUGGESTED READINGS: Flender, *Rescue in Denmark*; Goldberger, *The Rescue of Danish Jews.*

Bettelheim, Bruno (1903–1990). German Jewish political prisoner and famous psychoanalyst. He was interned at **Dachau** in 1939 and later transferred to **Buchenwald**. In *The Informed Heart*, he criticized what he perceived as Jewish passivity to Nazi persecution. In particular, he attacked **Anne Frank's** father, Otto, for simply hiding his family. Bettelheim believed all Jews should have participated in **resistance** movements. According to Bettelheim, he attributed the Jewish failure to respond to a death instinct that paralyzed Jews during the **Holocaust**. Sick and confined to his house, he committed suicide at age 87.

SUGGESTED READING: Angress, ''Who Really Was Bruno Bettelheim?''

Bettnachzieher (G., bed-after-puller). Inmate who fixed bedding to meet Nazi requirements in **concentration camps**.

Bialystok. City in eastern **Poland**. On ''Red Friday'' soon after **Operation Barbarossa**, 2,000 Jews were murdered. Of the 40,000 Jews confined to the Bialystok **Ghetto** in August 1941, only 260 survived. The remaining Jews were subject to random murder by German soldiers. (See also **Grodno**.)

SUGGESTED READINGS: Eckman and Lazar, *The Jewish Resistance*; Trunk, *Judenrat.*

Bialystok Uprising. In February 1943, **Mordechai Tenenbaum** of the Jewish Anti-Fascist Fighting Group warned the **ghetto's** 35,000 Jews of the impending liquidation. The Jewish revolt in this eastern Polish city began on August 16, 1943, in response to mass **deportations** in the ghetto. The battles persisted for four days until Mordechai Tenenbaum and the **resisters** finally succumbed to the vastly superior **SS** forces. (See also **Haika Grossman**.)

SUGGESTED READINGS: Grossman, *The Underground Army*; Steinberg, *Jews Against Hitler.*

Biebow, Hans (1902–1947). German civilian administrator of the **Lodz Ghetto**. He kept the **SS** out of operational control; however, he exploited **slave labor**, robbed inhabitants of their resources, and set up **ghetto** factories. In 1944, Biebow organized **transports** to **Chelmno** and **Auschwitz**. Tried by a Polish court, he was sentenced to death.

SUGGESTED READING: Dobroszycki, *The Chronicle of the Lodz Ghetto, 1941–1944.*

Bielski, Alexander (1912–1995). Jewish **partisan**. He, along with his four brothers, organized the Bielski Brigade, which harassed German occupation forces in **Belorussia** and rescued hundreds of Jews. The partisan survived the war and immigrated to America. (See also **Tuvia Bielski** and **Lida**.)
   SUGGESTED READING: Tec, *Defiance, the Bielski Partisans*.

Bielski, Tuvia (1906–1987). Jewish **partisan** commander. He, along with his brothers, established a base called "Jerusalem" in the **Novogrudok** region of **Russia**. His unit invited families to join in Naliboki forest and thus established a family camp. The group of 300 fighters utilized captured German uniforms and weapons, raided **collaborators** forces in order to obtain supplies and arms, derailed troop trains, and blew up electric stations. The camp was relieved by the **Red Army**. He survived the war and came to America. (See also **Alexander Bielski** and **Lida**.)
   SUGGESTED READING: Eckman and Lazar, *The Jewish Resistance*.

"Big Fortress." (See **Theresienstadt**.)

Biltmore Programme (Resolution). An extraordinary **Zionist** conference was held May 6–11, 1943, at the Biltmore Hotel in New York City. The chairman of the **Jewish Agency** Executive Board, **David Ben-Gurion**, declared, "Jews cannot depend on Great Britain to establish a Jewish national home in **Palestine**, therefore, the Jewish Agency should replace the **British Mandatory** power as the government of Palestine." The **World Zionist Organization** delegates, for the first time, declared themselves openly, without obfuscation, to a Jewish state, with complete Jewish sovereignty and no immigration restrictions on Jews. The declaration was prompted by the increasing information of the mass murder of Europe's Jews and the British policy of enforcing the 1939 **White Paper**.
   SUGGESTED READING: Bauer, *From Diplomacy to Resistance*.

Binding, Karl. Jurist, **eugenist**. This Freiburg professor of law developed his **euthanasia** ideas in tandem with a psychiatrist, Alfred Hoche (1865–1943), in a 1920 polemical work entitled, *Authorization for the Destruction of Life Unworthy of Life*. Both professors were ultranationalists who rejected individual rights, and instead championed the rights of the national community, meaning the German people. Binding stated that physical and mental inferiors should be killed even if they could live painlessly for many years. A particular life was worth living if it had worth to society. The jurist argued that those with incurable feeble-mindedness had lives with no purpose and imposed a terribly difficult burden on both relations and society. Binding believed the care of such individuals was a total misappropriation of valuable human resources. Hoche believed the Hippocratic Oath was outdated. **Hitler** and the Nazi killers espoused

those ideas. They became the basis for the **T-4** program and later gassing. Jews were "unworthy of life." (See also **"Lebensunwertes Leben."**)
  SUGGESTED READING: Lifton, *The Nazi Doctors.*

Birkenau. Polish town of **Brzezinka** was razed to make room for **Auschwitz II**. The new camp was organized to incarcerate Jews and **Roma** and was the site of four **gas chambers** and **crematoria**. (See also **Auschwitz, Death camp**, and **Lothar Hartjenstein.**)
  SUGGESTED READING: Nahon, *Birkenau.*

Bitburg. Site of a military cemetery in **Germany** that also contained **Waffen-SS** graves along with **Wehrmacht** stones. President Reagan's visit in 1985 created an international controversy. The president didn't seem to understand the special nature of **SS** activities. (See also **Elie Wiesel**.)
  SUGGESTED READINGS: Hartman, *Bitburg in Moral and Political Perspective*; Levkov, *Bitburg and Beyond: Encounters in American, German and Jewish History.*

BJ. (See **Bastard Jews.**)

"Black Police" (G., Schwartzpolizei). **Dutch** auxiliary security force usually trained by Germans for a six-week period. The "Black Police" were actively deployed against Dutch **resistance** and played a supporting role in **Razzian** (**Aktionen**). (See also **"Green Police."**)

"Black Saturday." Mass roundup of Jews in **Rome** on October 16, 1943. The German police arrested 1,259 Jews and **deported** them to **Auschwitz** where they were gassed one week later. Forewarned, many Jews took refuge in Catholic institutions prior to the raid. (See also **Pope Pius XII** and **Vatican.**)
  SUGGESTED READINGS: Herzer, *The Italian Refuge*; Kurzman, *The Race for Rome.*

"Black Shirts." Term given to the **SS**. **Heinrich Himmler** ran the **SS** like the elite Jesuit order who wore black outfits. They were the promoters and bearers of the true faith, that is **National Socialism. Benito Mussolini's** paramilitary units wore black shirts, and the term referred to them also.

Black Triangle. Patch worn by **asocials** in the Nazi **concentration camp** system.

Black Wall/Block H. Wall at **Auschwitz** I where inmates were shot. The wall was used to muffle the sound of inmates executed by a single bullet to the head.

"Black Work." Back-breaking physical labor at the camps.

Bletchley Park. Site of British code and cipher school near London. Using a replica of the German code machine, **Enigma**, the experts at Bletchley were able to decode German High Command radio signals as early as 1940. After Pearl Harbor, **Enigma** became available to the Americans. The cryptologists deciphered reports of mass executions of Jews from June–September 1941. The method of gaining this information was a high-level secret—the **Ultra** Secret. The knowledge of Jewish **genocide** in **Belorussia** and the **Ukraine** was revealed on June 27, 1941, by breaking the code ''Vulture.'' The ''secret'' was not revealed during or after the war and not publicized until November 1996. (See also **Ordnungspolizei** and **Ostbahn**.)

   SUGGESTED READINGS: Gilbert, *The Second World War; New York Times*, November 19 and 25, 1996.

Blobel, Paul (1894–1951). **SS** colonel. He coordinated the **Babi Yar** massacres and was actively involved with **Einsatzgruppe** C. In 1942, Blobel was put in charge of **Aktion 1005** where he destroyed evidence of mass killings by digging up corpses and burning them in pyres. The mass murderer was sentenced to death at the **Nuremberg Einsatzkommando Trials** in 1948 and hanged in **Landsberg Prison** on June 8, 1951. (See also **Emil Otto Rasch** and **Sonderkommando 1005**.)

   SUGGESTED READINGS: Hilberg, *The Destruction of European Jews*; Wells, *The Death Brigade* (*The Janowska Road*).

Bloch, Marc (1886–1944). Teacher and historian. He joined the French army. In 1943, Bloch wrote *Strange Defeat* about the fall of **France** and the need for **resistance** and battling German occupation. In March 1944, he was executed by the **Gestapo** as a **resister**, not as a Jew.

   SUGGESTED READING: Bacque, *Just Raoul*.

Block (G., area). Section of a camp surrounded by barbed wire, containing one or two rows of barracks. This was instituted by **Heinrich Himmler** to discourage escapes.

Block 10. ''Medical research experiments'' and sterilizations in **Auschwitz** were conducted in this area. **Drs. Josef Mengele, Horst Schumann**, and **Carl Clauberg** were especially notorious on this **block**. (See also **Ravensbrueck**.)

Block 11 (also referred to as the ''bunker''). First successful test of **Zyklon-B** occurred in this area on **Soviet POWs**. This **block** contained the punishment and torture courtyard and barracks at **Auschwitz**.

Block 20. Isolation **block** at **Mauthausen**. Prisoners sent here were marked for execution. From the fall of 1942 through May 1945, much of **Aktion Kugelerlass** was carried out in this site.

Block 25. "Death block." This area was the collection point at **Auschwitz** for women chosen to be gassed.

Blockaelteste (G., barracks senior). Inmate **block** foreman or supervisor at **concentration camps**. Usually non-Jewish, "**Greens**" or "**Reds**" who helped to control inmates for the **SS** in exchange for better treatment. (See also **Kapo, Lageraelteste, Self-government, Stubenaelteste**, and **Stubendienst**.)

Blockfuehrer (G., block leader). **SS** noncommissioned officer in charge of a number of barracks at **concentration camps**.

Blockschreiber (G., area registrar). Inmate **block** registrar at **concentration camps**.

Blocksperre (G., area prohibition). An order for inmates to remain in their barracks. This event usually occurred prior to a **selection**.

Blood and Soil. Nazi concept of the German community of people rooted to the soil. Promoted by **Richard Walther Darre**, this ideal was codified in the **Reich** Hereditary Farm Law (September 1933), which mandated only a person of **Aryan** blood could be a landowner. **Lebensraum** was an outgrowth of this precept.

"Blood for Trucks." Proposed plan negotiated between **Joel Brand** (on behalf of the Budapest **Judenrat**) and **Adolf Eichmann**, in spring 1944. The plan called for the Nazis to stop **deporting** Hungarian Jews and release up to 1 million people in exchange for 10,000 trucks, as well as sugar, coffee, and tea. Brand met with **Yishuv** and British leaders, but Britain rejected the deal. The **Allies** dismissed the whole idea believing it was a ruse to alienate the **Soviet Union** and make a separate peace with the West. Brand was later arrested in Syria by the British, but later released. **Dr. Rezso Kasztner** took over direct negotiations with Eichmann after Brand's arrest. The deliberations came to nothing. (See also **Bandi Grosz**.)
   SUGGESTED READINGS: Bauer, Jews for Sale?; Weissberg, Desperate Mission: Joel Brand's Story.

Blood Libel. Anti-Semitic myth, particularly popular in Eastern Europe and **Greece**. It falsely accused Jews of killing Christians, especially their children, for blood to be used during religious rituals, for example, using blood in matzoh at Passover. (See also "**Der Stuermer**" and **Kielce**.)

"Blood Squad." (See **Landwacht**.)

"Bloody Friday." On the evening of April 18, 1942, the Nazis swept through several towns in the **Generalgouvernement** murdering Jews in **Krakow**, Tarnow, Czestochowa, **Radom, Kielce**, and Ostroweic.

SUGGESTED READING: Gutman, *Resistance: The Warsaw Ghetto Uprising.*

"Bloody Wednesday." On November 3, 1943, the Germans murdered 18,400 Jews at **Majdanek** and marked the beginning of "Operation Erntefest." The camp was surrounded by an additional 500 **SS**; the watchtower guard increased from one to three. The Jews were shot in groups of 100 with the loudspeakers blaring the "Beer Barrel Polka" to drown out the screams and reduce the noise from the shootings. Most of the 13,000 victims were **selected** in Majdanek and the rest of the Jews came from **Lublin**. (See also **Operation Harvest Festival**.)

SUGGESTED READING: Arad, *Belzec, Sobibor, Treblinka.*

"Blue Police" (P., Policja Granatowa). Polish police under German (**Ordnungspolizei**) control in the **Generalgouvernement**. Their nickname was derived from the color of their uniforms, and they were loyal German employees. The "Blues" guarded **ghettos** in **Poland**, extorted money from smugglers, fought **partisans** beginning in 1942, and assisted the **Jewish Police** in taking Jews to the **Umschlagsplatz**. (See also **Heinz Auerswald, Freiwillige**, and **Joseph Szerynski**.)

SUGGESTED READING: Gutman, *The Jews of Warsaw, 1939–1943.*

Blum, Abraham ("Abrasha") 1905–1943). **Bundist** leader. He organized soup kitchens and cultural activities in the **Warsaw Ghetto**. Blum advocated **resistance** and led the Bund into **ZOB**. He died in the **Warsaw Ghetto Uprising**. (See also **Dr. Marek Edelman**.)

SUGGESTED READING: Gutman, *The Jews of Warsaw, 1939–1943.*

BMW (Bavarian Motor Works). German automobile company that exploited **concentration camp** labor.

Boegner, Marc. Head of the French Protestant Church in France. He was an ardent opponent of Jewish **deportations** (1942–1943). (See also **Cardinal Pierre-Marie Gerlier**.)

SUGGESTED READING: Zuccotti, *The Holocaust, the French, and the Jews.*

Bohemia-Moravia. (See **Protectorate of Bohemia-Moravia**.)

Bohr, Niels (1885–1962). Danish physicist. He was awarded the Nobel prize for his work on quantum theory, radioactivity, and nuclear fusion. Born to a Jewish mother, Bohr escaped the Nazis in 1943 and went to **Sweden**. He lobbied

the Swedes to provide haven to Danish Jews. The physicist became a consultant for the U.S. atomic bomb project at Los Alamos. (See also **Lise Meitner.**)
   SUGGESTED READING: Rhodes, *The Making of the Atomic Bomb.*

Bonhoeffer, Dietrich (1906–1945). Anti-Nazi theologian. He helped establish a **Confessional Church** in Germany to counter the Nazification of the Protestant Churches. Bonhoeffer opposed **Hitler's** military policies and persecution of Jews and sought theological friendship between Jews and Christians. Bonhoeffer was arrested and taken to **Buchenwald** in 1943. After the **July 20, 1944 Bomb Plot**, he was transferred to **Flossenbuerg**, sentenced by an **SS** tribunal and hanged on April 9, 1945. (See also **Admiral Wilhelm Canaris.**)
   SUGGESTED READINGS: Robertson, *The Shame and the Sacrifice*; Snyder, *Hitler's German Enemies.*

Book Burning. On May 10, 1933, **Dr. Joseph Goebbels** ordered the public burning of books. The Nazis targeted works by Bolsheviks, internationalists, Jews, humanists, and internationally renowned authors like **Thomas Mann** and Jack London. This event signaled the complete censoring and monitoring of the educational system to conform with Nazi views. Book burning originated in fifteenth- and sixteenth-century **Germany** and **Italy**. (See also **Talmud** and **Torah.**)
   SUGGESTED READING: Friedman, *Roads to Extinction.*

Border Patrol. Jewish Police squad formed in June 1942 to prevent smuggling in the **Warsaw Ghetto**. This force replaced the Polish Border Patrol and guarded the wall between **Aryan** (non-Jewish) and Jewish Warsaw.

Bor-Komorowski, Tadeusz (1895–1966). Commander of the **Polish Home Army (AK)** and the **Warsaw Polish Uprising**. Some Jews fought under his command in the Warsaw Polish Uprising. Bor-Komorowski grossly overstated the AK's rescue attempts on behalf of Jews after the war.
   SUGGESTED READINGS: Lukas, *Forgotten Holocaust*; Zawodny, *Nothing But Honour.*

Bormann, Martin (1900–1945?). Secretary of the **Reich** Chancellery. Formerly a secretary to **Rudolf Hess**, he became **Hitler's** private secretary. As Reichsleiter, he had control over **Gauleiter**. As the war turned against the Nazis, Bormann controlled access to Hitler and was detested by the Nazi elite, for example, **Dr. Joseph Goebbels, Albert Speer**, and **Heinrich Himmler**. He was tried in absentia at the **Nuremberg Trials**. Bormann is presumed to have died in Hitler's bunker, but rumors persist that he is living in South America. (See also **Walter Buch** and **Karl Kaufmann.**)
   SUGGESTED READINGS: Farago, *Aftermath*; Fest, *The Face of the Third Reich;* Snyder, *Hitler's Elite.*

Borowski, Tadeusz (1922–1951). Polish writer. Born to Polish parents in **Zhi-tomer, Soviet Ukraine**, Borowski endured famine, collectivization, and the **deportation** of his parents to Soviet penal colonies. He was trapped by the Germans in Warsaw and deported to **Auschwitz** and then **Dachau** from 1943–1945. Borowski wrote prolifically about his **Holocaust** experience and is best known for *This Way for the Gas, Ladies and Gentlemen*. He committed suicide in Warsaw.

Borzykowski, Tuvia (1911–1959). Underground Polish Jewish fighter. He was an important member of the **ZOB** in the **Warsaw Ghetto**. Borzykowski was involved in the armed **resistance** of January 18, 1943, and the general uprising of April 1943. He escaped through the sewers with **Yitzhak Zuckerman** and **Zivia Lubetkin** and fought in the **Warsaw Polish Uprising** in August 1944. He immigrated to Israel in 1949.
  SUGGESTED READING: Borzykowski, *Between Tumbling Walls.*

Bosnian-Herzogovinan Muslims. German **collaborators**. The **Grand Mufti of Jerusalem** recruited 20,000 Muslim to form the **SS Handzar** division, in 1943. They cooperated with the **Ustashi** in killing Serbs and most of the Jewish population of **Croatia** and Bosnia-Herzegovina. Muslims, Germans, and Croats burned down the ancient **Sephardic** Jewish Center in Sarajevo on April 17, 1941. (See also **Yugoslavia**.)
  SUGGESTED READING: Schechtman, *The Mufti and the Fuehrer.*

Bothmann, Hans (1911–1946). Kommandant of **Chelmno (Kulmhof)**. He committed suicide by hanging in 1946. Kogon, Langbein, and Ruckerl, Nazi Mass Murder.

Bouhler, Philipp (1899–1945). Chief of the **Fuehrer Chancellery (T-4)** and principal in directing the **euthanasia** program. He cooperated with **Heinrich Himmler** to murder **concentration camp** inmates as part of **"special treatment" 14 f 13**. Bouhler also placed T-4 services at the disposal of the SS. He committed suicide in May 1945.
  SUGGESTED READING: Friedlander, *The Origins of Nazi Genocide.*

Bousquet, Rene (1910–1993). Secretary-general of the French National Police in **Vichy**. Appointed by **Pierre Laval**, Bousquet ordered the **Velodrome d'Hiver** (1942) roundup and was involved in sending 60,000 Jews to their deaths in the East. He was sentenced by the French High Court to five years "national degradation," which was immediately suspended, and his role in Jewish **deportations** was never examined. The Frenchman became a director of the Bank of Indochina and the *Depeche du Midi* (French newspaper) after the war. His retrial was opposed by French President Mitterand. Bousquet was assassinated on June 9, 1993, before he could be tried for **crimes against humanity**. (See also **Jean Leguay, SS General Carl Albrecht Oberg**, and **Paul Touvier**.)
  SUGGESTED READING: Golsan, *Memory, the Holocaust and French Justice.*

Boycott of Nazi Germany. On March 27, 1933, a massive anti-German boycott protest rally took place in New York City. It was sponsored by the **American Jewish Congress**. The rally was held in response to sporadic killings and attacks by Nazis on Jews. The Nazi authorities, headed by **Julius Streicher**, responded to the boycott by posting **SA** members in front of Jewish shops for one day— April 1, 1933. Their orders were to keep out gentile customers. (See also **Anti-Jewish Boycott**.)

SUGGESTED READINGS: Poliakov, *Harvest of Hate*; Webster, *Petain's Crime*.

BRABAG (Braunkohle-Benzin A.G.). German mining company that was one of the largest and deadliest exploiters of **concentration camp** labor at **Auschwitz** and **Buchenwald**.

SUGGESTED READING: Ferencz, *Less Than Slaves*.

Brack, Dr. Victor (1904–1948). **Hitler's** special advisor on the **euthanasia** program. He created an administrative structure for adult euthanasia. Brack was one of three Nazis (Erhard Wetzel and **Adolf Eichmann**) who decided to use gas for the destruction of the Jews (October 5, 1941) and sent experienced **T-4** personnel to the **Generalgouvernement**. He was tried, convicted, and sentenced to death at the **Doctors' Trial**.

SUGGESTED READING: Friedlander, *The Origins of Nazi Genocide*.

Brand, Joel (1906–1964). Member of **Budapest Rescue Committee** and head of the **Tiyul**. He was approached by **Heinrich Himmler** to exchange Jewish lives for 10,000 trucks, that is, **"Blood for Trucks."** Brand was sent to Turkey in July 1944 (with approval of the **SS**), to negotiate the release of Hungarian Jews. The proposal was rejected by the **Allies**, and he was arrested by the British in Syria. He also suggested to the Allies that they bomb the tracks from **Hungary** to **Auschwitz**. This proposal was also rejected. In October 1944, Brand joined the **Stern Group** and fought the **Jewish Agency**, calling them **"quislings."** (See also **Chaim Weizmann**.)

SUGGESTED READING: Bauer, *Jews for Sale?*; Weissberg, *Desperate Mission: Joel Brand's Story*.

Brandt, Dr. Karl (1904–1948). **Hitler's** surgeon and confidant and surgeon-general of the **Waffen-SS**. As **Reich** commissioner for Health and Sanitation, he supervised the **T-4** program. Brandt also conducted dietary experiments at **Mauthausen**. He was sentenced to death by an American Military Tribunal and hanged in **Landsberg** prison on June 2, 1948. (See also **Philipp Bouhler, Dr. Leonardo Conti, Doctors' Trial**, and **Dr. Joseph Mayer**.)

SUGGESTED READINGS: Aziz, *Doctors of Death*; Friedlander, *The Origins of Nazi Genocide*.

Brandt, Dr. Rudolf (1909–1947). Physician and **war criminal**. He was charged at the **Doctor's Trial** with **crimes against humanity** for his part in inhumane, nonconsensual experiments on **concentration camp** inmates, particularly at **Dachau**. Prisoners suffered and died during research dealing with air pressure, freezing, mustard gas, and sea water. Brandt was convicted and hanged.

SUGGESTED READING: Annas and Grodin, *The Nazi Doctors and the Nuremberg Code.*

Braun, Wernher von (1912–1977). Rocket engineer and leading German scientist. He worked on the V-2 rocket, was a **Nazi Party** member and an honorary **SS** officer. Von Braun personally searched for skilled workers at **Buchenwald**; this undertaking exploited **concentration camp** labor leading to the death of 10,000 to 20,000 inmates. The scientist was arrested by the SS in March 1944 and briefly interned for ''defeatist'' remarks. He was brought to America as part of **Project Paperclip**. (See also **Dora-Nordhausen, General Walter Dornberger, Hans Kammler, Mittelbau-Mittelwerk**, and **Arthur Rudolph**.)

SUGGESTED READINGS: Hunt, *Secret Agenda*; Michel, *Dora*; Neufeld, *The Rocket and the Reich.*

Brausebad (G., shower bath). Euphemism frequently used for **gas chambers**, at **Dachau**.

Breendonck. Fortress south of Antwerp and the main Belgian **internment camp**. Jews were **transported** from this site to **Mechelen transit camp** and from there to extermination camps. From 1942, non-Jewish underground inmates formed the majority. The camp is now a museum and memorial.

SUGGESTED READING: United States Holocaust Memorial Museum, *Historical Atlas of the Holocaust.*

Bricha (H., ''flight'' or ''escape''). Movement of 250,000 Jewish **Holocaust** survivors (1944–1948), mostly Eastern European, from **DP camps** in Western Europe and on to Jewish settlements in **Palestine (Yishuv)**. The term applies to the organization and mass movement. Bricha was greatly helped by the **Jewish Brigade-Infantry** and emissaries of the **Haganah** and **Aliya Bet**. Due to the British **White Paper**, Bricha was forced to operate clandestinely. (See also **Yitzhak Arad, Yehuda Arazi, Shaul Avigur, Haika Grossman, Abba Kovner, Zivia Lubetkin, Jan Masaryk, Abraham Polonski, Rescue Committee of the Jewish Agency in Turkey**, and **Yitzhak Zuckerman**.)

SUGGESTED READINGS: Bauer, *Flight and Rescue: Bricha*; Szule, *The Secret Alliance.*

Brigadefuehrer. SS major general.

British Foreign Office. Along with the BBC, it refused to broadcast in **Yiddish** to occupied **Poland**. This department consistently suppressed news about the **Holocaust** during the war and insisted that reports of mass extermination were exaggerated. (See also *Struma* and **SWIT**.)

British Mandate. After World War I, the British were given a charge by the **League of Nations** to govern territory belonging to the former Ottoman Empire. **Palestine**, which included present-day Jordan, was to be the Jewish national homeland. The purpose of the mandate—to bring about a self-governing Jewish homeland—was betrayed by the British in May 1939, that is, the **White Paper**, to appease the Arabs in preparation for war with **Germany** and **Italy**. Immigration was reduced to a trickle, and the Jewish national home plan was abandoned in favor of an Arab State. This betrayal entrapped the Jews of Europe who now had no place to escape. (See also **Appeasement, Balfour Declaration, Menachem Begin, Neville Chamberlain, Abraham Stern**, and **Josiah Clement Wedgwood**.)
    SUGGESTED READINGS: Bell, *Terror Out of Zion*; Gilbert, *Exile and Return*.

"Brown Shirts." **SA** uniform, which consisted of inexpensive, leftover shirts from the German African colonies; hence, the term became the popular name for the **Sturmabteilung** or Stormtroppers.

"Brown Sisters." German women charged with identifying racially qualified Polish children to be abducted and taken to **Germany**. (See also **Lebensborn**.)

Brundridge, Avery (1887–1975). Head of the U.S. Olympic Committee. He was sympathetic to the Nazi cause and successfully fought for American participation in the 1936 **Berlin** Olympics. Brundridge insisted the boycott lobby was led by Jewish "special interests." His efforts were instrumental in getting American participation in the Berlin Olympics.
    SUGGESTED READING: Herzstein, *Roosevelt and Hitler*.

Brunner, Alois (b. 1912). **SS** major and **Eichmann's** assistant. He was appointed head of the **Reich Central Office for Jewish Immigration** in **Vienna** in 1938. Brunner was responsible for organizing the **deportation** of 47,000 Viennese Jews to the East from October 1939–1942. He organized the deportation of 44,000 Jews from **Salonika** to **Auschwitz** from March to June 1943. As head of **Drancy**, Brunner deported 23,500 Jews from **France** to Auschwitz, **Bergen-Belsen**, and **Buchenwald**. At the end of the war, he moved to **Slovakia** and deported an additional 14,500 Jews through March 1945. Eichmann called Brunner "one of my best." A proud and defiant Nazi, he lived in exile in Syria. Brunner is now believed to be in South America. The German government has offered a $338,000 reward for information leading to his arrest. (See also **Nice, Franz Rademacher**, and **Heinz Rothke**.)

SUGGESTED READINGS: Frieder, *To Deliver Their Souls*; Simpson, *Blowback*.

Brunner, Anton (d. 1946). **Obergruppenfuehrer** (general) for Jewish matters. Cruel and sadistic head of the **Gestapo** in **Vienna**, Brunner was involved with the first **deportations** to **Terezin**. He was hanged in May 1946 as a **war criminal** in the Russian Sector by the Vienna People's Court.

SUGGESTED READING: Hilberg, *The Destruction of European Jews*.

Brunner, Emil. Swiss Protestant leader. Along with **Karl Barth**, he publicized reports of the **Holocaust** in **Switzerland**. (See also **Auschwitz Protocols**.)

Brzezinka (P., Polish Village). Village razed by the Nazis to make room for **Birkenau**.

Buber, Martin (1878–1965). Austrian-born German Jewish theologian and philosopher. He was the central figure in establishing the Jewish Center for Adult Education (1934) and providing education to Jewish children after they were expelled from public schools. An ardent **Zionist**, Buber fled to **Palestine** in 1938. (See also **Otto Hirsch**.)

SUGGESTED READINGS: Friedman, *Martin Buber's Life and Work*; Levin, *The Holocaust: The Destruction of European Jewry, 1933–1945*.

Buch, Walter (1883–1949). Chief Justice of the Supreme Party Court in Nazi **Germany**. Buch was involved in the **Night of the Long Knives** and was **Martin Bormann's** father-in-law. He committed suicide at an **Allied internment camp** while awaiting trial.

SUGGESTED READING: Hilberg, *The Destruction of European Jews*.

Buchenwald. It was one of the first major **concentration camps**. Located outside of **Weimar**, in central **Germany**, near the graves of Goethe and Schiller. Former French Prime Minister Leon Blum was interned at this site, and 10,000 Jewish men were imprisoned there following **Kristallnacht**. This camp opened on July 15, 1937, and was designed to hold up to 120,000 inmates. Until 1943, most of the population were German criminals, but as political prisoners and Jews outpaced Germans, two bottom castes were created: **homosexuals** and Jews. A smaller camp was set aside for children. Subcamps included **Dora-Nordhausen** and **Ohrdruf**. Some **Soviet POWs** were identified by a tattoo on the chest. This camp supplied **slave labor** to **BRABAG, Krupp Works, I. G. Farben, Junkers, Siemens**, Reg, **Rheinmetall**, and other German companies. Many of these companies tested vaccines, diseases, chemicals, and weapons on inmates; most of whom died. **Typhus** experiments were carried out in Ward 46 under the aegis of **Dr. Erwin Ding-Schuler** and **Dr. Waldemar Hoven**. Inmates were executed by injection in Block 61. **Dr. Carl Vaernet** (Carl Peter Jensen) conducted hormone experiments on homosexuals.

Of the 238,980 inmates interned at the camp, 56,545 perished. The **death march** took place from April 6–10, 1945. This site was liberated by the Americans on April 11, 1945. German villagers were forced to walk through the camp after **liberation**. (See also **Wernher von Braun, Alois Brunner, CROW-CASS, Ebensee, Hans Kammler, J. A. Topf und Joehne, Ilse Koch, Karl Koch, Eugene Kogon, Kugel, Arthur Roedl**, and **Roma**.)

SUGGESTED READINGS: Hackett, *The Buchenwald Report*; Kogon, *The Theory and Practice of Hell*; United States Holocaust Memorial Museum, *Darkness before Dawn*; United States Holocaust Memorial Museum, *1945, The Year of Liberation*.

Budapest March of Death. Beginning on November 8, 1944, and lasting to December 29, 1944; about 70,000 Jews were gathered by the **SS** in Budapest and marched toward the Austrian border accompanied by the **Arrow Cross**. The Jews walked 30 km per day and approximately 5,000 died before reaching **Austria**. (See also **Raoul Wallenberg**.)

SUGGESTED READING: Braham, *The Politics of Genocide*.

Budapest Rescue Committee. (See **Relief and Rescue Committee of Budapest**).

Bukovina. Northern province of **Romania**, south of **Bessarabia**, and north of **Hungary**. Once a part of the Austro-Hungarian Empire, many of its citizens spoke German as a mother tongue, particularly in **Czernowitz (Cernauti)**, its principal city with a Jewish population of 47,932. In 1940, the **Soviets** occupied the area, closed Jewish institutions, and exiled so-called "capitalist" Jews. In the summer of 1941, the province was overrun by joint Romanian-German forces. Jews were uprooted from 100 communities and forced on a **death march** to **Transnistria**. In less than one year, more than 120,000 died. (See also **Traiah Popovici**.)

SUGGESTED READING: Fischer, *Transnistria*.

Bulgaria. Balkan country bordered by **Romania** and **Yugoslavia** in the north, **Greece** and Turkey in the south, and the Black Sea on the east coast. It was allied with **Germany** during World War II. The nation was the home of 50,000 **Sephardic** Jews, 10 percent of the population. In Sophia, Christian workers marched in the streets to denounce anti-Jewish edicts. Although Jews in Bulgaria proper were not persecuted, a joint effort by the clergy, monarchy, and parliament frustrated the **deportation** attempts of the **SS**. Protests by King Cyril and the papal **nuncio** in Turkey and **Angelo Roncalli** (Pope John XXIII) and the Bulgarian Orthodox church resulted in the Bulgarian Parliament voting unanimously against deportation. However, 11,384 Jews from **Thrace** and **Macedo-**

nia were rounded up and sent to **Treblinka**. Fourteen percent of Bulgaria's 50,000 Jews died in the **Holocaust**.

SUGGESTED READING: Chary, *The Bulgarian Jews and the Final Solution, 1940–1944.*

Buna (G., synthetic rubber; literally a contraction of Butadien and Natrium, two essential ingredients in synthetic rubber). Established in 1941 by **I. G. Farben**, this factory near **Auschwitz** utilized **slave labor** from their own camp called **Monowice**. This term, and Auschwitz III, applies to the camp.

SUGGESTED READING: Borkin, *The Crime and Punishment of I. G. Farben.*

Bund (G., organization). Non-**Zionist**, Jewish socialist organization mainly active in **Poland**. It cared for at least 2,000 Jews in the Warsaw area. It was a union and Jewish cultural organization. It believed in building Jewish culture within nations where Jews resided. The Bund underground first reported the **Final Solution** to the **Polish Government-in-Exile**. It joined the **ZOB** and fought in the **Warsaw Ghetto Uprising**. (See also **Abraham Blum, Dr. Marek Edelman, Leon Feiner, Jewish National Committee (ZKN), Vitebsk, Zegota**, and **Schmuel Artur Zygielbojm**.)

SUGGESTED READINGS: Dawidowicz, *The War Against the Jews, 1933–1945*; Levin, *While the Messiah Tarried.*

Bund deutscher Maedel (BdM) (G., **League of German Girls**). Paralleled male **Hitler Youth**. This organization, formed in 1930, indoctrinated girls ages 14–17 with Nazi racial policies. The League's main mission, as prescribed by the Nazis, was to procreate for the **Reich**. Their slogan was, "Your Body Belongs to Your Nation," and they were expected to perform one year of labor on a farm or domestic setting. In 1937, **Baldur von Schirach** created **Glaube und Schoenheit**, an extension of BdM for mature girls when they turned 17. (See also **Frauenschaft, Jungmaedel, Jungvolk**, and **Reich Labor Service**.)

SUGGESTED READINGS: Koch, *Hitler Youth*; Owings, *Frauen.*

Bunker. Underground room or cellar area set aside for **ghetto** fighters during the **Warsaw Ghetto Uprising**. (See also **Melina**.)

Burger, Anton (b. 1911). Former Austrian schoolteacher and commandant at **Theresienstadt**, fate unknown.

SUGGESTED READING: Troller, *Theresienstadt.*

Burkhardt, Carl Jacob (1891–1974). Vice-chairman of the International Committee of the **Red Cross** stationed in Geneva. He confirmed the **Riegner** cable in November 1942. Burkhardt negotiated with **Walter Schellenberg** late in the war to release Jewish inmates from **concentration camps**. (See also **Count Folke Bernadotte** and **Jean-Marie Musy**.)

SUGGESTED READING: Reitlinger, *The Final Solution.*

"Burned." To have one's contraband confiscated; to be denounced; to have a "safe" house exposed.

"Butcher of Lyon." (See **Klaus Barbie**.)

Bydgoszcz Affair. Fictitious prewar event in **Warthegau** created by Nazi propaganda in which Jews and Poles **collaborated** in the murder of 60,000 Germans.

Byelorussia (Ro.). (See **Belorussia**.)

C

Camoufles (F., snub). French Jews who hid as gentiles with the help of false papers. These people were aided by clandestine organizations across the Alps to **Switzerland** and across the Pyrenees to **Spain**.

Camp Brigade. (See **Aussenkommando**.)

Camp "Families." Close, intimate support groups maintained by some **concentration camp** inmates. These nonblood related bonds proved essential for survival.

Camp Orchestra. Inmates at **concentration camps** who performed music for the **Aussenkommandos**. Sometimes the orchestra played when gassing took place or an inmate was executed. (See also "**Death Tango**.")

Canada I and II (G., **Kanada**). Area of **Birkenau** where the worldly goods of arriving **deportees** were stored. This was a favorable work detail for securing food. It was named after the "vast" and "wealthy" nation. (See also **Mexico**.)

Canaris, Admiral Wilhelm (1887–1945). Intelligence chief and head of the **Abwehr** (1934–1944). He gradually became disenchanted with **National Socialism** and the drift toward war in 1938. He opposed **Hitler** and plotted against the regime. The admiral protected anti-Nazi **resisters** by giving them positions in the Abwehr, for example, **Dietrich Bonhoeffer**, and used **Confessional Church** members as couriers. Canaris was hanged slowly by a piano-wire noose in **Flossenbuerg** on April 9, 1945. (See also **Hans von Dohnany** and **July 20, 1944 Bomb Plot**.)

SUGGESTED READINGS: Gill, *An Honorable Defeat*; Manvell and Heinrich, *The Canaris Conspiracy.*

"Canteen." Clandestine Jewish school in the **Warsaw Ghetto**. (See also **Komplets** and **Tarbut**.)

Carbon Monoxide. Gas used for murdering mental patients in the **T-4** program. Jews were first gassed in sealed vans (**"Sonderwagons"**) at **Chelmno** using carbon monoxide. Later, carbon monoxide fumes were used at **Belzec, Treblinka**, and **Sobibor**. At **Birkenau**, the use of **Zyklon-B** was introduced under the direction of Kommandant **Rudolf Hoess**.

Caritas. Catholic charities; a Catholic social aid organization formed first in **Germany** to help non-**Aryan** (mainly converted Jews) Christians. An important leader in Germany in the Nazi period was **Dr. Gertrud Lueknor**. The Czech Caritas sheltered Jewish children in hostels and orphanages.
SUGGESTED READINGS: Block and Drucker, *Rescuers*; Friedman, *Their Brothers' Keepers.*

Casablanca Conference. Meeting held January 14–23, 1943, between President **Franklin Delano Roosevelt**, Prime Minister **Winston Churchill**, French Generals **Charles de Gaulle**, Giraud, and Nogu (**Vichy's** Resident General of **Morocco**.) The principle of total, unconditional surrender was promulgated at Casablanca. North African Jews were disappointed that restrictive racial laws were not abrogated. President Roosevelt accepted the principle of **Numerus Clausus** and proposed that "the number of Jews engaged in the practice of professions . . . should be definitely limited to the percentage that the Jewish population bears to the whole North African population." In October 1943, de Gaulle rescinded anti-Jewish legislation. (See also **Tripartite Conference**.)
SUGGESTED READING: Wyman, *The Abandonment of the Jews.*

"Catcher" (G., **Greifer**). Jews who **collaborated** with the **Gestapo** to denounce fellow Jews in hiding. This system was most effectively exploited in **Berlin**. (See also **"Submarine."**)
SUGGESTED READING: Wyden, *Stella.*

Cattle Cars. (See **Freight Cars**.)

Celler, Emanuel (1888–1981). Jewish congressman from New York. He sought liberalization of U.S. immigration laws during the 1930s to 1940s, particularly to admit Jewish **refugees**. Mainstream Jewish organizations gave his proposals very little support. The bills died in the House of Representatives. (See also

American Jewish Committee, American Jewish Congress, Samuel Dickstein, and **Breckinridge Long**.)

SUGGESTED READING: Medoff, *The Deafening Silence.*

CENTOS. (See **Central Agency for Care of Orphans**.)

Central Agency for Care of Orphans (CENTOS). Jewish children's welfare organization in **Poland** headed by **Adolf Abraham Berman**. This organization operated thirty orphanages and boarding homes in Warsaw and was involved with providing food for the needy. It was criticized by **Emmanuel Ringelblum** for failing to use its resources to aid street children in the **Warsaw Ghetto**. (See also **Jewish Self-Help Society, Janusz Korczak, Krakow**, and **ORT**.)

SUGGESTED READING: Tomaszewski and Werbowski, *Zegota.*

Central Council Law Number 10. Promulgated on December 20, 1945, by the United States, Britain, **France**, and the **Soviet Union**. It established the principle of **crimes against humanity**, which were distinctly different from crimes against peace and **war crimes**. It extended the indictments to include the entire Nazi era, 1933–1945, and it empowered each **Allied** nation to hold military and civilian trials of violators. The International Military Tribunal charter limited indictments relating to crimes against humanity to those committed after September 1, 1939, when the war in Europe began. During these trials, acts of cruelty and annihilation of Jews were used as evidence of criminality. (See also **Allied Control Council Law Number 10** and **London Charter Conference**.)

SUGGESTED READING: Annas and Grodin, *The Nazi Doctors and the Nuremberg Code.*

Central Museum of the Extinguished Jewish Race. The Nazis gathered religious artifacts and placed them in the Pincus Synagogue in Prague in August 1942. Jews cooperated with the project hoping to save the sacred objects. The Nazi motive for such a collection was based on their erroneous belief that they would win the war and annihilate all the Jews. Hence, they called the collection ''the artifacts of the extinct Jewish race.'' The religious pieces have been distributed among a number of synagogues.

Central Planning Board. Created in 1942 to help coordinate and alleviate labor shortages in **Germany**. Officially under the command of **Hermann Goering** (who quickly lost interest), **Albert Speer** took control of the Board.

Central Registry of War Criminals and Security Suspects (CROWCASS). This agency effectively located thousands of **war criminals**, especially those who committed atrocities at **Buchenwald, Dachau**, and **Mauthausen**. Established in Paris on April 14, 1945, by the **Supreme Headquarters Allied Ex-**

peditionary Forces, it was also used to recruit former Nazis as intelligence agents for the Counter Intelligence Corps until its closing in 1948.
SUGGESTED READING: Simpson, *Blowback.*

Cernauti (Ro.). (See **Czernowitz**.)

Chalutz(im). (See **He-Halutz**.)

Chamberlain, Houston Stewart (1855–1927). British **anti-Semite**, who authored *The Foundations of the Nineteenth Century*. He married one of **Richard Wagner's** daughters and became a German citizen. Chamberlain's racist writings contained ideas that greatly influenced **Hitler**, that is, race war between **Aryans** and Jews and the glorification of Germanic history at the expense of other nationalities. (See also **Guido von List, Lance von Liebenfels**, and **Voelkerchaos**.)
SUGGESTED READINGS: Mosse, *Toward the Final Solution*; Snyder, *Encyclopedia of the Third Reich.*

Chamberlain, Neville (1869–1940). Prime minister of Britain from 1937 to May 10, 1940. Under his **appeasement** policy, **Czechoslovakia** was dismembered at the **Munich** Conference held in September 1938. The policy was extended to the Arabs in **Palestine** and led to the **White Paper** in 1939.
SUGGESTED READING: Weitz, *Hitler's Diplomat.*

Le Chambon-sur-Lignon. Small French farming town 40 miles south of **Vichy**, 200 miles west of the **Switzerland** border, composed mostly of 5,000 Huguenot descendants. The townspeople and the network of surrounding farms, hamlets, and parishes took **refugees** from the Spanish Civil War, freedom fighters during World War II, and thousands of Jews. The people of Le Chambon, acting on their own initiative and led by Pastor **Andre Trocme**, hid, smuggled, and saved 5,000 Jews between 1940–1945. "Old Testament" was the coded reference for Jews. Thirty-five area residents have been recognized as **Righteous Gentiles** at **Yad Vashem**. (See also **CIMADE**.)
SUGGESTED READING: Hallie, *Lest Innocent Blood Be Shed.*

Channel Islands. British islands off the coast of **France**. This was the only portion of Great Britain occupied by **Germany**. On Jersey, Jews were registered, banned from holding certain jobs, and their property was expropriated. On Aldernay, approximately 1,000 Jews were conscripted to work for the **Todt Organization**. The location and the number of Jews **deported** to the continent is unknown, but at least three Jewish women deported from Gurnsey to **Auschwitz** were murdered. On August 15, 1943, about 1,000 French Jews (mostly Polish born) were deported to Aldernay where hundreds perished. In addition, several

hundred intermarried French Jews interned at **Drancy** were taken to this island chain for **slave labor**. (See also **Isle of Man**.)
SUGGESTED READING: Briggs, *The Channel Islands*.

Chaver (H., friend, comrade). A frequent greeting to a fellow **Zionist** or Jewish **Bund** member.

Chelmno (P.), **Kulmhof** (G.). Extermination camp geographically isolated in central **Poland**. Of the 250,000 victims murdered at Chelmno, 99 percent were Jews (primarily from **Warthegau**) and 5,000 were **Lalleri (Gypsies.)** The first of five Polish killing centers, Chelmno utilized **carbon monoxide** from "**Sonderwagon**" motor exhaust to murder their victims. Chelmno was operational on December 8, 1941, temporarily closed in the fall of 1942, but resumed gassings from May to August 1944. This site was razed by the Nazis on January 17–18, 1945. (See also **Aktion 1005, Hans Bothmann, Death camps, Artur Greiser, Walter Rauff**, and **Saurer**.)
SUGGESTED READING: Feig, *Hitler's Death Camps*.

Chernovtsy (Ru.). (See **Czernowitz**.)

Chetniks. Diverse group of irregular, pro-Royalist Serbian paramilitary forces under the leadership of General Draja Mikajlovic. They **resisted** German occupation but became preoccupied with anticommunism so much so that the Chetniks **collaborated** with the Germans against **Marshal Tito's partisans**. The Chetniks fought the Italians and **Ustashi**.
SUGGESTED READING: Hehn, *The German Struggle in World War II*.

Christian Friendship. (See **Alexandre Glasberg**.)

King Christian X (1870–1947). Danish monarch. He refused to institutionalize anti-Jewish decrees sponsored by the Nazis (such as the **Yellow Badge**). The king became the symbol of national **resistance** to Nazi occupation and inspired the Danish people to aid Jews.
SUGGESTED READINGS: Flender, *Rescue in Denmark*; Yahil, *The Rescue of Danish Jewry*.

Churban (Y., destruction). Term applied to the destruction of the two ancient temples in antiquity. This term was frequently used after the war to refer to the **Holocaust**. (See also **Porraimos** and **Shoah**.)

Churchill, Winston (1874–1965). British prime minister from May 1940 to July 1945. He foresaw the dangers of **Hitler** and **appeasement** in the 1930s and led his nation against the Nazis. Churchill was sympathetic to **Zionist** aspirations, but placed British imperialist interests above all else, refusing to ease immigration restrictions for Jews to enter **Palestine**. (See also **Casablanca Conference, Lord Moyne, Stern Group, Tripartite Conference**, and **Yalta Conference**.)

SUGGESTED READINGS: Cohen, *Churchill and the Jews*; Wasserstein, *Britain and the Jews of Europe, 1939–1945*.

CIMADE (F., Comite inter-mouvements auproge des evacues, Intermovement Committee for Refugees.) Rescue and relief group started in 1936 to help displaced French Alascians relieve suffering in **internment camps**. This French clandestine organization was involved in volunteer work in internment camps and the rescue of Jews in **Le Chambon-sur-Lignon**. Madeleine Barot, a Protestant social worker, hid Jews in the family residence. Eduard Theis served as a guide who escorted **refugees** to **Switzerland**. He was involved in Le Chambon, hid refugees, and allowed social workers in **Vichy** camps. Madame Eyraud ran one of the most dangerous and largest safe houses. Her **partisans** were important figures in the **resistance**. (See also **French Internment and Transit Camps**.)

SUGGESTED READING: Block and Drucker, *Rescuers*.

CIO (Congress of Industrial Organizations). Along with the **AFL**, the CIO endorsed Jewish organizations' appeals for rescue. (See also **AFL**.)

Circle of Friends of Himmler. Group of influential businessmen including **I. G. Farben, Siemens**, and **Rheinmetall** executives, as well as **Friedrich Flick**. They met on the second Wednesday of every month from 1933–1945. The group extended financial support to Himmler, exchanged "ideas" and worked cooperatively with the **RSHA** and **WVHA Hauptamt**, and solicited for **slave labor**.

SUGGESTED READINGS: Ferencz, *Less Than Slaves*; Lumsden, *The Black Corps*; Ruerup, *Topography of Terror*.

Class I, II, or III Concentration Camps. On August 19, 1941, **Reinhard Heydrich** issued an edict classifying concentration camps by severity of harshness. Class I was designated as a **labor camp**, for example, **Dachau**; Class II a hard labor camp, for example, **Plaszow** or **Dora-Nordhausen**; Class III was a **death camp**, for example, **Auschwitz-Birkenau**. A camp's classification did not necessarily restrict or define its role. **Mauthausen** was classified as Class III, a hard labor camp with an extremely high death rate.

Clauberg, Dr. Carl (1898–1957). **SS** obstetrics physician. He began performing sterilizations on women in 1934. Clauberg was notorious for conducting sterilizations at **Auschwitz** (including X-rays) and **Ravensbrueck**, but never perfected any of the sterilization methods he initiated. Clauberg died in 1957 while awaiting trial. (See also **Block 10** and **Dr. Horst Schumann**.)

SUGGESTED READINGS: Kater, *Doctors Under Hitler*; Lifton, *The Nazi Doctors*.

Clay, General Lucius D. (1898–1978). Deputy military governor from 1945–1947. He was military governor of Germany from 1947–1949. The general denied **Pope Pius XII's** plea for mercy of Nazi **war criminals**. (Clay only lifted the death sentence for **Ilse Koch**.) He transferred **denazification** functions to the German government, but expressed disappointment with the progress they made. (See also **John McCloy**).

SUGGESTED READINGS: Bird, The Chairman; Smith, Lucius D. Clay: An American Life.

Clemency Act of 1951. **John McCloy**, who succeeded **General Lucius D. Clay** as United States High Commissioner for **Germany**, succumbed to cold war politics and German political and religious pressure regarding the treatment of high-ranking Nazi war criminals. He commuted the death sentences of twelve out of twenty-five convicted Nazi war criminals. McCloy also reduced the sentences and released numerous Nazis complicit in **war crimes, crimes against humanity** and/or **genocide**. Most of the Nazi war criminals resumed their professional careers or retired and were entitled to pensions from the West German government. (See also **August Frank**, **Dr. Franz W. Six**, and **Edmund Veesenmayer**.)

SUGGESTED READING: Bird, The Chairman.

Collaboration. Cooperation between citizens of an occupied country and the Germans. Economic collaborators did business for the Nazis; administrative collaborators, such as civil servants and police, carried out anti-Jewish laws; and military collaborators included those who volunteered for **concentration camp**, military, or police duty. (See also **Vidkum Quisling**.)

Collection Camp. Camps in **Vichy**, for example, **Gurs**, run by French police. Inmates were held at these camps and then sent to **distribution centers** in the north of **France**, for example, **Drancy**. Approximately 3,000 Jews died in French collection and distribution camps.

Collective Responsibility. The Nazis imposed harsh retribution upon Jews and gentiles under their control for a single act of **resistance**. An act of sabotage in a factory could bring death to all workers. Escape by an inmate could lead to execution of members of his unit, family, or victims picked randomly. Resistance by **partisans** could bring death to hundreds inside **ghettos**. (See also **Ardeantine Caves, Kristallnacht**, and **Partisan Order**.)

Comite de Defense des Juifs (CDJ) (F., Committee for the Defense of the Jews). Belgian aid organization. The CDJ was founded by Gerts Jospa, with his wife Yvonne, to aid the 57,000 Belgian Jews under German occupation in 1940. The two became key figures in Jewish **resistance**. This organization helped by providing false **Aryan** papers and money for hiding. It saved 3,000 Jewish children aided by the general resistance group, Front Independence. The Front had burned all lists of Jews. CDJ also had the cooperation of the non-Nazi Belgian state officials and the church. (See also **Association of Jews of Belgium.**)

Comite Representatit des Israelites de France (F., Committee Representing Jews of France). French organization founded in Lyon in 1943 to represent principal Jewish institutions.

Commissar Order (G., **Kommissarbefehr**). Decree issued by **Hitler** on June 6, 1941, prior to **Operation Barbarossa**. All **Soviet** Commissar soldiers captured were to be summarily executed. This Order was often interpreted to include Jews since they were "carriers of Bolshevism." This was considered a **war crime**, in direct violation of the **Hague** and **Geneva Conventions**. This order facilitated the complicity of the **Wehrmacht** in Nazi crimes. (See also **Alfred Jodl, Wilhelm Keitel, Oberkommando der Wehrmacht**, and **Partisan Order.**)
    SUGGESTED READINGS: Bartov, *Hitler's Army*; Conot, *Justice at Nuremberg*.

Committee of Children of Deportees. French organization involved in pursuing French **collaborationists**, for example, **Klaus Barbie, Rene Bousquet, Jean Leguay**, and **Paul Touvier**, and bringing them to justice. (See also **Serge and Beate Klarsfeld.**)

Compiegne. Town in northern **France** where the French surrendered to the Germans in June 1940. This was the same site where the Germans surrendered to the French in World War I. It later became an assembly center and **transit camp** where 12,000 Jews were **deported** to **Buchenwald** and **Dachau**. The camp held French and Jewish political prisoners as **hostages**.

Concentration Camps. Despite the differing designations—**Class I, II** and **III**—most camps were primarily **labor**, holding, or **transit** centers. In some instances, that is, **Operation Heydrich**, concentration camps served only to kill Jews and are listed under a separate category: **death camp (Vernichtungslager)**. Due to the prevalent starvation type of diet, brutality, lack of sanitation and proper medical care, most inmates died after three months. The **SS** operated 1,800 concentration camps throughout Europe. (See also **Class I, II** or **III Concentration Camps.**)

Concentration Camp Uprisings. Inmate revolts took place at **Treblinka, Sobibor**, and **Birkenau**. The uprising at **death camp** Treblinka against Ukrainian guards and Germans occurred on August 2, 1943. Of the 600 **deportees** who rebelled, several dozen escaped. This revolt hastened Treblinka's demise. A well-prepared uprising took place in Sobibor on October 14, 1943. Ten **SS** officers were killed, but most of the rebels were murdered and some of the escapees joined **partisans**. The uprising at Birkenau took place from October 6–7, 1944. It was led by a **Sonderkommando** in charge of cremating corpses and several SS guards were killed. All of the participants were killed. The rebellion, particularly the blowing up of a **crematoria**, was made possible by female prisoners working at an ammunition works, most notably **Roza Robota**. (See also **Resistance**.)

SUGGESTED READING: Suhl, *They Fought Back.*

Concordat (Latin, agreement). Diplomatic accord between the **Vatican** and foreign governments. **Pope Pius XI** signed one in 1929 with **Italy**, and Nazi **Germany** signed a treaty July 20, 1933. German Vice-Chancellor **Franz von Papen** and Vatican Secretary of State **Cardinal Eugenio Pacelli** settled the rights and responsibilities of the Catholic Church in relation to the Nazi regime. The Church was guaranteed freedom of religion and the right to administer its own affairs and church property. No sooner was the ink dry, when the Nazis began a campaign to undermine the authority of the Church and terrorize Catholic parents into sending their children to state schools and youth organizations. (See also **Hitler Youth, Bishop Alois Hudal**, and **Bonito Mussolini**.)

SUGGESTED READINGS: Lewy, *The Catholic Church and Nazi Germany*; Rhodes, *The Vatican in the Age of Dictators.*

Conducator (Ro., Leader). **Ion Antonescu's** title.

Conference on Jewish Material Claims. International aid agency founded in 1951. Headed by **Nahum Goldmann**, it sought laws by the German government to secure funds for relief rehabilitation and resettlement of Jewish victims of Nazism. It also has sponsored educational, welfare, youth, and medical institutions. (See also **Luxembourg Agreement** and **Reparations and Restitution**.

SUGGESTED READINGS: Ferencz, *Less Than Slaves*; Goldmann, *The Jewish Paradox.*

Confessional or Confessing Church (G., **Bekenntniskirche**). Composed of traditional Protestants, it broke with the Protestant Evangelical Church because it refused to accept the primacy of the Nazi state over the church, racial superiority, and the **Aryan Paragraph**. In 1934, the Confessional Church, composed of Lutheran and Reform members, issued the Barman Declaration (which was the confession) accusing the Nazi government of idolatry. While attacking racial concepts, it did not protest formally against Nazi **anti-Semitic** policies. (See also **Karl Barth, Dietrich Bonhoeffer, Admiral Wilhelm Canaris, Kurt Gerstein, Dr. Heinrich Grueber, Ludwig Mueller, Pastor Martin Niemoeller**, and **Reichkirsche**.)

SUGGESTED READINGS: Bergen, *The German Christian Movement in the Third Reich*; Littell, *The Crucifixion of the Jews.*

Consistoire (F., consistory). **Jewish Council** in **Luxembourg**. The Council was well organized and provided relief to Jews, but dutifully implemented German decrees. (See also **Judenrat**.)

Conti, Dr. Leonardo (1900–1945). Chief physician of the **Reich** and **SS** major general. He was intimately involved in the **euthanasia** program, "medical experiments" at **concentration camps**, and racial **genocide**. He advocated murder by gassing. Conti joined the **SA** in 1923, the **Nazi Party** in 1927, and in 1939, succeeded **Dr. Gerhart Wagner**. His power and influence diminished as **Dr. Karl Brandt's** clout over **Hitler** increased. Arrested by the Americans in May 1945, Conti committed suicide in his prison cell at **Nuremberg**. (See also **Alter Kaempfer, 14 f 13, Dr. Ernst Schenck**, and **Dr. Claus Schilling**.)
SUGGESTED READINGS: Kater, *Doctors Under Hitler*; Proctor, *Racial Hygiene*.

Coordination. (See **Gleichschaltung**.)

Corfu. **Greek** island which included 2,000 Jews, initially under Italian rule during the war. The Germans occupied Corfu in September 1943, and most of the island's Jews were murdered at **Auschwitz**. Two hundred Jews returned after the war.
SUGGESTED READING: Novitch, *The Passage of the Barbarians*.

Coughlin, Reverend Charles E. Roman (1891–1979). Roman Catholic priest. An influential American radio broadcaster, Coughlin aired **anti-Semitic** speeches to a weekly audience of approximately 16 million listeners during his program "The Golden Hour of the Shrine of the Little Flower." He secretly supported the Nazis and openly endorsed **Francisco Franco, Benito Mussolini**, and **Pierre Laval**. Coughlin was involved in the formation of the anti-Semitic, paramilitary Christian Front. Coughlin urged the Front's members to attack Jewish Americans. Father Coughlin created the National Union for Social Justice in 1934 and began publishing a weekly newspaper, *Social Justice*, in 1936. He blamed the Jews for their persecution at the hands of the Nazis and reprinted the *Protocols of the Learned Elders of Zion* in his newspaper. Coughlin was finally forced to stop broadcasting in May 1942 or face sedition charges from Attorney General Francis B. Biddle. (See also **German-American Bund**.)
SUGGESTED READING: Warren, *Radio Priest*.

Council for Aid to Jews. (See **Zegota**.)

Council of Elders. (See **Aeltestenrat** and **Judenrat**.)

Cracow. (See **Krakow**.)

Crematorium; Cremo Building. (See **Krematorium-Kremchy**.)

Cremieux Decree. Issued for French government on October 24, 1870, by Isaac Adolph Cremieux. It conferred French citizenship on the Jews of **Algeria**. The **Vichy** government rescinded the decree in 1940. It was restored in 1943 by **General Charles de Gaulle**.

SUGGESTED READING: American Jewish Committee, *American Jewish Yearbook, Vol. 45, 1943–1944.*

CRIF. (See **Comite Representatit des Israelites de France**.)

Crimes Against Humanity. The last of three charges against the accused at the **Nuremberg Trials** and **Subsequent Nuremberg Trials** brought about by the **London Charter Conference** and **Central Council Law Number 10**. It was most relevant in relation to the **genocide** of the Jews by the Nazis and encompassed enslavement, extermination, **deportation**, and maltreatment not directly connected to warfare. This indictment was first introduced in 1919 by the French in reference to the Ottoman (Turkish) mass murder of the Armenians. This charge was unique because it accused the defendants of crimes against their own minorities, once considered the prerogative of a sovereign state. However, the **International Military Tribunal** and other military tribunals could only prosecute criminals for actions that occurred after September 1939. (See also **Murray C. Bernays, Fuehrerbefehl, Robert Jackson**, and **United Nations Resolution, December 11, 1946**.)

SUGGESTED READING: Falk, Kolko, and Lifton, *Crimes of War.*

Croatia. Area in pre–World War II **Yugoslavia** bordering **Hungary** in the north, **Romania** and Serbia in the east and south, and a western shoreline with the Adriatic Sea. It came into existence after German armies overran Yugoslavia in April 1941 and lasted until May 1945. The satellite, pro-Nazi state, permitted by **Hitler** to dismember Yugoslavia, annexed Bosnia and Herzegovina. It had a population of 3.3 million Roman Catholic Croats, 1.9 million Greek Orthodox Serbs, 700,000 Moslems, 170,000 Germans, 75,000 Hungarians, 40,000 Jews, and 30,000 **Roma**. The **fascistic** ruling Ustasha regime under dictator **Anton Pavelic** and Interior Minister **Andrija Artukovic** instituted a genocidal campaign against the Serbs, Roma, and Jews. A number of **concentration camps** were set up, the most infamous was **Jasenovac**, where hundreds of thousands were murdered. The attack on non-Croats took the lives of 700,000 Serbs and 30,000 Jews. Under the cover of anti**partisan** actions in the summer of 1942, in the Kozara District, over 60,000 Serbs were driven into Jasenovac where they were brutally murdered. **Kurt Waldheim** was part of this effort. Eighty percent of Croatia's Jews perished. The survivors owe their lives to the protection of the Italian occupation army on the Dalmation coast, the Papal **Nuncio's** protection of Jews in mixed marriages, and partisans. In May 1945, **Tito's** partisans, along with the **Red Army**, liberated the region. (See also **Father Krunoslav Dragonovic, Hundzar, Italy, General Mario Roatta**, and **Semlin**.)

SUGGESTED READINGS: Berenbaum, *A Mosaic of Victims*; Kendall, *The Yugoslav Auschwitz*; Rhodes, *The Vatican in the Age of Dictators.*

CROWCASS. (See **Central Registry of War Criminals and Security Suspects**.)

Cukierman, Yitzhak. (See **Yitzhak Zuckerman**.)

Czechoslovakia. Before the **Munich Pact**, this central European republic was one of the most progressive and democratic in the region. It bordered on **Germany** in the west and the **Soviet Union** on the east, **Hungary** and **Austria** to the south. Czechoslovakia's population in 1930 was 14,729,538 with a Jewish population of 350,000. Once a part of the Austro-Hungarian Empire, with that kingdom's breakup after World War I in 1918, this new republic was formed. It consisted of the **Sudetenland, Bohemia-Moravia**, a small part of Silesia, **Slovakia**, and **Ruthenia**. The state contained **Slavic** people (Czechs and Slovaks) and, in Ruthenia, many Ukrainians and Hungarians. Large numbers of ethnic Germans, forming a majority, lived in the Sudetenland, the area adjacent to Germany. With the support of the victorious British, French, and Americans, **Allies** in World War I, Thomas Masaryk assumed the presidency (1918–1935). **Eduard Benes** became president after him (1935–1938). Jews were granted full civic and economic rights.

The Munich Pact doomed the Jews. In 1938 the Sudetenland was annexed to Germany. In March 1939, the **Wehrmacht** marched into the rest of Czechoslovakia. By a **Hitler** decree of March 16, 1939, the Protectorate of Bohemia-Moravia was created, meaning it was under military rule and was considered part of the **Greater Reich**. It had a prewar Jewish population of 117,551. The Prague Jewish population of 56,000 was decimated. Over 73,600 Jews from Bohemia-Moravia were **deported** to **Theresienstadt**, the **ghetto** and **concentration camp** near Prague.

On March 14, 1939, Slovakia declared itself a separate republic under **Dr. Josef Tiso**, a Catholic priest with the "protection" of Nazi Germany. Its deputy premier was **Vojtech Tuka**. Its Jewish population was 135,000. Jewish victims in Ruthenia, taken from Slovakia and given to **Hungary** in 1939, numbered 80,000–90,000 out of 102,000 Jews. They suffered the fate of Hungarian Jews in 1944. The **Red Army liberated** Czechoslovakia in May 1945, however, some units of the American army reached the borders near Pilsen. An estimated 200,000 to 300,000 Czech Jews lost their lives. (See also **Appeasement, Kurt Becher, Konrad Henlein, Hlinka Guard, Sano Mach, Heinrich Schwartz Dieter Wislicency**, and **Working Group**.)

Czerniakow, Adam (1880–1942). **Obman** (chief elder) of the **Jewish Council** in the **Warsaw Ghetto**. He committed suicide on July 23, 1942, shortly after the Nazis began **resettling** Jewish children and announced an increase in the daily resettlement **quota** from 5,000 to 7,000. Eventually, the figure peaked at

10,000 daily **deportations**. After Czerniakow's death, Marek Lichtenbojm, an engineer, became chairman. (See also **Heinz Auerswald** and **"Work as a Means of Rescue."**)

SUGGESTED READING: Tushnet, *The Pavement of Hell.*

Czernowitz (G.), Cernauti (Ro.). **Bukovina's** capital where 50,000 Jews resided or were 40 percent of the total population. Formerly part of the Austro-Hungarian Empire, it was ceded to **Romania** after World War I. The city was taken over by the **Soviet Union** in 1939. Jewish businessmen were **deported** to **Siberia**, and Jewish communal life was severely restricted. With the attack by German and Romanian troops in July 1941, it reverted back to Romania. **Einsatzgruppe** commander **Otto Ohlendorf** was headquartered in the city. Its Jewish population was deported to **concentration camps** and killing centers in **Transnistria** in October 1941 on orders from **Ion Antonescu**. Few Jews remained, or returned, after **liberation** by the **Red Army** in late 1944. (See also **Traian Popovici**.)

SUGGESTED READING: Butnaru, *The Silent Holocaust.*

D

"D" (Deutscher; German inmate.) These inmates enjoyed special privileges and usually dominated the inmate hierarchy. Nazi racial policy favoring Nordics was practiced in the **concentration camps**. German prisoners were usually distinguished by a "D" on a red or green triangle. (See also **Kapo**.)

Dachau. **Himmler's** model camp located outside Munich. It was the first major **concentration camp** to open (March 20, 1933). Dachau was initially designed to hold political opponents of the Nazis. However, 10,000 Jewish men were imprisoned at this site following **Kristallnacht**. **Theodor Eicke** oversaw the ruthless training of the **SS's Death's Head Brigade** at Dachau. The camp was constructed for 5,000 inmates, peaked at 30,000, and after 1942, there were never less than 12,000. From 1933–1945, 206,000 inmates were interned at this site including **Bruno Bettelheim** and **Pastor Martin Niemoeller**. Of the 2,771 Catholic priests incarcerated 1,770 were Polish.

About 507,000 inmates died at the site, including 6,000 **Soviet POWs** executed at the SS rifle range.

"Medical research" was conducted at Dachau, coordinated by **Dr. Sigmund Rascher** who was infamous for his high-altitude and freezing experiments. **Dr. Claus Schilling** specialized in tropical medicine, and was later executed for conducting malaria experiments. **Drs. Wilhelm Beigelboeck** and **Hans Eppinger** of the Medical Faculty of **Vienna** conducted experiments to see how long humans could survive on a seawater diet.

The **crematorium** was located in Barracks X; however, the **Brausebad (gas chambers)** was infrequently used (only experimentally) and most inmates who were gassed were sent to **Hartheim Castle** as part of **14 f 13**. Dachau was occupied by the American Army on April 29, 1945. (See also **Dr. Rudolf**

Brandt, Buchenwald, CROWCASS, J. A. Topf und Soehne, Sachsenhausen-Oranienburg, and **Martin Weiss**.)
SUGGESTED READINGS: Aziz, *Doctors of Death*; Feig, *Hitler's Death Camps*; United States Holocaust Memorial Museum, *1945: The Year of Liberation.*

DAG (G., Dynamit–**Aktion**–Gesellschaft). (See **Dynamite Nobel**.)

Daimler-Benz. German automobile company that exploited **concentration camp** labor.

Daladier, Edouard (1884–1970). French prime minister and signatory to the **Munich Pact**. As war minister under the Republic, he was arrested and charged in September 1940 for **France's** military defeat. The hypocrisy of the trial at Riom (1942) by **Vichy** officials was apparent and the proceeding was suspended. Before he was sent to **Austria** in 1943, Daladier expressed despair in his prison journal concerning the fate of French Jewry. (See also **Appeasement**.)
SUGGESTED READING: Shirer, *The Rise and Fall of the Third Reich.*

Daluege, Kurt (1887–1946). **Orpo** head and military governor. This high Nazi official was a virulent **anti-Semite** and close aide to **Heinrich Himmler** who ardently advocated the **Final Solution**. Daluege, a police general, was head of regular police (Orpo or Order Police), which included firemen, coast guard, and civilian defense forces. They comprised occupation military police. He oversaw mass executions in the **Soviet Union** in September 1941. Daluege was appointed **Reichsprotektor** of **Bohemia-Moravia** from 1942–1945 and was responsible for the massacre at **Lidice**. The **war criminal** was executed by the Czechs in 1946. (See also **Ultra**.)
SUGGESTED READING: Crankshaw, *Gestapo.*

Dannecker, Theodor (1913–1945). Attorney and **SS** officer. **Eichmann's** most efficient and zealous aide, he coordinated the **deportation** of French, Bulgarian (**Macedonia** and **Thrace**), and Italian Jewry. Dannecker committed suicide in an American prison camp in December 1945. (See also **Otto Abetz**.)
SUGGESTED READING: Adler, *The Jews of Paris.*

Danzig (G.). Polish city of Gdansk on the Baltic Sea. The port was declared free after World War I by the **Versailles Treaty**. A corridor was added attaching Danzig to **Poland** and separating East Prussia from **Germany** proper. **Kristallnacht** was especially brutal in this city even though it was delayed until November 11–12, 1938. The Nazis considered Danzig and the corridor part of **Greater Germany**. **Hitler** demanded the Danzig area be annexed to the **Reich** in 1939 claiming this would be his last demand and would thereafter keep the peace. Great Britain and **France** pledged to assist Poland if attacked by the Germans. Germany attacked Poland and quickly overran Danzig. This was the trigger for World War II in Europe. Danzig's Jewish population of approximately 10,500 was **deported** to **ghettos**. A **nebenlager** was opened in 1944, which contained 800 Jewish inmates. (See also **Artur Greiser** and **Stutthof**.)

SUGGESTED READINGS: American Jewish Committee, *American Jewish Yearbook, Vol. 41, 1939–1940*; Bethell, *The War Hitler Won.*

Darlan, Admiral Francois (1881–1942). **Vichy** proconsul. He was commander-in-chief of the French navy and head of troops in North Africa. Headquartered in Algiers he was captured by **Aboulker's** group. Darlan negotiated with Robert Murphy and agreed to a cease-fire saving the American forces from attacking **Algeria**. The admiral was assassinated December 24, 1942, by a Frenchman in Algiers. (See also **Jose Aboulker**.)

SUGGESTED READING: Hoisington, *The Casablanca Connection.*

Darnand, Joseph (d. 1945). **Vichy** official. He founded the **Milice**, a paramilitary organization on January 10, 1943. Darnand tracked down members of the **resistance** and was blamed for the poor conditions in the **internment camps** in North Africa. In January 1944, he became Vichy's minister of security. Darnand was tried and executed by the French government on October 10, 1945.

SUGGESTED READING: Morgan, *An Uncertain Hour.*

Darre, Richard Walther (1895–1953). Nazi minister of agriculture and head of the **Race and Resettlement Main Office**. He promoted **Blood and Soil**, a strong German farming community, and advocated breeding people like animals to attain a master race. Like **Heinrich Himmler**, he reasoned that too much urbanization and separation from farming was detrimental to German society. The strong peasant-farmer was an **Aryan** ideal. His ideas reinforced the **Lebensraum** concept. Darre was convicted and sentenced at the **Nuremberg Trials**, but returned to civilian life and died of natural causes. (See also **Reichsnahrstrand**.)

SUGGESTED READING: Tenenbaum, *Race and Reich.*

Daven (Y., praying). **Concentration camp** work details used the term to look busy when a **kapo** or **SS** approached.

DAW (G., German Armament Works). **SS** enterprise founded in May 1939, headquartered in **Berlin** and headed by Walter Salpeter. This organization exploited **slave labor** from **Dachau, Sachsenhausen-Oranieburg, Buchenwald, Auschwitz, Lublin, Janowska, Stutthof, Ravensbrueck**, and **Neuengamme**. Most laborers were killed by **"Destruction Through Work."**

SUGGESTED READING: Ferencz, *Less Than Slaves.*

Death Camps. Six camps built exclusively for the extermination of Jews. Three camps were constructed as part of **Operation Heydrich: Treblinka, So-**

bibor, and **Belzec. Chelmno** was the other death camp. **Auschwitz** and **Maj-danek** were camp complexes that included death camps. These killing centers placed an overwhelming majority of deportees immediately into the **gas chambers**. They are to be distinguished from the rest of the **concentration camps**, which were intended to work inmates to death. (See also **Class I, II, or III, Concentration Camps, Deportation, Odilo Globocnik**, and **Vernichtungslager**.)

SUGGESTED READINGS: Arad, *Treblinka, Sobibor, Belzec: The Operation Reinhard Death Camps*; Reitlinger, *The Final Solution.*

Death Marches. As the Eastern Front collapsed from late 1944–May 1945, the **SS** marched **concentration camp** inmates on long treks, up to several months, toward the heart of **Germany-Austria**. Of the estimated 750,000 prisoners forced to march, 250,000 died of hunger, exhaustion, privation, or were shot when they walked too slow or fell down. (See also **Death Trains**.)

SUGGESTED READING: Goldhagen, *Hitler's Willing Executioners.*

Death's Head Brigades (SS Totenkopfverbaende). **Concentration** and **death camp** guards and officers who ran the concentration camp system. This branch of the SS was the brainchild of **Theodor Eicke** who trained all potential Death's Head candidates not to show mercy or human kindness. The Brigade first saw military action in northeastern Europe in spring 1940. (See also **Dehumanization**.)

SUGGESTED READING: Sydnor, *Soldiers of Destruction.*

"Death Tango." Music the inmate **camp orchestra** played prior to execution in some **concentration camps**.

Death Trains. In the final months of the war, the Nazis sent thousands of inmates of **concentration** and **labor** camps on long train trips inside of **Germany-Austria**. Many of the trains were strafed by **Allied** gunfire and deportees were executed or wandered aimlessly for days and weeks before being abandoned or **liberated**. (See also **Death Marches** and **Deportation**.)

de Gaulle, General Charles (1890–1970). Leader of the Free French movement and the **French Forces of the Interior**. Unlike the **Vichy** government, which was **anti-Semitic**, he accepted Jews into his ranks. De Gaulle rescinded anti-Jewish laws in North Africa. His niece, Genevieve de Gaulle was imprisoned in **Ravensbrueck** during the war. (See also **Casablanca Conference** and **FTPF**.)

SUGGESTED READINGS: Rousso, *The Vichy Syndrome*; Webster, *Petain's Crime.*

DEGESCH (G., Vermin-combating Corporation). Subsidiary of **I. G. Farben**, responsible for the production of **Zyklon-B**. In 1943, the sale of Zyklon-B represented 70 percent of DEGESCH's business. The text of an invoice found after

the war reminded the Nazis that adding odors to the gas would impede exter-
mination. (See also **Bauleitung, J. A. und Soehne Topf, Hans Kammler**, and
SS.)
   SUGGESTED READING: Borkin, *The Crime and Punishment of I. G. Farben.*

Degrelle, Leon (1906–1994). Belgian **anti-Semitic** politician. He was the founder and head of the **fascist Rexist** party. He led his party into active **collaboration** with the Germans after **Belgium**'s defeat in 1940. Degrelle, and the
Waffen-SS unit he founded, fought on the Eastern Front. After the war, Degrelle
escaped to **Spain** and died in exile.
   SUGGESTED READING: Conway, *Collaboration in Belgium: Leon Degrelle and the
Rexist Movement, 1940–1944.*

Dehumanization. The Nazis tried to eliminate human individuality by cruelty
to those they considered "inferior," particularly Jews, **Roma, Soviet POWs**,
and other "enemies of the state." The **Death's Head Brigades** divested themselves of human qualities as they reduced inmates to objects in the **concentration camps**. Techniques included: calling inmates by numbers; shaving all body
hair; stripping deportees naked; and clothing inmates with ill-fitting uniforms.
This was augmented by arbitrary brutality; whippings; unconditional obedience;
sleep and food deprivation; and meaningless labor. (See also **Deportation,
Theodor Eicke, Fuenfundzwanzig am Arsch, "Going into the Wire," Jewish Spiritual Resistance, "Pieces,"** and **"Stucke."**)

Delagatura (P., Delegates' Office). This office represented the underground in
the **Polish Government-in-Exile**. It was a conduit for information from **Poland**
to London and received and transmitted data concerning German activities
against Jews. On behalf of the **ZOB**, it relayed information to the world during
the **Warsaw Ghetto Uprising**.
   SUGGESTED READING: Gutman and Krakowski, *Unequal Victims.*

DELASEM (It., Delegation to Assess Emigrants). Jewish welfare agency
founded in December 1939 to help Jewish **refugees** in **Italy**. It operated until
September 8, 1943. (See also **Abbe Marie Benoit**.)
   SUGGESTED READING: Caracciolo, *Uncertain Refuge.*

Delousing Certificate. Paper required in several **ghettos** as proof that the bearer
was free of lice. Lice were carriers of **typhus**. The certificates could be easily
bought by the wealthy who wanted to forego long lines and delousing steam
baths.

Demjanjuk, John (b. 1920). **Concentration camp** guard. He was a graduate
of **Trawniki** and a Ukrainian **SS** guard at **Flossenbuerg, Sobibor**, and **Treblinka**. He was only the second **war criminal** to be tried in Israel. (**Adolf**

Eichmann was the first.) He was released by the Israeli Supreme Court (1993) over the issue of mistaken identity, that is, "Ivan the Terrible." Currently the **Office of Special Investigations** is considering **denaturalization** and **deportation** proceedings. Demjanjuk resides in Cleveland.

SUGGESTED READINGS: Danner, "How Terrible was Ivan?"; Sereny, "John Demjanjuk and the Failure of Justice"; Simon Wiesenthal Center, *Response*.

Denaturalization. A legal procedure conducted at a U.S. immigration court against suspected Nazi **war criminals** who received their citizenship papers by lying on their naturalization papers. If found guilty, the accused is deprived of his/her citizenship and **deportation** proceedings ensue. (See also **Office of Special Investigations**.)

Denazification. Screening process to eliminate former **Nazi Party** members from responsible positions in German society by **Allied** occupation officials. This included dissolution of Nazi organizations and Nazi activity, an end of all Nazi laws, and removal of Nazi personnel from public and important private offices. Suspected individuals were rated according to their responsibility in the **Hitler** regime by levels 1, 2, and 3. Many former Nazis escaped the net and resumed important posts in West Germany. The program in general was a failure due to lack of zeal and the desire to promote **Germany** as a bulwark against communism. (See also **General Lucius D. Clay, John McCloy, Occupation Zones, Persil-Schein**, and **Yalta Conference**.)

SUGGESTED READING: Hilberg, *The Destruction of European Jews*.

Denmark. Scandinavian country, north of **Germany**, jutting into the Baltic Sea. It was occupied by the Nazis in 1940, and ruled as a "model protectorate" because the Danes were Nordic. They retained much of their autonomy and pursued a policy of negotiation with the Nazis until August 1943. From October 1 until the end of November 1943, the people of Denmark smuggled between 6,500–7,000 Jews across the Oresund Strait to **Sweden**. After November 1943, members of the Danish **resistance** also transported Jews on fishing boats to safety in Sweden. Another 400 Jews were hidden by Christian protectors. The total Jewish population of Denmark was 7,800. The clergy, especially Lutheran **Bishop H. Fugslang-Damgaard** in Copenhagen and Kai Munk (who was murdered by the Nazis), took a lead in physical and spiritual resistance. On October 3, 1943, a joint pastoral letter was read in all Danish churches demanding Danes aid Jews. As a result, very few of Denmark's Jews perished during the Nazi occupation. The entire nation is recognized as **Righteous Gentiles** at **Yad Vashem**. (See also **Dr. Werner Best, King Christian X, DNSAP, Georg Ferdinand Duckwitz, "Helsinger Sewing Club," Chief Rabbi Marcus Melchoir**, and **Schalburg Corps**.)

SUGGESTED READINGS: Goldberger, *The Rescue of Danish Jews*; Yahil, *The Rescue of Danish Jewry*.

Deportation. Forced relocation of Jews, Polish Catholics, and **Roma** from their homes to **ghettos, labor, concentration**, or **death camps**. The Nazis used the euphemism **"resettlement."** Another meaning has to do with immigration policy. The **Office of Special Investigations** has deported suspected Nazi **war criminals** after trials in immigration courts for entering the United States under false statements. The convicted criminals may be sent to their native lands or another country. (See also **Denaturalization**.)

Deppner, Erich. (b. 1910). Kommandant of **Westerbork** from summer 1942 to the fall. He instituted a harsher regime than the one implemented by the **Dutch**, but conditions were not as severe as **concentration camps** in **Germany** or the East. Deppner was dismissed from his post because of alcoholism and incompetence. He was succeeded by SS Lt. **Albert Konrad Gemmeker** during the summer of 1942. He was tried and convicted at **Nuremberg**, served some time in prison, and was released early.
SUGGESTED READING: Boas, *Boulevard des Miseres*.

DEST. (See **German Earth and Stone Works, Ltd**.)

"Destruction Through Work" (G., **Zur Vernichtung durch Arbeit**). An agreement between **Heinrich Himmler** and Minister of Justice **Otto Thierack** on September 18, 1942, stating that all Jewish inmates in regular prisons and certain non-Jewish inmates would be transferred to the **SS** to be worked to death. This policy was often opposed by the **Wehrmacht**, which wanted to use skilled Jews in military support roles. (See also **DAW, Night and Fog**, and **Vernichtungslager**.)

Deutsche Arbeitsfront (G., German Labor Organization). Founded on May 10, 1933, under the leadership of **Dr. Robert Ley**, the German Labor Front supplanted labor unions. This arm of the Nazi government comprised 20 million workers. Wages were frozen, strikes prohibited, independent unions banned, and working conditions were controlled by the government.
SUGGESTED READING: Burleigh and Wipperman, *The Racial State*.

Deutsche Ausruestungswerke/DAW (G., German Armaments Works).

Deutsche Reichsbahn (G., German State Railroad). This system and its administration played a vital role in the implementation of the **Final Solution**. The Polish **Ostbahn** was forced to assist in the destruction of European Jewry and other nations, that is, **France, Hungary**, and **Slovakia** signed cooperative rail agreements.

Initially each **transport** carried 2,000 **deportees**; however, as the war turned against the Germans, trains carried up to 5,000 Jews. The trains traveled at an average speed of 31 mph and were often sidetracked. Armed guards made escape difficult. The **freight cars** were shut tight with little or no provisions for food, water, or sanitation. The railroad, within the **Greater Reich**, charged the state for each passenger over 12, and some Jews paid for their tickets.

SUGGESTED READING: Hilberg, *The Destruction of European Jews.*

"Deutschland erwache! Juda verrecke!" (G., "Germany awake! Jews croak!") Incantation and slogan used mostly by the **SA** in anti-Jewish campaigns in the early years of Nazi rule.

Diaspora. Refers to the worldwide dispersal of Jews outside the land of Israel. (See also **Golus**.)

Dickstein, Samuel (1885–1934). Democratic U.S. representative from New York. The congressman repeatedly introduced bills to liberalize the immigration laws to admit **refugees**, but the bills did not get out of committee, nor did mainstream Jewish organizations—such as the **American Jewish Committee**, the **American Jewish Congress**, or B'nai B'rith—support these measures. (See also **Emanuel Celler**.)

SUGGESTED READING: Lookstein, *Were We Our Brothers' Keepers?*

Ding-Schuler, Dr. Erwin (d. 1945). **SS** major and deputy to **Dr. Joachim Mrugrowsky**. He conducted **typhus** experiments, killing 600 inmates at **Buchenwald** by order of the surgeon general of the **Waffen-SS**. He also performed sterilizations on inmates at **Auschwitz** and poison bullet experiments at **Sachsenhausen-Oranienburg**. Ding-Schuler committed suicide.

SUGGESTED READING: Aziz, *Doctors of Death.*

Displaced Person (DP). One who did not wish to return to his/her native land. The reasons why Jews who survived in Nazi Europe did not wish to be **repatriated** were largely these: their families and friends were annihilated; their former communities—the economic and social basis of existence—was destroyed; the continued **anti-Semitic** hostility, particularly in Eastern Europe of large sections of the population; and the fear of living under **Soviet** or communist rule. Many Jews languished in **Displaced Person camps** waiting for immigration restrictions to ease. (See also **Displaced Persons' Act, Earl Harrison, Kielce, General George S. Patton, Repatriation, Supreme Headquarters Allied Expeditionary Forces, Union of Jewish Survivors**, and **United Nations Relief and Rehabilitation Agency**.

Displaced Persons' Act. On December 22, 1945, President **Harry S. Truman** granted preferential treatment by executive order to **Displaced Persons** who wanted to emigrate to the United States. Within eighteen months 22,950 **DPs** were admitted into America (15,478 of whom were Jewish). In 1948, Congress enacted the Displaced Persons' Act and only 40,000 of the 365,223 DPs admitted were Jews. Many Nazis and **collaborators** came to America due to lax immigration review. In 1949, Congress adjusted the Act to permit 50,000 DPs to enter annually through 1952, after President Truman assailed the 1948 law for being "flagrantly discriminatory against Jews." (See also **Kielce**.)

SUGGESTED READINGS: Dinnerstein, *America and the Survivors of the Holocaust*; Sanders, *Shores of Refuge*.

Displaced Persons' Camps. Camps where stateless persons, **DPs**, were kept after World War II in the different zones of **Allied** occupation. They were located in **Germany, France, Italy**, and **Belgium** from 1945–1957. Ironically, the camps were often at former **concentration camps**. Because of maltreatment and **anti-Semitism**, separate DP camps were established for Jews away from disguised Nazis, **Volksdeutsche**, and **collaborators**. Of the 2 million **refugees** in camps 200,000 were Jews. (See also **American Zone of Occupation, General Dwight David Eisenhower, Ira Hirschmann, Landsberg**, and **Harry S. Truman**.

Distribution Centers. Located in occupied France, inmates were interned at these sites prior to **deportation** to the **death** and **concentration camps**. (See also **Vichy**.)

DNSAP. Danish **Nazi Party** with a membership of 22,000. (See also **Schalburg Corps**.)

Doctors' Trial. From December 9, 1946–August 20, 1947, twenty-three **SS** physicians were tried before an American **International Military Tribunal**, the first of the twelve **Subsequent Nuremberg Proceedings**. The accused were charged with conducting inhumane experiments and **crimes against humanity** on nonconsenting inmates. Nazi "medical experiments" involved high-altitude, hypothermia, sulfa drugs, infectious diseases, bone grafting, and mustard gas research. Other crimes included **euthanasia** and skull collection. Sixteen physicians were found guilty, seven were acquitted. **Victor Brack, Karl Brandt, Karl Gebhardt, Dr. Waldemar Hoven, Joachim Mrugrowsky**, and **Wolfram Sievers** were sentenced to death. The only woman tried, **Herta Oberhauser**, received twenty years. (See also **Leo Alexander, Bayer, Dr. Wilhelm Beigelboeck, Nuremberg Trials**, and **General Telford Taylor**.)

SUGGESTED READING: Annas and Grodin, *The Nazi Doctors and the Nuremberg Code*.

Dodd, William (1869–1940). American ambassador to **Germany** from 1933–1937. He was unable to influence **Hitler** to ease the persecution of German Jews. The ambassador warned President **Franklin Delano Roosevelt** of Hitler's obsession against Jews and the Nazi ambition for aggression and war.

SUGGESTED READING: Herzstein, *Roosevelt and Hitler*.

Doenitz, Admiral Karl (1891–1980). Grand admiral and **Hitler's** successor. He was the architect of Nazi U-boat warfare and **Fuehrer** of the **Reich** for twenty-three days. He surrendered to the British. Convicted of **war crimes**, Doenitz served ten years at Spandau prison and was released on October 1, 1956. (See also **Otto Kranzbuehler** and **Field Marshal Bernard Law Montgomery**.)
   SUGGESTED READING: Davidson, *The Trial of the Germans*.

Dog Tags. Metal squares worn around the necks of American soldiers to identify them. Included were symbols of the wearers' religion: H–Hebrew, P–Protestant, and C–Catholic. American Jewish soldiers in Europe were not made aware of the dangers if one were to be captured and become a POW. Some Jewish soldiers were taken to **concentration camps**, while others were singled out for persecution. American authorities abandoned these servicemen. (See also **"H."**)
   SUGGESTED READING: Bard, *Forgotten Victims*.

Dohnany, Hans Johann von (1902–1945). German jurist and **resister**. He participated in a plot against **Hitler** while involved in intelligence service with **Admiral Wilhelm Canaris**. He was arrested initially for helping Jews transfer their assets to **Switzerland**, then executed by the **Gestapo**.
   SUGGESTED READINGS: Gill, *An Honorable Defeat*; Snyder, *Hitler's German Enemies*.

Dolchstoss (G., "Stab-in-the-back"). **Hitler** was convinced that the German army was still intact and there was no reason to surrender and sue for an armistice on November 11, 1918. He believed that the Jews and the other **"Novemberbrecher"** sold **Germany** out in the 1918 armistice ending World War I and at Versailles. (See also **Walther Rathenau** and **Weimar Republic**.)
   SUGGESTED READING: Flood, *Hitler, the Path to Power*.

Dollfuss, Engelbert (1892–1934). Austrian chancellor. He promulgated a new **fascist** constitution in 1934. However, Dollfuss favored an independent **Austria** and opposed an **Anschluss**. He was assassinated by Austrian Nazis.
   SUGGESTED READING: Toland, *Adolf Hitler*.

Dominican Republic. Located on the Caribbean island of Hispaniola. There were 640 Jews settled in **Sosua**, a seacoast town where **Rafael Trujillo** gave each Jew 80 acres, ten cows, a mule, and a horse. Funding for this planned community was provided by the **"Joint."** The Sosua settlement was a meager result of the unproductive **Evian Conference**. Between 1940 through 1945, the Dominican Republic issued 5,000 **visas** to trapped European Jews.
   SUGGESTED READING: Habe, *The Mission*.

Dora-Nordhausen. Originally a subcamp of **Buchenwald**. This secret camp (Geheimlager), located in the Hartz Mountains of western **Germany**, was established in August 1943 for the production of V-1 and V-2 rockets. Dora was the missile site located underground near Nordhausen. The camp became a major independent facility on October 28, 1944, with twenty-three satellite camps. Most of the prisoners were transferred from Buchenwald. Approximately 14,000 inmates lived in the tunnel system before barracks were constructed in 1944. Many of the prisoners were worked to death and lived in unspeakable filth. Emaciated Jewish inmates were sent to **Mauthausen** and **Auschwitz**. The majority of workers were French, Polish, and **Soviet POWs** who were shipped to **Majdanek** and **Bergen-Belsen** when they were debilitated. There were no **gas chambers**, although a **crematorium** was constructed to dispose of corpses. One quarter of the 32,532 prisoners were killed, primarily through **slave labor**. The camp was evacuated by the Nazis and **liberated** by the Americans on April 9, 1945. (See also **Wernher von Braun, General Walter Dornberger, Otto Forschner, Homosexuals, Hans Kammler, Arthur Rudolph**, and **Albert Speer**.)

SUGGESTED READINGS: Michel, *Dora*; Neufeld, *The Rocket and the Reich*.

Dornberger, General Walter (1895–1980). **Wehrmacht's** rocket development chief for the V-2. **Wernher von Braun's** mentor, he approved of using **slave labor** for the Nazi rocket program. Dornberger was rescued by the U.S. Air Force in 1947 through **"Project Paperclip."** (See also **Dora-Nordhausen**, and **Peenemuende Aerodynamics Institute**.)

SUGGESTED READINGS: Hunt, *Secret Agenda*; Neufeld, *The Rocket and the Reich*.

DP (Displaced Person). A person who was unable or unwilling to return to his/her native land after the war. There were 6.34 million Jews, POWs, **collaborators**, disguised-Nazis, stateless persons, and others who were kept (or hidden) at Displaced Person camps in the different zones of **Allied** occupation from 1945–1957. Most gentile DPs returned to their native lands. After the war, in the **American zone of occupation**, separate camps were established for Jews. Ironically, many **concentration camps** served as **DP camps**. The fear of communism drove many Eastern Europeans into DP camps. It was not uncommon for a **Volksdeutsche** to become a DP in order to avoid retribution in his native land. Reasons why uprooted Jews did not wish to be **repatriated** included: the annihilation of family and friends; the destruction of the social and economic bases of existence; and the continuing hostility of large sections of the local population, which for many years had been under the influence of **anti-Semitic** propaganda. Of the 2 million **refugees** in the camps, 200,000 were Jewish. (See also **David Ben-Gurion, General Dwight David Eisenhower, Earl Harrison, Kielce, Fiorello La Guardia, Ira Hirschmann, Rabbi Judah Nadich**, Occupation Zones, General George S. Patton, Rabbi Solomon Schonfeld, Supreme Headquarters Allied Expeditionary Forces, Harry S. Truman, Union of Jewish Survivors, United Nations Relief and Rehabilitation Agency, and Youth Aliya.)

SUGGESTED READINGS: Dinnerstein, *America and the Survivors of the Holocaust*; Gutman and Saf, *She'erit Hapletah 1944–1948*.

Dragonovic, Father Krunoslav (d. 1983). Croatian priest. He was the principal founder of the **Ratline**, which helped **Ustashi** members, Nazis, including **Klaus Barbie**, and other **collaborators** escape to South America. Working for U.S. intelligence, he eventually returned to **Yugoslavia** where he died of natural causes. (See also **Croatia**.)

SUGGESTED READING: Aarons and Loftus, *Unholy Trinity: The Vatican, The Nazis, and Soviet Intelligence.*

Drancy. Internment camp and assembly point outside of Paris (1940) where Jews from **France** were shipped directly from **collection camps**. The first **transport** from Drancy to **Auschwitz** took place on March 28, 1942. Approximately 74,000 Jews, including 11,000 children, were **deported** to Auschwitz, **Majdanek**, and **Sobibor**; including 5,000 Belgian Jews. Only 2,190 of the inmates interned at Drancy returned to France. The camp was run by the French police until July 1943, when the Germans took administrative control. On August 17, 1944, the Consul General of **Sweden** and the French **Red Cross** took control of this site and the 1,542 prisoners. (See also **Alois Brunner, Channel Islands**, and **Vittel**.)

SUGGESTED READING: Adler, *The Jews of Paris.*

Drang nach Osten (G., ''Drive to the East''). **Lebensraum** grew out of the German perennial desire to acquire more territory from the peoples of **Poland, Russia**, and the Baltics.

Drexler, Anton (1884–1942). Tool maker and founder of supernationalist **German Workers Party. Hitler** joined this party in Munich on September 19, 1919, as member number seven. Drexler greatly influenced Hitler's ideas pitting a Jewish, capitalist-Masonic conspiracy against the innocent German worker, farmer, and soldier. He eventually yielded his position as head of the party to Hitler. (See also **Nazi Party** and **Thule Society**.)

SUGGESTED READING: Flood, *Hitler, Path to Power.*

Drobitski Yar (Ro., **Drobitski Ravine**). There were 21,685 Kharkov Jews murdered and buried in this ravine in the **Ukraine**.

Dror (H., freedom). Youth movement. **Socialist Zionist** movement popular in **Poland**. Under the leadership of **Zivia Lubetkin** and **Yitzhak Zuckerman**, it countered the **Judenrat** in Warsaw by sponsoring cultural activities, running weapons, and distributing food. Prior to the war, it prepared young people for **aliya** to **Palestine** and communal life. The Dror formed the nucleus of the **ZOB** during the **Warsaw Ghetto Uprisings**.

Dubnow, Simon (1869–1941). Jewish historian. He conceived of the idea of autonomy, that is, Jews should engage in self-government living as citizens within a state. Dubnow returned to **Lithuania** urging Jews to record Nazi persecution. He was murdered by a Nazi, a former pupil, in **Riga** on December 8, 1941, during an **Aktion**. (See also **Hermann Fritz Graebe** and **Emmanuel Ringelblum**.)

SUGGESTED READINGS: Dubnow-Erlich, *Life and Work of S. M. Dubnow*; Levin, *Fighting Back*.

DuBois, Josiah (1912–1983). Treasury Department lawyer. He obtained knowledge of the **Final Solution** from information provided by Donald Hiss, head of Foreign Funds Control (State Department). DuBois documented the State Department's willful failure to act on behalf of European Jewry in his **Report to the Secretary on the Acquiescence of this Government on the Murder of the Jews**, which triggered Treasury Secretary **Henry Morganthau Jr**. to push for the creation of the **War Refugee Board**. After the war, DuBois served as chief counsel in the prosecution of **I. G. Farben**. He documented that firm's complicity in the Final Solution in his book *The Devil's Chemists*.

SUGGESTED READINGS: Gruber, *Haven*; Morse, *While Six Million Died*.

Duckwitz, Georg Ferdinand (1901–1973). Shipping attaché in the German embassy of Copenhagen. He played a crucial role in alerting Danish leaders on September 28, 1943, of the impending roundup of Jews. **Dr. Werner Best** apprised him of the **Aktion** in mid-September 1943. Duckwitz was recognized as a **Righteous Gentile**. (See also **Denmark** and **Chief Rabbi Marcus Melchoir**.)

SUGGESTED READINGS: Flender, *Rescue in Denmark*; Goldberger, *The Rescue of Danish Jews*.

Durchfall (G., diarrhea). Common diarrhea in the **concentration camps**, which usually proved fatal. Most victims remained lucid until death.

Durchgangslager (G.) (See **Transit camp**.)

"Durchschlesung" (G., "transportation to another world"). **Heinrich Himmler** forbade the use of **"Sonderbehandelt"** ("**special treatment**") on April 10, 1943, and suggested this term as a replacement.

Dutch. Pertains to peoples of the **Netherlands**, often called **Holland**. (See also **Aryan, "Black Police," "Green Police," Landwacht, Anton Mussert**, NSB, and **Sperre**.)

Dutch Workingmans' Strike. On February 19, 1941, the Germans surrounded the Jewish quarter and **deported** 425 young Jewish men to **Mauthausen**. In response, 2,200 dock workers went on strike and paralyzed Amsterdam. The Nazis broke the strike with a reign of terror. During German occupation, 20,000

Dutch Christians were deported to **concentration camps** for opposing Nazi racial policies. About 80 percent or 124,000 of **Holland**'s prewar Jewish population were deported to concentration camps. Less than 5,000 returned.

SUGGESTED READING: Presser, *Ashes in the Wind.*

Dynamit Nobel (DAG). German munitions company that utilized **concentration camp** labor. Part of **Flick** Enterprises, it was the leading manufacturer of explosives during World War II and employed female **slave laborers**.

SUGGESTED READINGS: Ferencz, *Less Than Slaves*; Owings, *Frauen.*

E

Early Number. A low number tattooed on the left forearm of an inmate at **Auschwitz**. This number indicated the inmate was a veteran and was accorded more status. Higher numbers (tattooed under the left forearm) and those without numbers were more likely to be gassed.

Eastern Territories (G., **Ostland**). Areas of **Poland**, the **Soviet Union**, and the Baltics conquered by the Germans, but not incorporated into the **Reich**. (See also **Aktion, General Gottlob Berger, Einsatzgruppen, Dr. Alfred Rosenberg**, and **Vernichtungskommando**.)

East Germany. From 1945–1987, the Democratic Republic of Germany, once a communist satellite, tried 12,877 **war criminals**, sentencing 127 to death and 267 to life imprisonment. When it was a communist satellite, it did not pay **reparations** or **restitution** to persecuted Jews.

Ebensee. Subcamp of **Mauthausen** located in an Austrian mountain retreat town. Inmates from **Buchenwald** and **Dachau** dreaded a transfer to this camp where they were forced to work in an underground factory. An armament plant was built into the mountains by 18,000 **slave laborers**. The Americans **liberated** Ebensee on May 5, 1945.
   SUGGESTED READING: Abzug, *Inside the Vicious Heart: Americans and the Liberation of Nazi Concentration Camps*.

Eberl, Dr. Irmfried (1919–1948). **SS** physician involved in the **T-4** program. He was director of Bernburg killing center, then transferred to medical duty in **Minsk**. Eberl was commandant of **Treblinka** for two months before being transferred back to Bernburg. The SS physician committed suicide in his cell in 1948. (See also **Euthanasia.**)

SUGGESTED READING: Friedlander, *The Origins of Nazi Genocide.*

Ebner, Dr. Gregor (b. 1882). Medical director of **Lebensborn.** A close friend of **Heinrich Himmler**, he signed orders for sterilization of non-Nordic children in 1936 and later ordered these children **deported** to **concentration camps.**

SUGGESTED READING: Hillel and Henry, *Of Pure Blood.*

Economic and Administrative Main Office. (See **WVHA.**)

Edelman, Dr. Marek (b. 1921). Polish **Bundist resister.** He represented the group in the **ZOB**. This underground fighter was one of the last to leave the command bunker at **Mila 18** with **Yitzhak Zuckerman** and **Zivia Lubetkin** through the sewers of Warsaw. One of two ZOB commanders to survive the **Warsaw Ghetto Uprising**, Edelman also fought in the **Warsaw Polish Uprising**. A devoted socialist, he remained in **Poland** and became a cardiologist. Edelman currently lives in Lodz. (See also **Abraham Blum.**)

SUGGESTED READINGS: Borzykowski, *Between Tumbling Walls*; Krall, *Shielding the Flame.*

Edelstein, Jacob (1907–1944). Czech Jew and **Judenaeltesten** of the Jewish Council in **Theresienstadt.** He attempted to make the **ghetto** economically viable, but also composed **deportation** lists for the Nazis. He was replaced in January 1943 by **Dr. Paul Eppstein** as camp demographics shifted in favor of German and Austrian Jews. Edelstein and his family were shot in **Auschwitz** in December 1943. (See also "**Work as a Means of Rescue.**")

SUGGESTED READINGS: Bondy, *"Elder of the Jews"*; Trunk, *Judenrat.*

Edelweiss Pirates. German youth gangs composed of 14-to 17-year-old males. They rejected **Hitler Youth** membership, rebelled against authoritarianism, and were called delinquents by the Nazi regime. They aided deserters, POWs, and **concentration camp** ecapees in **Germany**. The Pirates were active in the fall of 1944, mainly in the Cologne area. The Nazis publicly hanged twelve members in Cologne in November 1944 as a warning to other young people.

SUGGESTED READING: Burleigh and Wipperman, *The Racial State.*

Eden, Anthony (1897–1977). British Foreign Secretary under **Winston Churchill.** He did not use his office to assist European Jews, held fast to the **White Paper** policy, and refused to bomb **Auschwitz-Birkenau**. (See also **Jan Karski, John McCloy**, and **Chaim Weizmann**).

SUGGESTED READING: Wasserstein, *Britain and the Jews of Europe.*

Ehrenburg, Ilya Grigorovitch (1891–1967). Jewish Soviet writer. He was a novelist, essayist, and poet who wrote about the mass murder of Jews in German-occupied **Soviet Union**. He authored the *Black Book*, also referred to as the *Murderers of Nations*, detailing Nazi crimes against Jews in **Poland** and the Soviet Union. Ehrenburg was also a member of the **Jewish Anti-Fascist Committee**.
SUGGESTED READING: Vaksberg, *Stalin Against the Jews*.

Eichmann, Adolf (1906–1962). Lt. Colonel in the **SS** and infamous mass murderer. Eichmann was an "expert" on Jewish issues (**Judenreferent**) in the **SD**'s Jewish Department (II-112). He was appointed by **Reinhard Heydrich** to head the **RSHA** section IV A 4B. Eichmann was in charge of **deporting** and **transporting** Jews to **ghettos, labor**, and **death camps**. The Lt. Colonel was an efficient administrator who relished his work. He made sure his office got its allotment of trains and **freight cars**, even after the war turned against **Germany**. Utilizing a **Vatican** passport, he escaped to Argentina. In May 1960, the Israeli secret service kidnapped Eichmann from South America. Eichmann was tried in Israel, the first **war criminal** to be tried in the Jewish state, and hanged on May 31–June 1, 1962. (See also **Hannah Arendt, "Blood for Trucks," Dr. Victor Brack, Alois Brunner, Theodor Dannecker, Grand Mufti of Jerusalem, Dr. Heinrich Gruber, Gideon Hausner, Richard Korherr, Josef Loewenherz, Zivia Lubetkin, Madagascar Deportation Plan, Heinrich Mueller, Franz Novak, Franz Rademacher, Ratline, Reich Central Office for Jewish Emigration, Gustav Richter, Dr. Franz W. Six, Edmund Veesenmayer, Dr. David Wdowinski**, and **Dieter Wisliceny**.)
SUGGESTED READINGS: Arendt, *Eichmann in Jerusalem*; von Lang, *Eichmann Interrogated*.

Eicke, Theodor (1892–1943). Kommandant of **Dachau**. He was founder and trainer of the **Death's Head Brigade** and inspector of **concentration camps**. Brutal, hard, terroristic, and uncompromising, he successfully transmitted these traits to concentration camp guards. Eicke originated the term "**Arbeit Macht Frei**." The commandant was killed in a plane crash on the Eastern Front on February 16, 1943. (See also **Dehumanization, Richard Gluecks, Rudolf Hoess**, and **Ernst Roehm**.)
SUGGESTED READING: Segev, *Soldiers of Evil*.

Einbinder, Isaac. Organizer of **partisan** detail. In 1942, he was sent to Moscow to study guerrilla warfare. He then returned to the forests near **Vilna**. Nicknamed "The Fearless," Einbinder derailed sixteen trains and took the lives of many Germans before he was captured and killed. The Soviets awarded the partisan with the "Hero of the **Soviet Union**," its highest honor.
SUGGESTED READING: Eckman and Lazar, *The Jewish Resistance*.

Eindeutschung (G., Germanization). Reclaiming **Volksdeutsche** peoples and areas once dominated by the Germanic Holy Roman Empire.

"Eine Laus, dein Tod" (G., "One louse, your death"). Common refrain in **concentration camps**. Lice were the major cause of **typhus**. Lack of proper sanitation facilities in **ghettos** and camps facilitated the spread of lice.

Einkesselung (G., Encirclement). This **Aktion** took place in the **Warsaw Ghetto** from September 5–12 (**Rosh Hashana**), 1942. Approximately 70,000 Jews were **deported** during Einkesselung. Prior to this Aktion, 200,000 Jews living in the Warsaw Ghetto had been deported.

Einsatzgruppe H (G., Special Action Squad). Operated **Sered concentration camp** during the second phase of the liquidation of Slovakian Jewry in winter 1944–April 1945. (See also **Slovakia**.)

Einsatzgruppe(n)-Einstazkommando (G., intervention or **"Special Action Squad[s]"**). **SS** units, specially trained assassins, assigned terror tasks for the political administration in the **Soviet Union** and other **Eastern Territories**. Einsatzkommandos were subgroups (15) of Einsatzgruppen, which varies in strength from 100–150 men. The Einsatzgruppen worked behind the lines and murdered political opposition. For instance, the Einsatzgruppen entered **Poland** and annihilated the Polish intelligentsia. The **Wehrmacht** was directed to hand Jews, communists, and other political opponents over to the Special Action Squads for slaughter. **Heinrich Himmler** ordered these units to begin murdering Jewish men, women, children, and the elderly on August 15, 1941. Indigenous auxiliary units from Poland, the **Ukraine, Lithuania, Latvia,** and other regions helped identify and execute Jews. Their cooperation was essential to the Einsatzgruppe's effectiveness. Generally, the victims were forced to march to a secluded area, instructed to dig a pit, and were executed.

The Einsatzgruppen made up of 3,000 men were divided into four groups: Group A operated in the Balkans; Group B operated in parts of eastern Poland and the Eastern Territories; Group C operated in the Ukraine and other Eastern Territories; and Group D operated in the Eastern Territories almost reaching Stalingrad (Volograd) in the East and penetrating **Odessa** and the Crimea in the south. The Einsatzgruppen murdered between 1.25–2 million Jews and tens of thousands of Soviet citizens and **Soviet POWs**.

The task of the Einsatzgruppen was determined to be too haphazard and inefficient, so **death camps** replaced these roving squads of mass murderers. Himmler also felt the mass killings were having a "demoralizing" impact on the Einsatzgruppen. **Elie Wiesel** and his students conducted research on the makeup of the Special Squad, and "discovered that many of the killers of the four Einsatzkommando (killing squads) had college degrees. They had Ph.D. degrees in philosophy and literature, in the sciences and medicine. There were two opera singers, and one of them, may God save us all, had a Ph.D. in Divinity.'' (See also **Viktor Arajis, Babi Yar, Paul Blobel, Freiwillige, Odilo Globocnik, Hilfswillige, Italy, Karl Jaeger, Wilhelm Keitel, Krimchaks, Dr. Rudolf Lange, Latvian SS Legion, Lithuanian Activist Front, Arthur Nebe, Otto Ohlendorf, Omakaitse, Ostbataillone, Perkonkrust, Pinsk, Emil Otto Rasch, Walter Rauff, Schuma, Dr. Franz W. Six, "Sonderbehandelt," Sonderkommando, Special Echelon, Franz Stahlecker, Todt Organization, Transnistria**, and **Waffen-SS**.)

SUGGESTED READINGS: Arad, Krakowski, and Spector, *The Einsatzgruppen Reports*; Dawidowicz, *The War Against the Jews*; Hilberg, *The Destruction of European Jews.*

Einsatzkommando Trial. Held in Ulm, **Soviet Union**, in 1958. The Trial revealed evidence of mass atrocities in Nazi occupied **Lithuania**. (See also **Paul Blobel, Einsatzgruppen, Lithuanian Activist Front, Subsequent Nuremberg Trials**, and **Vernictungskommando**.)

Einsatzstab Rosenberg (G., Special Operational Staff Rosenberg). Created on September 17, 1940, and run by **Dr. Alfred Rosenberg**. This organization expropriated Jewish cultural property. The booty was taken back to the **Reich** and some of the stolen material found its way back into the homes of **Hitler, Hermann Goering**, Rosenberg, and other Nazi leaders. (See also **Aryanization**.)

SUGGESTED READING: Persico, *Nuremberg: Infamy on Trial.*

Einstein, Albert (1879–1955). German-born Jewish physicist and Nobel laureate. He was visiting the United States in 1933, the year **Hitler** came to power, and decided to remain in America. The Nazis stripped him of his honors and publicly burned his books. Hitler called Einstein's advances and physics in general, ''Jew science.'' The internationally known physicist urged **President Franklin Delano Roosevelt** to embark on the atomic bomb project. (See also **Lise Meitner, Dr. Bernard Rust**, and **Dr. Johannes Stark**.)

SUGGESTED READING: Einstein, *Out of My Later Years.*

"Ein Volk, ein Reich, ein Fuehrer" (G., ''One people, one state, one leader''). Nazi propaganda slogan that underscored the racial, organic, and dictatorial nature of the party and regime.

Eisenhower, General Dwight David (1890–1969). Supreme commander of **Allied** troops on the Western Front in Europe. The American general believed his primary task was to destroy Nazi forces. There were no plans for **liberating concentration camps**. In September 1944, he decreed that all German laws in liberated areas involving discrimination of race, religion, and political affiliation void. The general warned the Germans not to discriminate against American Jewish POWs. For the most part, the Germans honored the warning. Eisenhower and **General George S. Patton** visited **Ohrdruf** eight days after the camp was liberated and ordered Allied soldiers and the media to view the horrors of the concentration camps. The supreme commander also requested congressional and Parliamentary investigations into the atrocities. President **Harry S. Truman** ordered Eisenhower to improve conditions of Jewish **Displaced Persons**. After conducting his own investigation on August 22, 1945, separate camps were established with improved living conditions for Jews. (See also **CROWCASS, DPs, Dog Tags, Earl Harrison, Liberation, Rabbi Judah Nadich**, and **Witness to Liberation**.)

SUGGESTED READINGS: Sachar, *The Redemption of the Unwanted;* United States Holocaust Memorial Museum, *1945: The Year of Liberation.*

Elkes, Dr. Elchanan (1879–1944). Renowned physician and chairman of the **Kovno Aeltestenrat**. Eikes supported underground efforts to hide the Jews. On July 2, 1944, with the **Red Army** closing in, he suggested to Kovno **ghetto** kommandant Wilhelm Gocke that **deportations** cease. The ghetto was evacuated several days later. Elkes was deported to **Landsberg** where he died of illness on October 17, 1944.

SUGGESTED READING: Tory, *Surviving the Holocaust.*

El Salvador. The Foreign Ministry of this country, through its consulate in Geneva, **George Mandel Mantello**, issued thousands of **visas** and **Schutzpaesse** to Hungarian Jews.

Emalia. (See **Bergen-Belsen** and **Oskar Schindler**.)

Emergency Committee to Save the Jewish People of Europe. Bergson related group created by the Committee for the Jewish Army in June 1943; it emerged as a major force in bringing the **Holocaust** to the attention of the public. The Committee lobbied for rescue action from the United States, specifically, the creation of a rescue organization that materialized into the **War Refugee Board**, and later, the establishment of free ports. The executive director was **Samuel Merlin. Ben Hecht** and Will Rogers, Jr., were co-chairs. (See also **Fort Ontario**.)

SUGGESTED READINGS: Finger, *American Jewry During the Holocaust;* Medoff, *The Deafening Silence.*

Emergency Refugee Shelter. (See **Fort Ontario**.)

Emergency Rescue Committee (ERC). Committee, formed in New York, concerned with **refugee** writers, artists, and intellectuals. The committee grew out of an idea by **Hamilton Fish Armstrong**, editor of *Foreign Affairs*, who cabled the White House in mid-July 1940. He sent a list to President **Franklin Delano Roosevelt** that contained the names of prominent anti-Nazis. The information was relayed to the State Department, which sent the list to the American Emergency Rescue Committee in Marseilles and Lisbon. The instructions were to grant these people emergency visitor **visas**. Many Jewish organizations sent lists, including the **Jewish Labor Committee** and the **Union of Orthodox Rabbis of America**, as well as concerned individuals like **Rabbi Stephen S. Wise**. The ERC coordinated its work with the President's Advisory Committee on Political Refugees, created after the **Evian Conference**, under the direction of **James Grover McDonald**. The latter took over the task of coordinating this emergency visa effort. (See also **Hannah Arendt** and **Varian Fry**.)

SUGGESTED READINGS: Herzstein, *Roosevelt and Hitler*; United States Holocaust Memorial Museum, *Assignment Rescue*.

Enabling Act. Legislation passed by the **Reichstag** on March 23, 1933. It was based on Article 48 of the **Weimar** Constitution that allowed the chancellor to rule by decree to protect the security of the state. **Hitler** used the burning of the Reichstag as a pretense that a state of emergency existed in **Germany**. The Enabling Act facilitated the consolidation of power into the hands of Hitler and the **Nazi Party**. This Act "enabled" Hitler to suppress all opposition and rule by decree. It precluded the Reichstag from proposing legislation that didn't originate from the Nazis. **Anti-Semitic** legislation quickly followed the passage of the Act. (See also **Numerus Clausus** and **Nuremberg Laws**.)

SUGGESTED READING: Shirer, *The Rise and Fall of the Third Reich*.

Endloesung (G., **Final Solution**). Euphemism for the annihilation of the Jews. (See also **Hermann Goering** and **Wannsee Conference**.)

Enigma. Name of German coding machine used by the land, air, and sea forces of the German High Command. In July 1939, a copy of Enigma was sent to Britain by French intelligence. Polish cryptologists, Marian Rejewski, Jerzy Rozycki, and Henryk Zygalsk, succeeded in duplicating the German cipher machine. As early as 1930, the Poles provided British and French intelligence with models of the ciphering machine. A team of cryptologists, using primitive computers, broke the code in 1940. The British, and later the Americans, knew information concerning the **Final Solution**, including the movement of **deportation** as early as 1942. Foreknowledge of the plans of the German High Command by the deciphoring Enigma was known as the **Ultra** Secret. The decoding of the German's military codes gave the **Allies** a tremendous advantage in the war, on land, air, and sea. (See also **Bletchley Park** and **OSS**.)

SUGGESTED READING: Garlinski, *The Enigma War*.

Entjudung (G., de-Judification [of Europe]).

Entlausung (G., delousing [showers]). (See **Typhus**.)

Entress, Dr. Friedrich (1914–1947). **SS** physician and 2nd lieutenant. He conducted autopsies on the prisoners killed from "medical experiments" and recommended "sick inmates" for phenol injections at **Auschwitz**. Entrees sent sick inmates from **Mauthausen** to **Hartheim Castle** to be gassed.
SUGGESTED READING: Lifton, *The Nazi Doctors.*

"Entsprechend behandelt" (G., "Treated appropriately"). Euphemism for murder.

Entwesungstruppe (G., Delousing brigade). Unit that attempted to rid lice from clothing. (See also **Typhus**.)

Eppinger, Dr. Hans (1897–1945). Medical professor at the Medical Faculty of **Vienna**. He and **Dr. Wilhelm Beigelboeck** conducted seawater experiments on inmates from **Dachau**. Eppinger committed suicide after the war.
SUGGESTED READING: U.S. Government Printing Office, *Trials of War Criminals, Vol. 1, "The Medical Case."*

Eppstein, Dr. Paul (1901–1944). One of the leaders of the **Reich Association of Jews** in **Germany**. He became the second **Judenaeltesten** in **Terezin**. Eppstein was murdered at the **"Big Fortress"** in September 1944.
SUGGESTED READING: Ehrmann, *Terezin, 1941–1945.*

Erholungslager (G., "recuperation camp"). The Nazis represented to "prominent" German Jews (wealthy, intermarried, and World War I veterans) in the early 1940s that **Theresienstadt** was a spa.

Erntefest (G., Harvest Festival). (See **Operation Harvest Festival**.)

Ersatz (G., substitute). Poor or low-grade substitute commodity. Bread given to inmates in **concentration camps** contained sawdust rather than flour and colored water was called coffee.

Estonia. Northernmost Baltic republic on the Gulf of **Finland** bordering **Latvia** on the south and **Russia** in the north with a prewar Jewish population of 4,500 to 5,000 out of a general population of over 1.1 million. At the end of World War I, Estonia became an independent nation governed by a dictator. The **Soviet Union** annexed the country on August 3, 1940, and made it a Soviet Republic. Along with the invasion of the Soviet Union in June 1941, came the **Einsatzgruppen** and **Order Police**. Fortunately, the Estonian Jews were able to flee to the **USSR** for it took two months for the **Wehrmacht** to reach Estonia. Many Jews joined the **Red Army** and died fighting or were forced to go to **Siberia**. About 1,500 Jews returned between 1944–1950.
 Anti-Semitism was present in Estonia, however, widespread **pogroms** com-

mon in Latvia and **Lithuania** did not occur. Jews from Latvia and Lithuania were taken to **Klooga** and work camps for hard labor. Rich oil-bearing deposits owned by Kontinental Oel A. B. used hundreds of Jewish **slave laborers**.

By September 26, 1944, all of Estonia was retaken by the Red Army. (See also **Omakaitse** and **Franz Walter Stahlecker**.)

Eugenics. Term first used in 1883 by Francis Galton. The Nazis twisted this human improvement concept to mean that society should improve the human race by careful breeding to encourage the procreation of "superior races" (**Aryan** and Nordic) and discourage or murder inferior races (**Slavs**) and racial enemies (Jews and **Roma**) from procreating. Sterilization of Germans followed by **euthanasia** fell under this category. Nazi theory postulated that the Aryans and Jews were locked into a life or death struggle for blood purity; therefore, normal rules of civilized behavior did not apply during this epic conflict. The Nazis termed eugenics **racial hygiene** and believed destroying the Jews was imperative to Aryan survival. (See also **Karl Binding, Kaiser Wilhelm Institute, Dr. Alfred Ploetz, T-4,** and **Voelkerchaos**.)

SUGGESTED READING: Kuehl, *The Nazi Connection*.

Europa Plan. Program advanced by the **Working Group**, led by **Gisi Fleischmann** and **Rabbi Michael Dov Weissmandel** to halt the **deportation** of European Jewry. Through bribery of the **SS** and Slovakian officials, including a $50,000 bribe to **Dieter Wiscliceny**, Slovakian deportations of Jews were halted from the fall of 1942 through September 1944. In addition, communication with Jews in **Poland** was initiated. The Europa Plan was presented to Nazi officials via Wiscliceny, but failed to materialize due to a lack of support from Jewish organizations and the occupation of **Slovakia** by the **Wehrmacht** during the **Slovakian National Uprising**. (See also **Saly Mayer**.)

SUGGESTED READINGS: Finger, *American Jewry During the Holocaust*; Fuchs, *The Unheeded Cry*.

Euthanasia (T-4). The Nazis instituted a "medicalized" murder program for German citizens in the **Greater Reich** who they deemed mentally and physically unfit. The groundwork for this plan was laid in the "Law for the Prevention of Progeny of Sufferers From Hereditary Diseases" passed on July 14, 1933, and implemented six months later. The Nazis sterilized between 200,000 and 350,000 German citizens. These included **"Rhineland bastards,"** those with hereditary diseases, **"unproductive eaters,"** and habitual criminals. In late October 1939, **Hitler** authorized coercive euthanasia. (This order was actually backdated to September 1, 1939.) The medical murder of these victims by gassing (**carbon monoxide**) took place at former mental institutions or nursing homes: **Hartheim Castle**, Brandenburg, Bernburg, **Sonnenstein**, Grafeneck, and **Hademar**. Children were usually murdered by lethal injection. The decision to kill Jews in the T-4 program came in spring 1940. In June 1941, the German killing operation expanded to include the murder of all Jews in all areas controlled by **Germany**. The T-4 killers, sobered by the **Bishop Clemens von Galen** and other protests against the coerced euthanasia of the handicapped inside Germany, decided that the death factories would be in **Poland**, home of 3.3 million Jews. Approximately 70,000 German citizens were killed before the German clergy forced **Hitler** to formally suspend this program on August 24, 1941. The **Gestapo** forged and signed the death certificates of victims. However, the program continued to be implemented for **"special cases"** at Hartheim Castle, Sonnenstein, and **concentration camps** in Germany and expanded to the East from December 1941–1945, under the aegis of **Dr. Friedrich Mennecke**. **Heinrich Himmler** ordered (December 10, 1941) the establishment of commissions comprised of physicians from the euthanasia program to weed out concentration camp inmates who were mentally ill or physically unfit for labor in a program called **14 f 13**. By the end of the war, an estimated 200,000 Europeans were "euthanized." The T-4 program was the prototype for the mass gassing at the extermination camps. Key personnel were transferred to the **death camps**, for example, **Ernst Kaltenbrunner, SS Major Christian Wirth**, and **Franz Stangl**. The Americans discovered an active euthanasia facility on July 2, 1945, in Kaufbeuren, months after Germany's unconditional surrender. (See also **"Ballastexistenzen,"** **Belzec, Philipp Bouhler, Dr. Victor Brack, Dr. Karl Brandt, Dr. Leonardo Conti, Dr. Irmfried Eberl, Fuehrer Decree, Gross-Rosen**, *Mystici Corporis*, **Dr. Hermann Pfannmueller, Dr. Alfred Ploetz, Dr. Ernst Ruedin, Dr. Horst Schumann, Sobibor, "Special Cases," "Sterbehilfe,"** **Treblinka, Dr. Gerhardt Wagner**, and **Zyklon-B**.)

SUGGESTED READINGS: Friedlander, *The Origins of Nazi Genocide*; Sereny, *Into That Darkness*.

Evian Conference. An international meeting of thirty-two nations convened in Evian, a southern French resort town from July 6–15, 1938, to deal with the German Jewish immigration problem. Out of the thirty-three nations invited, only **Italy** refused to participate. The gathering was prompted at the suggestion of President **Franklin Delano Roosevelt**. Little was accomplished in the way of meaningful immigration reforms that would allow Jews to leave the **Greater Reich**. Most Western nations failed to meet their immigration **quotas** during the war, yet had no interest in accepting **refugees**. The conference was a wasted opportunity to rescue Jews and also reinforced in **Hitler's** mind that the West was unwilling to help Jews in any concrete way. (See also **Dominican Republic, Hans Habe, Intergovernmental Committee on Refugees**, and **Myron Taylor**.)

SUGGESTED READINGS: Feingold, *The Politics of Rescue*; Habe, *The Mission*; Morse, *While Six Million Died*.

Exchange Jews. **Privileged Jews** held by Nazi authorities to be exchanged for German nationals held by the **Allies**. (See also **Hotel Polski, George Mandel Mantello, Palestine Certificates**, and **Vittel**.)

SUGGESTED READING: Trunk, *Jewish Responses to Nazi Persecution*.

Extradition (of Nazi **war criminals**). The process of requesting the return of a war criminal residing in another nation for trial. Extradition treaties are formal agreements between two nation states. Many war criminals fled to South America for example, **Josef Mengele** and **Klaus Barbie**—with the help of the **Vatican** and American government—where they lived without fear of prosecution. (See also **Moscow Declaration, Erich Priebke, Dr. Horst Schumann, Joseph Schwammberger, Franz Stangl, Doeme Sztojay,** and **Dr. Josef Tiso.**)

F

Fabrikaktion (G., **Operation Factory**).

Fackenheim, Professor Emil (b. 1916). Jewish existentialist philosopher. He has written extensively on the evils of Nazism and the role of Jews and **Zionism** in a post-**Auschwitz** world. German-born, he was interned in **Sachsenhausen-Oranienburg** by the **Gestapo** in 1939, but released after three months. He then fled to England. The philosopher maintains that remembering the **Holocaust** is the 614th commandment. Fackenheim currently resides in Israel.
  SUGGESTED READING: Fackenheim, *The Jewish Return Into History.*

Fascism. Form of government predicated on a one-party dictatorship, super-militarism, ultranationalism, absolute conformity, and intolerance for civil liberties. The term is derived from the Italian fasces, or a bundle of roots with a projecting ax, a symbol of state authority in ancient **Rome**. Fascism utilized secret police to impose terror and repress dissent. It glorified the state and leader and used propaganda to promote nationalism, anticommunism, and hate. This form of government enjoys support from some segments of society, that is, reactionaries, antidemocrats, royalists, and alienated members of other groups. Although the government plays a prominent role in an individual's daily life, privately owned industry and commerce is normally permitted. All aspects of political, social, and cultural life are coordinated and subordinated to the state. (See also **Francisco Franco, Adolf Hitler, Benito Mussolini, Antonio de Oliveria Salazar**, **Sano Mach**, and **Horia Sima**.)

Feiner, Leon (1888–1945). Polish **Bundist** underground leader, deputy chairman of **Zegota** and an organizer for the **ZOB**. He gave **Jan Karski** a message

that pleaded for rescue to be dispatched to the **Allies** and drafted reports to London on the **Final Solution**. (See also **Adolf Abraham Berman**.)
  SUGGESTED READING: Tomaszewski and Werbowski, *Zegota.*

Feldhandler, Leon (1910–1945). Former **Judenrat** chairman of Zolkiew in southern **Poland**. He organized a Jewish underground at **Sobibor** and assisted **Aleksander Pechersky**, Jewish **Red Army** officer, in organizing the revolt at Sobibor on October 14, 1943. The rebellion influenced the Nazis to close the **death camp**.
  SUGGESTED READING: Novitch, *Sobibor, Martyrdom and Revolt.*

Fenelon, Fania (b. 1920). French Jewish cabaret singer, pianist, and member of the **resistance**. She was denounced in 1943, arrested, **deported** to **Drancy**, and later to **Auschwitz** in January 1944. Her life was spared as a member of the female orchestra. She recorded her experiences in *Playing for Time*, an autobiography. (See also **Camp Orchestra** and **Maria Mandel**.)

Ferenczy, Laszlo (d. 1946). Lt. colonel and Hungarian state secretary. Head of the Hungarian **Gendarmerie**, he oversaw the placement and **deportation** of Jews in **ghettos** in **Hungary** from May–July 1944. Ferenczy was executed in 1946. (See also **Vadasz Esendorok**.)
  SUGGESTED READING: Reitlinger, *The Final Solution.*

FFI. (See **French Forces of the Interior**.)

Filderman, Dr. Wilhelm (1882–1963). Lawyer and president of the Federation of Jewish Congregations in **Romania**. He appealed in vain to **Ion Antonescu** to halt **deportations**. As head of the Aid Committee, Filderman sought all avenues of relief and appealed to the West for **visas**. Romania was willing to let Jews go for a price, but the U.S. State Department withheld information and erected insurmountable barriers in 1943. (See also **Josiah DuBois, Cordell Hull, Breckinridge Long**, and **Henry Morganthau Jr.**)
  SUGGESTED READING: Butnaru, *The Silent Holocaust.*

Final Solution (G., Endloesung). Euphemism for **genocide** of Jews. For **Hitler**, the presence of Jews, or a "nation within a nation," required a resolution to what many in Europe had called the "Jewish question." The Nazi plan to destroy European Jewry was formalized at the **Wannsee Conference**, convened in a **Berlin** suburb, and chaired by **Reinhard Heydrich** on January 20, 1942. **Heinrich Himmler** revealed the plan to his deputies in **Posen** in 1943. Hitler and his aides used the terms **Ausrottung** and **Vernichtung** concerning the murder of Jews, and the reference to Endloesung was documented in a letter from **Hermann Goering** to Heydrich discovered in the files of Dr. Philip Hoffman. (See also **Churban, Grand Mufti of Jerusalem, Holocaust, Klessheim Castle,**

Shoah, Dr. Wilhelm Stuckart, and **United Nations Declaration of December 17, 1942**.)

SUGGESTED READINGS: Breitman, *The Architect of Genocide*: Browning, *Fateful Months: Essays on the Emergence of the Final Solution.*

Finland. The Jewish population in 1939 was between 1,900–2,300. Finnish divisions, including Jews, fought the **Soviets** with the help of Germans during the "Winter War" (1939–1940). The Finns signed on to the **Anti-Comintern Pact** and **Tripartite Pact**; however, Finland refused to cooperate with the **Final Solution** and successfully protected its Jewish citizens. Some 300 Finnish Jews served in the army, and 23 were killed. Finland's foreign policy was influenced by **Heinrich Himmler's** visit in the summer of 1942 and her dependence on German trade (over 90 percent). However, some foreign Jews were interned in hard **labor camps** and **deported** across the Gulf of Finland to Tallinn, **Estonia**. These Jews (mostly German and Austrian) also had their passport marked with a **"J"** and some were deported after 1938, due to Finland's immigration **quota** system. (See also **Arno Anthoni, Dr. Felix Kersten, Heinrich Lohse**, and **Valpo**.)

SUGGESTED READINGS: Cohen, *"Finland and The Holocaust"*; Rautkallio, *Finland and the Holocaust*; World Jewish Congress, *Dateline: World Jewry*. October 1996.

Finta, Imre. Hungarian **Gendarmerie** and captain in charge of 8,617 Jews imprisoned at the Szeged brickyard prior to **deportation** to **Auschwitz**. He was convicted by a Hungarian tribunal in 1948 of **war crimes**. Canadian courts cleared him of complicity in the **Holocaust** due to an "air of reality" defense developed in the appellate courts that supported his "obedience to order" defense (1989–1994). (Finta's attorney also noted the **Allies'** failure to prosecute **Kurt Becher**.) Finta, a wealthy restaurateur, remains free. The verdict virtually assured that Canadian courts will not be able to prosecute perpetrators of the Holocaust.

SUGGESTED READING: Braham, "Canada and the Perpetrators of the Holocaust: The Case of Regina v. Finta."

Fischer, Ludwig (1905–1947). Politician and **Gauleiter** of Warsaw. He was responsible for the establishment of the **Warsaw Ghetto** in 1940. He set up other **ghettos** in the Warsaw district and was personally involved in their liquidation. Fischer was arrested in West **Germany** and extradited to **Poland** in 1946. **Eric von dem Bach-Zelewski** testified against him at the Warsaw Trial. Fischer was hanged in 1947.

SUGGESTED READING: Gutman, *The Jews of Warsaw.*

Fisher, Dr. Fritz. (See **Ravensbrueck**.)

Fleischmann, Gisi (1897–1944). Underground Czech Jewish **resister**. Leader of the **Working Group, Zionist** activist, head of the **Jewish Center (UZ)** Emigration Department, Fleischmann also was **aliya** section leader of Women's International Zionist Organization in **Slovakia** in 1940. When **deportations** of Slovakian Jews began in March 1942, she attempted to bribe **Dieter Wisliceny**. Fleischmann and **Rabbi Michael Dov Weissmandel's Europa Plan** was rejected by the **Allies**. The resister established an underground escape route for survivors of Polish **ghettos** to Budapest where they were transported to **Palestine**. Fleischmann was arrested, deported to **Auschwitz**, where she was immediately killed in October 1944.

SUGGESTED READING: Campion, *In the Lion's Mouth.*

Flick. Large, diversified German conglomerate that owned **Daimler-Benz, Dynamit-Nobel**, and **Auto-Union**. Flick enterprises supported Nazi policies and exploited at least 40,000 **slave laborers**, of which 80 percent died.

SUGGESTED READING: Ferencz, *Less Than Slaves.*

Flick, Friedrich (1883–1972). Industrial **war criminal**. Ruthless, pro-Nazi patriarch of the **Flick** concern, whose friendship with **Hitler** and **Hermann Goering** yielded him **Aryanization** rights to Czech Jewish coal holdings, iron in Lorraine, and access to raw materials in the East. Flick was the **SS's** largest contributor and met frequently with **Heinrich Himmler**. He was tried and convicted at the **Subsequent Nuremberg Trials**. Flick adamantly refused to make **restitution** payments to any of his former slaves. (See also **Circle of Friends of Himmler**.)

SUGGESTED READING: Ferencz, *Less Than Slaves.*

Florstedt, Hermann (1895–1945). Third kommandant of **Majdanek**. He was convicted of fraud and corruption charges by an **SS** court and was executed in April 1945.

SUGGESTED READING: Segev, *Soldiers of Evil.*

Flossenbuerg. Special punishment **(Straflager)** camp composed mostly of German political prisoners, Czechs, Russians, French, Poles, and Jews. The camp held approximately 25,000 inmates and was located in south central **Germany** near **Czechoslovakia**. Kommandant **Karl Kuenstler** was dismissed by the **SS** in 1942 for drunkenness. Most inmates worked for **DEST** or underground at "**2004**" constructing **Messerschmidt** fighter planes. Other inmates worked at the dreaded Steinbruch Quarry. The site was exclusively staffed with SS. Flossenbuerg was equipped with a gassing barrack and **crematorium**. The camp also had a bordello for officers and inmates with special permits. Approximately 22,000 inmates were evacuated (1,700 Jews) by April 20, 1945, and were marched east, primarily to **Theresienstadt**. Flossenbuerg was **liberated** by the Americans on April 23, 1945. The Americans forced the "uninformed" towns-

people to view the 800 exhumed bodies. (See also **Arbeit Macht Frei, Dietrich Bonhoeffer, Admiral Wilhelm Canaris, John Demjanjuk, Karl Fritzsch, Hans Huettig, Homosexuals, "Jedem Das Seine," Max Koegel, "Pigs Corner,"** and **Egon Zill**.)
SUGGESTED READING: Feig, *Hitler's Death Camps.*

Forarbeiterin (G., work foreman; female); **Forarbeitmeister** (G., work foreman, male).

Forced Labor. While some of the 7 million foreign workers were nominally paid for their labor, as far as Jews were concerned, they were **slave labor**. A decree of March 21, 1942, called for the mobilization of foreign workers. Not obtaining enough workers, foreigners were **impressed** to meet demands of the Nazi war machine. As far as Jews were concerned, forced labor was slave labor. (See also **Fremdarbeiter, "Impressing," Ostarbeiter**, and **Fritz Sauckel**.)

Forschner, Otto (d. 1946). Kommandant of **Dora-Nordhausen-Mittelbau-Mittelwerk**. He was sentenced to death by an American military tribunal in May 1946.
SUGGESTED READING: Michel, *Dora.*

Forster, Albert (1902–1948). **Gauleiter** of **Danzig**. He ordered mass **deportations, forced labor**, and exterminations. Forster attempted to "Germanize" Polish children and destroyed Polish cultural treasures. He was hanged by a Polish Tribunal on April 28, 1948.
SUGGESTED READING: Levine, *Hitler's Free City: A History of the Nazi Party in Danzig.*

Fort Ontario. Old army site used to house **refugees** in **Oswego**, New York. (See also **Emergency Committee to Save the Jewish People of Europe**.)

Fossoli di Carpi. **Internment** and **transit camp** established in 1940 near Carpi, **Italy**. Initially this site was used for British and Maltese POWs. Approximately 3,200 Jews passed through this facility on the way to **Auschwitz**. Libyan Jews were also incarcerated at this camp before being **deported** to **Bergen-Belsen. Germany** assumed control of the facility in February 1944. Most inmates were transferred to Bolzano concentration camp in August 1944.
SUGGESTED READING: Zuccotti, *The Italians and the Holocaust.*

IVB4. Jewish Office headed by **Adolf Eichmann** within the jurisdiction of the **RSHA. Dieter Wiscliceny** served as deputy to Eichmann.

14 f 13. Code name for the continued **T-4** coerced **euthanasia** program from 1941–1945. Victims were placed at the killing centers of Bernburg, **Hadamar, Hartheim Castle**, and **Sonnenstein**. This included a program for **concentration**

camps (**Auschwitz, Buchenwald, Dachau, Flossenbuerg, Gross-Rosen, Mauthausen, Neuengamme**, and **Sachsenhausen-Oranienburg**) to kill prisoners no longer able to work, including **Ostarbeiter**, who suffered from infectious diseases. 14 f 13 was announced by the Inspectorate of Concentration Camps on December 10, 1941, after **Hitler** verbally ordered **Dr. Karl Brandt** to stop the Euthanasia program. **Dr. Friedrich Mennecke** was the chief **SS** doctor and coordinator of this program. (See also **"Lebensunwertes Leben"** and **"Wild Euthanasia."**)

SUGGESTED READING: Friedlander, *The Origins of Nazi Genocide.*

FPO (Y., Fareynitke Partisaner Organzatsye; United **Partisan** Organization). **Vilna ghetto** fighters' organization established on January 21, 1942. The FPO was composed of individuals from all political shades and led by **Yitzhak Arad, Hirsch Glick**, Shmerke Kaczeginski, **Josef Kaplan, Maria Rozka Korczak, Abba Kovner**, and **Yitzhak Wittenberg**. Its task was to prepare the ghetto for self-defense and spread the call for **resistance** since they recognized that the Germans meant to murder all the Jews. After September 24, 1943, these units fought in the forests.

SUGGESTED READING: Arad, *The Ghetto in Flames.*

France. Western European democracy bordering on the Atlantic Ocean in the west and **Germany** on the east, **Belgium** to the north, and **Spain** in the south. France was among the victorious **Allies** defeating Germany at the conclusion of World War I in 1918 and a signatory to the **Versailles Treaty**. The Third Republic, set up after the war, was beset by economic and political instability. Exhausted by losses during the war, it sought **appeasement** with Nazi Germany. It acquiesced to **Hitler's** violations of the Versailles Treaty: occupation of the Rhineland and German demands for the **Sudetenland**. However, on September 3, 1939, along with Great Britain, France declared war on Germany after Hitler attacked **Poland**, setting off World War II in Europe.

In 1939, the French Jewish population was 300,000 (200,000 in Paris) within the general population of 41,600,000. Jews were well integrated into French society. In 1936, Leon Blum was the first Jew and first socialist to become premier of France. He served until April 18, 1938. However, France had a history of **anti-Semitism**, and there were a number of people and groups sympathetic to the persecution of Jews.

German troops in a lightning war (Blitzkrieg) defeated France, and an armistice was signed in **Compiegne** on June 21, 1940. Under the terms, two-thirds of France was occupied by German troops, and a rump state, **Vichy**, was created under the head of World War I hero, **Marshal Henri Philippe Petain**. France kept its overseas colonies in North Africa and the Middle East. **General Charles de Gaulle** fled to London and vowed to fight on with his **Free French**.

The French state in the period June to September 1944 was called Vichy France, a **collaborationist** government. In 1942, Jews in **Unoccupied France** numbered 250,000, an additional 700,000 in French North Africa. In northern

France, occupied by German troops, the Jews numbered 165,000. Many foreign Jewish **refugees** fled to Vichy including 35,000 Belgian Jews and 20,000 Jews expelled from Alsace-Lorraine. All of France was liberated by British, Canadian, American, Free French forces, and interior French resistance forces by the beginning of September 1944. The French Provisional Government moved into Paris on September 7, 1944.

Because of the confusion of war and movement of people, it is difficult to ascertain the exact number of Jewish survivors. Approximately 180,000 French Jews survived, about 75 percent of those in the nation in 1940. Over 77,000 met their death in **concentration camps**, and 3,000 died in **French internment camps**. (See also **Otto Abetz, Jose Aboulker, Action Francaise, Algeria, CI-MADE, Comite Representatit des Israelites de France, Theodor Dannecker, Admiral Francois Darlan, Edouard Daladier, FFI, FTPF, Varian Fry, Robert Gamzon, Cardinal Pierre-Marie Gerlier, Duke Arthur Comte de Gobineau, La grande Rafle, Gurs, Pierre Laval, Jean Leguay, Lucien Lublin, Maquis, Rene Mayer, Leon Meiss, Pierre Mendes-France, Milice, Les Milles, Morocco, Munich Pact, SS General Carl Albrecht Oberg, Heinz Roethke, Trans-Sahara Railway**, and **Dr. Carltheo Zeitschel.**)

Franco, Francisco (1892–1975). **Fascist** dictator of **Spain**. He was aided by **Germany** and **Italy** during the Spanish Civil War, yet remained neutral during World War II. Franco believed the Jews were the power behind the **Allied** governments, but was also rumored to be a **Marrano**. The dictator tried to ingratiate Spain with the Allies by allowing Jews to cross the Pyrenees in transit to **Portugal**. Wealthy Jews in **Morocco** financed Franco during the Spanish Civil War. Some 40,000 Jews used Spain as a conduit to freedom, although some were detained in **Miranda de Ebro**. If a Jew could establish lineage to Spanish Jewish exiles, he was eligible to become a Spanish citizen, return to Spain, and was afforded protection by the Spanish government. A number of Greek Jews were saved due to this loophole. Spanish Blue Divisions in **Russia** fighting for the Germans offered some protection to Jews. (See also **Camoufles** and **Antonio de Oliveria Salazar.**)

SUGGESTED READING: Avni, Spain, the Jews and Franco.

Francs Tireurs et Partisans. (See **FTPF**.)

Frank, Anne (1929–1945). German-born Jewish teenager who resided in Amsterdam. Her diary was left behind after a police raid on her family's secret hideout. The journal was found by **Miep Gies**, a **Righteous Gentile**, who aided Anne's family. The *Diary of Anne Frank*, a document about her experiences in hiding and the anguish of being a teenager, was first published in 1947. She died in **Bergen-Belsen** on March 15, 1945, a month before **liberation** and several days after her sister, Margot, had succumbed to **typhus**. The diary became an international bestseller and a strong vehicle for **Holocaust** education, particularly for young people. (See also **Bruno Bettelheim** and **Netherlands**.)

SUGGESTED READINGS: Gies and Gold, *Anne Frank Remembered*; Lindwer, *The Last Seven Months of Anne Frank.*

Frank, August. Brigadier general and chief of **WVHA**. On September 26, 1942, he authorized Jewish property to be given away to **Volksdeutsche** and to the German military. Frank was sentenced by a U.S. Military Tribunal to life in prison, but the term was reduced by the clemency board to fifteen years. (See also **Aryanization** and **Clemency Act of 1951**.)

SUGGESTED READING: Hoess, *Death Dealer.*

Frank, Hans (1900–1946). Governor of the **Generalgouvernement** based in **Krakow, Poland**. An attorney, he wrote much of the anti-Jewish legislation for the Nazis and handled the sensitive matter of investigating **Hitler's** racial lineage. Frank was head of the National Socialist Lawyers Organization, president of the German Academy of Law, also **Reich** commissar for the Coordination of Justice in the States for the Reformation of the Law. He gradually fell out of favor with Hitler, but the **Fuehrer** refused to accept Frank's resignation as governor. Although his authority was undercut by **Heinrich Himmler** and the SS, Frank was an eager participant in the **Final Solution**. An observant Catholic prior to his Nazi conversion, Frank was one of the few Nazis to admit his guilt and comprehend the horrors of the **Third Reich** at the **Nuremberg Trials**: "A thousand years will pass and they will not take away this guilt of **Germany**." He returned to Catholicism during the trial and brought volumes of documents implicating himself and other Nazis. He was convicted of **war crimes** and hanged.

SUGGESTED READINGS: Davidson, *The Trial of the Germans;* Harris, *Tyranny on Trial.*

Frankfurt Trial (also referred to as the **Auschwitz Trial**). The longest legal case on file in **Germany**. The trial of chief **SS** officials, including Robert Mulka (adjunct to **Rudolf Hoess**), lasted from December 20, 1963, through August 20, 1965. All twenty-one defendants were charged with complicity in murder. Three were acquitted but none received the death penalty.

SUGGESTED READINGS: Gutman and Berenbaum, *Anatomy of the Auschwitz Death Camp*; Lifton, *The Nazi Doctors; New York Times*, December 21, 1963.

Frankl, Dr. Viktor (1905–1997). Viennese Jewish psychiatrist. He was arrested and **deported** to **Auschwitz**. While at the camp he pioneered logotherapy, basing healing on the idea that a sense of purpose and meaning is essential to mental health. His experiences are encapsulated in *Man's Search for Meaning.*

Franz, Kurt (b. 1914). Deputy kommandant of **Treblinka**. He lived in Dusseldorf under his own name until his arrest in 1959. When Franz was arrested, a photo album of his experience in Treblinka was located with the inscription: "The Best Years of My Life." Franz walked around Treblinka with his attack dog "Barry," crushed babies to death against walls, and practiced his boxing skills on inmates. He was tried from 1964–1965, convicted in the murder of 139 inmates and complicity in the extermination of 300,000 Jews. Franz was sentenced to life in prison, but released by the German government in 1993, at the age of 79. (See also **Franz Stangl**.)

SUGGESTED READING: Donat, *The Death Camp Treblinka.*

Frauenabteilung (G., women's section). Female work section established at **Auschwitz** in 1942. Women who survived **selections** were usually young, strong, and healthy, without children, and normally in their late teens to thirty.

Frauenlager (G., **concentration camp** for women). Approximately 300 such camps existed in the Nazi system. (See also **Bergen-Belsen, Bund deutscher Maedel (BdM), Lichtenburg, Moringen**, and **Ravensbrueck**.)

Frauenschaft (G., women's organization). Nazi women's league founded on October 1, 1931. After January 20, 1933, the Frauenschaft became the primary women's organization. Membership indicated loyalty to the Nazi regime. It actively discouraged feminism and sought to reinforce the female role as subordinate in Nazi society. The Nazis listed and limited the number of professions acceptable for women, for example, home economics and nursing. In addition, when a German woman bore five children she received an Honorable Mother's Cross from the Nazis. The original female **concentration camp** guards, the **SS Aufseherinnen**, were recruited from this organization. (See also **Bund deutscher Maedel (BdM), Bergen-Belsen, Irma Grese, Lichtenburg, Moringen**, and **Ravensbrueck**.)

SUGGESTED READING: Owings, *Frauen: German Women Recall the Third Reich.*

Free French. Movement headed by **General Charles de Gaulle** during World War II. Its purpose was to continue the fight against the German occupation of **France**. After the fall of the Third French Republic in June 1940, General de Gaulle continued the **resistance** from London, England. This was contrasted to the **collaborationist Vichy** government headed by **Marshal Henri Philippe Petain**. The Free French coordinated their resistance arm inside France, and the **French Forces of the Interior** welcomed Jews to their ranks wherever they were. In July 1942, the movement's name was changed to "Fighting France." By 1944, French armies swelled, particularly from their base in Algiers. On July 3, 1944, the movement became the Committee of National Liberation, and French forces aided the **Allies** in the **liberation** of Western Europe. (See also **Rene Mayer** and **Pierre Mendes-France**.)

Freemasons. Secret fraternal order founded in England in 1717. Antifreemasonry rhetoric was a staple of right-wing organizations since 1840. Masonic lodges were alleged to be a cover for a Jewish conspiracy to destroy Christianity and traditional, national society. The *Protocols of the Learned Elders of Zion* reasserted this view, and **Alfred Rosenberg** also shared this position. The organization's international links and belief in racial equality and humanitarianism made the order unwelcome to Nazis. Masonic Lodges were dissolved in **Germany** in September 1935.

 SUGGESTED READING: Robinson, *Born in Blood*.

Freight Cars. Term widely used for wagons of trains to transport Jews. Actually most Jews were deported in freight cars rather than cattle cars, although the latter was used. Jews from **Germany** and Western Europe often were **deported** in very crowded passenger cars **transporting** Jews to **ghettos** and from ghettos to **concentration camps**. The **SS** packed the Jews very tightly in each car (between 80–100 people) with no sanitary or water facilities. There was usually just a very small window that was covered with barbed wire. Many Jews perished in these cars. (See also **Deutsche Reichsbahn**.)

Freikorps (G., Free Corps). Right-wing, paramilitary group composed of World War I German veterans and unemployed youth. Formed in 1919, they blamed **Germany's** defeat on the **Social Democrats** and Jews. They crushed the Bavarian communist government and the Spartacists in **Berlin**. The Freikorps was formally dissolved in 1921. Many of its members joined the **Nazi Party** or **SA**, for example **Rudolf Hess** and **Erich Koch**. (See also **Thule Society**.)

 SUGGESTED READING: Jones, *Hitler's Heralds*.

Freisler, Dr. Roland (1893–1945). State secretary and president of the **People's Court** in **Germany** from 1942–1945. The appearance of legality was essential to Nazism, and Freisler, an ardent Nazi, oversaw a court system that sentenced thousands of political opponents, "race defilers," and "defeatists" to **concentration camps** or death. He presided over the "trials" of **Dietrich Bonhoeffer, Hans** and **Sophie Scholl**, and the members of the **July 20, 1944 Bomb Plot** to assassinate **Hitler**. The jurist represented the Justice Ministry at the **Wannsee Conference**. Freisler was killed in his courtroom during an American bombing in February 1945. (See also **Kreisau Circle**.)

 SUGGESTED READING: Mueller, *Hitler's Justice*.

Freiwillige (G., helper or volunteer). Non-Germans who joined the **Waffen-SS** or aided **Einsatzgruppen**. In military units, their assistance made mass murder of Jews possible. These units included Estonian, Latvian, Lithuanian, and Ukrainian **collaborators** and members of the Polish "**Blue Police**." (See also **Hilfswillige, Latvian SS Legion, Lithuanian Activist Front, Ostbataillone, Perkonkrust**, and **Schuma**.)

Freiwillige Schutzstaffel (G., volunteers protective squadron). Promoted by **Dieter Wisliceny, Adolf Eichmann's** representative in **Czechoslovakia**, this military force operated against Jews and was organized on the model of the German SS.

Fremdarbeiter (G., foreign laborers). Over 5 million workers were brought from Nazi-occupied Europe to work in the **Reich. Forced labor** applied to POWs, especially captured soldiers from the **Red Army**. Civilians were routinely "**impressed**" (kidnapped) to work for the **Todt Organization**. The **Geneva Convention** of 1929 prohibited the use of **slave labor**. Working conditions were poor and the mortality rate was high. (See also **Baron Gustav and Alfred von Krupp, Ostarbeiter, "P," Fritz Sauckel**, and **Albert Speer**.)
    SUGGESTED READING: Harris, *Tyranny on Trial.*

French Forces of the Interior (FFI). Noncommunist French **resistance** movement, based in **France**, loyal to **General Charles de Gaulle**. Inside France, they engaged in sabotage, espionage, and hit and run tactics against German and **Vichy collaborationist** forces. Their intelligence reports were especially important prior to the invasion at Normandy. Unlike **partisans** in the East, they were not **anti-Semitic** and accepted Jewish members. (See also **FPTF, Maquis**, and **Service de Travail Obligatoire**.)
    SUGGESTED READING: Marrus and Paxton, *Vichy France and the Jews.*

French Internment and **Transit Camps**. German Jews in the Rhineland and foreign Jews in **France** were sent to **internment camps** in the Pyrenees near the Spanish border. These camps included Beaune–la Rolande, **Gurs, Les Milles**, and **Rivesaltes. Drancy**, a transit camp near Paris, served as a staging area for foreign and indigenous Jews sent to **Auschwitz. Vichy** police cooperated with the Nazis in rounding up Jews for **deportation**. Approximately 3,000 Jews perished in these camps prior to deportation. (See also **Algeria, CIMADE, Alexandre Glasberg, Jean Leguay, Morocco**, and **Pithiviers**.)
    SUGGESTED READING: Zuccotti, *The Holocaust, the French, and the Jews.*

French Jewish Children's Aid Society. (See **Dr. Joseph Weill**.)

Frick, Wilhelm (1877–1946). **Reich** minister of interior. The legal mastermind behind mass murder in **Germany**. Frick was a jurist, intimate friend of **Hitler**, and participant in the Beer Hall Putsch in November 1923. He drew up laws, decrees, rules, and administrative charts that led to the enslavement of millions. As Reich minister of the interior, Frick was responsible for crafting most of the Nazis' racial laws designed to eliminate Jews from German life and the national economy. Frick's work provided the framework for the **Nuremberg Laws**. In June 1933, the interior minister delivered an influential policy pronouncement on "population and race policy." In 1935, he established advisory centers in every health center for genetic and racial care to carry out the Nuremberg Laws and determine who was fit for marriage. Frick was responsible for sending at least 100,000 persons to **concentration camps**. In August 1943, he became **Reichsprotektor** of the **Protectorate of Bohemia-Moravia** after **Heinrich Himmler** assumed his duties at Interior. Frick was convicted at the **Nuremberg Trials** on all counts, except planning aggressive war. He was hanged on October 16, 1946. (See also **Enabling Act, Euthanasia**, and "**Protective Custody**.")

SUGGESTED READING: Persico, *Nuremberg: Infamy on Trial.*

Friedman, Philip (1901–1960). Historian, father of **Holocaust** literature, and survivor from **Lvov**. *This is Oswiecim* (London 1946) was the first work to awaken the world about the magnitude of the Holocaust. Friedman was associated with the **Yiddish Scientific Institute** archives on the Holocaust.

Friends of the New Germany. Forerunner of the **German-American Bund**.

Friseur (G., barber). This position carried certain weight in the **concentration camp** universe. For instance, at **Mauthausen**, the **block** friseur was third in the block hierarchy after block chief and secretary.

Fritzche, Hans (1900–1953). Nazi broadcaster. Head of German radio broadcasts and responsible for wire services to foreign countries. He was the most popular radio commentator in Nazi **Germany** and creator of *Die Aktion (The Action)*, which emphasized the conspiracy of world Jewry. The **International Military Tribunal** at **Nuremberg** surprisingly found that his broadcasts did not incite **genocide**, and he was acquitted. He was arrested by the German police in 1947, convicted for inciting atrocities and sentenced to nine years by a **denazification** court, but pardoned in 1950.

SUGGESTED READING: Persico, *Nuremberg: Infamy on Trial.*

Fritzsch, Karl (1903–1945). Kommandant of **Flossenbuerg** and **Auschwitz**. He was killed during the Battle of **Berlin**.

SUGGESTED READING: Segev, *Soldiers of Evil.*

Fritz Schultz Company. German company that operated factories in **Trawniki** and the **Warsaw ghetto**.

Fromm, Erich (1900–1980). Psychoanalytic writer, social philosopher, and German **refugee**. His writings provide a psychoanalytic interpretation of why the Germans embraced **Hitler** (*Escape from Freedom*) and provided theoretical motivating forces behind mass murderers like **Heinrich Himmler** (*The Anatomy of Human Destructiveness.*)

SUGGESTED READING: Hughes, *The Sea Change.*

Fry, Varian (1917–1976). American rescuer and **Righteous Gentile**. President **Franklin Delano Roosevelt** yielded to his wife, **Eleanor**, and reluctantly allowed Fry to go to **France** with 200 **visas**. He was a representative of the **Emergency Rescue Committee** to Marseilles (**Vichy**) in 1940. Fry worked with the **American Friends Service Committee** and the Salvation Army. He purchased passports from other consuls, and when his **visas** ran out, he smuggled **refugees** over the Pyrenees to **Spain**. A young, Harvard-educated American photographer, he saved 4,000 people from the Nazis, including many prominent scholars, writers, and artists, for example, Heinrich Mann, Marc Chagall, **Hannah Arendt**, Andre Masson, Max Ernst, Marcel Duchamp, and Jacques Lipchitz. Fry was sent for a month, stayed for fourteen months (1940–1941) before the Vichy government expelled him to Spain in September 1941. Not only did the U.S. State Department approve of Fry's expulsion, it warned him to stop rescue activities. Fry was recognized at **Yad Vashem** almost thirty years after his death. He is the only American honored as a Righteous Gentile. (See also **Hamilton Fish Armstrong**.)

SUGGESTED READINGS: United States Holocaust Memorial Museum, *Darkness Before Dawn*, United States Holocaust Memorial Museum, *Assignment Rescue: The Story of Varian Fry and the Emergency Rescue Committee*.

FTPF (F., Francs Tireurs et Partisans French Sharpshooters and **Partisans**). Major French communist underground movement organized by **Marcel Rayman** that included many Jews. This organization did not coordinate activities with the **French Forces of the Interior** but harassed the occupying forces independently. (See also **Maquis** and **Service de Travail Obligatoire**.

SUGGESTED READING: La Couture, *De Gaulle, The Rebel, 1940–1945*.

Fuehrer (G., Leader). When **President Paul von Hindenburg** died on August 2, 1934, **Hitler** created the title of "Fuehrer," which incorporated the powers of the chancellor and the president. Hitler was now supreme ruler of an organic entity, and he demanded absolute obedience. All members of the armed forces pledged personal loyalty to Hitler. (See also **Fuehrer Prinzip**.)

Fuehrerbefehl (G., order or command from the leader). "Just following orders" was an excuse given by Nazi officials for **war crimes** and **crimes against humanity**. The **Nuremberg Principles** excluded this defense.

Fuehrer Chancellery (also referred to as the **Reich Chancellery**). Complex of buildings in **Berlin** from which the principal business of state was conducted and coordinated including **Hitler's** private affairs and the **T-4** program. (See also **Dr. Philipp Bouhler** and **Hans Heinrich Lammers**.)

Fuehrer Decree. In October 1939, **Hitler** paved the way for euthanizing German adults by instructing **Dr. Philipp Bouhler** and **Dr. Karl Brandt** to choose physicians to decide who "can be granted a mercy death" (**gnadentod**).

Fuehrer Prinzip (G., the leader principle). The Nazis viewed elections as wasteful, and natural leaders deserved unquestioning obedience in cultural, economic, and political spheres. **Hitler** was the supreme leader, that is, Der Fuehrer, but there were many lesser fuehrers who received their position by appointment in the **Third Reich. SS** positions had the suffix "fuehrer."

Fuenfundzwanzig am Arsch (G., Twenty-five on the ass). A **concentration camp** prisoner who committed an infraction of one of the numerous and petty camp rules would be bent over a trestle and whipped. An auspeitschtisch was a special whipping table used in the camps. Often the **SS** would chant "fuenfundzwanzig am arsch." This form of so-called discipline was part of the **dehumanization** process.

Fugslang-Damgaard, Bishop H. Lutheran bishop of Copenhagen. He prepared a written statement against persecution of Jews that he issued on behalf of all Danish churches on October 3, 1943. The text was sent to the German-occupation authorities. (See also **Denmark**.)
  SUGGESTED READING: Goldberger, *The Rescue of Danish Jews.*

Fugu Plan. Scheme by the Japanese government to influence the American government to accept Japanese aggression and their New Order by providing safe haven for Jewish **refugees**. They theorized that "World Jewry" would be grateful and persuade President **Franklin Delano Roosevelt** to adopt a hands-off policy toward Japanese expansion in the Far East. **Shanghai**, captured by Japan, was accepting Jews in 1938 and did not require an entry **visa**. Seventeen thousand European Jews reached safe haven in **Kobe** (Kyoto) Japan in February 1941 and eventually settled in Shanghai after Pearl Harbor. (See also **Mir Yeshiva**.)
  SUGGESTED READING: Tokayer and Swartz, *The Fugu Plan.*

Funk, Walther (1890–1960). Head of the Nazi banking system and minister of the economy. Funk facilitated financial support for the **Nazi Party** from industry, including **Baron Gustav and Alfred von Krupp** and **Fritz Thyssen**. He coined the term **Kristallnacht** and drew up the laws expelling Jews from economic life (1938). In 1942, Funk and **Heinrich Himmler** formed an alliance to distribute the booty taken from **concentration camp** inmates. Coins, bank notes, and gold extracted from eyeglasses and teeth of **gas chamber** victims were sent to the Reichsbank. Personal belongings, jewels, and watches were distributed to **Berlin** Municipal Pawn Shops. Funk was found guilty at the **Nuremberg Trials** of **crimes against humanity** and expropriation and looting of Jewish property.

Funk was given life imprisonment, but released in 1957. (See also **Aryanization**.)

SUGGESTED READINGS: Davidson, *The Trial of the Germans*; Pool and Pool, *Who Financed Hitler?*

G

Gailani, Kailani. (See **Rashid Ali al-Gaylani**.)

Galen, Bishop Clemens von ("Lion of Muenster") (1878–1946). Bishop of Muenster. He opposed the **euthanasia** program. von Galen's opposition climaxed with a speech he delivered on August 3, 1941. However, he did not openly oppose persecution of Jews. The religious leader was an outspoken critic of Nazi racial laws and penned a popular criticism of **Dr. Alfred Rosenberg's** *Myth of the Twentieth Century* in 1934. von Galen came from an aristocratic family and initially welcomed aspects of Nazi nationalism, for example, the occupation of the Rhineland (1936.) The bishop was imprisoned in **Sachsenhausen-Oranienburg** in July 1944 after the attempted assassination of **Hitler**, although he was not linked to the plot. The church official inspired the **White Rose resistance**. von Galen was released from prison in 1945, and in March 1945, he infuriated **Hitler** by surrendering Muenster to the **Allies**. (See also **Monsignor Bernhard Lichtenberg** and **Hans** and **Sophie Scholl**.)
   SUGGESTED READING: Rhodes, *The Vatican in the Age of Dictators.*

Galicia. Region in southeastern **Poland** and northwestern **Ukraine**, formerly part of the Austro-Hungarian empire. The **Soviet Union** annexed this territory in September 1939. In the summer of 1941, as part of the invasion of the Soviet Union, it was conquered by Nazi **Germany**. This area was incorporated into the **Generalgouvernement**. (See also **Belzec, Partition of Poland, Reserve Police Battalion 101**, and **Metropolitan Andrej Szeptyekyj**.)

Galician SS (14th Galizien). Division of 12,000 to 18,000 men formed early in 1943 from the ranks of **Ukrainian Nationalists**. They engaged in exceptional brutality in the **Ukraine**. The 14th Galizien were very badly mauled at the battle of Brody in 1944, losing 80 percent of their men. About 2,000 members are receiving a pension from the German government where they live peaceably in Canada. (See also **OUN**.)

SUGGESTED READINGS: Lumsden, The Black Corps; Sabin, Alliance for Murder.

Gamzon, Robert (1905–1961). French Jewish leader. He founded the Jewish Scout Movement in **France** and established **Maquis** units from this organization. As a **partisan** commander, Gamzon defeated a garrison of 3,500 Germans as part of his campaign to aid Americans (1944). He also spearheaded clandestine welfare and rescue operations. Gamzon settled in Israel in 1949.

SUGGESTED READING: Latour, The Jewish Resistance in France.

Garel Network. French underground organization that placed Jewish children with Christian institutions and families.

Gas Chambers. Specially sealed rooms cloaked as showers or delousing facilities at various **concentration, labor**, and **death camps**. Victims were either **selected** as they came off **freight cars** or were sent to the gas chambers after their physical condition deteriorated. The victims, including children, were stripped of their clothing and belongings before the gassing operation. The booty became the property of the **WVHA**. The chamber was hermetically sealed and **Zyklon-B** crystals were introduced from a fake shower nozzle (**Majdanek** and **Birkenau**). Most killing centers used **carbon monoxide**, for example, **Belzec, Sobibor**, and **Treblinka**. Victims were removed by the **Sonderkommandos**, and depending on the camp, they were either burned in the **Krematorium-Kremchy**, burned in an open pit, or buried in mass graves. (See also **Bauleitung, Dr. Ernst von Grawitz, J. A. Topf und Soehne, Hans Kammler**, and **Muselmann**.)

SUGGESTED READINGS: Arad, Belzec, Sobibor, Treblinka: The Operation Reinhard Death Camps; Pressac, Auschwitz: Technique and Operation of the Gas Chambers.

Gau (G., district). The **Nazi Party** initially divided **Germany** into thirty-two regional districts called Gaugeblete run by **Gauleiter**. These geographical areas were similar to old **Reichstag** electoral districts. Frequently, bureaucratic turf fights erupted between the **SS**, the Nazi Party, and the government. Each Gau was divided and subdivided among Nazi Party members down to the street block level; all were responsible to **Martin Bormann** after 1941.

Gauleiter (G., district leader). Governor of **Gau** appointed by and accountable to **Hitler**. These forty-three men were responsible for the political, economic, and labor activities, civil defense, and some police duties. To some extent, Gauleiter posts were forms of political patronage handed out to the less able or older party members. Through its subdivision, control was exerted over German citizens. (See also **Martin Bormann, Albert Forster, Artur Greiser, Konrad Henlein, Erich Koch, Fritz Sauckel, Baldur von Schirach**, and **Julius Streicher**.)

SUGGESTED READING: Farago, *Aftermath.*

Gebhardt, Dr. Karl (1899–1948). **SS** physician. He believed in the curative powers of sulfamilamide, but failed to heal **Reinhard Heydrich** with the drug after the military governor was wounded. He conducted inhumane sterilizations at **Ravensbrueck**. Gebhardt was convicted at the **Doctors' Trial** and executed June 21, 1948. (See also **Irma Grese** and **Lapin**.)

SUGGESTED READING: Annas and Grodin, *The Nazi Doctors and the Nuremberg Code.*

Geheime Reichssache (G., Top State Secret). Order given by Nazis and kept secret by all parties. **Heinrich Himmler** informed only a small number of subordinates of the **Final Solution** to the **Jewish Problem** in this manner. (See also **Posen Speech**.)

Geheime Staatspolizei. (See **Gestapo**.)

Gehinnom (H., and Y., hell). Term used by Jewish inmates in referring to life and conditions in the **concentration camps**.

Gehlen, General Reinhard (1902–1979). Most senior military officer on the Eastern Front. Gehlen surrendered to the Americans with complete files of his activities while in charge of intelligence in the **Soviet Union**. He was recruited by American intelligence to aid the United States in the cold war. Gehlen hired former Nazis, including **RSHA** officers. He was the first president of the West German intelligence service, an organization that included former Nazis. (See also **Dr. Franz W. Six**.)

SUGGESTED READING: Simpson, *Blowback.*

Gemeinde (G., community). Official Jewish communal organization in **Romania** headed by **Dr. Wilhelm Filderman** in Bucharest.

Gemmeker, Albert Konrad (b. 1907). Austrian SS lieutenant and kommandant of **Westerbork** form October 12, 1942 until April 12, 1945. His regime was strict, but inmates were provided with basic needs, including limited forms of recreation. Gemmeker attempted to deceive approximately 100,000 **Dutch** Jews and **Roma** that they were being **deported** to the East for work. After the war, he was sentenced to ten years imprisonment by a Dutch court, but he was released early.

Gendarmerie (F., literally constables; regional or national police force). These forces, particularly in **France** and **Hungary, collaborated** with the Germans.

Gendarmerie helped to roundup and **deport** Jews. (See also **Laszlo Ferenczy, Vadasz Esendorok**, and **Vichy**.)

Generalgouvernement (GG) (G., General gouvernement). Part of eastern **Poland** not incorporated into **Germany** proper. It included five districts: **Galicia**, Radom, **Warsaw, Lublin**, and **Krakow**. Most of Poland's 3.3 million Jews were located in or **deported** to this area. The GG sent a representative to the **Wannsee Conference**. Although **Hans Frank** was the general-governor, the **SS** was the preeminent source of power and control. (See also **"Blue Police"** and **"Total Evacuation."**)
   SUGGESTED READING: Korbonski, *The Jews and the Poles in World War II.*

Generalplan Ost (G., General plan for the East). Nazi concept for a racial **New Order** that included the colonization of Eastern Europe and extermination of the Jews.

Genetic Health Courts. Established by the Nazi regime in 1935, these "courts," 181 in all, were set up to adjudicate issues raised by the Law for Compulsory Sterilization (1933). (In 1934, 90 percent of the petitions taken to the Special Court resulted in sterilization.) On October 8, 1935, the law to "safeguard the hereditary health of the German people" legalized abortion if any parent suffered from "hereditary" diseases. In 1935, **Wilhelm Frick** established advisory units in every health center for genetic and racial care to carry out the **Nuremberg Laws** and determine who was fit for marriage. In 1937, the advisory centers were also charged with sterilization, genetic registration, and anti-Jewish **miscegenation**. (See also **Euthanasia** and **Dr. Robert Ritter**.)
   SUGGESTED READINGS: Friedlander, *The Origins of Nazi Genocide*; Proctor, *Racial Hygiene.*

Geneva Convention. An international agreement ratified in Geneva, **Switzerland**, in 1864 by the United States, Britain, and many other nations. Additions were made in 1925 (outlawing the use of poison gas) and 1929 (which Germany signed). It established rules for the humane treatment of prisoners of war, the sick, wounded, and dead. The 1949 provision added humane treatment for civilians. (See also **Nuremberg Trials, Slave Labor**, and **Wehrmacht**.)
   SUGGESTED READING: Falk, Kolko, and Lifton, *Crimes of War.*

Genocide. Systematic killing of a religious, ethnic, or national group. The term was coined in 1943 by **Rafael Lemkin** in his book *Axis Rule in Europe*. He derived it from the Greek word "genos" (tribe) and the Latin word "cedere" (kill). The **Holocaust** was the particular Jewish genocide by the Nazis. (See also **Crimes Against Humanity**.)

Genocide Convention (1948). A UN treaty ratified by most member nations after World War II. It made **genocide**, its planning, and execution an international crime and enabled the UN to punish those who perpetuate genocide within a sovereign nation. The Convention also provided for an ad hoc international tribunal to hear cases. The United States finally became a member on November 4, 1988, making genocide a federal crime in America. (See also **Rafael Lemkin.**)

SUGGESTED READING: Katz, *The Holocaust in Historical Context.*

Gens, Jacob (1905–1943). Chairman of the **Vilna ghetto Judenrat**. He promoted "work for life." While he did participate in **selecting** Jews for **deportation**, Gens actively aided **partisan** efforts to save Jews. Gens turned down an offer to escape. He was shot by the **Gestapo** on September 4, 1943. (See also **"Work as a Means of Rescue."**)

SUGGESTED READING: Tushnet, *The Pavement of Hell.*

Gerlier, Cardinal Pierre-Marie (1880–1968). **Righteous Gentile**. Archbishop of Lyon. Sympathetic to the Jewish plight, the prelate actively pressured **Marshal Henri Philippe Petain**, in vain, to halt Jewish **deportations**. He ordered Catholic institutions to hide Jewish children and attacked the Nazi **New Order** as based on hatred and violence. (See also **Marc Boegner.**)

SUGGESTED READING: Rhodes, *The Vatican in the Age of Dictators.*

German-American Bund (Friends of the New Germany). Anti-Semitic, U.S. pro-Nazi organization. Founded in 1933 as the **Friends of the New Germany**, comprised of 10,000–20,000 members, it became the **Bund** in 1935 under the leadership of Fritz Kuhn. This organization sponsored rallies, distributed literature, and advocated the boycott of Jewish owned businesses in the United States. **Hitler** officially disavowed the group because he feared an anti-German backlash. The Bund disappeared when the United States entered the war in December 1941. (See also **Reverend Charles E. Roman Coughlin.**)

SUGGESTED READING: Herzstein, *Roosevelt and Hitler.*

German Earth and Stone Works, Ltd. (**DEST**). SS corporation charged with overseeing construction and related enterprises at **concentration camps**. (See also **Flossenbuerg, Mauthausen, Messerschmidt, Natzweiler**, and **Sachsenhausen.**)

German Labor Front. (See **Deutsche Arbeitsfront.**)

German Workers Party (G., Deutsche Arbeiterpartiei). Grew out of the **Thule Society**; it was the forerunner of the **Nazi Party. Hitler** was sent as an army spy to watch this group. He ended up joining and becoming its leader. (See also **Anton Drexler** and **Nazi [NSDAP].**)

Germany. Highly industrialized and scientifically advanced country in central Europe lying between **France** and **Poland** sharing borders with the **Netherlands, Belgium, Switzerland, Austria, Czechoslovakia**, and **Denmark**. On the eve of **Hitler's** ascension to power 503,000 Jews lived in Germany among 65 million people. About 99,000 or almost 20 percent were East European Jewish nationals. The Jews were emancipated in 1871, meaning there were no special restrictions against them directed against their integration into Germany's political and economic life. Jews enjoyed a middle- to upper middle-class status supplying Germany with many professionals and Nobel Prize winners. They were very active in the **Social Democratic** Party and in the **Weimar Republic**. Hitler used Jewish participation in Weimar for his "**stabbed-in-the-back**" myth. When Hitler became chancellor and the Nazis dominated the **Reichstag**, a wave of **anti-Semitic** measures overtook German Jews. Rabbi **Leo Baeck** correctly predicted in 1933, "The end of a 1000 year history of German Jewry." The strong anti-Semitic programs developed by thinkers prior to World War I now became the policy of a new **National Socialist** state. Between April 1933 and May 1939, 304,500 German Jews emigrated from Germany largely to the following countries: United States (63,000); **Palestine** (55,000); Great Britain (40,000); France (30,000); and Argentina (25,000). However, in 1939, there were still 215,000 Jews left. The world's nations did not generously open their gates to these **refugees**. In October 1941, Nazi officials stopped emigration.

Nazi Germany unleashed a war of aggression. In September 1939 it attacked Poland starting World War II in Europe. It invaded Norway, Denmark and the Low Countries, and defeated France. The **Wehrmacht** invaded the Balkans and on June 22, 1941, attacked the **Soviet Union**. On December 11, 1941, Hitler declared war on the United States. At the end of World War II and the defeat of Germany by the **Allies** in May 1945, statistics revealed that Germany had lost 160,000 Jews. However, there were 330,000 German Jews who survived, consisting largely of those who had emigrated. Germany was occupied by the four victorious powers: France, the United States, Great Britain, and the **USSR**. The country was divided into **occupation zones**. Jewish **displaced persons** sought to be placed in American **DP camps** in the **American Zone of Occupation**. A **denazification** program was instituted by the occupying powers, but it was aborted during the cold war. (See also **Konrad Adenauer, Hermann Ahlwardt, Ahnenerbe, Anschluss, Arbeitsdienst, Aryan, Aryanization, Aryan Paragraph, Axis, Berlin, Book Burning, Boycott, Martin Buber, Houston Stewart Chamberlain, Drang nach Osten, Eugenics, Evian Conference, "J," Kristallnacht, John McCloy, Nuremberg, Operation Barbarossa, Walther Rathenau, Reich, Reichsvertretung der Deutschen Juden, Reichswehr, Reich Union of Jewish Front Line Soldiers, Reparations and Restitution,** *Saint Louis*, **Thule Society**, and **Richard Wagner**.)

Gerstein, Kurt (1905–1945). **SS** officer and head of the **Waffen-SS** Institute of Hygiene in **Berlin**. He joined the **Nazi Party** in 1933 and later became a member of the **Confessional Church**. For this, he was dismissed from state service in 1938 and thrown into a **concentration camp**. He volunteered for the Waffen-SS in 1941 and became chief Disinfection Officer in the Office of Health and Technology. As such, Gerstein served as a ''contamination expert'' and worked with **Zyklon-B**. In August 1941, Gerstein viewed the murder process at **Treblinka, Belzec**, and **Sobibor** and timed it with a stop watch. He tried to alert the papal **nuncio** in **Berlin**, church leaders, and diplomats about the **Final Solution** without success. The SS officer allegedly committed suicide in a French prison after the war; however, it was rumored that he was murdered by SS inmates.

SUGGESTED READINGS: Friedlander, *Kurt Gerstein: The Ambiguity of Good*; United States Holocaust Memorial Museum, *Darkness Before Dawn*.

Gestapo (acronym for **Geheime Staatsapolizei**) (G., German Secret State Police). Formerly the state police of Prussia under **Hermann Goering** in 1933. Placed under **Heinrich Himmler**'s control in April 1934, this police force maintained internal **Reich** security and eliminated real and perceived enemies of Nazism. The Gestapo was incorporated into the **SS** in 1936 and later combined with **SD** and SS intelligence branch under **Reinhard Heydrich**. It had enormous powers of incarceration without judicial review. **Heinrich Mueller** maintained operational control of the Gestapo. A subsection, **IVB4**, under **Adolf Eichmann** dealt with the **Jewish Question** and the **Final Solution**. The Gestapo assumed the role of the political police and was the most feared entity in Nazi occupied areas. (See also ''**Black Police**,'' **Euthanasia**, ''**Greifer**,'' **Hotel Polski, July 20, 1944 Bomb Plot, Kreisau Circle, Kripo, Landwacht, Political Department-Section**, ''**Protective Custody**,'' and **Sofort Vernichtet**.)

SUGGESTED READING: Crankshaw, *Gestapo*.

GG (See **Generalgouvernement**.)

Ghetto. Restriction of Jews to physically segregated and isolated areas of a town or city. This concept, together with book burning, had roots in fifteenth- and sixteenth-century **Germany** and **Italy**. The first ghetto mandated exclusively for Jews was created in Venice in 1516. The Nazis created 400 ghettos for Jews, mostly in Eastern Europe, where the conditions were squalid and privation prevailed. By the summer of 1942, 2 million Jews and 8,000 **Roma** were confined to ghettos. The ghettos served to contain, exploit, degrade, and eventually **deport** Jews to the **concentration camp** complex. The German euphemism was **Juedischer Wohnbezirk**—''Jewish residential district.'' (See also **Judenrat, Lodz Ghetto, Vilna**, and **Warsaw Ghetto**.)

Ghetto Cleaners. Underlings of the Germans who supervised the destruction of Jewish **ghettos** in Polish cities. Many **Soviet POWs** were trained for this job at **Trawniki**. These **collaborators** performed the most inhumane tasks including

house to house searches, sealing off the ghetto, and herding the victims to **transport** centers. (See also **Umschlagsplatz**).
SUGGESTED READING: Dobroszycki, The Chronicle of the Lodz Ghetto.

Ghetto Fighters' House. **Resistance** museum near Acre, Israel. Its exhibits include dioramas of the **Warsaw** and **Vilna Ghetto Uprisings**. It is a publishing arm for **Holocaust** resistance books. The museum was founded by **Yitzhak Zuckerman** and **Zivia Lubetkin**. (See also **Ghetto Fighters' Kibbutz**.)

Ghetto Fighters' Kibbutz. Located one mile north of Acre in Israel. Communal farm started by **Zivia Lubetkin** and **Yitzhak Zuckerman** for ghetto fighters and **partisans**. Most members are from **Socialist-Zionist** organizations. The kibbutz houses a museum and a large amphitheater where the **Warsaw Ghetto Uprising** is reenacted each year. (See also **Ghetto Fighters' House**.)

Gies, Miep (b. 1909). Dutch **Righteous Gentile**. Secretary to Otto Frank, she aided the Frank family in hiding. Gies rescued **Anne Frank**'s writings after the family was arrested. Only Otto Frank (Anne's father) survived the war. Gies returned Anne's diary to Otto.
SUGGESTED READING: Gies and Gold, Anne Frank Remembered.

Gildenman, Misha (''Uncle Misha'') (1898–1958). Soviet Jewish **resister**. An engineer from Koretz, **Poland**, Gildenman was a popular Polish **partisan** commander who organized Jews into a division in the forests of **Zhitomer**. Later, he joined the Soviets as a regular soldier and fought far into **Germany**.

Gingold, Dr. Nandor (d. 1988?). Titular head of the Romanian Jewish Center. He supplied labor, names, and addresses to the **SS** and Romanian government. The **collaborator** was convicted as a major **war criminal**, but released to practice medicine in Bucharest. Gingold converted to Christianity after the war. (See also **Romania**.)
SUGGESTED READING: Fischer, Transnistria.

Gitterman, Isaac (1889–1943). Director of the **American Joint Distribution Committee** in **Poland**. He made his way to **Vilna** and set up the **Jewish Self-Help Society**, which supplied money for arms to **ghetto resistance**. Gitterman was killed on January 18, 1943, by the **SS** during the initial **Warsaw Ghetto Uprising**.
SUGGESTED READING: Gutman, Resistance.

Glasberg, Alexandre (Abbe) (1902–1981). Catholic priest (converted from Judaism) in Lyon who established **Christian Friendship**, an organization that helped Jews. He sheltered hundreds of Jewish prisoners released from **French internment camps**. After 1942, the priest coordinated rescue efforts with Jewish organizations and worked closely with the **Society for the Rescue of Jewish Children**. Later, he joined the **partisans**. After the war Glasberg was active in **Mossad le Aliya Bet**.

SUGGESTED READING: Zuccotti, *The Holocaust, the French, and the Jews.*

Glaube und Schoenheit (G., "Faith and Beauty"). (See **Bund deutscher Maedel [BdM]**.)

Glazer, Gesja (d. 1944). Underground fighter in **Kovno**. She fled to Moscow in June 1941 and was later dropped by parachute back into Kovno to lead Jewish fighters in forests. Glazer was involved in the **Vilna resistance** in 1944 until she was trapped by the Nazis and committed suicide.

SUGGESTED READING: Arad, *The Ghetto in Flames.*

Glazman, Josef (1907–1943.) **Partisan** leader, head of **Beitar** and a founder of **FPO**. He was the first fighter out of the **Vilna Ghetto** and formed a Jewish partisan unit in the Naroch Forest. On October 7, 1943, encircled by Germans, Glazman and his entire unit were wiped out.

SUGGESTED READING: Eckman and Lazar, *The Jewish Resistance.*

Gleichschaltung (G., coordination or synchronization). Legal consolidation of Nazi power after **Hitler** took office. Its object was to create a central, one-party **Reich** and destroy the traditions and privileges of the old German **laender**. This Nazification process eliminated the Jews from German political, cultural, economic, and social institutions and consolidated the **National Socialist** perspective. (See also **Law for the Restoration of Professional Civil Service**.)

SUGGESTED READING: Fischer, *Nazi Germany: A New History.*

Gleiwitz. (1) Subcamps operated by German railroads at the **Auschwitz** complex; (2) The Gleiwitz Radio Station "assault" by "Polish" troops was a staged Nazi ruse. This "provocation" was used by **Hitler** to justify the invasion on **Poland**. (See also **Deutsche Reichsbahn** and **Otto Moll**.)

Glick, Hirsh (1922–1944). Poet and **partisan** member of the **FPO**. While **ghettoized** in **Vilna**, he wrote "Song of the Partisans" or "Zog nit Kainmul" ["Never Say"]. Glick was sent to a **concentration camp** in **Estonia** and killed during an attempted escape in the summer of 1944.

SUGGESTED READING: United States Holocaust Memorial Museum, *Revolt Amid the Darkness.*

Globke, Dr. Hans (1898–1973). Nazi jurist. He co-authored influential commentary on the **Nuremberg Laws** with **Dr. Wilhelm Stuckart** and drafted the **Reich** Citizenship Law (1935) and the Law for the Protection of German Blood and Honor (1935). These laws sought to exclude and separate Jews and other racial aliens from German society. He also wrote legislation that forced all Jews to use the middle names of "**Sarah**" or "**Israel**" if they didn't have a distinct Jewish name already (January 1939). The jurist crafted legislation that allowed the Reich to expropriate property from Jews sent to **concentration camps** (1944). Globke was arrested after the war but released despite his Nazi activities and his close alliance with **Heinrich Himmler**. He became a leading figure in the Christian Democratic Party and was ultimately defended by Chancellor **Konrad Adenauer**. As state-secretary for Konrad Adenauer in the spring of 1962, the legal expert actively sought indemnification legislation for Jews exploited by German companies during the war. This effort was rejected by German industry. Globke retired to **Switzerland** and died on February 13, 1973.

SUGGESTED READING: Mueller, *Hitler's Justice.*

Globocnik, Odilo (1904–1945). **Gauleiter** of **Vienna** and chief of police of **Lublin**. He coordinated **resettlement** of Jews in the **Generalgouvernement** in 1941. Globocnik was actively involved with the **Einsatzgruppen** and was **Heinrich Himmler's** right-hand man in eastern and southern **Poland**. He established **Belzec, Sobibor**, and **Majdanek**. Globocnik introduced the gas van at Belzec and Sobibor. Captured by the British in **Austria**, the mass murderer committed suicide in May 1945. (See also **Avengers, Hans Hoefle, OST**, "**Sonderwagon**," and **Zamosc**.)

SUGGESTED READING: Levy, *The Wiesenthal File.*

Gluecks, Richard (1889–1945). Chief aide to **Theodor Eicke**, whom he eventually replaced as inspector of the **concentration camps**. He oversaw an increase in the number and function of concentration camps and advocated the establishment of **Auschwitz**. Gluecks apparently committed suicide in May 1945. (See also **Avengers**.)

SUGGESTED READING: Zentner and Friedemann, *The Encyclopedia of the Third Reich.*

Gnadentod (G., "mercy death"). (See **Euthanasia** and **Fuehrer Decree**.)

Gobineau, Arthur Comte de (1816–1882). French philosopher and aristocrat. His seminal work, *Essay on the Inequality of Human Races*, postulated that all history can be explained by racial characteristics of the world's three races and that Caucasians of the Teutonic strain were most advanced. The **Aryans** were supposedly superior due to their energy, intelligence, and instinct for order. He feared intermarriage would lead to the weakening of the Aryan race and degeneracy. While not **anti-Semitic**, Gobineau's ideas were incorporated into Nazi racial ideology. (See also **Richard Wagner**.)

SUGGESTED READING: Mosse, *Toward the Final Solution.*

Goebbels, Dr. Paul Joseph (1897–1945). **Gauleiter** of **Berlin** and minister of Propaganda and Popular Enlightenment. He published and edited *Der Angriff* from 1927–1945 and was a master propagandist. He was a powerful speaker, virulent **anti-Semite**, devoted to **Hitler**, and with the exception of **Albert Speer**, was the only close aide with a substantial education. The propaganda minister was well aware of the West's apathy toward European Jewry and remarked in 1942: "Both the English and the Americans are happy that we're eliminating the Jewish riff-raff." He took over **Fritz Sauckel's** role and became Special Plenipotentiary for Labor in July 1944. Goebbels wrote in his journal in the last days of the war: "The Jews must be slaughtered while we can still do it." He poisoned himself, his wife, and children in Hitler's bunker. (See also **Book burning**, "**Jud Suess**," and **Leni Riefenstahl**.)

SUGGESTED READINGS: Fest, *The Face of the Third Reich*; Goebbels, *Final Entries*; Reutin, *Goebbels*.

Goerdelor, Carl Frederick (1884–1945). Anti-Nazi, German resister. Lord Mayor of Leipzig until 1937, he resigned his office in protest to Nazi racial and church policies. Goerdelor became head of the conservative, political **resistance**. He was arrested and executed as a traitor on February 2, 1945.

SUGGESTED READING: Snyder, *Hitler's German Enemies*.

Goering, Hermann (1893–1946). Deputy **fuehrer**. He held an impressive array of posts during his Nazi tenure including head of the **SA**, president of the **Reichstag**, Prussian minister of justice, founder and head of the **Gestapo**, commissioner of the Four Year Plan, commander in chief of the **Luftwaffe**, and German minister of the interior. He created the **concentration camps** in Prussia for communists, supervised the **Anschluss**, and bullied **Czechoslovakia** to capitulate the **Sudetenland**. Goering announced the **Nuremberg Laws** as president of the Reichstag, convened the **Wannsee Conference** and charged **Reinhard Heydrich** with implementing **Endloesung**. A World War I flying ace, Goering lent credibility to the **Nazi Party**. The deputy fuehrer was an able politician, but slid into disfavor with **Hitler** when his much vaunted Luftwaffe failed to defeat England in the Battle of Britain (1940). He was the most prominent and challenging defendant at the **Nuremberg Trials**. Unrepentant, Goering committed suicide in his cell a day before he was to be hanged for **war crimes**. (See also **Central Planning Board, Kristallnacht, Dr. Sigmund Rascher**, and **Dr. Claus Schilling**.)

SUGGESTED READINGS: Mosely, *The Reich Marshall*; Persico, *Nuremberg, Infamy on Trial*.

Goeth, Amon (1908–1946). **SS** officer who coordinated liquidation of several **ghettos** including **Krakow**. He was the brutal and sadistic kommandant of **Pla-**

szow from February 1943 to September 1944. Goeth was tried and hanged in Krakow in 1946.
   SUGGESTED READING: Federber-Salz, *And the Sun Kept Shining.*

"Going into the Wire." Suicide by touching electric fencing in **concentration camps**. At **Auschwitz**, Jewish girls were the most frequent victims of desperation, isolation, and hopelessness. (See also **Dehumanization.**)

Goldmann, Nahum (1894–1982). **Zionist** leader and diplomat. He represented the **Jewish Agency** at the **League of Nations** in the 1930s. He negotiated (1950s) on behalf of the **World Jewish Congress**, which he headed from 1949–1977, with West **Germany's Konrad Adenauer** for $827 million in **reparations** for Israel and **Holocaust** survivors. (See also **Luxembourg Agreement.**)
   SUGGESTED READING: Goldmann, *The Jewish Paradox.*

Goldsmid, Dr. Henryk. (See **Janusz Korczak.**)

"Gold Train." In 1945, the U.S. Army seized a train containing valuables from **concentration camp** inmates including thousands of gold wedding rings. Much of this booty has not been returned to the heirs of deceased Jews, nor to the Jewish community. Some gold is stored in **Switzerland** and the Federal Reserve vaults in Manhattan.
   SUGGESTED READING: The Philadelphia Inquirer, November 3, 1996

Gollancz, Victor (1893–1967) English Jewish writer and publisher. He helped establish the Left Book Club, which exposed Nazism. The writer campaigned for the National Committee for Rescue from Nazi Terror. In 1945, Gollancz advocated admission of Jewish survivors to **Palestine**.
   SUGGESTED READING: Johnson, *The Intellectuals.*

Golus (Y., exile). Term used to describe the **Diaspora** or dispersion of Jews outside the land of Israel.

Goy (H. and Y., non-Jew or nation). Gentile. The occasional intent may be unflattering, but the word is neutral.

Graben. Subcamp for women at **Gross-Rosen**.

Graebe, Hermann Fritz (1900–1986). German businessman. Graebe employed hundreds of Jews whom he treated well and intervened to save their lives, particularly in **Kovno, Lithuania**. He witnessed the murder of **Simon Dubnow** and gave evidence at the **Nuremberg Trials**. Graebe was recognized as a **Righteous Gentile**.
   SUGGESTED READING: Huneke, *The Moses of Rovno.*

Granatowa Policja (P., **Blue Police**).

Grand Mufti of Jerusalem (Hajj Amin al Husseini) (1895–1974). Palestinian religious leader. He spent much of World War II in **Germany** and argued for the **Final Solution** to be extended to the Middle East and North Africa. The Mufti was an Arab nationalist and organizer who led a revolt against British and Jewish presence in **Palestine** from 1936 to 1939, which subsequently led to the British **White Paper**. He helped overthrow British rule in Iraq, then fled to **Berlin**. The Mufti met with **Hitler** and **Heinrich Himmler** and was closely allied with **Adolf Eichmann**. The Palestinian leader reportedly visited **Auschwitz, Mauthausen, Theresienstadt**, and **Bergen-Belsen**. On November 28, 1941, Hitler promised the Mufti that upon German conquest of Palestine, the entire Jewish population would be exterminated. He also helped to recruit 20,000 Moslems for the **SS** in Bosnia (**Handzar**) in the spring of 1943. Also, the Arab nationalist helped recruit Moslems for the **Wehrmacht** in the Caucasus. The Palestinian leader actively lobbied against Jewish immigration to Palestine, especially late in the war. He was never tried for **war crimes**, escaped from Egypt in 1946, then spent the remainder of his life in various Middle Eastern capitals. (See also **Croatia, Horthy Offer, Nuremberg Trials, Rashid Ali al-Gaylani, Dieter Wisliceny**, and **Yugoslavia**.)
SUGGESTED READING: Schechtman, *The Mufti and the Fuehrer.*

La grande Rafle (G., the great roundup). In July 1942, in **France**, 6,000 children and many adults were savagely sent to their deaths in German **concentration camps**. The roundup started in France with foreign Jews, particularly in the Paris area on July 16–17, when 12,884 Jews, including 4,000 children, were placed in **Velodrome d'Hiver**. Arrests spread to the unoccupied zone. French opinion became favorable to Jews after the German armed forces suffered major defeats in Africa and **Russia** in 1943, and arrests by the French subsided. (See also **Cardinal Pierre-Marie Gerlier, Monsignor Jules-Gerard Saliege**, and **Velodrome d'Hiver**.)
SUGGESTED READING: United States Holocaust Memorial Museum, *In the Depths of Darkness.*

Grawitz, Dr. Ernst von (1899–1945). Chief **SS** physician and president of German **Red Cross** (1936). He was responsible for choosing doctors for the **T-4** program. von Grawitz also pioneered "**special treatment**." The doctor advised **Heinrich Himmler** on the use of the **gas chambers** and "medical experiments" carried out at **concentration camps**. The SS doctor also conducted **selections** for gassing at **Auschwitz**. He committed suicide in 1945. (See also **Avengers**.)
SUGGESTED READING: Aziz, *Doctors of Death.*

Greater Reich or **Greater Germany** (G., Gross Deutsches Reich). Greater **Germany** included prewar Germany, **Austria** (1938), **Sudetenland** (1938), the **Protec-**

torate of **Bohemia-Moravia** (1939), Alsace-Lorraine, and parts of **Poland** (1939)—**Danzig**, Memel, West Prussia, Upper Silesia, and **Warthegau**.

Greece. Southern Balkan kingdom bordering **Albania, Yugoslavia, Bulgaria,** Turkey, and the Aegean Sea. Approximately 80 percent of 75,000 Greek Jews were killed during the **Holocaust**, mostly in Polish **death camps**. Greek Jews were also **deported** from Bulgaria-occupied **Thrace**, and **Macedonia**. The Italians protected Jews in areas they occupied until **Italy's** capitulation to the **Allies** in September 1943. The Italian Army saved 20,000 to 30,000 Jews in southern Greece. The Germans took over Italian army responsibilities. There were **Aktionen** in **Athens** and roundups in **Corfu** and **Rhodes**, as well as the large Jewish settlement at **Salonika**. (See also **Angelo Roncalli, Joseph J. Schwartz,** and **Dieter Wisliceny**.)
SUGGESTED READING: Novitch, *The Passage of the Barbarians*.

"Green Police" (Du., **Gruene Polizei**). Nazis and their Dutch **collaborators**. (Their name came from their green uniforms.) They arrested Jews, were involved directly in **Razzien**, and attacked **resistance** fighters. **Anne Frank** and her family were captured by this police unit. (See also **"Black Police," Landwacht, Netherlands,** and **Schuma**.)
SUGGESTED READING: Presser, *Ashes in the Wind: The Destruction of Dutch Jewry*.

"Greens." Criminal **concentration camp** inmates who wore a green triangle. The "Greens" and the **"Reds"** were the most powerful groups in the camps. Professional criminals from **Germany** were often given **kapo** status. However, the "Greens" lacked the political cohesiveness of the political groups ("Reds"), for example, communists, **Social Democrats,** and conservatives.

Greifelt, SS General Ulrich (b. 1896). Aide to **Heinrich Himmler**. He was the head of the Chief Staff Office of the **Reich Commission for the Strengthening of Germandom**. Greifelt was the **SS** officer responsible for **resettlement** to the East.
SUGGESTED READING: Tenenbaum, *Race and Reich*.

"Greifer" (G., **"catcher"**). Jew employed by the **Gestapo** to seek out other Jews in hiding. These **collaborators** were especially active in **Berlin**. (See also **"Submarine."**)
SUGGESTED READING: Wyden, *Stella*.

Greiser, Artur (1897–1946). **Gauleiter** of **Wartheland**. As president of the **Danzig** Senate (1938–1939), Greiser helped institute anti-Jewish laws. Upon the Nazi conquest of **Poland**, he became a powerful administrator and played a major role in Jewish **deportations** and murders. Greiser pressed for an **Aktion**

and killing center (**Chelmno**) within his **Gau**. He was executed in Poland in 1946. (See also **Avengers**.)
   SUGGESTED READING: Dobroszycki, *The Chronicle of the Lodz Ghetto*.

Grese, Irma (1921–1945). **SS Aufseherin**. Sadistic guard and reporting officer at **Auschwitz**. She worked at Hohenlychen, a convalescent home, as an assistant to **Drs. Karl Gebhardt** and **Herta Oberhauser**. Grese was trained at **Ravensbrueck**, transferred to Auschwitz (1943–1945), and finally for three-and-one half weeks at **Bergen-Belsen**. She was noted to beat prisoners without mercy, made "**sport**," and viewed so-called medical experiments. She was known as a "schadenfreude," a sadistic, malicious person. Grese was tried, convicted, and hanged by the British on December 13, 1945.
   SUGGESTED READINGS: Brown, *The Beautiful Beast*; Feig, *Hitler's Death Camps*.

Greuelpropaganda (G., horror or atrocity propaganda). The term the Nazis used to refer to foreign news reports on the **concentration** and **death camps**. This concept was used to dismiss the mass murder of Jews.

Grodno. City in **White Russia**, northeast of **Bialystok, Poland**. Its prewar Jewish population was 23,000, 43 percent of the general population. The area was taken by **Germany** in June 1941, soon after the attack on the **USSR**. Over 25,000 Jews from Grodno and the surrounding region were placed in **ghettos** in November 1941. By the end of 1943, most were wiped out by murder or **deportation** to **Treblinka**. The **Red Army** recaptured the city on July 16, 1944. (See also **Novogrudok**.)
   SUGGESTED READING: Wiesenthal, *Every Day Remembrance Day*.

Grossman, Haika (1919–1996). **Resistance** fighter. She was one of the organizers of the **Bialystok** underground in August 1943. Grossman tried to persuade 20,000 Jews not to assemble for **deportation**. With her fighters, she broke through the deportation assembly area and continued to fight the Nazis in a **partisan** band. Grossman was later active in **Bricha** and **Aliya Bet** and settled in **Palestine**.
   SUGGESTED READING: Grossman, *The Underground Army*.

Grossman, Mendel (1917–1945). Photographer. He took 10,000 photographs of daily life in the **Lodz Ghetto** and hid them underground. The photographs were published in *With a Camera in the Ghetto* (1977). Grossman was **deported** to a German work camp where he perished.
   SUGGESTED READING: Gribetz, Greenstein, and Stein, *The Timetables of Jewish History*.

Gross-Rosen. Camp initially established in Lower Silesia in August 1940 for Polish men. Scant records on this camp cloud its history. It was a satellite camp of **Sachsenhausen-Oranienburg** before it became an independent and integrated camp in May 1941. Designed for 10,000 to 12,000 inmates, this site held as many as 20,000 prisoners, many of whom were victims of the **Night and Fog** program. Inmates from this camp were distinguished by a shaven strip down the center of their scalp. In one six-month period, 65,000 **Soviet POWs** died of dysentery. A **euthanasia** program for the extermination of Jews and mentally ill children was conducted at Gross-Rosen. The **Red Army** arrived on May 8, 1945. (See also **Graben, Krupp Works**, and **Arthur Roedl**.)

SUGGESTED READINGS: Feig, *Hitler's Death Camps*; Laska, *Women in the Resistance*.

Grosz, Bandi (1905–1970s?). Converted Jew and multiple-agent for Hungarian intelligence, **Abwehr**, and the **Jewish Agency**. He was an opportunist whose allegiance was to money. Grosz traveled with **Joel Brand** during the ''**Blood for Trucks**'' mission. The **SS** sought to use him to negotiate with the Western **Allies** to end the war. He was arrested by the British in 1944 in **Palestine** and freed after the war. He left Israel in 1955 and died in Munich sometime in the 1970s.

SUGGESTED READING: Abrams, *Special Treatment*.

Grueber, Dr. Heinrich (1891–1975). German Protestant leader of the **Confessional Church**. He established an organization to support the emigration of ''Jewish'' Protestants. Grueber's efforts inspired other church leaders to get involved with the movement, but he felt God was responsible for the death of German Jews. The cleric was tolerated by the Nazis until 1940, when he was interned at **Dachau**. Grueber was the only German to testify against **Adolf Eichmann** and is honored as a **Righteous Gentile**.

Gruene Polizei (Du.) (See ''**Green Police**.'')

Grueninger, Paul (1891–1972). Police chief of St. Gallen, **Switzerland**. A **Righteous Gentile**, he was responsible for saving 3,000 Jews escaping **Austria** and **Germany** from 1938–1939. Grueninger was dismissed, convicted in court (1940) of breaking Swiss law (falsifying documents to save Jews), and stripped of his pension. He died penniless and a convicted criminal. Five pardon requests were rejected by Swiss authorities before the canton of St. Gallen rehabilitated Grueninger's honor in 1994. (See also ''**Lifeboat is Full**,'' Refoulement, Dr. **Heinrich Rothmund**, and **Eduard von Steiger**.)

SUGGESTED READINGS: Haesler, *The Lifeboat is Full: Switzerland and the Refugees*; Kranzler, *Heroine of Rescue*.

Gruppenfuehrer. SS major-general.

Grynszpan, Herschel (1921–1943?). Polish Jew residing in Paris. This teenager assassinated **Ernst vom Rath** in retaliation for his parents' expulsion from **Germany**. vom Rath's murder was used by the Nazis as a pretext for **Kristallnacht**. Grynszpan was handed over by the French police to the Nazis in 1943. **Dr. Paul Joseph Goebbels** had planned a show trial in Germany, which never materialized, and may be attributable to Grynszpan's contrived claim to have had a **homosexual** relationship with his victim. His fate is unknown, and he is presumed to have died during the war. His father testified at the trial of **Adolf Eichmann**. (See also **Dorothy Thompson** and **Zbaszyn**.)

  SUGGESTED READING: Read and Fisher, *Kristallnacht: The Nazi Night of Terror.*

Guernsey. (See **Channel Islands**.)

Gunskirchen. A satellite camp of **Mauthausen** for Jewish prisoners. It opened in March 1944 and was **liberated** on May 5, 1945, when units of the U.S. Third Army moved in. Almost 20,000 deportees were found in squalid conditions with low supplies of food and water.

  SUGGESTED READING: United States Holocaust Memorial Museum, *1945: Year of Liberation.*

Gurs. French **internment (collection) camp** created for Spanish Republicans (**Rotspanir**) in 1939. Housing conditions were on the par of those at **concentration camps** in the East. Gurs included Austrian and German citizens seeking refuge in **France** as well as **deported** Jews from northern France, Alsace, **Germany, Belgium**, and **Poland**. From June 1940 to the summer of 1943, Gurs housed non-French Jews before they were shipped to **Drancy** and then on to **Auschwitz**. (See also **October Deportation, OJE, Rivesaltes, and Society for the Rescue of Jewish Children**.)

  SUGGESTED READING: Zuccotti, *The Holocaust, the French, and the Jews.*

Gusen. Labor camps at **Mauthausen**. Gusen I (later equipped with a **gas chamber**) opened on March 9, 1940. Gusen II began operations on March 9, 1944, and Gusen III opened on December 16, 1944. Working conditions were harsh in local brick yards and quarries. Inmates (1,830) perished in the gas chambers at **Hartheim Castle** or were executed by phenol injections. Over 31,500 inmates died at this site from starvation, privation, malnutrition, and torture. The camp was **liberated** by the Americans on May 5, 1945; however, some 2,000 inmates died after **liberation** due to their degraded physical condition.

  SUGGESTED READING: Feig, *Hitler's Death Camps.*

Gwardia Ludowa (P., Peoples Guard). Polish communist underground established in April 1943, under Soviet sponsorship. This group, also known as the

Polish Peoples Army, welcomed Jews into their ranks. An estimated 1,700 Jews were killed fighting for the Guard. This army supplied small arms to the **ZOB** during the **Warsaw Ghetto Uprising**. The Peoples Guard never integrated with the **Armia Krajowa**. (See also **Zofia Yamaika**.)

  SUGGESTED READING: Ainsztein, *The Warsaw Ghetto Revolt.*

Gymnasium (G., high school). Secondary European school for students preparing for a university education. During the **Hitler** regime, **eugenics** and Nazi ideology were strongly emphasized in the schools run by the **Reich**.

Gypsy. Pejorative term for **Roma, Sinti**, or **Lalleri**.

H

"H." Marking on American **dog tag** identifying bearer as Hebrew. Nazis utilized this marking when searching for Jewish American POWs who were meted out harsher treatment. The Germans had no consistent policy on Jewish American POWs. In September 1995, the German government agreed to compensate Hugo Princz, the son of an American who was interned in a German **concentration camp** because he was Jewish.

Haagen, Eugene. Nazi scientist. As professor of hygiene at the **Strasbourg** Medical School, he initiated experiments with **SS** support in 1944 on involuntary **Natzweiler-Stutthof** inmates. His efforts concentrated on developing diseases of **typhus**, jaundice, and influenza, with the object of an effective vaccine. Haagen was sentenced by a French military court to twenty years imprisonment.
    SUGGESTED READING: Aziz, *Doctors of Death.*

Ha'apala (H., striving). The ''striving'' was to gain entrance to **Palestine**; hence, the term meant illegal immigration of those involved with **Aliya Bet**. Immigrants who reached Palestine illegally were called **Ma'apilim**. (See also **Hachsharot**.)

Haavara Agreement (H., **Transfer Agreement**). An arrangement between German economic authorities and the German **Zionist** Federation with the Anglo-**Palestine** Bank (1933–1939). It made possible the export of Jewish capital from **Germany** to Jewish Palestine. The Agreement encouraged Jewish emigration from Germany, and under its terms 60,000 Jews migrated to the **Yishuv**. (See also **Enzo Sereni**.)
    SUGGESTED READING: Black, *The Transfer Agreement.*

Habe, Hans (1911–1977). Hungarian-born German novelist. Habe's pseudonym was Janos Bekesy when he was a correspondent for a German-language newspaper in the 1930s covering the **League of Nations**. He covered the **Evian Conference** in 1938 and wrote a novel, *The Mission*, based on his observations. The appendix to this work was nonfiction, containing revealing facts on proposed rescue plans. The material indicated that the Germans were willing to ''sell'' Jews, but there were no takers. Habe joined the French Army in 1939 and fought the Germans. He escaped from a POW camp in 1940 and eventually served with U.S. forces.

Hacha, Emil (1872–1945). Czech politician. He was elected president of **Czechoslovakia** in November 1938, after the Germans annexed the **Sudeten-land**. Hacha was intimidated by **Hitler** to sign the Nazi occupation protocol in **Berlin** where he swore an oath of loyalty to the **Third Reich**. He was memorialized in his home town of Trhove Sviny in 1995. (See also **Eduard Benes** and **Jan Masaryk**.)

SUGGESTED READING: MacDonald, *The Killing of SS-Obergruppenfuerher Reinhard Heydrich*.

Hachsharot (H., preparation). Preparatory agricultural training farms for young **Zionists** outside **Palestine**. Members often became cadres for Jewish **resistance**. (See also **Ha'apala**.)

Hademar. Infamous killing center in central **Germany** during the **euthanasia** program. At this site, 11,000 people were murdered from 1941 to 1945. After the murder of 10,000 victims, the institution conducted a celebration ceremony. Originally a psychiatric hospital founded in 1901 for alcoholism, later renamed (1933) the State Psychiatric Hospital. From 1944 to 1945, the facility was used to murder sick **slave laborers**. The administrator, Alfons Klein, was sentenced to death by a U.S. Military Commission in October 1945. American troops **liberated** this site on March 26, 1945. In October 1945, several staff members of the facility were tried for the murders of 460 **Allied** nationals. The U.S. prosecution team, headed by Colonel Leon Jaworski, had hoped to prosecute the staff concerning the murder of 15,000 German mental patients at Hademar. Under international law, the prosecution was prohibited from indicting the staff because they were only a military commission and were limited to dealing with crimes committed during war against **Allied** nationals. Convictions were handed down for seven defendants; three were executed. (See also **Hartheim Castle, Sonnenstein**, and **War Crimes Trial**.)

SUGGESTED READINGS: Gallagher, *By Trust Betrayed*; United States Holocaust Memorial Museum, *1945: The Year of the Liberator*.

Haeftling (G., inmate). Prisoner in the **Nazi concentration camp** complex.

Haganah (H., defense force). Jewish underground military group founded in 1920 by the **Yishuv** to fend off Arab attacks. Its cautious policy led to a split and the creation of the **Irgun** in 1931. It accepted women into the movement for rescue of European Jews. During the war, many of its members joined the British Army to fight the Nazis. Many members also joined the **Jewish Brigade-Infantry**. After the war, Haganah fighters got involved in the **Bricha** movement. (See also **Yehuda Arazi, Mossad le Aliya Bet**, *Patria*, and **Hannah Szenes**.)

SUGGESTED READINGS: Offer, *Escaping the Holocaust*; Szule, *The Secret Alliance*.

Hague Convention. Two international conferences held at the Hague in the **Netherlands**, one in 1899, and the other in 1907 at Czar Nicholas' request. The major European powers, including **Germany**, signed treaties. The contents pledged the various governments to eliminate needless suffering of soldiers, prisoners, and noncombatants. The conventions made governments, not individuals, responsible for the soldiers' welfare. However, at the **Nuremberg Trials**, Nazi leaders were held on criminal responsibility and the Hague treaties were cited. (See also **Commissar Order**.)

SUGGESTED READING: Falk, Kolko, and Lifton, *Crimes of War*.

Hahn, Dr. Ludwig (b. 1908). **SS** officer. He headed the **Einsatzkommandos** in **Poland**; then became kommandant of the **Gestapo** in Warsaw (1941–1943). Under his command, 350,000 Jews were sent to their deaths in **Treblinka** and **Majdanek**. He murdered thousands in **Pawiak Street Prison** and participated in suppressing the **Warsaw Ghetto Uprising**. The **Allies** arrested Hahn several times, but he was released for health reasons in 1965. Hahn worked as an insurance salesman before he was sentenced to life imprisonment in Germany (1975).

SUGGESTED READING: Ainsztein, *The Warsaw Ghetto Revolt*.

Halakha (H., to go or to walk). Jewish law that was developed through the Hebrew Bible, the **Talmud**, and various commentators over the ages. Traditional **Orthodox** Jews sought out their rabbis for answers in Jewish law as how to behave in extreme conditions under Nazi brutality. (See also **Rabbi Ephraim Oshry** and **Pikuah Nefesh**.)

SUGGESTED READING: Rosenbaum, *The Holocaust and Halakha*.

Halifax, Lord (Edward Wood) (1881–1951). British ambassador to the United States during the war. He opposed sending food parcels to Jewish **ghettos** in **Poland**. Halifax argued the food supplements would be exploited by the Nazis. Jewish Orthodox groups favored sending aid to Polish Jews while mainstream American Jewish organizations supported the blockade, especially after America entered the war in December 1941. (See also **White Paper**.)

SUGGESTED READING: Schechtman, *The Mufti and the Fuehrer*.

Handzar. Moslem **SS** divisions from Bosnia who brutalized Serbs and Jews; by the end of 1943, there were 20,000 soldiers. It fought against Yugoslav **partisans** and committed atrocities against the Serb population. (See also **Croatia, Grand Mufti of Jerusalem, Serbia**, and **Yugoslavia**.)

SUGGESTED READING: Schechtman, *The Mufti and the Fuehrer.*

Harrison, Earl (1899–1955). Dean of the University of Pennsylvania Law School. This **refugee** expert was commissioned by President **Harry S. Truman** to report on the condition of the **Displaced Persons' camps** after the war. His mission was prompted by U.S. Treasury head **Henry Morganthau, Jr**. The Harrison Report was instrumental in improving living conditions for Jewish refugees. He also found that in some cases Jews were being guarded by former Nazi **collaborators**. (See also **General Dwight David Eisenhower, Ira Hirschmann, Fiorello La Guardia, Rabbi Judah Nadich**, and **General George S. Patton**.)

SUGGESTED READINGS: Sachar, *Redemption of the Unwanted*; United States Holocaust Memorial Museum, *1945: The Year of Liberation.*

Hartheim Castle. Mental institution near Linz, **Austria**, equipped with **gas chambers**. Hartheim was the center of the **T-4** Program. Inmates from **Mauthausen, Gusen** (invalids), and **Dachau** were also gassed at this site. Approximately 30,000 victims of the T-4 Program and **concentration camp** inmates were gassed here. **Hitler** ordered the gassing operations to cease December 12, 1944. (Hitler had led the German clergy to believe that the **euthanasia** program was officially over on August 24, 1941.) Gassings were halted on December 11, 1944, and the gas chambers were destroyed the following day. A detachment of inmates from Mauthausen restored the castle to its original condition from December 30, 1944, through January 1945. (See also Bishop Clemens von Galen, **Dr. Georg Renno, Franz Stangl**, and "**Wild Euthanasia**.")

SUGGESTED READING: Friedlander, *The Origins of Nazi Genocide.*

Hartjenstein, Lothar (1905–1945). **SS** major. Kommandant of **Birkenau** from November 1943–May 8, 1944, during the peak period of extermination. He was the last kommandant of **Natzweiler-Strutthof**. Tried by a French military court, Hartjenstein was sentenced to death in 1945, but died in prison. (See also **Egon Zill**.)

SUGGESTED READING: Smolen et al., *KL Auschwitz Seen by the SS.*

"Harvest Festival." (See **Erntefest**.)

Ha-Shomer ha-Tzair (H., Young Guardians). Left-wing, **Zionist** youth movement active in the **Yishuv** and Europe. This organization produced a number of underground fighters, both male and female including: Tossia Altman (1918–1943), **Mordecai Anielewicz, Heshek "Zvi" Bauminger, Haika Grossman**,

Haika Klinger (1917–1958), **Josef Kaplan, Maria Rozka Korczak, Abba Kovner, Roza Robota,** and **Arie Wilner**. (See also **Socialist Zionists**.)

Hasidei umot Ha'olam (H., Righteous Persons of the Nations). Non-Jewish rescuers. Taken from the **Talmud**, from a larger verse: "The Righteous Among the Nations of the World Have a Place in the World to Come." (See also **Righteous Gentiles** and **Yad Vashem**.)

Hasidism (H., piousness). A mystical and emotional movement in Judaism founded in mid–eighteenth century **Ukraine-Poland**. The distinctive garb of these Jews made them targets of abuse by German soldiers and **collaborators**. (See also **Kapote, Rabbi Joseph Isaac Schneersohn, Sokolow-Podlaski,** and **Vitebsk**.)

Haskala (H., enlightenment). Jewish enlightenment in **Poland, Russia,** and the Baltics in the late nineteenth century and first quarter of the twentieth century. The movement sought to incorporate secular along with **Torah** studies. (See also **Maskilim**.)

Hassebroek, Johannes (b. 1910). **SS** ideological trainer and kommandant of **Gross-Rosen**. He was arrested by the Czechs, Americans, and British. The British sentenced him to death, but commuted his sentence in 1954. Tried again in 1967, he was acquitted due to insufficient evidence. Charged once again in 1970, he was acquitted and retried as a businessman.
   SUGGESTED READING: Segev, *Soldiers of Evil.*

Hauptamt. (See **WVHA**.)

Hauptscharfuehrer. SS master sergeant.

Hauptsturmfuehrer. SS captain.

Hausner, Gideon (1915–1990). Jurist and former attorney general of Israel. He successfully prosecuted **Adolf Eichmann** in Israel and wrote *Justice in Jerusalem.* In 1968, Hausner was appointed chairman of the **Yad Vashem** council. (See also **Yad Vashem**.)
   SUGGESTED READING: Arendt, *Eichmann in Jerusalem.*

Hautval, Dr. Adelaide (1906–1988). French **Righteous Gentile**. She protested **Vichy's** harsh treatment of Jews and was sent to **Auschwitz** as a result. The French doctor refused to participate in medical experiments. She secretly helped the inmates and minimized their suffering. Hautval testified against an English doctor in a libel trial (*Dering* v. *Uris,* 1964) and documented Nazi sterilization experiments.

SUGGESTED READINGS: Block and Drucker, *Rescuers*; Sachar, *The Redemption of the Unwanted.*

Hebrew Immigrant Aid Society (HIAS). American Jewish organization established in 1909 to facilitate immigration from countries that persecuted Jews. This group helped Jewish **refugees** throughout Europe as **Hitler's** policies accelerated in **Germany**. HIAS also helped to settle Jews after the war. (See also **HICEM** and **Portugal**.)
   SUGGESTED READINGS: Sanders, *Shores of Refuge*; Szule, *The Secret Alliance.*

Hecht, Ben (1894–1964). Playwright and writer. He drafted ads calling attention to the **Holocaust** for the **Bergson Group**. He also organized a pageant that alluded to the Holocaust entitled ''**We Shall Never Die!**'' which took place in March 1943 at Madison Square Garden and was attended by approximately 50,000 people. (See also **Emergency Committee to Save the Jewish People of Europe** and **Hollywood Jews**.)
   SUGGESTED READING: Hecht, *Child of the Century.*

Heder (H., room). Traditional Jewish religious school for boys common in Eastern Europe. Jews attempted to continue their **Talmudic** education clandestinely inside **ghettos** under penalty of death. (See also ''**Canteen**'' and **Komplets**.)

He-Halutz/Halutz (H., pioneer). **Zionist** pioneer farmer in **Palestine** and Zionist youth organization that encouraged an agrarian way of life and immigration to Palestine. Many of its members formed the core of the **resistance** in the **ghettos** and forests. (See also **Ha'apala, Roza Robota, Enzo Sereni, Socialist Zionists, Mordechai Tenenbaum**, and **Joop Westerweel**.)

Heidegger, Martin (1889–1976). German philosopher and prominent existentialist. **Hannah Arendt** studied under him, and they had a brief romance. He was a **Nazi Party** member from 1933–1945. Heidigger was one of the leading intellectuals who lent their name to the Nazi regime and failed to repudiate the racist **genocidal** state after the war. (See also **Hannah Arendt** and **Carl Jung**.)
   SUGGESTED READING: Neske and Kettering, *Martin Heidegger and National Socialism.*

Heimeinkaufvertrag (G., home buyer agreement). Agreement on sale of home used by the Nazis to legally expropriate property, especially elderly German Jews relocated to **Theresienstadt**. (See also **Aryanization**.)

Heinkel Werke. German aircraft company that exploited **concentration camp** labor from **Sachsenhausen-Oranienburg, Ravensbrueck, Mauthausen**, and **Plaszow** as well as the **Krakow Ghetto**.

Helferinnen (G., auxiliaries). **SS** women guards at **Ravensbrueck**.

"Helsinger Sewing Club." Initiated early rescue efforts of Jews in **Denmark**, which continued through 1943. Their escape route, the "Kaiser Line," was named after the group's founder, Erling Kaiser, who was betrayed and arrested in May 1944.

Henlein, Konrad (1898–1945). Head of the pro-Nazi Sudeten German Party, **Gauleiter** of the **Sudetenland**, and militia leader. His agitation and impossible demands on behalf of **Hitler** in the spring of 1938 gave the Nazis the excuse to demand annexation of the Sudetenland. Henlein committed suicide in an **Allied** internment camp. (See also **Munich Pact**.)
  SUGGESTED READING: Shirer, *The Rise and Fall of the Third Reich*.

Hereditary Courts. (See **Genetic Health Courts**.)

Hermann Goering Werke. Company set up by **Hermann Goering** in 1937 to mine and smelt low-grade iron ore. Its assets included properties stolen from Baron Rothchild (**Austria**). The company expanded into other fields, exploited **slave labor** at **Auschwitz**, but was poorly managed. This enterprise owned by the Nazis was an anomaly in that the Nazis left most companies in the hands of private industry.

Herrenvolk (G., lordly people). Nazi term for German master race. (See also *Mein Kampf* and **Uebermenschen**.)

Herzog, Chaim (1918–1997). Israeli nationalist. Born in Ireland, Herzog served as a captain in the British Army. He was part of the force that occupied Achen, Germany, in 1944. Although he was an intelligence officer, Herzog was instructed not to interrogate **Heinrich Himmler**. However, during a brief encounter, Himmler offered the **SS** to the **Allies** to fight the Soviets. Herzog confronted Himmler about the **concentration camps** and the SS chief represented that they were regular POW camps.

Herzog, Yitzhak Halevi (1888–1959). Israeli rabbinical scholar. Born in **Poland**, he became chief rabbi of Ireland in 1925 and chief rabbi of Palestine in 1936. During the **Holocaust**, he attempted to rescue Jews. After the war, he traveled throughout Europe to locate orphaned and hidden Jewish children. He received from the **USSR** (1940) permits for staff and students of Lithuanian and Polish **yeshivot** stranded in **Vilna** to cross **Russia** to the Far East. (See also **Chaim Herzog**.)
  SUGGESTED READING: Wein, *Triumph of Survival*.

Hess, Rudolf (1894–1987). (*Not to be confused with* **Rudolf Hoess**.) Deputy **fuehrer**. Former member of the **Freikorps**, he was one of **Hitler's** oldest and closest aides. He transcribed *Mein Kampf* as Hitler dictated to him in **Landsberg** Prison (1924). As Hitler's deputy, Hess signed all of the **Nuremberg Laws**. He was involved in the **Roehm** purge and participated in the plans to invade **Poland** and **Czechoslovakia**. He was gradually marginalized, and his power and authority were acquired by **Martin Bormann**. Hess flew to Scotland in 1941 to arrange a peace with Britain, and was incarcerated until the end of the war. Hess was supposedly mentally ill and stood trial in **Nuremberg** where he was sentenced to life in prison. At age 93, the inmate committed suicide at Spandau Prison outside **Berlin** in 1987. (See also **Berlin** and **Dr. Gerhart Wagner**.)

SUGGESTED READINGS: Davidson, *The Trial of the Germans*; Posner, *Hitler's Children*.

Hevra Kaddisha (H., holy society). Jewish burial society. The Hevra was active in **ghettos** and tried to bury Jews traditionally with as much dignity as possible.

Heydrich, Reinhard (1904–1942). **SS** lieutenant general. He was selected by **Heinrich Himmler** to head the **SD** and eventually became the head of the **Reich Security Main Office (RSHA)** and the **Gestapo**. Heydrich replaced **Konstantin von Neurath** as **Reich** protector of the **Protectorate of Bohemia-Moravia**. He was also intimately involved in the **Lublin** Reservation, headed the **Einsatzgruppen** in 1939, and was instructed by Himmler to organize mobile extermination units in the East. He oversaw the **Wannsee Conference**. Heydrich was arguably the third most powerful man in the Reich when he was assassinated in Prague, **Czechoslovakia**, on May 27, 1942. Even in death Heydrich haunted the Jews. The expedited **resettlement** of Jews in the **Generalgouvernement** and the plundering of Jewish property was named **Aktion Reinhard** or **Operation Heydrich**. (See also **Dr. Werner Best, Lezaky**, and **Lidice**.)

SUGGESTED READINGS: Crankshaw, *Gestapo*; MacDonald, *The Killing of SS-Obergruppenfuehrer Reinhard Heydrich*.

HIAS. (See **Hebrew Immigrant Aid Society**.)

HICEM. Acronym for combined immigration agency of **Jewish Colonization Association** and **HIAS**, which extended systematic aid to international Jewish **refugees** especially in **Spain**. Initially headquartered in Paris before Nazi occupation, it moved to Lisbon but financial activities were handled by the ''**Joint**.'' It refused to engage in illegal welfare and rescue efforts, yet approximately 90,000 Jews escaped the **Holocaust** through Lisbon with HICEM assistance. (See also **Antonio de Olivera Salazar** and **Aristide de Sousa Mendes**.)

SUGGESTED READINGS: Avni, *Spain, the Jews and Franco*; Sanders, *Shores of Refuge*.

Hilfpolizei. (G., auxiliary or "help" police). Ukrainian units that participated in the murdering of Jews.

Hilfsverein der Deutschen Juden (G., Relief Organization of German Jews). Organization of German Jews that was involved in emigration and sought havens in all locales except **Palestine**. This entity maintained offices throughout **Germany** and functioned as an independent organization until 1939 before becoming a section of **Reich Association of Jews in Germany**. Hilfsverein operated until 1941, when Jewish emigration was prohibited.

Hilfswillige (**Hiwis**) (G., volunteer helpers). Auxiliary units of **Soviet POWs**, Cossack, Belorussian, Tartar, Latvian, Lithuanian, and Ukrainian residents in German-occupied areas. They volunteered, or were drafted, into the **Wehrmacht**. The Hiwis were issued German uniforms and received a pay scale comparable to native Germans. They also aided the **Einsatzgruppen** in the murder of the Jews. (See also **Freiwillige, Latvian SS Legion, Lithuanian Activist Front, Ostbataillone, Perkonkrust, Schuma**, and **Ukraine**.)

"Himmelstrasse" (G., "heavenly road"). Doomed members of **deportation transports** were forced to walk this path to **gas chambers**, especially at **Treblinka**.

Himmler, Heinrich (1900–1945). **Reichsfuehrer SS**. He was the second most powerful man in the **Nazi** regime. Himmler was frail, near-sighted, cool, calculating, and of average intelligence. As head of the SS, Himmler was responsible for making it the most feared institution in the **Greater Reich** and occupied Europe. He methodically and cunningly developed an extensive police state apparatus. The Reichsfuehrer was a racial fanatic and agronomist who believed in the ultimate race war (**Voelkerchaos**) between **Aryans** and Jews. Himmler was appointed by **Hitler** (August 1942) to an additional post: chief of anti-**partisan** warfare. He reported to Hitler (December 20, 1942) that 663,000 Jews were executed in the East from August to November 1942. In a meeting with SS officials in Posen, October 4, 1943, the Reich leader laid out the **Final Solution**, of which he was the architect: "We had the moral right, and the duty, toward our nation to kill this people which wished to kill us." In a speech to **Gauleiter** on October 6, 1943, he said: "I didn't think it would be wise to exterminate the adult Jewish men . . . leaving their children to grow into avengers against our sons and grandsons. . . . The decision had to be made to make this people disappear from earth. This is being accomplished." Himmler disguised himself after the war, but was captured by the British and committed suicide before he could stand trial. (See also **Ahnenerbe, Einsatzgruppen,**

Chaim Herzog, Dr. Felix Kersten, Lodz Ghetto, Jean-Marie Musy, Posen (Poznan) Speech, Dr. Ernst Schenck, and **Warsaw Ghetto Uprising**.)
   SUGGESTED READING: Breitman, *The Architect of Genocide: Himmler and the Final Solution.*

von Hindenburg, Paul (1847–1934). German general, war hero, and president of the **Weimar Republic** from 1925–1934. On April 4, 1933, he wrote to **Hitler** to exempt Jewish war veterans, who were either wounded or served on the front during World War I, from anti-Jewish legislation, for example, civil servants, judges, teachers, and lawyers. Hitler honored his request until the president's death, at which time he assumed all powers of the presidency and began to pass more strident anti-Jewish legislation. After von Hindenburg's death, all soldiers swore an unconditional oath to Adolf Hitler. (See also **Fuehrer, Law for the Restoration of Professional Civil Service**, and **Franz von Papen**.)
   SUGGESTED READING: Toland, *Adolf Hitler.*

Hirsch, Freddy (d. 1944). Jewish youth leader. German Jew who organized Jewish youth in Prague and **Terezin**. He was the leader of the **Auschwitz-Birkenau "Family Camp"** and committed suicide when the camp was liquidated in July 1944.
   SUGGESTED READING: Czech, *Auschwitz Chronicle.*

Hirsch, Otto (1885–1941). Lay Chairman of **Reich Association of German Jews**. He oversaw economic aid, vocational training and schooling, and Jewish emigration. He assisted **Martin Buber** with Jewish Adult Education. Hirsch was arrested and tortured to death in **Mauthausen** in 1941. (See also **Leo Baeck**.)
   SUGGESTED READING: Kulka, "The 'Reichsvereinigung' and the Fate of German Jews, 1938/1939–1943: Continuity or Discontinuity?"

Hirschmann, Ira (1901–1989). American businessman, vice-president of Bloomingdales. He was appointed the **War Refugee Board's** special attaché in **Romania** and charged to negotiate, cajole, bribe, and/or influence the Romanian government not to **deport** or murder Jewish children from **Transnistria**. Hirschmann did convince the Romanians to transfer 48,000 Jews from Transnistria to safety in the Romanian interior. He also persuaded **Angelo Roncalli** to issue baptismal certificates to Jews in hiding. He played an active role in assisting the War Refugee Board in Turkey and saved thousands of Romanian, Bulgarian, and Hungarian Jews by securing safe-passage to **Palestine**. After the war he was appointed special inspector general for **UNRRA** to examine the conditions of Jewish **DPs** in **Germany**. (See also **Earl Harrison** and **Fiorello La Guardia**.)
   SUGGESTED READINGS: Hirschmann, *Caution to the Winds;* Hirschmann, *Lifeline to a Promised Land.*

Hirszfeld, Professor Ludwig (1884–1954). Biology professor, writer, and renowned Jewish bacteriologist. He taught classes in the **Warsaw Ghetto** and conducted important research into the theory and cause of hunger. Hirszfeld correctly perceived the **ghetto** as a Nazi means of exterminating Jews. He incorporated details of ghetto life in his book *Story of a Life*. He, his wife, and daughter escaped the ghetto. After the war, he founded an institute of immunology at Wroclaw University.

SUGGESTED READING: Iranek-Osmecki, *He Who Saves One Life*.

Hirt, Dr. August (b. 1898–?). Professor of anatomy at **Reich** University of **Strasbourg**. He was affiliated with **Ahnenerbe**, collected Jewish skulls and skeletons from **Auschwitz**, and conducted mustard gas experiments on inmates at **Natzweiler-Stutthof**. He also requested the bodies of eighty-seven gassing victims from Natzweiler to be sent to Strasbourg. He disappeared after the war, and his whereabouts were never determined. (See also **Dr. Wolfram Sievers**.)

SUGGESTED READING: Aziz, *Doctors of Death*.

Hitler, Adolf (1889–1945). The **Fuehrer, Nazi Party** leader from 1919–1945 and dictator of the **Third Reich** from 1933–1945. Hitler outlined his plans for territorial conquest (**Lebensraum**) and his hatred for Jews in his autobiography *Mein Kampf* (1924). He was the architect of the German racist state, the enslavement of non-**Aryan** peoples, and the central figure behind the instigation of World War II. Hitler adapted the Nazi philosophy into an appealing plan for the resurrection of the German people. On January 30, 1942 (the ninth anniversary of the Nazi seizure of power), Hitler proclaimed "the result of this war will be the total annihilation of the Jews." (The **Wannsee Conference** had been concluded ten days earlier.) His personality and will created the Nazi horror that lead to the death of over 40 million people. Hitler committed suicide in **Berlin** on April 30, 1945. (See also **Fascism** and **Klessheim Castle**.)

SUGGESTED READINGS: Bullock, *Hitler and Stalin*; Flood, *Hitler, The Path to Power*; Toland, *Adolf Hitler*.

Hitler Youth (G., Hitlerjugend). Nazi paramilitary and social club for German youths from 14–18. (From ages 10–14, boys belonged to the **Jungvolk**.) The organization was founded in 1922 and renamed Hitler Youth in 1926. It expanded to a parallel organization for girls. **Baldur von Schirach** was appointed **Reich** youth leader in 1931. By 1935, 60 percent of **Germany's** youth belonged to this entity. The organization indoctrinated German youth with **National Socialism** and **anti-Semitic** fervor, and it encouraged children to spy on their parents. Both boys and girls were kept busy with body-building and military training. In December 1936 all other youth groups were banned by the Hitlerjugend Law. Enrollment was compulsory for all racially pure boys 10 years and older as of March 25, 1939. Late in the war, they were used as front-line soldiers. Many of the young men and women became agents of mass mur-

der. (See also **Edelweiss Pirates, Jungmaedel, Junkerschulen**, and **League of German Girls**.)
SUGGESTED READING: Koch, *Hitler Youth.*

HJ. (See **Hitler Youth**.)

Hlinka, Andrej (1864–1938). **Anti-Semitic** and fervent Slovakian nationalist. He reestablished the Slovak Peoples' Party, founded in 1905, whose purpose was autonomy for **Slovakia**. Jewish leaders successfully protested Bratislava's plan (1994) to rename one of its central squares after Hlinka. (See also **Hlinka People's Party**.)
SUGGESTED READING: Frieder, *To Deliver Their Souls.*

Hlinka Guard. Militia maintained by the Slovak Peoples' Party from 1938–1945. It was the party's military wing commanded by **Sano Mach** that operated against Jews, Czechs, and leftists. In 1942, the Guard and other **collaboration-ists** aided local police and German authorities in **deporting** Jews to **Poland**. After the **Slovakian National Revolt** in August 1944, the **SS** took control of this group.
SUGGESTED READING: Frieder, *To Deliver Their Souls.*

Hlinka People's Party. Right-wing, Slovakian Catholic organization named af-ter **Andrej Hlinka**. Led by a Catholic priest, **Dr. Josef Tiso**, this party estab-lished a puppet government formed in March 1939. The party was actively involved in **deporting** and slaughtering 85,000 (nearly 80 percent of **Slovakia's** 90,000 Jews. (See also **Vojtech Tuka**.)
SUGGESTED READING: Frieder, *To Deliver Their Souls.*

Hoefle, Hans (1898–1945). Aide to **Odilo Globocnik**. Officer in charge of **Operation Heydrich**. As the **Resettlement** commissioner for the **Warsaw Ghetto**, he drew up the **deportation** plans.
SUGGESTED READING: Gutman, *Resistance.*

Hoess, Rudolf (1900–1947). (*Not to be confused with* **Hitler's** *aide* **Rudolf Hess**). **SS** lieutenant colonel who trained under **Theodor Eicke**. The komman-dant of **Auschwitz** I, Hoess was responsible for enlarging the camp's capacity and introducing **Zyklon-B** into the arena of mass murder. Hoess was also the deputy inspector of the **WVHA**. In May 1944, he was brought back to Ausch-witz to oversee the murder of 430,000 Hungarian Jews in fifty-six days at **Bir-kenau**. The **war criminal** was a major prosecution witness providing corroborating testimony to the **International Military Tribunal** on the destruc-tion of European Jewry. Hoess was hanged in Auschwitz I by the Poles on April 16, 1947. (See also **Otto Moll**.)
SUGGESTED READINGS: Fest, *The Face of the Third Reich*; Hoess, *Death Dealer.*

Hoessler, Franz (1906–1945). SS captain. Appointed **Lagerfuehrer** of **Auschwitz** I and the women's camp in Auschwitz II in June 1944. Hoessler was executed as a **war criminal** on December 13, 1945.
SUGGESTED READING: Czech, *Auschwitz Chronicle.*

Hoherer SS-und Polizeifuehrer (G., Higher SS and Police Leader). Senior SS and police officer in an occupied area who acted as **Heinrich Himmler's** personal emissary. **Erich von dem Bach-Zelewski** was one who served in the occupied **Soviet Union**.

Holland. (See **Netherlands**.)

Hollerith Machine. Data processing device used by the German government to track and compute census of Jews, **Roma**, and the handicapped. The **SS** used the electrochemical machines to record and process prisoner information at **concentration camps**. The Hollerith was produced by DEHUMAG, a German subsidiary of IBM. This device was also used in **Austria** to help expropriate businesses and property. The computer may have been used to coordinate **deportations** from **ghettos**.

Hollywood Jews. Jews were a major presence in the motion picture industry, yet remained defensive and fearful about their religious roots. They were silent during the **Holocaust** with the exception of **Ben Hecht**. This group opposed **Hitler** and the Nazis, but Hollywood films never portrayed the full barbarism of the Holocaust.
SUGGESTED READING: Hecht, *Child of the Century.*

Holocaust. Term applied to the destruction of European Jews under the Nazis. A Greek term (meaning burning) taken from the Bible (1: Samuel 7–9), which refers to a consuming fiery sacrifice. Holocaust was first used by **Elie Wiesel** in his book *And the World was Silent*. The term is applied to the destruction of 6 million European Jews under the Nazis. In Hebrew, the annihilation of European Jewry is referred to as **Shoah**. The **Yiddish** term **Churban** is also used to denote this event, placing it with the destruction of the First and Second Temples in Jerusalem. (See also **Porraimos**.)

Holtzman Amendment of the Immigration and Naturalization Acts. Legislation authored by Congresswoman Elizabeth Holtzman barring Nazi **war criminals** from entering the United States. To lie about complicity in **genocide** constitutes grounds for **deportation**. This amendment was used to ban **Kurt Waldheim** from entering America. It was used by the Department of Justice to ban the infamous Japanese Unit 731 Army detachment, which performed inhumane experiments on civilian and military persons during World War II.

SUGGESTED READINGS: New York Times, July 30, 1978: Saidel, The Outraged Conscience.

Homosexuals. The Nazis were homophobic for they considered homosexuality a contagious disease. Antihomosexual decrees had been passed as early as 1871. From 1933–1944, between 50,000–63,000 German male homosexuals were arrested of which 4,000 were juveniles. Homosexuals were among the first inmates imprisoned in **Dachau**. On October 26, 1936, the **RSHA** created the Federal Security Department for Combating Abortion and Homosexuality. In April 1938, the Nazis decreed that men engaging in homosexual activities could be sent to **concentration camps**. Approximately 15,000 male homosexuals were incarcerated and at least 12,000 (75 percent) were murdered. Persecution of homosexuals was limited to the **Greater Reich**. Lesbians were considered acceptable "breeding stock" if their blood line was **Aryan**.

Despite the disdain, "politically correct" homosexuals such as high Nazis, **SS** officers, officials in **Hitler Youth** had their sexual preferences ignored. **Baldur von Schirach** and Rudolf Lange were suspected homosexuals. Male homosexuals had the option to "volunteer" for front-line military duty.

Homosexuals were vulnerable at the camps and targeted for harsh treatment. Many were sent to the **Sachsenhausen-Oranienburg** Brickworks where the life expectancy was thirty days. Homosexuals were also disproportionally **deported** to **Dora-Nordhausen**. At **Buchenwald, SS** physician, **Dr. Carl Vaernet** conducted inhumane hormone experiments on male homosexuals. In addition, many homosexuals were castrated. The Nazis attempted to "cure" homosexuality by bringing prostitutes from **Ravensbrueck** to "treat" male homosexuals in **Flossenbuerg**. Many homosexuals remained in jail after the war. (See also **Asocials**, "**175er**," **Pink Triangle**, and **Ernst Roehm**.)

SUGGESTED READINGS: Plant, The Pink Triangle; Rector, The Nazi Extermination of Homosexuals.

Hoppe, Paul Werner (1910–1974). Kommandant of **Stutthof**. He used **gas chambers** (1942) to execute Polish **partisans** and shot Jews in the nape of the neck. He escaped from the British and lived in **Switzerland** under an assumed name as a landscape designer. Hoppe rejoined his family in 1952 and was arrested in 1953. He was sentenced by a West German court in 1957 to nine years in prison but was released in 1962. The former kommandant worked for an insurance company before his death in 1974.

SUGGESTED READING: Segev, Soldiers of Evil.

"Horst Wessel" (G., song). Supposedly written after 1923 and dedicated to the memory of an early Nazi street fighter who died in a clash with communists in 1930. The official song of the **Nazi Party** included a phrase that inspired the **SA** to attack Jews: "When Jewish blood flows from the knife, things will go

much better.'' This verse was from a poem Horst Wessel had published in *Der Angriff* as early as September 24, 1929. (See also **Night of the Long Knives**.)
   SUGGESTED READING: Wistrich, *Who's Who in Nazi Germany.*

Horthy, Admiral Miklos (1868–1957). Regent of **Hungary** from 1920–1944. Though he passed anti-Jewish legislation from 1938–1941, he rejected **Hitler's** demands to impose the **Final Solution** between 1942–1944, even after the German occupation on March 19, 1944. Horthy was forced to relinquish power to **Doeme Sztojay** after the admiral flirted with the idea of negotiating a separate peace with the **Allies**. After the war, the Allies permitted him to live in **Portugal**. Horthy's remains were reburied in Hungary on September 4, 1993. (See also **Cordell Hull, Miklos Kallay, Klessheim Castle**, and **Ferenc Szalasi**.)
   SUGGESTED READING: Hilberg, *The Destruction of European Jewry.*

Horthy Offer. In July 1944, Admiral Horthy proposed safe transit for 7,000 Hungarian Jews prompted by the intervention of **Pope Pius XII**, President **Franklin Delano Roosevelt**, and **Sweden's** King Gustav. The proposal would have placed the Jews under international protection. The program was thwarted by **Heinrich Himmler** out of consideration for the **Grand Mufti of Jerusalem** who wanted to prevent Jews from going to **Palestine**.
   SUGGESTED READING: Finger, *American Jewry During the Holocaust.*

Hostages. Nazis took Jewish and Gentile innocent civilians and incarcerated them as a means to extort money or cooperation. Also, many hostages were killed in retaliation for rebellion by others. This violation of international law was considered a **crime against humanity**. (See also **Ardeantine Caves, Exchange Jews, Wilhelm Keitel**, and **Wehrmacht**.)

Hotel Polski. Plan initiated by the **Gestapo** in the summer of 1943 to trade Jews from neutral nations (mostly Latin America) for German nationals detained by the **Allies**. The hotel, located on Dluga Street in Warsaw, housed approximately 3,000 Jews. The Nazis treated their guests well and exploited Jewish relatives outside of **Poland** for money. In addition, the Office to Combat Usury and Profit (''Jewish Gestapo'') sold false nationality papers to Jews in hiding. The guests of the hotel were taken to **Pawiak** in September 1943. South American nations did not honor the documents, and most of the Jews were **deported** to **Auschwitz, Bergen-Belsen**, or **Vittel**. (See **Exchange Jews** and **George Mandel Mantello**.)
   SUGGESTED READING: Shulman, *The Case of Hotel Polski.*

House Committees. Rival authority to **Judenraete** in Eastern European **ghettos** who provided welfare services to Jews. The Committees sent delegates to a central commission. These Committees were more sympathetic and active in aiding the disadvantaged than organized Judenrat. They were comprised of diverse elements from both sexes. Women gained prominence as more men were "**impressed**" for **forced labor**, executed, or **deported**. (See also **Emmanuel Ringelblum**.)

SUGGESTED READINGS: Dawidowicz, *The War Against the Jews*; Ringelblum, *Notes From the Warsaw Ghetto*.

Hoven, Dr. Waldemar (1903–1948). SS camp physician at **Buchenwald**. He conducted inhumane **typhus** experiments on inmates and murdered them by lethal injections. Hoven was tried and sentenced to death by a U.S. **International Military Tribunal** at the **Doctors' Trial**. (See also **Dr. Erwin Ding-Schuler**.)

SUGGESTED READING: Aziz, *Doctors of Death*.

Hudal, Bishop Alois (1885–1963). Pro-Nazi prelate. He was a virulent **anti-Semite** and Catholic bishop of the German community in **Rome**. He prayed for German victory. Hudal was close to **Cardinal Eugenio Pacelli**, with whom he helped negotiate the **Concordat** with Nazi **Germany**. After the war, he was the first priest to run the **Ratline**, which supplied false papers and hiding places to fleeing Nazis. The Bishop's memoirs define his unrepentant role in helping Nazi **war criminals**. (See also **Walter Rauff, Franz Stangl**, and **Gustav Wagner**.)

SUGGESTED READINGS: Farago, *Aftermath*; Simpson, *Blowback*.

Huettig, Hans (1894–1980?). Kommandant of **Natzweiler, Flossenbuerg, Sachsenhausen-Oranienburg**, and **Vught**. He was sentenced to life by the French, but was pardoned and released in March 1956.

Hugo Schneider A. G. (HASAG). German construction company that utilized **concentration camp** labor. One of its camps was a **Judenlager**, an armaments works near **Radom** from 1943–1944.

Hull, Cordell (1871–1955). U.S. secretary of state from 1933–1944. Prior to the war, he declined to rescue Jews because he felt they were a German "internal affair." He opposed relaxing immigration laws and promoted the ideal of winning the war first as a means of rescuing Jews during the **Holocaust**. Hull played a passive role in immigration policies, deferring to **Breckinridge Long**. He opposed the creation of the **War Refugee Board**. Ironically, his wife was Jewish, a fact he kept secret. He did send a note to **Admiral Miklos Horthy** through the Swiss legation in June 1944 threatening reprisals against those responsible for Hungarian Jewish **deportations**. (See also **Henry Morgenthau Jr., Moscow Declaration**, and **Franklin Delano Roosevelt**.)

SUGGESTED READINGS: Wyman, *The Abandonment of the Jews*; Wyman, *Paper Walls*.

Hundestaffel (G., trained dog echelons). Vicious dogs who bit inmates and were used to manage **deportees**. Upon leaving the **transport** and entering the **concentration camp**, the deportees were confronted with German shepherds or dobermans. (See also **Juden, Rause!**)

Hungary. Landlocked country in east central Europe bordered in the north and west by **Austria, Czechoslovakia**, and the **USSR**, and the south by **Yugoslavia** and **Romania**. It was part of the Austro-Hungarian Dual Monarchy until the defeat of the Hapsburg Empire in World War I (1918). Hungary became an independent republic after the war. By the Treaty of Trianon (1920), Hungary lost two-thirds of its territory, including Transylvania, which was awarded to Romania. **Ruthenia** was awarded to the new state of Czechoslovakia. **Admiral Miklos Horthy** was installed as regent with the help of Romanian forces, who expelled dictator Bela Kuhn. Anxious to regain lost territory, Hungary drew close to Nazi **Germany** in the 1930s. Soon after the **Munich Pact**, it received South **Slovakia** (Felvivek) and Ruthenia in 1938. In 1940, Hungary received nearly half of Transylvania. Hungary joined the **Axis** in 1939, declared war on the United States in December 1941, and in January 1942, sent troops to fight against the **Soviet Union**. On March 19, 1944, suspicious that Admiral Horthy was looking for a separate peace, German troops occupied Hungary. On April 4, 1945, the last German forces left the country.

In 1939, there were 403,000 to 445,000 Jews in Hungary out of a population of 9,106,000. However, with the acquisition of former Czech and Romanian lands, the Jewish population jumped to close to 650,000 to 700,000. The general Hungarian population increased to 15 million. There were 500,000 ethnic Germans (**Volksdeutsche**). The Horthy regime, while **anti-Semitic**, did not want to deport or murder Jews. Jews were placed in special army labor battalions called **Munkaszolgalat**. Many of these laborers were sent to the Russian front and met with mistreatment and death. The **Red Army** saw them as the enemy.

The Jews constituted the major part of Hungary's middle class. They were subject to *Numerus Clausus* and **Aryanization**, but managed to survive until the German invasion on March 19, 1944. With the occupation came the **SS, Adolf Eichmann**, and the **Final Solution**. For the first time, **Pope Pius XII** and the **Red Cross** spoke out against Jewish **deportation**. President **Franklin Delano Roosevelt** sent a direct message to Horthy opposing deportation. The regent resigned in October 1944, and the viciously anti-Semitic and Nazi sympathetic **Arrow Cross** took over the reins of government. Deportations of 435,350 Jews (often sent directly to **Auschwitz**) were facilitated by the Hungarian **Gendarmerie**. Deportation was delayed by the embassies of **Sweden, Switzerland**, the **Vatican**, and the intervention of **Raoul Wallenberg** and **Carl Lutz**. The Red Army moved into Pest, part of Budapest on January 17, 1945, relieving the threat of mass murder of 120,000 Jews.

About 400,000 Hungarian Jews died at Auschwitz, while 30,000 Budapest Jews died on **death marches** to Germany and Austria ostensibly for labor. All told, 569,000 Hungarian Jews perished. Hungarian Jews were the last large group of Jews in Europe deported, and the Nazis were eager to carry out the Final Solution before their war was lost. (See also **Backa, Laszlo Baky, Kurt Becher, "Blood for Trucks," Joel Brand, Anton Brunner, Budapest Rescue Committee, Laszlo Ferenczy, Cordell Hull, Miklos Kallay, Dr. Rezso Kasztner, Martin Luther, Otto Moll, Munkacs, Franz Novak, Operation Margarethe, Angelo Roncalli, Monsignor Angelo Rotta, Miguel Angel Sanz-Briz, Dr. Siegfried Seidl, Ferenc Szalasi, Doeme Sztojay, Edmund Veesenmayer, Vienna, "Waldsee"** and **Weiss-Manfred Works**.)

Hungerhausen (G., starvation houses). Part of the "**Wild Euthanasia**" program after 1943. Two special "dietary" houses were operated for older citizens of the **Reich**. (See also **Dr. Hermann Pfannmueller** and **T-4**.)

Husseini, Hajj Amin al. (See **Grand Mufti of Jerusalem**.)

I

Iasi (G., Jassy). City in **Bessarabia** (Moldavia) that belonged, in 1941, to **Romania**. It was located close to the **USSR** frontier and had a population of 50,000 Jews. On June 29, 1941, roundups initiated by **Iron Guard** Legionaires led to the deaths of many Jews. Mere travel in **freight cars** on a pointless five-day journey without proper sanitation or food led to the death of 2,430 Jews. All told, 8,000 Iasi Jews were murdered in the city. There was a trial for **war criminals** (1948) in the Iasi **pogrom**; forty-six Romanians were found guilty. No German soldiers came to trial.
   SUGGESTED READING: Butnaru, *The Silent Holocaust.*

Ickes, Harold L. (1874–1952). Secretary of the Interior (1933–1946) under **Franklin Delano Roosevelt**. He attempted to save European Jews by introducing the **Alaskan Development Bill** in Congress. Ickes favored a liberal **refugee** policy and played a leading role in establishing **Oswego**.
   SUGGESTED READINGS: Watkins, *Righteous Pilgrim;* Wyman, *Paper Walls.*

ICRC. (See **Red Cross**.)

IGCR. (See **Intergovernmental Committee on Refugees**.)

I. G. Farben (IGF). Chemical giant comprised of eight German chemical companies that utilized **slave labor** at its **Buna/Monowice** (Auszchwitz III) site and other camps. All told, Farben exploited 350,000 slave laborers. Farben also produced **Zyklon-B (DEGESCH)** for the **gas chambers**. This corporate entity, affiliated for years with Standard Oil and DuPont, strove to help make Nazi **Germany** self-sufficient before and during the war. They profited handsomely from Hitler's Four-Year Plan. Farben was broken up after the war and divided into six corporations including **Bayer**, BASF, and Hoecsht. Corporate witnesses at Nuremberg claimed they were unaware of **selections** at Auschwitz and that the food served at Auschwitz III, that is, "Buna soup," was "delicious." The directors were tried after the war as part of the subsequent **Nuremberg Trials**. Karl Krauch and other Farben executives claimed ignorance and were given light sentences. **Josiah DuBois**, American prosecutor of the case, said of the July 1948 sentence (six years): "It was light enough to please a chicken thief." (See also **Circle of Friends of Himmler**.)

SUGGESTED READINGS: Borkin, *The Crime and Punishment of I. G. Farben*; Ferencz, *Less Than Slaves*.

"Illegal." Person without a work permit.

Impressing. Kidnapping and seizing Jews, Poles, and other non-**Aryans** for **forced labor**.

IMT. (See **International Military Tribunal**.)

Institute for the Study of Jewish Questions (Einsatzstab). Founded in March 1941, the Institute was headed by **Alfred Rosenberg** and focused on "researching" Jewish racial issues. It also had the right to seize cultural assets of Jews in occupied territories of the East. (See also **Aryanization**.)

SUGGESTED READING: Davidson, *The Trial of the Germans*.

Intergovernmental Committee on Refugees (IGCR). Rescue organization set up as a result of the **Evian Conference** to search for new areas of large-scale Jewish settlements, find ways of pressuring the German government to release Jews, and prompt Evian nations (thirty-two) to accept Jews. The Committee was headed by George Rublee (1939) and based in London. The Committee's lukewarm rescue efforts were ineffective and did not lower immigration barriers. Its very existence, a mere token, frustrated other rescue plans and was replaced by the **War Refugee Board**. (See also **Myron Taylor**.)

SUGGESTED READINGS: Feingold, *The Politics of Rescue*; Wyman, *Paper Walls*.

Internationale Vereinigung Bibelforsche (International Bible Students Association). (See **Jehovah's Witnesses**.)

International Military Tribunal (IMT). Coordinated prosecution of major Nazi **war criminals** by the **Allies**. Two judicial bodies were established at the end of the war to conduct trials of war criminals: one in **Nuremberg** and the other in Tokyo. It was chartered at the **London Charter Conference** on August 8, 1945. The participating nations included the United States, **France**, Great Britain, and the **Soviet Union**. Each nation sent two judges to each tribunal.

Senior judges were Lord Justice Lawrence from Great Britain, Frances Biddle from the United States, Professor Donnedieu de Vabras from France, and Major General I. T. Nikitehenko from the Soviet Union. (See also **Potsdam Conference, United Nations War Crimes Commission**, and **Yalta Conference**.)

   SUGGESTED READINGS: Persico, *Nuremberg, Infamy on Trial*; Taylor, *The Anatomy of the Nuremberg Trials*.

Internment Camps. In Western Europe, these camps (e.g., **Gurs**) served as the first stop on the road to **concentration camps**. Typically, foreign Jews (followed by indigenous Jews) would be sent to internment camps then to **transit camps** (e.g., **Westerbork** or **distribution centers**, e.g., **Drancy**) before arriving at concentration camps. (See also **Joseph Darnand, French Internment and Transit Camps,** and **Switzerland**.)

"Inventorization" (also referred to as "furniture action"). Euphemism for the expropriation of Jewish property. Nazis and their **collaborators** would enter a Jewish property (usually in Western Europe) prior to plundering it and establish a record of possessions. If a Jew concealed his property prior to Nazi expropriation, the penalty was **deportation**. A very small percentage of Jewish belongings was recovered after the war. (See also **Aryanization, Jewish Restitution Successor Organization**, and **Reparations and Restitution**.)

Irgun Zvai Leumi (H., National Military Organization). Underground movement founded by dissident **Haganah** members and followers of the **Zionist Revisionist** Movement in 1931. It founded Af-Al-Pi ("In Spite of Everything") in 1937, an organization that assisted **Aliya Bet** from Europe throughout the 1930s–1940s. During the war, this group aided the British in anti-Nazi operations. However, in January 1944, the Irgun attacked British military targets in **Palestine** for its **White Paper** policy, which it considered complicity to the **Holocaust**. (See also **Menachem Begin, Peter Bergson, Ze'ev Jabotinsky, David Raziel**, and *Struma*.)

   SUGGESTED READINGS: Bell, *Terror Out of Zion*; Ben-Ami, *Years of Wrath*.

Iron Guard (Ro., Garda de Fier). Romanian **fascist** party. A political and paramilitary organization, it was established in July 1927 as the **Legion of the Archangel Michael** by Corneliu Codreanu. It became the Iron Guard in 1929. The Guard wore green shirts, revered the peasant, and subscribed to murder as a means of purifying the country of politicians and Jews. They were closely allied with the Nazis. It was officially disbanded in 1933, but continued to operate clandestinely and became the third largest political party after elections in 1937. In the summer of 1940, **Horia Sima**, leader of the Iron Guard, and **Ion Antonescu**, Romanian politician, formed the **anti-Semitic National Legionary Government**. The Iron Guard attempted a coup in January 1941. The coup failed, due in large part to the Romanian Army's support of Prime Minister

Antonescu. **Hitler** also supported Antonescu. The Guard instituted anti-Jewish riots in Bucharest (January 1941), before fleeing to **Germany**. After the Romanian government's surrender, Sima established a government-in-exile (December 1944). (See also **Romania**.)

SUGGESTED READINGS: Butnaru, The Silent Holocaust; Ioanid, The Sword of the Archangel.

Iron Wolf. Lithuanian **fascist** organization headed by **Augustinas Voldemaras**. (See also **Lithuanian Activist Front**.)

Isaac, Jules (1872–1963). French Jewish historian. He saw **anti-Semitism** rooted in Christian teaching of contempt for Jews. Under the French Republic, he was an inspector of history and later escaped the Nazis. After the war, he presented his book, Teaching of Contempt, to **Pope Pius XII**. The historian argued that Nazi anti-Semitic terror was the secular radicalization of anti-Jewish impulses of historic Christianity. Later, anti-Jewish phraseology was deleted from Good Friday liturgy by **Pope John XXIII**.

Isle of Man. British island in the Irish Sea. During the war, approximately 3,000 German Jewish women were interned, isolated, and segregated on this island. (See also **Channel Islands**.)

"Israel." Mandatory middle name the Nazis assigned to all German Jewish males promulgated on August 17, 1938. It went into effect on January 1, 1939. This middle name was required on all IDs and **passports** if the bearer did not have an already very distinct Jewish name. (See also **"J"** and **"Sarah."**)

Italy. Kingdom in southern Europe comprising a boot-shaped peninsula that extended into the Mediterranean Sea. It included the islands of Sicily and Sardinia. It borders **Austria** on the north and west to east, **France, Switzerland**, and **Yugoslavia**. In 1922, **Benito Mussolini** and his **Fascist "Black Shirts"** marched on **Rome** and assumed power. The Fascists abolished parliamentary government and institutions. In 1939, Italy became an **Axis** partner with Nazi **Germany**. The dictatorship entered World War II by attacking France in June 1940. The Italians, along with their powerful ally, the German Afrika Korps, lost North Africa in 1943, and the **Allies** then moved on to Sicily. After the fall of Sicily and landings on the southern coast, Mussolini and the Fascists were overthrown in September 1943, and an Italian government soon joined the Allies. Mussolini was rescued by Nazi commandos, and a puppet state, **Salo Republic**, was created. German troops moved into northern Italy and Rome in September 1943. After very hard fighting, with the Germans still lodged in far northern Italy, the **Wehrmacht** surrendered in April 1945, and the Salo Republic was destroyed.

Italy's Jewry numbered only 45,000 when the March on Rome (1922) occurred. Many Jews supported the Fascists. One-third of Italy's Jewish adults were party members, some becoming high military officers and government officials. By 1938, Jews numbered 57,000 in an Italian population of 45,600,000. Italian Jews played an important role in the state, contributing to its cultural, political, and scientific life. They were assimilated. As Mussolini moved closer to Nazi Germany, a change took place. **Nuremberg**-type laws were passed against the Jews in 1938. By 1939 severe laws restricting employment and commerce impoverished the Jewish community. Ten percent emigrated and another 10 percent converted to Catholicism.

While Italy was formally allied with Germany, the Italian people had no interest in the war and were friendly to the Jewish people. In those sections of Europe occupied by the Italian Army, they protected the Jews, preventing murder and **deportations**. This happened in southern France and the coastal areas of Yugoslavia and in **Greece**. It was only after the Italians changed sides (September 8, 1943) and the Germans took over both formerly Italian-occupied areas and northern Italy (September 9, 1943) did conditions change drastically for the worse for Italian Jews. Internment and deportation (10,271 Jews) took place under German occupation. At World War II's end, 7,500 to 8,000 Italian Jews had perished. (See also **Albania, Anti-Comintern Pact, Athens, Bricha, Concordat, Croatia, Fascism, Fossoli de Carpi, Ghetto, Jewish Brigade-Infantry, Herbert Kappler, Libya, Benito Mussolini, Pope Pius XI, Pope Pius XII, Erich Priebke, Rab, Walter Reder, Rhodes, La Risiera di San Sabba, Joseph Schwammberger, Enzo Sereni, SS Colonel Otto Skorzeny, Spain, Vatican, Karl Wolff,** and **Rabbi Israel Zolli.**)

SUGGESTED READINGS: Cohen, *The Neppi Modena Diaries*; Herzer, *The Italian Refuge.*

J

"J." Stamped on German passports, ration, and identification cards to identify the owner as a Jew. The "J" was initiated in October 1938, at the bequest of the **Swiss** government. German ID cards without the "J" were expensive but available on the black market. (See also **Finland, Kennkarte, Refoulement, Dr. Heinrich Rothmund, Eduard von Steiger**, and **Theresienstadt**.)

Jabotinsky, Ze'ev (Vladimir) (1880–1940). Russian-born **Zionist**. He founded the **Zionist Revisionists** and initiated the Jewish Legion, which fought with the British in **Palestine** during World War I. Jabotinsky distrusted the British, a position that eventually led to a break with mainstream Zionists. He favored self-defense with Jewish legionnaires in the **Yishuv** in 1920. Jabotinsky founded the youth scout movement, **Beitar**. The **Irgun** was the military arm of Jabotinsky Revisionists. He advocated a Jewish state in Palestine on both sides of the Jordan and promoted immigration of European Jews prior to the **Holocaust**, an event that he had predicted. (See also **Menachem Begin, Abraham Stern**, and **Josiah Clement Wedgwood**.)
   SUGGESTED READING: Schechtman, *Rebel and Statesman.*

Jackson, Robert (1892–1954). Associate Justice of the U.S. Supreme Court (1942–1954) and chief prosecutor during the initial **Nuremberg Trial** of twenty-four Nazi **war criminals**. He is credited with developing the concept of **crimes against humanity**, which included the **genocide** of Jews. (See also **Murray C. Bernays** and **Rafael Lemkin**.)
   SUGGESTED READINGS: Harris, *Tyranny on Trial*; Persico, *Nuremberg: Infamy on Trial.*

Jaeger, Karl (1888–1959). **SS** colonel and head of Einsatzkommando 3 of **Einsatzgruppe** A. As head of the **SD** in **Lithuania**, he set up the **ghetto** in Slovoda, a suburb of **Kovno**. He was the initiator of numerous **Aktionen**, particularly shooting Jews into pits. He was charged with the **genocide** of Lithuanian Jewry, but committed suicide before his trial in 1959. (See also **Dr. Rudolf Lange**.)

SUGGESTED READING: Tory, *Surviving the Holocaust.*

Jagendorf, Siegfried (1885–1970). Engineer and head of the transplanted Jewish community in Romanian-occupied **Mogilev-Podolski**. He employed harsh methods, but as promised, he repaired and maintained the electrical system and iron works in Mogilev. He saved 1,500 Jews in this manner. Jagendorf died in the United States. (See also **Romania** and "**Work as a Means of Rescue**.")

SUGGESTED READING: Jagendorf, *Jagendorf's Foundry.*

"**Jan.**" Jewish code for **Warsaw Ghetto Uprising**.

Janowska (Road). Major **labor** and **concentration camp** outside of **Lvov**. It operated from September 1941 to September 1945. Those Jews who were exhausted or sick were forced to dig their own graves at nearby areas. A separate area served as a **transit camp** for those **selected** for **Belzec**. Tens of thousands of Jews were killed in this camp. (See also **Sonderkommando 1005**.)

SUGGESTED READING: Wells, *The Death Brigade.*

Jasenovac. **Concentration** and **death camp** complex sixty miles south of **Zagreb, Croatia**, established in August 1941, and operated by the **Ustashi**. Of the 200,000 Serbs, Jews, political opponents, and **Roma** murdered in Croatian concentration camps, 70,000 perished at this site, of whom 20,000 were Jews. An additional 300,000 to 400,000 Serbs and thousands of Jews and Roma were murdered by the Ustashi. This camp did not possess a **gas chamber**. Contests were held to see which Ustashi could execute victims the fastest. (The Ustashi used a long, curved knife called a graviso.) Jasenovac was liberated by the 4th Serbian Brigade of the First Yugoslavian Army (**partisans**) on May 2, 1945. (See also **Andrija Artukovic, Anton Pavelic, Sarajevo, Serbia, Marshal Tito,** and **Yugoslavia**.)

SUGGESTED READINGS: Berenbaum, *A Mosaic of Victims*; Romans, *The Jews of Yugoslavia.*

Jaspers, Karl (1883–1969). German philosopher and psychiatrist. After the war, he acknowledged Nazi crimes, collective German political guilt, and urged serious attention to the lessons of the pre-Nazi and Nazi periods. (See also **Pastor Martin Niemoeller**.)

SUGGESTED READING: Dawidowicz, *The Holocaust and the Historians.*

J. A. Topf und Soehne. German company based in Ehrford. They designed the huge furnaces at **Auschwitz**. The moving force behind increasing the capacity of the ovens up to 2,200 bodies per day was Topf engineer, Kurt Prufer. Topf built ovens with limited capacity at **Dachau** and **Buchenwald**. The company's owner, Ernst-Wolfgang Topf, started a new company in West **Germany** (1950) and applied for a patent to burn corpses and cadavers. Topf's heirs have launched a bid to reclaim the old factory sites and other family property. (See also **Bauleitung SS, DEGESCH,** and **Heinz Kammler**.)
   SUGGESTED READING: Pressac, *Auschwitz*.

Jazz. Condemned by the Nazis, especially **Dr. Paul Joseph Goebbels**, as a modern, decadent, American, black-Jewish cultural manifestation aimed at seducing German women. German youth who clandestinely listened to this music were called "swing youth."
   SUGGESTED READING: Kater, *Different Drummers*.

"Jedem Das Seine. Arbeit Macht Frei" (G., "To Each What He Deserves. Work Makes Free"). Sign erected at the entrance to **Flossenbuerg** and the first portion of the phrase was used at the entrance of **Buchenwald**. "Work Makes Free" was a slogan used at **Birkenau** and other **concentration camps**. Interned Jews had indeterminate sentences and were not slated to be freed. The slogan was a tragic hoax.

Jehovah's Witnesses (G., **Internationale Bibelforscher**). International Bible Students Association and referred to as **"voluntary prisoners"** by the Nazis. Approximately 20,000 Jehovah's Witnesses lived in **Germany** when **Hitler** came to power. The Nazis banned the activities of the Jehovah's Witnesses in 1933 and forced them out of the civil service in April 1935. Mass arrests were made on April 7, 1939. Their members (including Austrians, Belgians, Czechs, Poles, Norwegians, and Dutch) were sent to **concentration camps** for their refusal to make the "Heil Hitler" salute or fight for the **Third Reich**. The Jehovah Witnesses' population at any given camp was usually several hundred, and approximately 2,500 died in the camps, including **Auschwitz**. They were identified by a purple triangle. Their strong solidarity and faith, cleanliness, isolation (less they convert other inmates), and native German tongue contributed to their high survival rate. The Witnesses did not actively resist the Nazis or try to escape and were, therefore, afforded preferential treatment. They were at times allowed to work outside concentration camps without supervision. (See also **Lichtenburg** and **Moringen**.)
   SUGGESTED READING: Berenbaum, *A Mosaic of Victims*.

Jewish Agency. Established in the **Yishuv** to promote Jewish self-government as part of the **British Mandate** (1921) by the **League of Nations**. In 1941, it set up a Joint Rescue Committee and maintained operational centers in Geneva and Istanbul. The Agency was reluctant to expend funds on rescue, arguing moneys should be provided by international Jewish communities. However, some funding was spent on modest rescue efforts. This group tried to rescue Jews in **Transnistria**, urged the **Allies** to save Jews from **concentration camps**, advocated the bombing of railway hubs, and brought orphans to **Palestine**. However, the Agency refused to fund the **Europa Plan** or "**Blood for Trucks.**" (See also **David Ben-Gurion, Joel Brand, Nahum Goldmann, Bandi Grosz, Dr. Isaac Lewin, Richard Lichtheim, Moshe Shertok, Socialist Zionists, World Zionist Organization**, and **Abraham L. Zissu.**)

SUGGESTED READINGS: Cohen, *Churchill and the Jews*; Szule, *The Secret Alliance*.

Jewish Anti-Fascist Committee. Soviet propaganda and information agency established in Moscow in 1941. It sought to gain American Jewish support for the **Soviet Union**. Headed by Soviet-**Yiddish** literary figures, Ber Mark (Jewish historian), **Ilya Grigorovitch Ehrenburg** (editor of *Murderers of Nations*), Itzik Fefer, and **Shlomo Mikhoels**. Its magazine, *Eynikayt*, publicized Nazi atrocities in Yiddish and distributed information on Jewish life in the Soviet Union. The Committee was disbanded in 1948, when **Josef Stalin** purged Jewish intellectuals, including Fefer and Mikhoels.

SUGGESTED READING: Vaksberg, *Stalin Against the Jews*.

Jewish Atonement Fine. (See **Kristallnacht**.)

Jewish Badge. The badge featured a six-pointed Yellow Star with the word "Jew" in the local language or a white armband imprinted with a blue Star of David (**Poland**) that the Nazis and their **collaborators** ordered Jews to wear. The star had to be sewn on visible garments. Failure to wear the star resulted in immediate punishment or **deportation**. (See also **Robert Weltsch** and **Yellow Badge-Triangle**.)

Jewish Brigade-Infantry. After much agitation, this organization was formed in September 26, 1944, comprising 5,000 men. These soldiers, mostly from the **Yishuv**, served in **Italy** in November 1944 as part of the British 8th Army. The Brigade were also an important part of the **Bricha** movement and served as a training ground for **Haganah** and Palmach (Palestine Jewish commandos). (See also **Allies, Lord Moyne**, "**Parachutists**," and **Moshe Shertok**.)

SUGGESTED READINGS: Szule, *The Secret Alliance*; Wasserstein, *Britain and the Jews of Europe 1939–1945*.

Jewish Center. (See **Ustredna Zidov**.)

Jewish Colonization Association. Founded in London in 1891 by Baron Maurice de Hirsch, its purpose was to facilitate emigration from urban population centers to rural areas and encourage farming. During the **Holocaust**, the Association joined with other immigrant aid societies to rescue **refugees**. (See also **HICEM**.)

SUGGESTED READING: Avni, *Spain, the Jews and Franco.*

Jewish Combat Organization. (See **ZOB**.)

Jewish Communal Self-Help (Society). Social welfare organization. During the German occupation of **Poland**, it provided cash relief, clothing, medicine, and maintained soup kitchens. By 1942, this organization had 412 branches in Poland. In Warsaw, it aided 30 percent of Warsaw Jewry and was called the Jewish Society for Social Welfare. (See also **Central Agency for Care of Orphans, Isaac Gitterman, Jewish National Committee, ORT, TOZ**, and **Warsaw Ghetto**.)

SUGGESTED READING: Dawidowicz, *The War Against the Jews.*

Jewish Council. (See **Judenrat**.)

Jewish Cultural Reconstruction. International agency founded in 1945 to deal with cultural and religious property seized by the Nazis and received by the U.S. military government. Established in 1947 in New York by the **World Zionist Organization**, it operated in **Germany** from 1948–1950. (See **Reparations and Restitution**.)

Jewish Documentation Center. (See **Simon Wiesenthal**.)

Jewish Fighting Organization. (See **ZOB**.)

Jewish Labor Committee. New York–based social democratic organization, founded in 1934 to represent Jewish workers in the American labor movement. It joined with the **American Jewish Congress** to establish the **Joint Boycott Council** (1935). It often allied itself with Orthodox rescue organizations to raise funds and relief for European Jews and exploited its connections with the Soviets to enable **Va'ad ha-Hatzala** to send food packages to incarcerated Jews in **Siberia**. Despite its secularism, this organization aided rabbis and **yeshivas**, particularly in the **Shanghai** enclave. The Committee served as a conduit in Warsaw and rescued leading Jewish and non-Jewish labor leaders, intellectuals, artists, and writers. In 1940, it obtained 2,500 Emergency Visitor **visas** from the U.S. government with **AFL** support for this purpose. (See also **Jewish National Committee** and **Joint Emergency Committee for European Jewish Affairs**.)

SUGGESTED READING: Finger, *American Jewry During the Holocaust.*

Jewish Military Resistance. Jews *did* fight back in the **ghettos** (twenty), forests, and even in the **death** and **concentration camps** (five). An estimated 20,000 to 30,000 Jews fought in **partisan** groups in the forests of Eastern Europe. However, military **resistance** was hampered by a number of factors: lack of arms; lack of cadre of soldiers and officers; lack of friendly populace; lack of support by **Allies** or underground movement; lack of a Jewish homeland; German policy of **collective responsibility**—down to noncombatant loved ones—failure to grasp the depth of Nazi murder plans and the nature of Nazi barbarism; and **anti-Semitic collaborators**. (See also **Concentration camp uprisings**.)

SUGGESTED READING: United States Holocaust Memorial Museum, *Resistance during the Holocaust.*

Jewish Military Union. (See **Beitar Revisionists** and **ZZW**.)

Jewish National Committee (ZKN). Umbrella body of **Zionist** and youth movements. It provided the political framework for the **ghetto** underground. The Committee provided aid and assistance to approximately 5,600 Jews in the Warsaw area and gave funds to the **ZOB** and **Zegota**. Money was provided by the "**Joint**" and the **Jewish Labor Committee**. (See also **Jewish Communal Self-Help [Society]** and **Zegota**.)

SUGGESTED READING: Gutman, *The Jews of Warsaw 1939–1943: Ghetto, Underground, Revolt.*

Jewish Observer. (See *Juedische Rundschau*.)

Jewish Office. (See **IVB4**.)

Jewish Police. (See **Jewish Service to Maintain Order** and **Red Card/permit**.)

Jewish Problem/Jewish Question. (See **Judenfrage**.)

Jewish Restitution Successor Organization (JRSO). Between 1945–1947, the **Allies** enacted legislation for the return of expropriated real estate. U.S. Military Government in the **American Zone of Occupation** established the JRSO to recover seized heirless Jewish properties and assets. This organization did not deal with Jewish **forced labor** claims. (See also **Reparations and Restitution**.)

SUGGESTED READING: Bird, *The Chairman.*

Jewish Self-Help Society. (See **Central Agency for Care of Orphans, Isaac Gitterman, ORT**, and **TOZ**.)

Jewish Service to Maintain Order (G., **Juedischer Ordnungsdienst**). Jewish **police** force within the **ghetto** affiliated with the **Judenrat**. These Jews assisted the Nazis in rounding up other Jews for **selections** and **deportations** to **death** and **concentration camps**. Their activities caused great enmity among ghetto residents. (See also **Joseph Szerynski**.)

SUGGESTED READINGS: Perechodnik, *Am I a Murderer?*; Trunk, *Judenrat.*

Jewish Special Courts. Jewish court system in the **ghettos**.

Jewish Spiritual Resistance. Jews attempted to keep their humanity and culture in both the **ghettos** and **concentration camps**. This was done through clandestine religious services, study groups, and holiday observances. Within the ghettos, plays, musical events, Jewish celebrations, and educational activities, including **Zionist** instruction, were conducted. (See also **Dehumanization, Oneg Shabbat Group**, and **Resistance**.)

JFO. (See **Jewish Fighting Organization; ZOB**.)

Jodl, Alfred (1890–1946). Chief of Military Operations of High Command of **Wehrmacht** and **Hitler's** personal military advisor. He signed **Germany's** surrender at Rhiems on May 7, 1945. At the **Nuremberg Trials** he was held responsible for military atrocities, **war crimes**, and planning and implementing aggressive war. Jodl was convicted by the **International Military Tribunal** and hanged on October 16, 1946. (See also **Nacht und Nebel**.)
 SUGGESTED READING: Davidson, *The Trial of the Germans*.

"Joint." (See **American Joint Distribution Committee**.)

Joint Boycott Council. Organized in 1936, it was an unsuccessful effort by the **Jewish Labor Committee** and the **American Jewish Congress** to boycott German goods and services. The State Department affirmed the idea (summer 1941), saying shipments of goods were "against interests of **Allies**." **Agudat Israel** sought to defy the Boycott Council in order to feed Polish Jews in the summer of 1941. (See also **Boycott of Nazi Germany**.)
 SUGGESTED READING: Finger, *American Jewry During the Holocaust*.

Joint Emergency Committee for European Jewish Affairs. Comprised of **Agudat Israel**, American Emergency Committee for Zionist Affairs, **American Jewish Congress**, American Jurist Committee, B'nai B'rith, **Jewish Labor Committee**, Synagogue Council of America, and **Union of Orthodox Rabbis of America**. This umbrella organization submitted a Jewish rescue proposal to the attendees of the **Bermuda Conference**, but all its ideas were ignored.
 SUGGESTED READINGS: Finger, *American Jewry During the Holocaust*; Wyman, *The Abandonment of the Jews*.

Jood (Du., Jew). **Dutch** word for Jew placed on Jewish star mandated on April 29, 1942.

Joodse Raad (Du., Jewish **Council of Elders**). In the **Netherlands**, similar to **Judenrat** of Eastern Europe. (See also **Lodewijk Ernst Visser**.)

JRSO. (See **Jewish Restitution Successor Organization**.)

Juda verrecke! (G., May Jewry Perish!) **Nazi Party** slogan dating back to the 1920s.

Jude (G., Jew). This word was put on the **Yellow Badge** in September 19, 1941, and was affixed to the clothing of Jews in the **Reich**.

Juden, Rause! (G., Jews, out!). Nazi orders barked at Jews as they were rounded up and then unloaded from **freight cars** at **death** and **concentration camps**. (See also **Hundestaffel**.)

Judenaeltesten (G., Jewish elders or leaders). Term applied to the German appointed leaders of a **Judenrat**. These men were expected to provide information on the number of Jews and their property, supply labor, and participate in **deportations**. Their degree of culpability in Nazi crimes varied. (See also **Aeltestenrat, Adam Czerniakow, Jacob Gens, Siegfried Jagendorf, Mordechai Chaim Rumkowski**, and "**Work as a Means of Rescue**.")

"**Judenaktion**" (G., "Jewish operation"). Euphemism for organized murder of Jews. (See also **Aktion**.)

Judenfrage (G., Jewish question). The presence of Jews in **Germany** and Europe was a "problem" that had to be solved by **Hitler**. The **Fuehrer** saw Jews as a contaminating element, and the **Final Solution** was the Nazi resolution to the "question." (See also **Franz Rademacher** and **Voelkerchaos**.)

"**Judenfrei**" (G., "free of Jews"). Nazi euphemism for making an area "free of Jews" by **deportation** or murder. (See also **Judenrein**.)

"**Judenhaus**" (G., "Jewish House") Jews were put into select houses in **Germany**, which made them easy targets for harassment and **deportation**. Instituted after **Allied** bombing, Judenhause was not a **ghetto** or designated in any one particular part of town. (See also **Karl Kaufmann, Privileged Jews**, and **Albert Speer**.)

Judenlager (G., Jewish camp). (See **Hugo Schneider A. G. [HASAG]** and **Zivilabeitslager**.)

Judenmischlinge (G., Jewish half-breed). (See **Mischlinge**.)

Judenrat (G., Jewish council). Set up to organize all facets of Jewish **ghetto** life. Members of the Judenrat were called Elders. These councils were used by the Nazis to implement the **Final Solution**, although the degree of **collaboration**

varied. Judenraete were established in **Poland**, the Baltics, portions of Western Europe, and the western **Soviet Union. Jewish police (Juedischer Ordnungsdiesnt)** were attached to the Judenrat. (See also **Aeltestenrat, Hannah Arendt, Consistoire, Adam Czerniakow, Jacob Gens, House Committees, Siegfried Jagendorf, Joodse Raad, Judenaeltesten, Juedischer Arbeitseinsatz, Mordechai Chaim Rumkowski**, and **"Work as a Means of Rescue."**)

   SUGGESTED READINGS: Trunk, *Judenrat*; Tushnet, *The Pavement of Hell*.

Judenreferent (G., expert on Jewish affairs). (See **Adolf Eichmann**.)

Judenrein (G., cleansed of Jews). Nazi euphemism for making an area "cleansed of Jews" by **deportation** or murder. (See also **Estonia, "Judenfrei,"** and **Radom Ghetto**.)

"Die Juden sind unser Unglueck" (G., "The Jews are Our Misfortune"). Phrase conceived by German historian and nationalist Heinrich von Treitschke in 1879. This slogan, printed on the cover of **Julius Streicher's** newspaper *Der Stuermer*, was used frequently by the Nazis.

Judeophobia. A fear of Jews characterized by Christian leaders who saw them as a challenge to the "true faith." The Jews were religious sinners who could earn redemption by conversion. Unlike **anti-Semitism**, it had no racial component, but it provided the floor of hate upon which the Nazis could build. (See also **Jules Isaac**.)

Jude Suess (G., *Jew Suess*). A 1938 propaganda movie ordered by **Dr. Paul Joseph Goebbels**. It was based on the life of Joseph Oppenheimer, an eighteenth-century Swiss Jewish financier. The script, a highly distorted version of the truth, has Suess extort, torture, and rape in a most depraved way. In the end, the townspeople and the government execute the Jew. This motion picture prepared German opinion for future atrocities against Jews.

   SUGGESTED READING: Rentschler, *The Ministry of Illusion*.

Juedischer Arbeitseinsatz (G., Jewish labor employment). The labor registries of **Judenraete**. Most of the **forced labor** was carried out in numerous camps the Germans set up.

Juedischer Ordnungsdienst (G., **Jewish Service to Maintain Order) Jewish police** in **ghettos**. Their activities caused much resentment by ghetto residents since the service aided in roundups and **deportation**. (See also **Judenrat**.)

Juedische Rundschau (G., *Jewish Observer*). Official weekly of German **Zionists** published from 1897–1938. Its most famous edition ran on April 1, 1933, and bore the headline by journalists **Robert Weltsch**: ''Wear it with pride, the **Jewish badge**.'' Although the badge had not yet been issued, Jewish businesses were targeted during the **Anti-Jewish Boycott**.

Juedischer Wohnbezirk (G., Jewish quarter). Nazi euphemism for Jewish **ghetto**.

Jugendschutzlager (JULAG) (G., youth ''protection'' camps). Located outside of some **concentration camps**, for example, **Buchenwald**.

Juif (F., Jew). Pejorative term marked on the **Yellow Badge-Triangle** in **France**. Decreed June 7, 1942, just for German-occupied France. **Vichy** did not force Jews to wear the badge. (See also **Statue des Juifs**.)

July 20, 1944 Bomb Plot. Assassination attempt on **Hitler** led by Count Claus Schenk von Stauffenberg at Rastenberg (''Wolf's Lair'') in East Prussia. The bomb was planted under a wooden table, but failed to kill Hitler. Quick action by **Dr. Paul Joseph Goebbels** in **Berlin** foiled a coup. The rebellion involved senior military officers and was motivated by the **Third Reich's** excesses, imminent defeat, and **Allied** bombing of **Germany's** cities. After brutal investigations by the **Gestapo**, and a mock trial before the **People's Court**, 21 generals, 33 colonels, 7 ministers, 3 state secretaries, 2 ambassadors, and 141 other figures were executed. (See also **Kreisau Circle, Arthur Nebe**, and **Operation Valkyrie**.)
    SUGGESTED READINGS: Galante, *Operation Valkyrie*; Posner, *Hitler's Children*.

Jung, Carl (1875–1961). Swiss psychoanalyst. He investigated anthropology and the occult. Jung developed a theory of archetypes or universal symbols present in what he called humankind's collective unconscious. Before the advent of the Nazis, he was an associate of Sigmund Freud. He viewed Nazism favorably as an ecstatic phenomenon, a return of repressed pagan mystical tendencies. Jung lived in **Germany** during World War II. (See also **Martin Heidigger**.)
    SUGGESTED READING: Cox, *Psychotherapy and the Third Reich*.

Jungfernhof. Killing center in **Riga**. (See also **Kaiserwald**.)

Jungmaedel (G., young girl or maiden). Girls between 10–14 were inculcated with Nazi values through this youth organization. (See also **Bund deutschen Maedel [BdM], Hitler Youth**, and **Jungvolk**.)

Jungvolk (G., young people). Boys between 10–14 were indoctrinated into Nazi doctrine and **anti-Semitism** through this youth organization. (See also **Bund deutscher Maedel [BdM], Hitler Youth, Jungmaedel**, and **Pimpf**.)

Junkers. German aircraft company that utilized **concentration camp** labor from **Buchenwald**.

Junkerschulen/Junkerschools. SS training schools and indoctrination facilities for **Hitler Youth**.

K

Kaddish (Aramaic). Special Jewish prayer praising God, said in honor of the dead. Recited at burial and anniversary of the date of death. After **liberation**, one of the first acts performed by Jews at **crematorium** sites was saying the Kaddish.

Kaindl, Anton (1902–1947). Kommandant of **Sachsenhausen-Oranienburg**. Sentenced to life imprisonment by the Soviets.

Kaiserwald. **Concentration camp** outside of **Riga** interning Jews from the **Greater Reich, Latvia, Hungary, Vilna**, and **Lodz**. The camp exploited **slave labor**, particularly at the **Allgemeine Elektrizitaets-Gessellschaft (AEG)**. As the **Red Army** approached in September 1944, Jews under 18 and over 30 were murdered and most of the evacuees were **transported** to **Stutthof**. (See also **Jungfernhof** and **Liepaja**.)

   SUGGEST READINGS: Penny, *I Was There*; United States Holocaust Memorial Museum, *Darkness Before Dawn*.

Kaiser Wilhelm Institute. Research facility established for the study of anthropology, human genetics, and **eugenics**. The facility was initially headed by Eugen Fischer (1927), a specialist in the study of twins, who coined the term ''erblehre'' (genetics). **Otmar von Verschuer** was a prominent member of this body and stayed on until war's end. His pupil, **Dr. Josef Mengele**, fed the Institute with blood samples and skeletons of **concentration camp** inmates. The Institute illustrates the danger of research in medical science without regard for ethical, moral, or humanitarian considerations. (See also **Lise Meitner, Nuremberg Principles**, and **Dr. Ernst Ruedin**.)

SUGGESTED READING: Proctor, *Racial Hygiene.*

Kallay, Miklos (1887–1967). Prime Minister of **Hungary** from March 1942 to March 1944. He implemented anti-Jewish measures, but **resisted** the **Final Solution** and attempted to negotiate a separate peace with the **Allies** in Turkey. His actions facilitated the German occupation of Hungary on March 19, 1944. Kallay was deposed and **deported** to **Mauthausen**. The ex-prime minister survived and settled in New York City. (See also **Admiral Miklos Horthy** and **Munkaszolgalat**.)

SUGGESTED READING: Braham, *The Politics of Genocide.*

Kaltenbrunner, Ernst (1903–1946). **SS** lieutenant general and police administrator. He was an attorney, then chief of police in **Vienna**. He was **Reinhard Heydrich's** replacement in January 1943, as chief of the Security Police, **RSHA**, and **SD**. Kaltenbrunner was head of the Austrian SS and became state secretary of Security after the **Anschluss**. As chief of the RHSA, Kaltenbrunner ordered the **Gestapo** to execute captured "**parachutists**." He was involved in the **euthanasia** program, a major player in **Aktion Reinhard**, and instigator of the **deportation** of Jews from **Theresienstadt** to **Auschwitz**. He was promoted above other senior and more capable SS, for example, **Walter Schellenberg**. Kaltenbrunner was efficient, but unlike Heydrich, subservient to **Heinrich Himmler**, due to his alcoholism and extravagant lifestyle. However, after the assassination attempt on **Hitler** on **July 20, 1944**, Kaltenbrunner gained direct access to Hitler, increased his power, and became more independent from Himmler. The **International Military Tribunal** convicted him of **war crimes, crimes against humanity**, and complicity in the murder of millions at the **Nuremberg Trials**. Kaltenbrunner was hanged on October 16, 1946. (See also **Rassenschande**.)

SUGGESTED READINGS: Black, *Ernst Kaltenbrunner;* Persico, *Nuremberg: Infamy on Trial.*

Kammler, Dr. Hans (1901–1945). **SS** general and construction chief. He was instrumental in attaching armaments production to **concentration camps**. Kammler helped to build **gas chambers** at **Auschwitz** and other **death camps**. After mid–1944, he became director of **Mittelbau-Mittelwerk**, where he oversaw the ruthless exploitation of 170,000 concentration camp inmates from **Buchenwald, Dora-Nordhausen**, and other camps. Kammler supervised the construction of the tunnels for the production of the V-2 missiles. He committed suicide at the war's end. (See also **Bauleitung SS, J. A. Topf und Soehne**, and **WVHA**.)

SUGGESTED READING: Michel, *Dora.*

Kanada (G.). (See **Canada I and II.**)

Kaplan, Chaim Aaron (1880–1942). Polish Jewish author. In his journal, *Warsaw Ghetto Diary* (September 1939–August 1942), he recorded critical data and observations of Nazi occupation, Jewish responses, and the destruction of Jews in the **ghetto**. His diary was preserved in a kerosene can. Kaplan was murdered in **Treblinka**. (See also **Emmanuel Ringelblum**.)
   SUGGESTED READING: Gutman, *The Jews of Warsaw.*

Kaplan, Josef (1913–1942). Founder of the **Jewish Fighting Organization** in **Vilna**. The underground grew out of his leadership in **Zionist HaShomer ha-Tzair**. He published an underground newspaper and encouraged guerrilla movements. Kaplan was captured and killed on September 3, 1942.
   SUGGESTED READING: Gutman, *The Jews of Warsaw.*

Kaplinski, Hirsch (1910–1942). Jewish **partisan** commander. Operating in the **Novogrudok** district of **Poland**, he founded the Kaplinski Battalion of 120 men who fought in the Lipiezary Forest. Kaplinski was wounded by the Germans, escaped, but was killed by Russian partisans.
   SUGGESTED READING: Yad Vashem, *Jewish Resistance During the Holocaust.*

Kapo (I., head). The **block** or barracks's leader in **concentration camps**. This inmate assisted in the administration of a camp in return for more rations and better living conditions. Many were renown for their sadism and brutality. In February 1944, **Heinrich Himmler** issued an order prohibiting Jewish kapos. (See also **Blockaelteste, Lageraelteste, Self-government, Stubenaelteste**, and **Stubendienst**.)

Kapote (Y., gabardine). Traditional black outer-garments (long coats) worn by pious male Jews. The Nazis were particularly brutal with ultraorthodox Jews. (See also **Hasidism**.)

Kappler, Herbert (1907–1978). Lt. colonel and head of **Gestapo** in **Rome**. He was involved in the **Ardeantine Cave** massacre and was ordered by **Hitler** to deport Rome's 8,000 Jews to **Mauthausen**. Kappler was sentenced to life imprisonment by an Italian military court. He was smuggled out of jail (1978) in the trunk of his wife's car and died of cancer shortly after arriving in **Germany**.
   SUGGESTED READINGS: Kurzman, *Race for Rome; New York Times,* August 16–27, 1978.

Karaites. Jews who broke away from **Talmudic** Judaism in eighth-century Babylonia. They were considered heretics by mainstream Jews because they did not accept the vast rabbinical tradition. The Karaite prewar population of approximately 12,000 was based mostly in the Crimea (10,000) and **Lithuania**. In **Germany**, they requested exemption from the **Nuremberg Laws**. On January 9,

1939, the German Ministry declared that their "racial psychology" was not Jewish and they were rarely persecuted anywhere in Nazi-occupied Europe. (See also **Krimchaks**.)

SUGGESTED READINGS: Ben-Zvi, *The Exiled and the Redeemed; Encyclopedia Judaica.*

Karski, Jan (b. 1914). **Righteous Gentile** and Polish courier of the **Armia Krajowa (AK)**. He was smuggled into the **Warsaw Ghetto** by two Jews. He entered **Belzec**, or a nearby camp, posing as a guard and observed the mass murder process. Escaping to England in November 1942, he made his way to the United States. Karski personally informed **Winston Churchill, Anthony Eden, Cordell Hull, Henry Louis Stimson, Rabbi Stephen S. Wise**, Judge Felix Frankfurter, **Shmuel Artur Zygielbojm**, and President **Franklin Delano Roosevelt** about the **Final Solution**. In 1943, fearing arrest by the NKVD (Soviet secret police), Karski remained in the United States and wrote about his experiences in the *Secret State* (1944), which documented the **Holocaust** in **Poland** and Polish underground activities. He lectures widely on his wartime experiences. (See also **Leon Feiner**.)

SUGGESTED READINGS: Block and Drucker, *Rescuers*; Laqueur, *The Terrible Secret*; Wood and Jankowski, *Karski: How One Man Tried to Stop the Holocaust.*

Kasztner, Dr. Rezso (Rudolph) (1906–1957). Controversial head of the **Budapest Rescue Committee**. He negotiated with the **SS** in the spring of 1944 for the release of Hungarian Jews. Kasztner organized a train that brought 1,685 Jews from Budapest to **Bergen-Belsen** and eventually to safe haven in **Switzerland**. He was also involved in the "**Blood for Trucks**" deliberations. Kasztner and **Kurt Becher** were instrumental in negotiating the peaceful transfer of Bergen-Belsen inmates from German to British control. Maikiel Greenwald accused Kasztner of **collaborating** with the Nazis and not warning Hungarian Jews of the **Final Solution**. Kasztner sued Greenwald in Israel for libel. The court implicated Kasztner, but the decision was overturned by the Israeli Supreme court in 1958, a year after his assassination in Tel Aviv. (See also **Saly Mayer** and **Rabbi Michael Dov Weissmandel**.)

SUGGESTED READINGS: Bauer, *American Jewry and the Holocaust*; Hilberg, *The Destruction of European Jews.*

Katzet (KZ). (See **Konzentrationslager**.)

Katzenelson, Itzkhak (1886–1944). Poet, educator, and writer. He bewailed the murder of Jewish people. The poet founded and directed a **Yiddish** drama group and wrote plays for children in the **Warsaw Ghetto**. Katzenelson and his son, Zvi, were to be **deported** to **Treblinka**, then sent to **Vittel** (May 1943) because they possessed Honduran passports. Their passports were invalidated in 1944, and father and son were murdered in **Auschwitz**.

SUGGESTED READINGS: Bauer, *From Diplomacy to Resistance*; Katznelson, *Vittel Diary*.

Katzetnik (Y., **concentration camp** inmate). From German term **KZ** meaning concentration camp.

Kaufmann, Karl (1900–?). **Gauleiter** of Hamburg. A close friend of **Martin Bormann**, he wrote **Hitler** directly on September 16, 1941, following a British bombing raid. He requested the evacuation of Jews from their homes to accommodate the critical housing shortage. Hitler responded by personally issuing an order to evacuate Jews to the East except for the old and sick. This order set in motion the **deportation** of Jews to the East from **Austria**, the **Protectorate of Bohemia-Moravia, Germany**, and **Luxembourg**. This development was a reversal in policy. Hitler had initially wanted to resolve the **Greater Reich's Jewish Problem** after the conquest of the **Soviet Union. Riga** and **Minsk** were two cities absorbing Jews from the Greater Reich. From 1948 on, he was tried three times, incarcerated, but freed in 1953. The former **Gauleiter** became a Hamburg businessman. (See also **Judenhause**.)

SUGGESTED READING: Witte, "Two Decisions Concerning the 'Final Solution to the Jewish Question.' "

Kaunas (L.). Polish name for **Kovno**.

"Keeping Cats." Hiding Jews by Poles.

Keitel, Wilhelm (1882–1946). Field marshal and head of the **Oberkommando der Wehrmacht** from 1938–1945. He was a faithful, unquestioning follower of **Hitler** who violated the conventions of war. Keitel was intimately involved in planning the annexation of **Austria** and **Czechoslovakia**, the invasions of **Poland, France**, the **Netherlands, Belgium**, and **Luxembourg**. Keitel signed orders for the execution of prisoners of war, **hostages**, civilians (approximately 70,000 in Western Europe alone), endorsed the **Night and Fog** campaign, and permitted the **Einsatzgruppen** to operate with army support. He signed the surrender of Germany on May 8, 1945. His defense at the **Nuremberg Trials**— that he merely carried out orders of the state—was rejected by the International Military Tribunal. Keitel was convicted as a **war criminal** and hanged on October 16, 1946. (See also **Anschluss, Commissar Order, Hague Convention, Alfred Jodl, Partisan Order**, and **Sudetenland**.)

SUGGESTED READING: Harris, *Tyranny on Trial*.

Kempner, Dr. Robert M. (b. 1900). Prosecutor of Nazis. Authority on the pursuit and punishment of Nazi **war criminals**. A prosecutor at the **Nuremberg Trials** and a co-author of the **Martin Bormann** indictment, he charged that too many **SS** officers convicted of murder at **Subsequent Nuremberg Trials** were

prematurely pardoned. He also revealed that gold, particularly from the teeth of Jews, was hidden outside **Germany**, which included **Allied** lands, with no compensation to heirs. (See also **John McCloy**.)
  SUGGESTED READING: Farago, *Aftermath*.

Kennedy, Joseph P. (1888–1969). American ambassador to the Court of St. James in England from 1937–1940. He advocated an isolationist policy in the face of what he perceived to be a certain German victory. He proposed settling 600,000 Jews in sparsely populated areas controlled by Western democracies. President **Franklin Delano Roosevelt** rejected the plan. He unsuccessfully lobbied the British and their dominions to provide a safe haven for Jews.
  SUGGESTED READINGS: Beschloss, *Kennedy and Roosevelt*; Herzstein, *Roosevelt and Hitler: Prelude to War*.

Kennkarte (G., identification card). This document had to be carried by all Jews at all times and produced on demand to German officials. It had a red "**J**" denoting a Jew on German IDs and **passports**. It was implemented on December 31, 1938, for Jews at the request of **Dr. Heinrich Rothmund**.

Kersten, Dr. Felix (1898–1960). **Heinrich Himmler's** personal physician and masseur. He was instrumental in brokering the release of thousands of Danish, Dutch, Norwegian, Polish, and French Jews from **concentration camps**. Kersten also advised the Finns on how to resist **deportations** of Jews. Kersten's influence over Himmler was largely due to his ability to relieve Himmler's acute stomach pains. His efforts to help Jews began in the winter of 1943. Kersten lobbied Himmler not to evacuate any more concentration camps in April 1945, and he arranged for a meeting between Himmler and **Norbert Masur** to release Jewish women from **Ravensbrueck**. His efforts to free Jews from German concentration camps was recognized by the **World Jewish Congress**, which estimated that he saved 3,500 Jewish lives. (See also **Count Folke Bernadotte** and **Valpo**.)
  SUGGESTED READINGS: Kersten, *The Kersten Memoirs, 1940–1945*; Schwarz, *Walking With the Damned*.

"Kesselwascher" (G., pot washer). Coveted inmate job of washing the food vats at the camps.

Kibbutz (H., collective farm). A farm mainly in the **Yishuv** where members own property in common. **Socialist Zionist** organizations espoused this form of agriculture.

Kiddush ha Hayyim (H., sanctifying life). Used by Jews during the **Holocaust** as a response to Nazis as a means of spiritual **resistance**. The concept was attributed to Rabbi Yitzhak Nissenbaum who demanded Jews should preserve their bodies, stay alive, maintain the Jewish community, and cling to ritual and tradition. Rabbi Issacher Shlomo Teichthal believed that the term meant to re-create a Jewish homeland in Israel.

Kiddush ha-Shem (H., sanctification of God's name). A person who died sim-ply because he is Jewish is a martyr. The 6 million who perished exemplify this term. (See also **Zachor Institute**.)

Kielce. Southeastern Polish city with a prewar Jewish population of 24,000. Approximately 150–250 **Holocaust** survivors returned, and a postwar **pogrom** was perpetrated on July 4, 1946. Polish Catholics brutally murdered forty-two Jews, including children, and wounded approximately fifty others. The pogrom was set off by the accusation that Jews used Christian blood to make unleavened bread. This event helped to convince Polish Jews who survived the Holocaust to leave **Poland**. (See also **Blood Libel** and **Displaced Persons**.)
   SUGGESTED READINGS: Blumenfeld, "Fifty Years After the Lie"; Zuckerman, *A Surplus of Memory*.

Kiev. Capital of the **Ukraine**. It was occupied by the Germans on September 19, 1941. The slaughter of the city's 175,000 Jews began a week after occu-pation. **Einsatzkommando** 4 D, aided by Ukrainian militiamen, shot 33,000 Jews at **Babi Yar**. The Nazis murdered 100,000 Jews, **Roma, Soviet POWs**, and disabled persons. Kiev was **liberated** in November 1943, two months after Jewish inmates revolted at the Babi Yar camp.
   SUGGESTED READING: Hilberg, *The Destruction of European Jews*.

Kinderaktion (G., childrens' operation). Rounding up and murdering of Jewish children. Over 1.5 million Jewish children died during the **Holocaust**.

Kindertransport (G., childrens' **transport**). Successful transports of 9,354 German, Austrian, and Czech Jewish children to private homes and institutions in England from 1938–1939. The children were unescorted and their parents were left behind. Jewish **refugee** organizations provided funds to maintain the children. Pensions for children involved in these transports were made available by the German government in 1995. (See also **American Friends Service Com-mittee** and **Rabbi Solomon Schonfeld**.)
   SUGGESTED READING: Drucker, *Kindertransport*.

Kishinev. Capital of **Bessarabia**, now called Moldavia. Annexed by Czarist **Russia** at the turn of the century, ceded to **Romania** after World War I, it was awarded to the **Soviet Union** following the **Molotov-Ribbentrop Pact** in 1939. The 41,405 Jews were **ghettoized** by German Romanian forces in July 1941; 10,000 were murdered before the ghetto was established; 20,000 were murdered and 10,000 joined retreating Soviet forces. This city was **liberated** by the **Red Army** in August 1944.

SUGGESTED READING: Braham, *The Tragedy of Rumanian Jewry.*

Klarsfeld, Serge (b. 1935) and **Beate** (b. 1939). Nazi hunters and head of the **Committee of Children of Deportees**. Their most noted success was the discovery and apprehension of **Klaus Barbie** in 1972. This husband and wife team kept the issue of justice for Nazi **war criminals** alive in cases involving **Paul Touvier, Jean Leguay**, and **Rene Bousquet**.

SUGGESTED READING: Paris, *Unhealed Wounds.*

Klausner, Rabbi Abraham. Organized the book containing names and locations of **concentration camp** survivors entitled *She'erit ha-Peletah*, first published on June 1, 1945.

Klein, Julius (d. 1984). Retired American brigadier general and former commander of Jewish War Veterans of America. He was retained after the war by **I. G. Farben** and **Rheinmetall** as their public relations agent in America. Klein was repudiated by the Jewish War Veterans for his association with Rheinmetall.

SUGGESTED READING: Ferencz, *Less Than Slaves.*

Klessheim Castle. Site of conference in **Germany** April 17–18, 1943, between Regent **Niklos Horthy** and **Hitler**. Hitler told the Hungarian leader "Nations that did not eliminate Jews perished." It was a rare occasion when Hitler betrayed himself about the true purposes behind **deportation** and the **Final Solution**.

SUGGESTED READING: Braham, *The Destruction of Hungarian Jewry.*

Klinker Brickworks/Project. Brick works and ship loading facilities at **Sachsenhausen-Oranienburg**. Assignment to these facilities were dreaded and often meant death. **Homosexuals** were often assigned to the Brickworks where the average life-expectancy was thirty days.

Klooga. **Labor camp** established in 1943 in northern **Estonia** near Tallinn. The camp held 3,000 Jews who lived under deplorable conditions, often in a cement factory. The **SS** murdered 2,400 Jewish prisoners before the **Red Army liberated** the camp on September 20, 1944, and found eighty-five prisoners in hiding.

SUGGESTED READING: United States Holocaust Memorial Museum, *Darkness Before Dawn.*

Kobe. Japanese city on the southern coast of West Honshu. Between 3,500 to 5,000 Lithuanian and Polish Jews found sanctuary there. Most of the Jews received travel **visas** from **Sempo Sugihara** and **Jan Zwartendijk** in **Lithuania** and traveled the Trans-Siberian Railway (July 1940–August 1941) to Vladivostok. From there they took a boat to Japan and paid a minimal processing charge. The Jews were welcomed warmly by the city, which contained a small Jewish community of forty families. They helped to resettle the entire **Mir Yeshiva**. In 1941, with the advent of an expanded war in Europe and the Pacific, the Japanese did not extend the **visas** for the Jews, but assisted the **refugees** in their passage to **Shanghai**. (See also **Dr. Abraham Silberschein**.)

SUGGESTED READING: Tokayer and Swartz, *The Fugu Plan.*

Koch, Erich (1896–1986). Member of the **Freikorps, Gauleiter** of Konigsberg and **Reichskommissar** for the **Ukraine**. He boasted he would give the Ukrainians, even if anticommunist and pro-German, "Not national **liberation** but the whip." He was responsible for the mass murder of Ukrainians and the destruction of the Ukrainian independence movement. Tried in Warsaw in 1959, Koch was sentenced to death, but spared due to "poor health." He died in a Polish prison in 1986.

SUGGESTED READING: Aziz, *Doctors of Death.*

Koch, Ilse (1906–1967) ("**Bitch of Buchenwald**,"). Wife of **Buchenwald** kommandant. She was infamous for lashing inmates as she rode through the camp on horseback. However, it was Koch's hobby of selecting victims for her husband, Karl, to construct lampshades from the tattooed skin of inmates that gained her international notoriety. Koch was tried by an **SS** court for improprieties and acquitted. She was captured by the U.S. Army and sentenced to life imprisonment in August 1945, but, soon after, was released. Koch was sentenced to life imprisonment again after a new trial in West **Germany**, but committed suicide in jail in September 1967. (See also **General Lucius D. Clay**.)

SUGGESTED READING: Snyder, *Hitler's Elite.*

Koch, Karl (1897–1945). First kommandant of **Sachsenhausen-Oranienburg**, first kommandant of **Buchenwald**, and first kommandant of **Majdanek**. He had a hobby of collecting skulls and tattooed skin. Koch was tried by the **SS** for a number of crimes including murder, sexual offenses, alcoholism, corruption, and fraud. He was executed by the SS in April 1945. (See also **Ilse Koch** and **Arthur Roedl**.)

SUGGESTED READING: Snyder, *Hitler's Elite.*

Koegel, Max (1895–1946). First kommandant of **Ravensbrueck** (May 1939–August 1942), then commanded **Majdanek** (1942), and **Flossenbuerg** (1943). Kogel was trained in **Dachau** where he worked from 1934–1937. He assumed control of the women's camp at **Lichtenburg** on September 1, 1938. The **Lagerfuehrer** was arrested by the U.S. Army, but later found dead in his cell in 1946.

SUGGESTED READING: Segev, *Soldiers of Evil.*

Kogon, Eugene (1903–1987). Writer and Catholic prisoner at **Buchenwald**. He was arrested in 1938 for anti-Nazi activity. As a medical clerk, he gained insight into Nazi medical experiments and the structure of the camp, which he documented in *The Theory and Practice of Hell* (1950), a seminal work on the camps.

Kolbe, Father Maximilian (1884–1941). Catholic priest. In July 1941, he took the place of a Polish peasant with seven children who was sentenced to be starved to death by the Nazis. Kobe survived over fourteen days in a starvation bunker at **Auschwitz** before the Nazis murdered him by lethal injection in August 1941. Kobe was canonized by Pope John Paul in 1982. However, prior to the war his publications and preachings were **anti-Semitic** identifying Jews as "the hand guiding **Freemasons** who want to destroy the church."
   SUGGESTED READINGS: Modras, "Of Saints and Anti-Semitism"; Treece, *A Man for Others.*

Kommando (G., detail). **Slave labor** detail.

Kommandofuehrer (G., detail leader). **SS** officer in charge of labor gangs at **concentration camps**.

Kommissarbefehl. (See **Commissar Order**.)

Komoly, Otto (1892–1945). A Hungarian **Zionist** who worked with the **Budapest Rescue Committee**. He headed the **Red Cross** offices in **Hungary** in 1944. In that capacity, Komoly organized rescue activities that provided food, shelter, heat, and protection for Jews. This included children's houses under international protection. Komoly was murdered by the **Arrow Cross** in January 1945.
   SUGGESTED READING: Cohen, *The Halutz Resistance in Hungary.*

Komplets (Y., **ghetto** schools). Over 20 percent of former Jewish high school students studied in "illegal" ghetto schools taking academic subjects. This was a form of **spiritual resistance**. (See also "**Canteen**" and **Tarbut**.)

Konrad, Franz (1906–1951). Commander of the **Werterfassung** (confiscatory agency) in the **Warsaw Ghetto**. Captured, tried, and convicted of **war crimes** in **Poland**, he was hanged in Warsaw in 1951.

Konzentrationslager (G., **KZ/Katzet**). **Concentration camp**.

Kook, Hillel (b. 1915). The real name of **Peter Bergson**, who used an alias to protect his uncle, Abraham Kook, the Chief Rabbi of **Palestine**. He headed the **Bergson Group** in America whose purpose, at first, was to promote the formation of a Jewish army. Kook, recognizing the **Holocaust**, concentrated on rescuing the Jews of Europe. (See also **Ben Hecht**.)

SUGGESTED READING: Ben-Ami, *Years of Wrath.*

Korczak, Janusz (1879–1942) (pseudonym for **Dr. Henryk Goldsmid**). Jewish pediatrician and famous author of children's books. He became the beloved director of the Jewish orphanage on Krochmania Street in the **Warsaw Ghetto**. Dr. Korczak, an elderly man, turned down asylum on the Polish side of the **ghetto** many times. He garnered respect and admiration for accompanying his children to the **Umschlagsplatz** on August 5, 1942, and **Treblinka**. The children remained composed and dignified as they faced certain death.

SUGGESTED READINGS: Berhaim, *Father of Orphans*; Korczak, *Ghetto Diary.*

Korczak, Maria Rozka (1921–1988). **Zionist** underground and **partisan** leader. She was active in the **FPO** in the **Vilna ghetto** with **Abba Kovner**. Korczak was among the first to fight in **Rudninkai Forest** and organized autonomous partisan units. After liberation by the **Red Army**, she moved to **Palestine** and helped establish **Holocaust** study centers.

SUGGESTED READING: Kowalski, *Anthology of Armed Jewish Resistance, 1939–1945.*

Korherr, Richard (b. 1903). Chief Inspector of the Statistical Bureaus in the **SS**. He was the statistician who provided figures on the destruction of the Jews. The *Korherr Report*, completed in March 1943, was the first empirical analysis of the number of Jews murdered by the Nazis. He updated the report every three months. The statistician also served **Adolf Eichmann** in organizing liquidations of Jews by indicating the number of Jews in certain areas. Korherr remained unpunished after the war.

SUGGESTED READING: Poliakov, *Harvest of Hate.*

Kosher (H., and Y., sanitary). Food that is permitted by Jewish tradition. In regard to meat, it is ritually slaughtered and prepared. The rabbis gave permission to eat unkosher meat if they felt that the person was sick, or if it was necessary for survival during the **Holocaust**. (See also **Halakha, Pikuah Nefesh, Shechitah**, and **Shochet**.)

SUGGESTED READING: Braham, *The Politics of Genocide.*

Kosice. City in southeast **Slovakia** annexed by **Hungary** in 1938. It was the site where Hungarians handed over Jews to the Germans. Jews were **ghettoized** in April 1944, and only 1,300 Jewish inhabitants of the 12,000 (1940) survived the war.

SUGGESTED READING: Braham, *The Politics of Genocide.*

Kossack, Zofia Szczuska (1890–1968). Polish Catholic novelist and a founder of **Zegota**. She helped Polish Jews hide. The Nazis arrested and interned her at **Auschwitz**. Later Kossack wrote a chronicle of the period entitled *From the Abyss*.

SUGGESTED READING: Bartoszewski and Lewin, *Righteous Among Nations: How Poles Helped Jews, 1939–1945*.

Kovner, Abba (1918–1988). Lithuanian Jewish **partisan** commander of **FPO**. A leader of **Ha-Shomer ha-Tzair**, he succeeded **Yitzhak Wittenberg**. He urged the Jews of **Vilna** to resist: "Do not go like sheep to slaughter." Kovner headed the fighting organization (FPO) of Vilna, which worked both inside the **ghetto** and in the woods. Later, as the architect of **Bricha**, he offered leadership in the secret flight to **Palestine** where he settled. (See also **Avengers, Josef Kaplan, Maria Rozka Korczak**, and **Resistance**.)

SUGGESTED READING: Arad, *The Ghetto in Flames*.

Kovno (L.)/**Kaunas** (P.). Jewish cultural and spiritual center in **Lithuania** and home to 40,000 Jews or 25 percent of the city's prewar population. German occupation began in June 1941. Between June–July 1941, 10,000 Jews were murdered by Lithuanians and Germans. The **ghetto** was sealed in August 1941, with 30,000 Jewish inhabitants. **Partisans** helped some Jews escape to the woods. On October 28, 1941, during the "big **Aktion**," 9,000 Jews were murdered, half of them children. In the fall of 1943, the Kovno ghetto was converted into a **concentration camp** for Austrian and French Jews. **Sonderkommando 1005**, comprised of sixty-four Jewish prisoners, escaped their captors after exhuming bodies of Jews murdered at the **Ninth Fort**. On March 27, 1944, 1,800 infants and women were murdered. The ghetto was liquidated on July 8, 1944, and on August 1, 1944, the Soviets arrived. Approximately 2 percent of the prewar Jewish population survived the **Holocaust**. (See also **Dr. Elchanan Elkes, Gesja Glazer, Hermann Fritz Graebe, Karl Jaeger, Rabbi Ephraim Oshry, Sempo Sugihara, Twelfth Lithuanian Auxiliary Battalion, Hiam Yelin, Henrik Ziman**, and **Jan Zwartendijk**.)

SUGGESTED READINGS: Eckman and Lazar, *The Jewish Resistance*; Tory, *Surviving the Holocaust*.

Kowalski, Wladyslaw (1895–1971). Retired Polish colonel and rescuer. The Warsaw representative of Philips, a Dutch corporation, Kowalski aided Jews from the **Warsaw Ghetto**. He found safe-havens on the **Aryan** side, including his own home. He also restored the basement of a bombed out building where forty-nine Jews were placed. After the war, he emigrated to Israel and was recognized as a **Righteous Gentile** in 1967.

SUGGESTED READING: Bartoszewski and Lewin, *Righteous Among Nations*.

Krakow (Cracow). City in southern **Poland** with a prewar (1938) Jewish population of 57,000 and capital of the **Generalgouvernement** (1939). Despite being **ghettoized** in March 1941, **Zionist** youth movements vigorously and immediately opposed Nazi rule. These **partisans** fought through the fall of 1944, and some made their way to the **resistance** in Budapest. The **Central Agency for Care of Orphans** and **Zegota** were active in this area. Notable resistance fighters included **Heshek "Zvi" Bauminger**, Tova Draenger, Shomshon Drachser, and **Aharon Liebskind**. Jews were **deported** to **Belzec** and **Plaszow**. (See also **Hans Frank, Amon Goeth, Heinkel Werke**, and **Tadeusz Pankiewicz**.)

SUGGESTED READINGS: Kowalski, *Anthology of Armed Jewish Resistance 1939–1945*; Pankiewicz, *The Crakow Ghetto Pharmacy*.

Kramer, Josef. (1906–1945). Kommandant at **Natzweiler, Auschwitz-Birkenau** (May–November 1944) and **Bergen-Belsen** (December 1944–April 1945). He was known as the "Beast of Belsen," and also held high-level posts at **Auschwitz, Sachsenhausen-Oranienburg**, and **Mauthausen**. The **Lagerfuehrer** was tried by a British Tribunal for **war crimes** in the fall of 1945 and hanged on December 13, 1945.

SUGGESTED READINGS: Snyder, *Hitler's Elite*; United States Holocaust Memorial Museum, *1945: The Year of Liberation*.

Krankenbau (G., hospital)/**Krankenlager** (G., camp hospital or infirmary). At **Auschwitz** the hospital was called the Krankenbau. Placement in a hospital made the inmate vulnerable to **selection**. The main infirmary at **Mauthausen** was referred to as the Krankenlager. (See also **Lazarett, Revier**, and **Westerbork**.)

Kranzbuehler, Otto. Captain and German naval judge. He defended **Admiral Karl Doenitz** at the **Nuremberg Trials** and **Alfred Krupp, I. G. Farben** executives, and other German corporations during the **Subsequent Proceedings** at the Nuremberg Trials. Kransbuehler argued that **war crimes** could only be assessed against those directly engaged in hostility. He was also vice-chairman of **Rheinmetall**; as such, he was not interested in **reparations and restitution** for **slave laborers**.

SUGGESTED READINGS: Davidson, *The Trial of the Germans*; Ferencz, *Less Than Slaves*.

Kreisau Circle. A group of prominent Germans who believed the Nazis should be removed from power and replaced by a new social order. They met at the estate of **Helmuth James Graf von Moltke** at Kreisau in Silesia. The group's membership peaked at thirty-two between 1940–1943. Most members were pacifists, but several participants began to endorse the concept of assassinating

Hitler. The Circle was implicated in the **July 20, 1944 Bomb Plot** assassination attempt on Hitler, tracked down by the **Gestapo**, tried by **Dr. Roland Freisler**, and sentenced to death.

SUGGESTED READINGS: Carsten, *The German Resistance*; Nicosia and Stokes, *Germans Against Nazism: Nonconformity, Opposition and Resistance in the Third Reich*.

Krematorium-Kremchy (G., **crematorium**). Building at **concentration camps** that housed the ovens that burned murdered inmates.

Kriegsgefangener-lager (G., prisoner of war/prisoner of war camp).

Krimchaks. Crimean Jews, which included some **Karaites**, were murdered by **Einsatzgruppe D**.

Kriminalabteilung; **Kriminalpolizei**. (See **Kripo**.)

Kripo (G., criminal police; acronym for **Kriminalpolizei**). Plainclothes police inside of the **Reich** headed by **Arthur Nebe**. They eventually came under control of the **SD**. In the occupied areas these men wore **SS** uniforms. Their duties related mainly to nonpolitical crimes, but on occasion they would lend support to the **Gestapo** in operations against Jews joining the **Einsatzgruppen**. (See also **SS Major Christian Wirth**.)

SUGGESTED READING: Ruerup, *Topography of Terror*.

Kristallnacht (G., Night of Crystal) (**Night of Broken Glass**). Between November 9–10, 1938 (anniversary of the Beer Hall Putsch) **Nazis** ravaged Jewish communities in **Germany, Austria**, the **Sudetenland**, and **Danzig** in "retaliation" for the slaying of **Ernst vom Rath**, third-secretary of the German Embassy in Paris by **Herschel Grynszpan**. Approximately 400 synagogues and 7,000 shops were looted, set ablaze, desecrated, or completely destroyed. Ninety-two Jews were murdered. In addition, 20,000 to 30,000 Jewish men were interned at **Dachau, Sachsenhausen-Oranienburg**, and **Buchenwald**. A number of these internees died from maltreatment. Despite the Nazi warning against **Rassenschande**, numerous Jewish women were raped. The **pogrom** got its name from the shattered shop windows of Jewish businesses. In January 1939, the German government levied the **Jewish Atonement Fine** of 1 billion marks ($400 million) on German Jews making them financially responsible for the Nazi rampage. On November 12, 1938, **Hermann Goering** ordered Jews to clean up and pay for the damages they caused during Kristallnacht. In addition, Jews were stripped of radios. On January 21, 1939, all Jewish men 18 or younger arrested during the pogrom were released from **concentration camps**. Soon after the event, commercial activity by Jews was prohibited. On August 24, 1945, a German court convicted Richard Lang of blowing up the Forcheim synagogue.

He was the first person tried and convicted for the pogrom. (See also **Walther Funk, "November Jews," Dorothy Thompson**, and **Zbaszyn.**)
SUGGESTED READING: Thalmann and Feinerman, *Crystal Night.*

Krupp, Baron Gustav von (1870–1950) and **Alfred** (1907–1967). Patriarchs of Krupp armaments. Alfred was an eager Nazi who joined the **SS** in 1931 and led the firm after the war started. His father, Gustav, reluctantly supported **Hitler** and later became chairman of the **Reich** Association of German Industry. Krupp Works, under the leadership of Baron Gustav and Alfred Krupp, profited handsomely from the Nazis' war machine. Wages were locked at Depression Era rates. Krupp Works utilized **forced labor** from **Auschwitz, Buchenwald, Gross-Rosen**, and the **Lodz Ghetto**. Alfred favored extermination through work. In addition, Krupp Works made a great deal of money from expropriated Jewish businesses. Alfred Krupp was convicted of **war crimes** by an American Tribunal and was sentenced to twelve years. His sentence was commuted and his entire fortune was returned. Gustav was deemed mentally and physically incompetent to stand trial. (See also **Aryanization, Otto Kranzbuehler**, and **John McCloy.**)
SUGGESTED READING: Manchester, *The Arms of Krupp.*

Krupp Works. (See **Baron Gustav and Alfred von Krupp.**)

Kube, Wilhelm (1887–1943). Generalkommissar of **Belorussia** and **Gauleiter** of **Ostmark**. He opposed the mass murder policy of the **SS** and **transports** of Jews from the **Reich** to the **Minsk** ghetto because they undermined his authority. Kube was assassinated by a Soviet **partisan** on September 22, 1943. (See also **Eliyahu Mushkin.**)
SUGGESTED READING: Steinberg, *The Jews Against Hitler.*

Kuenstler, Karl (1901–1945). Kommandant of **Flossenbuerg**. His drinking led to his dismissal by the **SS** in 1942. Kuenstler was transferred to the **Waffen-SS** and killed in the Battle of Nuremberg in April 1945.
SUGGESTED READING: Segev, *Soldiers of Evil.*

Kugel (G., bullet). Jews, **Soviet POWs**, and other inmates at **concentration camps** were frequently murdered by a single shot to the back of the head. At **Buchenwald**, under the pretense of measuring an inmate's head, the **SS** shot the victim through a hole in the wall. A similar charade was played out at **Mauthausen**. This practice was considered a major **war crime** by the **Nuremberg Tribunal**. (See also **Aktion Kugelerlass.**)
SUGGESTED READING: Harris, *Tyranny on Trial.*

Kugelerlass (G., bullet ordinance). (See **Aktion Kugelerlass.**)

Kuhl, Dr. Julius. (See **Aleksander Lados**.)

Kulmhof (G., **Chelmno**.)

Kulturbund (G., Culture Society of [German Jews]). Established in spring 1933 by Dr. Kurt Singer to help thousands of Jewish actors and musicians who were dismissed by the Nazis. The Kulturbund supported theater companies, symphony orchestras, operas, singers, and lectures. This organization gave comfort to persecuted Jews before it was closed in September 1941. (See also **Reich Representation of German Jews**.)

KZ (G., **concentration camp**). (See **Konzentrationslager**.)

L

Labor Camp. **Concentration camp** that exploited the **slave labor** of inmates. Many large German corporations took advantage of this captive labor pool. (See also **Allgemeine Elektrizitaets-Gesselschaft, Auto-Union, BMW, Class I, II, and III Concentration Camps, Daimler-Benz, Dynamit Nobel, I. G. Farben, Flick, Heinkel Werke, Junkers, Baron Gustav and Alfred von Krupp, Gerhard Maurer, Messerschmidt, Oswald Pohl, Rheinmetall, Siemens, Telefunken, Fritz Thyssen, Toebbens**, and **Union Werke**.)

Labor Zionists. (See **Socialist Zionists**.)

Ladino. Language of **Sephardic** Jews composed of a mixture of medieval Spanish and Hebrew. (See also **Morocco, Salonika**, and **Spain**.)
   SUGGESTED READING: Ben-Zvi, *The Exiled and the Redeemed.*

Lados, Aleksander. Polish diplomat and humanitarian. As head of the legation in **Switzerland**, he issued 7,000 **visas** for Jews. He was assisted by Dr. Julius Kuhl, a Jew, and allowed **Rita and Isaac Sternbuch** to use his office for rescue efforts. In September 1942, the Sternbuchs used Lados' facilities to aid **refugees** and relay a message about the **Final Solution** to **Agudat Israel**.
   SUGGESTED READING: Kranzler, *Heroine of Rescue.*

Laender (G., States). The fifteen German states or regional governing districts in the **Weimar Republic**. (See also **Gau, Gleichschaltung**, and **Ludwigsburger Zentralstelle**.)

Laeufer (G., runner). Courier in a **ghetto, labor**, or **concentration camp**.

Lager (G., camp). Reference to **concentration camp**.

Lageraelteste (G., inmate camp elder or head of **concentration camp**). (See **Blockaelteste, Kapo, Self-government, Stubenaelteste**, and **Stubendienst**.)

Lagerfuehrer (G., kommandant or commander of **concentration, labor**, or **death camp**).

Lagergeld (G., camp scrip). In some **concentration camps**, inmates could purchase items from the canteen using this money, for example, **Buchenwald** and **Vught**. The funds were derived from the possessions confiscated from inmates and theoretically held in escrow. The Nazis were inconsistent in honoring the scrip.

Lagerschreiber (G., camp writer). Inmate registrar at **concentration camps**.

Lagerschwester (G., camp sister). Isolated Jewish women, who didn't have anyone else in the camps, developed this support system for survival. The women would look for some sort of connection or bond with other women who then became their lagersister.

Lagerstrasse (G., camp street). (1) Main (and only paved) street in **Birkenau**. reserved for **SS**. (2) Main camp road at **Dachau**.

La Guardia, Fiorello (1882–1947). General Director of the **United Nations Relief and Rehabilitation Agency (UNRRA)**. He used his post with UNRRA to aid Jewish **DPs**. La Guardia was an outspoken supporter of Jewish causes during the war. His mother was Jewish and his sister was held captive by the Nazis during the war. (See also **Earl Harrison** and **Ira Hirschmann**.)
   SUGGESTED READING: United States Holocaust Memorial Museum, *Darkness Before Dawn.*

Lalleri. Austrian "**Gypsies**." Initially persecuted and sent to **concentration camps**, they were spared from further persecution by an order from **Heinrich Himmler**. (See also **Asocial, Mischlinge, Nuremberg Laws, Porraimos, Dr. Robert Ritter, Roma**, and **Sinti**.)
   SUGGESTED READING: Proctor, *Racial Hygiene.*

Lammers, Hans Heinrich (1879–1962). Jurist. He was a close aide to **Hitler** and state secretary in the **Reich (Fuehrer) Chancellery** (1933–1944). Every anti-Jewish measure passed through his desk. Lammers was sentenced to twenty years imprisonment at the **Nuremberg Trials**, but was pardoned in 1954.

SUGGESTED READINGS: Hilberg, *Destruction of European Jews*; Speer, *Inside the Third Reich*.

Landsberg. Prison where **Hitler** wrote *Mein Kampf* after the Nazis' failed Putsch in 1923. This site was converted to a **concentration camp**, mostly for Jews. Prior to **liberation** (April 27, 1945), guards went on a killing spree. After the war, Nazi **war criminals** such as **Oswald Pohl** and **Otto Ohlendorf** were incarcerated and hanged at this prison. Later a **DP camp** was set up in this area. (See also **Rudolf Hess**.)

SUGGESTED READING: United States Holocaust Memorial Museum, *1945: The Year of Liberation*.

Landsman (G. and Y., fellow countryman). Jewish immigrant who comes from a common area in Europe.

Landwacht (Du., ''Home Guard''). **Dutch** volunteer militia. These **collaborators** hunted Jews and members of the Dutch **resistance** for the **Gestapo**. (See also ''**Black Police**'' and ''**Green Police**.'')

Langbein, Hermann (1912–1995). Physician and rescuer. He was an Austrian volunteer to the International Brigade (1938), which aided the Republicans during the Spanish Civil War (1936–1939). He was interned in **France**, moved to **Dachau** in 1941, transferred to **Auschwitz** in 1942 (where he aided Jewish inmates), and **liberated** from **Neuengamme**. Langbein was secretary of the International **Concentration Camps** Committee and a prolific writer on **Auschwitz**. (See also **Francisco Franco** and **Rotspanir**.)

SUGGESTED READING: Lifton, *The Nazi Doctors*.

Lange, Dr. Rudolf (b. 1909) (also referred to as Otto). **SS** officer in charge of **Einsatzgruppe** A. He supervised Viennese and German Jews **deported** to **Riga**. Lange was in attendance at the **Wannsee Conference** and involved with the development of the ''**Sonderwagon**.'' He escaped British detention in 1949 and relocated to Buenos Aires. (See also **Karl Jaeger**.)

SUGGESTED READING: Ehrenburg and Grossman, *The Black Book*.

Lapin (G., rabbit). Reference to Polish Catholic women from **Lublin**. They were victims of ''medical experiments'' at **Ravensbrueck**. They were deliberately infected with gangrene by **Drs. Rail Gebhardt** and **Fritz Fisher**, who then administered sulfa treatments. (See also **Herta Oberhauser**.)

Latvia. Baltic republic located between **Lithuania, Estonia, Belorussia**, and **Russia** with a seacoast along the Baltic Sea. It had a prewar population of about 2 million with a Jewish population estimated between 93,000 to 95,000, centered largely in **Riga**. Latvia, a people of Littish back-ground, with Lithuanian,

German, and Russian minorities, once was part of the Russian Tsarist empire. It detached itself from the **Soviet Union** after World War I (1919) and was recognized by the **League of Nations** as an independent state. On August 3, 1940, the country was annexed by the **USSR**. Prior to the annexation, the dictatorship was **anti-Semitic** and anti-Soviet. In June 1941, Latvia was overrun by German forces as part of **Operation Barbarossa**. Many Latvians welcomed the occupation believing that Nazi Germany would grant Latvians autonomy, if not independence again, but this was not to be. **Einsatzgruppen** A, joined by Latvian volunteers and local anti-Semites, murdered thousands of Jews. Latvia was incorporated into the **Reichskommissariat Ostland** headed by **Heinrich Lohse**. The country was retaken by the **Red Army** in late 1944 to early 1945. Over 70,000 Latvian Jews were annihilated, 70 percent of its prewar population. (See also **Viktor Arajis, Kaiserwald, Latvian SS Legion, Janus Lipke, Perkonkrust, Schuma**, and **Franz Walter Stahlecker**.)

Latvian SS Legion. Native force very active in liquidating Jews in the **Riga** area. The Legion, comprised of 80,000 men, **collaborated** with the **Waffen-SS**. Some men were conscripted into service. (See also **Viktor Arajis, Ostbataillone, Schuma**, and **Franz Walter Stahlecker**.)
   SUGGESTED READING: Schneider, *The Unfinished Road.*

Lause-Kontrolle/Lausekontrolle (G., louse control). Lice were equated with **typhus** and their absence or presence could mean life or death for a **concentration camp** inmate or **ghetto** residents.

Lausestrasse (G., lice boulevard). Part of an inmate's head where a stripe was shaved down the middle. It was used as a device to discourage escape, especially among inmates on labor details. In **Mauthausen**, this haircut was referred to as the ''autostrade.'' (See also **Typhus**.)

Laval, Pierre (1883–1945). **Vichy** vice-premier who was appointed chief of Government in May 1942. He coordinated Jewish **deportations** between the French police and the Nazis. Although the Nazis did not request Jewish children, Laval, **Marshal Henri Philippe Petain**, and **Rene Bousquet** encouraged the deportation of Jews under 16 in the spring of 1942. Laval (1942–1943) offered ''his Jews'' to any country that wanted them; there were no takers. A pragmatist, he began to be less accommodating with the Nazis in 1943 when **Germany** suffered major defeats. Laval was tried by a French court and hanged in October 1945, after a failed suicide attempt.
   SUGGESTED READING: Poliakov, *Harvest of Hate.*

Law for the Restoration of Professional Civil Service. Early major anti-Jewish law passed April 7, 1933. It dismissed Jewish teachers and administrators. This was followed by dismissal of Jewish judges, lawyers, and physicians in public service. Front-line Jewish soldiers in World War I were exempt as a favor to President **Paul von Hindenburg** who requested that the veterans not be subject to the anti-Jewish law.

SUGGESTED READING: United States Holocaust Memorial Council, *Fifty Years After the Eve of Destruction.*

Lazarett (G., military infirmary). Term used for military or **concentration camp** infirmary. (See also **Krankenbau** and **Revier**.

League of German Girls. (See **Bund deutscher Maedel**.)

League of Nations. International peacekeeping organization set up as part of the **Versailles Treaty** in 1919, with headquarters in Geneva. Appeals by German Jews regarding human rights in the **Reich** were not adjudicated. Its High Commission for **Refugees** was ineffectual, leading **James Grover McDonald** to resign. Insincerity of the great powers lead to the League's impotency. The High Commissioner for Refugees revealed, as early as 1939, the fate of Jewry in various countries and the persecutions and gross violations of human rights. Although the League existed until 1946, it was replaced by the United Nations. (See also **Balfour Declaration, Bernheim Petition, British Mandate, Maksim Maksimovich Litvinov, Minorities Treaties, Nansen Passport, Silesian Convention**, and **Sudetenland**.)

SUGGESTED READINGS: Feingold, *The Politics of Rescue*; Johnson, *Modern Times.*

Lebensborn (G., fountain of life). Program of selective breeding to improve the German nation into a super race. German women, particularly the **Bund deutscher Maedel**, were encouraged, without benefit of marriage, to become pregnant by **SS** men. After conception, the women were sent to maternity centers. Many were established from expropriated Jewish homes. There were six centers in **Germany**, nine in **Norway**, one in **France**, and one in **Belgium**. The special program did not induce increased birth rates; in fact, infant mortality was higher than average. Beginning in 1942, Lebensborn was used as a cover for the kidnapping of **Aryan**-looking Polish children. Thousands were taken from their families (who had usually been murdered or **deported**) and placed in indoctrination centers in the **Greater Reich** before being adopted by "racially trustworthy families." This was considered a **war crime** by the **International Military Tribunal** and a form of **genocide** later described in the **Genocide Convention**. The SS, **Wehrmacht**, and **Sipo** actively participated in the abductions. Investigations after the war found that SS-related children and kidnapped "Aryans" did not adhere to Nordic or Aryan characteristics. (See also **"Brown Sisters," Dr. Gregor Ebner, Lidice, Racial Hygiene**, and **RuSHA**.)

SUGGESTED READINGS: Clay and Leapman, *Master Race*: Hillel and Henry, *Of Pure Blood.*

Lebensraum (G., living space). Guiding principle of German foreign policy. The Nazis believed they were entitled to regain former German European areas (Holy Roman Empire) and absorb **Slavic** territories into the **Third Reich** in order to accommodate the needs of the **Aryan** race. (See also **Blood and Soil, Richard-Walther Darre, Drang nach Osten, Adolf Hitler, Werner Lorenz,** *Mein Kampf*, **Reich Commission for the Strengthening of Germandom**, and **Volk Ohne Raum**.)

"Lebensunwertes Leben" (G., "life unworthy of life"). Term applied to mentally and physically handicapped Germans slated for medical murder, **euthanasia**. The term first appeared in a book by two German professors—**Karl Binding**, a jurist, and Alfred Hoche, a psychiatrist—who both wrote *The Permission to Destroy Life Unworthy of Life* (1920). It later applied to anyone not capable of work, particularly in **labor** and **concentration camps**. (See **14 f 13, T-4, "Unproductive Eaters,"** and **"Wild Euthanasia."**)
  SUGGESTED READING: Lifton, *The Nazi Doctors*.

Lecca, Radu (1902–1980). Romanian commissar for Jewish Affairs. As director of Security Services and liaison with the German legation, he coordinated the government's anti-Jewish policies that included stripping assets, **forced labor**, and the general impoverishment and **deportation** of Romanian Jewry. However, Lecca balked at deporting Jews to **Poland**. After the war, he was tried, convicted, and given life in prison. Lecca only served a couple of years of his sentence. (See also **Ion Antonescu, Gustav Richter, Romania**, and **Horia Sima**.)
  SUGGESTED READINGS: Butnaru, *Waiting for Jerusalem*; Finger, *American Jewry During the Holocaust*.

Lederer, Viteslav (Siegfried). Polish Jewish escapee. He escaped from **Auschwitz** on March 8, 1944, disguised in an **SS** uniform and aided by an SS guard. He conveyed his experience at Auschwitz to inmates at **Terezin (ghetto)** who did not believe him and rejected his appeal for an uprising. The general population at Terezin never learned of his report.
  SUGGESTED READING: Czech, *Auschwitz Chronicle*.

Legion of the Archangel Michael. (See **Iron Guard**.)

Leguay, Jean. **Vichy** police chief. Director of **transit camps** in the occupied zone of **France**. He was **Rene Bousquet's** representative in the occupied zone involved with **deportation** of Jews in 1942.
  SUGGESTED READING: Rousso, *The Vichy Syndrome*.

LEHI. (See **Lohamei Herut Israel**.)

Lemberg (G., Lvov).

Lemkin, Rafael (1901–1959). Jewish Polish jurist and writer. A **resistance** member who escaped from **Poland**, he documented the biological nature of the Nazi's preoccupation with their racial theories. He is credited with coining the term **genocide** in his book *Axis Rule in Occupied Europe* (1941). The work is basic to the study of Nazi racist legislation. Lemkin served in the **war crimes** section of military headquarters in **Germany**. The jurist acted as Chief Counsel to Justice **Robert Jackson** for the prosecution at the **Nuremberg Trials**. He was instrumental in developing the concept of **crimes against humanity**. Lemkin was also the architect of the **Genocide Convention**.

SUGGESTED READING: *Current Biography, 1951.*

Leo Baeck Institute. **Holocaust** archival organization. Founded in 1955, it focuses on the history of German-speaking Jewry. The Institute has branches located in Jerusalem, London, and New York. (See also **Robert Weltsch**.)

Les Milles. Detention camp in southern **France**. Originally a tileworks factory, this French **internment camp** opened in September 1939, primarily for prominent German and Austrian Jewish **refugees**. Two thousand inmates transferred to **Drancy** were **deported** to **Auschwitz**. The camp closed on December 12, 1942.

Levi, Primo (1919–1987). Italian chemist, **partisan**, and prolific author. He was captured in 1943 and **deported** to **Auschwitz III/Monowice**. Levi wrote of his ten-month **concentration camp** experiences in *If This be a Man* (*Survival at Auschwitz*.) He is alleged to have committed suicide.

SUGGESTED READING: Cicioni, *Primo Levi, Bridges of Knowledge.*

Lewin, Dr. Isaac (1894–1971). Orthodox rescue activist. Stationed in Washington, D.C., he warned American Jews not to give up on the rescue of their European brethren. Lewin deplored the lack of urgency by mainstream Jewish organizations for rescue and their overconcern with postwar Jewry. He urged the **American Jewish Conference** to put rescue foremost on its agenda and soften **Palestinian** state resolutions. Lewin played a crucial role as the intermediary between the **Orthodox** and the **Polish Government-in-Exile** in Washington and London after his escape from Warsaw in 1940. All messages sent by diplomatic Polish pouch came into Dr. Lewin's hands. He not only conveyed that information, but developed a strategy of rescue that included bribery. Dr. Lewin represented Orthodox organizations meeting with other Jewish organizations, such as the London-based Representation of Polish Jewry and the **Jewish Agency**. (See also **Rita and Isaac Sternbuch** and **Union of Orthodox Rabbis**.)

SUGGESTED READING: Kranzler, *Thy Brother's Blood.*

Ley, Dr. Robert (1890–1945). Chemist and leader of the **Nazi Labor Front**. He equated Jews with the bubonic plague. Ley was outflanked and outmaneuvered by **Albert Speer** over the use of German "voluntary" **forced labor**. He was convinced that the extermination of the Jews was a proper policy and assisted with anti-Jewish propaganda: "The struggle will not be abandoned until the last Jew in Europe has been exterminated and is actually dead." Ley committed suicide in his jail cell at Nuremberg awaiting trial by the **International Military Tribunal**.

SUGGESTED READINGS: Fest, *The Face of the Third Reich*; Speer, *Inside the Third Reich*.

Lezaky. Czech village near Prague destroyed on June 10, 1942, in retaliation for **Reinhard Heydrich's** assassination. This village was targeted because it harbored a member of Heydrich's assassination team. (See also **Lidice**.)

Liberation. Term used when **concentration** and **death camps** were overrun by the Soviet, American, British, Canadian, or French armies. Most of the camps were captured or turned over to **Allied** control between January–April 1945, although there was no direct Allied order to capture these sites. **Majdanek** was the first camp to be **liberated** in July 1944 by the **Red Army**. **Mauthausen** was the last camp liberated by the West on May 5, 1945, just two days before the German surrender. The last camp liberated in the war was **Theresienstadt** on May 8, 1945, by the Soviets. (See also **Witness to Liberation**.)

SUGGESTED READINGS: Bridgman, *The End of the Holocaust*; United States Holocaust Memorial Museum, *1945: The Year of Liberation*.

Liberators. An official term by the U.S. Army for American soldiers who overran the **concentration camps** within the first forty-eight hours. Those who came later were called **Witnesses to Liberation**. The soldiers were unprepared for the horror they encountered. One serious mistake the medics made was giving the inmates regular food. The food was too rich for their contracted stomachs, and many died as a result.

Libya. North African colony bordered the Mediterranean Sea on the north, Egypt on the west, and Tunisia and **Algeria** on the east. It was under Italian rule until 1943 with a prewar Jewish population of 30,000. Anti-Jewish decrees and racial laws were passed as early as 1938. These measures were strongly supported by the indigenous Muslim population. **Internment** and **forced labor** camps for Jews were established in Giado, Sidi Azaz, and Bukbok. Some Libyan Jews were **deported** to **Fossoli di Carpi** in **Italy**.

Lichtenberg, Monsignor Bernhard (1875–1943). Canon of St. Hedwig's church in **Berlin**. Influenced by **Bishop Clemens von Galen**, he opposed the **T-4** program and publicly prayed against **Kristallnacht**. Lichtenberg openly preached against maltreatment of Jews and hid several Jews. He died enroute to **Dachau** in the fall of 1943. The Monsignor was beatified by Pope John Paul II in June 1996.

SUGGESTED READING: Rhodes, *The Vatican in the Age of Dictators.*

Lichtenburg. Women's **concentration camp** located in Saxony, **Germany**. A sixteenth-century fort converted into a prison until 1928, Lichtenburg was a men's concentration camp from June 1933 until the summer of 1937. The camp was closed from 1937–1938, but reopened as a **Frauenlager** from March 1938–May 1939. The camp was operated by the **SS** and contained approximately 1,500 prisoners, including **Jehovah's Witnesses**, "race defilers," **asocials**, and criminals. (See also **Max Koegel, Moringen**, and **Ravensbrueck**.)

SUGGESTED READING: Owings, *Frauen.*

Lichtheim, Richard (1895–1963). Representative of the **Jewish Agency** in Geneva during World War II. An associate of **Dr. Gerhart Riegner**, he was one of the few observers in neutral nations who relayed information about the **Holocaust** to London, New York, and Jerusalem.

SUGGESTED READINGS: Laqueur, *The Terrible Secret*; Wyman, *The Abandonment of the Jews.*

Lida. City in **Belorussia** where Jews had lived for over 400 years. In 1941 Lida had a Jewish population of 9,000. Germans assembled Jews from surrounding areas into the Lida ghetto. By June 25, 1942, 5,000 Jews were murdered despite **partisan** activity. After liberation by the **Red Army** in the summer of 1944, 300 Jews returned, mainly those who had joined **Alexander Bielski's** camp.

SUGGESTED READING: Tec, *Defiance, the Bielski Partisans.*

Lidice. Czech village. Hitler ordered the destruction of this town on June 9, 1942. The following day, in retaliation for the assassination of **Reinhard Heydrich**, the Nazis razed this village near Prague and murdered all 192 adult men and 71 women. Additionally, 198 women and 98 children were **deported**. Many of the children were sent to **SS** foster homes to be "Germanized." The Nazis also organized and deported a special penal transport to **Poland** consisting of 1,000 Prague Jews. (See also **Kurt Daluege, Lebensborn, Lezaky**, and **Werner Lorenz**.)

SUGGESTED READING: United States Holocaust Memorial Museum, *Darkness Before Dawn.*

Liebehenschel, Arthur (1901–1948). **SS** officer and kommandant. As director of the **WVHA**, he oversaw the plundering of inmates' property. Liebehenschel became **Lagerfuehrer** of **Auschwitz** I in November 1943 and later **Majdanek**. He was executed by a Polish tribunal in January 1948.

SUGGESTED READINGS: Czech, *Auschwitz Chronicle*; Hilberg, *The Destruction of European Jews.*

Liebenfels, Lance von (1874–1954). Viennese writer. A pagan, he wanted to breed blond supermen and favored sun worship through the goddess, Ostara. According to von Liebenfels, the enemies of the **Aryans** were dark people whose physical extermination was desirable. His newspaper, *Ostara Journal for Blond People*, was published from 1905–1914 and greatly influenced young **Adolf Hitler**. In *Mein Kampf*, Hitler alludes to Liebenfels.
SUGGESTED READING: Mosse, *Toward the Final Solution.*

Liebeskind, Aharon (1912–1942). Jewish underground leader in **Krakow**. "Dolek" headed vocational and agricultural training of the **Jewish Self-Help Society** in the United **Zionist** Movement. In December 1942, members of his **partisan** group launched and attacked Germans and Liebeskind was killed in the fighting.

Liepaja. Port city in **Latvia** with a prewar Jewish population of 7,400. It was the site of the massacre of 2,800 Jews perpetrated by **Einsatzgruppe** and Latvian militiamen from December 15–17, 1941. The city contained a **ghetto** headed by an **Aeltestenrat** with a **Jewish police** force. The ghetto was liquidated, and surviving Jews were deported to **Kaiserwald** on October 8, 1943.
SUGGESTED READING: Ezergailis, *The Holocaust in Latvia.*

"Lifeboat is Full." Excuse given by neutral countries for not admitting Jews, particularly refers to **Switzerland**. (See also **Paul Grueninger, Dr. Heinrich Rothmund**, and **Eduard von Steiger**.)

Life Tickets. Forty thousand numbered cards for "needed" workers in the **Warsaw Ghetto**. Those who were issued these passes were promised survival by the Nazis. (See also **Arbeitskarten**.)

"Life Unworthy of Life." (See **"Lebensunwertes Leben."**)

Links (G., left). (See **Rechts**.)

Lipke, Janus (d. 1987). **Luftwaffe** representative. He was instrumental in saving hundreds of Jews in **Riga** by providing jobs and workpasses. Lipke survived the war and was honored, along with his wife Johnna, as **Righteous Gentiles** at **Yad Vashem**.
SUGGESTED READING: United States Holocaust Memorial Museum, *From Terror to Systematic Murder, 1941–1991.*

List, Guido von (1848–1919). Expert on Rune alphabet, he publicized the **SS** symbol and the concept of an elite militaristic body of pure **Aryans**. In 1911, he formed an elitist occult organization known as The Higher Armonen Order. The Order, which **Hitler** may have been a member of, had great influence on the Nazis. It called for a pan-German empire and ruthless subjection of non-Aryans to Aryan masters in a highly structured hierarchical state. Racial purity was a major qualification for membership and leadership. Its philosophy anticipated the SS. List was infatuated with the Rune SS lightning bolt symbol and an order of militaristic male supremacy.

SUGGESTED READING: Mosse, *Toward the Final Solution: A History of European Racism.*

Lithuania. Most westerly of the Baltic states adjacent to **Poland.** In 1938, Lithuania had a general population of 2,575,363 with a Jewish population of 155,000. It proclaimed itself a republic on February 16, 1918. The **USSR** annexed Lithuania on August 3, 1940. It was overrun by **Germany** in 1941 and occupied by the **Red Army** in the fall of 1944. About 220,000 Jews were murdered in the Baltic country, giving it the highest victimology rate (94 percent) in occupied Europe. Massive **collaboration** in the **Final Solution** was perpetrated by all strata of Lithuanian society. The Lithuanian Security Police were particularly active in **Vilnius (Vilna)** where tens of thousands of Jews were annihilated. (See also **Einsatzkommando Trial, Iron Wolf, Kurt Jaeger, Kovno, Lithuanian Activist Front, Litvak, Memel, Ponary, Franz Walter Stahlecker, Twelfth Lithuanian Auxiliary Battalion, Union of Orthodox Rabbis of America,** and **Augustinas Voldemaras.**)

Lithuanian Activist Front. Underground, nationalist pro-Nazi group active from 1939–1941. This organization called for the annihilation of Lithuanian Jewry prior to the German invasion and was stridently opposed to Soviet rule. Upon the German invasion in the summer of 1941, this group instigated a **pogrom** against Lithuanian Jews. After **Germany** refused to establish an independent **Lithuania,** the Front resolved to aid the **SS** and the **Einsatzgruppen.** In 1995, Kazys Skirpa, a leader of the Front and **collaborator,** was given an official state burial. (See also **Freiwillige, Hilfswillige, Iron Wolf, Ostbataillone,** and **Schuma.**)

Litomerice. Labor camp attached to **Theresienstadt.**

Litvak (Y.). **Lithuanian** Jew.

Litvinov, Maksim Maksimovich (1876–1954). Soviet Jewish diplomat. He became an expert on foreign policy. Litvinov championed collective security at the **League of Nations** and played a pivotal role in American recognition of the **Soviet Union.** The Nazis claimed that **Russia** was controlled by the Jews and offered Litvinov as proof. He was dismissed by **Stalin** prior to the Nazi-Soviet pact of Non-Aggression on August 23, 1939, and replaced by **Molotov.**

Litvinov became the Soviet Ambassador to the United States in 1941. (See also **Molotov-Ribbentrop Pact**.)
SUGGESTED READING: Vaksberg, Stalin Against the Jews.

Litzmannstadt (P., **Lodz**).

Lodz Ghetto (G., Litzmannstadt). First major **ghetto** to be established on December 10, 1939, and the last to be destroyed. The second largest ghetto after **Warsaw** located in **Warthegau, Poland**. Thousands of Jews were relocated from **Austria, Bohemia-Moravia, Germany**, and **Luxembourg** (1941–1942). The first victims of mass extermination were 4,600 **Lalleri** ("**Gypsies**") in January 1942. In mid-April 1942, **Heinrich Himmler** ordered the liquidation of 10,000 Jews (in **Chelmno**) "resettled" from Western Europe. From January–May 1942, 55,000 Jews and 5,000 **Roma** were sent to Chelmno. The lists for the **transports** were drawn up by **Mordechai Rumkowski** and the **Aeltestenrat**. The ghetto functioned as a **labor camp** from October 1942 through May 1944. During this "quiet period" **deportations** ceased, and 77,000 Jews remained in Lodz. From May to mid-July 1944, over 7,100 Jews were deported to Chelmno. Deportations resumed on August 7 and the destination was now **Auschwitz**. By August 30, 1944, 74,000 people had been transported to Auschwitz. **Resistance** was negligible. Of the 220,000 Jewish residents of Lodz, 870 survived the ghetto and were **liberated** by the **Soviets** on January 16, 1945. An additional 5,000 to 7,000 survived the Nazi **concentration camp** system. (See also **Hans Biebow, Mendel Grossman, Baron Gustav and Alfred von Krupp**, and "**Work as a Means of Rescue**.")
SUGGESTED READING: Dobroszycki, The Chronicle of the Lodz Ghetto.

Loesener, Bernard (1890–1952). German jurist. He contributed to many racial laws including the **Nuremberg Laws**. He strongly advocated **Mischlinge** be excluded from anti-Jewish measures. His Nazi past was forgiven because he tried to help Jews during the war and resigned from his post as racial expert upon learning of the **Holocaust**. Loesener was employed by the "**Joint**" after the war.
SUGGESTED READING: Hilberg, The Destruction of European Jews.

Loewenherz, Josef (1884–1946). Head of the **Vienna** Jewish community. He worked with **Adolf Eichmann** (with the support of the "**Joint**") to encourage emigration. Loewenherz tried to save prominent Jews from **deportation** and remained in Vienna until the arrival of the **Red Army** in 1945. He immigrated to the United States.
SUGGESTED READING: Berkley, Vienna and the Jews.

Lohamei Herut Israel (**LEHI**) (H., Fighters for the Freedom of Israel). (See **Stern Group**.)

Lohse, Heinrich (1896–1964). **Reichskommissar** feur **Ostland**. He supervised the implementation of the **Final Solution** in the Baltic and **Belorussian** areas. Lohse was arrested in 1945, but released by West **Germany** in 1951 due to poor health. (See also **Viktor Arajis, Finland, Latvian SS Legion, Lithuanian Activist Front, Ostbattaillone, Dr. Alfred Rosenberg**, and **Franz Walter Stahlecker**.)

SUGGESTED READING: Ezergailis, The Holocaust in Latvia.

London Charter Conference. Agreement signed on August 8, 1945, by America, **France**, Great Britain, and the **Soviet Union** outlining the charges against Nazi **war criminals**. The alleged crimes included: crimes against the peace (planning and making an aggressive war); **war crimes**, and **crimes against humanity** (crimes against civilians not related to war and directed against racial, religious, or political groups). The charges were the basis for the **Nuremberg Trials**. The London Conference was an outgrowth of the **Yalta Conference**. (See also **Allied Control Council Law Number 10** and **International Military Tribunal**.)

SUGGESTED READING: Taylor, The Anatomy of the Nuremberg Trials.

Long, Breckinridge (1881–1958). American undersecretary of state for European Affairs, which included the **Visa** Division. He was responsible for orchestrating restrictive policies, including **quotas**, designed to prevent European Jews from coming to the United States. Long refused Britain's offer to divert some of its immigration space for Jews. He successfully argued at the **Bermuda Conference** against making special considerations for Jews. Long misled Congress on November 26, 1943, in testimony concerning legislation that would have set up a commission to deal with the rescue of Jews. The undersecretary's claim that the United States had admitted 580,000 **refugees** was refuted. The diplomat eventually was removed from his refugee responsibilities in the State Department. (See also **Hamilton Fish Armstrong, Emanuel Celler, Cordell Hull, Harold L. Ickes, Robert Borden Reams, War Refugee Board**, and **Sumner Welles**.)

SUGGESTED READINGS: Feingold, The Politics of Rescue; Wyman, Paper Walls.

Lorenz, Werner (1891–1974). Lt. General **SS** head of the Main Office for the Welfare of Ethnic Germans (1937–1945). Lorenz was responsible for the "Germanization" of ethnic Germans. **Volksdeutsche** were given special privileges in occupied areas who, in turn, aided in the persecution of Jews and non-Germans. Lorenz was tried and convicted by a U.S. military tribunal. He was sentenced to twenty years imprisonment in 1948, but was released in 1955. (See also **Lebensraum**.)

SUGGESTED READING: Reitlinger, SS: Alibi of a Nation.

Loritz, Hans (1895–1946). Kommandant of Esterwegen, **Dachau**, and lastly **Sachsenhausen-Oranienburg** from 1940 to August 1942. He committed suicide in 1946.
SUGGESTED READING: Segev, *Soldiers of Evil.*

Lubetkin, Zivia (1914–1976). **Ghetto** fighter. Lubetkin was one of the prominent leaders and founders of the **Jewish Fighting Organization** in Warsaw. She participated in the initial **Warsaw Ghetto Uprising** (January 1943) as a commander and fought through April and May 1943 in the major Warsaw Ghetto Uprising. The ghetto fighter escaped through the sewers and fought in the **Warsaw Polish Uprising** in August 1944. After the war, she became active in **Bricha**, moved to **Palestine**, and founded the **Ghetto Fighters' House** with her husband **Yitzhak Zuckerman**. Lubetkin also testified against **Adolf Eichmann**.
SUGGESTED READING: Lubetkin, *In the Days of Destruction and Revolt.*

Lublin, Lucien (b. 1909). Underground organizer and co-founder of the **Armee juive**. He recruited French and **Dutch** Jewish youths to fight with the **partisans** while others immigrated to **Palestine**. After the war, he set up an organization to assist French children who survived the **Holocaust**—the Society for the Protection of Children.
SUGGESTED READING: Latour, *The Jewish Resistance in France.*

Lublin(land). City in eastern **Poland** with a Jewish population of 40,000. The Germans planned a "reservation" for up to 400,000 Jews to perform agricultural work in a pocket of eastern Poland. In 1939, 100,000 German and Polish Jews were **deported** to this area and 20,000 died in less than four months. The idea of using Lublin as a "reservation" was dropped by the Nazis in the spring of 1940. It was designated as the capital of a Jewish "state" and flooded with 200,000 deportees. This area also served as the administrative headquarters for **Aktion Reinhard**. Jews from this city were the first victims **selected** for **Belzec** and later **Majdanek**. (See also "**Bloody Wednesday**," **Erntefest, OST, Poniatowa, Reserve Police Battalion 101, Dr. Alfred Rosenberg, Jacob Sporrenberg**, and **Trawniki**.)
SUGGESTED READING: Tenenbaum, *Race and Reich.*

Ludendorff, General Erich (1865–1937). German general and politician. He led the Germans to military victories over the Russians in 1914. After the war, Ludendorff identified with ultranationalist groups and lent credibility to the **Nazi Party**. He participated in the Beer Hall Putsch (an unsuccessful Nazi revolution in Munich) (1923) with **Hitler** and served in the **Reichstag** from 1924–1928 as a deputy for the Nazi Party. Ludendorff frequently denounced the "Jewish-Masonic-Bolshevik international conspiracy" and sponsored publication of ***Pro-***

tocols of the Learned Elders of Zion in the **Weimar Republic**. (See also **Freemasons**.)
 SUGGESTED READING: Flood, *Hitler, The Path to Power.*

Ludwigsburger Zentralstelle (G., Ludwigsburg Central Office). Established December 1, 1958, as a judicial administrative office of eleven **laender** (states) making up the Federal Republic. It was charged with investigating crimes of the Nazi era. This office collected and turned over information of alleged criminals connected directly with Nazi ideology to public prosecutors.

Lueknor, Dr. Gertrud (b. 1900). **Righteous Gentile**. She was born in England, but lived in **Germany**. During the war, she worked for the German Welfare Association as a leader in **Caritas**. Lueknor assisted all victims of Nazism, primarily by providing financial help to Jews and Germans from mixed marriages, for which she was arrested in 1943 and sent to **Ravensbrueck**. After the war, she remained active in Caritas and formed the Freiburg Circle, a Catholic group intent on combating **anti-Semitism** in Germany. Although her group unsuccessfully pressed the **Vatican** to support **reparations and restitution** for **Holocaust** victims, it did succeed in removing some anti-Semitic tracts from German Catholic liturgy.
 SUGGESTED READING: Block and Drucker, *Rescuers.*

Luftwaffe (G., armed air wing). The German Air Force in World War II headed by **Hermann Goering**. (See also **Janus Lipke, Dr. Sigmund Rascher**, and **Dr. Hubertus Strughold**.)

Luther, Martin (1483–1546) (*Not to be confused with entry below*). Leader of the Protestant Reformation. He believed the Catholic Church's policies of alienation and exclusion prevented Jews from converting to Christianity. However, after his split from the Catholic Church, he railed against Jews when they continued to practice their faith. His virulent denunciation of Jewry in 1543, "On the Jews and Their Lies," was incorporated into Nazi propaganda. The Evangelical Lutheran Church of America rejected Luther's **anti-Semitic** writings in 1994. (See also **Julius Streicher**.)
 SUGGESTED READING: Johnson, *A History of the Jews.*

Luther, Martin (1896–1945) (*Not to be confused with the above entry*). Headed the Inland II, or the secret liaison between the Foreign Office and the **Reich Security Main Office** until the summer of 1943. Luther attended the **Wannsee Conference**. He wrote the Luther Memorandum on October 6, 1942, informing the Hungarian government they were not adequately persecuting Jews. Luther was sent to **Sachsenhausen-Oranienburg** in 1943 for plotting against **Joachim**

von Ribbentrop. The Russians captured him after liberating Sachsenhausen-Oranienburg. He died soon after, in May 1945. (See also **Hungary**.)
SUGGESTED READING: Weitz, *Hitler's Diplomat*.

Lutz, Carl (Charles) (1895–1975). Swedish diplomat. He issued approximately 50,000 **Schutzbriefe** (protective letters) guaranteeing the holders of safety until their departure to **Palestine**. He served as a model for **Raoul Wallenberg** and other diplomats in Budapest. Along with Wallenberg and other envoys, Lutz was responsible for saving over 100,000 Hungarian Jews in 1944. The diplomat was in charge of foreign interests in the Swiss Legation in Budapest and represented the United States and Great Britain. He helped Jews get entry **visas** to America, permits to Palestine, Swiss safe-conduct passes, and offered protection at the Legation. Lutz was honored as a **Righteous Gentile** in **Yad Vashem**. (See also **El Salvador, Hungary, Red Cross, Sweden**, and **Vatican**.)
SUGGESTED READING: Paldiel, *The Path of the Righteous*.

Lutze, Viktor (1890–1943). **Roehm's** replacement as head of the **SA** in 1934. Ineffectual with diminished police powers, he remained until he was killed in an automobile accident May 2, 1943.
SUGGESTED READING: Breitman, *The Architect of Genocide*.

Luxembourg. Western European duchy situated between southeast **Belgium** and western **Germany**. The Jewish population during the war was 3,500, including a large number of Austrian and German **refugees**. After the German invasion in May 1940, a civilian government under the administration of **Gauleiter Gustav Simon** was installed in August 1940. From 1940–1941. **Nuremberg Laws** (September 1940) were introduced, anti-Jewish laws decreed, and **forced labor** mandated for Jews. **Deportations** began in October 1941, and by war's end, 1,945 Jews had been murdered. Most Jews were taken to the Fuenfbrunnen **transit camp**. The Germans left Luxembourg on September 1, 1944. (See also **Consistoire, Lodz Ghetto, Villa Pauly, Volksdeutsche Bewegung**, and **Volksjugend**.)
SUGGESTED READING: Zarez, "The Jews of Luxembourg During the Second World War."

Luxembourg Agreement. **Reparations** agreement signed on September 10, 1952, between Jewish representatives, primarily the **World Jewish Congress**, and the government of West **Germany**. The agreement yielded a small stipend to survivors who could prove they suffered physical, mental, and educational losses as a result of Nazi activities. (See also **Conference on Jewish Material Claims** and **Nahum Goldmann**.)
SUGGESTED READING: Balabkins, *West German Reparations to Israel*.

Lvov (G., **Lemburg**; UK., Lviv). City in eastern **Galicia** with a prewar Jewish population of 100,000. The Germans occupied the city on June 30, 1941. Anti-Jewish riots soon followed known as **Petliura Days** because so many Ukrainians were involved. The **Aktion** was undertaken by members of the Ukrainian Militia called Nachtigall Battalion under **Gestapo** direction. Seven thousand Jews were slaughtered between July 1–3, 1941. A **ghetto** was established in 1941, which was converted to a **labor camp** in January 1943. In June 1943, Jews staged an armed rebellion and thousands were **deported** to **Janowska**. (See also **Father Klemens Szeptyekyj, Metropolitan Andrej Szeptyekyj, Ukraine**, and **Zegota**.)

  SUGGESTED READING: Kahana, *Lvov: Ghetto Diary.*

M

Ma'apilim (H., strivers). Jews who sought to immigrate to **Palestine**. (See also **Socialist Zionists**.)

Maccabi. Nonpolitical movement of **Zionists** in Europe, which attracted non-Socialists who favored a **Palestinian** homeland. The Maccabi World Union took the form of gymnastic clubs.

Macedonia. Region of southern **Yugoslavia** (Skopjc and Bitola) with a Jewish population of 7,800, mostly **Sephardic**. In April 1941, this area was awarded (annexed) to **Bulgaria**. Jews were subsequently prohibited from becoming citizens. **Theodor Dannecker** arranged for the **deportation** of 20,000 Jews from this region and **Thrace**. A number of Jews, including women, joined the Macedonian **partisan** brigade. The Bulgarian police seized the Jews and deported them in March 1943. Only 200 Macedonian Jews survived the war.
   SUGGESTED READING: Romans, The Jews of Yugoslavia.

Mach, Sano (Alexander) (b. 1902). Slovak **fascist** leader, commander of the **Hlinka Guard** and Minister of Internal Affairs. He and **Dr. Josef Tiso** met with **Hitler** in July 1940 to establish a Slovakian pro-Nazi state. The fascist leader advocated the expulsion of Jews from **Slovakia** and arranged for the **deportation** of 58,000 Slovakian Jews. Mach's plan was initially thwarted by the **Working Group**. The commander was convicted of **war crimes** by the National Tribunal in Bratislava and sentenced to thirty years. (See also **Anton Vasek**.)
   SUGGESTED READING: Frieder, To Deliver Their Souls.

Machtergreifung (G., seizure of power). Nazi ascent to power in **Germany** with **Hitler** as chancellor on January 30, 1933. The term meant the **Nazi Socialist** "revolution" from the democratic **Weimar Republic**.
SUGGESTED READING: Shirer, The Rise and Fall of the Third Reich.

Madagascar Deportation Plan. Madagascar is an island in the Indian Ocean off the east coast of Africa. Between the World Wars, two British **anti-Semites**, Henry Hamilton Beamish and Arnold Leese, and Egon van Winghene from the **Netherlands**, proposed **deporting** Jews to this island. In 1937, the Polish government sent a commission to this French colony to investigate the practicality of the concept. The Nazis theorized they could solve their **Jewish Problem** by shipping 4 million European Jews to Madagascar. The Germans never consulted with the French colonial government. The Plan was approved by **Hitler** in 1940 after the defeat of **France**, supported by **Heinrich Himmler**, and assigned to **Adolf Eichmann**. British naval presence, a lack of enthusiasm from the German government, the number of years for implementation and the ensuing invasion of the **Soviet Union** made the Plan unrealistic and unfeasible. (See also **Franz Rademacher** and **Dr. Alfred Rosenberg**.)
SUGGESTED READING: Breitman, The Architect of Genocide.

Magyar Zhid (Hu., Hungarian Jew). Derisive reference to Jews used by Eastern European Gentiles.

Majdanek. Hard **labor** and **death camp** complex located outside of **Lublin** in eastern **Poland**. It was also the repository for looted goods from **Aktion Reinhard**. The camp was run by the **Waffen-SS** who were aided by Lithuanian **collaborators**. Established on July 21, 1941, as a POW camp, it was patterned after **Dachau** and divided into five parts. **Soviet POWs** were the first to be interned at the camp. Over 360,000 (out of 500,000 inmates) from twenty-eight nations were murdered at this site.

Most deaths (60 percent) were attributable to malnutrition, poor hygiene, illness, beatings, and/or overwork. This included 122,000 Jews, 80,000 Polish Catholics, and a substantial number of Soviet POWs. An additional 25 percent of the inmate population was gassed.

Majdanek was equipped with seven **gas chambers**, gassing vans, and two gallows. The **SS** at this camp were notoriously sadistic—killing infants and children before their mothers' eyes. This death camp (Section 5) utilized gas vans and gas chambers. In addition, 18,400 Jewish inmates were shot on November 3, 1943, as part of the **Erntefest** program. One thousand inmates were **liberated** by the **Red Army** on July 23, 1944. (See also "**Bloody Wednesday**," **Arthur Liebehenschel, Mittelbau**, and "**Sonderwagon**.")
SUGGESTED READING: United States Holocaust Memorial Museum, Darkness Before the Dawn.

Maly Trostinets. Village and **concentration camp** near **Minsk** opened on May 7–8, 1942. This was the location of the mass murder (1942) of 200,000 **Soviet POWs** and citizens, **partisans** and Jews. Victims were forced to dig their own graves before being executed. Approximately 65,000 Jews were murdered there, including Jews who were **transported** from the **Greater Reich, Bohemia-Moravia**, the **Netherlands**, and **Poland**.

SUGGESTED READING: Smolar, *The Minsk Ghetto.*

Mandel, Maria (1912–1947). Chief **SS** supervisor (**Aufseherin**) for the women's camp at **Birkenau** beginning in 1942. She succeeded Johanna Langfeldt. Mandel, known as "The Beast," took part in **selections**, and instituted the innovation of a camp orchestra. She was also a supervisor at **Lichtenburg** from 1938–1939 and at **Ravensbrueck** from 1939–1942. After 1942, the cruel matron was tried by the Supreme People's Court in **Poland** and executed. (See also **Fania Fenelon** and **Irma Grese**.)

SUGGESTED READING: Czech, *Auschwitz Chronicle, 1939–1945.*

Mann, Thomas (1875–1955). German novelist awarded the Nobel Prize for literature in 1929. He left the **Reich** for England where he became an outspoken opponent of the Nazis. The famous author broadcasted for the BBC, and he was one of the few who told Europeans of the **Final Solution**. (See also **Book Burning**.)

SUGGESTED READING: Drexel, *Encyclopedia of the 20th Century.*

Manstein, Field Marshal Erich von (1887–1973). German general. He led the attack on the southern Russian Front and assisted **Otto Ohlendorf** in mass shootings of Jews and Russians. After the war, the field marshal was sentenced by the British to eighteen years in prison for **war crimes** in the East, but was released in 1953. (See also **Operation Barbarossa** and **Soviet POWs**.)

SUGGESTED READING: Davidson, *The Trial of the Germans.*

Mantello, George Mandel (1901–1993). **El Salvadoran** diplomat in Geneva. A businessman and former Orthodox Romanian Jew, he became a Salvadoran citizen in 1939. Mantello became secretary general of the Salvadoran consulate in Bern and honorary consul for **Hungary, Czechoslovakia**, and **Yugoslavia**. He issued thousands of Salvadoran documents similar to **Raoul Wallenberg's Schutzpaesse**. Although the papers were bogus, it gave the Germans a bargaining chip to exchange Jews for German nationals. Mantello rescued numerous Hungarian Jews. He received and published the **Auschwitz Protocols** from **Rabbi Michael Dov Weissmandel** via **Monsignor Filippo Bernardini**. The diplomat distributed the Protocols along with letters attached from four prominent theologians. The Protocols were then published in 500 Swiss newspapers. (See also **Karl Barth, Exchange Jews**, and **Hotel Polski**.)

SUGGESTED READINGS: Kranzler, *Thy Brother's Blood*; Kranzler and Gevirtz, *To Save a World.*

Maquis/Maquisards. French underground and **partisan** fighters of varied political persuasions. Before 1943, up to 25 percent of its membership was Jewish. They were extremely active in south central **France** in the mountainous region known as Massif Central. The French communists operated independently. (See also **French Forces of the Interior**, **FTPF**, **Robert Gamzon**, and **Service de Travail Obligatoire**.

SUGGESTED READING: Schoenbrun, *Soldiers of the Night.*

Marmalade. (1) Jews were enticed to volunteer for **deportation** through a German offer of marmalade and bread. (2) Reference by Warsaw Jews to the German casualty list in the newspaper.

Marr, Wilhelm (1819–1904). German essayist and political theorist. He coined the term **anti-Semitism** (1879), which defined being Jewish as racial rather than membership in the Jewish religion. His view was most significant, for now hatred was based on ''innate'' characteristics, rather than the Jewish religion. Marr allegedly was of Jewish extraction.

SUGGESTED READING: Goldhagen, *Hitler's Willing Executioners.*

Marrano (Sp., pig). Pejorative term for Spanish and Portuguese Jews who were forced to convert to Catholicism during the Inquisition but secretly observed Jewish rituals. (See also **Francisco Franco, Portugal**, and **Spain**.)

Marzgefallene (G., March opportunists). Germans who joined the **Nazi Party** after **Hitler** came to power on January 30, 1933. (See also **Machtergreifung**.)

Masaryk, Jan (1886–1948). Czech statesman. He was foreign minister of **Czechoslovakia** prior to the **Munich Pact**. A committed democrat, Masaryk was revered in the Czech Jewish community. His father, Tomas, was the former president and a supporter of Jewish rights. Jan Masaryk retained the title of foreign minister of the Czech Government-in-Exile (1940–1945), and actively publicized the Jewish plight. In October 1945, Masaryk aided **Bricha** by providing transportation to Jewish survivors to move from the Soviet zone to the **American Zone of Occupation**. He was deputy Prime Minister of Czechoslovakia from 1945 through 1948. Masaryk was murdered by communists in 1948. (See also **Eduard Benes, Emil Hacha**, and **Masaryk Transport**.)

SUGGESTED READING: Drexel, *Encyclopedia of the 20th Century.*

Masaryk Transport. On September 7, 1943, 5,000 Czech Jews were shipped from **Terezin** to **Auschwitz**. Named after the Czech Foreign Minister, the **deportations** were a ''present'' for **Hitler**. Upon arrival, the Nazis informed the

Czech Jews they would be gassed six months later. By March 7, 1944, only 2,800 people were alive. The victims sang Hatikva (Jewish National Anthem) and the Czech national anthem on their way to the **gas chambers** in **Birkenau**. (See also **Auschwitz-Birkenau "Family Camp"** and **Czechoslovakia**.)

Maskilim (H., enlighteners). Students of the **Haskala** who believed in secular combined with Jewish studies.

Massfeller, Franz. Authored a commentary on the **Nuremberg Laws**. He represented the **Reich** Ministry of Justice at the **Wannsee Conference** (1942). Massfeller was one of many former Nazi judges who found employment in the West German Federal Ministry of Justice.
SUGGESTED READING: Mueller, *Hitler's Justice.*

Masur, Norbert. World Jewish Congress Swedish representative. He met with **Heinrich Himmler** and **Walter Schellenberg** on April 20, 1945, to discuss the release of Jews from **concentration camps**. The meeting was arranged by **Dr. Felix Kersten**. Masur's bargaining led to 1,000 women being released from **Ravensbrueck** to Stockholm. (See also **Count Folke Bernadotte**.)
SUGGESTED READING: Finger, *American Jewry During the Holocaust.*

Maurer, Gerhard (1907–1951). **SS** colonel. As head of the **WVHA's** D II Department, he was responsible for processing German corporate requests for **forced labor**. Maurer became deputy to **Richard Gluecks** in 1943 and handled important meetings involving all the **concentration camps**. He was sentenced to death in December 1951. (See also **Labor camps, Nuremberg Trials**, and **Karl Sommer**.)
SUGGESTED READING: Czech, *Auschwitz Chronicle.*

Mauritius. Island in the Indian Ocean east of Madagascar. In 1941, the British interned over 1,500 Czech, German, and Austrian Jews, including 600 Jews released from German **concentration camps**. The internees were denied entry into **Palestine** after the *Patria* affair. Afterward, 124 succumbed to disease during the four-year incarceration in which families were separated. The surviving Jews arrived in Haifa on August 26, 1945. (See also **White Paper**.)
SUGGESTED READING: Wasserstein, *Britain and the Jews of Europe.*

Mauthausen. Hard **labor** and **concentration camp** located near Linz, **Austria**, with forty-nine subcamps. Established in 1938, Mauthausen recorded the highest percentage of inmate/death ratio and was the only concentration camp classified as a **Class III** (along with **Melk**) facility. This camp was equipped with **gas chambers** installed by an **SS** pharmacist, Dr. Wisicky (who also introduced the gas), and a **crematorium**. The gas chambers, also known as the "gas cell," had a capacity for 120 victims. Approximately 120,000 prisoners (of the

200,000 people interned) were murdered or worked to death at this camp; over 38,000 were Jews. **Deportees** came from a broad cross-section of Europe including: **Belgium, Bulgaria, Czechoslovakia, Denmark, France, Germany, Greece, Netherlands, Hungary, Luxembourg, Norway, Poland, Spain**, the **Soviet Union**, and **Yugoslavia**. The most organized prisoners were the Spanish Republicans and Czech politicals. Inmates who were to be executed were marked with a red spot on their clothing. According to the camp records, 28,000 prisoners were ''shot while attempting to escape.''

This camp had a brutal quarry where inmates perished at a very high rate. Inmates who were pushed over the edge of the **Wienergraben** quarry were called ''**parachutists**.'' Those who were regarded as ''cultured'' were singled out for extermination including those prisoners who wore eyeglasses. Spanish Republicans and **Dutch** Jews were targeted for harsh punishment. On February 3, 1945, 570 inmates, mostly **Soviet POWs**, staged a revolt and escaped from **Block 20**; only 17 eluded capture. The Isolation Building was a windowless structure where emaciated prisoners were taken, and it was not uncommon for dead inmates to lay for two or three days before being collected.

In addition, Mauthausen replaced **Oranienburg** as the test-tube camp for **Heinrich Himmler's** food experiments. **Dr. Ernst Schenck** oversaw these experiments at Block 16. **Dr. Helmut Vetter** conducted sulfa experiments for **Bayer**. Gold teeth were extracted by Drs. Henkel and Jutman, who were easily able to locate their victims by looking for a red ''X'' on the chests of gassed inmates. Most ''selected'' victims were sent to **Hartheim Castle** to be gassed. **Dr. Friedrich Entress**, the chief doctor from October 21, 1943–July 26, 1944, started to send sick inmates to Hartheim Castle in the spring of 1944. From 1944, Dr. Wolters was the chief doctor who conducted **selections** and had the ability to send sick inmates to the gas chambers. Drs. Krebsbach and Wasicky selected inmates for the ''auto car'' or gassing van. This camp was the hub of the SS industrial empire in Austria. Mauthausen and **Gusen** I were **liberated** on May 5, 1945, by the Americans. **Gunskirchen**, a subcamp, was liberated on May 4, 1945, by Americans. (See also **Auschwitz, DAW, Ebensee, German Earth and Stone Works, Ltd., Heinkel Werke, Primitivbauweise, Rotspanir, Albert Sauer**, and **Franz Ziereis**.)

SUGGESTED READINGS: Feig, *Hitler's Death Camps*; United States Holocaust Memorial Museum, *1945: The Year of Liberation.*

Mayer, Dr. Joseph. German moral theologian at the Catholic University at Paderhorn. Dr. Mayer was commissioned to write an Opinion on **euthanasia** and Christianity. He concluded the Christian church would not forcefully protest the ''mercy killing'' of German adults. After the Opinion, **Hitler** issued a **Fuehrer Decree** in October 1939 and charged **Philipp Bouhler** and **Karl Brandt** with coordinating ''mercy deaths'' (**gnadentod**). (See also **Bishop Clemens von Galen**, *Mystici Corporis*, and **T-4**.)

SUGGESTED READING: Fischel and Pinsker, "The Church's Response to the Holocaust."

Mayer, Rene (1895–1972). French Jew, statesman, and **resistance** leader. He escaped to **Algeria** and became a member of the **Free French** Committee for National Liberation in 1943. The following year **General Charles de Gaulle** appointed Mayer minister in the provisional government. In 1945, he became high commissioner for German Affairs.

SUGGESTED READING: Rousso, *The Vichy Syndrome.*

Mayer, Saly (1882–1950). Swiss Jewish leader. He was president of the Federation of Swiss Jewish Communities, member of the **World Jewish Congress**, and representative of the **American Joint Distribution Committee** in Bern, **Switzerland**. Mayer played a pivotal role in negotiations with **Heinrich Himmler** to ransom Jews. His skillful negotiations with **Kurt Becher** facilitated the release of 1,700 Hungarian Jews from **Bergen-Belsen** and allowed for the diversion of 18,000 Jews to **Vienna** who were destined for **Auschwitz**. Mayer was involved in the "**Blood for Trucks**" transaction. He was criticized by **Rita and Isaac Sternbuch** for refusing to operate outside of Swiss and American law. After the war, he used his influence and money to aid **Displaced Persons**. (See also **Dr. Rezso (Rudolph) Kasztner, Roswell McClelland, Refoulement, Dr. Heinrich Rothmund**, and **Eduard von Steiger**.)

SUGGESTED READINGS: Bauer, *American Jewry and the Holocaust*; Kranzler, *Thy Brother's Blood.*

McClelland, Roswell (b. 1914). American diplomat. As director of the **American Friends Service Committee** in southern **France**, he clandestinely provided financial aid to the **resistance**. McClelland was involved with saving Jews by using the underground taking them to **Switzerland** and **Spain**. The diplomat was appointed **War Refugee Board** representative in Switzerland where he continued rescue work; most notably, sending the **Auschwitz Protocols** to Washington. However, he was criticized by **Orthodox Jewry** for being too legalistic, because he would not pass money to stop **deportations**. He also refused to tamper with the Swiss policy of **Refoulement** and argued, as did **Saly Mayer**, that such illegal activities would jeopardize their mission in Switzerland. (See also **Dr. Heinrich Rothmund, Eduard von Steiger**, and **Rita and Isaac Sternbuch**.)

SUGGESTED READINGS: Bauer, *American Jewry and the Holocaust*; Kranzler, *Thy Brother's Blood.*

McCloy, John (1895–1989). American lawyer and diplomat. As assistant secretary of War, he opposed rescue and relief pleas of Jews in favor of an all-out effort to defeat **Germany**. He rebuffed the **War Refugee Board** and successfully argued against bombing the **gas chambers** and railroad tracks leading to **Auschwitz**, insisting that such actions were military unfeasible. After the war, he was appointed United States high commissioner for Germany (1949–1952). McCloy issued the **Clemency Act of January 1951**, which pardoned many Nazi **war criminals** and industrialists in the hope of building up West Germany as a bulwark against Soviet expansion. Under his administration, only three death sentences were carried out. McCloy encouraged German corporations to make payments to former **forced laborers**, a request that yielded mixed results. (See also **General Gottlob Berger, General Lucius D. Clay, Anthony Eden, Dr. Robert M. Kempner, Baron Gustav and Alfred von Krupp, Henry Morgenthau Jr., Dr. Franz W. Six**, and **Edmund Veesenmayer**.)

SUGGESTED READINGS: Bird, *The Chairman*; Manchester, *The Arms of Krupp*.

McDonald, James Grover (1886–1964). **League of Nations** high commissioner for **refugees** from **Germany**. The American resigned in 1935, in disgust with the West's failure to accept Jewish refugees. In his long letter of protest he attacked Nazi racial policies as a form of racial extermination. In 1938, McDonald was appointed to the President's Advisory Committee on Political Refugees. He took over the task of coordinating the emergency **visa** effort in 1940. He then served on the Anglo-American Committee of Inquiry on **Palestine** in 1945. McDonald became the first American ambassador to Israel from 1948–1951. (See also **Quota** and **War Refugee Board**.)

SUGGESTED READINGS: Breitman and Kraut, *American Refugee Policy and European Jewry 1933–1945*; Wyman, *Paper Walls*.

Mechelen (F., Malines.) Belgian **transit camp** operated by the Nazis. Between August 4, 1943, and July 31, 1944, 26,000 Jews were shipped in **freight cars** to **Auschwitz** from this **concentration camp** mostly for Jews. Most wore a distinctive marking—"T" for **Transportjuden**. (See also **Breendonck**.)

SUGGESTED READING: Tenenbaum, *Race and Reich*.

Meed, Vladka (Feigele Peltel) (b. 1922). Underground Polish Jewish activist. A courier for the **ZOB** on the **Aryan** side of Warsaw, she smuggled weapons into the Jewish side and helped Jews escape. She wrote about her experiences in *On Both Sides of the Wall*. Mrs. Meed resides in New York and is active in **Holocaust** education.

Mein Kampf (G., *My Struggle*). **Hitler's** autobiography written in 1924 with his secretary, **Rudolf Hess**, in **Landsberg** prison. This anti-Bolshevik, **anti-Semitic** political treatise blamed the Jews for **Germany's** suffering and defeat in World War I. Hitler first mentioned gassing of Jews in this book. The **Nazi Party** leader spelled out his reasons for aggressive conquest in the East based on his world-view that Germans were the **Herrenvolk** and needed **Lebensraum**. (See also **Lance von Liebenfels** and **Guido von List**.)

SUGGESTED READING: Staudinger, *The Inner Nazi*.

Meiss, Leon (1896–1966). Jewish leader. Active in the Central Consistory of French Jews, he intervened in **Vichy** on behalf of French Jews and aided French Jewish **resistance** groups.
   SUGGESTED READING: Lazare, *Rescue as Resistance.*

Meitner, Lise (1878–1968). Austrian Jewish physicist. Head of the radiation department at the **Kaiser Wilhelm Institute**, she left for **Sweden** after the **Anschluss**. In Stockholm, Meitner achieved fission, the key to making the atom bomb. However, she refused to work on the bomb project. **Hitler** was reluctant to allow his scientists to use the advances of nuclear physics, which he termed a "Jew science." (See also **Niels Bohr, Albert Einstein**, and **Dr. Johannes Stark**.)
   SUGGESTED READINGS: Drexel, *Encyclopedia of the 20th Century*; Sime, *Lise Meitner.*

Melchoir, Chief Rabbi Marcus (1897–1969). Head of the Danish Jewish community. He warned his people on September 29, 1943, of the planned **Aktion**. The rabbi and his family were transported to safety in **Sweden** by the Danish underground. (See also **Denmark** and **Georg Ferdinand Duckwitz**.)
   SUGGESTED READING: Goldberger, *The Rescue of Danish Jews.*

Melina (P., hideout). Safe hiding place; usually a **bunker** in the **Warsaw** or **Vilna ghettos**.

Melk. Subcamp of **Mauthausen** established on April 11, 1944. **Slave laborers** dug deep tunnels for munitions factories. Harsh conditions, cruelty, and accidents resulted in the death of 5,000 inmates.

Memel. Lithuanian port city with a prewar Jewish population of 9,000. On March 22, 1939, the Germans annexed the city; however, most of the Jews left after the 1938 elections swept the Nazis into power (see also **Lithuania**.)
   SUGGESTED READINGS: American Jewish Committee, *American Jewish Yearbook, Vol. 41, 1939–1940*; Goralski, *World War II Almanac.*

Menczer, Aron (1917–1943). Austrian **Aliya Bet** representative. He was sent to **Theresienstadt** where he cared for 1,200 children from **Bialystok**. Menczer and the children were gassed at **Birkenau** in October 1943.

Mendes-France, Pierre (1907–1982). French Jewish statesman. He was an active member of the **resistance**. Imprisoned by **Vichy**, Mendes-France escaped to Britain and joined the **Free French**. In 1954, he became Prime Minister of **France**. (See **French Forces of the Interior**.)
   SUGGESTED READING: Webster, *Petain's Crime.*

Mengele, Dr. Josef (1911–1978) (''**Angel of Death**''). SS physician and anthropologist. Mengele joined the **Stahlhelm** in 1931, the **SA** in 1934, and the **Nazi Party** and the SS in 1937. Initially, he was deployed to the Eastern Front as a **Waffen-SS** physician. The doctor was wounded and awarded the Iron Cross first and second degree. His injury prompted a transfer to **Auschwitz** in the spring of 1943. An ardent **eugenicist** and disciple of **Otmar von Verschuer**, the physician was infamous for his sadistic ''medical experiments'' at Auschwitz and **Mauthausen** on Jews, and the ease and pleasure with which he made **selections**. He was especially interested in twins, dwarfs, and people with physical abnormalities at Auschwitz. After the war, he was initially able to elude capture and detention in POW camps due to the absence of the SS **tattoo** under his left armpit. Mengele actually lived with some farmers in West **Germany** for several years after the war. He escaped to South America with a falsified **Red Cross** ID. The fugitive lived extravagantly in Argentina before fleeing to Paraguay and Brazil. While in South America, his family provided him with financial assistance. The **war criminal** is presumed to have drowned in Brazil in 1978. (See also **Barrack 11**, and **Block 10**.)
   SUGGESTED READINGS: Lifton, *The Nazi Doctors*; Posner, *Mengele*.

Mennecke, Dr. Friedrich (1904–1947). Nazi **euthanasia** expert. He coordinated the ''**special treatment**'' **14 f 13** policy at **Gross-Rosen, Buchenwald**, and most probably **Dachau, Sachsenhausen-Oranienburg, Mauthausen, Auschwitz, Flossenbuerg**, and **Neuengamme**. Tried and convicted at the **Nuremberg Trials**, Mennecke died in prison of TB, which he contracted during his participation in the **T-4** program. (See also **Philipp Bouhler, Dr. Karl Brandt, Doctors' Trial**, and **Dr. Ernst von Grawitz**.)
   SUGGESTED READING: Friedlander, *The Origins of Nazi Genocide*.

Menschlichkeit (Y., humaness). Humane activities.

Merin, Moshe (1906–1943). Chairman of the regional **Judenrat** (1940–1943) in Eastern Upper Silesia, which contained forty-five communities and 100,000 Jews. He cooperated with the **Nazis** in selecting Jews for **deportation** in order to save segments of his community. The Jewish underground passed a death sentence on Merin after he denounced members of the **Zionist youth** group and communist **resistance**. In June 1943, Merin was deported to his death at **Auschwitz**. (See also ''**Work as a Means of Rescue**.'')
   SUGGESTED READING: Trunk, *Judenrat*.

Merlin, Samuel. Executive Director of the **Emergency Committee to Save the Jewish People of Europe**, an organization affiliated with the **Bergson Group**. This committee actively publicized the **Holocaust** in America, for example, full-page ads in the *New York Times*. Merlin was often the writer, and he lobbied

for Jewish rescue from 1943–1944. He now lives in New York City. (See also **Oswego** [Fort Ontario] and **War Refugee Board**.)
    SUGGESTED READING: Ben-Ami, *Years of Wrath.*

Messerschmidt. German aircraft company that exploited **concentration camp** laborers in **Flossenbuerg, Mauthausen**, and **Dachau**. In 1944, the company produced aircraft in tunnels near Mauthausen. Ninety thousand inmates worked in the aircraft industry. The firm never paid any **reparations** to camp survivors. (See also **German Earth and Stone Works, Ltd**.)

Mexico. Proposed warehouse complex for inmate loot at **Auschwitz-Birkenau**. This site was never built. However, in the summer of 1944, Mexico housed Hungarian Jewish women slated for extermination. (See also **Block 25** and **Canada I and II**.)

Mezuzah (H., doorpost). Jewish ritual rectangular box placed on doorposts that contained parchment with Biblical passages, particularly Deuteronomy 6:9.

Mikhoels, Shlomo (1890–1948). Director of the Jewish State Theater in Moscow. He later became chairman of the **Jewish Anti-Fascist Committee**. During his visit to the United States in 1943, Mikhoels publicized the **Holocaust**. He was murdered by **Stalin's** secret police in January 1948.
    SUGGESTED READING: Vaksberg, *Stalin Against the Jews.*

Mikvah (H., "gathering" of water). Ritual bath immersion by Jewish women, particularly married women after completion of their menstrual cycle. Some Orthodox men immerse themselves in the mikvah before the Sabbath and after intimate relations.

Mila 18. Address in the **Warsaw Ghetto** of the **bunker** and headquarters of the **Jewish Fighting Organization (ZOB)** from April–May 1943. Over 100 fighters died there including **Mordecai Anielewicz**.
    SUGGESTED READING: Zuckerman, *A Surplus of Memory.*

Milejkowski, Dr. Joseph (d. 1943?). Director of the **Judenrat's** Health Department in the **Warsaw Ghetto**. He coordinated scientific research with other Jewish doctors on the clinical effects of starvation. Milejkowski also organized hiding places for the medical research. By August 1942, almost every doctor involved in the experiments was dead.
    SUGGESTED READING: Gutman, *The Jews of Warsaw, 1939–1943: Ghetto, Underground, Revolt.*

Milice (F., militia). Pro-Nazi, **Vichy** French paramilitary of 30,000 formed in 1943 to support German occupation and **Marshal Henri Philippe Petain's col-**

laborationist government. Headed by **Joseph Darnand** and later **Paul Touvier** (Lyons), the militia rounded up Jews for **deportation**.

SUGGESTED READING: Marrus and Paxton, *Vichy France and the Jews.*

Mindszenty, Cardinal Josef (1892–1975). Hungarian Roman Catholic prelate appointed Bishop of Vezprem in 1944 during Nazi occupation. He opposed Jewish persecution, which led to his arrest and imprisonment by the **Arrow Cross** from 1944–1945. (See also **Hungary**.)

SUGGESTED READING: Szule, *The Secret Alliance.*

Minorities Treaties. The **League of Nations** in the 1920s declared Jews to be a national minority. In a series of treaties filed with the League pertaining to East European states created from the **Versailles Treaty, anti-Semitic** legislation was prohibited, and equal treatment of Jews guaranteed. However, for the most part; the victorious **Allied** nations of World War I did nothing to enforce the treaties. (See also **Bernheim Petition**.)

SUGGESTED READING: Heller, *On the Edge of Destruction.*

Minsk. Capital of **Belorussia** and a center of Russian Jewish culture. The Jewish population swelled to 80,000 in June 1941, one-third of the population after German occupation. It was headquarters for the Generalkommissar **Wilhelm Kube**. The **ghetto** was established in July 1941. A separate ghetto was created for German Jews. Although many **Aktionen** were carried out, the Jews of this city formed seven **partisan** groups. The head of **Judenrat, Eliyahu Mushkin**, actively aided **resistance** movements. Many residents were saved by the partisans. (See also **Maly Trostinets, Hersh Smolar, and Shalom Zorin**.)

SUGGESTED READINGS: Eckman and Lazar, *The Jewish Resistance*; Smolar, *The Minsk Ghetto.*

Minyan (H., quorum). A minimum of ten Jewish adult males needed to recite certain prayers. Religious Jews, even at **Auschwitz**, would clandestinely gather at work to recite morning and/or afternoon, evening or holiday prayers. (See also **Spiritual Resistance**.)

Mir. Belorussian town with a Jewish population of 2,500. Occupied by the **Red Army** in 1940, after the **Molotov-Ribbentrop Pact**, the entire **Mir Yeshiva** was transplanted to **Shanghai**. The Germans entered on June 26, 1941, and initiated **Aktionen**, which resulted in the murder of 1,500 Jews. A Jewish underground formed ties to **Shmuel Rufeisen**, a district commander. Some Jews escaped but most were murdered on August 13, 1941. (See also **Belorussia**.)

SUGGESTED READING: Kowalski, *Secret Press in Nazi Europe.*

Miranda de Ebro. Concentration camp in north central **Spain**. It was built during the Spanish Civil War for enemies of **Francisco Franco** and used to house Jewish **refugees** fleeing Nazi rule. Although conditions were squalid, there was no organized systematic torture of Jews or other inmates. (See also **Rotspanir**.)

SUGGESTED READING: Avni, *Spain, the Jews and Franco*.

Mir Yeshiva. Over 500 students from this Talmudic academy were stranded in **Lithuania**. They were granted safe passage through the **Soviet Union**, via **Siberia** to **Kobe**, Japan. Soon afterward, they were transported by the Japanese to **Shanghai**. They remained in Shanghai throughout the war, with the support of Rabbi Kalmanowitz (former President of Mir Yeshiva and rescue activist) and the **Va'ad ha-Hatzala**. (See also **Sempo Sugihara, Talmud**, and **Jan Zwartendijk**.)

SUGGESTED READINGS: Kranzler and Gevirtz, *To Save a World*; Lipschitz, *The Shanghai Connection*.

Miscegenation. Pejorative term for intermarriage between races. According to Nazi racial theory, such a marriage, and the children born from this union, were a disgrace to the **Aryan** race and contributed to the impurity of the **Volk**. (See also **Mischlinge, Nuremberg Laws, Rassenschande**, and **Voelkerchaos**.)

Mischlinge (G., hybrid/half-breed). Persons born of intermarriage, partly Jewish or **Roma**, as defined by the **Nuremberg Laws**. Intermarriage between an **Aryan** and a Jew was strictly prohibited. A Mischlinge of the first degree had two Jewish or Roma grandparents. One Jewish grandparent qualified a person as a Mischlinge of the second degree. In **Germany** (1935), there were approximately 350,000 persons classified as Mischlinge: 50,000 converts from Judaism; 210,000 half-Jews, and 80,000 quarter-Jews. On July 7, 1940, Mischlinge of the first degree were released from the military. (See also **Bernard Loesener, Miscegenation**, and **Reichssippenamt**.)

SUGGESTED READING: Proctor, *Racial Hygiene*.

Mit brennender Sorge (G., ''With Burning Concern''). Encyclical written by **Pope Pius XI** on March 14, 1937 (Palm Sunday). It became one of the greatest condemnations of the regime ever expounded by the **Vatican**. A long section was devoted to disproving the Nazi theory of **Blood and Soil** and the Nazi claim that faith in **Germany** was equal to religious faith in God. The letter, written in German, sent out clandestinely to hundreds of towns and villages where it was printed locally, attacked **Dr. Alfred Rosenberg's** *Myth of the Twentieth Century* (race theories), as ''The Cult of Idols.'' Recent findings say that before his death, Pius XI was preparing a scathing attack on Nazi persecution of Jews.

SUGGESTED READING: Rhodes, *The Vatican in the Age of Dictators*.

Mittelbau-Mittelwerk. Underground factory near **Dora-Nordhausen** dedicated to Nazi rocket construction; primarily the V-2. Most of the inmates were not

Jewish, but Soviet, Polish, and French **POWs**. Approximately 20,000 laborers were worked to death or executed. This site utilized a portable **crematorium** and debilitated inmates were sent to **Majdanek** or **Bergen-Belsen** to be gassed. (See also **Wernher von Braun, General Walter Dornberger, Dr. Hans Kammler, Peenemuende Aerodynamics Institute, Project Paperclip**, and **Arthur Rudolph**.)

SUGGESTED READINGS: Michel, *Dora*; Neufeld, *The Rocket and the Reich*.

Mizrachi (H., East). Worldwide religious organization of **Zionists** dedicated to rebuilding Israel according to **Orthodox Jewish** law. Its youth group was B'nai Akiva.

Mogilev-Podolski. Town on the Dniester River in **Ukraine**. By 1942, 15,000 Jews were concentrated in Urba, the assembly point for **Bessarabian** and **Bukovinian** Jews expelled to **Transnistria**. The **transit camp** was operated by Romanian **Gendarmerie**. **Siegfried Jagendorf** established a foundry in the area employing Jewish workers. Large numbers of Jews survived due to their proximity to **Romania** and the aid furnished by Jews from Bucharest. The **Soviets liberated** the camp on March 20, 1944, and immediately drafted 20,000 Jewish men into the **Red Army**. (See also **Dr. Albert Widmann**.)

SUGGESTED READING: Fischer, *Transnistria*.

Mohel (H. and Y.). Religious Jew who performs ritual circumcision. During the **Holocaust**, Jews were virtually the only men circumcised, making them vulnerable to humiliating and deadly inspections by Nazis and their **collaborators**.

Moll. German construction company that utilized **concentration camp** labor.

SUGGESTED READING: Smolen et al., *KL Auschwitz Seen by the SS*.

Moll, Otto (1915–1946). **SS** captain. He supervised the murder of Hungarian Jewry in **Birkenau** and managed the **crematoria** and **gas chambers** at **Auschwitz**. Moll designed the pits at Auschwitz that collected the fat draining off of burning corpses. He thought it was more efficient to throw live babies and small children into the gutters of scalding fat. In 1945, the **war criminal** managed **Gleiwitz** until it was **liberated**. An American military court sentenced him to death in 1945. Moll was executed after the war.

SUGGESTED READING: Smolen et al., *KL Auschwitz Seen by the SS*.

Molotov, Viachoslav Mikhailovitch (1890–1980). Soviet Foreign Minister who replaced **Maksim Maksimovich Litvinov** prior to the signing of the **Nazi-Soviet Pact** in August 1939. Later, he informed the American Embassy and other **Allied** governments on January 6, 1942, and April 27, 1942, of the mass murder of Jews in Nazi-occupied Soviet territories. Molotov supported the creation of the Jewish state in **Palestine** in the United Nations in 1947.

SUGGESTED READING: Vaksberg, *Stalin Against the Jews.*

Molotov-Ribbentrop Pact (August 23, 1939). Signed by the respective Soviet and German foreign ministers in Moscow. The public provisions called for a nonaggression pact and various trade relations neutralizing the **Soviet Union** in the coming war with the **Allies**. Its secret protocols called for the division and annexation of **Poland** and the apportionment of Eastern Europe into spheres of interest. The agreement had an adverse impact on Jews, in that the Soviets did not publicize Nazi persecution, and Jews were unprepared for the German onslaught. However, Jews were evacuated into the Soviet interior (400,000 to **Siberia**) prior to the Nazi attack of June 1941, saving tens of thousands of lives. (See also **Maksim Maksimovich Litvinov**.)

SUGGESTED READING: Weitz, *Hitler's Diplomat.*

Moltke, Helmuth James Graf von (1907–1945). German **resister**. As legal advisor to the German High Command, he communicated with the British during the war. He was a member of the **Kreisau Circle**, which met at his estate in Silesia. Moltke was suspected by the Nazis as early as 1941, as evidenced by the failure of his department to receive an invitation to the **Wannsee Conference**. He was implicated in the **July 20, 1944 Bomb Plot**, tried for treason before the **People's Court**, and executed in Plotzensee Prison.

SUGGESTED READINGS: Gill, *An Honorable Defeat*; Snyder, *Hitler's German Enemies.*

Monowice (G., Monowitz). Polish town close to **Auschwitz**. A **slave labor** factory operated by **I. G. Farben** (starting in the fall of 1943) was located in this area. (See also **Buna** and **Heinrich Schwarz**.)

SUGGESTED READINGS: Borkin, *The Crime and Punishment of I. G. Farben*; Gutman and Berenbaum, *Anatomy of the Auschwitz Death Camp.*

Montgomery, Field Marshal Bernard Law (1887–1976). Commander of the British 8th Army. He defeated Erwin Rommel's Africa Korps at El Alamein in late 1941 and pursued the Korps across **Libya** and Tunisia. His victories prevented the implementation of the **Final Solution** on North Africa's **Sephardic** Jews. Montgomery accepted the surrender of **Admiral Karl Doenitz's** representatives in northwest **Germany, Denmark**, and **Holland**. He rejected all appeals by **SS** guards at **Bergen-Belsen** facing execution. (See also **Irma Grese** and **Josef Kramer**.)

SUGGESTED READING: Wasserstein, *Britain and the Jews of Europe.*

Morganthau, Henry Jr. (1891–1967). Jewish secretary of Treasury under President **Franklin Delano Roosevelt** from 1933–1945. Morganthau maintained a fractious relationship with **Cordell Hull** over what he felt was obstructionist policies blocking European Jews from reaching America. The State Department believed the Treasury Department was encroaching on foreign policy. After the revelations of **Josiah DuBois**, he used his influence to establish the **War Refugee Board** in January 1944. The Board saved over 200,000 Jews. After the war, he advocated the "pastoralization" of **Germany**, known as the Morganthau Plan, which was rejected in favor of an industrialized Germany as a bulwark against communist expansion. (See also **John McCloy, John Pehle**, and **Wallenberg Bank**.)

SUGGESTED READING: Morganthau, *Mostly Morganthaus.*

Moringen. Small **concentration camp** for women located near Hanover, **Germany**. From March-June 1933, the site was used for German male political opponents of the Nazis, but designated a **Frauenlager** on October 28, 1933. The camp was not run by the **SS**, but by a civil servant who utilized female guards drawn from the **Fraueneschaft**. On March 21, 1938, Moringen ceased to be a women's camp and inmates were dispatched to **Lichtenburg**. (See also **Bergen-Belsen** and **Ravensbrueck**.)

SUGGESTED READING: Owing, *Frauen.*

Morocco. North African country near **Spain**. One hundred and fifty thousand Jews were interned in hard **labor camps** in this North African French colony controlled by **Vichy**. Approximately 4,000 Moroccan Jews volunteered for the French army in 1939. Many Jews were also forced to work on the **Trans-Sahara Railway**. The **Allied** invasion in 1942 saved these Jews from the **Final Solution**. (See also **Casablanca Conference, Francisco Franco**, and **Statut des Juifs**.)

SUGGESTED READING: Laskier, "Between Vichy Anti-Semitism and German Harassment."

Morrell, Dr. Theodor (1890–1948). **Hitler's** personal physician until 1944. He contributed to Hitler's physical deterioration using alternative medical treatments with an emphasis on vitamin remedies. Considered a quack, **Hermann Goering** labeled him the "Herr **Reich** Injection Master."

SUGGESTED READING: Aziz, *Doctors of Death.*

Moscow Declaration. Negotiated by U.S. Secretary of State **Cordell Hull** in October 1943, and signed by **Winston Churchill, Josef Stalin**, and **Franklin Delano Roosevelt**. The document stated that at the end of the war, those who participated in atrocities would be **extradited** to the country where the crime was committed. No mention of the **genocide** against European Jewry was made. (See also **Allied Control Council Law Number 10** and **London Charter Conference**.)

SUGGESTED READING: Annas, *The Nazi Doctors and the Nuremberg Code.*

Mosrim (H., snitches or squealers). Informing on fellow Jews is considered a major religious transgression. (See also **Greifer**.)

Mossad le Aliya Bet (H., organization for secret illegal immigration). Arm of the **Haganah**, which during the war outfitted "illegal" ships, bringing European Jewish **refugees** to **Palestine**. After May 1939–May 1948, it cooperated with **Bricha** and continued clandestine voyages. (See also **Shaul Avigur**, *Patria*, and **White Paper**.)
   SUGGESTED READINGS: Bauer, *From Diplomacy to Resistance*; Offer, *Escaping the Holocaust*.

Moyne, Lord (Walter Edward) (Eric Guiness) (1880–1944). British deputy minister of state for the Middle East. Before the war, he opposed Jewish settlements in British Guinea. Moyne refused any dispensation for passengers aboard *Struma*, upheld the **White Paper** throughout the war, opposed the **Jewish Brigade-Infantry** and any plans to provide safe havens in North Africa. He was assassinated in Cairo in 1944 by **Stern Group** (LIHI) members Eliahu Hakin and Aliahu Ben Tzuri.
   SUGGESTED READING: Wasserstein, *Britain and the Jews of Europe*.

Mrugrowsky, Dr. Joachim (1905–1948). SS general and chief of the SS Institute of Hygiene. He was responsible for "medical experiments" carried out at **concentration camps**. He supervised the distribution of **Zyklon-B**. Mrugrowsky carried out experiments on Jews and **Roma** at **Oranienburg**, infected inmates with **typhus** at **Buchenwald**, assisted **Dr. Karl Gebhardt** in infecting inmates with sulfa during experiments at **Ravensbrueck**, and conducted poison bullet experiments at **Sachsenhausen**. He was convicted by an American **International Military Tribunal**. Mrugrowsky was hanged on June 2, 1948. (See also **Dr. Erwin Ding-Schuler, Doctors' Trial,** and **Dr. Albert Widmann**.)
   SUGGESTED READING: Annas, *The Nazi Doctors and the Nuremberg Code*.

Muellabfuhrkommando (G., rubbish). Refuse transport in the **concentration camps** that often hauled food. Inmates coveted this job assignment.

Mueller, Heinrich (1900–?) (**"Gestapo Mueller"**). SS major-general. From 1939 to 1940, Mueller was head of Department IV, which investigated and indicted enemies for the **Reich Security Main Office**. He ordered "**protective custody**" and had the authority to transfer a suspect on the flimsiest pretense to a **concentration camp**. Mueller built up a network of spies and informants. The major-general supervised **Adolf Eichmann**. He disappeared from **Hitler's** bunker in April 1945.
   SUGGESTED READING: Crankshaw, *Gestapo*.

Mueller, Ludwig (1883–1945). Evangelical theologian. He was appointed **Reich** Bishop of **Germany** in 1933 to unite the Protestant Church into a unified Nazi entity. A vigorous racist and **anti-Semite**, Mueller was a central figure in the clash between the German Faith Movement, backed by **Hitler**, and the **Confessional Church**, led by **Pastor Martin Niemoeller**. By 1935, his influence declined. Hitler said, ''The difference between the church and me [on the **Jewish Problem**] is that I'm finishing the job.''
    SUGGESTED READING: Bergen, *The German Christian Movement in the Third Reich.*

Munich Pact. Agreement in September 1938 among **Germany (Adolf Hitler), Italy (Benito Mussolini), France (Edouard Daladier)**, and Britain (**Neville Chamberlain**) to dismember the **Sudetenland** from **Czechoslovakia** and add it to the **Greater Reich**. The Pact was brokered by Mussolini, but not a single Czech leader was invited to attend. (See also **Appeasement, Eduard Benes, Jan Masaryk**, and **Hungary**.)
    SUGGESTED READINGS: Shirer, *The Rise and Fall of the Third Reich*; Weitz, *Hitler's Diplomat.*

Munkacs (Hu.,) **Munkacevo** (Cz.). City in eastern **Czechoslovakia** bordering **Hungary**. This center of **Hasidic** and **Orthodox Jewry** was transferred from Czechoslovakia to Hungary in November 1938. Over 40 percent of the city's population of 13,500 were Jewish. Most Jews were sent to **Auschwitz** in the spring of 1944 after the Germans occupied Hungary.
    SUGGESTED READING: Braham, *The Destruction of Hungarian Jewry.*

Munkaszolgalat (Hu., Hungarian Labor Service System). After the **anti-Semitic** laws of 1939, over 100,000 Jewish men of military age were drafted into the labor service (Jewish Labor Brigade); a division of the Hungarian Army. Over half of the conscripts served outside of Hungarian borders, often in the **Ukraine**, where they were subjected to inhumane conditions and the terror of German units. On the Eastern Front, 43,000 Jewish men were killed while they were attached to the Hungarian Army. The **Red Army** interned these Jews as enemies. However, those who served inside **Hungary** usually avoided the horrors of **ghettoization** and **deportation**. (See also **Miklos Kallay** and **Rabbi Pinchas Tibor Rosenbaum.**)
    SUGGESTED READING: Braham, *The Hungarian Labor Service System.*

Muselmann (G., Muslim). Term used by **concentration camp** inmates to refer to the most physically and emotionally run-down prisoners who looked like a praying Moslem. These inmates were so weak and emaciated they could not walk, work, or stand erect. Once an inmate became a Muselmann, his fate was sealed.

Mushkin, Eliyahu (d. 1942). Chairman of the **Minsk Judenrat**. He supported the underground and local **partisans** and aided Jews trying to escape the **ghetto**. Mushkin was arrested and hanged by the Nazis. (See also **Wilhelm Kube**.)
SUGGESTED READING: Smolar, *The Minsk Ghetto*.

Mussert, Anton (1892–1945). **Dutch fascist** leader. He founded the Dutch **National Socialist** Party **(NSB)** in 1931, but never had a mass following. Mussert **collaborated** with the Germans during occupation. He was executed by a Dutch firing squad after the war. (See also **Netherlands**.)
SUGGESTED READING: Davidson, *The Trial of the Germans*.

Mussolini, Benito (1883–1945). Dictator of **Italy** from 1922–1943, the architect of **fascism**, and an ally of **Hitler**. He negotiated a **Concordat** with **Pope Pius XI**, establishing **Vatican** City and friendly co-existence between the Catholic Church and fascist Italy in 1929. He introduced anti-Jewish legislation in 1938. Mussolini did not actively enforce **anti-Semitic** laws and permitted the Italian Army to protect 40,000 Jews within their zones of occupation in **France, Greece**, Tunisia, and **Yugoslavia**. However, after the **Allied** invasion of Italy, and the German occupation of northern Italy, the Italian government **deported** Jews. The dictator was executed by Italian **partisans** on April 28, 1945. (See also **Axis, Munich Pact, OVRA, Pope Pius XII, General Mario Roatta, Salo Republic**, and **SS Colonel Otto Skorzeny**.)
SUGGESTED READINGS: Michaels, *Mussolini and the Jews*; Zuccotti, *The Italians and the Holocaust*.

Musy, Jean-Marie. Rightist Swiss banker and former president of the Swiss Confederation. Pro-Nazi and a personal friend of **Heinrich Himmler**, Musy served as a conduit between **Germany** and the Western **Allies** to discuss a separate surrender. He met with **Walter Schellenberg** and Himmler in late 1944 and early 1945 and arranged a deal where foreign currency was exchanged for Jewish **concentration camp** inmates. The proposal discussed would involve the ransom and release of 1,200 Jews to **Switzerland** every two weeks. Only one **transport** from **Theresienstadt** (February 4, 1945) took place before **Hitler** stopped the deliberations. **Heinrich Mueller** and **Ernst Kaltenbrunner** were opposed to the negotiations and influenced Hitler to issue a directive against such dealings. Musy's son, Jean Batiste, was also involved with negotiations. (See also **Count Folke Bernadotte, Rita and Isaac Sternbuch**, and **Rabbi Michael Dov Weissmandel**.)
SUGGESTED READING: Bauer, *Jews for Sale*?

Mystici Corporis (Latin, Mystic Body). Papal encyclical issued by **Pope Pius XII** on June 27, 1943, condemning **euthanasia**. The Pope condemned the murder of the deformed, handicapped, and incurable as a violation of divine and natural law. He never condemned, by name, the mass murder of Jews. (See also **Dr. Joseph Mayer** and **T-4**.)

    SUGGESTED READING: Rhodes, *The Vatican in the Age of Dictators*.

N

Nacht und Nebel (G., **Night and Fog**). **Hitler's** secret order issued on December 7, 1941, which mandated the arrest of anyone suspected of underground activities against the **Reich**. The Decree was prompted by anti-German **resistance** in Western Europe, particularly occupied **France**. Suspects were made to "disappear" by work, execution, or gassing. Military courts could impose the death sentence and turn the suspect over to the **SS**. The Decree implicated the **Wehrmacht** in **war crimes**. (See also **"Destruction Through Work,"** Gross-Rosen, Alfred Jodl, Wilhelm Keitel,** and **Natzweiler-Strutthof.**)

SUGGESTED READINGS: Harris, *Tyranny on Trial*; Mueller, *Hitler's Justice*.

Nadich, Rabbi Judah (1912–1995). Chaplain of U.S. Army in Europe from 1942–1946. Shocked by revelations contained in **Earl Harrison's** report, President **Harry S. Truman** designated Nadich special advisor on Jewish affairs to **General Dwight David Eisenhower** on the advice of **Rabbi Stephen S. Wise**. Eisenhower followed Nadich's advice and greatly improved conditions for Jewish **DPs**, providing separate Jewish self-governing camps. On August 29, 1945, he was appointed to the Civil Affairs Division. After the war, Nadich described his postwar experiences in *Eisenhower and the Jews*.

Nansen Passport. Passport named after Fridtjof Nansen, **refugee** overseer for the **League of Nations**. The passes were issued by the League to stateless persons after World War I. The United States refused to recognize its legal validity for Jewish refugees after 1933.

Narodowe Sily Zbrojne. (See **NSZ.**)

National Legionary Government. Pro-**fascist, anti-Semitic** government established in **Romania** on September 6, 1940, by **Ion Antonescu** and **Horia Sima**.

National Military Organization. (See **Irgun Zvai Leumi**.)

National Socialism. **Hitler's** political movement. It was predicated on the state carrying out the will of the **Volk** and included: obedience to the **Fuehrer**, expansion, and militarism. National "socialism" was anti-Marxist and rejected class struggle, but advocated the right of the state to exercise great power on the individual and economy in order to improve the health of the Volk. (See also **Fascism, Lebensraum**, and **Nazi Party**.)
   SUGGESTED READING: Fischer, *Nazi Germany*.

National Socialist German Students' League. Arm of the **Nazi Party** dedicated to spreading Nazism among German university students even before **Hitler's** seizure of power. This organization was influential and popular among students.

National Socialist German Workers Party (NSDAP; Nazi Party). Started as an appendage of the **Thule Society** formed in 1917. In 1918, Thule organized the Political Workers Circle; out of that **Anton Drexler** and other railroad workers founded the **German Workers Party**, which often held meetings in Thule quarters. In 1919, **Hitler** was sent by army intelligence to spy on the party and quickly became its chairman of propaganda and soon its leader. He added the term **National Socialist** to German Workers Party, which became "Nazi" in common vernacular. By 1932, it was the largest single party in **Germany**, but not the majority. In the election that year, Nazis polled 38 percent of the vote. Its popularity was due to a number of factors: fear of the Bolsheviks, economic chaos, political and social instability, supernationalism, and **anti-Semitism**. Hitler was carefully portrayed as Germany's savior.
   SUGGESTED READINGS: Bullock, *Hitler and Stalin*; Flood, *Hitler, the Path to Power*.

National Socialist Physicians' League. Formed by medical doctors in 1929 to coordinate Nazi medical policy and "purify" the German medical community of "Jewish Bolshevism." (See also **Dr. Gerhart Wagner**.)
   SUGGESTED READING: Proctor, *Racial Hygiene*.

Nationalsozilistische Volkswohlfahrt (NSV). **Nazi Party** welfare organization.

Natzweiler-Strutthof. Small, forced **labor camp** for men in Alsace, **France** with numerous satellite facilities attached to it. The camp was built in 1940 to accommodate Western prisoners. Members of the French **Resistance** were brought to this site as part of the **Night and Fog** program. Most of these prisoners perished from the horrid living conditions. Mustard gas experiments were carried out by **Dr. August Hirt** and **Dr. Wolfram Sievers**. An "experimental" **gas chamber** was erected. This camp was in operation from May 1941 through September 1944, when the Germans evacuated. The French and Americans occupied the deserted camp on November 23, 1944. (See also **Lothar Hartjenstein** and **Egon Zill**.)

SUGGESTED READINGS: Annas, *The Nazi Doctors and the Nuremberg Code*; Feig, *Hitler's Death Camps*.

Nazi (NSDAP). An acronym formed from the syllables of the words "NAtional" and "SoZIalist." While the term applied at first to the **Nazi Party**, it became the common name for **Germany** during World War II. Konrad Heiden (1906–1966), an authority on National Socialism, is alleged to have coined the term. (See also **National Socialism** and **National Socialist German Workers Party**.)

Nazi Labor Front. Umbrella organization for Nazi-controlled labor unions, founded on May 10, 1933. All traditional unions were abolished and their leaders imprisoned. The Front was led by **Dr. Robert Ley** and included more than 20 million workers. It tried to persuade the working class to see the merits of the Nazi way of life. (See also **Deutsche Arbeitsfront**.)

Nazi Party. (See **National Socialist German Workers Party**.)

Nazi-Soviet Pact. (See **Molotov-Ribbentrop Pact**.)

Nebe, Arthur (1894–1945). **SS** lt. general. Commander of **Einsatzgruppen** B in 1941 and later the head of **Kripo**. He suggested **Roma** be used for saltwater experiments. Fearing defeat, he joined the **July 20, 1944 Bomb Plot** against **Hitler**. Nebe was tried and executed by a Nazi court on April 3, 1945. (See also **Dr. Albert Widmann**.)

SUGGESTED READING: Crankshaw, *Gestapo*.

Nebenlager (G., subcamp). Smaller **labor camp** attached to a **Stammlager**. (See also **Danzig**.)

Netherlands (also called **Holland**). Kingdom located in northwestern Europe bounded by the North Sea in the west, **Belgium** in the south, and in the east by **Germany**. The **Dutch** language, a Germanic tongue, is spoken. Its prewar Jewish population was 140,000 in a general population of 8,828,680. Native Dutch Jews numbered 110,000, and 30,000 were **refugees** from Germany and **Austria**. The Jews played an important role in the country's economic and political life. Civil rights for Jews were granted as early as 1796. Ten percent of Netherland's Jews worked in the diamond industry.

Holland was invaded by the Germans in May 1940, and Queen Wilhelmina fled to London with her government-in-exile. The Austrian, **Artur Seyss-Inquart**, was made governor (**Reichskommissar**). He subordinated all the civil administration to his German authority. Seyss-Inquart had local Nazis to aid him: **Anton Mussert** and members of the **Dutch Nazi Party (NSB)** were given posts. The Dutch Police were re-organized into a new body, Communal Police, trained by the **SS**. In 1943, **Landwacht** Nederland (Dutch Home Guard) wearing Germanic SS uniforms fought against Dutch **resistance**. Holland produced 50,000 volunteers for front-line **Waffen-SS**. Over 3,000 fought on the Eastern Front. This is not surprising since 50,000 Germans lived and worked in Holland during World War II.

There were numerous Dutch friendly to Jews. In Amsterdam for two February days in 1941, dockworkers and others went on strike, protesting the **deportation** of Jewish young men who fought back at Dutch Nazi police. It was ruthlessly put down. The Dutch underground was one of the most effective in Europe. **Onderduikers** were active in rescuing Jews.

With the advent of Nazi control, a series of **Nuremberg**-type laws ensued, demolishing Jewish civil and economic activity. In January 1942, **forced labor** camps were set up. By April, Jews were wearing Yellow Stars and under curfew. On May 21, 1942, complete expropriation of Jewish property was enforced. By July, **transit camps Westerbork** and **Vught** were filled with Jews slated for deportation to **concentration camps**. September 29, 1943, found the last roundup of Jews (5,000) for deportation to **Auschwitz**. It included the **Jewish Council** members who were carrying out Nazi orders for all Dutch Jews.

In September 1944, **Allied**, particularly British, airmen tried to liberate Holland. They succeeded only to occupy the southern half. The Dutch **resistance** attempted a railway strike supported by the Allies. It failed to cripple the transport of **Wehrmacht** troops. The German retaliation was very harsh. Famine and starvation followed in a bitter cold winter (Hunger Winter) from 1944–1945. There was an Allied airborne supply to the Dutch permitted by the Germans. On May 6, Queen Wilhelmina returned to her throne after all German forces surrendered to the British. Jewish losses were about 106,000, 78 percent of Dutch Jewry. This number included 30,000 refugees from Austria and Germany. (See also "**Black Police,**" **Collaboration, Dutch Workingman's Strike, Eindeutschung, Anne Frank, Miep Gies, "Green Police," Joodse Raad, Marion Pritchard, Hans Rauter, Sonderreferet, Edith Stein, Lodewijk Ernst Visser, Joop Woortman**, and **Jan Zwartendijk**.)

Neuengamme. Concentration camp opened outside of Hamburg in 1938. Originally a satellite camp of **Sachenhausen-Oranienburg**, this site became an independent camp in 1940. The camp supplied **slave labor** to local industry. Between 40,000 to 55,000 of the approximately 90,000 internees were worked to death or murdered. Woebbelin, a satellite camp, was **liberated** on May 2, 1945, by the Americans, who forced the villagers to view the camp's atrocities. During the last days of the war, the **SS** placed approximately 10,000 inmates on three unseaworthy vessels, which were destroyed by a British air raid on May 3, killing 7,300 inmates. Another 8,000 inmates were murdered one day before **Germany's** unconditional surrender to the British on May 4, 1945. The Hamburg government refused to build a memorial at this site for thirty-five years. (See also **Richard Baer, "Destruction Through Work,"** and **Max Pauly.**)

SUGGESTED READING: Feig, *Hitler's Death Camps.*

Neurath, Konstantin von (1873–1956). German diplomat. He led **Germany's** foreign office from 1932–1938, until he was replaced by **Joachim von Ribbentrop**. von Neurath resigned from the cabinet on February 4, 1938, yet accepted the post of **Reich** Minister Without Portfolio. He was the first **Reichkommissar** for the **Protectorate of Bohemia-Moravia** when **Aryanization** began in 1939. von Neurath implemented anti-Jewish measures identical to those in Germany. Tried at **Nuremberg** and sentenced to fifteen years, he was released in 1954 due to health problems.

SUGGESTED READING: Davidson, *The Trial of the Germans.*

New Order. Nazi concept of a thousand year **Reich** with the end of all Jewish influence and the establishment of a Teutonic brand of Christianity. The West and Scandinavian countries would be Nazified and **Slavs** would be used as slaves for Germanic peoples. Every phase of living in the **Third Reich** would be coordinated with **National Socialist** principles. (See also **Generalplan Ost**.)

SUGGESTED READING: Shirer, *The Rise and Fall of the Third Reich.*

Nice. City on the Mediterranean French Riviera occupied by Italian troops in 1940. The Italian Army protected 50,000 indigenous Jews and Jewish **refugees** from the **Vichy** government and German anti-Nazi political opponents who had clustered in Nice at the end of 1942. French Vichy officials ordered all foreign Jews shipped to the Northern Zone, German-occupied **France**. The Italian consul in Nice, with the backing of the Italian Foreign Ministry, protected the Jews in the area. They remained safe until September 1943, when **Italy** surrendered to the **Allies**, and the Germans occupied former Italian zones of occupation, including Nice. Thousands of Jews in this area were rounded up and **deported** to **Auschwitz**. (See also **Pere Benoit, Alois Brunner, Italy**, and **Heinz Rothke**.)

SUGGESTED READINGS: Poliakov and Sabille, *Jews Under the Italian Occupation*; Zuccotti, *The Holocaust, the French, and the Jews.*

Niemoeller, Pastor Martin (1892–1984). German **resister**. A submarine captain in World War I, he initially supported the Nazis, but opposed **Hitler** when the **Fuehrer** institutionalized the primacy of the state over the church. By December 1933, 6,000 other pastors of the Protestant Evangelical Church joined him in opposing the German Christians who argued Christ was an **Aryan** and the church should conform to **National Socialist** principles. They formed the **Confessional Church** (Bekenntniskirche). He spent 1937–1945 in **concentration camps**, including **Sachsenhausen-Oranienburg** and **Dachau**. Niemoeller was **liberated** in 1945 and subsequently issued the Stuttgart Confession of Guilt, which declared the collective guilt of the German people for the war. (See also **Dietrich Bonhoeffer, Karl Jaspers**, and **Ludwig Mueller**.)

SUGGESTED READINGS: Goldhagen, *Hitler's Willing Executioners*; Gutteridge, *Open Thy Mouth for the Dumb: The German Evangelical Church and the Jews, 1879–1950*.

Nietzsche, Friedrich (1844–1900). Mid–nineteenth-century German philosopher. He introduced the concept of a superman or a hero who transcended Christian morality. Although Nietzsche was not an **anti-Semite, Hitler** adapted his concepts to justify **Aryan** superiority and discard the Christian concepts of humaneness and morality. (See also **Uebermenschen**.)

SUGGESTED READING: Macintyre, *Forgotten Fatherland*.

Night and Fog. (See **Nacht und Nebel**.)

Night of Broken Glass. (See **Kristallnacht**.)

Night of the Long Knives. On June 30, 1934, **Hitler** ordered the **SS** to purge the **SA**. His motivation was to honor the "Deutschland Pact," an agreement he concluded with German generals to establish the supremacy of the **Reichswehr**. A murder spree took place for three days and many prominent SA were murdered, including **Ernst Roehm**, Gregor Strasser, and sixteen of their lieutenants. This purge marginalized the SA and marked the beginning of the supremacy of the SS. German Jews were lulled into believing this event marked the end of Nazi barbarism. The term of "Long Knives" is taken from a stanza of the song "**Horst Wessel**." (See also **Walter Buch** and **Viktor Lutze**.)

SUGGESTED READINGS: Snyder, *Hitler's Elite*; Toland, *Adolf Hitler*.

Ninth Fort. Killing site in **Kovno** where 10,000 Jews were murdered by Germans and Lithuanians in October 1941.

SUGGESTED READING: Elkins, *Forged in Fury*.

Norway. Scandinavian nation adjacent to **Sweden**, invaded by the Germans on April 8–9, 1940. By June 9, 1940, the Germans had defeated the combined Norwegian, Polish, French, and British forces. The **collaborationist** government headed by **Vidkun Quisling** participated in rounding up and **deporting** Jews beginning in October–November 1942. The Lutheran Church protested deportations and sent a protest letter to Quisling. The underground smuggled approximately 900 out of Norway's 1,700 Jews to Sweden. **Internment–transit camps** were located in Falstad, Grini, Tromso, Berg, and Bredveit. (See also **Bishop**

Eivind Berggrav, Count Folke Bernadotte, Lebensborn, Franz Stahlecker, and **Josef Terboven**.)
SUGGESTED READING: Abrahamsen, *Norway's Response to the Holocaust.*

Novak, Franz (b. 1913). SS captain, aide to **Adolf Eichmann**. He served in **Vienna** in the **Reichszentrale fuer Juedische Auswanderung (Reich Central Office for Jewish Emigration)**. Novak set up Jewish Immigration offices in Prague and **Berlin**. He was a member of the **Hitler Youth, SA**, and **RSHA**, and played a key role in the liquidation of Hungarian Jewry as a transportation expert. He lived in **Austria** under an assumed name before reverting back to his real name in 1957. Tried and convicted in 1964 for his role in the **Final Solution**, he was acquitted in 1966 after a re-trial at the behest of the Austrian Supreme Court.
SUGGESTED READING: Hilberg, *Destruction of European Jews.*

Novaky. Forced labor and **concentration camp** in **Slovakia**. (See also **Us-tredna Zidov**.)

"Novemberbrecher" (G., "November criminals"). Pejorative Nazi term describing German leaders who signed the armistice on November 11, 1918. The Nazis alleged that it was the **Social Democrats** and Jews who stabbed **Germany** in the back. (See also **Dolchstoss, Slovakian National Revolt**, and **Weimar Republic**.)

"November Jews." Reference to 20,000 to 30,000 Jewish men taken to **concentration camps** during **Kristallnacht**.

Novitch, Miriam (d. 1994). French Jewish **resistance** fighter. She devoted her life to **Holocaust** documentation. Novitch was interned at **Vittel** along with the poet **Itzkhak Katzenelson**. She immigrated to the **Ghetto Fighters' Kibbutz** in Israel and authored a number of books on Jewish Resistance.
SUGGESTED READING: Novitch, *Spiritual Resistance.*

Novogrudok (P., Nowogrodek). **Belorussian** town, formerly in **Poland**, in the **Grodno** District. At the outbreak of World War II, 6,000 Jews lived there, many refugees from German-occupied Poland. It was occupied by the **Red Army** in September 1939 and captured by the Nazis in 1941. The Germans carried out **Aktionen** against Jews. On April 15, 1943, a tunnel was completed. Many Jews broke out, but only 100 survived to join the **Bielski partisans**; who came back to aid in **liberation** of the town. (See also **Hirsch Kaplinski** and **Molotov-Ribbentrop Pact**.)
SUGGESTED READINGS: Trunk, *Jewish Responses to Nazi Persecution*; Wiesenthal, *Every Day Remembrance Day.*

NSB (Du., Nationale Socialistische Beweging). Highly **anti-Semitic**, National Socialist Movement founded in the **Netherlands** in 1931 by **Anton Mussert**. With the German occupation, the NSB hounded Jews and were involved in **razzia**. After the war, the party was disbanded. (See also "**Black Police**," "**Green Police**," and **Landwacht**.)
SUGGESTED READING: Presser, *Ashes in the Wind.*

NSDAP. (National Socialist German Workers Party). Nazi Party.

NS-Frauenschaft (G., National Socialist Women's Organization). (See **Frauenschaft**.)

NSV. Nationalsozilistische Volkswohlfahrt.

NSZ (Narodowe Sily Zbrojne) (P., National Armed Force). Right-wing, nationalist Polish **resistance** group that hated Jews, communists, and liberals. They refused to recognize the authority of the **Armia Krajowa** and operated independently. During the war, they murdered hundreds of Jewish **partisans** and others seeking asylum. NSZ terrorized and killed Jewish survivors after the war.
SUGGESTED READING: Gutman and Krakowski, *Unequal Victims.*

Numerus Clausus (Latin, restrictive number). **Quota** of Jews, supposedly equal to their proportion of the general population, permitted to attend a university. It was official, **anti-Semitic** state policy in a number of countries prior to the **Holocaust** and instituted by the Nazi regime in April 1933. For example, "The Decree Against Overcrowding of German Schools" had an admission quota for Jews of 1,590. (See also **Casablanca Conference** and **Hungary**.)

Nuncio (I., messenger). The highest ranking diplomatic envoy of the Pope and **Vatican** placed in a civil government. (See also **Monsignor Angelo Rotta**.)

Nuremberg Code. Human Rights Document dealing with medical experimentation. The Code was formulated by U.S. judges at the end of the trial of twenty-three Nazi physicians (**Doctors' Trial** in 1947). These experiments involved murder and torture and were systematic and barbarous acts with the death of the subjects often in mind. The test victims were **concentration camp** prisoners, mainly Jews, **Roma, Slavs**, and **Soviet POWs**. The Code was a response to the evidence that the experiments were nontherapeutic and nonconsensual. Embodied in it are ten principles that protect the rights of subjects. A major principle states that all experiments must have the voluntary, informed, competent, and understanding consent of the subject. The Nuremberg Code is the most important ethical, moral, and legal document on the practice of human medical experimentation. (See also **Leo Alexander** and **Kaiser Wilhelm Institute**.)

SUGGESTED READING: Annas and Grodin, *The Nazi Doctors and the Nuremberg Code.*

Nuremberg Laws. Restrictive, anti-Jewish legislation passed on September 15, 1935, defining who was a Jew. These Laws denied citizenship to Jews and forbade intermarriage. They were announced at the annual **Nazi Party** rally in Nuremberg. Based on bogus racial assumptions, the primary authors were **Dr. Hans Globke** and **Dr. Wilhelm Stuckart**. The U.S. State Department weakly protested. The Laws were extended to Nazi-occupied countries and the definition often was a matter of life and death to individuals. The Nazis instituted 400 anti-Jewish laws between 1933–1939. (See also **Aryan Paragraph, Bastard Jews, Enabling Act, Wilhelm Frick, Genetic Health Courts, Karaites, Franz Massfeller, Miscegenation, Mischlinge, Reichssippenamt**, and **Dr. Gerhart Wagner**.)

SUGGESTED READING: Mueller, *Hitler's Justice.*

Nuremberg Principles. A summary of what was decided at the **Nuremberg Trials**. The Principles were formulated by the International Law Commission, technical law experts set up by the United Nations General Assembly in 1946. Basically, any person, head of state or soldier, even acting under orders, who commits a crime under international law is responsible and liable for punishment. The crimes listed are: crimes against the peace, **war crimes**, and **crimes against humanity**.

SUGGESTED READING: Falk, Kolko, and Lifton, *Crimes of War.*

Nuremberg Trial(s). Main trial of twenty-two major Nazi **war criminals** held from November 20, 1945–October 1946. The attorneys for the defense argued that the charges were ex post facto, in that no international law was formulated prior to 1945 dealing with the four main charges. The defense counsel maintained the legal right of a sovereign state to wage war and argued that nations could treat its minorities any way they saw fit within its borders. However, the German Military Penal Code (Paragraph 47, Clause 3), in effect during World War II, stipulated that the extermination of civilians was a criminal order and could be refused. The **International Military Tribunal (IMT)** held the **Hague** and **Geneva Conventions**; the Kellogg-Briand Pact, the League Charter, and Locardo Pact banned aggressive war. **Crimes against humanity**, such as slavery, **deportations**, and murder were part of a civil law and customs among nations for generations, and the Allies acted in accordance with international custom. Prosecution witnesses included **Dieter Wisliceny, Erich von dem Bach-Zelewski, Hermann Fritz Graebe**, and **Rudolf Hoess**. The verdicts were delivered on **Yom Kippur**, and eleven Nazi leaders were sentenced to death by hanging on October 16, 1946. Those executed were cremated at **Dachau**, and their ashes were deposited in the Iser River.

The Nazis were tried by an IMT composed of two judges from Britain,

France, the **Soviet Union**, and the United States; the United States was the primary prosecutor. Unprecedented in history, these trials held individuals responsible for crimes of war. There were twelve additional trials from 1946–1949 at Nuremberg. Only American judges were involved, and they meted out 12 death sentences, 25 life imprisonments, and 177 convictions. These proceedings dealt with ''medical experiments,'' camp kommandants, membership in a criminal organization, German corporate complicity, and **Einsatzgruppen** leaders. These trials established four charges that in turn established principles of international law including: crimes against the peace, waging an aggressive war, **war crimes**, and crimes against humanity. In 1951, most convictions were subject to a liberal pardon policy. Among Jewish groups, there was little enthusiasm for the trials. The **American Jewish Conference** only called for one—the ex– **Grand Mufti of Jerusalem**. (See also **Murray C. Bernays, General Lucius D. Clay, Doctors' Trial, Otto Kranzbuehler, Rafael Lemkin, London Charter Conference, John McCloy**, and **Subsequent Nuremberg Trials**.)

SUGGESTED READINGS: Conot, *Justice at Nuremberg*; Taylor, *The Anatomy of the Nuremberg Trials*.

Nyilas Part (Hu.). (See **Arrow Cross**.)

O

Oberfuehrer. **SS** senior colonel.

Oberg, SS General Carl Albrecht (1897–1965). Obergruppenfuehrer first chief of the **SS** in **France**. He secured an agreement with **Rene Bousquet**; whereby, the Vichy French would aggressively pursue enemies of the **Reich** in return for the autonomy of French police. In addition, the Germans would assume responsibility for selecting **hostages** to be shot. Oberg was tried and sentenced to death on October 9, 1954, by the French. Four years later his sentence was commuted to life imprisonment, and in 1965 he was pardoned by **General Charles de Gaulle**. Oberg was returned to Germany.
  SUGGESTED READING: Webster, *Petain's Crime.*

Obergruppenfuehrer. **SS** lieutenant-general.

Oberhauser, Herta (b. 1911). Physician and **war criminal**. She was a doctor at **Ravensbrueck** and assistant physician to **Dr. Karl Gerhardt** at Hohenlyohen Hospital. Oberhauser conducted inhuman, nonconsensual experiments on inmates causing death or permanent injury, particularly in 1942 and 1943. She was the only female defendant at the **Nuremberg Trials** and was sentenced to twenty years imprisonment by the American Military Tribunal **Doctors' Trial** in 1947. (See also **Irma Greese** and **Lapin**.)
  SUGGESTED READING: Aziz, *Doctors of Death.*

Oberjude (G., Jewish foreman). Jews who headed work brigades. (See also **Labor camp**.)

Oberkommando de Herres (OKH) (G., Supreme Army High Command). In 1941, **Hitler** gave them control of the war in the **Soviet Union** and told them they did not have to abide by the rules of war. (See also **Aktion Kugelerlass, Commissar Order,** and **Partisan Order.**)

Oberkommando der Wehrmacht (OKW) (G., Supreme Command of German Armed Forces). This body issued the directive for the war on the **Soviet Union** on June 4, 1941: "The total elimination of all **resistance** passive or active." This was a mandate for mass murder against military and civilian targets contravening all traditional rules of war. (See also **Aktion Kugelerlass, Commissar Order, Alfred Jodl, Wilhelm Keitel, Helmuth James Graf von Moltke, Partisan Order,** and **Field Marshal Walter von Reichenau.**)

Oberscharfuehrer. SS quartermaster or technical sergeant.

Oberschutze. SS private first class.

Oberstgruppenfuehrer. SS general.

Obersturmbannfuehrer. SS lieutenant-colonel.

Obersturmfuehrer. SS lieutenant.

Obman (G., chairman). Chief elder of a Jewish Council. (See **Judenaeltesten** and **Judenrat.**)

Oboz Narodowo Radykalny (E., Radical Nationalist Camp). (See **ONR.**)

Occupation Zones. After the capitulation of **Nazi Germany**, the country, along with **Austria**, was divided into American, British, French, and Soviet military occupation zones. Jews sought out **DP camps** in the **American Zone** believing they would be afforded better treatment. Military tribunals were established in all zones to try Nazi **war criminals** and to implement **denazification** proceedings. (See also **Earl Harrison** and **General George S. Patton.**)

October Deportation. On October 22, 1940, approximately 6,500 Jews from Baden (of which 3,800 were women) and 500 from Palatinate were deported to **Gurs** for "**resettlement.**" Out of this experimental **deportation**, only 550 survived.
  SUGGESTED READING: Zuccotti, *The Holocaust, the French, and the Jews.*

Odessa. (1) Port on the Black Sea in the **Ukraine** with a prewar Jewish population of 153,000. The city was conquered by the Romanians in October 1941. There was a large-scale massacre by Romanians of 60,000 Jews. Jews were assembled in the **ghetto** of **Slobodka,** near Odessa, where thousands more perished as a result of starvation, hypothermia, and execution. On April 10, 1944, the **Red Army liberated** the city. Its Jewish population gradually recovered to two-thirds of its prewar population (102,000 in 1959). (2) Term given to secret **SS** underground escape route after the war. (See **Ratline, Romania, SS Colonel Otto Skorzeny**, and **Transnistria**.)

SUGGESTED READINGS: Fisher, *Transnistria*; Wiesenthal, *The Murderers Among Us.*

Oeuvre de Secours aux Enfants Israelites (OSE) (Society for the Rescue of Jewish Children).

Office of Special Investigations (OSI). Established in 1979 as a branch of the Justice Department, as a result of investigations by the Congressional Committee on Immigration dealing with Nazi **war criminals** in the United States. Its agents investigated falsified immigration forms and statements by aliens upon entering this country. This office can prosecute war criminals in immigration court in order to **denaturalize, extradite**, or **deport** those who hid their participation in the **Final Solution**. (See also **Holtzman Amendment of the Immigration and Naturalization Acts**.)

SUGGESTED READINGS: Blum, *Wanted! The Search for Nazi War Criminals*; Saidel, *The Outraged Conscience.*

Office of Strategic Services. (See **OSS**.)

Ohlendorf, Otto (1907–1951). Senior Nazi official with **RSHA**. He was responsible for the mass murder of 90,000 Jews as commander of **Einsatzgruppe** D and acknowledged his instructions were issued in May 1941 "based on secret oral orders." He was headquartered in **Czernowitz**. Ohlendorf gave testimony at the initial **Nuremberg Trial** implicating the Einsatzgruppen of the murder of 90,000 Jews. He was the chief defendant at the **Subsequent Nuremberg Trials** (Einsatzkommando) sentenced to death, and hanged on June 8, 1951. (See also **Transnistria**.)

SUGGESTED READING: Hoehne, *The Order of the Death's Head.*

Ohrdruf ("S III"). Opened on November 6, 1944, as a sub-**concentration camp** of **Buchenwald**. Most of the 10,000 inmates at this site were transferred from other camps and used to build underground housing for the **SS** and German government officials. It was the first Nazi concentration camp **liberated** on the Western Front (April 4, 1945) and the first camp visited by **Generals Dwight David Eisenhower** and **George S. Patton** (April 12). The Americans who liberated the camp forced villagers to bury corpses in the center of town.

SUGGESTED READINGS: Abzug, *Inside the Vicious Heart*; Hackett, *The Buchenwald Report.*

OKH. (See **Oberkommando de Herres**.)

OKW. (See **Oberkommando der Wehrmacht**.)

Old Kingdom of Romania (Regat: old spelling Rumania or Roumania). Central and south central portion of **Romania** composed of Moldavia and Wallachia. Jews were not as harshly persecuted in this area, that is, of the 300,000 Romanian Jews exterminated, 20,000 were from this vicinity.

Omakaitse. Estonian nationalists. They assisted **Einsatzgruppe** A in the extermination of Jews and Soviet citizens. (See also **Estonia**.)

Onderduikers (Du., "Divers"). Name given to one faction of Dutch **resistance**. Most were "diving" to avoid labor in **Germany**. They did much to aid Jews. However, nearly 50 percent were denounced and tracked down. (See also **Netherlands**.)

186. The number of steps in the **Wienergraben** quarry at **Mauthausen**. Also referred to as the "**staircase of death**."

Oneg Shabbat (archivists) (H. and Y., Joy of Sabbath). Jewish social historians. They compiled notes, data, and documentation of **Warsaw Ghetto** life and the process of annihilation. The group was led by **Emmanuel Ringelblum** and collected 100 volumes of material. After the war, two milk cans and ten cases of records, documents, journals, and notes were unearthed. Historical documentation of **ghetto** conditions was forbidden by the Nazis and punishable by death.

"175er." Homosexual inmate. The number is derived from Paragraph 175, which was enacted in 1871 and amended in 1935. This statute criminalized male **homosexual** behavior in Germany. This law remained intact for several decades *after* the war.
    SUGGESTED READING: Plant, *The Pink Triangle*.

ONR (P., **Oboz Narodowo Radykalny**) (**Radical Nationalist Camp**). Ultra, right-wing Polish underground group. ONR opposed the **Polish Government-in-Exile** and was rabidly **anti-Semitic**. Its newspaper, *Ramparts*, approved of the German **genocide** of Polish Jews. ONR units attacked Jewish **partisans** and Jews in hiding.
    SUGGESTED READING: Gutman and Krakowski, *Unequal Victims*.

Operation Barbarossa. Code for German invasion of the **Soviet Union**, which began on June 22, 1941. The name is derived from a famous medieval German emperor, Frederick Barbarossa. The invasion encompassed a 930-mile front from the Baltic to Black Seas and was supported by **Albania, Finland, Hungary, Italy, Romania**, and **Slovakia. Hitler**, in direct violation of the **Geneva Convention** of War, issued a **Commissar Order**, which encouraged the summary execution of Soviet officers and Jews. Following closely behind the **Wehrmacht**, was the **Einsatzgruppen** and **Order Police** whose activities represent the beginning of the **Holocaust**. (See also **Partisan Order.**)

SUGGESTED READING: Dallin, *German Rule in Russia, 1941–1945*.

Operation Factory (G., **Fabrikaktion**). In February 1943, the **SS** entered workshops and factories in **Berlin**, seizing 2,000 Jewish men for **deportation** to **Auschwitz**. Over 6,000 German "**Aryan**" women married to the Jews staged a protest for six days outside of **Gestapo** headquarters. The men were released and the demonstrators were not prosecuted. On this rare occasion, a **transport** to Auschwitz was returned to Berlin. (See also **Privileged Jews** and **Operation Factory**.)

SUGGESTED READING: Prager, "Love Prevailed on the Street of Roses."

Operation Harvest Festival (G., **Erntefest**). The code term for a shooting massacre of Jews working in the **Generalgouvernement**. On November 3–4, 1943, **SS** and Ukrainian units organized by **Jacob Sporrenberg** started their mass murder on "**Bloody Wednesday**." At **Trawniki**, 8,000 to 10,000 Jews were shot, and at **Poniatowa** camp, 15,000 Jewish **resistance** prisoners were shot. At **Majdanek**, 18,400 were shot on November 3, 1945. A German report written May 24, 1944, estimated 90,000 to 150,000 Jews were annihilated by the **Aktion** that the Germans euphemistically called their "**Harvest Festival**." (See also **Jacob Sporrenberg**.)

SUGGESTED READING: Goldhagen, *Hitler's Willing Executioners*.

Operation Margarethe. German military code for the occupation of **Hungary**. Beginning March 19, 1944, the Germans occupied Hungary based on **Hitler's** correct suspicion that **Admiral Miklos Horthy** was negotiating peace terms with the **Allies**. The Germans installed a new prime minister, **Doeme Sztojay**, who intensified repression of Jews and allowed **transports** to proceed to **Auschwitz** on May 15, 1944.

SUGGESTED READING: Braham, *The Politics of Genocide*.

Operation Reinhard. (See **Aktion Reinhard**.)

Operation Valkyrie. The failed assassination attempt on **Hitler** on **July 20, 1944** (bomb plot), led by Colonel von Stauffenberg and General Beck. (See also **Sippenhaftung**.)

SUGGESTED READING: Galante, *Operation Valkyrie*.

Oranienburg. Small punishment camp near **Berlin** for political dissidents established on March 31, 1933. One of the first **concentration camps** in **Germany**, this site was closed by **Hermann Goering** around March 1935. However, the concentration camp **Sachsenhausen** was located in the town of Oranienburg, near Berlin. Oranienburg became a subcamp of Sachsenhausen. (See also **Heinkel Werke**, and **Sippenhaftung**.)

SUGGESTED READING: Gutman and Saf, *The Nazi Concentration Camps*.

Order Police. (See **Ordnungspolizei**.)

Ordnungsdienst (G., Order Service). (See **Jewish Service to Maintain Order**.)

Ordnungspolizei (G., **Order Police; Orpo**). Reserve police battalions under the control of Police General **Kurt Daluege**. Order Police, a terroristic and murderous group, were used to secure and hold down occupied areas in the East, particularly **Poland** and **Russia**. They guarded **ghettos** and controlled **Schutzpolizei**. They engaged in horrendous atrocities. The **Bletchley Park** decoders using **Ultra** material reported that German Order Police engaged in mass killing of Jews as early as July 1941 in the **Soviet Union**. Recent data has revealed that these **genocidal** activities of ordinary men, not front-line caliber soldiers, preceded even the **Einsatzgruppen**. (They are not to be confused with the **Wehrmacht's** military police Feldengendenmerie.) (See also **Erich von dem Bach-Zelewski**,"**Blue Police**," and **Enigma**.)

SUGGESTED READING: Browning, *Ordinary Men*; Goldhagen, *Hitler's Willing Executioners*.

Organizing. Theft, bartering, or stealing within the camps. A good organizer was admired and respected by inmates and Nazis. At **Auschwitz**, for example, an organizer could trade one day's bread for three cigarettes. For example, 200 cigarettes could be traded for one bottle of vodka. The vodka was for a bribe or an **arrangement**. However, a ration of bread was roughly equal to one day of life.

Orpo. (See **Ordnungspolizei**.)

ORT (Organization for Rehabilitation Through Training). Organization dedicated to providing Jews with trade and farm skills. Founded in **Russia** in 1880, it intended to replace traditional Jewish employment such as peddling, petty commerce, and liberal professions, for example, medicine and law, with vocational skills. After World War II, ORT set up free schools, vocational, and cooperative workshops in Europe and North Africa for displaced Jews. (See also **Displaced Persons**.)

SUGGESTED READING: Shamir and Shavit, *Encyclopedia of Jewish History*.

Orthodox Judaism. Denomination of religious thought that adheres to the belief of the divine origin of the Bible and the sacredness of the **Talmud**. It insists on strict adherence to the Code of Jewish Law (**Halakha**). Orthodox Judaism was dealt a terrible blow by the mass murder of most of its members in Eastern and Central Europe and the destruction of its learning centers. In America, its institutions criticized the **Zionist** organizations in the United States and **Yishuv** and diaspora mainstream Jewish organizations for their inadequate efforts to rescue Europe's Jews. (See also **Dr. Isaac Lewin, Mizrachi, Rabbi Joseph Isaac Schneersohn, Rabbi Solomon Schonfeld, Rita and Isaac Sternbuch, Union of Orthodox Rabbis of America,** and **Simon Zucker.**)

Ortsgruppenleiter (G., local German leader). **Nazi Party** official, subordinate to a Kreisleiter (a subordinate of a **Gauleiter.**) Until 1935, this official also served as a mayor of a town.

OSE (F., **Oeuvre de Secours aux Enfants Israelites**). (See **Society for the Rescue of Jewish Children**).
  SUGGESTED READINGS: Adler, *The Jews of Paris and the Final Solution*; Cohen, *The Burden of Conscience.*

Oshry, Rabbi Ephraim. A **Halakhic** (Jewish law) authority from **Kovno**. During the Nazi occupation of Kovno (June 1941–August 1944), he maintained that to fight the Germans until defeated was an obligation, thus encouraging support for Jewish **partisan** forces. He also reasoned that in order to save lives, one was released from most Jewish commandments. (See also **Pikuah Nefesh**.)
  SUGGESTED READING: Rosenbaum, *The Holocaust and the Halakhah.*

OSS (Office of Strategic Services). American intelligence organization. Created by President **Franklin Delano Roosevelt** in July 1942, it was charged with the collection and analysis of foreign information. The OSS worked with the British on **Ultra** to break the code of the German High Command **Enigma**. It knew of the **Final Solution**; photographs had been taken on April 4, 1944, of the **gas chambers** and **crematoria** at **Auschwitz**. The office ignored the photo documentation and hid the photographs in CIA archives until 1979. (See also **Special Operations Executive**.)
  SUGGESTED READING: Smith, *OSS.*

OST (G., Ostindustrie GmbH) (Eastern Industries, Ltd.). **SS** enterprises in the **Lublin** district that included brush and fur factories, iron works, and peat mines. Founded by the SS in March 1943, under **Oswold Pohl** in the **WVHA**, the Chief Executive Officer was **Odilo Globocnik**. When the 6,000 Jewish and 1,000 Polish **forced laborers** were **deported** to **death camps**, these industries ceased to exist.
  SUGGESTED READING: Hilberg, *The Destruction of European Jews.*

Ostarbeiter (G., Eastern worker). **Forced** or **slave laborer** from Nazi-occupied territories in the East **transported** to work in **Germany**. As of December 31, 1944, there were 2.5 million Russians, 911,000 Poles, and 1.8 million POWs.

Many Ostarbeiter were killed by lethal injection in 1944–1945 when they contracted TB. However, unlike the Jews, they were not slated for **genocide**. (See also **14 f 13, Fritz Sauckel**, and "**Special treatment**.")

Ostbahn (G., East railroad). East or Polish railroad system. During the war, **Bletchley Park** became aware of wide-scale rail deportations of Jews to the East. (See also **Deutsche Reichsbahn**.)

Ostbataillone (G., Eastern battalion). Units in the **Wehrmacht** composed of **Soviet collaborators** and **POWs**. Many of the units were trained in the **Generalgouvernement**, and in 1943, under **Hitler's** orders, most were sent to the Western Front. An estimated 1 million members were handed over to the Soviet government after the war where they were either executed or sent to gulags. (See also **Einsatzgruppen, Freiwillige, Hilfswillige, Latvian SS Legion, Lithuanian Activist Front, Perkonkrust**, and **Schuma**.)

Ostindustrie GmbH (G., **Eastern Territories** Industries, Ltd.). An **SS** company founded in 1943 under **Oswald Pohl** in **WVHA** with **Odilo Globocnik** as its director. Jewish prisoners worked as **slave laborers** in the **Lublin** area.

Ostjuden (G., East European Jews). Jews who emigrated from the East to **Germany**. These Jews comprised 20 percent of the German Jewish population. Ostjuden were more outwardly Jewish, religiously observant, spoke **Yiddish** rather than German, and worked lower level occupations such as artisans and peddlers. They were resented by Jewish and Gentile Germans alike. (See also **Kristallnacht** and **Yekkes**.)

Ostland (G., **Eastern Territories**). Nazi term for the occupied territories of **Estonia, Latvia, Lithuania**, and western **Belorussia**. The administration came under **Reichskommissariat Ostland**, headed by **Heinrich Lohse**.

Ostmark (G., Nazi term for occupied **Austria**). (See **Wilhelm Kube** and **Artur Seyss-Inquart**.)

Ostmensch (G., Eastern person). A **Slavic** person had an inferior **Aryan** status in the Nazi view; hence they were slated by Nazis for hard labor, virtual slave status. (See also **Herrenvolk**.)

Oswego, New York (**Fort Ontario**). Only free port established by President **Franklin Delano Roosevelt** as an **Emergency Refugee Shelter**. Free ports were advocated by the **War Refugee Board** to be part of a larger plan of rescue, but Oswego proved to be merely a political gesture. In August 1944, 982 European **refugees** (874 Jews) under **Allied** control in **Italy** were put aboard the army transport *Henry Gibbins* and shipped to America. The refugees signed papers promising to return to Europe at war's end. The refugees included Catholics, Protestants, Greek Orthodox, as well as Jews. Although they were warmly welcomed by the townspeople, they were housed behind barbed wire in the former Fort Ontario military base. President **Harry S. Truman** granted the refugees permanent citizenship. (See also **Emergency Committee to Save the Jewish People of Europe, Harold L. Ickes, John Pehle, Rescue Committee of the Jewish Agency in Turkey**, and **Eleanor Roosevelt**.)

SUGGESTED READING: Gruber, *Haven*.

Oswiecim (P.) (G., **Auschwitz**.) (1) Polish city located next to Auschwitz. Forty percent of the city's prewar inhabitants were Jewish. (2) Poles used this term to refer to the **concentration camp** complex.

OUN (Uk., Orhanizatsyia Ukrainsaykh Nationalistiv) (Nationalist Ukranian Organization). **Anti-Semitic** independence movement in the **Ukraine** and **Poland**. After the German occupation of Poland, it cooperated with the Nazis and formed two battalions in the German Army. The **Stefan Bandera** (1909–1959) faction, created in 1940 (OUN-Bandera) became the majority. Frustrated by the failure of Germans to recognize Ukrainian independence, it resisted both occupation and the **Soviet Union**. This group existed into the 1950s when they were crushed by the Soviets. (See also **Galicia** and **Galician SS**.)

SUGGESTED READING: Sabin, *Alliance for Murder*.

Outworkers (also referred to as ''the outposts''). Jews who worked on the **Aryan** side of the **Warsaw Ghetto**. These Jews were required to wear an armband with the Star of David while they labored outside the **ghetto** walls.

OVRA (I., Operazione di Vigilanza per la Repressione dell' Antifascismo). **Fascist** secret police in **Italy**. Counterpart to the **Gestapo**, they were charged with investigating and arresting antifascists. A disproportionate number of Jews were arrested by OVRA.

P

"P." Marking on triangle denoting Polish Christian inmate in the **concentration camps**. It was also found on the badge of Polish **forced laborers**.

Pacelli, Cardinal Eugenio. (See **Pope Pius XII.**)

Pale (Pale of Settlement). Refers to land in Czarist **Russia** from the Baltic to Black Sea where Jews were confined in the **Partition of Poland** in the 1790s. **Poland** inherited most of this area when it gained its independence in 1918. The rich Jewish cultural and religious institutions were wiped out by the Nazis. (See also **Shtetl**.)

Palestine. Mideastern region, south of Lebanon and Syria, bordering the Mediterranean Sea. It was the site of the Jewish National Homeland promised by the **Balfour Declaration, League of Nations**, and **British Mandate**. From 1933–1939, 215,232 Jews, mostly European **refugees**, immigrated to the Jewish homeland. After May 1939, the British sealed Palestine and prohibited Jewish immigration based on their 1939 **White Paper** policies. Approximately 25,000 **Yishuv** Jews joined the British forces to fight the Nazis. In 1948, part of the region became Israel. The western part was the Kingdom of Jordan. (See also **Appeasement, Grand Mufti of Jerusalem, Haganah, Irgun Zvai Leumi, Ze'ev Jabotinsky, Jewish Agency, Jewish Brigade, "Parachutists," Rescue Committee of the Jewish Agency in Turkey, Moshe Shertok, Youth Aliyah, Zionism**, and **Zionist Revisionists**.)

Palestine Certificates (or immigration permits). Restrictions were placed on Jewish entry into **Palestine** by the **White Paper** of 1939. The immigration

documents or **visas** were issued by the **British Mandatory** government permitting the bearer to enter Palestine. They were extremely difficult to obtain. People who possessed Palestine certificates were held by Germans for possible exchange with German nationals living in Palestine. The **Jewish Agency** was responsible for issuing Palestinian certificates through its network of Palestine offices at various places (even in Nazi Europe). It often meant life or death. From May 17, 1939–May 13, 1949, the restrictive British policy was in effect. Only 1,500 legal certificates a year were permitted. By the end of August 1943, Jews who reached Turkey on their own were issued a **visa**, a gesture of the British after widespread **Holocaust** publicity. The Agency official, in addition to administering legal immigration, also organized "illegal" or uncertified immigration. (See also **Aliya Bet**, **Bricha**, and **Exchange Jews**.)
SUGGESTED READING: Wasserstein, *Britain and the Jews of Europe*.

Pankiewicz, Tadeusz. Polish **Righteous Gentile**. He maintained a pharmacy within the confines of the **Krakow Ghetto**, thus being in a position to witness events. He assisted Jews in many ways. His book *The Krakow Ghetto Pharmacy* (1947) sheds light on the end of the Jewish community of that city and the **Plaszow concentration camp**.

Papen, Franz von (1879–1969). German diplomat. He urged **Paul von Hindenburg** to appoint **Hitler** chancellor, thinking that he and other conservative politicians could control the Nazis. von Papen served as Vice-Chancellor under Hitler and negotiated the **Concordat** with the **Vatican**. After he witnessed Nazi excesses, von Papen protested the Nazi dictatorship in the Marburg Address (1934). He was arrested, his assistant was murdered, and **Dr. Paul Joseph Goebbels** suppressed the protest speech. His resignation was rejected by **Hitler**. von Papen attempted to resign again after the **Ernst Roehm** purge and was rebuffed by Hitler. The diplomat was ambassador to **Austria** during the **Anschluss** and an ambassador to Turkey: He kept that nation neutral during the war. He was tried by the **International Military Tribunal**, but acquitted.
SUGGESTED READINGS: Fest, *The Face of the Third Reich*; Taylor, *The Anatomy of the Nuremberg Trials*.

Papon, Maurice (b. 1910). **Vichy** official and French budget minister (1970s.) He was ordered to stand trial for **crimes against humanity**. Papon was involved in **deporting** 1,690 Jews between 1942–1944; most of those deported were murdered at **Auschwitz**. Charges against Papon are now pending in **France**, and he will probably be the last Frenchman tried for crimes against humanity. (See also **Rene Bousquet** and **Paul Touvier**.)
SUGGESTED READING: Webster, *Petain's Crime*.

"Parachutists." (1) Thirty-two Jews from the **Yishuv**, originally from Eastern Europe, deployed in the Balkans and **Austria** to rescue Jews and spy for the

British. (2) Term used when a Nazi pushed an inmate over the edge of the **Wienergraben** quarry in **Mauthausen**. (See also **Haganah, Ernst Kaltenbrunner, Haviva Reik, Enzo Sereni**, and **Hannah Szenes**.)

Partial Solution. Term applied to **France's** initial policy of allowing only non-French Jews to be **deported**. (See also **Bulgaria**.)

Partisan. Indigenous, underground armed **resistance** to Nazi rule based in rural areas. Jews were often rebuffed from joining regular military forces in **Poland, Lithuania**, and **Russia**; hence, many formed separate units. However, due in part to Jewish resistance, **Heinrich Himmler** prohibited the use of the term ''partisan'' in the summer of 1942. (See also **Tuvia Bielski, Croatia**, and **Tito**.)

Partisan Order. General **Wilhelm Keitel**, at **Hitler's** behest, issued the order upon the invasion of the **USSR**. This was a gross violation of international law. ''Every case of rebellion against German occupation forces . . . must be of communistic origin. . . . As atonement for the life of one German soldier, the death penalty for fifty to one hundred Communists is generally considered proper.'' Most often it was difficult to identify communists. Field Marshall **Walter von Reichenau** interpreted the Order to murder Jews. ''The army must annihilate revolts in the hinterlands, which as experience proves, have always been caused by Jews.'' The mass murder at **Babi Yar** was based on this interpretation. (See also **Commissar Order**.)
　　SUGGESTED READING: Conot, *Justice at Nuremberg*.

Partition of Poland. In September 1939, the German army moving from west to east, and the **Red Army** moving west to east, crushed **Poland**. As agreed to by the **Molotov-Ribbentrop Pact** of August 1939, the country was partitioned between the two powers. **Germany** annexed into the **Greater Reich** the western part of its section (**Warthegau**) and created a **Generalgouvernement**, which it ruled militarily. The Soviets incorporated its half using the Bug and San Rivers as boundaries. An independent Poland ceased to exist. The Jewish population of Poland was 3.3 million in a Polish population of 34.7 million. Two million Jews lived in the German zone of 73,000 square miles, while in the Soviet zone the Jewish population was 1.3 million. The Nazis instituted almost immediately a torrent of persecution against Jews and random **Aktionen**, as well as **deportation** to the Generalgouvernement. The Soviets deported so-called Jewish ''capitalists'' to **Siberia** and curtailed Jewish religious and communal organizations. About 250,000 Jews fled to the Soviet area. (See also **Danzig**.)
　　SUGGESTED READING: Bethell, *The War Hitler Won*.

Passeur (F., ferryman). In **France**, an individual who was paid to help someone escape to **Vichy** France or a Nazi-free area, that is **Spain, Switzerland, Italy**, or the Italian zone in Vichy.

Passierschein (G., safe-conduct pass). Document issued to **ghetto** dwellers who had special business valuable to the Germans and who had to leave the ghetto in order to perform these duties.

Passport (G., **Reispass**). A formal document issued by one's native country to travel outside the country. It certifies the identity of the bearer. The **Reich** added a big red "**J**" at the request of the Swiss government. The Nazis added a middle name "**Israel**" or "**Sarah**" to German Jewish passports (January 1, 1939). A major problem for Jews was obtaining a **visa**. (See also **Dr. Heinrich Rothmund**.)

Patria. Jewish **refugee** ship outside of Haifa. It was used by the British to **deport** "illegals," but was sunk by the **Haganah** on November 25, 1940. The Haganah had aimed to cripple the ship, but the operation was poorly planned and executed, and 250 passengers drowned. Some 1,900 survivors were granted amnesty and admitted into **Palestine** by the British; however, 1,600 refugees scheduled to be transferred to the *Patria* went to **Mauritius**. (See also **Mossad le Aliya Bet** and **White Paper**.)
SUGGESTED READING: Steiner, *The Story of the Patria*.

Patton, General George S. (1885–1945). American general and commander of the U.S. Third Army. His men overran several **concentration camps** in Germany. After the war, Patton was appointed military governor of Bavaria. He was an **anti-Semite** who opposed the prosecution of Nazi **war criminals**. He countermanded **General Dwight David Eisenhower's** orders and hired ex-Nazis for civil posts. Patton also sought to keep Jewish **DPs** out of the **American Zone of Occupation**. He stated "[The] Jewish type of DP is, in the majority of cases, a sub-human species without any of the cultural or social refinements of our time." (See also **Ohrdruf**.)
SUGGESTED READINGS: Blumenson, *The Patton Papers*; United States Holocaust Memorial Museum, *1945: The Year of Liberation*.

Pauly, Max (1907–1946). Kommandant of **Stutthof** (1939–1942) and **Neuengamme** (1942–1945). He was sentenced to death by the American Military Tribunal and executed in October 1946.
SUGGESTED READING: Segev, *Soldiers of Evil*.

Pavelic, Anton (1889–1959). **Ustashi** leader and Croatian chief of state from 1941–1945. Under his regime, Jews lost their possessions, rights, and eventually were murdered. He escaped justice by fleeing to Argentina. (See also **Andrija Artukovic, Croatia**, **Jasenovac,** and **Ratline**.)
SUGGESTED READING: Rhodes, *The Vatican in the Age of Dictators*.

Pawiak (Pawia) **Street Prison**. Old prison in Warsaw used by Nazis to incarcerate and torture Poles and Jews suspected of underground activities. Of the 100,000 Polish citizens incarcerated at this site, 85 percent were Catholic and the remainder were Jews. Approximately 37,000 inmates were executed on the prison grounds, and 60,000 were sent to **concentration camps**, particularly **Auschwitz**. Death certificates were only issued for Catholic inmates. An antechamber was set up for Jews caught hiding in **Aryan** Warsaw during the **Warsaw Polish Uprising**. Forty Jewish inmates successfully escaped from the prison. (See also **Dr. Ludwig Hahn, Hotel Polski**, and **Irena Sendler**.)
  SUGGESTED READING: Hirshaut, *Jewish Martyrs of Pawiak.*

Pechersky, Aleksander (1909–1996). Officer in the **Red Army**. A POW, he and **Leon Feldhandler**, both Jews, established a clandestine revolt organization at **Sobibor**. The uprising occurred on October 14, 1943, and facilitated the closure of the **death camp**. About 350 rebels participated and 600 inmates broke out. Although most were captured and killed, Pechersky and about sixty remained free and joined various **partisan** groups.
  SUGGESTED READING: Novitch, *Sobibor, Martyrdom and Revolt.*

Peenemuende Aerodynamics Institute. German long-range, rocket testing site in the Baltic Sea. After severe bombing in 1943, the facility was transferred to the Hartz Mountains. The German government has been criticized for proposing a "space center" at this site in 1994. (See also **Wernher von Braun, Dora-Nordhausen, Mittelbau-Mittelwerk**, and **Arthur Rudolph**.)
  SUGGESTED READING: Neufeld, *The Rocket and the Reich.*

Pehle, John (b. 1909). Head of the Foreign Funds Control section in the U.S. Treasury Department. He was sympathetic to the rescue of Jews. He and **Henry Morganthau Jr**. met with **Franklin Delano Roosevelt** and handed the president a version of the memorandum drawn up by **Josiah DuBois**. This led to the creation of the **War Refugee Board** (1944). As director of the War Refugee Board, he strongly supported the establishment of **Oswego (Fort Ontario)**, published the **Auschwitz Protocols** (for which he was criticized by the Office of War Information), and advocated bombing the tracks and **crematoria** at **Auschwitz**. He and **Herbert Pell** argued that all persons who committed crimes against "**Axis** Jews" should be prosecuted as **war criminals**.
  SUGGESTED READINGS: Feingold, *The Politics of Rescue*: Morse, *While Six Million Died.*

Pell, Herbert (1884–1961). American diplomat. Appointed by President **Franklin Delano Roosevelt** in June 1943 to the **United Nation War Crimes Commission**. He proposed that crimes against individuals in groups based on race be included as **war crimes** even if the crimes were committed by leaders against their own people. The State Department ousted Pell in January 1945, but his removal created a controversy that forced the agency to reverse its position and support holding Japanese and German leaders and their subordinates responsible for war crimes. (See also **John Pehle**.)

SUGGESTED READINGS: Blayner, ''Herbert Pell''; Wyman, *The Abandonment of the Jews.*

Pellepoix, Louis Darquier. **Vichy** official. He succeeded **Xavier Vallat** as chief of Jewish Affairs in the Vichy government from 1942–1944. Pellepoix coordinated the **deportation** of French Jewry and called the **Final Solution** a ''Jewish Invention'' from exile in Madrid (1978).

SUGGESTED READING: Marrus, ''Coming to Terms With Vichy.''

People's Court (G., Volksgerichtshof). Treason trial court for ''enemies of the **Reich**.'' From 1942 until February 1945, the Court was headed by **Dr. Roland Freisler**. The judicial panel contained two professional judges, five individuals selected by the **Nazi Party, SS**, and armed forces. Its proceedings were ideological, swift, and held *in cameria*. From 1934 to 1945, the People's Court condemned 12,000 civilians to death in **concentration camps**. The Germans the Court prosecuted included **Pastor Martin Niemoeller, Helmuth James Graf von Moltke**, members of the **White Rose**, and the **July 20, 1944 Bomb Plotters**. (See also **Otto Thierack**.)

SUGGESTED READING: Mueller, *Hitler's Justice.*

People's Youth. (See **Volksjugend**.)

Perkonkrust. (See **Thundercross**.)

Pernkopf, Dr. Eduard Dean of faculty at the Medical Faculty of **Vienna**. A pro-Nazi physician, he worked on an anatomical atlas utilizing data from children killed in a Viennese hospital. Pernkopf also used corpses of executed opponents of Nazism for teaching purposes. He was briefly imprisoned after the war, released, and allowed to complete his anatomical atlas. (See also **Dr. Wilhelm Beigelboeck** and **Dr. Hans Eppinger**.)

SUGGESTED READING: Ernst, ''A Leading Medical School Seriously Damaged.''

Persil-Schein (G., joke card). Slang for the **denazification** certificate distributed to ''repentant'' Nazis by the **Allies**.

Petain, Marshal Henri Philippe (1856–1951). Head of **collaborationist Vichy** government. A French war hero of World War I, he enjoyed immense prestige and public support in **France**. Petain signed several major decrees restricting Jewish rights and freedoms. He offered French police and militias to assist Nazis in the roundup of Jews for **deportation** and served the Germans until the end of the war. His death sentence was commuted to life in prison by **General Charles de Gaulle**. Petain died in prison. (See also **Pierre Laval**.)

SUGGESTED READINGS: Roy, *The Trial of Marshall Petain*; Webster, *Petain's Crime*.

Petliura, Simon (1879–1926). Military commander and Ukrainian head-of-state from 1917–1920. He was a fierce **anti-Semite** who coordinated large-scale **pogroms** that resulted in the deaths of 60,000 Jews. Petliura was assassinated in Paris on May 25, 1926, by a Ukrainian Jew who lost fifteen relatives during one of the pogroms. The anniversary date of his death was moved back to symbolically highlight these pogroms. In 1992, the Ukrainians named a street in **Lvov** after him. (See also **Ukraine**.)

SUGGESTED READING: Friedman, *Pogromchik*.

Petliura Days. Pogrom incited and carried out by Ukrainian nationalists against the Jews in **Lvov** from July 25–July 27, 1941. This pogrom was encouraged by the Nazis. The Jewish intelligentsia was wiped out based on lists supplied by Ukrainian police. All told, 2,000 Jews were murdered. The pogrom gets its name from the last premier of an independent **Ukraine**, General **Simon Petliura**.

SUGGESTED READING: Kahana, *Lvov Ghetto Diary*.

Pfannmueller, Dr. Hermann (1886–1961). Nazi physician and director of Eglfing-Haar State Hospital. An institutional psychiatrist closely associated with the **T-4** program, he was an early advocate of **euthanasia**. Pfannmueller boasted about starving children to death in **Hungerhausen**. He gave testimony at the **Nuremberg Trails** and also in a postwar West German court, but he was not tried at the **Doctors' Trial**.

SUGGESTED READING: Lifton, *The Nazi Doctors*.

Philipp Holzmann. German construction company that exploited **concentration camp** labor at **Stutthof**.

SUGGESTED READING: Ferencz, *Less Than Slaves*.

"Pieces" (G. and Y., stucke). Corpses. The Nazis never considered the humanity of their victims. (See also **Dehumanization**.)

"Pigs Corner." Area at **Flossenbuerg** where those **selected** for gassing were taken. Inmates assigned to this area were marked with a red cross on their foreheads.

Pikkolo (G., apprentice waiter). Inmate messenger and clerk in the **concentration camp**.

Pikuah Nefesh (H., for the sake of life). Jewish precept that permits rabbis in periods of extreme persecution to waive the observance of rituals and most commandments in order to preserve life. (See also **Halakha** and **Rabbi Ephraim Oshry**.)

Pilenko, Sister Elizabeth (d. 1945) (Mother Marie). Also known as **Elizabeta Skobtsova**, she became a nun after leading a secular life, including marriage. Pilenko embarked on her mission of aiding and rescuing Jews in Paris. She smuggled out children at the **Velodrome d'Hiver**. Pilenko was captured by the **Gestapo** in 1943 and sent to **Ravensbrueck**. At this **concentration camp**, Sister Pilenko exchanged her **Aryan** card with a Jewish woman. She saved the other woman's life, but she perished at the camp on March 31, 1945. Mother Marie was recognized by **Yad Vashem** as a **Righteous Gentile**.
SUGGESTED READING: Paldiel, *The Path of the Righteous.*

Pimpf (G., lad). German boys 10 to 14 years old who began entry-level indoctrination into the **Hitler Youth**. As members of the **Jungvolk** they had to learn Nazi dogma, pass vigorous athletic feats, and participate in small arms drills.

Pink Triangle. Patch worn by **homosexual** inmates who were also known as "**175ers**." Prior to the pink triangles, homosexuals were identified by a black dot on a patch in the camp complex. The triangle's vertex was pointed down with an inmates' camp number sewn underneath. (See also **Asocials**.)

Pinsk. City in **Belorussia** located in Pripet marshes. It was the last and largest Jewish **ghetto** in German-occupied territory in the **USSR**. In 1941 it had a Jewish population of 30,000. It was the site of mass executions of 16,000 Jews by **Einsatzgruppe** A in October 1942.

Piorkowski, Alex (d. 1948). Kommandant of **Dachau**. He was condemned to death by the Americans and executed in October 1948.
SUGGESTED READING: Segev, *Soldiers of Evil.*

Pister, Hermann (1885–1948). Kommandant of **Buchenwald**. He ignored pleas to liquidate the camp and transferred 20,000 Jewish inmates to other camps from April 3–10, 1945. Most of the prisoners died in transit. He was condemned to death by an American tribunal. Pister committed suicide in September 1948.
SUGGESTED READING: Hackett, *The Buchenwald Report.*

Pithiviers. First French **internment** and **transit camp** opened in May 1941, 65 miles south of Paris. (Beaune-la-Rolande was created at about the same time). Conditions were poor, but better than in **concentration camps**. The **Vichy** government **transported** 3,700 Jews to **Auschwitz** from this site. A separate camp

for **Roma** children was also maintained at Pithiviers. (See also **French Internment and Transit Camps**.)
SUGGESTED READING: Zuccotti, *The Holocaust, the French and the Jews*.

Plaszow. **Labor camp** opened in 1942 outside of **Krakow** for Polish political and religious prisoners. The facility was "upgraded" to a **concentration camp** in January 1944. At this point, the **Death's Head Brigade** units replaced the Ukrainian guards and operated the facility. The camp was predominantly composed of Jewish inmates, but after the Polish revolt in Warsaw, the number of Polish political prisoners increased. The camp's population peaked in the spring of 1943 at around 24,000. The most barbarous crimes were committed under the leadership of **Amon Goeth**. On January 14, 1945, Plaszow's surviving prisoners were evacuated to **Auschwitz**. (See also **Heinkel Werke**.)
SUGGESTED READING: Gutman and Saf, *The Nazi Concentration Camps*.

"Pleasure Hours." Intimidation, harassment, and beating of Jews after the Nazi seizure of power in **Germany**.

Ploetz, Dr. Alfred (1860–1940). Father of "race hygiene" (1894) in **Germany** and co-founder of the German Society for **Racial Hygiene**. At first he viewed the Jews as **Aryans**, but after a long relationship with **Hitler**, he joined the **Nazi Party** and condemned the Jews. His ideas of sterilization, **euthanasia**, and state-controlled marriages were adopted by the **Third Reich**. (See also **Eugenics** and **Dr. Ernst Ruedin**.)
SUGGESTED READING: Proctor, *Racial Hygiene*.

Pogrom (Ru., attack). This term became synonymous with an organized riot and massacre of Jews with complicity of the authorities. In certain areas of **Poland**, the Baltics, and **Russia**, the entry of the German Army precipitated pogroms against Jews. A major pogrom occurred after the war in **Kielce**. (See also **Belorussia, Iasi, Kielce, Kristallnacht, Lithuanian Activist Front, Lvov, Petliura Days, Simon Petliura, Rashid Ali al-Gaylani, Sarajevo, Self-cleansing, Horia Sima, Ferenc Szalasi, Tarnopol**, and **Zolochev**.)

Pohl, Oswald (1892–1951). Head of the **SS's** powerful **Economic and Administrative Main Office (WVHA)** from 1942–1945. He managed the SS's multifaceted financial empire derived from the looted goods of **concentration camp** inmates sent back to **Germany**. Pohl's department was responsible for overseeing the construction of **death** and concentration camps, which meant he controlled a **slave labor** pool of over 500,000 to 600,000 concentration camp inmates. Pohl was tried by the U.S. Military Tribunal, convicted, and executed. (See also **Labor Camp**.)
SUGGESTED READINGS: Ferencz, *Less Than Slaves*; Tenenbaum, *Race and Reich*.

Poisoned Mushroom. **Anti-Semitic**, elementary school book published by **Julius Streicher** to instill hatred of Jews.

Poland. Nation located between the **Soviet Union** and **Germany**. The **Versailles Treaty** established a Polish corridor and made **Danzig** a free city under nominal Polish rule. This separated East Prussia, a part of Germany, from the heart of Germany. World War II in Europe started with the German invasion of Poland (September 1, 1939), which brought Great Britain and **France**, allied with Poland, into the fray. As early as September 21, 1939, all communities with less than 500 Jews had to dissolve, their residents to go to larger ones. As of December 12, 1939, all Jewish males age 14 to 60 were to serve two years of **forced labor**. About 10 percent (3.3 million) of the Polish population was Jewish. Over 3 million Polish Jews were murdered. The major **death camps**— **Treblinka, Sobibor, Belzec, Auschwitz, Chelmno**, and **Majdanek**—were located in the eastern part of the country. (See also **Armia Krajowa, Armia Ludowa, Bedzin, Hans Frank, Generalgouvernement, NSZ, Partition of Poland, Polish Government-in-Exile, Polish Workers' Party**, and **Warsaw Ghetto**.)

Polish Army in England. Remnants of Polish military who escaped and fled to England. After the fall of Poland they were under the aegis of the **Polish Government-in-Exile**. Hundreds of Jews asked to be transferred to the British Army due to **anti-Semitism**. However, Jews did fight alongside Polish Catholics when this army was engaged in the battle of Monte Cassino, **Italy**, in the winter of 1944.

SUGGESTED READING: Ainsztein, *"The Enemy Within: Anti-Semitism Among Polish Soldiers in War-Time Britain."*

Polish Government-in-Exile. Located in **France** after the German-Russian occupation in 1939 and relocated to London after the fall of France in 1940. Several Jews were affiliated with this body, which also supported **Zegota** and the **Jewish National Committee**. It received dispatches from the **Armia Krajowa** about the **Final Solution**. The Government-in-Exile was apprised of the fate of the Jews via a cable from the Polish underground in the summer of 1942. It urged the **Allies** to initiate a retaliation plan against Germany, but to no avail. It also encouraged the **Warsaw Polish Uprising**. Its diplomatic pouch from agents in **Switzerland** proved to be an invaluable source of information on the Jewish **genocide**. (See also **Bund, Delagatura, Dr. Isaac Lewin, ONR, Poland, Polish Army in England. Ignacy Isaac Schwarzbart, Wladyslaw Sikorski, SWIT**, and **Shmuel Artur Zygielbojm**.)

SUGGESTED READING: Lukas, *Forgotten Holocaust*.

Polish Home Army. (See **Armia Krajowa** and **Henryk "Waclaw" Wolinski**.)

Polish Workers Party (PPR). Established in January 1942, replacing the defunct Communist Party. It resisted Nazi occupation and favored an independent socialist **Poland** with ties to Stalinist Russia. PPR cooperated with the **ZOB** and supplied them with some arms during the **Warsaw Ghetto Uprising**. The party was sympathetic to Jews and some members worked with **Zegota**.
   SUGGESTED READING: Gutman and Krakowski, *Unequal Victims.*

Political Department-Section (G., Politische Abeteilung-amt). Feared **SS** entity within the **concentration camp** complex. This **Gestapo** department conducted interviews, prepared dossiers on camp inmates, and crushed attempts at escapes.

Politische Abeteilung-amt (G.). (See **Political Department-Section.**)

Polonski, Abraham (b. 1903). Engineer and co-founder of the **Armee juive** in **France**. He espoused a Jewish and **Zionist** ideology and argued that a Jewish army would be valuable after the war in the creation of a Jewish state. Polonski survived the war and became a member of **Bricha**.
   SUGGESTED READING: Latour, *The Jewish Resistance in France.*

Ponary (L., Paneriai). Site of "death pits" outside of **Vilna (Vilnus)** where 70,000 Jews were massacred between 1941–1944 during German occupation. The Nazis were aided by Lithuanian Security Police. The massacres led to the creation of Jewish **partisan** movements in Vilna. (See also **Abba Kovner, Lithuania**, and **Vilnius Sonderkommando.**)
   SUGGESTED READING: Arad, *The Ghetto in Flames.*

Poniatowa. Slave labor camp near **Lublin**. Approximately 10,000 Jews worked for **Toebbens** at this site. Most of the guards were Ukrainian **collaborators**. Despite a revolt by members of the underground on the night of November 3–4, 1943, 15,000 Jews were murdered at the camp as part of the **Erntefest** program. A few survivors managed to escape before the camp's liquidation. (See also **Emmanuel Ringelblum.**)
   SUGGESTED READING: Arad, *Belzec, Sobibor, and Treblinka.*

Pope John XXIII. (See **Angelo Roncalli.**)

Pope Pius XI (Achille Ratti) (1857–1939). Pope from 1922–1939. He negotiated the **Concordat** with **Benito Mussolini**. He authorized **Cardinal Eugenio Pacelli (Pope Pius XII)** to draw up the Concordat (1933) with **Germany**. Pope Pius XI soon realized **Hitler** had no intention of honoring the treaty. Pius condemned Nazi violations and issued an encyclical entitled *Mit brennender Sorge*. Recent revelations indicate that the Pope was prepared to condemn Nazi persecution of Jews. (See also **Franz von Papen** and **Edith Stein.**)

SUGGESTED READINGS: Lewy, *The Catholic Church and Nazi Germany*; Rhodes, *The Vatican in the Age of Dictators.*

Pope Pius XII (Monsignor Eugenio Pacelli) (1876–1958). Pope from 1939–1958. As **nuncio** to **Berlin**, he negotiated and signed the **Concordat** with the Nazis on July 20, 1933, in **Rome**. His vehement anticommunist beliefs led to his conviction that Nazi Germany was a bulwark against Godless Bolshevism. The **Vatican** was a source of diplomatic information for the United States and confirmed the destruction of European Jewry to U.S. envoys **Myron Taylor** and **Harold H. Tittman**. Pius permitted clergy to assist Jews and ordered various sanctuaries to shelter Jews (5,000 were given haven) during German **deportations** in Rome. He also pleaded with **Admiral Miklos Horthy** in 1944 to stop deporting Hungarian Jews to **Auschwitz** and asked **Dr. Josef Tiso** to spare Jews in **Slovakia** who had converted to Catholicism. In addition, he issued an encyclical condemning **euthanasia**. Many historians have questioned why Pope Pius XII was unwilling to use the full force of his moral authority to condemn the **Final Solution**. The pope maintained after the war that he spoke secretly to the College of Cardinals condemning the **Holocaust**. His conclusion was that any public proclamation would be futile and endanger the position of the Church. In 1948, he requested mercy for all Nazi **war criminals** condemned to death, a plea denied by **General Lucius D. Clay**. (See also **"Black Saturday," Bishop Alois Hudal, Hungary, Jules Isaac,** *Mystici Corporis*, **Franz von Papen, Pope Pius XI, Ratline, Angelo Roncalli, Metropolitan Andrej Szeptyekyj, Ernst von Weizsacker,** and **Rabbi Stephen S. Wise.**)

SUGGESTED READINGS: Friedlander, *Pius XII and the Third Reich*; Graham, *Vatican Diplomacy*; Lewy, *The Catholic Church and Nazi Germany.*

Popovici, Traian. Mayor of **Cernauti (Czernowitz), Romania**. He delayed **deportations** from **Bukovina**, issuing exemption documents, that is, "Popovici papers" for thousands of Jews from 1941–1942. He acted courageously while **Ion Antonescu** was in power. Popovici is credited with saving over 17,000 Jews. He lost his job due to his stance. Popovici was honored as a **Righteous Gentile**.

SUGGESTED READING: Butnaru, *Waiting for Jerusalem.*

Population Transfers. After the German surrender (1945), there were huge transfers of population based largely on ethnicity. The Czechs expelled 3 million **Sudeten** Germans and 700,000 Magyars (Hungarians). The Poles expelled 12 million Germans in the territories ceded to them after World War II. Poles were particularly angry at **Volksdeutsche** for their role during the Nazi occupation. The **USSR** and the reconstructed **Poland**, both having new boundaries, which moved them westward, exchanged populations.

Porraimos. (Romani, "the devouring"). Term for the destruction of approximately 500,000 European **Roma, Sinti**, and **Lalleri**. (See also **Churban, Gypsy, Holocaust**, and **Shoah**.)

Portugal. Neutral, **fascist** nation led by **Antonio de Oliveria Salazar**. Portugal adopted a vacillating policy toward the admittance of Jews and did not institute anti-Jewish laws against their small Jewish population of 3,000. However, thousands of **refugees** were able to escape to Portugal from **Vichy France** and through **Francisco Franco's Spain**. Lisbon was a base of operations for Jewish organizations on the Iberian peninsula. According to a **HICEM** report, between 1940 and the fall of 1942, 10,500 Jews sailed to freedom from Portuguese ports. In 1943, Portugal instituted a more liberal entry and transit policy. In July 1944, Portugal joined other nations in granting Jews consular protection from German occupation. In Budapest, the Portuguese issued 698 **Schutzpaesse**. However, Portugal's banking industry laundered gold from Nazi victims, gold sent from **Switzerland**. (See also **Hungary** and **Aristide de Sousa Mendes**.)
   SUGGESTED READING: Figueiredo, Portugal.

Posen (Poznan) Speech. On October 4, 1943, **Heinrich Himmler** addressed SS officers and other party officials, including **Albert Speer**. He admitted the mass murder of Jews and stated: "We had the moral right, and the duty, toward our nation to kill this people which wished to kill us." Himmler added he had no interest in the fate of **Slavs**, including Poles, Czechs, Russians, Ukrainians, and other conquered peoples. This speech, noted by officers, was a prime piece of evidence of the **Final Solution**. (See also **Sippenhaftung** and **Uentermenschem**.)
   SUGGESTED READING: Breitman, The Architect of Genocide.

Potsdam Conference. Summit meeting between **Winston Churchill, Josef Stalin**, and **Harry S. Truman** from July 17–August 2, 1945. Among the issues settled was the formation of an **International Military Tribunal** to try **war criminals**. The trial of the top Nazis at Nuremberg grew out of the Conference.
   SUGGESTED READING: Drexel, Encyclopedia of the 20th Century.

PPR. (See **Polish Workers Party**.)

Press Gangs. Men dragged off the street for **forced labor** by Germans and their **collaborators**.

Priebke, Erich (b. 1913). **SS** captain and second in command in Rome. He escaped from a British prison camp and later was **extradited** from Argentina to **Italy** for his participation in the **Ardeantine Caves** massacre. Priebke was acquitted of **war crimes** by an Italian military court on August 1, 1996. The Court reasoned he was following orders, and the statute of limitations was applicable. However, on October 15, 1996, Italy's highest court, the Court of Cassation, ordered a retrial based on the bias of the lead judge in the military court. However, after Italian public outrage he was convicted by another military court.

Priebke was given a five-year sentence of which he served only six months. (See also **Herbert Kappler** and **Joseph Schwammberger**.)

SUGGESTED READINGS: New York Times, October 16, 20, 1996; April 15, 1997.

Priesterblock (G., Priest block). **Block** 26 at **Dachau**. Incarcerated clergy, mostly Catholic priests, were imprisoned in this section of the camp. (See also **Dr. Claus Schilling**.)

Primitivbauweise (G., primitive way of construction). Concept formalized by **Albert Speer** after visiting **Mauthausen** in 1943. In a letter to **Heinrich Himmler**, he recommended camp inmates use poor materials and work with their bare hands.

Pritchard, Marion (b. 1920). **Dutch Righteous Gentile**. She found hiding places, provided medical care, and identity cards for Jews. In one instance, she killed a policeman to protect Jews she was hiding. Currently, she is a psychoanalyst practicing in the United States.

SUGGESTED READING: Block and Drucker, *Rescuers*.

Privileged Jews. Jews from large German cities with **Aryan** spouses or parents from "mixed" races. **Adolf Eichmann** temporarily postponed their murder after the **Wannsee Conference**. (See also **"Judenhause," Operation Factory**, and **Theresienstadt**.)

"Processed" (G., verarbeitet). Refers to a Jew who had been gassed in a truck (**"Sonderwagon"**).

"Productive Annihilation" (G., "producktive Vernichtung)." Euphemism for working **slave laborers** to death. At a meeting with **Heinrich Himmler** on September 14, 1942, **Otto Thierack**, minister of justice, agreed that Jews and "**asocial** elements" would be destroyed through work (**Vernichtung durch Arbeit**.)

SUGGESTED READING: Ferencz, *Less Than Slaves*.

Project Paperclip. American military program (1945–1990) designed and implemented to recruit German rocket scientists, including **war criminals** convicted at the **Nuremberg Trials**. American immigration laws were suspended for these scientists who were clandestinely smuggled into America to work on the Apollo and Saturn space projects. (See also **Wernher von Braun, General Walter Dornberger, Ratline, Arthur Rudolph**, and **Dr. Hubertus Strughold**.)

SUGGESTED READING: Hunt, *Secret Agenda*.

Project Reinhard. Reference to **Operation Heydrich** or **Aktion Reinhard** with a twist: Money from Project Reinhard was used to sustain Nazis hiding after the war. (See also **Odessa.**)

"Prominent" ("Kombinator" or "Organisator") (1) Privileged or resourceful inmate. These prisoners were better nourished and dressed than ordinary inmates and survived in the camps for extended periods of time. (2) Derogatory reference to Hungarian Jews on the **Kastzner transport**. (See also **"Organizing."**)

Property Collection Agency. (See **Werterfassung.**)

"Protective Custody." Nazi euphemism for imprisonment. The victim was arrested on any suspicion as an "enemy of the state." The prisoner was sent without a trial to a **concentration camp**. The practice, instituted in 1933, was legalized by **Wilhelm Frick**. (See also **Schutzhaftbefehl, Schutzhaftjuden**, and **Schutzhaftling.**)

Protectorate of Bohemia-Moravia. Two western provinces of **Czechoslovakia** occupied by the Nazis in March 1939 and placed under military rule. Its Jewish population was forced to wear the **Yellow Star** in September 1941. Out of a prewar Jewish population of 118,000, only 30,000 survived the **Holocaust**. (See also **Kurt Daluege, Wilhelm Frick, Reinhard Heydrich, Munich Pact, Konstantin von Neurath**, and **Theresienstadt.**)

Protocols of the Learned Elders of Zion. **Anti-Semitic** fraud and fabrication produced by **Russia's** Czarist Secret Police at the end of the nineteenth century. The book's main thrust was that a powerful cabal of Jews had a secret plan for world domination. The Jews were allegedly the central force behind Bolshevism and capitalism who sought to destroy Christian society. The **Freemasons**, acting as a front, were also implicated in this grand Jewish conspiracy. The *Protocols* had a profound impact on Nazi ideologists, including **Hitler**. It is still printed and distributed throughout the world. Henry Ford serialized this document and called it *The International Jew*. On November 29, 1993, a Russian court finally pronounced the *Protocols* a forgery. (See also **Reverend Charles E. Roman Coughlin, General Erich Ludendorff, Dr. Alfred Rosenberg**, and **Baldur von Schirach.**)
    SUGGESTED READING: Cohn, *Warrant for Genocide.*

Prussic Acid. (See **Zyklon-B.**)

Q

"Quisling." The term refers to a **collaborator** or traitor.

Quisling, Vidkun (1887–1945). Norwegian politician. He was the collaborationist prime minister during Nazi occupation. Quisling and the Germans began to persecute and roundup Jews in the fall and winter of 1942 despite protests from Protestant churches and the general populace. He was executed in **Norway** in 1945. Quisling has become synonymous with traitor. (See also **Collaborator** and **Josef Terboven**.)

   SUGGESTED READING: Abrahamsen, *Norway's Response to the Holocaust.*

Quota. (1) Number given by the U.S. State Department to a future immigrant who wanted to legally enter the country. A low number meant permission to immigrate was likely. A high number could mean years of waiting, and perhaps death for the **refugee** desperate to escape the Nazis. (2) Quota also meant the number of immigrants permitted annually to enter a nation. During the war, most Western countries, especially Britain and the United States, created artificial barriers to restrict the flow of Jewish refugees. (See also **Alaskan Development Bill, Bermuda Conference, Evian Conference, Breckinridge Long**, *Numerus Clauses*, **Oswego, Robert Borden Reams**, *Saint Louis*, **War Refugee Board**, and **White Paper**.)

   SUGGESTED READING: Feingold, *The Politics of Rescue.*

R

Rab. Island off Dalmatia, **Yugoslavia**, and **internment camp** established July 1942. It contained 15,000 inmates, mostly opponents of Italian occupation. The Italians also protected 3,577 Jewish **refugees**. Many Jews joined the Yugoslavian **partisans** in September 1943. In March 1944, 300 women and children were **deported** to Nazi-held areas. (See also **Yugoslavian Resistance Movement**.)

SUGGESTED READING: Romans, *The Jews of Yugoslavia.*

Race and Resettlement Main Office (RuSHA) (G., Rasse und Siedlungshauptamt). Nazi racial research office. This bureau compiled genealogical tables including racial statistics of families in **Germany** and the **Netherlands**. The RuSHA selected candidates for "Germanization," and kidnapped Polish children who were designated for the **Lebensborn** ("Fountain of Life"). It also determined **Aryan** fitness of ethnic Germans (**Volksdeutsche**) who wanted to settle in conquered Polish territory and checked the purity of the **SS** and their mates.

SUGGESTED READINGS: Lumsden, *The Black Corps*; Tenenbaum, *Race and Reich.*

Racial Hygiene (G., Rassenhygiene). Term coined by **Dr. Alfred Ploetz**, father of the German **eugenic** movement, near the end of the nineteenth century. The fear of the degeneration of the human race led to a belief in social control of human breeding to improve human germ plasma. Ploetz believed that the state should initiate measures to improve the Germanic peoples. **Hitler** adopted the concept in his world-view (**Weltanschauung**).

SUGGESTED READING: Proctor, *Racial Hygiene.*

Racial State. The primary objective of the Nazis was to realize a racially organized state and society. They believed the continued existence of **Aryan** culture, beauty, and order was threatened by inferior races, especially the Jews. German blood purity had to be protected against alien races, and it was eventually concluded that Jews had to be exterminated through the **Final Solution.** **Slavs** and **Uentermenschen** were to be used as servants of the Germanic Aryan. (See also **Mischlinge, Nuremberg Laws**, and **Volksgenossen**.)

Rada Pomosci Zydom. (See **Zegota**.)

Rademacher, Franz (1906–1973). **SS** general and administrator. He was head of the office in the German foreign ministry that dealt with the **Jewish Problem**. He suggested the Jews be expelled to **Madagascar** and worked with **Adolf Eichmann** to coordinate **deportations** from **Belgium, France, Slovakia**, and **Yugoslavia**. In the fall of 1941, Rademacher ordered mass execution of Jews in **Serbia**. He was arrested by German authorities, tried in 1949, skipped bail, and fled to Syria. Then he escaped to South America to avoid a prison term. However, he returned to **Germany** in 1966, was retried, and convicted. (See also **Alois Brunner**.)

SUGGESTED READING: Browning, *The Final Solution and the German Foreign Office.*

Radical Nationalist Camp (Oboz Navodowo Radykalny). (See **ONR**.)

Radom Ghetto. Located in central **Poland**, the city's prewar Jewish community numbered 25,000 Jews. The German Army occupied Radom on September 8, 1939. In March 1941, the community was **ghettoized** and split into two sections. A wave of **deportations** occurred in August 1942. On August 5, 1942, the "small ghetto" was liquidated by Germans and Ukrainians; 8,000 Jews were deported to **Treblinka** (including 2,000 from the "large ghetto.") From August 16–18, 1942, the "large ghetto" was liquidated, and 1,500 Jews were murdered for **resisting** deportation. There was no Jewish community by war's end. Radom was not repopulated in the postwar period. (See also "**Bloody Friday**.")

SUGGESTED READING: Yahil, *The Holocaust.*

Rahm, Karl (1907–1947). Austrian **SS** lt. colonel. He was the last kommandant of **Terezin**, officiating from February 1944–May 1945. Rahm allowed food parcels sent by the Danish government in 1944 to be given to Danish Jews. A hoax was perpetuated by his "beautification" program of the camp in preparation to deceive the Red Cross. Before and after the **International Committee of The Red Cross** visit, many Jews were sent to **Auschwitz**. He was hanged by a Czech Tribunal in 1947.

SUGGESTED READING: Troller, *Theresienstadt.*

Rampa (P., railway platform). This runway served arriving trains at **death** and **concentration camps**.

Rapaport, Nathan (1911–1994). Israeli sculptor born in Warsaw. He is renowned for his monument "Defenders of the **Warsaw Ghetto**" and his statue of **Mordecai Anielewicz** on the Yad Mordecai **kibbutz**.
SUGGESTED READING: Young, *The Texture of Memory.*

Rapportfuehrer (G., **SS** recording officer). This individual kept the records at **Appellplatz** in **concentration camps**.

Rasch, Emil Otto (1891–1948). commander of **Einsatzgruppe** C. He was in charge of the **Babi Yar** massacre. Rasch was involved in **Aktionen** where tens of thousands of Jews were murdered. He was a prime figure in the **Subsequent Nuremberg Trials (Einsatzkommando)**. Rasch died before a verdict was rendered.
SUGGESTED READING: Arad, Krakowski, and Spector, *The Einsatzgruppen Reports.*

Rascher, Dr. Sigmund (1909–1944). **Luftwaffe** physician and **SS** officer. He conducted and coordinated "medical experiments" at **Dachau** including high altitude, coagulation, and freezing tests on camp inmates. **Hermann Goering** thanked Rascher for his "research." He personally murdered some of his patients. Rascher was also associated with **Ahnenerbe**. The physician was killed in a bunker at Dachau by the SS for kidnapping babies.
SUGGESTED READING: Aziz, *Doctors of Death.*

Rashid Ali al-Gaylani (1882–1968). Lawyer and Iraqi political leader. He was assisted in his rise to power (1940) by the **Grand Mufti of Jerusalem** and seized power on April 1, 1941. He saw the war as an opportunity to end British occupation and gain German support. The British defeated the pro-Nazi Arab government led by Rashid two months after he seized power. Rashid fled to **Germany** with the Grand Mufti on May 30, 1941. In his absence, Rashid's followers carried out a **pogrom** in Baghdad's Jewish quarter in June 1941. Both men were leading pro-Nazi **collaborators** and propagandists in the Arab world. After the war, Rashid lived in exile in Arab countries before returning to Iraq in 1959.
SUGGESTED READING: Schechtman, *The Mufti and the Fuehrer.*

Rassenkampf (G., race struggle).

Rassenpolitik (G., racial policy). Its main thrust was to "purify" the **Aryan/ German Volk** and discourage relations between so-called Aryans and "lesser" peoples. (See also **Rassenschande** and **Dr. Alfred Rosenberg**.)

Rassenschande (G., race defilement). Sexual contact between a Jew and an **Aryan** was punishable by death. **Ernst Kaltenbrunner** made the death penalty ruling on February 10, 1944. The term applied to Slavic eastern workers as well. (See also **Kristallnacht, Nuremberg Laws, Racial State, Rassenpolitik, Ravensbrueck, Roma**, and **Slavs**.)

Rath, Ernst vom (1911–1938). German diplomat. Third secretary of the German embassy in Paris who was slain by **Herschel Grynszpan** on November 7, 1938. Vom Rath's death was the catalyst and excuse for **Kristallnacht**.
SUGGESTED READING: Read and Fisher, *Kristallnacht*.

Rathenau, Walther (1867–1922). German Jewish statesman, industrialist, and leading figure in the **Weimar Republic**. He helped to negotiate the **Versailles Treaty** (1919) and served as minister of reconstruction and foreign minister (1922) in the Weimar Republic. He was associated with the "**stab-in-the-back**" myth used by Nazis and racist nationalists, an association that led to his assassination by right-wing extremists on June 24, 1922.
SUGGESTED READING: Flood, *Hitler, the Path to Power*.

Ratline. An informal organization of Catholic clergy, American **OSS**, and **Vatican** representatives. This group aided Nazis after World War II to escape from Europe to South America, the United States, Australia, and Canada. **Passports** were most commonly obtained from the **Red Cross** and the Vatican. (See also **American Army's Counter Intelligence Corps, Andrija Artukovic, Klaus Barbie, Caritas, Father Krunoslav Dragonovic, Adolf Eichmann, Bishop Alois Hudal, Anton Pavelic, Walter Rauff, Joseph Schwammberger, SS Colonel Otto Skorzeny, Franz Stangl, Ustashi**, and **Gustav Wagner**.)
SUGGESTED READINGS: New York Times, January 26, 1984; Simpson, *Blowback*.

Ratti, Achille. (See **Pope Pius XI**.)

Rauff, Walter (1907–1984). Head of the **RSHA** section on technical affairs. He supervised the outfitting and dispatch of twenty gassing vans ("**Sonderwagons**" which murdered 200,000 people in late 1941–early 1942. He also led **Einsatzgruppe** commandos in **Tunis** and northern **Italy**. After the war, Rauff sought refuge in monasteries via the **Ratline** and was protected by the Chilean government. He died of natural causes. (See also **Chelmno** and **Bishop Alois Hudal**.)
SUGGESTED READINGS: Neufeld, *The Rocket and the Reich; New York Times*, May 15, 1984; May 16, 1984.

Rauter, Hans (1895–1947). **SS** general and commissioner for public safety in the **Netherlands**. A former Austrian **Freikorps** leader, Rauter instigated house-by-house searches for Jews in Holland. He arrested 10,000 intermarried Jews, and he transferred Jewish workers from thirty-six **labor camps** to **Westerbork**. Rauter was sentenced to death by a **Dutch** War Crimes Tribunal in 1947, one of five Nazis executed in the Netherlands for crimes committed during German occupation. (See also **Artur Seyss-Inquart** and **Sonderreferet**.)

SUGGESTED READING: Presser, *Ashes in the Wind.*

Ravensbrueck. **Concentration camp** for women outside of **Berlin**. Construction began in November 1938, and it opened on May 15, 1939. In April 1941, a camp was added for men, and **Uckermark**, a camp for 1,000 children was also established. (Between September 1944–April 1945, 560 births were recorded in Ravensbrueck.) The **SS** trained 3,000 female concentration camp guards at this site. Many of the trainees remained at Ravensbrueck, but hundreds of female SS were sent to **Auschwitz, Gross-Rosen, Neuengamme**, and **Oranienburg**. The camp was built by inmates from **Sachsenhausen** and had a capacity for 15,000 people. **Heinrich Himmler** allowed for corporal punishment of female inmates in 1940. Out of 132,000 prisoners, 92,000 women from twenty-three nations were murdered at this site. (Himmler's sister, Olga, was imprisoned at this site for having sex with a Pole [**Rassenschande**].) Ravensbrueck also supplied a small number of prostitutes for the bordellos in **Gusen** and **Mauthausen**.

Inmates were forced to work for the armaments industry, and **Siemens** built a factory adjacent to the camp. The **gas chambers** at Uckermark, for women unable to work, operated from December 1944–April 14, 1945, and at least 6,000 women were murdered. However, women and children were gassed at Bernberg and Auschwitz prior to the construction of on-site gassing capability. The Swedish rescue mission evacuated 21,000 "healthy" inmates from April 22, 1945, until the end of the war. However, by April 28, 15,000 inmates had been evacuated by the Nazis. The camp was **liberated** by the Soviets on April 30, 1945. The majority of the 106,000 women interned at this site were *not* Jewish (15 percent).

"Medical experiments," including the sterilization of **Roma** children were conducted at this site by **Dr. Horst Schumann, Dr. Karl Gebhardt** (an internationally renowned surgeon), and **Dr. Carl Clauberg**. Schumann's X-ray and sterilization experiments (January 1945) caused great pain and suffering. Dr. Rolf Rosenthal pioneered murder by injection of evipan in spring 1942. **Dr. Fritz Fisher** was the mainstay in the vivisection department while **Dr. Herta Oberhauser** carried out lethal injections. Clauberg and Oberhauser conducted sterilization experiments on women in July 1942, utilizing X-rays and injecting special substances into the uterus and oviducts. Drs. Gebhardt, Fisher, and **Joachim Mrugrowsky** conducted sulfa experiments on artificially induced wounds. Gebhardt also removed bones, muscles, and nerves for regeneration projects and cut off limbs for transplant experiments. In May 1944, Dr. Bruno

Orendi conducted an experiment ("Orendi Express") where he placed eighty women into a 9' by 9' cell. The Nazis referred to their victims as **Lapin**.

Ravensbrueck contained prominent inmates including **Sister Elizabeth Pilenko**, Gemma **La Guardia** Gluck, **Dr. Gertrud Lueknor**, and Genevieve **de Gaulle**. (See also **Bergen-Belsen, Count Folke Bernadotte, Doctors' Trial, Irma Grese, Heinkel Werke, Helferinnen, Homosexuals, Dr. Felix Kersten, Lichtenburg, Maria Mandel, Norbert Masur, Moringen, Sister Elizabeth Pilenko**, and **Fritz Suhren**.)

SUGGESTED READING: Tillion, *Ravensbrueck.*

Rayman, Marcel (1923–1944). French Jewish underground fighter with the **Francs Tireurs et Partisans**. He made numerous attacks on German military installations in Paris. Rayman was captured and killed by the **Gestapo** on February 21, 1944, after he staged a daring assassination of a high-level German official, Dr. Julias von Ritter.

SUGGESTED READING: Zuccotti, *The Holocaust, the French, and the Jews.*

Raziel, David (1910–1941). Underground **Yishuv Zionist Revisionist** leader. He was one of the founders of the **Irgun** in 1931; later he directed sabotage activities against the British. In 1941, he decided to volunteer for a British-sponsored mission to Iraq to sabotage oil installations. When he died under questionable circumstances in Iraq, Raziel was replaced as Irgun leader by **Menachem Begin**. (See also **Rashid Ali al-Gaylani**.)

SUGGESTED READING: Bell, *Terror Out of Zion.*

Razzia/Razzien (G., police raid). Term for roundup of Jews in several Western European nations, for example **Belgium** and the **Netherlands**. (See also **Aktion**.)

Reams, Robert Borden (b. 1904). Foreign service officer in the U.S. State Department specializing in the Division of European Affairs. He worked closely with **Breckinridge Long** to implement immigration **quotas** hostile to European Jews. Reams obstructed rescue proposals, bottlenecked **visas** and opposed the creation of the **War Refugee Board** during congressional testimony. Reams served as the principal delegate to the **Bermuda Conference** and acting-secretary of the **Intergovernmental Committee on Refugees**.

SUGGESTED READINGS: Wyman, *The Abandonment of the Jews*; Wyman, *Paper Walls.*

Rebbe (Y., my master). A version of rabbi used mainly by **Hasidim** to refer to their local leader or teacher. (See also **Rabbi Joseph Isaac Schneersohn**.)

Rechts/Links (G., right/left). During a **selection**, the mere pointing of a finger meant life or death. "Rechts" meant staying in the **ghetto** or barracks. "Links" meant **deportation** or death in the **gas chambers**.

Red Army. Military forces of the **USSR**. There was no **anti-Semitic** policy in effect in this army although historical anti-Jewish actions were displayed from time to time. Over 500,000 Jews fought in its ranks; 200,000 were killed in action. The **Wehrmacht** lost more than 2,100,000 men fighting in the **Soviet Union** and sustained more than 5 million wounded. The Red Army liberated also **Auschwitz, Chelmno, Gross-Rosen, Kaiserwald, Kiev, Klooga, Majdanek, Ravensbrueck, Sachenhausen-Oranienburg, Stutthof**, and **Theresienstadt**. The Soviets also liberated **Czernowitz, Kishinev, Kovno Liepaja, Novogrudok, Odessa, Transnistria, Tuchin, Vilna, Zamosc**, and **Zhitomir**. However, the Soviet military failed to provide aid to the Poles during the **Warsaw Polish Uprising**. **Soviet POWs** were also the target of German exploitation and extermination. The Red Army issued a directive forbidding anti-Semitism and mandated that Soviet **partisans** accept Jews into their ranks. (See also **General Wladyslaw Anders, Heshek "Zvi" Bauminger, Tuvia Bielski, Croatia, Leon Feldhandler, Fremdarbeiter, Kommissarbefehl, Maria Rozka Korczak, Josef Loewenherz, Mogilev-Podolski, Munkaszolgalat, OUN, Riga, Josef Stalin, Tarnopol, Vienna, Lt. General Andrei Vlasov, Henrik Ziman**, and **Shalom Zorin**.)

SUGGESTED READINGS: Gilbert, *The Day the War Ended*; Gilbert, *The Second World War*.

Red Card/permit. Temporarily exempted bearer from "**resettlement**" in Warsaw. Most of these cards belonged to the rich, members and families of the **Jewish Council**, and **Jewish Police**. These people were brutalized, **deported**, and murdered when the **Warsaw Ghetto** had been cleared out.

Red Cross (ICRC). (1) Founded in 1863 as a humanitarian organization to moderate between belligerents and to monitor application of humanitarian international law. This body was charged to oversee humane conditions in POW camps among civilian internees during wartime, but gained limited access to **concentration camps**. With the exception of two visits to **Dutch** inmates interned at **Buchenwald** in 1940, and the inspection of **Theresienstadt** at the behest of the Danish government (where they were fooled by the **SS** in 1944), the Red Cross was never able to enter concentration camps until late in the war. The ICRC did not take great initiatives to intervene on behalf of the Jews for fear of losing its credibility with the **Axis** Powers, thus losing its position to work on behalf of POWs and civilian internees. Jews and **Night and Fog** victims were exempt from help from the Red Cross by the Nazis. In the spring of 1944, the Red Cross urged the Hungarian government to suspend **deportations** of Jews, and it did assist in saving thousands of Jews from the **Arrow Cross**. Records and documents show that the Red Cross worked with the American

War Refugee Board to bring 3,000 orphaned children from the **Ukraine** to **Palestine** in 1944. In 1995, ICRC president, Cornelio Sommaruga, finally admitted his agency's inaction during the **Holocaust**. (2) The SS painted a "Red Cross" on trucks at concentration camps to deceive gassing victims, for example in **Auschwitz**. This guise was a carryover from **T-4** when the SS wore white coats over their uniforms and engaged in the sorting of clothing prior to gassing. (3) Marking used to identify inmates at **Flossenbuerg**. (See also **Auschwitz-Birkenau "Family Camp," Count Folke Bernadotte, Drancy, Dr. Ernst von Grawitz, Hungary, Otto Komoly, Night and Fog, Karl Rahm**, and **Ratline**.)

SUGGESTED READINGS: Gutman and Zuroff, Rescue Attempts; Perl, The Four-Front War.

Reder, Walter (b. 1915). Austrian **SS** officer. He oversaw the murder of 1,830 civilians, including women and children, in Tuscany, **Italy**, for allegedly giving aid to **partisans**. He was convicted as a **war criminal** and sentenced to life, but later was pardoned by the Italians due to his age and poor health. Reder was greeted warmly by the Austrian government upon repatriation.

SUGGESTED READING: Bassett, Waldheim and Austria.

Red Orchestra (G., **Rote Kapelle**). Name of an anti-Nazi spy ring, an arm of Soviet military intelligence in the occupied countries of Western Europe. The term was coined by the German security offices. The intelligence network was established by a Polish Jew, Leopold Trepper (1904–1983) an headquartered in Paris. Among its achievements was an advance report detailing the German invasion of the **Soviet Union**. Most of its members were discovered and executed in 1943.

SUGGESTED READINGS: Gilbert, The Second World War; Trepper, Great Game.

"Reds." Political inmates identified by a red triangle. These were the most powerful and privileged inmates in the **concentration camps** due to their political solidarity, for example, communists, socialists, and other political opponents of the Nazis. This group also included captured **resistance** fighters from various nations. (See also **"Greens."**)

Refoulement. Swiss policy of sealing their borders in 1938 to prevent illegal Jewish immigration. The **refugees** were shipped back to the **Greater Reich**. This policy was prompted by fear of Nazi aggression and **anti-Semitism**. Refoulement permitted entry of refugee families with children under 16 and adults over 60. Of the 200,000 refugees accepted by **Switzerland** and interned, 23,000 were Jews. The policy was ended by **Dr. Heinrich Rothmund** in July 1944. (See also **Monsignor Filippo Bernardini, Paul Grueninger, Roswell McClelland, Saly Mayer, Eduard von Steiger**, and **Rita and Isaac Sternbuch**.)

SUGGESTED READING: Kranzler, Heroine of Rescue.

Refugee. A person who is attempting to escape the danger of persecution because of his/her race, religion, ethnicity, or political beliefs. The term during the Hitler era was a code word for Jews seeking refuge from Nazi terror. For example, the special U.S. agency to rescue Jews was called the **War Refugee Board**. (See also **Bermuda Conference, Evian Conference, Breckinridge Long, Robert Borden Reams**, and **Refoulement**.)

Regat (Ro., the Old Kingdom lands). (See **Old Kingdom of Romania**.)

Reich (G., nation, state, or empire). Term most often used to refer to the German state from 1933–1945. (See also **Third Reich**.)

Reich, Wilhelm (1897–1957). Austrian-born Danish psychoanalyst and author. He fled Nazi **Germany** in 1939 for America. His book entitled *The Mass Psychology of Fascism* argued that Nazism was a rechanneling of repressed sexual energy.
   SUGGESTED READING: Rieff, ''World of Wilhelm Reich.''

Reich Association of Jews in Germany. (See **Reichsvereingung der Juden in Deutschland**.)

Reich Central Office for Jewish Emigration. (See **Reichszentrale fuer Juedische Auswanderung**.)

Reich Chancellery. (See **Fuehrer Chancellery**.)

Reich Commission for the Strengthening of Germandom. SS agency in charge of resettling ethnic Germans (**Volksdeutsche**) from areas formerly controlled by the **Soviet Union**. Headed by **SS General Ulrich Greifelt**, it was intended to be a crucial element to achieve **Lebensraum** through demographic engineering from 1939–1942. The Commission resettled 500,000 Germans from Soviet incorporated territories.

Reichenau, Field Marshal Walter von (1884–1942.) German commander of the Sixth Army. Devoted to **Hitler**, he facilitated the implementation of the loyalty oath to Hitler in the **Wehrmacht**. As commander of Army Group South in **Russia**, he issued a directive sanctioning the murder of **Soviet POWs** and Jews, which Hitler ordered to be sent to all Wehrmacht commanders. von Reichenau died of a heart attack. (See also **Oberkommando der Wehrmacht, Operation Barbarossa**, and **Partisan Order**.)
   SUGGESTED READING: Wistrich, *Who's Who in Nazi Germany.*

Reich Labor Service (G., Reichsarbeitsdienst). Mandatory paramilitary organization for German men, ages 18–25. The obligatory year of service was extended to women in 1939. This agency was a device for alleviating unemployment and preparing young Germans for the coming war. (See also **Bund deutscher Maedel** and **Hitler Youth**.)

Reichleitner, Franz (d. 1944). Third kommandant of **Sobibor**. In December 1943, the **SS** leader was sent to command a camp in Trieste. He was killed by **partisans** in the Trieste region.
SUGGESTED READING: Segev, *Soldiers of Evil*.

Reich Press Law. Mandated (1933) all media editors must be German citizens of **Aryan** descent and not married to a Jew.
SUGGESTED READING: Hale, *The Captive Press in the Third Reich*.

Reich Representation of Jews of Germany. (See **Reichsvertretung der Deutschen Juden**.)

Reich Security Main Office. (See **RSHA**.)

Reichsfuehrer (G., state or supreme leader). Title **Hitler** gave himself when he combined the duties of president and chancellor in 1934. (See also **Paul von Hindenburg**.)

Reichsfuehrer SS (G., leader of the SS). **Heinrich Himmler's** title.

Reichskirche (G., state church). German Protestant church sponsored by the Nazi government. It was paganized with a racial philosophy and anti–Old Testament, anti-Jewish philosophy. Its opposition was the **Confessional Church**. (See also **Ludwig Mueller** and **Pastor Martin Niemoeller**.)

Reichskommissar (G., Reich commissioner). German governor, head of large territorial area in the occupied **Soviet Union**. (See also **Erich Koch, Heinrich Lohse, Dr. Alfred Rosenberg**, and **Artur Seyss-Inquart**.)

Reichskommissariat Ukraine. Headed by **Erich Koch**, it was the German civil administration of occupied Ukraine.

Reichskommissariat Ostland (G., State Commission for Eastern Territories). Major component of the German civil administration in the Occupied Territories of the **Soviet Union**. Headed by **Dr. Alfred Rosenberg**, it included **Latvia, Lithuania, Estonia**, and **Belorussia**. The municipal administrations contained police forces consisting of volunteers operating under the direction of the German police. Local administrators were composed of **collaborators** who actively aided the Nazis in the murder of Jews. From July–September 1941, most of the Jews in the Baltics were shot to death (224,000), while the Jews of **Belorussia** were targeted in 1942. (See also **Heinrich Lohse**.)

Reichskreditkassenscheine (G., German occupation money).

Reichsnahrstrand (G., German agricultural organization). Headed by **Richard-Walther Darre**, this entity dealt with production, marketing, ''soil,'' and folk (**Volk**) life.

Reichsprotektor (G., military governor). Highest Nazi official of the Czech government under military occupation. The head of the **Protectorate of Bohemia-Moravia** (Czech lands) was given this title. (See also **Reinhard Heydrich, Wilhelm Frick**, and **Konstantin von Neurath**.)

Reichssippenamt (G., Reich Genealogical Office). This agency was charged with conducting investigations about being Jewish or of non-Jewish origin. It determined who was a **Mischlinge** and who was a pure **Aryan**.

Reichstag. Legislative building and lawmaking body of the **Weimar Republic**. The Nazis set fire to the building on February 27, 1933, setting in motion a chain of events that allowed **Hitler** to rule by decree and assume dictatorial powers. Although the Nazis allowed the Reichstag to continue to function, it was nothing more than a rubber stamp. (See also **Enabling Act** and **General Erich Ludendorff**.)

Reichstatthalter (G., Nazi governor of a territory).

Reichsvereingung der Juden in Deutschland (G., **Reich Association of Jews in Germany**). This successor entity to the **Reichsvertretung der Deutschen Juden** started July 4, 1939, charged by the Nazis as its major mission emigration of Jews from the **Reich**. It included all Jews as defined by the **Nuremberg Laws**, but its jurisdiction was confined to **Germany** and the **Sudetenland. Austria** and **Bohemia-Moravia** were excluded. The Reich Association came under the direct control of the **SS** who gave it tasks that eventually led to the **Final Solution**. It continued to provide Jewish welfare and schooling. The emigration aspects ended after October 1, 1941. The Emigration Section then became involved in **deportation**. A number of its leaders were executed as a result of the **Baum Gruppe** arrest. In the spring of 1943, the Reichsvereingung was dissolved. Leaders Rabbi **Leo Baeck** and **Dr. Paul Eppstein** were deported to **Theresienstadt**.

SUGGESTED READING: Friedlander, *Nazi Germany and the Jews.*

Reichsvertretung der Deutschen Juden (G., **Reich Representation of Jews of Germany**.) Body representing German Jews vis-à-vis the German government. This **Jewish Council** started as early as September 1933, and was headed by Reform Rabbi **Leo Baeck** and the Chief Executive Officer **Dr. Otto Hirsch**. The Reichsvertretung centralized the political aspects of the Jewish community in Germany, trying to enter open debate and dignify controversy with the Nazi administration. Its constituent arms handled most aspects of Jewish life in the **Reich**—emigration, welfare-relief, education, vocational training, and cultural activities. Attached to it were the Central Committee for Relief and Reconstruction, the Jewish Center for Adult Education, the German Jewish Aid Society, and the **Palestine** Office. Its advocates saw the Reichsvertretung doing its best to safeguard the German Jewish community's physical and moral existance. Its critics, such as **Robert Weltsch**, lamented that the organization lulled German Jews with false hopes and did not allocate enough resources for emigration. (See also **Martin Buber** and **Huavara Agreement**.

SUGGESTED READINGS: Black, *The Transfer Agreement*; Hilberg, *The Destruction of European Jews.*

Reichswehr (G., State Defense). Name for German Army from 1919–1935. It was officially limited to 100,000 men by the **Treaty of Versailles. Hitler** clandestinely augmented this force with irregulars and police training units. Its officers insisted that the **SA** be neutralized. After 1935, the regular army was known as the **Wehrmacht**. (See also **Night of the Long Knives** and **Ernst Roehm**.)

Reichszentrale fuer Juedische Auswanderung (G., **Reich Central Office for Jewish Emigration**). Established on August 26, 1938, and headed by **Adolf Eichmann**. It concentrated all the Jews of **Austria** in **Vienna**, set **quotas** and obligated the Jewish community to meet German demands for human chattel. This process was financed by wealthy Jews. These "innovative" methods were a model for **Reinhard Heydrich** in **Berlin** who exported the concepts to the East. This office dealt with Jewish emigration matters until October 1941, when Jewish emigration was prohibited. Eichmann's staff became part of the **RSHA**. (See also **Alois Brunner** and **Anton Brunner**.)

SUGGESTED READING: United States Holocaust Memorial Museum, *Fifty Years After the Eve of Destruction, 1939.*

Reich Union of Jewish Front Line Soldiers (**RJF**). Jewish war veterans union, which sought to counteract the widespread belief that Jews avoided military service in World War I. With the support of President **Paul von Hindenburg**, they were exempted from much of the Nazi racial legislation and obtained preferred treatment for its 30,000 members. The RJF's special status position was canceled in 1935 by the Nazis. (See also **Privileged Jews** and **Theresienstadt**.)

Reik, Haviva (1914–1944). **"Parachutist"** and **partisan** leader. As a representative of the **Haganah**, she was dropped in **Slovakia** in November 1944 to try to establish contact with the underground in Bratislava. Unable to establish contact, Reik and her comrades formed a partisan unit until she was captured and killed by a Ukrainian **SS** division in November 1944. (See also **Slovakian National Revolt**.)

SUGGESTED READING: Steinberg, *Jews Against Hitler.*

Reispass (G., **passport**).

RELICO. (See **Relief Committee for the War Stricken Jewish Population**.)

Relief and Rescue Committee of Budapest (H., Va'ad ha-Ezra ve-ha-Hatzala be-Budapest). Established in 1941 to rescue Jewish refugees by smuggling them into Hungary. When Germans occupied **Hungary** in March 1944 the Rescue Committee expanded. The Va'ad was apprised in April 1944 by the **Working Group** of increased capacity for gassing at **Auschwitz** and the cooperative agreement on transport by the railroads of **Germany**, Hungary, and **Slovakia**. The Rescue Committee became involved in controversial negotiations with the **SS** to prevent the **Final Solution** in Hungary known as the **"Blood for Trucks"** plan. It fell through; however, a small number of Jews including members of the Rescue Committee, were saved. The Va'ad was severely criticized for not warning Hungarian Jewry of impending doom. (See also **Auschwitz Protocols, Joel Brand, Dr. Rezso Kasztner, Otto Komoly, Tiyul**, and **Vrba-Wetzler Report**.)

SUGGESTED READING: Finger, *American Jewry During the Holocaust.*

Relief Committee for the War Stricken Jewish Population (RELICO). Established in Geneva in September 1939 by **Dr. Abraham Silberschein** under the aegis of the **World Jewish Congress**. He assisted Jewish **refugees** from **Germany** and later from **Poland** and **Lithuania** and other areas of Europe. This organization was instrumental in getting refugees to **Kobe**, Japan, and **Shanghai**, China. It was also one of the first to apprise the world of the **Chelmno** and **Treblinka death camps**. RELICO's attempt to obtain 10,000 South American passports for prominent Poles fell through due to U.S. State Department opposition.

SUGGESTED READING: Kranzler, *Thy Brother's Blood.*

Renno, Dr. Georg (b. 1907). German chief doctor and director of **Hartheim Castle**. He also served as a child killer at various **euthanasia** centers. In Renno's trial in Frankfurt (1965), he admitted that gassings of the mentally ill and invalids from **Mauthausen** occurred at Hartheim.

SUGGESTED READING: Friedlander, *The Origins of Nazi Genocide.*

Reparations and Restitution. (1) Money and goods paid by the West German government to the State of Israel. Israel argued that **Germany** was obligated to pay the Jewish state for the 500,000 Jews it absorbed who had been victims of Nazi persecution. **Konrad Adenauer**, first chancellor of the Federal Republic of Germany, made statements in September 1951 that the German people would make amends for crimes against Jews. The agreement was carried out by the West German government, which helped to provide a firm economic base for Israel. The **Conference on Jewish Material Claims** against Germany was formed to oversee reparation claims. Reparations were made from 1953–1965. All told, 8.5 million marks were paid in compensation. East Germany refused to make restitution. **Austria** has also held back payments. In September 1990, a unified Germany agreed to additional funding for victims but *did not* provide for Jews who lived in former communist countries in Eastern Europe. In 1996, the United States and Germany signed an agreement to compensate American citizens interned in Nazi **concentration camps**. The deal is limited to $2.1 million. In addition, several Eastern European nations are negotiating with Jewish agencies. For example, on July 3, 1996, the Hungarian Jewish Heritage Foundation was created to deal with expropriated Jewish properties.

(2) Restitution payments were made to individuals to compensate them for their suffering, loss of property, and lost opportunities during the Nazi period. A German court in Karlsrule ruled that **I. G. Farben** (which once had Jewish owners) and other property in East Germany, later seized and redistributed by Soviet occupation authorities, need not be returned to pre–World War II owners. Restitution is an ongoing process. However, in 1996, the German government refused to compensate individual **Holocaust** survivors from **Lithuania**. Instead, a one-time contribution of $1.3 million was paid in exchange for the Lithuanian government's agreement not to make any further claims. (See also **"Inventorization," Jewish Cultural Reconstruction, Jewish Restitution Successor Organization, Dr. Gertrud Lueknor, Luxembourg Agreement, Unification Treaty**, and **World Jewish Congress**.)

SUGGESTED READING: Balabkins, *West German Reparations to Israel*; Ferencz, *Less Than Slaves*; Nicholas, *The Rape of Europa*.

Repatriation. To restore or to return to one's country of origin. Millions of gentile **forced laborers** and **displaced persons** were repatriated. Jews were restored to citizenship in most Western countries, except **Germany** and **Austria**. Many Jews returning to Eastern Europe were met with **anti-Semitism**, even **pogroms**. Many decided to remain DPs. A number of ex-Nazis were repatriated. The **Volksdeutsche**, fearing reprisals, were permitted into Germany and granted citizenship. Germans from the **Sudetenland** were expelled to Germany. (See also **Kielce**.)

Report to the Secretary on the Acquiescence of this Government on the Murder of the Jews. Document handed to Secretary **Henry Morganthau Jr.**, prepared by **Josiah DuBois**, and signed by Randolph Paul in late December 1944, which outlined the perfidy of the U.S. State Department in preventing rescue. Secretary Morganthau toned down the language and presented it to President **Franklin Delano Roosevelt** in January, along with a model executive order creating a commission to rescue Jews, later called the **War Refugee Board**.

SUGGESTED READING: Feingold, *The Politics of Rescue*; Morse, *While Six Million Died.*

Rescue Committee of the Jewish Agency in Turkey. Operated in Istanbul from 1943–1945. The Committee had the three-fold task of establishing contact with Jews in the occupied countries of Europe and conveying to them the concern of **Yishuv**. The main object of its third charge, rescuing Jews, was to save the Jews from the Balkans from **deportation** and mass murder. Senior leaders of the **Palestine** Jewish Committee visited Istanbul to facilitate the transfer of funds to bribe Nazis and smuggle Jews, facilitate legal immigration from Turkey and the Balkans to Palestine, and encourage illegal immigration to Palestine. The Rescue Committee encouraged **Bricha** escape routes from Eastern European states and countries that would come to be under Soviet control.

SUGGESTED READING: Shaw, *Turkey and the Holocaust.*

Reserve Police Battalion 101. Mobile murder unit utilized mainly in the **Lublin** district and eastern **Galicia**. It was composed of ordinary, nonpolitical men and second-rate soldiers who moved into an area as **Order Police** after it was secured by the regular army. They willingly followed orders to murder Jews. (See also **Orpo**.)

SUGGESTED READING: Browning, *Ordinary Men.*

"Resettlement." Euphemism for **deportation**, which often meant death for Jews and **Roma**. (See also **SS General Ulrich Greifelt, Red Card/permit**, and **Werterfassung**.)

Resistance. Opposition to Nazi occupation. Jewish resistance took many forms. Military resistance occurred in the **ghettos**; the most famous was the **Warsaw Ghetto Uprising**, but there were also **concentration camp uprisings**. Resistance also took place in the forests and rural areas where Jews formed **partisan** units, for example, the **Vilna** and **Bielski partisans**. Jews also flocked to underground movements within the countries where they resided; an example was the **French Forces of the Interior** in France. Members of the Jewish underground assisted rescue efforts of Christian rescuers such as **Zegota**. They were part of a partisan and escape network along with non-Jews. Jews participated in national uprisings such as the **Warsaw Polish Uprising** in August 1944, the General Revolt, or the **Slovakian National Revolt**. In **Palestine**, Jews from the **Yishuv** joined the British Army, 35,000 strong. There were thirty-four "**para-**

chutists" who were dropped on British missions inside occupied Europe, where they also aided Jewish resistance.

In addition to military resistance, Jews practiced **spiritual resistance**. Rabbis taught and students learned clandestinely in ghettos. Jews prayed and observed holidays under the guns of the Germans. Cultural events went on in ghettos, even **concentration camps**, to uphold the humanity of the people.

Opposition to **collaborationist** governments was also considered resistance. Resistance forces consisted of those loyal to governments-in-exile, such as **Poland's Armia Krajowa**, the Communist Party, or ethnic organizations such as Slovakian or Ukrainian nationalists (**OUN**). The resisters had to be clandestine, thus they went underground. Military operations took place as guerrilla warfare. For example, in the forests and mountains of France, they were called **Maquis** or partisans.

SUGGESTED READINGS: Eckman and Lazar, *The Jewish Resistance*; Kohn and Tartakower, *Jewish Resistance during the Holocaust*; Steinberg, *The Jews Against Hitler*.

Restitution. (See **Reparations and Restitution**.)

Revier; Revierbaracken (G., infirmary or hospital). Term used in **concentration camps**. (See also **Krakenbau** and **Lazarett**.)

Rexist. Belgian **fascist** police force and political party founded by **Leon Degrelle**. Dominated by Flemish Belgians, it was particularly strong in Antwerp. Its members became the core of the Belgian **SS** and served as a puppet government for the **New Order** after **Belgium's** defeat in 1940.

SUGGESTED READING: Conway, *Collaboration in Belgium*.

Reynders, Father Bruno (Henry) (1903–1981). **Righteous Gentile**. A Benedictine monk who usually worked alone, Father Reynders hid approximately 300 Jewish children and 50 adults throughout **Belgium**. His activities were discovered by the **Gestapo**, and he was forced to leave his monastery and live under false papers. Father Reynders continued his work until the end of the war. He was recognized by **Yad Vashem** in 1964.

Rheinmetall. Second largest German munitions producer for the **Third Reich**. The company utilized **concentration camp** labor and assumed an industry leadership role with the **SS**. Twelve hundred Jewish women attached to **Buchenwald** were exploited by Rheinmetall. The company steadfastly refused to pay **reparations and restitution** after the war. (See also **Circle of Friends of Himmler, Dr. Hans Kammler, Julius Klein**, and **Otto Kranzbuehler**.)

SUGGESTED READING: Ferencz, *Less Than Slaves*.

"Rhineland Bastards" (G., Rheinland bastarde). Interracial German children from liaisons between German women and black men from French African colonies during the post–World War I Allied Rhineland occupation (1920–1930). Targeted later for the **T-4** program, these Germans were sterilized in 1937.

SUGGESTED READING: Proctor, *Racial Hygiene.*

Rhodes. Greek island in the Aegean Sea ceded to **Italy** by Turkey in 1923. The Germans occupied the island after the Italian surrender to the **Allies** in 1943. The Jewish population of 1,700 was **deported** to **Greece** en route to killing centers in the East; only 161 survived. (See also **Athens** and **Salonika**.)

SUGGESTED READING: Gaon and Serels, *Sephardim and the Holocaust.*

Ribbentrop, Joachim von (1893–1946). Minister Plenipotentiary at Large and German Foreign Minister from 1938–1945. He negotiated the German-Japanese **Anti-Comintern Pact**, the **Molotov-Ribbentrop Pact**, and was actively involved in planning all Nazi foreign aggressions. The foreign office was represented at **Wannsee** and was actively involved in the **deportations** of French, Slovak, and Hungarian Jews, but was frustrated by **General Mario Roatta** in **Croatia**. Ribbentrop was convicted of **war crimes** by the **International Military Tribunal** and hanged at **Nuremberg**. (See also **Martin Luther** and **Konstantin von Neurath**.)

SUGGESTED READING: Weitz, *Hitler's Diplomat.*

Richter, Gustav (1913–1982). **SS** captain and attorney. **Adolf Eichmann's** representative in Bucharest, **Romania**. As advisor on Jewish Affairs, he guided anti-Jewish legislation and established a **Judenrat** in Romania. He used **Radu Lecca** as his personal agent. Richter was unsuccessful in a last-ditch attempt to **deport** Jews to **Belzec**. Richter was apprehended on August 23, 1944, by the Romanians who handed him over to the Soviets. He served ten years in **Russia**, and in 1982 he was sentenced to four years in prison in **Germany**.

SUGGESTED READINGS: Butnaru, *Waiting for Jerusalem; New York Times*, January 12, 1983.

Riefenstahl, Leni (b. 1902). Filmmaker. She was most noted for *The Triumph of the Will* (1934) and *Olympiad* (1936), which glorified the Nazi regime. Her films were considered brilliant propaganda pieces, but she has consistently denied being a Nazi. (See also **Dr. Paul Josef Goebbels**.)

SUGGESTED READING: Riefenstahl, *A Memoir.*

Riegner, Dr. Gerhart (b. 1912). **World Jewish Congress** representative in **Switzerland**. A German Jewish **refugee**, he was informed indirectly by a German industrialist, **Eduard Schulte**, on August 1, 1942, that **Hitler** had ordered the extermination of European Jewry. He is credited with being the first person to publish reliable reports about the **Holocaust**. The "Riegner Cable" was sent through diplomatic channels to **Rabbi Stephen S. Wise**, head of the

American Jewish Congress, and British MP **Sidney Silverman** in Liverpool, England, on August 8, 1942. However, the State Department refused to pass on the cable. On August 28, 1942, Sidney Silverman sent Wise a copy. Riegner worked tirelessly to promote **Allied** rescue action, but was thwarted by the U.S. State Department. (See also **Carl Jacob Burkhardt, Cordell Hull, Richard Lichtheim, Breckinridge Long, Rita and Isaac Sternbuch, Myron Taylor**, and **War Refugee Board**.)

SUGGESTED READINGS: Browning, "A Final Hitler Decision"; Laqueur, *The Terrible Secret.*

Riga/Riga Ghetto. Latvian port city with a prewar Jewish population of 194,000. It was the largest Jewish center in **Latvia**. Riga was occupied by the Germans on July 1, 1941, whereupon Latvian volunteers arrested Jewish men. Two weeks later, 2,700 Jews were **deported** to their deaths in the Bikernieki Forest, and 30,000 Jews were sealed in a **ghetto**. In November 1941, a small ghetto was created for working Jews. Later in the month, Germans shot 28,000 Jews in the large ghetto, including **Simon Dubnow**. In December 1941, German Jews from the **Greater Reich** were "**resettled**" in the large ghetto, and 5,007 **Roma** were deported. The Riga Ghetto was liquidated on September 23, 1943. In December 1943, the remaining Jews were deported to **Kaiserwald**. Roma were also gassed at **Chelmno**. On October 22, 1944, the **Red Army liberated** the city. (See also **Jungfernhof, Dr. Rudolf Lange, Latvian SS Legion, Janus Lipke, Stutthof, Thundercross**, and **Jan Zwartendijk**.)

SUGGESTED READING: Ezergailis, *The Holocaust in Latvia, 1941–1944.*

Righteous Gentiles (H., **Hasidey Ummot Ha'olam**). Christians who risked their lives to save Jews, honored at **Yad Vashem** in Israel with a plaque and a carob tree in the Garden of the Righteous. Some were anti-Nazi patriots who interpreted rescue as opposing the hated occupier. Others rescued Nazi victims out of religious, humanitarian, or altruistic motives. As of October 1996, 13,668 people have been recognized for heroic efforts during the war. Of the thirty-three nationalities included, there were 4,478 Poles, 3,774 Dutch, 1,249 French, and 685 Belgians.

SUGGESTED READINGS: Bartoszewski and Lewin, *Righteous Among Nations;* Silver, *The Book of the Just;* Tec, *When Light Pierced the Darkness.*

Ringelblum, Emmanuel (1900–1944). Social historian, archivist, an organizer of **House Committees**. He was the author of *Notes from the Warsaw Ghetto* and leader of the **Oneg Shabbat** (archivists). The historian was captured by the Nazis in 1943 and sent to the **Poniatowa slave labor** camp. He was smuggled from the camp and taken to the **Aryan** side of Warsaw. In January 1944, Ringelblum rejected offers of safe passage and stayed in Warsaw where he, his wife and child, and thirty-five others were killed by the Nazis. After the war, ten file cases and two milk cans containing documentation of conditions in the

ghetto were discovered. (See also **Central Agency for Care of Orphans, Simon Dubnow**, and **Chaim Aaron Kaplan**.)

SUGGESTED READING: Ringelblum, *Notes from the Warsaw Ghetto*.

La Risiera di San Sabba. **Concentration camp** near Trieste. Of 20,000 inmates, over 3,000 Italian POWs and 620 Jews from Trieste were executed by the Nazis in the camp. Its first commander was **SS Major Christian Wirth**. From October 1943–March 1944, twenty-two **transports** carried deportees to **Auschwitz**. On February 25, 1945, the final **deportation** for **Bergen-Belsen** took place. The camp was **liberated** on April 30, 1945.

SUGGESTED READING: Zuccotti, *The Italians and the Holocaust*.

Ritter, Dr. Robert (b. 1901). Headed Eugenic and Criminal Biological Research Section of **Reich** Health Department. He was the German psychiatrist responsible for compiling a national Racial Census of **Roma** and **Sinti** beginning in 1936. These ''health'' surveys served to locate and isolate the Roma population. Convinced that the Roma ''social characteristics'' were hereditary and could not be changed by environmental means, he provided the intellectual and empirical underpinnings for **genocide**. Ritter was assisted by Eva Justin, a nurse and anthropologist. (See also **Wilhelm Frick, Genetic Health Courts**, and **Hollerith Machine**.)

SUGGESTED READING: Proctor, *Racial Hygiene*.

Rivesaltes. French **internment camp**. Located in unoccupied southern **France** near the Spanish border. Large numbers of German Jews from Baden, Palantine, and the Saar regions were rounded up by the Germans and dumped at the border between occupied and **Unoccupied France**. The **Vichy Gendarmerie** arrested these Jews and placed them at Rivesaltes and **Gurs**. About 3,000 Jews died in French internment camps. Most of the Jews were later **deported** to **death camps**. Spanish Republicans and **Roma** were also interned in Rivesaltes. (See also **October Deportation, Rotspanir**, and **Society for the Rescue of Jewish Children**.)

SUGGESTED READING: Zuccotti, *The Holocaust, the French, and the Jews*.

Roatta, General Mario (1887–1968). General and commander of the Second Italian Army stationed in **Croatia**. He refused **von Ribbentrop's** requests to turn Jews over for **deportation. Hitler** was enraged and asked **Benito Mussolini** to talk to Roatta; however, the general devised a scheme to temper Hitler's anger—internment of Jews under benign supervision. Roatta was transferred to **Italy** in May 1943, but his successor, General Rabotti, also protected the Jews.

SUGGESTED READINGS: Gutman, *Men and Ashes*; Herzer, *The Italian Refuge*; Zuccotti, *The Italians and the Holocaust*.

Robota, Roza (1921–1944). Jewish **resister**. She was an active member of **Ha-Shomer ha-Tzair** in Ciechanow, **Poland**, who was taken to **Auschwitz** in 1942.

She joined the underground in the camp in 1943 and smuggled gunpowder from the **Union Werke** factory in Auschwitz to the **Sonderkommandos** at **Birkenau**. After the October 1944 revolt in Birkenau, the resister was tortured and then hanged at roll call a few days before the camp was evacuated. Robota's last word was, "Nekama!" (Revenge!) (See also **Concentration Camp Uprisings, Mala Zimetbaum**, and **ZOX**.)

SUGGESTED READINGS: Suhl, *They Fought Back*; United States Holocaust Memorial Museum, *Darkness Before Dawn.*

Roedl, Arthur (1898–1945). Kommandant of **Gross-Rosen** and deputy to **Karl Koch** at **Buchenwald**. An alcoholic, at Gross-Rosen his conduct was marked by cruelty, sadism, and corruption. Roedl was dismissed as camp kommandant and placed with the occupation police in the **Ukraine** where he committed suicide in April 1945.

SUGGESTED READING: Segev, *Soldiers of Evil.*

Roehm, Ernst (1887–1934). Head of the **SA**. He was **Hitler's** superior in the **Reichswehr** who sent the corporal to investigate the **German Workers Party**. An old-line Nazi, he was primarily responsible for militarizing the **Nazi Party**. Roehm wanted the SA to supplant the **Reichswehr** as a "peoples" army. Hitler considered Roehm and the SA a challenge to his authority, and the German Army was also apprehensive about Roehm's 3 million man street militia. Hitler authorized the purging of the SA during the **Night of the Long Knives** in June 1934. Roehm was arrested on June 30, 1934, and executed in his cell two days later by an **SS** squad led by **Theodor Eicke**. The murder of the SA chief underlined the criminality of the Nazi state and squarely placed Hitler above the judiciary. After the purge, all German military swore a personal oath of allegiance to Adolf Hitler. (See also **Hermann Goering** and **Viktor Lutze**.)

SUGGESTED READINGS: Fest, *The Face of the Third Reich*; Snyder, *Hitler's Elite.*

Roethke, Heinz. SS first lieutenant in the **Gestapo** Bureau for Jewish Affairs in Paris. He planned the roundup (1943) of the Jews of Paris which involved the arrest (1943) of 4,500 foreign Jews in the occupied zone. Roethke worked with **Alois Brunner** in **Nice** hunting down Jews. Roethke succeeded **Theodor Dannecker** in **deporting** French Jews to the East. (See also **Velodrome d'Hiver**.)

SUGGESTED READING: Morgan, *An Uncertain Hour.*

Roma (G., **Zigeuner**) (also referred to as "**Gypsies**"). People living in Europe since the fifteenth century, bound by a common language and culture. The Roma were labeled **asocials** under the July 1933 Law for the Prevention of Offspring with Hereditary Defects. Ziguener were deemed "alien blood" in the race-based **Nuremberg Laws** (1935) and registered on racial grounds. After 1935, the Roma were arrested, sterilized, and **deported**. In 1936, the **Reich** Minister of the Interior, **Wilhelm Frick**, issued the guidelines, "On Combating the Gypsy Plague," which mandated fingerprinting and photographing of Roma and initiated the national racial census conducted by **Dr. Robert Ritter**. The following year, data gathered from this effort was used to send Roma to **concentration camps** where they were identified by a brown triangle. They were deported East for extermination in large numbers in early 1943. In early 1942, 5,000 Roma from the **Lodz Ghetto** were gassed at **Chelmno**. On June 1, 1942, the Nazis began arresting Roma in occupied **Poland. Heinrich Himmler** issued a declaration on December 16, 1942, to move all Ziguener to **Auschwitz-Birkenau;** the first **transport** arrived in Birkenau on February 26, 1943. Roma families were housed together in Camp II b, they kept their clothing, and were tattooed with a "**Z**." Most of the Roma were gassed in August 1944.

Roma were also deported to **Belzec, Buchenwald, Jasenovac, Majdanek, Pithiviers, Ravensbrueck, Sachsenhausen-Oranienburg, Sobibor, "Star Prison,"** Treblinka, and **Westerbork**. "Medical experiments" on Roma were conducted by **Drs. Joachim Mrugrowsky** and **Horst Schumann**. About 300,000 Roma of a total 872,000 were killed by Nazi barbarism during the war period. The major fatalities were in **Germany** (21,500), Poland (28,200), **USSR** (30,000), **Hungary** (28,000), **Romania** (36,000), and **Croatia** (28,000). The Roma received no compensation for their persecution and pain during the Nazi period. (See also **Ion Antonescu, Auschwitz, Babi Yar, "Black Saturday," Dehumanization, Eugenics, Genetic Health Courts, Hollerith Machine, Kiev, Lalleri, Mischlinge, Arthur Nebe, Porraimos, Ravensbrueck, Rome, Sinti, "Star Prison," Volksgemeinschaft**, and **The Yarnton Declaration**.)

SUGGESTED READINGS: Crowe and Kolsti, *The Gypsies of Eastern Europe*; Friedlander, *The Origins of Nazi Genocide*; Hancock, *The Pariah Syndrome*.

Romania (Rumania, Roumania). An Eastern European country and one of the Balkan kingdoms prior to World War II. It shared borders in the west with **Yugoslavia** and **Hungary**, in the east with the **USSR (Bessarabia)** and in the south with **Bulgaria** and the Black Sea. By entering World War I on the side of the **Allies**, it was rewarded (in 1919) with territory: **Bukovina**, northern Transylvania from **Austria**-Hungary, and Bessarabia (Moldavia) from the USSR. This award increased its Jewish population from 300,000 to 765,218 (1939) in a general population of 16.5 million. Romania was then made up of many minorities, including 500,000 **Volksdeutsche** and many Hungarians, particularly in Transylvania. The Jews in old Romania were assimilated and patriotic. The newly acquired provinces harbored two-thirds of the population of Greater Romania. **Anti-Semitism** was endemic. On November 23, 1940, the Baltic nation joined the **Axis** powers. **Hitler** arranged for northern Transylvania, a region northwest and in central Romania, to be annexed to his ally, Hungary. The 150,000 Transylvanian Hungarian Jews escaped the fate of their brothers until the summer of 1944 when they were **deported**. Three hundred thousand Jews of Bukovina and Bessarabia were under Soviet rule from 1940–1941. With the aggression of **Operation Barbarossa**, they met a terrible fate at the hands of both Romanian troops and **Einsatzgruppen**. Many were butchered in **Transnistria**. The Jews of Old Romania were spared—the Romanian government under **Ion Antonescu** considered using them for barter as the war went against **Germany**. There was a proposal in 1943 to release Jews to **Palestine** for $1,340 per head, a proposal hushed up and sabotaged by the U.S. State Department. The **Red Army** started offensives, and the fear of retribution saved many Romanian Jews. The victorious Red Army captured the capital city of Bucharest on February 13, 1945.

Of the 185,000 Jewish deportees from Transnistria, there were 51,000 survivors; of the 150,000 Transylvanian Jews (most deported to **Auschwitz**), there were 30,000 survivors. After the war, approximately 350,000 Jews remained in Romania. Today, there are 15,000 to 18,000 (See also **Conducator, Czernowitz, Josiah DuBois, Dr. Wilhelm Filderman, Dr. Nandor Gingold, Ira Hirschmann, Iasi, Iron Guard, Siegfried Jagendorf, Kishinev, Radu Lecca, Mogilev-Podolski, Odessa, Old Kingdom of Romania, Traian Popovici, Gustav Richter, Rabbi Alexandre Safran, Horia Sima, Special Echelon**, *Struma*, **Tuchin, War Refugee Board, Chaim Weizmann, Rabbi Stephen S. Wise**, and **Abraham L. Zissu**.)

Rome. Capital city of **Italy** and site of Europe's oldest Jewish community. In 1943, 8,000 Jews lived there in the shadow of the **Vatican**. In October, the Germans moved into the city by force and tried to implement the **Final Solution**. Lt. Colonel **Herbert Kappler** demanded a ransom of 50 kilos of gold ($56,254) with the threat of arresting 300 **hostages**. The Jewish community, whose wealthy members were in hiding, did not raise the sum. According to **Rabbi Israel Zolli**, the Vatican delivered 15 kilos of gold ($16,879). Notwithstanding, a roundup of Jews occurred on "**Black Saturday**," and 1,007 Jews were **deported** to **Auschwitz**. Nearly 7,000 Jews escaped the murderous net. The Vatican opened church institutions for hiding Jews; however, the pope himself did not protest the **Aktion**. In March 1944, a **resister's** bomb killed three German officers, which triggered the **Ardeantine Cave** incident. The Italian Committee of National **Liberation**, an umbrella organization of **resistance** to **fascism** was centered in Rome and gave the rescue of Jews a special role. (See also **Bishop Alois Hudal** and **Pope Pius XII**.)

SUGGESTED READINGS: Herzer, *The Italian Refuge*; Kurzman, *The Race for Rome*.

Roncalli, Angelo (Pope John XXIII) (1881–1963). Apostolic delegate to Turkey and **Greece** from 1935–1944 and **nuncio** to **France** from 1944–1953. He was elected pope in 1958. Roncalli was actively involved in saving thousands of Jews from **deportation** (particularly in **Hungary**) while apostolic delegaria at Istanbul, but he was uncomfortable with increased Jewish immigration to a potential Jewish state in **Palestine**. As Pope John XXIII, he initiated **Vatican**

reforms expurgating negative references to Jews. (See also **Bulgaria, Ira Hirschmann, Jules Isaac**, and **Pope Pius XII**.)

SUGGESTED READINGS: Hoffman, "Roncalli in the Second World War": Morse, *While Six Million Died*; Szule, *The Secret Alliance*.

Roosevelt, Eleanor (1884–1962). American humanitarian and wife of President **Franklin Delano Roosevelt**. She initially opposed active rescue of European Jews, although she supported emergency **visas** in 1940 until the war was won (June 1943). The First Lady visited **Oswego**, and was so moved that she wrote about her experiences in her syndicated column "My Day." Mrs. Roosevelt fought for Oswego **refugees** to become citizens and helped eight students enroll in college. After the war, she regretted she hadn't done enough to save European Jewry. She drafted the **United Nations Declaration of Human Rights** with the **Holocaust** in mind. Mrs. Roosevelt wrote the Introduction to the American edition of **Anne Frank's** diary. (See also **Varian Fry**.)

SUGGESTED READINGS: Gruber, *Haven*; Haveron, *Eleanor Roosevelt*; Herzstein, *Roosevelt and Hitler; New York Times*, November 7, 1945; December 11, 1962 (Obit.).

Roosevelt, Franklin Delano (1882–1945). American president from 1933–1945. He recognized early the great danger that the Nazis posed to the **Allies**, but was reluctant to tamper with restrictive immigration laws to help European Jews seeking refuge. However, he did order the State Department to admit as many **refugees** as legally possible in 1938. Roosevelt met with **Jan Karski**, who personally informed him of the **Final Solution**. He met only once (December 8, 1942) with a delegation of American Jews led by **Rabbi Stephen S. Wise** to discuss the persecution of European Jews. He did issue warnings to the **Axis** on crimes against Jews and others. The president was beloved by American Jews, a number of whom served in his administration, including Secretary of the Treasury **Henry Morganthau Jr**. He established the **War Refugee Board** by executive order in January 1944, an agency that saved 200,000 Jews. (See also **Casablanca Conference, William Dodd, Josiah DuBois, Albert Einstein, Evian Conference, Varian Fry, Horthy Offer, Cordell Hull, Hungary, Harold L. Ickes, Joseph D. Kennedy, Breckinridge Long, Moscow Declaration, Oswego, John Pehle**, *Saint Louis*, **Abba Hillel Silver, Tripartite Conference**, and **Yalta Conference**.)

SUGGESTED READINGS: Feingold, *The Politics of Rescue*; Herzstein, *Roosevelt and Hitler*; Pentower, *The Jews Were Expendable*.

Rosenbaum, Rabbi Pinchas Tibor. Rescuer. He founded a secret B'nai Akiva (**Mizrachi**) cell in the **forced labor (Munkaszolgalat)** unit of the Hungarian Army (1944). He obtained safe-conduct passes from the **Zionist** underground, which he used to help free Jews from **labor camps** and elsewhere transferring them to safe-houses in the Swiss legation buildings in Budapest. The rabbi also obtained **Arrow Cross** and **SS** uniforms to lead Jews away to safety.

SUGGESTED READING: Braham, *The Hungarian Labor Service System.*

Rosenberg, Dr. Alfred (1893–1946). Chief Nazi ideologist. He was a member of the **Thule Society** before joining the **Nazi Party**. Rosenberg edited the *Volk-ischer Beobachter* and *NS Monatshefte* and wrote many books on Nazi ideology. Later, Rosenberg headed the **Institute for the Study on Jewish Questions (Einsatzstab)** founded in Frankfurt in March 1941. Viruently **anti-Semitic**, he greatly influenced **Hitler** through his book *The Myth of the Twentieth Century*. Rosenberg was a member of the inner circle prior to the Nazi ascension to power. He originated the **Lublinland** concept and pushed for resettling Jews to **Madagascar**. Rosenberg was tapped to be the **Reich** Minister for the Occupied **Eastern Territories** on July 17, 1941, and given the important task of governing the Eastern Territories, which included the liquidation of Jews. However, his power in this capacity was limited. Rosenberg was convicted of **war crimes** at the **Nuremberg Trials** and hanged. (See also **Einsatzstab, Rosenberg, Heinrich Lohse, Mit brennenger Sorge**, and **Rassenpolitik**.)

SUGGESTED READINGS: Davidson, *The Trial of the Germans*; Fest, *The Face of the Third Reich.*

Rosenstrasse. (See **Operation Factory**.)

Rote Kapelle (G., **Red Orchestra**).

Rothmund, Dr. Heinrich. Chief of Federal Swiss Police. He "suggested" German Jewish **passports** be specially marked with a red "**J**". On September 29, 1938, a treaty was signed between **Germany** and **Switzerland**, adopting this measure. The agreement amounted to a de facto death sentence, especially after **Kristallnacht**, since it made escape from Germany extremely difficult. Thousands of Jews who escaped the **Reich** to Switzerland were returned to Germany (1944) based on this agreement. After the release of the **Auschwitz Protocols**, Rothmund relented on the policy of **refoulement**. (See also **Kennkarte, George Mandel Mantello, Saly Mayer, Roswell McClelland, Eduard von Steiger**, and **Rita and Isaac Sternbuch**.)

SUGGESTED READING: Haesler, *The Lifeboat is Full.*

Rotspanir (G., Red Spaniards). Spanish Republicans incacerated in several internment camps in **France** and then **deported** to camps within the **Reich**. The Republicans were well organized and miraculously adapted to the harsh conditions at **Mauthausen**. (See also **Le Chambon-sur-Lignon, Rivesaltes, Paul Touvier, Gurs**, and **Trans-Sahara Railway**.)

Rotta, Monsignor Angelo. Papal **nuncio** in Budapest. He intervened on behalf of Hungarian Jewry from June–September 1944. Rotta made numerous protests to authorities, informed the **Vatican**, coordinated with other rescue agencies by issuing numerous baptismal certificates, safe conduct passes, and other documents. Additionally, he sheltered 2,500 Jews on church property. (See also **Angel Miguel Sanz-Briz** and **Schutzpaesse**.)

SUGGESTED READINGS: Friedman, *Their Brothers' Keepers*; Morse, *While Six Million Died*.

Rottenfuehrer. SS corporal.

RSHA/Reich Security Main Office (Reichssicherheitshauptamt). The combined headquarters of the Nazi security police, security service, and **Gestapo** as of September 27, 1939. It was the principal office of the Nazi regime's political, ideological, and racial warfare. The RSHA's backbone was the Gestapo and was founded by **Reinhard Heydrich**. After his assassination, **Ernst Kaltenbrunner** assumed command on January 30, 1943. This branch of the **SS** issued a decree in 1940 containing a tacit order for the **Final Solution** and coordinated the activities of the **Einsatzgruppen**. (See also **Abwehr, Circle of Friends of Himmler, Adolf Eichmann, Homosexuals, Kripo, Martin Luther, Franz Novak, Otto Ohlendorf, Walter Rauff, Reich Central Office for Jewish Emigration, SD, Sipo, Dr. Franz W. Six, Franz Walter Stahlecker**, and **Dieter Wisliceny**.)

SUGGESTED READINGS: Breitman, *The Architect of Genocide*; Lumsden, *The Black Corps*.

Rudninkai Forest. Site of **partisan** activity, located near **Vilna**. (See also **Yitzhak Arad, Maria Rozka Korczak, Hiam Yelin**, and **Henrik Ziman**.)

Rudolph, Arthur (b. 1907). Rocket scientist and chief engineer at the V-2 site in **Peenemuende Aerodynamics Institute** (later in the Hartz mountains). This **Nazi Party** member advocated the use of **slave labor** on the rocket project resulting in the death of 10,000 **concentration camp** inmates. He was brought to the United States as part of **Project Paperclip**, then deported in 1984 when his wartime activities were publicly exposed. Rudolph is petitioning to return to the United States. (See also **Wernher von Braun, Dora-Nordhausen, General Walter Dornberger**, and **Hans Kammler**.)

SUGGESTED READINGS: Hunt, *Secret Agenda*; Neufeld, *The Rocket and the Reich*.

Rueckkehr unterwuenscht (G., "Return not desired"). An "RU" placed on an inmate's dossier by the **Gestapo** was a death sentence in a **concentration camp**. (See also **Nacht und Nebel**.)

Ruedin, Dr. Ernst (1874–1952). Swiss-born psychiatrist. He joined the **Nazi Party** in 1937, co-founded the German Society for **Racial Hygiene**, and became director of the **Kaiser Wilhelm Institute** for psychiatry. He received two awards from **Hitler** "as a pathfinder in the field of hereditary hygiene" and is also referred to as the "Father of Sterilization." Ruedin was not directly involved in killing. (See also **Euthanasia** and **Dr. Alfred Ploetz**.)

SUGGESTED READING: Proctor, *Racial Hygiene.*

Rufeisen, Shmuel ("Oswald"; also Father Daniel). Polish Jew who came to **Mir** from western **Galicia** using a dead person's papers. His knowledge of German enabled him to become an interpreter for the German police occupying the area. Rufeisen became commandant of the Mir police, and in that position, Rufeisen rescued Jews, aided, and helped to organize the **resistance**. He warned the resistance of impending **Aktionen** (1941–1942). After his arrest and escape, he hid in a monastery (1912–1945) where he converted to Catholicism. Father Daniel immigrated to Israel.

SUGGESTED READINGS: Suhl, *They Fought Back*; Trunk, *Jewish Responses.*

Rumkowski, Mordechai Chaim ("King Chaim") (1877–1944). Head of the Lodz **Judenrat**. He was shrewd, manipulative, egocentric, and ruled Lodz like a personal fiefdom. His philosophy was to save Jews by making the **ghetto** economically indispensable to the Nazis: "Work is our only way." Rumkowski was somewhat successful. The **Lodz Ghetto** was the last major ghetto to be liquidated. Unlike **Adam Czerniakow** in Warsaw, Rumkowski tried to accommodate and negotiate with the Nazis as Lodz was being "resettled." Most of the Jews were gassed in **Chelmno**. Eventually, he and his family were **deported** to **Auschwitz** and gassed. (See also **Hans Biebow, "Resettlement,"** and **"Work as a Means of Rescue."**)

SUGGESTED READINGS: Trunk, *Judenrat*; Tushnet, *The Pavement of Hell.*

RuSHA. (See **Race and Resettlement Main Office**.)

Russia. Inexact generic term applied to **Union of Soviet Socialist Republics (USSR)** during World War II period. At the time, Russia was the largest of fifteen Soviet Republics whose territory spread across Eastern Europe: bordering **Belorussia** and **Poland** on the east; the **Ukraine** on the south; north to **Siberia** and east into northern Asia bordering with China. Russia's Slavic European population in 1939 was 85 million; its Asian population east of the Ural Mountains was 5 million. The independence of the so-called "autonomous republics" was a facade. In reality, the USSR was a communist dictatorship, dominated by ethnic Russians, with the Russian language and culture permeating throughout the federation. The name "Russia" was inherited from the Tsarist empire, which was overthrown in 1917 when the Bolsheviks established one-party totalitarian rule.

About 3 million Jews were counted in the Soviet census of 1939. Two million

Jews came under dictator **Josef Stalin's** rule between September 1939 and June 1940. This included the Baltic states (**Latvia, Lithuania**, and **Estonia**) and the "return" to the USSR by **Romania** of **Bessarabia** and **Bukovina** and half of Poland acquired by force. About 200,000 **refugee** Jews crossed into Soviet territory with the outbreak of war with **Germany** (1941), and another 150,000 Polish Jews found refuge deep in central Russia. Soviet takeovers in 1939–1940 brought poverty and exile for middle-class Jews. Jewish religious, social, and cultural institutions were abolished. Those who rejected Soviet citizenship were **deported** to Siberia. Later, wartime practical considerations (**Stalin–Sikorski** Pact) made the authorities revoke this policy, and Polish Jews received amnesty. Many fled to Soviet central Asia. Jews under communist rule were not informed of the German atrocities against their brethren.

At no time during the war did Soviet authorities acknowledge the Nazi purpose was to destroy the Jews of Europe. There was no political or military offensive to support Jews, although thousands of Jews fled into the Russian interior. Indeed, when masses of Jews were killed, the term "Jew" was not mentioned. However, most Soviet **partisans** accepted Jews. The invasion of the Soviet Union by German forces unleashed the **Holocaust** in full fury. The figures for German-occupied Soviet areas show over 1.4 million Jewish victims. (See also **General Wladyslaw Anders, Menachem Begin, Ilya Grigorovitch Ehrenburg, Jewish Anti-Fascist Committee, Operation Barbarossa, Red Army, Vitebsk, Zhitomir, Henrik Ziman**, and **Zolochev**.)

Russian Liberation Army (Ru., **Russkaya Osvoboditelnaya Armiya**). Comprised of two divisions of pro-Nazi, Russian military personnel. Headed by **Lt. General Andrei Vlasov**, the first battalion was established on December 1, 1944, and the second on January 23, 1945. These soldiers assisted in the murder of Jews during anti-**partisan** atrocities. This Army surrendered to the Americans. They were turned over to the Soviets who executed these **collaborators**.

SUGGESTED READING: Andreyev, *Vlasov and the Russian Liberation Movement.*

Rust, Dr. Bernard (1883–1945). Nazi Minister of Education. He dismissed over 1,000 Jews from educational institutions, including **Albert Einstein**. He included a curriculum in schools that presented Jews as hereditary enemies of **Germany**, "a chosen people of criminals who endanger the existence of the **Third Reich**." (See also **Walter Schultze** and **Dr. Johannes Stark**.)

SUGGESTED READING: Wistrich, *Who's Who in Nazi Germany.*

Ruthenia. Area at the tail end of prewar **Czechoslovakia** near the **Ukraine**. About 104,000 Jews lived in **Slovakian** territories ceded to **Hungary** in 1939— Ruthenia and Subcarpathia. Their fate was sealed with Hungarian Jews.

S

SA (G., **Sturmabteilungen; "Stormtroopers"**; Storm Detachment). Also known as the "**Brown Shirts**." This was an old-line, Nazi paramilitary organization led by **Ernst Roehm**. A brutal street force, especially valuable from 1922–1933 in battling communists and socialists, its membership peaked at 4.5 million men and women. The organization was purged of its leadership during the **Night of the Long Knives** and faded from importance. (See also **Anti-Jewish Boycott, Viktor Lutze, Reichswehr**, and **Wilde Lager**.)

Sachs, Nelly (1891–1970). German Jewish poet of the **Holocaust**. She was best known for "O' The Chimneys." Sachs fled to **Sweden** in 1940 and won a Nobel Prize for literature in 1966.

Sachsenhausen-Oranienburg. Concentration camp for men outside of **Berlin**, which opened in 1933 as a **Wilde Lager**. Approximately 10,000 Jewish men were interned in Sachsenhausen after **Kristallnacht**. This facility had an eclectic array of inmates including **partisans**, political opponents, Poles, **Soviet POWs, Roma, homosexuals**, and Jews. Of the 204,000 inmates interned at this camp, approximately half were murdered or died from torture or starvation. The facility exploited **slave labor**. The most feared assignments were unloading ships at the **Klinker Project** or laboring at the **Klinker Brickworks**. Homosexuals were routinely sent to the Brickworks where the average life expectancy was thirty days. "Medical experiments" were conducted at the Pathologie by Drs. Werner Fisher and **Joachim Mrugrowsky** on Jews and Roma. Drs. **Erwin Ding-Schuler** and **Albert Widmann** conducted "poison bullet" experiments. In 1943, this camp was the scene of a major counterfeiting ring producing fake British pounds. The **SS** evacuation of over 30,000 inmates began on April 20,

1945. About 3,000 emaciated prisoners were present when the Soviets arrived on April 22, 1945. However, the Soviets did not free the inmates until early May. (See also **Hermann Baranowski, Berlin, Gross-Rosen, Heinkel Werke, Hans Loritz**, and **Martin Luther**.

SUGGESTED READINGS: Feig, *Hilter's Death Camps*; United States Holocaust Memorial Museum, *1945: The Year of Liberation.*

"Saeuberungsaktion" (G., "cleansing operation"). Killing prisoners in an area to make room for new ones, for example, **Block 11** at **Auschwitz**. It could also mean **deporting** Jewish communities to extermination centers.

Safran, Rabbi Alexandre (b. 1911). Chief rabbi of **Romania's** 750,000 Jews from 1940–1947. His residence was a focal point for underground activities and a center for aid to Jews during the war. The Rabbi beseeched the Catholic Church, Greek Orthodox Metropolitan Tit Siemdrea, and Queen Mother Elena, for assistance and relief from **anti-Semitic** laws and persecution against Romania's Jews. His pleas met with limited success and a brief respite in **deportations**. The Romanian policy initiative of selling Jews their permits and **visas** via Western nations was a result of Safran's activities, but was blocked by the U.S. State Department. The rabbi was expelled by the communists in 1947 and made his home in Geneva, **Switzerland**. (See also **Breckinridge Long**.)

SUGGESTED READINGS: Butnaru, *The Silent Holocaust*; Butnaru, *Waiting for Jerusalem*; Safran, *Resisting the Storm.*

Saint James Declaration. Statement by **Allied** governments, including governments-in-exile in London on January 17, 1942, concerning the punishment of criminal acts by the **Axis** against civilian populations. This declaration was supposed to be included among the principal war aims by the signatories. However, the statement did not include persecution of Jews and was followed by a policy of hushing up in regard to the **Final Solution**. (See also **Totschweigen**.)

SUGGESTED READING: Cohn, *Churchill and the Jews.*

Saint Louis. German cruise ship. Despite the fact that the passengers possessed Cuban landing papers, the president of Cuba invalidated their papers, claiming they were illegal. The passengers were denied entry into Havana. (The Cuban government asked for a $500,000 entry fee.) The vessel set sail for the Florida coast. President Franklin Delano **Roosevelt**, who ignored appeals and a cable from passengers, ordered the Coast Guard to prevent this ship from landing in the United States from June 4–6, 1939. This was done even though 734 of the Jewish passengers held valid U.S. **quota** numbers. No Latin American country would accept the refugees. The *St. Louis*, which started its journey in Bremen, docked at Antwerp on June 17, 1939. The European representative of the "**Joint**" arranged for the Jews to find temporary haven in England (287), **Bel-**

gium (214), **France** (224), and the **Netherlands** (181). Six people had proper credentials and disembarked in Cuba. Almost all of the 287 people who went to England survived. Only an estimated 240 of those who returned to the continent lived. Its voyage punctuated U.S. indifference to the plight of Jewish refugees. (See also **Evian Conference.**)

SUGGESTED READING: Thomas and Witt, *Voyage of the Damned.*

"Salami." **SS** term for Hungarian Jews arriving at **Auschwitz.**

Salazar, Antonio de Oliveria (1899–1970). **Fascist** dictator of **Portugal**. In 1933, one year after becoming premier, Salazar transferred Portugal into a dictatorship based on fascist principles. During World War II, he kept Portugal neutral, maintained cordial relations with Great Britain and the United States, and did not institute anti-Jewish laws against Portugal's 3,000 Jewish citizens. Lisbon was a base for Jewish refugees and rescue. (Ironically, the expulsion edict imposed under King Alphonso in 1510 was still in effect.) (See also **Francisco Franco** and **HICEM.**)

SUGGESTED READING: Figueiredo, *Portugal: Fifty Years of Dictatorship.*

Saliege, Monsignor Jules-Gerard (1870–1956). Archbishop of Toulouse. He actively opposed anti-Jewish measures in Vichy **France**. In August 1942, a pastoral letter, which became known as the "Saliege Bomb," demanded compassion for Jews and had a profound impact on French public opinion. He ordered Sister Denise Bergon to shelter sixty five Jewish children and eleven adults in a summer camp.

SUGGESTED READING: Webster, *Petain's Crime.*

Salonika. Main port of **Greek Macedonia** with an established **Sephardic** Jewish community of 56,000 people. Nazi occupation began on April 9, 1941. Jewish properties were marked and ghettos were created. **Deportations** began in February 1943. From March 14–August 7, 1943, most of the Jews (44,000) were deported to their deaths in **Birkenau**. Jews holding Italian, Spanish, and Turkish passports were protected. In 1945, the Salonikan Jewish population was 1,950. (See also **Athens, Alois Brunner, Italy, Ladino, Rhodes, Spain, General Juergen Stroop, Dieter Wisliceny,** and **Guelfo Zamboni.**)

SUGGESTED READINGS: Gaon and Serels, *Sephardim and the Holocaust*; Herzstein, *Waldheim, The Missing Years.*

Salo Republic. **Fascist** Italian puppet-state. Controlled by the Nazis, it was established under **Bonito Mussolini** after his rescue from captivity on September 12, 1943. The Republic had nominal control over northern **Italy** where German troops took over. Zealous fascists did arrest and **deport** an estimated 7,000 to 10,000 Jews in areas under their jurisdiction beginning on January 22, 1944. (See also **SS Colonel Otto Skorzeny.**)

SUGGESTED READING: Herzer, *The Italian Refugee.*

Sanz-Briz, Miguel Angel. Spanish diplomat in **Hungary**. He saved thousands of Jews in 1944, including 5,500 children and 60 adults who were issued Spanish citizenship papers. On November 17, 1944, together with **Monsignor Angelo Rotta** and other neutral representatives, they appealed to **Ferenc Szalasi** to halt Jewish **death marches**. Sanz-Briz left Hungary in early December 1944, but the Spanish embassy issued an additional 3,000 protective passes. (See also **Schutzpaesse** and **Spain**.)
    SUGGESTED READING: Avni, *Spain, the Jews and Franco.*

"Sarah." Middle name assigned to all Jewish women on their German ID cards and **passports** on January 1, 1939 if they did not have a distinct Jewish name. Jewish males were forced to adopt **"Israel"** as their middle name.

Sarajevo. City in Bosnia with a Jewish population of 10,000 in 1941. It was occupied by the Germans from April 1941–April 1945. Muslims engaged in a **pogrom** and destroyed the historic **Sephardic** Jewish synagogue during German occupation. Jews were deprived of their livelihood, subject to random arrests, and murdered. Mass **deportations** began in September 1941, mainly to **Jasenovac**. About 2,400 Jews were saved by the Italians, and 1,400 returned to Sarajevo. (See also **Italy** and **Yugoslavia**.)
    SUGGESTED READING: Friedenreich, *The Jews of Yugoslavia.*

"Sardine." **SS** slang for French Jews arriving in **Auschwitz**.

Sauckel, Fritz (1894–1946). Plenipotentiary General for Labor Mobilization from 1942–1945, **Reich** governor, and **Gauleiter** of Thuringia. Sauckel was a ruthless coordinator and supplier of foreign **forced labor** for the Nazi war machine. He was responsible for the deaths of thousands of Jewish workers in **Poland**. He bragged: "Of the five million foreign workers who came to **Germany**, less than 200,000 came voluntarily." He was pushed from power by **Joseph Goebbels** in July 1944. Sauckel received the death sentence at the **Nuremberg Trials** and was hanged with the major **war criminals** on October 16, 1946. (See also **Central Planning Board**, **Impressing**, and **Albert Speer**.)
    SUGGESTED READING: Davidson, *The Trial of the Germans.*

Saurer, Albert (1898–1945). First kommandant of **Mauthausen** and kommandant of **Ravensbrueck** for a few days. He was killed on May 3, 1945.

Saurer. German company that designed and built the gassing vans ("**sonderwagon**"). (See also **Chelmno** and **Walter Rauff**.)
    SUGGESTED READING: Berndac, *The 186 Steps.*

SCH (G., **Schutzhaftling**).

Schachmeister (G., chief foreman at work camp).

Schalburg Corps. Danish **collaborationist** police. They worked with the Germans to roundup Jews. (See also **DNSAP**.)

Scharfuehrer. **SS** staff sergeant.

Schein (G., work card). Permit issued to Jews working for German-owned companies or impressed into Nazi **forced labor**. The card "temporarily" exempted the bearer from **deportation**. (See also **Arbeitskarten, "Impressing," Labor Camp**, and **Sperre**.)

Scheissmeister (G., Latrine master). Orderlies who stayed in the latrine and noted time and frequency an inmate would spend there.

Schellenberg, Walther (1910–1952). **SS** general and intelligence officer. He was head of the SS office for counterespionage and was director of the German Political Information Office. Schellenberg sent a circular on May 20, 1941, to all departments of the German Security Police and all German consulates announcing that Jewish emigration from Europe was forbidden due to the "imminent **Final Solution** of the Jewish question." Young, bright, and an ex-law and medical student, Schellenberg became an SS major general at the age of 30. He was adored by **Heinrich Himmler** and blackmailed by **Reinhard Heydrich**. (His stepmother was Jewish.) As early as August 1942, he began negotiations with the British for a separate peace with the West with Himmler's approval. He conducted negotiations with **Jean-Marie Musy** in late 1944 to exchange inmates for foreign currency. Schellenberg also negotiated with **Count Folke Bernadotte** and **Carl Jacob Burkhardt** in October 1944. He was tried with **Ernst von Weizsacker**, acquitted of **genocide**, but found complicit in the murder of **Soviet POWs**. Schellenberg was sentenced to six years in prison and released in 1951 due to ill health. He retired to **Switzerland** where he wrote his memoirs.
SUGGESTED READING: Bauer, *Jews for Sale?*

Schenck, Dr. Ernst (b. 1904). **SS** lt. colonel, medical chief of the hospital of Munich and chairman of the Scientific Society for Natural Life and Therapy. He was Liekist, which meant he advocated noninterference with pain. He was **Dr. Leonardo Conti's** closest advisor on national health policies. Schenck worked to improve the diet of SS troops and was selected by **Heinrich Himmler** to carry out food and nutrition experiments on 370 inmates at **Mauthausen**. He became a full professor of physiology after the war.
SUGGESTED READING: Kater, *Doctors Under Hitler.*

Schilling, Dr. Claus (1871–1946). Established a malaria experiment facility at **Dachau** from 1942–1944. He never became a member of the **SS** or the **Nazi Party**. Schilling tested tropical medicine on approximately 1,200 inmates; many were Catholic priests. Approximately 400 prisoners died as a result of the experiments, many succumbing to medical overdoses. Schilling reported to **Heinrich Himmler** and **Dr. Ernst von Grawitz**. He was tried at a military court (1945) at Dachau and executed for his involvement in malaria experiments. (See also **Dr. Leonardo Conti, Priesterblock**, and **Dr. Wolfram Sievers**.)

   SUGGESTED READING: United States Holocaust Memorial Museum, *1945: The Year of Liberation.*

Schindler, Oskar (1908–1974). Sudeten-German and Jewish protector. He was a **Nazi Party** member and an agent of the **Abwehr** who operated an enamelware factory, **Emalia**, in **Krakow**. Schindler used his connections to secure humane conditions for his 900 Jewish workers. He was imprisoned several times by the **Gestapo**, accused of corruption, and released. The Jewish protector successfully transported 1,100 Jews from Krakow and **Plaszow** to work in his home town of Brunnlitz. Schindler was honored at **Yad Vashem** as a **Righteous Gentile**. He was was buried in the Catholic cemetery in Israel in 1974.

   SUGGESTED READING: Brecher, *Schindler's Legacy.*

Schirach, Baldur von (1907–1974). Head of the **Hitler Youth**, which included the supervision of the **Bund deutscher Maedel. The Reichstatthalter** of **Austria** (1933–1940), and **Gauleiter** of **Vienna** (1940–1945), von Schirach preached racism, which included a strong **anti-Semitic** component. At the **Nuremberg Trials** he maintained that he was strongly influenced by Henry Ford's *The International Jew.* As Gauleiter of Vienna, he arranged for the **deportation** of 50,000 Jews to **concentration camps** in **Poland**. In 1943, von Schirach fell from grace when he advocated moderate treatment for Eastern Europeans and better conditions for the Jews. A product of the German nobility, he announced: "If anyone reproaches me with having driven from this city, which was once the European metropolis of Jewry, tens of thousands upon tens of thousands into the **ghettos** of the East, I feel myself compelled to reply: I see in this an action contributing to European culture." The evidence used against him at the Nuremberg Trials included minutes of a meeting he attended with **Hitler** where they discussed the deportation of Jews. von Schirach was contrite at Nuremberg, sentenced to twenty years, then released in 1966. (See also *Protocols of the Learned Elders of Zion.*)

   SUGGESTED READINGS: Davidson, *The Trial of the Germans*; Koch, *Hitler Youth.*

Schmelt Organization. Economic agency of the **SS** operating in parts of Silesia and the **Sudetenland** from 1940–1943. Over 6,500 Jewish **forced laborers** were issued papers that temporarily exempted them from annihilation. (See also **Schein**.)

Schmid, Anton (1900–1942). **Righteous Gentile**. A German army sergeant, he helped Jewish **partisans** in **Vilna** by supplying them with papers, trucks, and guns from October 1941–March 1942. He was discovered smuggling Jews out of the Vilna **ghetto** by the **Gestapo** and executed on April 13, 1942.
   SUGGESTED READING: Elkins, *Forged in Fury.*

Schneersohn, Rabbi Joseph Isaac (1880–1950). The Grand **Rebbe** of the Lubavitch movement. He left the **USSR** and went to **Riga** in 1934. Eventually he settled in Warsaw, **Poland**. In 1940, he escaped to the United States with the aid of a half-Jewish German soldier, Major Ernst Flocks and a special appeal from the United States. Schneersohn eventually organized the Lubavitch **Hasidic** movement from his headquarters in Brooklyn. (See also **She'erit ha-Peletah**.)
   SUGGESTED READINGS: Jewish Exponent, January 2, 1997; Wein, *Triumph of Survival.*

Scholl, Hans (1918–1943) and **Sophie** (1921–1943). German student youth **resisters**. This brother and sister team formed the idealistic anti-Nazi group, **White Rose**, in Munich in 1942. This group published and distributed leaflets advocating the overthrow of the Nazis and labeled the regime mass murderers. They were inspired by **Bishop Clemens von Galen**. The Scholls were tried and convicted by the **People's Court**. They were beheaded on February 22, 1943.
   SUGGESTED READINGS: Dumbach and Newborn, *Shattering the German Night*; Jens, *At the Heart of the White Rose.*

Schonfeld, Rabbi Solomon (1912–1982). English rescue activist. Creator of the Chief Rabbi's Religious Emergency Council, a rescue organization active from 1938–1948, designed to bring Orthodox rabbis, teachers, and children to England. He obtained entry permits to rescue 3,700 Jews before and during the war. The rabbi also helped to rehabilitate **displaced persons** in the British sector of **Germany**. (See also **Kindertransport** and **Orthodox Judaism**.)
   SUGGESTED READING: Kranzler, *Thy Brother's Blood.*

"Schreibttischorder" (G., "desk murderer"). Bureaucrats who maintained the paper flow and schedule for the **Final Solution**. They did not perform the actual gassings, and many never saw their victims, for example, railroad dispatchers, agencies staff, corporate employees.

Schulte, Eduard (1891–1966). Anti-Nazi German industrialist. He revealed to a Swiss associate on July 30, 1942, credible information from **Hitler's** headquarters on the **Final Solution**. The information was relayed to **Dr. Gerhart Riegner** a few days later in Geneva.

SUGGESTED READING: Laquer and Breitman, *Breaking the Silence.*

Schultze, Walther (1894–1979). German leader of university lecturers. He was a member of the **Nazi Party** since its inception and participated in the Beer Hall Putsch (aborted Nazi revolution in Munich in 1923). As a national leader, he drove out Jews from universities and was involved in the **euthanasia** program. He was convicted of being complicit in the mercy killings of 380,000 and sentenced to four years in prison by a Military Tribunal. Schultze died of natural causes in his villa. (See also **Dr. Bernard Rust.**)

SUGGESTED READING: Friedlander, *The Origins of Nazi Genocide.*

Schuma (G., Schutzmannschaft de **Ordnungspolizei**). Detachments of Order Police, also referred to as Schupos); pro-German auxiliary police forces in occupied countries. They viewed Nazism as a liberating force. Their estimated strength in **Croatia**: 15,000; **Estonia**: 26,000; **Latvia**: 15,000; **Lithuania**: 13,000; and the **Ukraine**; 70,000. The Schuma committed atrocities against their own countrymen, **partisans**, and Jews. (See also **Einsatzgruppen, Freiwillige, Green Police, Hilfswillige, Latvian SS Legion, Lithuanian Activist Front, Ostbataillone, Perkonkrust**, and **Vilnius Sonderkommando.**)

Schumann, Dr. Horst (1906–1981). **SS** physician in charge of the **euthanasia** program. He was particularly active in the killing centers at Grafeneck and **Sonnenstein**. Schumann conducted cruel, painful, and unsuccessful sterilization experiments on approximately 1,200 inmates at **Auschwitz**. His attempts to sterilize inmates by using x-rays was found to be inefficient and many of the experimentees were sent to the **gas chambers**. Schumann continued his sterilization experiments on **Roma** girls at **Ravensbrueck**. Fleeing to Africa in 1951, Schumann evaded capture after the war. He was extradited to West **Germany** in 1966, served a prison term, and died in 1981. (See also **Dr. Carl Clauberg** and **Extradition.**)

SUGGESTED READINGS: Friedlander, *The Origins of Nazi Genocide*; Smolen et al., *KL Auschwitz Seen by the SS .*

Schutzbriefe (G., ''protective letters''). Extralegal letters of protection, created and issued by **Carl Lutz**, and other diplomats, to Jews in Budapest. The certificates stipulated that the bearers were to be given safe conduct for they were under the protection of the Swiss Embassy for one reason or another. Bearers were also boarded at apartment houses officially designated under Swiss protection. **Raoul Wallenberg** modeled his **Schutzpaesse** after the idea in the summer of 1944.

Schutze. **SS** private.

Schutzhaftbefehl (G., "**protective custody**" order). Procedure instituted by the **Gestapo** on February 28, 1933, and legalized by **Wilhelm Frick**. The Gestapo had the authority to arrest anyone, at any time—who they deemed a danger to public safety—without a warrant or hearing. The primary target, German dissidents, were usually sent to **concentration camps** and eventually murdered later in the war. (See also **Night and Fog, Schutzhaftling**, and **Social Democrats**.)

Schutzhaeftjuden (G., "**protective custody**" Jews). Jews sent to **concentration camps** for an alleged transgression.

Schutzhaeftling (G., inmate in "**protective custody**") (**SCH**). Prisoner marked for punishment or **death** in **concentration camps**.

Schutzjuden (G., "protected" Jews). In pre-Nazi **Germany**, this term referred to insulated Jews from the upper class. (See also **Privileged Jews**.)

Schutzpaesse (G., "protective passports"). An extralegal pass created by **Raoul Wallenberg** in the summer of 1944. These cards gave the impression that Jewish holders were on their way to **Sweden** under protection of the Royal Crown. Distribution of these documents is credited with saving 20,000 Jews in **Hungary**, mostly in Budapest. The **Vatican**, Spanish, Portuguese, Salvadoran, and Swiss diplomatic emissaries in Hungary also assisted in this campaign. (See also **Carl Lutz, George Mandel Mantello, Monsignor Angelo Rotta, Antonio de Oliveria Salazar**, and **Schutzbriefe**.)
   SUGGESTED READING: Anger, *With Raoul Wallenberg in Budapest.*

Schutzpolizei (G., protective police). City or municipal police.

Schutzstaffel (SS) ("Defense Echelon," Protection Squad, also known as the "**Black Shirts**"). A small detachment was formed in 1925 to provide security for **Hitler**. Beginning in 1929, under the tutelage of **Heinrich Himmler**, the SS was enlarged and became an independent entity (July 1944) within the **Nazi Party**. In 1934, it effectively eliminated its rival, the **SA**, during the **Night of the Long Knives**. The SS was composed of the **Gestapo, Kriminalpolizei, Waffen-SS**, and **Totenkopfverbaende**. All police agencies were brought under the control of the SS in 1936. The **Nuremberg** Tribunal declared the SS to be a criminal organization for the "persecution and extermination of Jews," brutality and murder of inmates in **concentration camps**, excesses in their administration of occupied territories, exploitation of **slave labor**, and mistreatment of POWs. (See also **Murray C. Bernays, Guido von List, Order Police, SD, Soviet POWs**, and **SS Central Office for Economy and Administration**.)
   SUGGESTED READINGS: Breitman, *The Architect of Genocide*: Sydnor, *Soldiers of Destruction.*

Schwammberger, Joseph (b. 1912). **Waffen-SS** sergeant. He was responsible for the death of 3,000 Jews, including inmates he killed at the Przemysl **ghetto** camp. Schwammberger eluded the **Allies** with the assistance of the **Red Cross**, then escaped to South America with the help of Catholic priests. He lived in Argentina for forty years before being extradited to **Germany** in 1990 for ordering the deaths of Jews in **slave labor** camps in **Poland**. Schwammberger was sentenced to life in prison. (See also **Extradition, Eric Priebke**, and **Ratline**.)

SUGGESTED READING: Freiwald and Mendelsohn, *The Last Nazi.*

Schwartz, Joseph J. (1899–1975). European Director of the "**Joint**." He was involved in rescue operations with the **War Refugee Board**. The director supported the French underground. He documented the **Velodrome d'Hiver** roundup, aided Jews in Central Asia and Teheran, and arranged for mass **aliya** from 1948–1950. Working with the War Refugee Board he negotiated with neutral countries for rescue of many Jews. He reported on April 19, 1945, that the Greek Jewish Population had been reduced from 77,00 (prewar) to 8,500. (See also **Greece** and **Salonika**.)

SUGGESTED READINGS: Bauer, *My Brother's Keeper*; Szule, *The Secret Alliance.*

Schwarz, Heinrich (1905–1947). **SS Death's Head** Formation's officer. He worked himself up the ranks at **Auschwitz** and became the only kommandant of **Auschwitz** III. Schwartz was tried and executed after the war. (See also **Monowice**.)

SUGGESTED READING: Czech, *Auschwitz Chronicle.*

Schwarzbart, Ignacy Isaac (1888–1961). Polish **Zionist** politician. He was a member of the executive committee of the **World Zionist Organization** and a leader of the **Krakow** Jewish community. Schwarzbart was elected to the Polish Parliament before the war, and after the German invasion, he served in the **Polish Government-in-Exile**. He published a Polish Jewish newspaper in London, *The Future*, which documented the **Holocaust** in **Poland** (1942), but had little impact on **Allied** officials. He opposed bombing **Auschwitz** fearing it would cause too many Jewish casualties.

SUGGESTED READING: Bartoszewski and Lewin, *Righteous Among Nations.*

Das Schwarze Korps (G., *The Black Corps*). Official weekly newspaper of the SS, named after the SS uniforms. It was started in 1935, and within four years its circulation was 500,000. The paper was the only uncensored organ in Nazi **Germany**. It railed against Catholicism and urged the mass murder of Jews as early as 1939. By 1945, the paper had degenerated to a propaganda sheet extolling war exploits.

SD (G., **Sicherheitsdienst**). Security Service, which included the **Gestapo**, headed by **Reinhard Heydrich**. This entity served as the intelligence gathering arm of the **SS**. The SD cemented the SS grip on power from 1932–1937. **Adolf Eichmann** began his career in the SD as head of the Scientific Museum of Jewish Affairs. (See also **Kripo**.)

Secret Reich Matter. (See **Geheime Reichssache**.)

Seidl, Dr. Siegfried (1911–1946). Austrian Nazi and first kommandant of **Theresienstadt** from November 1941–July 1943. He moved on to **Bergen-Belsen** and played a major role in **deporting** Hungarian Jewry to **Auschwitz**. He was tried and hanged by the Austrian government.
SUGGESTED READING: Hilberg, *The Destruction of European Jews.*

Selection (G., selektion). Jews chosen either to remain or to be **deported** from the **ghetto**. Selection was used in a "parade" process to weed out exhausted and sick inmates in camps with extermination in mind. Selection by an **SS** officer at the **concentration camps** meant life or death. (See also **Rechts/Links, Transportunfaehig, "Unproductive Eaters,"** and **Dr. Eduard Wirths**.)
SUGGESTED READING: Lifton, *The Nazi Doctors.*

Self-cleansing (G., Selbstreinigungsaktionen). Bloody **pogroms** encouraged by Nazis, which they euphemised as "reprisals by a wronged national population against oppressive Jews." (See also **Lvov**.)

Self-government. Special inmates chosen to handle day-to-day operations in a **concentration camp** in return for certain privileges. Generally, these inmates engaged in cruelty as a means of proving their worth to the **SS**. (See also **Blockaelteste, Kapo, Lageraelteste, Shtubhova, Stubenaelteste,** and **Stubendienste**.)

Semlin (G.), Sajmiste (Sl.). Death factory and German **concentration camp** outside of Belgrade with a Jewish population between 5,000 to 6,000. A "**Sonderwagon**" was used at these two sites. Mass murder was also by machine gunning. Bodies were dumped in huge pits. Later **Aktion 1005** was used to exhume corpses. (See also **Croatia** and **Handzar**.)

Sendler, Irena (b. 1916). Polish **Righteous Gentile** and a member of **Zegota**. Sendler aided Jews, particularly 2,500 children, in the **Warsaw Ghetto** where she found safe houses for them. Sendler survived imprisonment in **Pawiak Street Prison** and lives in Warsaw.
SUGGESTED READING: Tomaszewski and Werbowski, *Zegota.*

Sephardim/Sephardic. Jews of Spanish or Portuguese descent expelled in 1492 and 1510, respectively, during the Inquisition. Most Sephardim settled in North Africa, **Greece, Italy**, Turkey, and the **Netherlands. Salonika**, Greece, became the cultural capital for these displaced Jews. (See also **Algeria, Bulgaria, Ladino, Libya, Macedonia, Field Marshal Bernard Law Montgomery, Morocco, Sarajevo, and Thrace**.)

SUGGESTED READING: Gaon and Serels, *Sephardim and the Holocaust*.

Serbia. An independent nation prior to World War I (1914), located south of Bosnia in the Balkans. Following the war this kingdom of Greek Orthodox peoples became part of the kingdom of Serbs, Croats, and Slovenes, named **Yugoslavia** in 1929. From 1941 to 1945 it was occupied by Nazi **Germany**. Serbs suffered at the hands of the **Ustashi;** many were killed at **Jasenovac**. The portion of Serbia under German occupation included 12,000 Jews, most of whom were trapped in Belgrade. Six thousand Jews were gassed at **Semlin** by mobile gassing vans. (See also "**Sonderwagon.**")

SUGGESTED READING: Tenenbaum, *Race and Reich*.

Sered. Labor and **concentration camp** in **Slovakia** containing Jews and Slovak **partisans**. Jews were shipped to **Terezin** from this site from December 1944–April 1945. The camp kommandant was **SS** Lt. Colonel Witiska. (See also **Einsatzgruppen, Sano Mach, Dr. Josef Tiso, Vojtech Tuka**, and **Anton Vasek**.)

SUGGESTED READING: Frieder, *To Deliver Their Souls*.

Sereni, Enzo (1905–1944). Italian-born "**parachutist.**" **He-Halutz** leader in **Germany** in the late 1930s, active in **Youth Aliya**, he worked on the **Haavara Agreement**. Sereni was a liaison officer (1943) between parachutists and British trainers. Sereni worked as a secret agent for the British in Cairo and went to Iraq to protect the Jewish community in Baghdad. He was sent by both the **Yishuv** and British into northern **Italy** in May 1944 on a parachute mission and was captured, interned, and executed in **Dachau**. After his death, his wife, Ada, became one of the leaders of the **Bricha**.

SUGGESTED READINGS: Bondy, *The Emissary*; Herzer, *The Italian Refuge*.

Service du Travail Obligatoire (STO) (F., Compulsory Work Force). **Vichy** decree introduced in February 1943, drafting young French men to work in **Germany**. This order fermented opposition to Nazi rule and strengthened the French **resistance**, particularly the **Maquis**. (See also **French Forces of the Interior** and **FTPF**.)

Seyss-Inquart, Artur (1892–1946). Austrian Nazi political leader. He was appointed Chancellor of **Austria** during the **Anschluss** in March 1938 and later was appointed governor of **Ostmark** by **Hitler**. He was **Hans Frank's** deputy in **Poland** before being promoted **Reichskommissar** for the **Netherlands**. He oversaw the destruction of **Dutch** Jewry. Approximately 105,000 (78%) Dutch Jews perished in **Auschwitz** and other camps. Seyss-Inquart was convicted of **war crimes** at the **Nuremberg Trials** and hanged. (See **Hans Rauter**.)

SUGGESTED READINGS: Davidson, *The Trial of the Germans*; Miale and Selzer, *The Nuremberg Mind*.

SHAEF. (See **Supreme Headquarters Allied Expeditionary Forces**.)

Shammes (H. and Y., caretaker). Learned Jew and the person responsible for maintenance and use of ritual objects in a synagogue.

Shanghai. After Japanese occupation in 1938, this Chinese city was the only destination that did not require an entry **visa**. Over 17,000 European **refugees**, mostly from **Austria** and **Germany**, joined an established Jewish population of 10,000 and were afforded safe haven during World War II. Many refugees came as religious school students, including the entire **Mir Yeshiva**. The Japanese occupied this port city in November 1937 and wanted world Jewry to use their influence, especially in America, to persuade the West to accept Japanese aggression. In July 1942, Colonel Joseph Mesinger of the **Gestapo** in Japan sought the Shanghai Jewish population for the **Final Solution**. He was rebuffed by Japanese authorities. The Jewish refugees were declared stateless, and a **ghetto** was created on February 18, 1943. Approximately 8,000 Jews were dependent on welfare from groups including **HICEM** (''Kitchen Fund''), the ''**Joint**,'' and **Va'ad ha-Hatzala**. About half of the Jewish population immigrated to the State of Israel in 1948. The remaining Jews left Shanghai for various destinations in the 1950s. (See also **Fugu Plan, Jewish Labor Committee** and **Relief Committee for The War Stricken Jewish Population**.

SUGGESTED READING: Ross, *Escape to Shanghai*; Tokayer and Swartz, *The Fugu Plan*.

Shechitah (H. and Y., ritual slaughter). One of the first anti-Jewish decrees in **Germany** promulgated on April 21, 1933, prohibited **kosher** slaughter. Jewish butchers risked their lives to provide Jews with kosher meat. (See also **Shochet**.)

She'erit ha-Peletah (H., ''Surviving Remnant''). Biblical term used to refer to **Holocaust** survivors. The inherent implication is that these people would revive Judaism. (See also **Rabbi Abraham Klausner** and **Rabbi Joseph Isaac Schneersohn**.)

Shertok (Sharett), **Moshe** (1894–1965). Head of the **Jewish Agency's** Political Department in **Palestine** in the 1940s. He insisted that rescue efforts be tied to immigration by **refugees** to the **Yishuv**. Shertok was reluctant to allocate funds for rescue since he believed it had little chance of succeeding and preferred to save funds and energy for the Yishuv. The official also promoted the **Jewish Brigade**, which brought survivors to Palestine after the war.

SUGGESTED READING: Wasserstein, *Britain and the Jews of Europe.*

Shirer, William (1904–1995). American journalist and author. He reported on the **Anschluss** and German atrocities against Jews. Shirer authored the acclaimed *Berlin Diary* (1941) and *The Rise and Fall of the Third Reich* (1959), which documented Nazi persecution.

Sh'ma Yisroel (H., Hear O Israel). Central Jewish prayer uttered each morning and evening by religious Jews. When a Jew approaches death, this is the last confession of faith.

Shoah (H., catastrophe). Preferred term in Israel for the **Holocaust**. Found in the Bible (Isaiah 10:3), this passage refers to a Holocaust; destruction, complete ruination. (See also **Churban** and **Porraimos**.)

Shochet (H. and Y.). Jewish ritual slaughterer or butcher. Many risked their lives to provide **kosher** meat to Jews under Nazi rule. (See also **Shechitah**.)

Shostakovich, Dimitri (1906–1975). Major **Soviet** composer of the twentieth century. His thirteenth symphony, "**Babi Yar**" (1962), was a choral rendition of a poem by Yevgeni Yevtaushenko. This work was banned by Soviet authorities because of its implications of Soviet **anti-Semitism**.

SUGGESTED READING: Vaksberg, *Stalin Against the Jews.*

Shtetl (Y., town). Jewish village in the **Pale** of Eastern Europe.

Shul (Y., school). This term refers to a synagogue.

Shutzpolizei. (See **Schuma**.)

Siberia. Over 400,000 Jews from **Poland, Lithuania**, and western **Russia** were sent by the NKVD (Soviet Secret Police) to **labor camps** in this desolate area of Russia. This process was accelerated after the German invasion of the **Soviet Union** in June 1941. Polish Jews were granted amnesty following the **Sikorski-Stalin** Agreement signed on August 12, 1941. Many Siberian Jews were sent to camps or areas in Tashkent or Samarkan, but most Jews remained in Siberian exile until the end of the war. Care packages were sent from the United States by **Va'ad ha-Hatzala**. The forced **deportations** saved most of the Jews from the **Einsatzgruppen** and deportation to **death camps**. (See also **Partition of Poland and Union of Orthodox Rabbis of America**.)

SUGGESTED READING: Bullock, *Hitler and Stalin.*

Sicherheitsdienst. (See **SD**.)

Sicherheitspolizei. (See **Sipo**.)

Siddur (H., order). Prayer book, daily order of prayers. Some religious Jews memorized most of its prayers and would recite them clandestinely while in labor gangs and inside **concentration camps**. (See also **Spiritual Resistance**.)

"Sieg Heil!" (G., "Hail to Victory!"). Salute and triumphal saying used at Nazi gatherings. (See also **Jehovah's Witnesses**.)

Siemens. German electrical concern that utilized **concentration camp** labor and assumed an industry leadership role with the **SS**. The company paid out 7 million Deutschmarks in **reparations** for use of concentration camp labor and pain and suffering. Two thousand people qualified for claims, each claimant received $825. (See also **Circle of Friends of Himmler** and **Ravensbrueck**.)
  SUGGESTED READING: Ferencz, *Less Than Slaves*.

Sievers, Dr. Wolfram (1900–1948). **SS** colonel and medical officer. A Nazi student leader, he joined the **SA** in 1923 and the **SS** in 1930. He was chief of the Institute for Military and Scientific Research and administrator of **Ahnenerbe** in 1942. Sievers oversaw "medical experiments" in the **concentration camp** system, infected healthy inmates for malaria experiments, and tested mustard gas on inmates at **Natzweiler-Stutthof**. Sievers also collected skeletons and he donated the corpses to Ahnenerbe. He was tried and convicted at the **Doctors' Trial**, then hanged on June 2, 1948. (See also **Altreich** and **Dr. Claus Schilling**.)
  SUGGESTED READINGS: Annas and Grodin, *The Nazi Doctors*; Aziz, *Doctors of Death*.

Sighet. City close to the Hungarian-Romanian border with a prewar Jewish population of 10,000. In 1928, it was part of **Romania** in the Maramurset District. From 1940–1945, it was annexed to the sub-Carpathian zone of **Hungary**. When **Germany** invaded Hungary in the spring in 1944, Jews were **deported** to **Auschwitz**, including **Elie Wiesel** and his family.
  SUGGESTED READING: Braham, *The Tragedy of Rumanian Jewry*.

Sikorski, Wladyslaw (1881–1943). Prime minister of the **Polish Government-in-Exile**. He condemned Nazi atrocities in **Poland** and lobbied in vain for retaliation. He negotiated the Sikorski-**Stalin** Pact on July 30, 1941, which included relief activities for Polish Jews in the **Soviet Union** and allowed Polish Jews to join **General Wladylsaw Anders'** Army. Sikorski was killed in a plane crash on July 4, 1943. (See also **Menachem Begin** and **Siberia**.)

SUGGESTED READINGS: Gutman and Krakowski, *Unequal Victims*; Lukas, *Forgotten Holocaust*.

Silberschein, Dr. Abraham (d. 1951). Representative of the **World Jewish Congress**. He was one of the first to document **forced labor** and the annihilation of Polish Jewry. Silberschein assisted Jewish **refugees** from **Germany, Lithuania**, Japan, and other parts of Europe. When he died, his archives were transferred to **Yad Vashem**. (See also **Kobe** and **Relief Committee for the War Stricken Jewish Population**.)
   SUGGESTED READING: Eck, ''The Rescue of Jews.''

Silesian Convention (1922) Treaty signed by **Germany** regarding the disposition of Upper Silesia including a provision providing full equality for all German citizens. Franz Bernheim, a Silesian Jew, presented the petition to the **League of Nations** on May 12, 1933. Germany honored the provision exempting Silesian Jews from **anti-Semitic** legislation until it expired in 1937. (See also **Bernheim Petition, Minority Treaties**, and **Moshe Merin**.)
   SUGGESTED READING: Johnson, *Modern Times*.

Silver, Rabbi Abba Hillel (1893–1963). **Zionist** reform rabbi. He was elected chairman of the **Zionist Emergency Council** (1943). Silver tried to convince American officials and Congress of the need for a Jewish state and the rescue of European Jews to attain this goal. He opposed **Rabbi Stephen S. Wise** because the latter did not demand more from President **Franklin Delano Roosevelt**.
   SUGGESTED READING: Urofsky, *American Zionism from Herzl to the Holocaust*.

Silverman, Sidney (1895–1968). British member of Parliament and a member of the **World Jewish Congress**, who received news about the **Holocaust** from **Dr. Gerhart Riegner**. On August 28, 1942, Silverman transmitted this information to **Rabbi Stephen S. Wise**. The Riegner Message was suppressed by the U.S. States Department.
   SUGGESTED READINGS: Laqueur, *The Terrible Secret*; Wyman, *The Abandonment of the Jews*.

Sima, Horia (b. 1906). Commander of the **Iron Guard** in **Romania**. He returned from exile in **Germany** in 1940 and staged an unsuccessful coup against his former superior, **Ion Antonescu**. He also instigated a **pogrom** against the Jews of Bucharest during this period. In late 1940, he retreated to **Vienna**. Sima established a government-in-exile in December 1944 after the Romanian government's surrender to the **Allies**. Sima was tried and sentenced to death *in absentia* in 1946. After the war, he found refuge in **Spain**. (See also **Fascism** and **Radu Lecca**.)
   SUGGESTED READING: Butnaru, *The Silent Holocaust*.

Simaito, Ona (1899–1970). Lithuanian **Righteous Gentile**. A librarian at the University of **Vilna**, she brought supplies into the **ghetto** and aided the Vilna **partisans** from 1941–1944. Simaito was sent to **Dachau, liberated**, and went to live on a **kibbutz** in Israel in 1953.

SUGGESTED READINGS: Paldiel, *The Path of the Righteous*; Sachar, *The Redemption of the Unwanted.*

Simon, Gustav (1900–1945). Nazi **Gauleiter** of the Koblenz-Trier district. He was later appointed chief of the German civil administration in **Luxembourg** on August 7, 1940.

SUGGEST READING: Zarez, ''The Jews of Luxembourg.''

Sinti. German tribe of **''Gypies.''** By order of **Heinrich Himmler** on October 13, 1942, they were supposed to be spared, but sterilized. Large scale **deportation** of Sinti to the East for extermination began in early 1943. (See also **Asocials, Auschwitz, Lalleri, Mischlinge, Nuremberg Laws, Porraimos, Dr. Robert Ritter**, and **Roma**.)

SUGGESTED READING: Crowe, *History of the Gypsies of Eastern Europe.*

Sipo (G., **Sicherheitspolizei**) (SRE) (Security Police). Consisting of the **Gestapo** (political police) and **Kripo** (criminal police), Sipo was merged with the **SD** to form the **RSHA** on September 27, 1939. **Reinhard Heydrich** became Chief of Sipo and the SD. (See also **Lebensborn**.)

Sippenhaftung/Sippenhaft (G., kinship responsibility). At **Posen** in 1944, **Heinrich Himmler** introduced a legal concept for guilt—punishing families for the guilt of one of its members. ''This man has committed treason; his blood is bad; there is a traitor's blood in him; that must be wiped out. And in the blood feud the entire clan was wiped out down to the last member.'' Over 5,000 family members of senior **Wehrmacht** officers were murdered for the officers' role in **Operation Valkyrie**.

SUGGESTED READING: Fest, *Plotting Hitler's Death.*

Six, Dr. Franz W. (1909–1975). Author, professor of Political Science, dean of faculty at the University of **Berlin** and **SS** general. He was chief of the Cultural Policy Division of the **RSHA**, which focused on Jewish issues. Six was Commander of **Einsatzgruppe** B. He was sentenced in April 1948 to twenty years in prison, but served only seven years. Six received clemency from **John McCoy** and was employed in counterintelligence by the U.S. government. The former mass murderer testified in defense of **Adolf Eichmann**. (See also **Clemency Act of 1951**.)

SUGGESTED READING: Simpson, *Blowback.*

Skobtsova, Elizabeta. (See **Sister Elizabeth Pilenko**.)

Skorzeny, SS Colonel Otto (1908–1975). German commando. He rescued **Benito Mussolini** on September 12, 1943, from Italian guards and kidnapped **Admiral Miklos Horthy's** son, who was eventually interned at **Mauthausen**. The commando headed a large group at the Battle of the Bulge who donned **Allied** uniforms and mislead U.S. troops. He fled with the help of the **Vatican** after the war. Skorzeny founded **Odessa** and became a leader in the German–Latin American community. He died of natural causes in Madrid. (See also **Ratline**.)
    SUGGESTED READING: Whiting, *Otto Skorzeny.*

Slave Labor. Term often used for **forced labor**. Technically workers were not slaves. The Nazi **concentration camp** system exploited foreign labor. In this system the camp inmates went unpaid for work they did. When inmates were loaned out to German corporations, such as **I. G. Farben, BMW, Flick** industries, and **Daimler-Benz**, the corporation was charged a set fee for each inmate by the **SS**. However, there were SS industries that also employed unpaid laborers. **Soviet POWs** were forced into armaments industries, which was a direct violation of the **Geneva Convention**. Of the 2 million Jews used as slaves in German war production, only 200,000 survived. (See also **Central Planning Board, Circle of Friends of Himmler, Labor Camp, Gerhard Maurer, Ostarbeiter, Karl Sommer, Soviet POWs, WVHA**.)
    SUGGESTED READING: Borkin, *The Crime and Punishment of I. G. Farben.*

Slavs. Largest ethnic-linguistic group of peoples inhabiting mainly eastern, southeastern, and east central Europe. Religiously, they belong to either the Roman Catholic or Eastern Orthodox church. Eastern Slavs (such as Russians) use the Cyrillic alphabet. The Nazis considered them as subhuman and worthy only of domination by Nordic **Aryans**. (See also **Poland, Soviet POWs**, and **Untermenschen**.)

Slobodka. (See **Odessa**.)

Slovakia. Rump state created soon after the dismemberment of **Czechoslovakia** in 1939. The **fascist** dictatorship was headed by **Dr. Josef Tiso**, a Catholic priest. **Sano Mach** controlled the police and the Interior Ministry. The state lasted as a satellite until 1944, when, due to the **Slovakian National Revolt, Germany** occupied the entire country. There were 89,000 Jews in ''independent'' Slovakia. **Deportations** of 66,000 Slovakian Jews occurred as early as 1942. Over 58,000 Jews were deported to **Auschwitz**. About 28,000 to 35,000 Slovakian Jews survived. In April 1945, the country was **liberated** from German occupation by the **Red Army**. Over 136,739 Jews lived in Slovakian territory. This included **Ruthenia** and Subcarpathia, which was ceded to **Hungary** in 1939. Their fate was sealed with Hungarian Jews. (See also **Einsatzgruppe H, Gisi Fleischmann, Hlinka Guard, Munich Pact, Novaky Sered, Rabbi Michael Dov Weissmandel**, and **Working Group**.)

SUGGESTED READINGS: Campion, *In the Lion's Mouth*; Reitlinger, *The Final Solution.*

Slovakian National Revolt. In August 1944, in response to a call to arms by the Czech Government-in-Exile, a revolt occurred. The fighters consisted of units of the regular Slovakian army, 16,000 strong, inmates of camps in **Novaky** and all sorts of **partisans**. Jews in **labor camps** in the Novaky area joined, as well as members of the **Zionist** and communist units. Palestinian Jews, **Haviva Reik,** and Zvi Benjudkov, parachuted in and led camps of fighting Jews. Outmanned and outnumbered, the general revolt failed by October 1994. Over 2,000 Jews retreated into the mountains to hide. (See also **General Gottlob Berger** and **Svoboda Army.**)

"Small Fortress." (See **Theresienstadt.**)

Smolar, Hersh (b. 1905). Polish Jewish leader active in the communist underground. After 1939 and the **Partition of Poland**, he went to Soviet-occupied **Bialystok** and founded a **Yiddish** newspaper. Later, he went to **Minsk** where he played a central role in **resistance**, organizing and fighting with the **partisans**. He survived the war and became chairman of the Cultural Social Union of Jews in **Poland** and editor of a Yiddish newspaper in the communist-controlled government. Smolar immigrated to Israel in 1971. (See also **Shalom Zorin.**)
SUGGESTED READING: Smolar, *The Minsk Ghetto.*

Sobibor. One of three **death camps** dedicated to the extermination of Jews. Located in eastern **Poland,** this camp operated from May 1942–October 1943. Sobibor was staffed by **euthanasia** veterans and Ukrainian guards. Approximately 250,000 Jews were gassed at this site. An inmate insurrection on October 14, 1943, forced the closure of Sobibor. By the end of 1943, the Nazis completely destroyed the death camp and converted it to a farm. (See also **Aktion Reinhard, Leon Feldhandler, Aleksander Pechersky, Franz Reichleitner, Franz Stangl, Richard Thomalia, Vught, Gustav Wagner**, and **Zamosc.**)
SUGGESTED READING: Novitch, *Sobibor.*

Social Darwinism. Theory about society that applied Charles Darwin's struggle for survival to human affairs. Ernst Haekel, a German biologist, ranked the **Aryans** as "fit," superior, and atop the racial pyramid, while Jews, the "unfit," were at the bottom. The Nazis adopted this concept together with **eugenics** in an attempt to breed a super race of Aryans. (See also **Untermenschen.**)

Social Democrats. Largest political party in the **Weimar Republic** until 1932. Many Jews belonged to this organization, which favored liberal democratic ideals. Members of this party were staunch opponents of Nazism and were persecuted and imprisoned in **concentration camps** after the Nazis came to power.

Socialist Zionists or **Labor Zionists**. Jews who believed in a communal society. Labor Zionists were the main founders of the **Kibbutz[im]** in the **Yishuv**. They also dominated the **Jewish Agency**. Their youth groups included **Dror** and **Ha-Shomer Ha-Tzair**. In Europe, they were the vanguard of underground **resistance** in the **ghettos** and the forests. (See **He-Halutz** and **Ma'apilim**.)

Society for the Rescue of Jewish Children (OSE). Incorporated in March 1942 under **Vichy**, it set up a children's home. This Jewish welfare organization was actively involved in saving Jewish children and adults in Vichy **France**. It rescued at least 5,000 children. OSE became part of the **UGIF** and gave assistance to Jews in French **internment camps**, particularly **Gurs** and **Rivesaltes**. (See also **Alexandre Glasberg**.)
    SUGGESTED READING: Zuccotti, *The Holocaust, the French, and the Jews*.

SOE. (See **Special Operations Executive**.)

Sofort Vernichtet (G., immediate killing). **Gestapo** designation of inmates to be instantly exterminated.

Sokolow-Podlaski. Town located in central **Poland**. With a Jewish population of 4,000, this locale was a center of **Hasidism**. A **ghetto** was established in 1941, which prompted a number of Jewish youths to join the **partisans**. Jews were **deported** to **Treblinka** in 1942, and by war's end, the Jewish community was annihilated.

Sommer, Karl (b. 1915). **SS** general. He worked with **Gerhard Maurer** to coordinate and distribute **slave labor** to German corporations. He testified at the **Nuremberg Trials** in January 1947 that **forced labor** could only be obtained upon a request by German corporations. After May–June 1944, such requests had to be approved by **Albert Speer**. Sommer stated that German companies utilized 600,000 slave laborers. The general was sentenced to death, but that was later commuted to life in prison and eventually reduced to twenty years. (See also **I. G. Farben, Krupp, Labor camps**, and **WVHA**.)
    SUGGESTED READING: Hilberg, *The Destruction of European Jews*.

"Sonderaktion" (G., "special operation"). Refers to **Einsatzgruppe** activity or **Aktionen** directed against Jews.

"Sonderbehandelt" (G., "specially treated" or handled). Euphemism for person or group to be killed. **Einsatzgruppen** reports often bragged that Jews in a village had been "handled," meaning destroyed.

Sondergericht (G., Special Court). (1) Nazi courts for political crimes. There were no appeals and its decisions were enforced immediately. (2) Jewish court system in the **ghetto** accountable to the Nazis. Death sentences were frequent punishments meted out to Jews for the slightest infractions.
SUGGESTED READING: Mueller, *Hitler's Justice.*

Sonderkommando (G., special squads). (1) Jews assigned to do the most degrading work in the camps and in the killing vans. Tasks included: cleaning up a **ghetto** after it had been emptied of Jews, emptying and cleaning a truck after victims had been gassed, sorting the possessions of Jews after their arrival in the camps, clearing and cleaning the **gas chambers**, and shoveling bodies into the ovens. The Nazis normally killed off Sonderkommandos every three months. (2) Term also applied to **SS** squads on special assignment to eliminate target groups in the **Soviet Union**. They were attached to the **Einsatzgruppen**. (See also **Aktion 1005, Ash Brigade, Auschwitz, Concentration Camp Uprisings, Roza Robota, "Sonderwagon," "Special Ones,"** and **Zwiazek Organizaci Wojskowej**.)
SUGGESTED READING: Gutman and Berenbaum, *Anatomy of the Auschwitz Death Camp.*

Sonderkommando 1005. (See **Aktion 1005** and **Janowska**.)

"Sonderkost" (G., special diet). Nutritional experiments applied to mentally and physically disabled adults and children. (See also **Euthanasia**.)

Sonderreferet (G., Special Office). Established in the **Netherlands** under direct command of **Hans Rauter**. This office managed **Westerbork** and dealt with all matters pertaining to Jews in **Holland** including preparation for future evacuation.

"Sonderwagon" (G., "special car"). Killing van that circulated exhaust from the vehicle into a compartment containing humans. The first prototype was pioneered on instructions from **Heinrich Himmler** by **Arthur Nebe** and **Dr. Albert Widmann** in Mogilev. Time of death was anywhere from fifteen minutes to one hour. In many instances, victims survived and were executed by a bullet. The Sonderwagons were most rigorously utilized at **Chelmno**. At **Mauthausen**, the vehicle was known as an "auto car." This means of mass murder was found to be sloppy, traumatic, and inefficient by the Nazis who perfected **gas chambers** for mass extermination. (See also **Dr. Rudolf Lange, "Processed," Walter Rauff, Saurer**, and **Semlin**.)

Sonnenstein. Austrian gassing facility. This site was utilized during the **T-4** program and throughout the war. (See also **Euthanasia** and **Dr. Horst Schumann**.)

So Oder So (G., one way or the other). Term used by **Hermann Goering** and **Hitler** referring to the resolution of the "**Jewish Question**" by any means.

Sosua. A colony for German and Austrian Jewish **refugees** in the Dominican Republic. Initiated by President Generalissimo **Rafael Trujillo** who had bought a 26,000-acre tract from the United Fruit Company. Funds for the settlement of 635 people came from the "**Joint**" (See also **Evian Conference**).
  SUGGESTED READING: Sanders, *Shores of Refuge*.

Sousa Mendes, Aristide de (1885–1954). Portuguese counsel in Bordeaux, **France**. From May–June 1940, Sousa Mendes defied the Portuguese government and issued up to 10,000 **visas** to Jewish and non-Jewish **refugees** before his expulsion. Sousa Mendes was assisted by his sons, Jose and Pedro; they accepted no payment, and when Sousa Mendes ran out of visas, he issued de facto **passports** on ordinary paper. The diplomat was recalled to **Portugal**, but on his way to **Spain**, he ordered the legation in Bayonne, France to issue special visas to Jewish refugees. Sousa Mendes was dismissed by the Portuguese government and died in poverty on April 3, 1954. He was honored as a **Righteous Gentile** by **Yad Vashem** in 1966 and has since received posthumous honors from Portugal. (See also **HICEM** and **Antonio de Oliveria Salazar**.)
  SUGGESTED READING: Sachar, *The Redemption of the Unwanted*.

Soviet POWs (Prisoners of War). The Germans did not abide by traditional rules of war concerning treatment of POWs. Over 3.5 million Soviet POWs were executed or perished in German **death** and **concentration camps**. These inmates were subject to **dehumanization** and were the victims of the first "successful" **Zyklon-B** tests at **Auschwitz-Birkenau**. (See also **Aktion 1005, Aktion Kugelerlass, Babi Yar, Bergen-Belsen, Buchenwald, Commissar Order, Dachau, Dora-Nordhausen, Forced Labor, Geneva Convention, Ghetto Cleaners, Gross-Rosen, Hilfswillige, Kiev, Majdanek, Maly Trostinets, Field Marshal Erich von Manstein, Mauthausen, Partisan Order, Field Marshal Walter von Reichenau, Sachsenhausen, Walter Schellenberg, Slave Labor**, and **Yarnton Declaration**.)
  SUGGESTED READING: Berenbaum, *A Mosaic of Victims*.

Soviet Union. (See **Union of Soviet Socialist Republics**.)

Spain. Nonbelligerent, but pro-German fascistic nation on the Iberian peninsula, south of **France** and west of **Portugal**. From the fall of France in 1940, to the summer of 1942, 20,000 Jewish **refugees** passed through Spain en route to Portugal. These Jews were serviced by American relief organizations. Approximately 1,000 Jews were detained at **Miranda de Ebro**, and 10,500 were assisted by **HICEM** in Lisbon. Spain showed some sympathy for Jews with **Sephardic** heritage. In the summer of 1944, **Francisco Franco's** government gave 2,750 **Schutzpaesse** to Jews in **Hungary**. Some estimates have put the total number of Jews, mostly Sephardic, rescued by Spanish diplomats and given safe-passage through Spain to be 40,000 to 50,000. Ironically, the Spanish Inquisition enacted in 1492 was still in force. (See also **Anti-Cominterm Pact, Armee Juive, Varian Fry, Miguel Angel Sanz-Briz**, and **Aristide de Sousa Mendes**.)

SPD. (See **Social Democrats**.)
   SUGGESTED READING: Avni, Spain, the Jews and Franco.

"Special Cases." Mentally ill patients gassed after the **euthanasia** program was suspended. (See also **14 f 13, "Special Treatment,"** and **"Wild Euthanasia."**)

Special Echelon. Mobile killing teams in **Romania**. These units performed the same function as the **Einsatzgruppen**.

"Special Ones." (See **Vilnius Sonderkommando**.)

Special Operations Executive (SOE). An agency established by the British in 1940 in London to organize and carry out sabotage in Nazi-occupied Europe. Many operations were carried out with the various undergrounds in occupied Europe, often in coordination with the **OSS**. However, it gave no assistance to Jewish underground forces.
   SUGGESTED READING: Benovet, SOE: Recollections and Reflections.

Special Task Forces. (See **Einsatzgruppen**.)

"Special Treatment" (G., **"Sonderbehandlung"**). Euphemism for killing Jews and other enemies of the Nazis. This concept was pioneered by **T-4** physicians **Drs. Karl Brandt, Ernst von Grawitz**, and **Friedrich Mennecke**, and was utilized by **Einsatzgruppen**. (See also **Durchschlesung**.)
   SUGGESTED READING: Friedlander, The Origins of Nazi Genocide.

Special Treatment 14 f 13. (See **14 f 13**.)

Speer, Albert (1905–1981). Nazi minister of armaments and munitions. He joined the **Nazi Party** at the university (1931) and quickly rose to become one of **Hitler**'s closest aides. Speer was appointed **Reich** Party architect in 1934 and minister of armaments and munitions after **Dr. Fritz Todt's** death (1942). He was also the dominant member of the **Central Planning Board**, which oversaw and coordinated the **forced labor** supply. He ruthlessly exploited forced labor including inmates from **concentration camps**. From 1938 through January 1942, Speer's office expelled 75,000 **Berlin** Jews from their homes. Speer visited Dnepropetrovsk in March 1941, after the **Einsatzkommando** had murdered 100,000 Jews. He attended **Heinrich Himmler's Posen** speech on October 4, 1943, and personally inspected **Dora-Nordhausen** in early 1944. He was convicted of exploiting slave labor, but since he had taken steps to countermand Hitler's orders to destroy the German infrastructure at the end of the war, he was sentenced to twenty years in prison. His autobiography, *Inside the Third Reich*, does not discuss his complicity in the **Holocaust**, although a share of the royalties were donated to Jewish organizations. (See also **Berlin, Primitivbau-weise, Fritz Sauckel**, and **Karl Sommer**.)

SUGGESTED READINGS: Davidson, *The Trial of the Germans*; Speer, *Inside the Third Reich*.

Sperre (G., blockade). Nazis and their assistants, which often included **Jewish Police**, rounded up **ghetto** residents who did not have **scheinen** or protective permits.

Spiritual Resistance. Jews continued to pray, hold services, honor the holidays as best they could, hold religious classes, and learn from sacred texts. Other educational and cultural activities ensued in **ghettos** and even at the camps. Smuggling of food, medicines, and vital supplies needed for survival occurred. Writers and historians recorded Nazi atrocities and artists produced musical and theatrical performances. (See also **"Canteen," Dehumanization, Kiddush ha Hayyim, Komplets, Oneg Shabbat, Talmud**, and **Terezin**.)

Sporrenberg, Jacob (1902–1952). **SS** general. He became the SS and police leader in the **Lublin** District in August 1943. As such, he organized **Operation Erntefest** in which 43,000 Jews were killed at **Majdanek, Trawniki**, and **Poniatowa**. Sporrenberg was arrested by the British, **extradited** to **Poland**, and hanged.

SUGGESTED READING: Hilberg, *The Destruction of European Jews*.

"Sport." Form of torture of **concentration camp** inmates by Nazi guards. Severe penal exercises designed to inflict pain and induce exhaustion, often resulted in death. (See also **Irma Grese** and **Maria Mandel**.)

Sprachregelung (G., speech control). Use of terminology to hide the true purpose of Nazi activity. For example; **deportation** to **death camps** was called **"resettlement"** (umsiedlung). (See also **"Protective Custody"** and **"Special Treatment."**)

SS. (See **Schutzstaffel**.)

SS Central Office for Economy and Administration (WVHA) (G., **Wirtschfts und Verwaltungshauptamt**). (See **WVHA**.)

SS-und Polizeifuehrer (G., **SS** and police leader).

"Stab-in-the-Back." (See **Dolchstoss**.)

Stahlecker, Franz Walter (1900–1942). **SS** police official. He commanded **Einsatzgruppe** A in **Estonia, Latvia, Lithuania**, and **Belorussia**. Stahlecker boasted of killing 2,000 Estonian Jews; 60,000 Latvian Jews; 130,000 Lithuanian Jews; and, "only" 41,000 Belorussian Jews. His was killed on March 23, 1942, in a battle with Soviet **partisans**. (See also **Viktor Arajis, Latvian SS Legion, Lithuanian Activist Front, Heinrich Lohse, Ostabataillone, Perkonkrust**, and **Schuma**.)
   SUGGESTED READING: Ezergailis, *The Holocaust in Latvia.*

Stahlhelm (G., **"Steel Helmet party"**). German nationalist organization of ex-soldiers formed on September 23, 1918. Their purpose was to oppose a German revolution, and by 1923, the group claimed 1 million members. Followers indoctrinated themselves in the concept of the **Volk**. Its leader and co-founder, Franz Seldte, was appointed minister of Labor by **Hitler**, 1933–1948. Stahlhelm was absorbed into the **SA** in June 1933. (See also **Weimar Republic**.)
   SUGGESTED READING: Jones, *Hitler's Heralds.*

"Staircase of Death." (See **186**.)

Stalin, Josef (1879–1953). Dictator of the **Soviet Union** from 1928–1953. His pact with the Nazis (**Molotov-Ribbentrop**) paved the way for German aggression and trapped over 3 million Polish and Baltic Jews. The Soviet press suppressed all information relating to Nazi persecution and atrocities, therefore depriving Jews in the Baltics and **Russia** of any information on the coming storm. When the **Wehrmacht** invaded the Soviet Union in June 1941, most Jews did not try to escape. Stalin forced "capitalist Jews" to relocate to Gulags (punishment camps) in **Siberia**, and while conditions were severe, their lives were spared. These so-called "capitalist Jews" were mainly from Soviet-occupied **Poland**. Jews from **Latvia, Lithuania**, and **Estonia** were not normally permitted to immigrate to Russia. When Soviet authorities learned of the terrible fate of Jews during the process of the war or **liberation** of the **concentration camps**, they never mentioned Jews in their reports or publicity. During a purge in 1948, Stalin executed members of the **Jewish Anti-Fascist Committee** in an **anti-Semitic** phase that lasted until his death. (See also **Stefan Bandera, Moscow Declaration, OUN, Polish Workers Party, Potsdam Conference, Wladyslaw Sikorski, Tripartite Conference, Warsaw Polish Uprising**, and **Yalta Conference**.)
   SUGGESTED READINGS: Bullock, *Hitler and Stalin*; Vaksberg, *Stalin Against the Jews.*

Stammlager (G., main camp). Central facility in **concentration camp** complex.

Standartenfuehrer. SS colonel.

Stangl, Franz (1908–1971). Austrian police officer and kommandant. He was superintendent of **Hartheim Castle** (1940) and kommandant of **Sobibor** (1942). Stangl finished construction of the Sobibor **death camp**. He later moved on to **Treblinka** from September 1942–August 1943 where he oversaw the murder of 870,000 Jews. The genocidist escaped to Syria with the help of **Bishop Alois Hudal** and then on to Brazil in 1948. Stangl was **extradited** to **Germany** in 1967 and sentenced to life in prison in 1970. Prison interviews detailing his descent into mass murder were documented by Gita Sereny in *Into That Darkness*. Stangl died of a heart attack in prison on June 28, 1971. (See also **Extradiction, Kurt Franz, T-4, Gustave Wagner**, and **Simon Wiesenthal**.)
   SUGGESTED READING: Sereny, *Into That Darkness.*

Stanislaw. City in western **Ukraine**, part of **Poland** in 1939, with a prewar Jewish population of 24,823. Soviet occupiers closed Jewish communal and religious institutions. The Germans occupied the city in July 1941 and **deported** Jews to **Belzec**. The remaining Jewish population was murdered on February 22, 1943, at the Jewish cemetery. Oskar Friedlender and Anna Luft formed **partisan** units in the area.
   SUGGESTED READING: Gilbert, *Atlas of the Holocaust.*

Star Camp. Camp II for Jews at **Bergen-Belsen**.

Stark, Dr. Johannes (1874–1951). German physicist. He labeled physics "Jewish physics" and was instrumental in pushing out scientists from German universities. Stark was tried at **Nuremberg** in 1947, but given a suspended sentence. (See also **Albert Einstein, Lise Meitner**, and **Dr. Bernard Rust**.)
   SUGGESTED READING: Beyerchen, *Scientists Under Hitler.*

"Star Prison" (Hu., Csillag). Prison in Komaron, **Hungary**, converted to an assembly point for Hungarian **Roma**.

Statut des Juifs (F., Statute upon the Jews). Anti-Jewish legislation enacted by the **Vichy** government on October 3, 1940, and extended the following year (summer 1941), without German pressure. These provisions were then applied to **Algeria, Morocco**, and Tunisia. This legislation forced Jews to register, wear a **Jewish Badge**, essentially removed all Jews from French public life, and resulted in the **Aryanization** of 42,000 Jewish buildings, businesses, and properties. (See also **Louis Darquier Pellepoix, Service de Travail Obligatiore, Tunis**, and **Xavier Vallat**.)
   SUGGESTED READING: Marrus and Paxton, *Vichy France and the Jews.*

Steel Helmet Party. (See **Stahlhelm**.)

Stehzelle (G., standing cell). Cramped punishment cell for captured, **concentration camp** escapees. At **Auschwitz**, sixteen inmates were forced into a small cell where they could not stand upright. Food, water, and air were grossly inadequate; the result was often death or execution. (See also **Block 11**.)

Steiger, Eduard von. Federal counselor of **Switzerland**. He referred to Switzerland as "crowded as a lifeboat." While the Swiss had admitted 28,512 Jews for refuge, their borders were sealed from 1938 to July 1944. (See also "**Lifeboat is Full**" **Saly Mayer, Roswell McClelland, Refoulement, Dr. Heinrich Rothmund**, and **Rita and Isaac Sternbuch**.)
   SUGGESTED READING: Haesler, *The Lifeboat is Full*.

Stein, Edith (1891–1942). Philosopher and nun. A German Jew who converted to Catholicism, she wrote to **Pope Pius XI** in April 1933 asking him to write an encyclical condemning Nazi **anti-Semitism**. Stein was arrested by the **Gestapo** in a **Dutch** monastery in July 1942. She was taken to **Auschwitz** in August 1942 and gassed as a reprisal against a Dutch Catholic Church official's condemnation of Nazi anti-Semitism. The philosopher was beatified by the Catholic Church.
   SUGGESTED READINGS: Braybrooke, "Simone Wgol and Edith Stein"; Cargas, "The Unnecessary Problem of Edith Stein."

"Sterbehilfe" (G., "aide to the dying"). Nazi term for **euthanasia**.

Stern, Abraham ("Yair") (1907–1942). Charismatic leader of the **Stern Group (LEHI)**. A former **Irgun** member, he correctly perceived British pro-Arab, anti-Jewish sentiments. **Ze'ev Jabotinsky** favored suspension of hostilities with Britain while they were fighting the Nazis, whereas Stern continued violent agitation. He was shot by **British Mandate** detectives in February 1942. (See also **Count Folke Bernadotte** and **White Paper**.)
   SUGGESTED READING: Bell, *Terror Out of Zion*.

Sternbuch, Rita (1905–1971) and **Isaac** (1903–1971). Swiss representatives of the **Va'ad ha-Hatzala**. They sent cables to Orthodox rabbis at the same time as the **Riegner** cable confirming the **Final Solution**. The couple managed to get relief packages to Jews in **Theresienstadt** and helped to rescue and smuggle 2,300 Jews illegally into **Switzerland**. The Sternbuchs bribed officials (despite objections from the "**Joint**"), smuggled Latin American **passports** for Jews to claim protection, and recovered Jewish children from Christian orphanages after the war. (See also **Monsignor Filippo Bernardini, Aleksander Lados, Saly Mayer, Roswell McClelland, Jean-Marie Musy, Dr. Heinrich Rothmund, Eduard von Steiger**, and **Union of Orthodox Rabbis of America**.)
   SUGGESTED READINGS: Kranzler, *Heroine of Rescue*; Kranzler, *Thy Brother's Blood*.

Stern Group (H., **Lohamei Herut Israel [LEHI]** (Fighters for Freedom of Israel). Dissident **Yishuv** underground movement. It broke away from the **Irgun** in June 1940. The 300 fighters opposed compromise with Great Britain and declared war on the **British Mandate** power. This organization made overtures to the **Axis** in 1939. The Group received its name from its leader, **Abraham Stern**. Members assassinated **Lord Moyne** (which alienated **Winston Churchill**) in Cairo for his role in the *Struma* affair. After Stern's death, the underground continued its military struggle until the formation of the State of Israel in 1948.

SUGGESTED READING: Bell, *Terror Out of Zion.*

"S III." (See **Ohrdruf.**)

Stimson, Henry Louis (1867–1950). American Secretary of War from 1940–1945. He supported intervention against Nazi **Germany** and the development of the atomic bomb. However, he was not interested in Jewish rescue and opposed the creation of the **War Refugee Board**. Stimson took part in major **Allied** conferences, but ignored Jewish issues. (See also **Jan Karski** and **John McCloy.**)

SUGGESTED READING: Bird, *The Chairman.*

STO. (See **Service de Travail Obligatoire.**)

"Stormtroopers." (See **SA.**)

Strafappell (G., punishment roll call). Procedure ordered after an inmate escaped. This roll call could last an evening and half of the next day. Failure to stand erect, regardless of the climate, was punishable by death.

Strafblocke (G., penal barrack in the camps).

Strafkompanie (G., punishment company [at **concentration camps**]). Hard labor crews. Inmates were assigned to these details for the slightest infraction. Most prisoners usually died from exhaustion.

Straflager (G., special punishment camp). Prison for enemies of the Nazis, often **resistance** fighters. They were usually sent to **Flossenbuerg** or **Stutthof**. (See also **Nacht und Nebel.**)

Strasbourg. City in Alsace, **France.** The population was removed to central France (Limoge) after the German takeover in 1940. Displaced Jews organized many institutions, especially at the relocated Strasbourg University, located at Clermont Ferrand. About 8,000 Jews returned to the reconstituted city after the war.

Streicher, Julius (1885–1946). Editor, founder, and publisher of *Der Stuermer*. A fanatical and pornographic **anti-Semite**, and close friend of **Hitler**, he became **Gauleiter** of Fraconia where he embezzled large portions of Aryanized Jewish property. In addition to publishing *Der Stuermer*, Streicher edited other anti-Semitic publications, for example, *The Mushroom* (a children's book). His carousing and corruption led Hitler to discipline his friend, and he eventually placed a speaking ban on Streicher. He was dismissed from his party posts after a commission reporting to **Hermann Goering** examined his personal and financial activities. At the **Nuremberg Trials**, he claimed he only behaved in accordance with **Martin Luther's** preachings. Unrepentant, Streicher was convicted of **war crime** charges and hanged. (See also **Aryanization**.)

SUGGESTED READINGS: Davidson, *Trial of the Germans*; Snyder, *Hitler's Elite*.

Stroop, General Juergen (1895–1952). Higher **SS** officer and police leader and veteran antiguerrilla fighter. He directed the destruction of the **Warsaw Ghetto**. In the "Stroop Report," he related that 13,920 Jews were exterminated and 5,000 to 6,000 were killed in shelling and fighting. Stroop alleged only 400 German casualties, but Polish Catholic and Jewish **resistance** figures placed losses much higher. He was sent to **Athens**, as the Higher SS and police leader, to organize the **deportation** of the remaining Jews. Stroop was only able to deport 800 Jews out of an estimated 5,000 to 7,000 Greek, Italian, and Spanish Jews. He was captured and sentenced to death by the United States for killing nine American POWs and for his leadership in a criminal organization (SS). Stroop was handed over to the Poles, and tried, convicted, and sentenced to death for the liquidation of the Warsaw Ghetto and persecution of Poles in **Warthegau**. He was hanged in Warsaw on March 6, 1952.

SUGGESTED READINGS: Ainsztein, *The Warsaw Ghetto Revolt*; Stroop, *The Stroop Report*.

Strughold, Dr. Hubertus. Nazi scientist. Proclaimed as the "Father of U.S. Space Medicine," this former head of the **Luftwaffe's** Institute for Aviation Medicine attended a conference on medical experiments on inmates at **Dachau** in 1942. Strughold was smuggled into America in 1945. In 1995, his name was removed from the U.S. Air Force Library's School of Aerospace Medicine in Texas. (See also **Project Paperclip**.)

SUGGESTED READING: Hunt, *Secret Agenda*.

Struma. **Refugee** ship. Sponsored by **Irgun**, this unseaworthy ship, carrying 769 Romanian Jews who feared **deportation** to **Transnistria**, arrived in Istanbul on December 16, 1941. They were refused permission to land and on February 24, 1942, they were forced out to sea by Turkish officials at the urging of the **British Foreign Office**. An explosion cost the lives of all but one passenger. The incident confirmed British intransigence. However, there were conflicting

reports that a Soviet submarine sank the vessel. (See also **Lord Moyne**, the **Stern Group**, and **White Paper**.)
    SUGGESTED READING: Hirschmann, *Lifeline to a Promised Land.*

Stubenaelteste (G., room elder). Senior inmate in charge of the **block** at **concentration camps**. (See also **Blockaelteste, Lageraelteste, Self-government, Stubhova**, and **Stubendienst**.)

Stubendienst (G., [quarters] service). Assistant and subservient to **Blockaelteste**. (See also **Lageraelteste, Self-government, Stubenaelteste**, and **Stubhova**.)

Stubhova (G., female inmate supervisor). Headed a section of barracks in **concentration camps**.

Stuckart, Dr. Wilhelm (1902–1953). Nazi jurist. He was a member of the **Freikorps** and **SS**, later as minister of the interior, he played a key role in the drafting and implementing of the **Nuremberg Laws**. Stuckart was the only attendee of the **Wannsee Conference** sentenced for planning the **Final Solution**. He was arrested in 1945, tried, and sentenced to four years in prison. He was released in 1949 and restored to office as Managing Director of the Institute for Promotion of Economy in Lower Saxony. He may have been a victim of revenge when he died in a car accident. (See also **Avengers** and **Dr. Hans Globke**.)
    SUGGESTED READING: Tenenbaum, *Race and Reich.*

"Stucke" (G., "pieces"). This term for inmates indicated German contempt for the humanity of their prisoners. (See also **Dehumanization**.)

Der Stuermer (**The Attack**). Crude, pornographic **anti-Semitic** paper published first in 1923 by **Julius Streicher**. This paper enjoyed a wide readership (500,000) in Nazi **Germany** and proudly broadcast "The Jews Are Our Disaster" on the front-page of every issue. It called for the extermination of Jews in 1939 and printed accusations of Jewish ritual murder. (See also **Blood Libel**, *Der Angriff*, and "**Die Juden sind unser Unglueck**.")

Sturmabteilung. (See **SA**.)

Sturmbannfuehrer (G., SS major).

Sturmmann (G., SS lance-corporal).

Sturmscharfuehrer (G., SS sergeant-major).

Stutthof (G., **Danzig**). **Forced labor**, punishment, and extermination camp in Gdansk. It began operation on September 2, 1939. Sixteen nationalities constituting 115,000 inmates were interned there; the majority of deportees were Polish Catholic. Jews were transferred from **Riga**. Its **gas chambers** worked at full capacity, and more than 65,000 victims were murdered. Most of the inmates were evacuated on **death marches**, which began on January 25, 1945. The Baltic camp was **liberated** by the **Red Army** on May 10, 1945. (See also **Paul-Werner Hoppe** and **Kaiserwald**.)

SUGGESTED READINGS: Picleholz-Bernitsch, ''Evaluation of Stutthof Concentration Camp''; Yahil, The *Holocaust*.

''Submarine.'' Term for German Jews who removed the **Jewish Badge** and went underground, disguised as Gentiles. (See also **Greifer**.)

Subsequent Nuremberg Trials. Twelve cases of **war criminals** held at **Nuremberg's** Palace of Justice after the major cases were tried before the **International Military Tribunal**. The first case was *U.S. vs. Karl Brandt, et al.* (Doctors' case). Other cases were: *U.S. vs. Erhard Milch* (Milch Case); *U.S. vs. Josef Altstoetter, et al.* (Justice Case); *U.S. vs. Oswald Pohl, et al.* (Pohl Case); *U.S. vs. Frederick Flick, et al.* (Flick Case); *U.S. vs. Carl Krauch, et al.* (I. G.Farben Case); *U.S. vs. Wilhelm List, et al.* (Hostage Case); *U.S. vs. Ulrich Greifelt, et al.* (RuSHA Case); *U.S. vs. Otto Ohlendorf, et al.* (Einsatzgruppen Case); *U.S. vs. Alfred Krupp, et al.* (Krupp Case); and *U.S. vs. Wilhelm von Leeb, et al.* (High Command Case). (See also **Dr. Robert M. Kempner, Otto Kranzbuehler**, and **General Telford Taylor**.)

SUGGESTED READING: Annas and Grodin, *The Nazi Doctors and the Nuremberg Code*.

Sudetenland. Western **Czechoslovakia** annexed by the Nazis. This region, carved out of the Austro-Hungarian Empire after World War I by the **League of Nations** to form Czechoslovakia, was never a part of the German Empire. This area contained 3.5 million Sudeten Germans and 40,000 Jews. The Sudetenland was strategically valuable due to its fortifications and industrial armaments plants. After World War II, reconstituted Czechoslovakia retrieved the Sudetenland and threw out the Germans living there. (See also **Appeasement, Emil Hacha, Konrad Henlein, Kristallnacht, Population Transfers, Repatriation**, and **Schmelt Organization**.)

SUGGESTED READING: Shirer, *The Rise and Fall of the Third Reich*.

Sugihara, Sempo (Chiune) (1900–1986). Japanese vice-counsel general in **Kovno, Lithuania**. He defied diplomatic orders from the Ministry of Foreign Affairs and issued 1,600–3,500 transit **visas** from August 1940–September 1, 1940, to Polish and Lithuanian Jews. From December 1940 to November 1941, over 2,200 Jews found sanctuary in **Kobe**, Japan, and an additional 1,000 found haven in America, Australia, **Palestine**, and South America. Sugihara was aware many of the visas were forged. He worked in concert with the **Dutch** counsel, **Jan Zwartendijk**, who issued destination visas to Curaco. The Russians ordered the counsel closed three times and delivered an ultimatum in August 1940. He returned to Japan in 1947 and was dismissed from the diplomatic corps. Sugihara was recognized as a **Righteous Gentile** by **Yad Vashem**. (See also **Mir Yeshiva**.)

SUGGESTED READING: Levine, In Search of Sugihara.

Suhren, Fritz (1908–1950). **Waffen-SS** officer. Stationed at **Sachsenhausen**, he became kommandant of **Ravensbrueck** in July 1942. Under his administration, conditions deteriorated, brutality increased, and inhumane medical experiments ensued. Suhren was directly responsible for the murder of several thousand women who were worked to death. He was executed by the French in June 1950.

SUGGESTED READING: Tillion, Ravensbrueck.

Supreme Headquarters Allied Expeditionary Forces (**SHAEF**). Established in London (1943) to oversee and direct the planning, preparation, and launching of the D-Day invasion. Their course of attack was in Western Europe. In Administrative Memorandum Number 35, it set forth regulations dealing with **Displaced Persons**. Included in the term were stateless persons and those who were outside their country and could not return. The latter category included thousands of Jews who feared **anti-Semitic** hostility in Eastern Europe. (See also **CROWCASS** and **Kielce**.)

SUGGESTED READING: United States Holocaust Memorial Museum, 1945: The Year of Liberation.

"S" Van. (See "**Sonderwagon**.")

Svoboda Army. Czech military force under Soviet control and under the command of General Jan Svoboda. Formed in **Poland** in 1939, about one-third of its members were Jews. Units of the Independent Parachute Brigade fought in the **Slovakian National Revolt**.

Swastika. Symbol of Nazi **Germany** and centerpiece of the German flag (officially made the German flag in 1935) designed by **Hitler**. The twisted cross dates back to Indian antiquity where the **Aryan** symbol is considered a sign of good luck. The swastika was widely used by racist precursors of Hitler such as **Lance von Liebenfels**, **Guido von List**, and the **Thule Society**.

SUGGESTED READING: Lutzer, Hitler's Cross.

Sweden. Kingdom in Scandinavia with a prewar Jewish population of 8,000. It was a haven for half of Norwegian Jewry and virtually all of **Denmark's**

Jewry. The nation began accepting Jewish **refugees** in the winter of 1943. The **Horthy Offer** was prompted, in part, by the instigation of King Gustav. The Swedish Legation in Budapest, inspired by **Carl Lutz** and **Raoul Wallenberg**, saved thousands of Jews. In the spring of 1945, prodded by **Count Folke Bernadotte**, Sweden accepted thousands of **concentration camp** victims for treatment and recuperation. (See also **Bergen-Belsen, Hungary, Dr. Felix Kersten**, **Norbert Masur**, and **Wallenberg Bank**.)

SUGGESTED READING: Koblik, *The Stones Cry Out.*

SWIT ("Anusia"). Clandestine radio communication from the **Polish Government-in-Exile** in London. It received reports from the **Armia Krajowa** and broadcast the **Warsaw Ghetto Uprising**. Most Poles and Germans believed the radio station headquarters was in **Poland**, and the **Gestapo** was never able to locate the facility. Although it was subject to BBC censorship, it revealed the destruction of the Polish Jews.

Switzerland. Central European nation with a prewar Jewish population of 12,000. Switzerland was a neutral country and traditional refuge for persecuted peoples. However, after a large influx of Jews from **Germany** and **Austria**, it sealed its borders implementing a policy known as **refoulement** in 1938. In mid-1944, **Monsignor Filippo Bernardini**, papal **nuncio** in Switzerland, persuaded officials at the Swiss-Italian border to allow Jewish **refugees** to enter the nation. After receiving information about the **Holocaust** and the publication of the **Auschwitz Protocols**, the Swiss press publicized the destruction of European Jewry. On July 7, 1944, **Dr. Heinrich Rothmund** revoked refoulement. The Swiss did accept many **concentration camp** inmates after the war. Although the Swiss government allowed numerous Jewish relief agencies to operate, the administrative and banking industry actively laundered gold and money for the Nazis. This included assets confiscated from persecuted Jews. German assets deposited in Swiss banks have ballooned to between $3.3 and $3.5 billion. Class action legal suits have been filed in federal court against Swiss banks. (See also **Karl Barth, Emil Brunner, Le Chambon-sur-Lignon, CIMADE, Hans Johann von Dohnany, "Gold Train," Paul Grueninger, Hungary, Dr. Robert M. Kempner, Aleksander Lados, "Lifeboat is Full," Carl Lutz, Saly Mayer, Roswell McClelland, Jean-Marie Musy, Portugal, Dr. Gerhart Riegner, Eduard von Steiger, Rita and Isaac Sternbuch**, and **Theresienstadt**.)

SUGGESTED READING: Haesler, *The Lifeboat is Full.*

Szalasi, Ferenc (1897–1946). Hungarian fascist, founder, and leader of the **Arrow Cross**. He headed the Hungarian government from October 15, 1944–January 1945, soon after the Germans removed **Admiral Miklos Horthy**. On the day he came to power, a **pogrom** was carried out in which thousands of Jews were massacred in Budapest. He was captured by the Americans, extradited to

Hungary in October 1945, convicted of **war crimes**, and executed on March 12, 1946. (See also **Extradition, Miguel Angel Sanz-Briz**, and **Doeme Szto-jay.**)

SUGGESTED READINGS: Braham, *The Politics of Genocide; World Jewish Congress Report*, July-August 1996.

Szaulis. Units of **Lithuanian collaborators**. They assisted in the destruction of the **Warsaw Ghetto**.

Szenes, Hannah (1921–1944). Hungarian **"parachutist."** She became a **kib-butznik** (collective farmer) in the **Yishuv** and joined the British Army. Origi-nally from Budapest, she was dropped into **Yugoslavia** (March 1944) and fought with **Marshal Tito's partisans** for three months. Her mission was to assist Jews to escape Nazi persecution in **Hungary**. Szenes was arrested on June 9, 1944, and executed by the **Arrow Cross** on November 7, 1944. She is also noted for the poem, "Blessed is the Match," written in 1944. (See also **Palestine**.)

SUGGESTED READING: Syrkin, *Blessed is the Match.*

Szeptyekyj, Father Klemens (1869–1950). Greek Catholic priest and **Right-eous Gentile**. He worked with his brother **Metropolitan Andrej Szeptyekyj** in hiding Jews, setting up a chain of safe houses, and publically protesting the mistreatment of Jews. (See also **Lvov**.)

SUGGESTED READINGS: Friedman, *Their Brothers' Keepers; National Catholic Register*, January 26, 1997.

Szeptyekyj, Metropolitan Andrej (1865–1945). Greek Catholic leader of East-ern rite in the **Ukraine (Lvov)**. He initially welcomed German occupation, but protested the murder of Jews in **Galicia** and the Ukrainian territories. Szeptyekyj wrote a letter of outrage to **Heinrich Himmler** and **Pope Pius XII** about the murder of the Jews in August 1942. He chastised Ukrainian militia men for aiding German forces in massacring Jews, particularly around **Kiev**. The Met-ropolitan hid Jewish children and stored **Torah** scrolls. However, his friendship to German forces precluded his award as a **Righteous Gentile**. (See also **Greece**.)

SUGGESTED READING: Kahana, *Lvov Ghetto Diary.*

Szerynski, Joseph (d. 1943). Chief of **Jewish Police** in the **Warsaw Ghetto**. A Catholic convert chosen by **Adam Czerniakow**, he was corrupt and detested by **ghetto** residents. Threatened with death by the Nazis, Szerynski ordered the Jewish Police to prepare the execution of smugglers. But the actual arrest and execution was carried out by the Polish police. He was attacked and wounded on August 20, 1942, and subsequently hid from the **JFO**. The police chief committed suicide. (See also **Heinz Auerswald, Jewish Service to Maintain Order**, and ''**Blue Police**.'')

SUGGESTED READING: Gutman, *The Jews of Warsaw*.

Szmalcownik (P., blackmailer). Polish Catholics living in **Aryan** Warsaw who extorted money from Jews in hiding or their protectors. Failure to pay the ransom resulted in denouncement to the **Gestapo**. Frequently these **collaborators** would take the loot and betray Jews in hiding. Even when the blackmailers kept silent, they left their victims destitute. (See also ''**Keeping Cats**'' and **Warsaw Ghetto**.)

Szold, Henrietta (1860–1945). Director of **Youth Aliya** from 1933–1945. She arranged for German Jewish youth to go to **Palestine**. Later, Szold was stationed in the **Yishuv** where she helped to absorb Arab and European Jews. It is estimated she saved 20,000 young lives.

SUGGESTED READING: Krantz, *Daughter of My People*.

Sztojay, Doeme (1883–1946). Hungarian diplomat and head of the Hungarian **collaborationist** government from March–July 1944. This government implemented **ghettoization** and **deportation** during the German occupation. Sztojay fled to **Germany**, but was captured by the Americans. Extradited to Budapest and convicted of **war crimes**, he was executed on March 22, 1946. (See also **Extradition, Admiral Miklos Horthy, Operation Margarethe**, and **Ferenc Szalasi**.)

SUGGESTED READING: Braham, *The Politics of Genocide*.

Szultz. German company that operated a huge factory inside the **Warsaw Ghetto**.

T

Tallis/Tallith (Y. and H., prayer). Prayer shawl worn by Jewish men during morning services. In **ghettos**, religious Jews clandestinely continued their practices. This was a form of **spiritual resistance**.

Talmud (H., research). Oral commentaries on the Hebrew Bible along with the code of Jewish Law (**Halakha**). The Talmud and the **Torah** scroll were targets of **book burning** and desecration. (See also **Heder, Orthodox Judaism, Spiritual Resistance**, and **Yeshiva**.)

Tarbut (H., culture). **Zionist**-oriented secular school in **Poland** and **Lithuania**.

Tarnopol (also Ternopol). City in the **Ukraine** located east of **Lvov** with a prewar Jewish population of 14,000. The Ukrainians welcomed the Nazis when they entered on July 2, 1941. On July 7, 1941, random killings took place, synagogues were destroyed, and 500 Jews were driven into one of the synagogues as it was set aflame. Ukrainian nationalists brought hundreds of Jews to Tarnopol and murdered them. Over 8,000 Jews were murdered in these **pogroms**. In September 1941, a Jewish **ghetto** formed with 12,500 people. The Tarnopol ghetto revolted on July 21, 1943. Of 18,000 Tarnopol Jews, only 139 remained when the **Red Army** liberated it in spring 1944.
  SUGGESTED READING: Sabin, Alliance for Murder.

Tattoo. (1) A number tattooed on the left forearm of an inmate at **Auschwitz**. A low number indicated the inmate was a veteran and was accorded more status. Higher numbers (tattooed under the left forearm), and those without numbers, were more likely to be gassed. Out of the 1.6 million inmates at Auschwitz, most were registered or tattooed. (2) All **SS** were branded with their numbers under their left armpit. This marking provided confirmation of **Adolf Eichmann's** identity when he was captured by the Israelis in Argentina. (3) Some **Soviet POWs** were tattooed on their chest at **Mauthausen**. (See also **Josef Mengele**.)

Taylor, Myron (1874–1959). President **Franklin Delano Roosevelt's** personal envoy to the **Vatican**. A businessman turned diplomat, he was tapped by FDR to chair the **Evian Conference**. Taylor was sincerely interested in saving Jewish **refugees** and sought to revitalize the **Intergovernmental Committee on Refugees**. He was upset by consistent British and American stonewalling. It was Taylor who confirmed (September 1942) inquiries made by **Sumner Welles** that the Vatican had reliable data on the Jewish **genocide**. Taylor and his deputy, **Harold H. Tittman**, spoke frequently with **Pope Pius XII**, but failed to convince him to condemn Nazi atrocities. They also sent reports of the **Holocaust** back to the United States to no avail. (See also **Dr. Gerhart Riegner** and **Rabbi Stephen S. Wise**.)
   SUGGESTED READING: Wyman, *The Abandonment of the Jews.*

Taylor, Telford (b. 1908). American brigadier general and prosecutor at the **Nuremberg Trials**. He was involved with the **Ultra** code-breaking operation. Taylor took over the prosecution of the German High Command at Nuremberg **International Military Tribunal** and became chief prosecutor at the **Subsequent Nuremberg Trials** on March 29, 1946. (See also **Leo Alexander**.)
   SUGGESTED READINGS: Annas and Grodin, *The Nazi Doctors and the Nuremberg Code*; Taylor, *The Anatomy of the Nuremberg Trials.*

Teffilin (H., prayer phylacteries). Two boxes, one with strips wrapped around a man's arms, and the other worn attached to the head. Inside these boxes are selections from Scriptures (Exodus 13:1–10, 11:16; Deuteronomy 6:4–9, 11:13–21). Teffilin were highly desirable in the **ghetto**, and even more so in the **concentration camps** when inmates wore them secretly and prayed in the morning. (See also **Spiritual Resistance**.)

Teheran Conference. (See **Tripartite Conference**.)

Telefunken. German electrical company that utilized **concentration camp** labor.

ten Boom, Corrie (1892–1983). **Righteous Gentile**, rescuer. Based on her Christian evangelical beliefs, she hid Jews in her house in Amsterdam. Detected by the Germans, she was sent to **Vught** and **Ravensbrueck**. She wrote a book about her experiences called *The Hiding Place*.
   SUGGESTED READING: ten Boom and Sherrill, *The Hiding Place.*

Tenenbaum, Mordechai (1916–1943). Member of **He-Halutz** and key underground leader in **Bedzin, Bialystok, Vilna**, and Warsaw. He gave the signal to initiate the **Warsaw Ghetto Uprising** on April 16, 1943, and died during the battle.
SUGGESTED READING: Eckman and Lazar, *The Jewish Resistance.*

Terboven, Josef (1898–1944). **Reichskommissar** for **Norway** starting in 1940. Terboven was the real power in Norway, placed there because **Hitler** distrusted local Norwegian Nazis. He was very involved in the persecution of Jews. He committed suicide in May 1945. (See also **Vidkun Quisling**.)

Terezin (Cz.).

Tesch & Stabenow, International Vermin Extermination Corporation Ltd. (**TESTA**). Subsidiary of **I. G. Farben**, based in Hamburg and responsible for supplying **Zyklon-B** to **death** and **concentration camps**. Bruno Tesch and Karl Weinbacher were sentenced to death by a British Military Tribunal (1946) for manufacturing gas to kill prisoners.
SUGGESTED READING: Borkin, *The Crime and Punishment of I. G. Farben.*

TESTA. (See **Tesch & Stabenow, International Vermin Extermination Corporation Ltd.**)

Teutonic Tendency. Germanic peoples since Immanuel Kant, including Jews, tended to obey the state regardless of the moral consequences. This helps to explain, in part, why most Germans followed **Hitler**, and Jews within the **Greater Reich** registered with the state.

T-4 (Tierggartenstrasse 4). Acronym for headquarters of the **euthanasia** program. The name is derived from the address of a building located in the **Fuehrer Chancellery**, the complex of government buildings in **Berlin**. (See also **Dr. Irmfried Eberl** and **Dr. Albert Widmann**.)

Theresienstadt (G.). **Transit Ghetto**, also known as the "**big fortress**," this former army barracks site contained a Jewish ghetto. It opened on November 24, 1941. About one mile away was the site of the Prague **Gestapo** prison, known as the "**small fortress**," which first received prisoners on June 14, 1940, and held 32,000 inmates during the war.
The first internees and 50 percent of the inmates were Czech Jews. The second wave of deportees were **privileged** [German] **Jews**, that is, World War I veterans and spouses of mixed marriages. They began to arrive in the summer of 1942, believing they were being sent to an old-age ghetto and spa. Some prominent German Jews bribed the **SS** for the privilege to be sent to this model camp. In

addition, Danes and **Dutch** were interned at this site. The class system brutalized the old and sick who were always the first to be victimized by the **Council of Elders**. The ghetto's population reached 53,000 despite being built for 3,700. All Jews wore a red "**J.**" **Transports** to the East began on January 9, 1942, and continued through October 28, 1944. Destinations included **Riga, Minsk**, Polish ghettos, **Belzec, Sobibor, Treblinka**, and **Auschwitz**.

The first **Judenaeltester** at Terezin, **Jacob Edelstein**, was shot in Auschwitz, with his wife and son in December 1943. He was succeeded by **Dr. Paul Eppstein** who was murdered in Theresienstadt in September 1944. The last Jewish leader was Benjamin Murmelstein. The Ghettowache, Jewish guard, were equipped with wooden truncheons and were replaced by the Ordenwache (military guard) in May 1942. The camp also supplied labor to **Flossenbuerg** and the nearby underground factory known as "Richard." The **crematorium** was completed on September 7, 1942. On February 5, 1945, **Jean-Marie Musy** negotiated a transfer of Jews to **Switzerland**. A **typhus** epidemic engulfed the ghetto in April–May 1945, as transports (12,000 inmates) poured in from **Dachau, Buchenwald, Bergen-Belsen**, and Flossenbuerg.

The **Red Cross** and other agencies were paraded through this so-called "recuperation camp" (**Erholungslager**) after the Nazis instituted a "beautification" campaign. The most famous Red Cross visit occurred in June 1944, at the behest of the Danish government. After the tour, the Red Cross issued a favorable report.

Of the 140,000 inmates from thirty nations, 90,000 were shipped to **death camps** (primarily Auschwitz-**Birkenau**). Additionally, 33,430 inmates perished at Terezin, and only 100 of the 15,000 children survived. Approximately 30,000 inmates survived when the camp was turned over to the International Red Cross on May 3, 1945. The **Red Army** arrived on May 8, 1945. (See also **Anton Burger, Freddy Hirsch, Ernst Kaltenbrunner, Viteslav Lederer, Aron Menczer, Netherlands, Dr. Siegfried Seidl, Sered, Rita and Isaac Sternbuch**, and **Vedem**.)

SUGGESTED READINGS: Gilbert, *Final Journey*; Troller, *Theresienstadt: Hitler's Gift to the Jews*.

Thierack, Otto (1889–1946). President of the **People's Court** and later **Reich** minister of Justice. He signed the "**Destruction Through Work**" agreement with **Heinrich Himmler**. Thierack hanged himself before he could be brought to trial at **Nuremberg**.

SUGGESTED READING: Mueller, *Hitler's Justice*.

Third Reich (G., Dritten Reich—Third Empire). Term given to **Hitler's** regime (1933–1945). The first **Reich** was the Holy Roman Empire; the second Reich was the Bismarck-Kaiser period. Hitler envisioned that the Nazis would rule for a thousand years. (See also **New Order**.)

Thomalia, Richard (b. 1903). Lt. general **SS**, began construction at **Sobibor** and was the camp's first kommandant. He was killed in the war.
SUGGESTED READING: Arad, *Belzec, Sobibor, Treblinka.*

Thompson, Dorothy (1894–1961). Prominent, American anti-Nazi journalist. In her "General Electric" radio hour on November 14, 1938, she publicized the plight of **Herschel Grynszpan**. Soon after, Thompson established a Journalists' Defense Fund for Grynszpan. She called for the destruction of the Nazi regime and sympathized with the plight of the Jews. (See also **Kristallnacht**.)
SUGGESTED READING: Read and Fisher, *Kristallnacht.*

Thrace. Region located between European Turkey on the east and **Bulgaria** and **Greece**, north and west. In 1941, the former Greek province was annexed to Bulgaria (with the exception of eastern Thrace, which came under German occupation). By March 1943, most Jews were either **deported** or detained. **Sephardic** Jews were gathered and **transported** to **Treblinka**. Over 4,000 were deported. Only 242 Jews survived, sheltered by a sympathetic gentile local population. A number of Jews found safe haven in Italian occupied areas from 1941 to 1942. (See also **Macedonia**.)
SUGGESTED READINGS: Nahon, *Birkenau: The Camp of Death.*

Thule Society. Literary circle of upper-class supernationalists founded in **Berlin** in 1912. Its name was taken from Ultima Thule: the Land at the End of the World and the mythical birthplace of the Germanic race. They believed in the superiority of the Teutonic race. It promoted the old Germanic religion by examining ruins and studying Norse script, northern German stories, folk beliefs, and festivals. It spawned what was later to be known as the **German Workers Party** in 1918. After 1918, the organization accepted some workers and became zealously anti-Bolshevik and **anti-Semitic**. Its members included **Rudolph Hess** and **Adolf Hitler**. The Thule Society financed and guided the **Freikorps** and its symbol was the sunwheel **swastika**. (See also **Anton Drexler** and **Dr. Alfred Rosenberg**.)
SUGGESTED READINGS: Berman, *Coming to Our Senses*; Levenda, *Unholy Alliance.*

Thundercross (La., **Perkonkrust**). Latvian **fascist** organization. It **collaborated** with the German Army and rounded up thousands of Jews from **Riga** and murdered them in the Bikerniecki Forest on July 1, 1941. (See also **Latvia, Latvian SS Legion**, and **Schuma**.)
SUGGESTED READING: Ezergailis, *The Holocaust in Latvia.*

Thyssen, Fritz (1873–1951). German industrialist. He was appointed Prussian state counselor in September 1933 by Hermann **Goering**. The industrialist helped finance the Nazis up to 1939, but was upset by the Nazis' anti-

Catholicism and persecution of Jews. He was particularly dismayed by Nazi brutality during **Kristallnacht**. Thyssen fled **Germany** on December 28, 1939, but later was captured by the **Vichy** government and turned over to the Nazis. He was imprisoned for the duration of the war.

SUGGESTED READING: Pool and Pool, *Who Financed Hitler?*

Tiso, Dr. Josef (1887–1947). Catholic priest and head of **Slovakia's Hlinka People's Party**. He was the pro-Nazi president of Slovakia from March 1939–1945. Tiso introduced anti-Jewish legislation, expropriated Jewish property, established **forced labor camps**, and supported **deportations.** **Pope Pius XII** appealed to Tiso not to deport Jews who converted to Catholicism. The plea had only a temporary effect. Out of Slovakia's pre-**Final Solution** Jewish population of 90,000, only 15,000 survived the war. Caught and extradited by the Americans in 1945, he was convicted of **war crimes** and hanged by the Czechs in 1947. Members of the Slovak National Party (1995) continue to lobby for the restoration of Tiso's honor. (See also **Extradiction, Sano Mach, Sered, Vojtech Tuka**, and **Anton Vasek.**)

SUGGESTED READING: Reitlinger, *The Final Solution.*

Tito, Marshal (Josip Broz) (1892–1980). Yugoslavian communist leader. He commanded 300,000 **partisans** during the war, and by 1943, kept twenty Nazi divisions occupied. Tito tried to unify all ethnic and religious partisans and rescued many Jews. Tito ordered his men to assist escaping Jews. Over 2,000 Jews fought with Tito's partisans. (See also **Croatia, Serbia, Hannah Szenes**, and **Yugoslavia.**)

SUGGESTED READING: Hehn, *The German Struggle in World War II.*

Tittman, Harold H. American Charge d'Affairs to the **Vatican**. He received news of the **Final Solution** from the Holy See. The pope didn't want to worsen the situation of Catholics in Germany and occupied countries with an *ex cathedra* (pope speaking as official doctrine) approach (September 1942). In October 1942, he received Vatican reports on the mass murder of the Jews. Tittman expressed great surprise at the apathy of the pope: "The Holy Father adopts an ostrich like policy toward notorious atrocities." (See also **Myron Taylor** and **Ernst von Weizsacker.**)

SUGGESTED READING: Rhodes, *The Vatican in the Age of Dictators.*

Tiyul (H., "excursion"). Hungarian Jewish rescue organization headed by **Joel Brand**. This group operated as an arm of the **Relief and Rescue Committee of Budapest** and rescued 1,100 Polish Jews.

Todt, Dr. Fritz (1891–1942). German minister of armaments and munitions (1938–1943). He was killed in a plane crash in January 1942 and was succeeded by **Albert Speer**. (See also **Todt Organization.**)

Todt Organization (Organization Todt; OT). Nazi-sponsored, paramilitary labor battalions. This German military organization was dedicated to heavy construction and utilized **concentration camp** labor. OT also operated in the rearguard of **Einsatzgruppen** activity. It was headed by **Dr. Fritz Todt** until his death in 1942. (See also **Channel Islands, Forced Labor, Fremdarbeiter, Impressing**, and **Albert Speer**.)

   SUGGESTED READINGS: Speer, *Inside the Third Reich*; Yahil, *The Holocaust*.

Toebbens. German company that operated brush factories in the **Warsaw Ghetto** and employed Jewish **slave labor** in **Poniatowa**.

   SUGGESTED READING: Ainsztein, *The Warsaw Ghetto Revolt*.

Torah (H., instruction). Specifically refers to the Five Books of Moses. These books are placed on a scroll, Sefer Torah, and are an essential part of the holy objects of every synagogue. The Nazis took special joy in desecrating and destroying the Sefer Torah. Jews risked their lives to save Torah scrolls burnt by the Nazis. This term is also a generic reference to all Jewish learning.

"Total Evacuation." Nazi euphemism for the murder of Jews in the **Generalgouvernement** and **Warthegau**.

Totenkopfverbaende (G., **Death's Head Brigades**). Division of **SS** later incorporated into the **Waffen-SS**. Headed by **Theodor Eicke**, it was responsible for training and guarding **death** and **concentration camps**. Founded by Eicke in July 1934, the Death's Head became independent of the SS in March 1936, and by September 1939, this force totaled 24,000. In October 1939, Eicke created the Totenkampfverbaende. By April 1941, the division was fully assimilated into Waffen-SS, and, by the end of the war, this force totaled 40,000 men. These units were responsible for committing atrocities in **France** in 1944. (See also **Wehrmacht**.)

   SUGGESTED READING: Hoehne, *The Order of the Death's Head*.

Totschweigen (G., hushing up). Policy of not mentioning Jews. (See also **Moscow Declaration** and **Saint James Declaration**.)

Touvier, Paul (1915–1996). Director of the **Milice** in Lyons. A French official who took an oath to destroy "Jewish leprosy" in **France**, Touvier rounded up Jews and Spanish Republicans for **deportation** from 1943 to 1944. He ordered the execution of seven Jewish **hostages** in June 1944. Touvier was sentenced to death *in absentia* in 1946 and 1947, but was pardoned by Georges Pompidou in 1971, and was consistently sheltered by sympathetic Catholic prelates. He was jailed in 1994, after forty years on the run. He was the first Frenchman tried and convicted of **crimes against humanity** (reprisal executions of seven Jews) in April 1994. (The trial was opposed by French Prime Minister, Francois

Mitterrand.) Touvier died of prostate cancer in his prison cell in 1996. (See also **Rene Bousquet, Maurice Papon,** and **Rotspanir**.)

SUGGESTED READINGS: Golsan, Memory, the Holocaust and French Justice; Webster, *Petain's Crime.*

TOZ (Society for the Protection of the Health of Jews). Self-help organizations, particularly involved in medical aid in Polish **ghettos**. Active and independent of the **Judenraete**, it affiliated with the **Jewish Self-Help Society**. (See also **Central Agency for Care of Orphans** and **ORT**.)

Transfer Agreement. (See **Haavara Agreement**.)

Transferstelle (G., transfer agency). Nazi entity in Warsaw that coordinated the **ghetto's** economic affairs and the exchange of goods between the ghetto and the **Aryan** side. (See also **Warsaw Ghetto**.)

Transit Camps. Temporary **concentration camps** for Western Jews prior to **deportation** to **death** and/or **slave labor** camps. Deportation in **internment camps** could precede incarceration in **transit camps**, for example, **Compiegne, Drancy, French Internment** and **Transit Camps**, and **Westerbork**.

Transit Ghetto. (See **Theresienstadt**.)

Transnistria. Province carved out of the **Ukraine** between the Bug and Dneister Rivers, after German and Romanian victories against the **Soviet Union** in the summer of 1941. In the summer of 1941, **Einsatzgruppe** D, under the command of **Otto Ohlendorf**, perpetrated large-scale massacres of thousands of Jews. On November 11, 1941, **Ion Antonescu** assigned this area as a penal colony. Approximately 185,000 indigenous Ukrainian Jews were murdered by March 1943. An additional 90,000 Jews **deported** from **Bukovina** and western **Romania** were killed in Transnistria. Romanian political prisoners were also deported to the region. Transnistria contained five camps devoted to murder: Peciora, Bogdanovka, Mostovoi, Acmececta, and Berezowka. The **Red Army** recaptured this region in March 1944. (See also **Bessarabia, Ira Hirshmann, Czernowitz, Siegfried Jagendorf, Jewish Agency, Radu Lecca, Mogilev-Podolski, Odessa, *Struma*,** and **Vapniarca**.)

SUGGESTED READING: Fischer, Transnistria, The Forgotten Cemetery.

Transport. **Deportation** to **labor, concentration**, or **death camps**. The deportees usually arrived on **freight cars** attached to trains.

Transportjuden (G., Jewish transport). Jewish **deportation**.

Transportunfaehig (G., not for transportation). Those who were "unfit" for **transport**; mostly the sick, elderly, and small children. All were summarily executed. (See also **Selection**.)

Trans-Sahara Railway. Construction of this route in **Algeria** was authorized in March 1941. More than 1,500 Jews serving in the French Foreign Legion were sent to **labor camps** in Algeria and **Morocco**, then under French control. The railway was completed between 1941–1942. It went from Abadla labor camp to Oran, the large port city in Algeria. The harsh conditions imposed took a toll on the Jews as well as Spanish Republican internees. (See also **Rotspanir**.)
   SUGGESTED READING: Gilbert, *Atlas of the Holocaust.*

Trawniki. Labor camp, SS training facility, and industrial site. Established in 1941 outside of **Lublin**, the **Fritz Schultz Company** exploited 10,000 **slave laborers**. Peat was also harvested from this area. SS graduates, including **John Demjanjuk**, became guards of **labor, concentration**, and **death camps** in the **Generalgouvernement**. Trawniki SS also served as **ghetto cleaners** and fought against Jews in the **Warsaw Ghetto to Uprising**. Members of the **ZOB** and **Emmanuel Ringelblum** were imprisoned here. On November 5, 1943, 10,000 Jews were murdered in this camp as part of **Operation Erntefest**. However, the Jewish underground, surprised by the **Aktion**, resisted and were murdered. (See also **Belzec, OST, Sobibor**, and **Treblinka**.)
   SUGGESTED READING: Arad, *Belzec, Sobibor, Treblinka.*

Treblinka. Death camp. Located in **Poland** near the town of Malkinia (125 km northeast of Warsaw), this **death concentration camp**/complex was patterned after **Sobibor** and staffed by veterans of the **euthanasia** program. The largest of the three **Operation Heydrich** killing centers, most of the Jews from **Radom** and Warsaw were murdered here. In 1941, Treblinka I, a penal camp (dulag) was established to exploit raw materials from the quarry. Treblinka II, the death camp, operated from July 22, 1942–August 1943. It was run by Nazis with the help of Ukrainian guards. About 870,000 Jews were killed at Treblinka. An armed inmate insurrection on August 2, 1943 hastened Treblinka's demise. The Nazis razed the facility under **Heinrich Himmler's** orders, and by November 1943, all visible signs of the killing camp were gone. The site was quickly converted to a farm. (See also **Dr. Irmfried Eberl, Kurt Franz, Grodno, "Himmelstrasse," Franz Stangl, Warsaw Ghetto, Karl Wolff**, and **(Zalman) Friedrych "Zygmunt."**)
   SUGGESTED READING: Donat, *The Death Camp Treblinka.*

Treuhander (G., trustee). Individual who operated a formerly owned Jewish business in occupied **Poland**.

Tripartite Conference. From November 29–30, 1943, in Teheran, the **Allies** (**Franklin Delano Roosevelt, Winston Churchill**, and **Josef Stalin**) formalized their commitment to unconditional surrender, adopted at the **Casablanca Conference**, and agreed not to engage in separate negotiations with the Nazis.

Tripartite Pact. Signed in **Berlin** on September 27, 1940, among Japan, **Germany**, and **Italy**. It provided for mutual assistance should any signatory be attacked by the United States. In November 1940, **Hungary, Romania**, and **Slovakia** joined, as did **Bulgaria** in February 1941. **Finland** and **Albania** joined these powers in the war with the Soviets in the summer of 1941.

Trocme, Andre (1901–1971). French Protestant rescuer. He was the pastor of the village of **Le Chambon-sur-Lignon**, who urged the Huguenot townspeople to hide Jews and escort them to safety to **Switzerland**. Trocme was assisted by his wife Magda, cousin Daniel, and the **CIMADE** rescue group. He is honored as a **Righteous Gentile** at **Yad Vashem** and credited with saving 5,000 Jews.
  SUGGESTED READING: Hallie, *Lest Innocent Blood Be Shed.*

Trujillo, Rafael (1891–1961). Dictator of the **Dominican Republic**. He offered a safe haven for 100,000 Jews at the **Evian Conference**. Although only 645 German and Austrian Jews made it to the Caribbean city of **Sousa** between 1940–1945, the 5,000 **visas** issued by this nation provided a safety net for many more.
  SUGGESTED READING: Sanders, *Shores of Refuge.*

Truman, Harry S. (1884–1972). President of the United States from 1945–1953. He was sympathetic to the plight of Jewish **Holocaust** survivors and allowed the **American Zone of Occupation** in **Germany** to remain open to accommodate the flood of Jewish **refugees**. Truman commissioned **Earl Harrison** to investigate the conditions of **DP camps**. He also pushed Congress to liberalize U.S. immigration laws so that more Jews might be able to enter. Truman's actions were crucial to the creation of the State of Israel. (See also **Displaced Persons' Act, Rabbi Judah Nadich**, and **Potsdam Conference**.)
  SUGGESTED READING: Sachar, *The Redemption of the Unwanted.*

Tryszynska, Luba (''**Angel of Belsen**''). Jewish inmate who nursed, protected, and saved forty-four **Dutch** children in **Bergen-Belsen**. Shipped to Belsen in the summer of 1944 from **Auschwitz**, she came upon forty-six **Dutch** children in a barrack, all younger than 14 years of age. Her husband and son were murdered at Auschwitz.

Tuchin (G.); **Tyczyn** (P.). Ukrainian town annexed by the Soviets and occupied by the Nazis on July 6, 1941. The **Judenrat**, with the help of the local Ukrainian population, helped 4,000 Jews resist the Germans. Some of the Jews escaped and joined Soviet **partisans** after the **ghetto** was liquidated on September 23, 1942. Only twenty Jews who resisted survived the war. A **concentration camp** was located outside of town. The **Red Army liberated** Tyczyn on January 16, 1944.

   SUGGESTED READING: Fischer, *Transnistria, The Forgotten Cemetery.*

Tuka, Vojtech (1880–1946). Law professor, active in the **Hlinka People's Party** and Prime Minister of **Slovakia**. He was the main force behind Jewish persecution and requested German assistance in June 1942 to facilitate Jewish **deportations**. Tuka was condemned to death after the war by the National Tribunal in Bratislava, but died in prison. (See also **Sano Mach, Sered, Dr. Josef Tiso, Anton Vasek**, and **Working Group**.)

   SUGGESTED READING: Frieder, *To Deliver Their Souls.*

Tunis. Capital of Tunisia with a Jewish population of 50,000. Jews were forced to wear the **Yellow Badge** and sell their property when the city fell under German control in March 1942. In December 1942, 2,000 Jews were assigned to **forced labor**, and 4,000 were sent to the front lines as the British and Americans approached. In May 1943, **Allied** armies drove out the Germans and prevented the **deportation** of Tunisian Jews to Polish **death camps**. Most of Tunisia's 85,000 Jews resided in Tunis. (See **Aryanization, Italy**, **Walter Rauff**, and **Statut des Juifs**.)

   SUGGESTED READING: Abitol, *The Jews of North Africa.*

Twelfth Lithuanian Auxiliary Battalion. Guarded Jewish **ghetto** in Kaunas (**Kovno**) and murdered 47,000 Jews in **Lithuania** and **Belorussia**. This unit specialized in brutality and mass murder. This battalion, one of ten known to the Germans as Schutzmannschaft, aided **Einsatzgruppen** III in murdering 136,000 Jews. Individuals who served in this unit are entitled to receive compensation for being convicted by Soviet courts.

   SUGGESTED READING: Tory, *Surviving the Holocaust.*

"Twins' Father" (G., Zvilingefater). **Josef Mengele** was enamored by twins for he sought to find the secret of the phenomenon so that **Germany** could populate faster. He appointed an inmate twin, Zvi Spigel, to care for twin boys. He became known as the "Twins' Father." Zvi had to inform the children of the fate of their parents and prepare the children for experiments by making sure they were clean and spotless. Mengele had a fetish for cleanliness. He supervised the children when they were not serving as guinea pigs. Spigel survived the war. However, out of 3,000 sets of twins at **Auschwitz**, only 100 survived.

   SUGGESTED READING: Lagnado and Dekel, *Children of the Flames.*

"2004." Underground factory where inmates from **Flossenbuerg** built **Messerschmidt** fighter planes.

Typhus. Infectious disease very common in the **concentration camps** and a common cause of death. It was characterized by exhaustion, nervous symptoms, and the eruption of reddish spots on the body, as well as a high fever. The microorganisms are transmitted by lice and fleas and thrive under unsanitary, crowded conditions. (See also **Bath certificate, Bergen-Belsen, Delousing certificate, Dr. Erwin Ding-Schuler, "Eine Laus, dein Tod," Entlausung, Anne Frank, Eugene Haagen, Dr. Waldemar Hoven, Lause-Kontrolle, Lausestrasse, Dr. Joachim Mrugrowsky, Terezin, Weil Felix Reaction**, and **Dr. Eduard Wirths**.)

U

Uckermark. Youth **concentration camp** at **Ravensbrueck**. In December 1944, this camp was converted to a killing center for women who were no longer able to work. (See also **Herrenvolk**.)

Uebermenschen (G., supermen). The Nazis depicted themselves, the **Aryans**, particularly Germans, as above all the rest of mankind. The Nazis borrowed the term from a book by **Friedrich Nietzsche**.

UGIF (F., Union General des Israelites de France; General Union of French Jews). Established on November 29, 1941, by the **Vichy** government, it aided Jews to escape to the Italian Zone. Membership was compulsory for all Jews in **France**. The UGIF was divided into a northern and southern section. It operated hospitals, old age homes, orphanages, and other local service organizations. It did not aid in **deportations**. (See also **Society for the Rescue of Jewish Children**.)

SUGGESTED READINGS: Adler, *The Jews of Paris*; Bauer, *American Jewry and the Holocaust*.

Ukraine. **Slavic** country bounded in the north by **Belorussia** and **Russia**, in the south by the Black Sea and **Bessarabia**, and in the west by **Poland** and **Czechoslovakia**. The Ukrainians are a separate cultural people distinct from Russians. It was once a province of Tsarist Russia, but became independent for a short time after the Bolshevik Revolution of 1917–1918. After the victory of the **Red Army** over anticommunist forces, the Ukraine was subdued and made a republic within the **USSR**. It lost its western part, **Galicia**, to Poland, and **Ruthenia** was awarded to Czechoslovakia. Ukrainian nationalism remained strong. Since Ukrainian farmers resisted collectivization, the Soviet dictator **Josef Stalin** induced a famine **genocide** in the early 1930s. In June 1941, with the advance of the German armies in the Soviet Union, Ukrainians hoped that **Germany** would restore their independence, but **Hitler** had no such plans. His **Generalplan Ost** was to colonize the Ukraine with Germanic peoples, decimate the local **Slavs**, and enslave the rest. However, many Ukrainians joined the **Wehrmacht** volunteer forces. Over 100,000 applied for the **Waffen-SS** and 30,000 were accepted.

Realizing that Nazi occupation was more brutal than the communists, the Ukrainian divisions in the Red Army fought well. By November 6, 1943, the Red Army reoccupied **Kiev**, the former capital of the Ukraine. On July 27, 1944, the Soviets took **Lvov**, the principal city in Galicia (western Ukraine).

There were a million and a half Jews living in the Soviet Ukraine in 1939, along with a total population of 40 million. When the USSR swallowed up half of Poland in 1939, 568,000 Galician Jews came under their rule; in that area 80 percent remained. But in the USSR proper, over 75 percent of the Jewish population fled before the Nazis reached them. The Soviets had no interest in Jews as Jews but as workers, and sought to save their working force to continue beyond the German reach. Nevertheless, the **Einsatzgruppen** that cut into the Ukraine, aided by the **Order Police** and many Ukrainian **anti-Semites**, exacted a terrible toll on Jews. In four short months in the summer of 1941, 350,000 Jews met their death. Ukrainian militias and bands inflicted terrible mayhem, instituting **pogroms**. Statistics on the number of Jews who died by genocide are difficult to come by. Many Hungarian and Romanian Jews were murdered in **Transnistria**. More than 1.4 million Jews from the USSR were killed in the Holocaust. (See also **Babi Yar, Erich von dem Bach-Zelewski, Stefan Bandera, Bletchley Park, Paul Blobel, Collaboration, John Demjanjuk, Galician SS, Hilfswillige, Erich Koch, Field Marshal Erich von Manstein, Mogilev-Podolski, Munkaszolgalat, Odessa, Ostabatallione, Ostarbeiter, Ostmensch, OUN, Partition of Poland, Petliura Days, Pogrom, Poniatowa, Emil Otto Rasch, Field Marshal Walter von Reichenau, Schuma, Sonderkommando 1005, Stanislaw, Father Klemens Szeptyekyj, Metropolitan Andrej Szeptyekyj, Tarnopol, Treblinka, Untermenschen, Ukrainian Liberation Army**, and **Zolochev**.)

Ukrainian Liberation Army. Auxiliary, part-time military forces under **Wehrmacht** control. It had many **OUN** members. At its height it boasted 180,000 members.

Ukrainian Nationalist Organization (OUN). **Anti-Semitic** independence movement in the **Ukraine** and **Poland**. The **Stefan Bandera** faction created in 1940 (OUN-Bandera) became the majority. At first, they supported the Nazis, hoping such **collaboration** would bring about an independent Ukraine. Many manned the **Galician SS** division. They were disappointed by German unwillingness to form a separate Ukrainian entity. Fervent nationalists were sent to **concentration camps**. Many OUN members were involved with the roundup and murder of Jews and complicity in **pogroms**. In 1944, the Ukrainian Nationalist Supreme Liberation Council offered Jews (mostly dead) "full rights to cultivate their culture." Eventually, the **Red Army** destroyed the OUN in the 1950s. (See also **Lvov**.)

   SUGGESTED READINGS: Potichny and Astor, *Ukrainian Jewish Relations*; Sabin, *Alliance for Murder.*

Ultra. Code name given by British for deciphered material gained by **Enigma** machines at **Bletchley Park**. From 1940 on through the war, cryptoanalysts decoded messages from the German air, land, and naval high commands. The eavesdropping on the Nazis was shared with the United States. Ultra provided information on the mass murder of Jews, but the **Allies** failed to act. (See also **Order Police, OSS,** and **General Telford Taylor**.)

   SUGGESTED READINGS: Lewin, *Ultra Goes to War*; Rymkiewicz, *The Final Station.*

Umschlagsplatz; Umschlag (G., transfer or assembly point). This area, also referred to as the "Trading Place," separated the Jewish **ghetto** from **Aryan Poland** on Zamenhoff and Niskla Streets. A railway siding and transfer office in this plaza were located in the **Warsaw Ghetto**, where 300,000 Jews were loaded on a train for "**resettlement**." The final destination for most Jews was **Treblinka. Deportations** began on July 22, 1942. (See also **Blue Police**.)

"Uncle." (See **American Joint Distribution Committee**.)

Unification Treaty. Agreement made when East **Germany** reunited with West Germany. Article Two of the treaty signed on September 18, 1990, extended the laws of restitution to the former East Germany. This included retroactive pension for members of the German civil service, payments to the State of Israel, compensation to **Holocaust** survivors for "lost" and stolen property. (See also **Konrad Adenauer** and **Reparations and Restitution**.)

Union of Jewish Survivors. Established on June 20, 1945, by the First Congress of Bavaria, this organization aided **DPs** and represented and protected their interests.

Union of Orthodox Rabbis of America. Its rescue arm, **Va'ad ha-Hatzala**, sent funds to **Siberia** and **Lithuania** for rabbis, students, and their families to escape to Japan and China. This organization supported **Rita and Isaac Sternbuch** and joined the **Bergson Group** in holding the only march (October 6, 1943) on Washington to demand rescue for European Jews. The Union was at odds with the "**Joint**" concerning the rescue of Jews because the former avoided illegal means of rescue such as bribery and trading with the enemy. (See also **Joint Emergency Committee for European Jewish Affairs, Kobe, Dr. Isaac Lewin, Orthodox Judaism**, and **Shanghai**.)

SUGGESTED READING: Kranzler, *Thy Brother's Blood.*

Union of Soviet Socialist Republics (USSR). Official name of the **Soviet Union**. It existed as a single entity from 1919–1991. The huge territory, a totalitarian state, encompassed the Old Tsarist Russian Empire, stretching from the Baltic and Black Seas across to **Siberia**, Asia, and the Pacific. Its Jewish population in 1939 was 3,060,000 out of a total population of 167,300,000. Over 500,000 Jews served in the armed forces, and 200,000 lost their lives. Jews were concentrated in the largest republics—**Russia, Belorussia**, and the **Ukraine**. In 1939, half of **Poland** was incorporated into the USSR. In 1940, the Baltic countries of **Lithuania, Latvia**, and **Estonia** were annexed as Soviet Republics; they had a Jewish population of 260,000. Also in that year, **Bukovina** and **Bessarabia** were broken off from **Romania** and made into a Soviet Republic, Moldavia. Just before the German invasion of the USSR in June 1941, and immediately afterward, 1.5 million Jews fled from these areas into the Soviet interior. Most were saved from the Holocaust Nazi **genocide**. (See also **Jewish Anti-Fascist Committee, Molotov-Ribbentrop Pact, Operation Barbarossa, Red Army, Soviet POWs, Josef Stalin**, and **Raoul Wallenberg**.)

Union Werke. German armaments factory that utilized **slave labor** from **Auschwitz** I.

United Nations Declaration of December 17, 1942. Official statement of eleven **Allied** nations indicting the Nazi leadership in the "extermination of the Jews." The Declaration pledged that "retribution would be taken." This announcement to the media recognized, for the first time, the Nazis' systematic destruction of European Jewry.

SUGGESTED READING: United States Holocaust Memorial Museum, *Darkness Before Dawn.*

United Nations Declaration of Human Rights. A nonbinding statement of basic principles signed by UN General Assembly members in December 1946. It prohibited torture of prisoners, unfair trials, **slave labor**, and persecution on a political, ethnic, or racial basis. (See also **Eleanor Roosevelt**.)

United Nations Relief and Rehabilitation Agency (UNRRA) (1943–1948). Formed in 1943 by the **Allies**, three-quarters of the money came from the United States. This entity aided in the rehabilitation of **refugees**. Its general director was **Fiorello La Guardia**. Surviving Jews received a great deal of help at **DP camps** from the UNRRA. (See also **Ira Hirschmann**.)

SUGGESTED READING: United States Holocaust Memorial Museum, 1945: *The Year of Liberation.*

United Nations Resolution, December 11, 1946. Affirmed principles established by the **London Charter Conference** and judgments of the **Nuremberg Tribunal**. This included making extermination of people on the basis of race and religion an international **crime against humanity**. (See also **Genocide Convention.**)

SUGGESTED READING: Falk, Kolko, and Lifton, *Crimes of War.*

United Nations War Crimes Commission (UNWCC). Agency formed on December 17, 1942, by the **Allies** (except the **Soviet Union**) to examine atrocities committed by the **Axis** powers. The Commission was represented by fifteen nations and initially led by **Herbert Pell**. The U.S. State Department obstructed the Commission's efforts and objected to the inclusion of **crimes against humanity**, arguing there was no precedent in international law. However, this body did publish reports about killing centers in **Poland** in 1944. Between 1944–1948, it amassed files on 36,000 criminals and organizations, including **Kurt Waldheim**. (See also **International Military Tribunal.**)

SUGGESTED READINGS: Blayner, "Herbert Pell"; United States Holocaust Memorial Museum, *Darkness Before Dawn.*

United Partisan Organization. (See **FPO.**)

Unoccupied France. The Nazi armies crushed **France** in June 1940, forcing the French government to sign an armistice on June 21, 1940. One provision allowed France independence in a large central and southern section, a sovereign country with its own army and police force, and a capital at the town of **Vichy**. This southern part was called the "Free Zone" or Unoccupied France, while the northern section of France and a long strip next to the Atlantic Ocean was occupied by German troops. French Jews, as well as **refugees** from other places, particularly **Belgium**, streamed into the Unoccupied Zone. The United States recognized the Vichy government, and refugee aid organizations were able to operate there. However, with the **Allied** invasion of French North Africa on November 8, 1942, German troops on November 11, 1942, moved into the unoccupied zone, except the Mediterranean coast. The Italians were given jurisdiction over this area, and their army protected Jews along the Cote D'Azur. (See also **CIMADE, Varian Fry, Gurs**, and **Italy.**)

SUGGESTED READING: Adler, *The Jews of Paris.*

"Unproductive Eaters." Nazi euphemism for people who ate but did not work, for example, those mentally and terminally ill. These Germans were targeted for the **T-4** program and later **14 f 13**. (See also **Euthanasia, "Lebensunwertes Leben,"** and **Selection.**)

UNRRA. (See **United Nations Relief and Rehabilitation Agency**.)

Unterkapo (G., assistant to **Kapo**).

Untermenschen (G., subhuman). Slave element in Nazi racial theory. This racial category was reserved for **Slavs** and most ruthlessly employed against Polish civilians and **Soviet POWs**. Although Jews also fell into this category, the Nazis believed the Jews to be a pestilence with no redeeming value. The German government published a pamphlet with this title in several languages. It glorified the heroic, handsome, Nordic **Aryan** and degraded other peoples. (See also **General Gottlob Berger, Roma**, and **Social Darwinism**.)

Unterscharfuehrer (G., **SS** sergeant).

Untersturmfuehrer (G., **SS** second lieutenant).

Unvolkungspolitik (G., population policy). Forced relocation of eastern and southeastern Europeans.

UNWCC. (See **United Nations War Crimes Commission**.)

USSR. (See **Union of Soviet Socialist Republics**.)

Ustasha/Ustashi (Cr., "insurgent" or "upright"). Croatian **fascist** movement, Croatian political party and paramilitary created in 1930. It **collaborated** with the Nazis to set up an "independent" state in April 1941 after **Yugoslavia** was overrun by the **Wehrmacht**. The Ustashi, headed by **Anton Pavelic**, was largely responsible for the murder of 700,000 Orthodox Serbs, 60,000 Jews, 30,000 **Roma**, and thousands of communists. Archbishop Aloysius Stepinac denounced the murder of Jews. (See also **Chetniks, Croatia, Ratline, Schuma, Semlin, Serbia, Edmund Veesenmayer, Kurt Waldheim**, and **Zagreb**.)
   SUGGESTED READING: Berenbaum, *A Mosaic of Victims.*

Ustredna Zidov (UZ) (Sl., Jewish Center). Slovakian version of the **Judenrat** headed by Heinrich Schwartz, created in 1940. The UZ established **Novaky**, a **labor camp**, in the hope of saving Jews through "**Work as a Means of Rescue**." The **Working Group** broke with the Center when **deportations** began in March 1942. (See also **Gisi Fleischmann** and **Rabbi Michael Dov Weissmandel**.)
   SUGGESTED READING: Rothkirchen, "The Dual Role of the 'Jewish Center' in Slovakia."

UZ. (See **Ustredna Zidov**.)

V

Va'ad ha-Ezra ve-ha-Hatzala be-Budapest (H., **Relief and Rescue Committee of Budapest**). (See **Joel Brand** and **Dr. Rezso Kasztner**.)

Va'ad ha-Hatzala (H., Rescue Committee). Arm of **Union of Orthodox Rabbis of America** established in 1939 with the express purpose of saving rabbis and their families. This group supported relief and rescue activities despite a ban on bribery of Nazis. It sent funds, food, and clothing to Polish Jews incarcerated in **Siberia** and Jews trapped in **Shanghai**. Va'ad spearheaded the only public demonstration against American apathy on October 6, 1943. About 400 Orthodox rabbis protested at the White House. In January 1944, Va'ad decided to rescue all Jews, regardless of affiliation. After the war, they played an active role in rehabilitating survivors. (See also **Agudat Israel, American Jewish Congress, Peter Bergson, Kobe, Jewish Labor Committee, Orthodox Judaism, Rita and Isaac Sternbuch**.)
  SUGGESTED READINGS: Dinnerstein, *America and the Survivors*; Kranzler, *Thy Brother's Blood*.

Vadasz Esendorok (Hu., **Gendarmerie**). The National Police of **Hungary**. They were a significant force largely responsible for the **deportation** of Jews to **Auschwitz** in spring 1944. (See also **Laszlo Ferenczy**.)

Vaernet, Dr. Carl. Danish **SS** major and physician. He attempted to cure male **homosexuals** of their "disease" by implanting a hormone on the right side of the groin (1944). No medical gains were attained from these experiments in **Buchenwald**.
  SUGGESTED READING: Burleigh and Wipperman, *The Racial State*.

Vajas, Albert (1905–1964). Jewish **partisan** leader in **Yugoslavia**. He was captured by the Germans, however, and he survived the war. He became a member of the State **War Crimes** Commission and deputy head of Yugoslavia's delegation to the **International Military Tribunal**.
SUGGESTED READING: Romans, *The Jews of Yugoslavia*.

Vallat, Xavier (1891–1972). **Vichy** administrator. As Commissioner for Jewish Affairs, he coordinated Vichy's anti-Jewish program from 1941–1942, which included "**Aryanization**" of Jewish economic life. However, his anti-Jewish stance was tempered by an anti-German attitude, and the Nazis forced him out of office in May 1942 when they began the **deportation** and liquidation of French Jewry. After the war he was sentenced to ten years in prison, but was released after serving only two years in 1950. (See also **Gurs, Louis Darquier Pellepoix**, and **Statut des Juifs**.)
SUGGESTED READINGS: Adler, *The Jews of Paris*; Marrus, "Coming to Terms With Vichy."

Valpo. Finnish state police headed by **Arno Anthoni**. It worked with the **Gestapo** and German authorities. Both treated foreign Jews harshly. (See also **Finland** and **Dr. Felix Kersten**.)
SUGGESTED READING: Cohen and Svensson, "Finland and the Holocaust."

Vapniarca. Infamous camp for Jewish political prisoners in **Transnistria**. The camp operated from October 1941–March 1944.

Vasek, Anton ("King of the Jews") (1905–1946). Pro-Nazi Slovakian minister. He coordinated Jewish **deportation**; however, Vasek was successfully bribed by the **Working Group** to temporarily stall the process. He was hanged after the war by the Czech National Tribunal in Bratislava.
SUGGESTED READING: Frieder, *To Deliver Their Souls*.

Vatican. Papal headquarters in **Rome**. The Papal Holy government is recognized by the world as a sovereign state. Sometimes the term "Holy See" is used for the Vatican's diplomatic arm; ambassadors are called **nuncios**. (See also **Monsignor Filippo Bernardini, Blood and Soil, Concordat, Extradition, Galician SS, Bishop Alois Hudal, Hungary, Dr. Gertrud Lueknor, Carl Lutz, Benito Mussolini, Franz von Papen, Pope Pius XI, Pope Pius XII, Pope John XXIII, Priesterblock, Ratline, Monsignor Angelo Rotta, Schutzpaesse, Edith Stein, Myron Taylor, Harold H. Tittman, Kurt Waldheim, Ernst von Weizsacker,** and **Rabbi Israel Zolli**.)

VDB. (See **Volksdeutsche Bewegung**.)

Vedem (Cz., *Let's go!*). Secret magazine of Jewish boys ages 13–15 at **Theresienstadt**. The magazine was produced between 1942–1944. Of the 15,000 children **deported** to this **ghetto**, only about 100 survived.
   SUGGESTED READING: Krizkova, Kurt, and Ornest, *We Are the Children*.

Veesenmayer, Edmund (b. 1894). **SS** brigadier general and German minister. A strident **anti-Semite**, he was an envoy in **Serbia** during the **deportations** (1942) and **Reich** plenipotentiary of **Hungary** during the deportation of Hungarian Jewry to **Auschwitz**. The minister pressured Hungarian officials to participate in the **Final Solution**. Sentenced to twenty years in prison (1949), Vessenmeyer's sentence was commuted by **John McCloy**, and he was released in 1951. (See also **Adolf Eichmann, Clemency Act of 1951, Ustashi**, and **Zagreb**.)
   SUGGESTED READING: Browning, *The Final Solution*.

Veil, Simone (b. 1927). French Jewish political leader. **Deported** from **Drancy** to **Auschwitz**, she survived the war. In 1979, Veil was elected president of the Council of Europe.
   SUGGESTED READING: Webster, *Petain's Crime*.

Velodrome d'Hiver. Sports stadium outside of Paris. On July 16–17, 1942, 9,000 French police under **Rene Bousquet's** orders rounded up 13,000 French and foreign Jews and took them to this stadium. Approximately 4,000 of the victims were children. There was inadequate food, water, or sanitary facilities. (See also **Theodor Dannecker, La grande Rafle, Sister Elizabeth Pilenko, Heinz Roethke, Joseph J. Schwartz**, and **Vichy**.)
   SUGGESTED READINGS: United States Holocaust Memorial Museum, *Darkness Before Dawn*; Zuccotti, *The Holocaust, the French, and the Jews*.

Verboten (G., forbidden). A maze of rules and regulations posted in **ghettos** and **concentration camps** forbidding Jews to conduct a normal life. Punishment for infringement of these rules was severe.

Verbraucht (G., to consume). "Use up" or destroy a person.

Vernichtung durch Arbeit (G., "Destruction Through Work"). Policy of killing workers in camps by brutality, starvation, and **slave labor**. (See also "**Productive Annihilation**.")
   SUGGESTED READING: Ferencz, *Less Than Slaves*.

Vernichtungsanstalt (G., extermination facility). (See **Death Camps**.)

Vernichtungskommando (G., annihilation or death squads). Large ad hoc **SS** formations that murdered Jews in the **Eastern Territories**. (See also **Einsatzkommando**.)

Vernichtungslager (G., **death camp**). **Sobibor, Majdanek, Belzec, Auschwitz-Birkenau, Treblinka**, and **Chelmno**. The great majority of deportees were quickly gassed.

Versailles Treaty. Treaty signed at the Paris Peace Conference between **Germany** and Britain, **France, Italy**, and the United States on June 28, 1919, in the Hall of Mirrors at Versailles. (This was the same locale where Bismarck proclaimed the German empire in 1871.) The terms included: Germany admit war guilt; make reparations, accept occupation of the Rhineland; the loss of **Danzig** and a corridor for **Poland** to the Baltics; and surrender of Alsace-Lorraine, African colonies, and other territories. **Hitler** condemned the treaty as a "**stab-in-the-back**," and successfully exploited the terms of the treaty and anti-**Weimar** sentiment for propaganda purposes. He accused aristocratic Jews of betraying the German people at Versailles because some Jewish leaders signed the Treaty. (See also **Walther Rathenau, Third Reich**, and **Josiah Clement Wedgwood**.)
   SUGGESTED READING: Flood, Hitler, The Path to Power.

Verschuer, Otmar von (1896–1969). German **eugenicist**. He was **Josef Mengele's** mentor at the Institute for Racial Purity at the University of Frankfurt. In 1942, he headed the **Kaiser Wilhelm Institute** for Anthropology. Von Verschuer encouraged Mengele to conduct experiments on twins. He received specimens and reports from **Auschwitz** at his office in the Kaiser Wilhelm Institute. Unrepentant after the war, von Verschuer resumed lecturing on human genetics at the University of Munster in 1951 until his death in an automobile accident.
   SUGGESTED READING: Proctor, Racial Hygiene.

Vetter, Dr. Helmut (1910–1949). **SS** first lieutenant. He worked for **Bayer** and conducted inhumane sulfa experiments on inmates at **Auschwitz** and **Mauthausen**. In 1947, Vetter was indicted by an American military court. Two years later, he was convicted and executed. (See also **Dr. Eduard Wirths**.)
   SUGGESTED READING: Czech, Auschwitz Chronicle.

Vichy. Capital of **Unoccupied France**. A pro-Nazi French government was set up after the defeat of France in June 1940. French Jewry numbered 350,000 in 1940. After 1940, over 46,000 Jews served in the **Free French** forces. The Vichy government was headed by **Marshal Henri Philippe Petain** and **Pierre Laval** and operated as an autonomous state in south central France until the German occupation in November 1942. Theoretically, it still had some autonomy over all France. The Vichy civil service and police were active in identifying, rounding up, and **deporting** 76,000 Jews. The **Allies** liberated France in September 1944. On the 53rd anniversary of the **Velodrome d'Hiver** roundup, President Jacques Chirac finally acknowledged French complicity in the **Holo-**

caust. (See also **Otto Abetz, Alois Brunner, Le Chambon-sur-Lignon, Cremieux Decree, Theodor Dannecker, French Internment** and **Transit Camps, Gendarmerie, Pierre Laval, Milice, Jean Leguay, Leon Meiss, Nice, Louis Darquier Pellepoix, Heinz Roethke, Statut de Juifs, Service de Travail Obligatoire, Transit Camps, UGIF, Xavier Vallat, Dr. Joseph Weill,** and **Dr. Carltheo Zeitschel.**)

SUGGESTED READING: Marrus and Paxton, *Vichy France and the Jews.*

Vienna. Capital of **Austria** with a 1939 Jewish population of 91,500 (in 1933 it was 178,000). Out of sixty synagogues, twenty-four were destroyed on **Kristallnacht**, and none survived the war. After the **Anschluss**, Jews were forced to clean the gutters and streets. **Adolf Eichmann** set up his **Zentralstelle fuer Juedische Auswanderung** there in 1939. The city was **liberated** by the **Red Army** on April 12, 1945. About 300 Jews survived Nazi occupation. (See also **Alois Brunner, Anton Brunner, Josef Loewenherz, Baldur von Schirach,** and **Zentralstelle fuer Juedische Auswanderung.**)

SUGGESTED READING: Berkley, *Vienna and Its Jews.*

"Viking" Nordic **SS** units from **Norway** and **Denmark.** (See also **Schalburg Corps.**)

Villa Pauly. Gestapo headquarters in **Luxembourg**.

Vilna (Ru.); **Vilnius** (L.); **Wilno** (P.). **Ghetto.** Medieval capital of **Lithuania** seized by Polish forces in a war with the **Soviet Union** in October 1920. With a prewar Jewish population of 57,000, Vilna was also referred to as the ''Jerusalem of Europe.'' The city was returned to Lithuania by the Soviets in October 1939 and became part of the **USSR** in 1940. Vilna was occupied by the German army on June 24, 1941, and ghettoized on September 6, 1941. Vilna was split into two **ghettos**: Ghetto I housed 30,000 ''productive'' (skilled) Jews, and Ghetto II included 11,000 ''unproductive'' (unskilled) Jews. Even before the ghettoization, 20,000 of Vilna's 57,000 Jews had been butchered by the **Einsatzgruppen.** By the end of 1941, 35,500 Vilna Jews had been murdered. Numerous **Aktionen** triggered a major ghetto uprising on September 24, 1943, led by the Yehiel **partisans.** The final liquidation of the ghetto began on September 23–24, 1943. The remaining 3,700 Jews were **deported**: men and women were sent to **concentration camps** in **Estonia** and **Latvia**. Women, children, and the elderly were sent to **Sobibor.** An estimated 200,000 Lithuanian Jews were murdered during the **Holocaust.** The **Red Army** arrived on July 13, 1944. (See also **Irene Adamowicz, Jacob Gens, Isaac Gitterman, Josef Glazman, Hirsch Glick, Josef Kaplan, Maria Rozka Korczak, Abba Kovner, Ponary, Anton Schmid, Ona Simaito, Mordechai Tenenbaum, Vilnius Sonderkommando, Yitzhak Wittenberg, Yiddish Scientific Institute,** and **Henrik Ziman.**)

SUGGESTED READINGS: Kowalski, *A Secret Press in Nazi Europe*; Trunk, *Judenrat.*

Vilnius Sonderkommando (G., Special Vilna Task Force) (also referred to as the "Special Ones"). Lithuanian volunteers who **collaborated** with the Germans and participated in the shooting of approximately 5,000 Jews at **Ponary**, outside of **Vilna** in July 1941. (See also **Lithuania** and **Schuma**.)
SUGGESTED READING: Arad, *The Ghetto in Flames.*

Vilnius Uprising. The **United Partisan Organization** met in the home of **Josef Glazman**. **Abba Kovner** proclaimed, "Let us not go like sheep to slaughter." It was finally decided that it was better to fight in the forests, rather than in the **ghetto** where there was little support. The Uprising occurred in the forest in September 1940. The revolt in the ghetto was put down in 1943, but **partisans** continued in the forest. (See also **Isaac Einbinder, Gesja Glazer**, and **Rudninkai Forest**.)
SUGGESTED READINGS: Kowalski, *A Secret Press in Nazi Europe*; Suhl, *They Fought Back.*

Visa. Permission by a country when an immigrant (or **refugee**) wishes to enter that country. It is an endorsement to a **passport**. Consular officers of the United States who were employed by the State Department were reluctant to give visas to Jews wishing to escape the Nazis. The excuse given was that an alien was a "security threat." (See also **Adolf Berle, Emergency Rescue Committee, Evian Conference, Breckinridge Long, James Grover McDonald, Quota, Robert Borden Reams, Shanghai, Sempo Sugihara**, and **Jan Zwartendijk**

Visser, Lodewijk Ernst (1871–1942). Jurist and Jewish communal leader in the **Netherlands**. He founded the Jewish Aid Committee for German Jews. Visser opposed the **Joodse Raad's** policy of issuing identity cards and secretly supported Jewish **resistance**. Visser's wife and son perished in the camps.
SUGGESTED READING: Presser, *Ashes in the Wind.*

Vitebsk. **Belorussian** city. It contained a prominent and active **Hasidic** and Jewish **Bund** population and was well known for its art school, which graduated Marc Chagall. A large portion of the city's Jewish population of 37,000 fled into the Russian interior where they were protected during the Nazi invasion. The **ghetto** held 16,000 Jews who were systematically murdered by the Germans.
SUGGESTED READING: Dallin, *German Rule in Russia.*

Vittel. **Internment camp** in French resort town near **Drancy**. Germans attempted to exchange Jews for German nationals under **Allied** control. Jews with Latin American **visas** or documents, often false, were detained at this site. The game was played from May 1943 to March 1944. The camp was eventually disbanded and inmates, including 300 Jews, were sent to Drancy and from there to **Auschwitz**. (See also **French Internment and Transit camps, Hotel Polski, Itzkhak Katzenelson**, and **Miriam Novitch**.)

SUGGESTED READINGS: Katznelson, *The Song of the Murdered Jewish People*; Katznelson, *Vittel Diary*; United States Holocaust Memorial Museum, *Darkness Before Dawn*.

Vlasov, Lt. General Andrei (1900–1946). Head of the German-created **Russian Liberation Army**. He was captured by the Germans in May 1942 at Sevastopol while serving in the **Red Army**. His puppet-army was restricted by **Hitler**, but did attack Jewish **partisans** in the **Belorussian** forests. He attempted to switch sides at the end of the war in Prague, but was turned over to the **Soviets** and hanged. (See also **Galician SS**.)

SUGGESTED READING: Andreyev, *Vlasov and the Russian Liberation Movement*.

Voelkerchaos (G., Chaos of the Peoples). Epitomized the struggle of blood purity between the **Aryan** and "infectious" Jewish race. (See also **Houston Stewart Chamberlain, Miscegenation**, and **Volkstod**.)

Voelkischer Beobachter (G., *Peoples Observer*). The daily official newspaper of the **Nazi Party** published from 1921–1945. The paper was banned in 1924; however, it was reinstated the following year. **Dr. Alfred Rosenberg** edited the *Voelkischer* in 1923; **Dr. Paul Joseph Goebbels** frequently contributed columns. From 1933–1945, it was the official organ of the **Third Reich**.

Voldemaras, Augustinas (1883–1942). Prime minister of **Lithuania**. He founded the **fascist, anti-Semitic Iron Wolf** organization. He supported and **collaborated** with the Nazis and was actively involved in murdering Jews. Voldemaras died in a Soviet prison.

SUGGESTED READING: Sabaliunas, *Lithuania in Crisis*.

Volk (G., people). Romanticized notion of a German nation, a mystical union of people with an essence, developed in the nineteenth century. The group's essence is linked to the individual's innermost nature and is the source of his creativity. Each individual has a unity with other members of their racial group. **Hitler** saw the state as promoting the German Volk. The Jews, **Roma**, and the **Slavs** were considered impure and alien. (See also **Aryan**.)

Volk ohne Raum (G., People without a Space). This concept led to the **Lebensraum** policy. The term originated from the nationalist author, Hans Grimm

(1875–1951), who wrote a political novel by the same title. (See also **Richard-Walther Darre** and **Volksliste**.)

SUGGESTED READING: Zentner and Friedemann, *The Encyclopedia of the Third Reich.*

Volksdeutsche (G., ethnic Germans). In occupied areas, for the most part, they supported and **collaborated** with the Nazis. Fearing retribution after the war, ethnic Germans fled in large numbers to **DP camps**. (See also **Werner Lorenz, Repatriation, Sudetenland, Volksliste**, and **Volksdeutsche Mittelstelle**.)

Volksdeutsche Bewegung (VDB) (G., German Racial Movement). This organization spearheaded Nazi propaganda in occupied **Luxembourg** and was run by the **collaborationist**, Professor Kratzenberg. (See also **Volksjugend**.)

SUGGESTED READING: Krier, *Luxembourg Under German Occupation.*

Volksdeutsche Mittelstelle (VoMi) (G., Ethnic Germans Welfare Office). **SS** welfare and **repatriation** office for ethnic Germans headed by **Werner Lorenz**. It organized the large-scale looting of Jewish property in occupied areas. This office also encouraged membership in the **Waffen-SS** (300,000 joined) and police units. (See also **Volksdeutsche**.)

Volksgemeinschaft (G., national community). "Folk community" of ethnic Germans united by blood, race, and a common world-view (**Weltenschauung**). Jews, **Roma**, mentally and physically handicapped, and those of mixed "racial" blood were excluded. (See also **Volkstod**.)

Volksgenossen (G., national comrades). A member of the German national community under Nazi rule presumed **Aryan** and expected to be genetically healthy, socially efficient, and ideologically reliable. Those outside of the community, particularly Jews, **Roma**, and **asocials**, were persecuted. (See also **Racial State**.)

Volksgerichtshof. (See **People's Court**.)

Volksjugend (G., People's Youth). **Hitler Youth** movement in **Luxembourg**. Even in this small nation, Nazi indoctrination and persecution of Jews were priorities. (See also **Volksdeutsche Bewegung**.)

Volksliste (G., Peoples List). Document signed by **Volksdeutsche** pledging allegiance to the **Third Reich**.

Volkssturm (G., People's Army). German or Austrian civilians in arms between the ages of 16–60, akin to local militias, were called upon to defend **Germany** by a decree from **Hitler** on September 25, 1944.

Volkstod (G., Death of the People). Nazi racial policy that led to sterilization and later **euthanasia. Hitler** believed that if the German people lost their battle for racial purity (**Voelkerchaos**) with the Jews, the **Aryan** race would be destroyed. (See also **Volksgemeinschaft**.)

"Voluntary Prisoners." Euphemism for **Jehovah's Witnesses**. Incarcerated at **concentration camps**, these inmates were afforded the opportunity to be released if they signed a declaration renouncing their religion.
 SUGGESTED READING: Berenbaum, *A Mosaic of Victims.*

Vrba-Wetzler Report. Rudolf Vrba (b. 1924) (Walter Rosenberg) and Alfred Wetzler successfully escaped from **Birkenau** on April 7, 1944. They wrote detailed reports on the operation of the camp. (See also **Auschwitz Protocols**.)

Vught (G., Hertogenlosch). **Transit** and punishment camp located at a former police detention center in the southern **Netherlands**. Set up late in 1942 as a model camp with a theater, schools, library, orchestra, and sporting events, the first **Dutch** Jews arrived on January 16, 1943. Over 12,000 were **deported** to **Westerbork**. Other inmates included **resistance** fighters, **homosexuals**, and **Jehovah's Witnesses**. Conditions were poor, privileged inmates were employed in workshops by Philips. The camp was dismantled on June 2, 1944, and internees were sent to Westerbork and then to **Auschwitz**. The non-Jewish resistance prisoners stayed on until September 6, 1944, when most were evacuated to **Ravensbrueck** and **Sachsenhausen-Oranienburg**. The camp was **liberated** by Scottish infantry and English tanks in October 1944. (See also **Hans Huettig** and **Sobibor**.)
 SUGGESTED READING: Presser, *Ashes in the Wind.*

W

Wachman (G., watchman). Privileged **SS** status for **death camp** guards. SS guards receive pensions to this day for their service. (See also **John Demjanjuk.**)

Wachturme (G., guard towers).

Waffen-SS (G., armed SS). **SS** military units. The Waffen was the largest branch of the SS (thirty-nine divisions) reaching its peak strength of 900,000 soldiers in October 1944. Steeped in Nazi ideology and composed of many nationalities, this political army participated in the **Anschluss**, the occupation of the **Sudetenland**, and invasion of **Poland, Greece**, and **Yugoslavia**. It captured thousands of prisoners, especially in the Baltics and **Russia**, and aided the **Einsatzgruppen** when called upon to do so. They also operated the **Majdanek concentration camp** complex. As the Waffen-SS retreated from the Western Front, many were assigned to guard several concentration camps including **Bergen-Belsen**. Some 180,000 were killed, 70,000 missing, and 400,000 were wounded in action. (See also **Bitburg, Leon Degrelle, Freiwillige, Hilfswillige, Latvian SS Legion, Josef Mengele, Ostbattaillone, Perkonkrust, Schuma, Fritz Suhren, Totenkopfverbaende, Volksdeutsche Mittelstelle**, and **Wehrmacht.**)
SUGGESTED READINGS: Keegan, *Waffen SS*; Lumsden, *The Black Corps*.

Wagner, Dr. Gerhart (1892–1938). Chief physician of the **Reich**. He was a member of **Freikorps** and the **SA**, also a disciple of **Rudolph Hess**. Wagner was first to head the pro-Nazi Reich Physicians Chamber (1929). He distrusted academic medicine and pure science and advocated a racist and ideological "people's medicine." On September 12, 1935, he announced his intention to enact a law for the protection of German blood. Wagner was also referred to as the "Godfather of **Euthanasia**." (See also **Dr. Leonardo Conti, National Socialist Physicians' League,** and **Nuremberg Laws**.)

SUGGESTED READING: Lifton, *The Nazi Doctors*.

Wagner, Gustav (1911–1980). Deputy kommandant of **Sobibor**. He illegally joined the **Nazi Party** in **Austria** in 1931 and later became a member of the **euthanasia** program. Wagner was known as the "Human Beast" at Sobibor for his enjoyment of murder. He received an Iron Cross from **Heinrich Himmler** for his genocidal proficiency. The **Lagerfuehrer** was sentenced to death *in absentia* at the **Nuremberg Trials**. Wagner, along with **Franz Stangl**, escaped to Brazil through the **Ratline**. Unrepentant, Wagner committed suicide in Sao Paolo, Brazil, in 1980. (See also **Bishop Alois Hudal**.)

SUGGESTED READING: Kater, *Doctors Under Hitler*.

Wagner, Richard (1813–1883). Famous composer and vicious **anti-Semite**. He borrowed the **Aryan** superiority notion from his friend, **Arthur Comte de Gobineau**. He worried that **Germany** was not keeping her race pure and degeneracy was setting in. Intensely interested in Teutonic legends, myths, and runes, he wanted these to replace Christianity. **Hitler** believed that Wagner's operas and ideas expressed the German **Volk** soul. Wagner's wife formed the Bayrouth Circle after his death, a German racist group that Hitler joined and from which he developed many of his ideas.

Waldheim, Kurt (b. 1918). German intelligence officer and member of the Austrian **SA**. He served in the Balkans as an intelligence officer in Bosnia. Waldheim was awarded the Order of the Crown of St. Zvonimir, the highest award of the **Ustashi**, and was involved with **deporting** Greek Jews and Yugoslav **partisans** to **concentration camps**. As former secretary general of the UN from 1972–1982, Waldheim was praised by Pope John Paul for "safeguarding human rights" and was awarded a Papal knighthood on July 6, 1994. He is currently banned from entering the United States under the **Holtzman Amendment of the Immigration and Naturalization Acts**. In his autobiography, Waldheim blames his situation on a conspiracy organized by the **World Jewish Congress**. (See also **Croatia, Greece, United Nations War Crimes Commission,** and **Yugoslavia**.)

SUGGESTED READINGS: Herzstein, *Waldheim: The Missing Years*; Levy, *The Wiesenthal File*.

"Waldsee." The first wave of **deported** Hungarian Jews. They were forced to send letters from this nonexistent place to lull Hungarian Jews into a false sense of security that deportation did not mean death.

Wallenberg, Raoul (1912–1947?). Swedish diplomat and rescuer. Recruited by the **War Refugee Board** as a member of the Swedish legation, he arrived in Budapest in July 1944. He rescued approximately 100,000 Hungarian Jews between July–December 1944, primarily through the devices of **Schutzpaesse**, hostels, and protected houses. Wallenberg boarded **deportation** trains, interrupted **death marches**, and convinced Nazis that Jews had Swedish protection. In December 1944, prior to the Russian occupation, Wallenberg persuaded and threatened the **Wehrmacht** to protect the Budapest **ghetto** from **Arrow Cross** destruction. He was kidnapped by the Soviets on January 17, 1945. The following day 80,000 Jews were **liberated** from the Budapest Ghetto. Despite numerous alleged sightings, Wallenberg's passport was returned to his family by Mikhail Gorbachev who insisted the rescuer was dead. He is the most celebrated **Righteous Gentile** honored at **Yad Vashem**. (See also **Carl Lutz, George Mandel Mantello, Schutzbriefe, Sweden**, and **Zsido Tanacs**.)

SUGGESTED READINGS: Anger, *With Raoul Wallenberg in Budapest*; Handler, *A Man For All Connections.*

Wallenberg Bank. In February 1996, previously secret U.S. documents of wartime Secretary of the Treasury **Henry Morganthau Jr**. revealed that the Wallenberg Bank was **collaborating** with the Nazis. Enskilca, the Swedish bank, was making loans to German industry without receiving collateral and was connected with large black market operations and with deposits of money by German officers. The documents were discovered in the *U.S. National Archives* by the **World Jewish Congress** and implicated **Raoul Wallenberg's** uncles, Marcus and Jacob. The 1948 documents include a note by Morganthau to acting Secretary of State Joseph Grew. The data throws more light on why Raoul Wallenberg was arrested by **Soviet** authorities. (See also **Sweden**.)

SUGGESTED READING: Barbash, "Accounting for the Sins of Neutrality."

Wannsee Conference. Meeting held on January 20, 1942 in a villa outside **Berlin**. Chaired by **Reinhard Heydrich**, the purpose of the Conference was to inform and coordinate elements of the German bureaucracy to participate in the **SS** extermination of Jews. On July 31, 1941, **Hermann Goering** issued orders to Heydrich to implement the **Final Solution**. The mass murder of Jews in the East had already begun. The meeting was originally scheduled for December 9, 1941, but the Japanese attack on Pearl Harbor caused a postponement. In ninety minutes, a plan was laid out to convert several **concentration camps** into institutions of **slave labor** and systematic, industrialized murder, otherwise known as the Final Solution. Jews from all corners of Europe were to be shipped to these centers where the Nazis believed they could exterminate 11 million Jews. Eight out of the fifteen participants held Ph.D.s The following Germans attended: Josef Buhler, **Adolf Eichmann, Dr. Roland Freisler**, Otto Hoffmann (**Race and Settlement Office**), Wilhelm Krutzinger (Secretary of **Reich** chancellors), **Dr. Rudolf Lange**, Georg Leibbrandt (**Political Department**), **Martin**

Luther, Erich Neumann (Secretary of Four Year Plan), **Dr. Alfred Rosenberg**, Karl Schongarth (SS General **SD** and **Gestapo** in the **Generalgouvernement**), and **Dr. Wilhelm Stuckart**. (See also **Berlin** and **Einsatzgruppen**.)

SUGGESTED READINGS: Breitman, *Architect of Genocide*; United States Holocaust Memorial Museum, *Darkness Before Dawn*.

War Crimes. The violation of rules of war established by international law, that is, murder, **deportation** of native populations, enslavement, bombing civilians, wanton destruction of nonmilitary targets, and maltreatment of prisoners of war. The charges did not include **crimes against humanity** or **genocide**. (See also **Geneva Convention, Hague Convention, Herbert Pell**, and **United Nations War Crimes Commission**.)

War Crimes Act. Passed in 1991 by Great Britain. Allows the prosecution of **war criminals** even though they were not British citizens at the time they committed the act.

War Crimes Trials. Compilation of charges leveled against Nazi leaders, **SS** officers, **collaborators**, and German physicians and businessmen from 1946–1949. The most famous trials took place in **Nuremberg, Germany** by the **International Military Tribunal**. There were **Subsequent Trials** at Nuremberg and in military zones and European nations. There were also trials of Japanese high officials in Tokyo. Germany has convicted about 7,000 of its citizens for the murder of foreigners or minorities while the Nazis were in power. (See also **Denazification, Doctors' Trial, I. G. Farben, Herbert Pell**, and **Nuremberg Trials**.)

SUGGESTED READINGS: Davidson, *The Trial of the Germans*; Harris, *Tyranny on Trial*.

War Refugee Board. Ad hoc agency created on January 22, 1944, by Presidential Executive Order 9417. Its purpose was to circumvent obstruction by the U.S. State Department and rescue Jews. The impetus for the Board came from **Josiah DuBois, John Pehle**, and Randolph Paul. President **Franklin Delano Roosevelt** had been lobbied by Secretary of the Treasury **Henry Morganthau Jr**. to create the Board. This proposal was opposed by Secretary of War **Henry Louis Stimson** and Secretary of State **Cordell Hull**. In addition, rescue legislation was pending in the Senate, crafted by the **Bergson Group**. The Board was funded largely by the **"Joint"** and not by the government. Approximately 200,000 Jews and other victims of Nazi persecution were rescued through the Board's efforts. Under John Pehle's leadership, this entity encouraged liberal immigration policies, pushed neutral nations to promote rescue, and advocated havens in the hopes of mitigating Nazi atrocities. In vain, it urged the bombing of **Auschwitz**. This WRB was aided by **Ira Hirschmann** in Turkey and **Roswell McClelland** in **Switzerland** and **Portugal**. The Board's chief counsel was

DuBois. (See also **Emergency Committee to Save the Jewish People of Europe, Intergovernmental Committee on Refugees, Breckinridge Long, John McCloy, Oswego, Robert Borden Reams, Red Cross**, and **Joseph J. Schwartz**.)

SUGGESTED READINGS: Morse, *While Six Million Died*; Wyman, *The Abandonment of the Jews.*

Warsaw Ghetto. Warsaw had a 1939 prewar Jewish population of 365,000, almost 30 percent of the city's population. Warsaw Jews were enclosed in approximately 100 square city blocks, roughly the same size as New York's Central Park, beginning in November 1940. The Wall (or **Hans Frank's** Line) that separated Jewish and **Aryan** Warsaw was 11.5 feet high, 10.6 inches thick, topped with barbed wire and stretched for eleven miles. Five hundred thousand Jews lost their lives in the course of three years by starvation, privation, execution, torture, **slave labor**, and finally "**resettlement**." Prior to ghettoization, thousands of Polish Jews sought refuge or were forced to relocate to Warsaw. Ukrainian guards (who were especially brutal), "**Blue Police**," and **Jewish Police** supplemented Nazi rule in the **ghetto**. From July–September 1942, over 300,000 Jews were **deported** to **death camps**—primarily **Treblinka**—including the Jewish Police and their families. The authorities intended to close all ghettos by the end of 1942, but the **Warsaw Ghetto Uprising** staved off destruction until mid-May 1943. On July 19, 1943, the Germans established a **concentration camp** on the former ghetto site and used **forced labor** and four German firms to recover anything of value. In July 1944, the camp was evacuated. (See also **Heinz Auerswald, Adolf Abraham Berman, Border Patrol, Caritas, Einkesselung, Fritz Schultz Company, Professor Ludwig Hirszfeld, Hans Hoefle, Jewish Communal Self-Help (Society), Jan Karski, Itzkhak Katzenelson, Franz Konrad, Life Tickets, Majdanek. Dr. Joseph Milejkowski, Outworkers, Emmanuel Ringelblum, General Juergen Stroop, Joseph Szerynski, Szmalcownik, Szultz, Toebbens, Transferstelle, Treblinka**, and **Michael Weichert**.)

SUGGESTED READING: Meed, *On Both Sides of the Wall*; Trunk, *Judenrat.*

Warsaw Ghetto Uprising. Began on the first day of Passover (April 19, 1943), after 90 percent of the **Ghetto's** residents had been "liquidated." This tenacious uprising by 800 to 1,000 young Jews was a reaction to the final phase of the "voluntary **resettlement**" of Warsaw's remaining 56,000 Jews. The Polish underground provided 90 pistols, 500 grenades, explosives, and aided some ghetto fighters through the sewers. The Nazis were forced to call on the regular army to subdue the Jewish **resistance**. The greatest resistance took place at Muranowski Square. The uprising surprised the Nazis who suffered heavy casualties; nevertheless, few Jews survived the battle, which ended on May 16, 1943. This uprising was preceded by a smaller scale insurrection on January 18, 1943. The

initial uprising occurred after a visit by **Heinrich Himmler** in January 1943. Himmler was irate that the ghetto still existed and ordered its immediate liquidation. Auxiliary Lithuanian and Ukrainian troops aided in putting down the rebellion. The **SS** guerrilla specialist, **General Juergen Stroop**, estimated that 13,929 Jews were "exterminated; 5,000–6,000 were killed during the assault and the survivors were **deported** to **concentration** and **death camps**. (See **Mordecai Anielewicz, Armia Krajowa, Armia Ludowa, Erich von dem Bach-Zelewski, Abraham Blum, Tuvia Borzykowski, Bund, Bunker, Delagatura, Dror, Dr. Marek Edelman, Isaac Gitterman, Gwardia Ludowa, Dr. Ludwig Hahn, Janusz Korczak, Zivia Lubetkin, Mila 18, Polish Workers Party, SWIT, Szaulis, Mordechai Tenenbaum, Trawniki, Warsaw Polish Uprising, Dr. David Wdowinski, Arie Wilner, Henryk "Waclaw" Wolinski, Yom Hashoa, Rabbi Menachem Ziemba, ZOB, Jan Zubindsk, Yitzhak Zuckerman, Freidrych Zygmunt**, and **ZZW**.)
    SUGGESTED READINGS: Gutman, *Resistance*; Krall, *Shielding the Flame.*

Warsaw Polish Uprising. The **Armia Krajowa** rose up against the **SS** in Warsaw on August 1, 1944, encouraged by the **Polish Government-in-Exile**. The Polish commander, General **Tadeusz Bor-Komorowski** surrendered to **SS** General **Erich von dem Bach-Zelewski** on October 2, 1944, after a gallant fight against overwhelming odds. The **Red Army** was encamped on the other side of the Vistula River and failed to come to the aid of the Poles. Additionally, the **Allies** were only able to offer limited aid due to **Stalin's** intransigence. Over 15,000 Poles and 10,000 Germans were killed, and 200,000 Polish civilians subsequently met their death in **concentration camps**. A small number of Jewish survivors of the **Warsaw Ghetto Uprising** joined the Polish resisters. (See also **Dr. Marek Edelman, Gwardia Ludowa, Zivia Lubetkin, Dr. David Wdowinski, Jan Zubindk**, and **Yitzhak Zuckerman**.)
    SUGGESTED READING: Lukas, *Forgotten Holocaust.*

Warthegau/Wartheland. Largest Nazi administrative district in western **Poland**. Annexed into the **Reich** in autumn 1939, this district included the **Lodz Ghetto**. **Artur Greiser** divided the people into superior and inferior persons; Germans were the former and the Poles, Jews, and **Roma** were the latter. The Jews of the area were eventually annihilated, particularly at **Chelmno**. (See also **Partition of Poland, General Juergen Stroop**, and "**Total Evacuation**.")

Wascherel. (G., camp laundry).

Wdowinski, Dr. David (1895–1970). **Zionist Revisionist** and psychiatrist. He was the founder of the **Jewish Military Union (ZZW)** in the **Warsaw Ghetto**. Before the war, he was President of the Zionist Revisionist Organization in **Poland** and organized **Aliya Bet** to **Palestine**. He was captured during the **War-**

saw **Ghetto Uprising**, imprisoned, but nevertheless, survived and testified against **Adolf Eichmann** in 1961.

SUGGESTED READING: Wdowinski, *And We Are Not Saved.*

Wedgwood, Josiah Clement (1872–1942). Pro-**Zionist** British statesman. He participated in efforts leading to the **Balfour Declaration** and influenced American delegates at Versailles to support the idea of a Jewish homeland. He was close to **Ze'ev Jabotinsky** and the **Zionist Revisionists** and recognized that the United Kingdom was betraying the **British Mandate**. Wedgwood called for illegal immigration to the **Yishuv** and **resistance** to British authority. He also supported a special Jewish fighting force in the British Army. (See also **Versailles Treaty** and **White Paper**.)

SUGGESTED READING: Wasserstein, *Britain and the Jews of Europe.*

Wehrmacht (G., Defense Might). Name for the German army after 1935. Often in competition for supplies and authority with the **Waffen-SS**, the Wehrmacht also assisted the **SS** in carrying out the **Final Solution**. It was involved in activities in **Poland** and the **Soviet Union**, which violated the **Geneva Convention**, such as mass killings of **hostages**, innocent civilians, and prisoners of war. The Wehrmacht also kidnapped children in **Ruthenia** for **Lebensborn**. (See also **Einsatzgruppen, Grand Mufti of Jerusalem, Alfred Jodl, Wilhelm Keitel, Kommissarbefehl, Field Marshal Erich von Manstein, Nacht und Nebel, Operation Barbarossa, Ostbataillone, OUN, Field Marshal Walter von Reichenau, Reichswehr, Semlin**, and **Sippenhaftung**.)

SUGGESTED READING: Bartov, *Hitler's Army.*

Weichert, Michael (1890–1967). **Yiddish** theater producer. He organized cultural events in the **Warsaw Ghetto**. Weichert's two-volume work, *Jewish Self-Help*, revealed much about life in the **ghetto**. He settled in Israel. (See also **Spiritual Resistance**.)

Weil Felix Reaction. Test for **typhus**. A positive reaction meant death for **ghetto** and **concentration camp** inhabitants.

Weill, Dr. Joseph (1902–1988). Jewish physician and medical advisor to the **French Jewish Children's Aid Society**. He alerted Swiss and American humanitarian organizations about the plight of Jewish children in **Vichy**, provided forged papers and Christian identity cards to Jewish children, and also set up rescue groups to place Jewish children in Christian homes. Weill continued his work in **Switzerland** after fleeing **France** in May 1943. He is credited with saving 4,000 children.

SUGGESTED READING: Block and Drucker, *Rescuers.*

Weimar Republic. Freely elected, democratic government of **Germany** from 1919–1933. Located in Weimar, Goethe's birthplace, the Nazis and Nationalists bitterly opposed the Republic and associated it with weakness. The Weimar constitution was drafted by Hugo Preuss, a German Jew. Some Jewish intellectuals were involved with its inception, a fact that provided **Hitler** with another excuse to denounce the budding democracy. (See also **Dolchstoss, Enabling Act, Paul von Hindenburg, Laender, Machtergreifung, "Novemberbrecher," Walther Rathenau, Reichstag**, and **Social Democrats**.)
    SUGGESTED READING: Flood, Hitler, the Path to Power.

Weiner, Alfred (1885–1964). General Secretary of the Central Organization of German Citizens of the Jewish Faith. He fled to London in 1933 and established one of the most comprehensive **Holocaust** libraries in the world.

Weiss-Manfred Works. Named after the family. Forty-seven family members were allowed to leave **Hungary** in return for transferring the Weiss-Manfred Works (1944), Hungary's largest industrial armaments company, to the **SS** for twenty-five years. (See also **Kurt Becher**.)
    SUGGESTED READING: Arendt, Eichmann in Jerusalem.

Weiss, Martin (1905–1946). Kommandant of **Dachau, Neuengamme**, and **Majdanek**. Weiss was one of forty defendants in the 1945 Dachau trial. He was sentenced to death by the Americans and executed in May 1946.
    SUGGESTED READING: United States Holocaust Memorial Museum, 1945: The Year of Liberation.

Weissmandel, Rabbi Michael Dov (1903–1951). Leading figure in the **Working Group**. This Orthodox rabbi was head of a **Yeshiva** in Bratislava and began rescue work in 1938. His couriers brought the message of the **Holocaust** to Orthodox circles in the West. He urged, in vain, **Allied** bombing of rail hubs to and **crematoria** in **Auschwitz**. Through his efforts, the **Auschwitz Protocols** was published. Weissmandel was rescued via the **Kasztner** Transport. He came to America after the war, and headed a Yeshiva in Mt. Kisco, New York. (See also **Monsignor Filippo Bernadini, Europa Plan, Gisi Fleischmann, George Mandel Mantello, Union of Orthodox Rabbis of America**, and **Ustredna Zidov**.)
    SUGGESTED READINGS: Finger, American Jewry During the Holocaust; Fuchs, The Unheeded Cry; Kranzler, Thy Brother's Blood.

Weizmann, Chaim (1874–1952). **Zionist** statesman and Polish-born Jewish leader. He was president of the **World Zionist Organization** and first president of Israel (1949). Weizmann, a British subject, pleaded with British leaders for a separate Jewish fighting force within the British Army, suspension of the **White Paper** for fleeing Jews, acceptance of the Romanian offer to transfer 70,000 Jews, and for a positive response to the **Joel Brand** mission. His pleas were ignored. Weizmann lobbied, in vain, the British Foreign Secretary to bomb **Birkenau** and the rail line leading to the **death camp** on July 6, 1944, to save Hungarian Jews. **Anthony Eden** stated that "technical difficulties" precluded such a bombing.

SUGGESTED READING: Cohn, *Churchill and the Jews*; Rose, *Chaim Weizmann*; Weizmann, *Trial and Error*.

Weizsacker, Ernst von (1882–1951). German diplomat. Opportunistic and pragmatic state secretary to the Foreign Office, von Weizsacker opposed many Nazi policies, but faithfully served **Joachim von Ribbentrop**. Later, as the German envoy to the **Vatican**, he noted the remarkable indifference of **Pope Pius XII** to act on the **deportation** of the Jews from **Rome** on October 16, 1943. Von Weizsacker was tried and convicted of **war crimes** at **Nuremberg**, but served only eighteen months. His son, Richard, became president of the Federal Republic of **Germany** in 1984, and denounced Nazism at the United States **Holocaust** Memorial Museum in May 1993. (See also "**Black Saturday**," **Rome, Walter Schellenberg**, and **Harold H. Tittman**.)

SUGGESTED READING: Browning, *The Final Solution and the German Foreign Office*.

Welles, Sumner (1892–1961). Undersecretary of State for Latin American Affairs under President **Franklin Delano Roosevelt** from 1937–1943. He was involved in discussions with American Jewish leaders, particularly **Rabbi Stephen S. Wise**, about reports of Jewish **genocide**, but did nothing, and urged delay. He did rescind an order barring Rabbi Wise from receiving messages from the **Jewish Agency** and the **World Jewish Congress** in Bern, **Switzerland**. (See also **Dr. Gerhart Riegner, Sidney Silverman**, and **Myron Taylor**.)

SUGGESTED READINGS: Feingold, *The Politics of Rescue*; Gellman, *Secret Affairs*.

Weltanschaulich (G., ideological fitness). One had to be a **National Socialist** believer, an **Aryan**, to qualify for **Reich** clubs, including sports. It was a means of excluding Jews, particularly during the **Berlin** Olympics in 1936.

Weltanschauung (G., world-view). One's broad philosophical, political, and social view. (See also **Racial State** and **Volksgemeinschaft**.)

Weltsch, Robert (1891–1982). German **Zionist** leader and journalist. He wrote in *Juedische Rundschau* (*Jewish Observer*) on April 4, 1933, "Wear **Yellow Badge** with Pride," urging Jews to face Nazi oppression with dignity. He immigrated to **Palestine** in 1936 and later helped to establish the **Leo Baeck Institute**. (See also **Reich Representation of German Jews**.)

SUGGESTED READING: Black, *The Transfer Agreement*.

"Wenn das Judenblut vom messer spritzt, demn gehts nochal do gut" (G., "When Jewish blood flows from the knife, things will go better"). A major verse from the "**Horst Wessel**" song widely sung by "**Stormtroopers**" and other Nazi groups. (See also *Der Angriff*.)
   SUGGESTED READING: Morse, *While Six Million Died.*

Werterfassung (G., Property Collection Agency). **SS** agency responsible for confiscating Jewish property after "**resettlement**." (See also **Aryanization** and **Franz Konrad**.)

"We Shall Never Die!" Pageant organized by the Committee for a Jewish Army, a **Bergson Group** organization. This event, written by **Ben Hecht**, was staged at Madison Square Garden on March 9, 1943, and taken on the road to several American cities. The pageant was a memorial to the slain Jews of Europe and a means to publicize the Nazi mass murder. American Jewry responded apathetically, believing little could be done after the **Bermuda Conference** failure.
   SUGGESTED READING: Ben-Ami, *Years of Wrath.*

Westerbork. An **internment camp** for German Jewish **refugees** opened in 1939 by the **Dutch** in northeastern **Netherlands**. On July 1, 1942, the administration of the camp passed from Dutch to German hands, and it became the primary **transit camp** to **Theresienstadt, Auschwitz, Sobibor**, and **Bergen-Belsen** for Dutch Jewry. Conditions were decent and communications with the outside world were permitted. Out of 107,000 Jewish inmates that passed through the camp, less than 5,000 survived. There were 245 **Roma** and **Sinti** interned; only 30 survived. Inmates wore their own clothing with a **Yellow Badge. Anne Frank** left on the last **transport** (September 3, 1944). The first transport to Auschwitz occurred on July 15, 1942. **SS** Lieutenant **Albert Gemmeker** served as kommandant from November 1942 to April 1945. **Deportations** ceased in 1944, and the camp was **liberated** by the Canadians and the British on April 12, 1945. Westerbork had been evacuated earlier in the day, but 909 Jewish inmates were left behind. (See also **Erich Deppner, Hans Rauter, Sonderreferet**, and **Vught**.)
   SUGGESTED READINGS: Boas, *Boulevard des Miseres*; Gilbert, *Final Journey.*

Westerweel, Joop (1899–1944). Christian **Dutch** educator and underground rescuer. He smuggled Jewish youths from **France** through the Pyrennes to **Spain**. He worked with Halutz leader Joachim Simon. Westerweel was shot to death by the Germans in 1944. He was named a **Righteous Gentile** by **Yad Vashem**.
   SUGGESTED READINGS: Friedman, *Their Brothers' Keepers*; Paldiel, *Path of the Righteous.*

"White Death." (1) Death of an individual fleeing Nazi rule. (2) Death of an individual working in **labor camps** characterized by the person dying alone in the snow.

White Paper. British foreign policy position (May 17, 1939–May 14, 1948) severely limiting Jewish immigration to 1,500 per year for five years to **Palestine**. The paper also included the creation of an Arab state in 1949. This was in direct violation of the **British Mandate**. The British committed a great deal of naval resources to implement the White Paper. In effect, it trapped the Jews of Europe, leaving them vulnerable to the coming Nazi onslaught. (See also **Aliya Bet, Appeasement, Bricha, Winston Churchill, Anthony Eden, Grand Mufti of Jerusalem, Lord Halifax, Irgun, Mauritius, Mossad le Aliya Bet, Palestine Certificates**, *Patria*, **Rashid Ali al-Gaylani, Abraham Stern**, *Struma*, **Josiah Clement Wedgwood, Chaim Weizmann**, and **Yishuv**.
SUGGESTED READING: Wasserstein, *Britain and the Jews of Europe.*

White Rose. Small group of University of Munich students opposed to Nazism and persecution of Jews from 1942–1943. The group was also active in Hamburg. They dropped leaflets denouncing the regime. The group's leaders, **Hans** and **Sophie Scholl**, were beheaded on February 18, 1943 for distributing anti-Nazi leaflets. (See also **Bishop Clemens von Galen** and **People's Court**.)
SUGGESTED READING: Dumbach and Newborn, *Shattering the German Night.*

White Russia. (See **Belorussia**.)

Widmann, Dr. Albert (b. 1912). **SS** chemist. He was involved with **T-4** gassing and "poison bullet" experiments in **Sachsenhausen-Oranienburg**. Widmann and **Arthur Nebe** carried out gassing of handicapped victims using a "**Sonderwagon**" prototype in **Mogilev-Podolski** on September 8, 1941.
SUGGESTED READING: Friedlander, *The Origins of Nazi Genocide.*

Wienergraben. Quarry at **Mauthausen**. Inmates were usually worked to death. Many other prisoners, known as "**parachutists**," were forced to jump to their deaths. (See also "**Destruction Through Work**" and **186**.)

Wiesel, Elie (b. 1928). **Holocaust** survivor and novelist. Hungarian Jew from **Sighet**, he is the major spokesman for Holocaust awareness. He provided the moral compass for the United States Holocaust Memorial Museum and was awarded the Congressional Medal in 1985 and the Nobel Peace Prize in 1986. Wiesel has written twenty-five novels on the Holocaust, including his groundbreaking work entitled *Night*. (See also **Bitburg** and **Einsatzgruppen**.)
SUGGESTED READING: Stern, *Elie Wiesel: Spokesman for Humanity.*

Wiesenthal, Simon (b. 1908). Nazi hunter. Polish Jew and survivor of five **concentration camps**. After his **liberation** from **Mauthausen**, he became a successful Nazi hunter. In the postwar period, Wiesenthal saw a lack of interest by the **Allies**, Jews, and gentiles alike, to pursue and prosecute Nazi **war criminals**. He established the **Jewish Documentation Center** in **Vienna**, which helped to track 1,000 Nazis, including **Franz Stangl**. The Center received little aid from Jewish organizations. Wiesenthal has written several books on the **Holocaust**. In 1977, the Los Angeles Wiesenthal Center was established in his honor. (See also **Franz Ziereis**.)

SUGGESTED READINGS: Levy, *The Wiesenthal File*; Wiesenthal, *The Murderers Among Us.*

Wilde Lager (G., Wild Camp). Independent and unauthorized German prisons converted into a temporary **labor** or **concentration camp** by individual Nazis. These facilities built in the early Nazi period 1933 were manned by the **SA** and incarcerated **Hitler's** political enemies. (See also **Sachenhausen-Oranienburg**.)

SUGGESTED READING: Lifton, *The Nazi Doctors.*

"Wild Euthanasia." "Mercy killing" after August 1941. Physicians were allowed more freedom in **selecting** victims in this phase. (See also **14 f 13, Hartheim Castle, Hungerhausen, "Lebensunwertes Leben,"** and **"Special Cases."**)

SUGGESTED READING: Lifton, *The Nazi Doctors.*

Wilner, Arie (1917–1943). **ZOB** representative. He made contact with **Armia Krajowa** and **Armia Ludowa** and brought arms into the **Warsaw Ghetto**. Wilner was active in both the January and April **Warsaw Ghetto Uprisings**. He died in the ZOB command bunker **Mila 18**.

SUGGESTED READING: Ainsztein, *The Warsaw Ghetto Revolt.*

Winter Aid (G., Winterhilfe). The **Nazi Party** relief organization. The Germans confiscated, or forced Jews to "donate," winter apparel for the war effort.

Wirth, SS Major Christian (1885–1944). **Kripo** officer (1931–1939) and head of the **concentration camps** in **Poland**. He innovated the use of gas as an efficient means of murder during the **euthanasia** program. Wirth was inspector of euthanasia in **Germany** and used his expertise and knowledge of industrialized mass murder at **Chelmno**. Wirth was also the first kommandant of **Bergen-Belsen** and a **Lagerfuehrer** of **Belzec**. He was killed by **partisans** in Fiume, **Italy**, in May 1944. (See also **La Risiera di San Sabba**.)

SUGGESTED READINGS: Ainsztein, *The Warsaw Ghetto Revolt*; Friedlander, *The Origins of Nazi Genocide.*

Wirths, Dr. Eduard (1909–1945). Chief **SS** physician at **Auschwitz**. He established **selections** and initiated and oversaw medical killings. Wirths, and his brother, Helmut, were preoccupied with medical experiments on the cervix. Wirths also assisted Dr. **Helmut Vetter** in sulfa experiments and infected some Jewish inmates with **typhus**. However, he was humane to favored inmates. Wirths committed suicide soon after surrendering to the British in September 1945. (See also **Avengers**.)

SUGGESTED READING: Lifton, *The Nazi Doctors*.

Wise, Rabbi S. Stephen (1884–1949). Head of the **American Jewish Congress, Zionist**, and a lifelong Democrat with close ties to President **Franklin Delano Roosevelt**. He received news of the **Final Solution** from **Sidney Silverman**, who heard it from **Dr. Gerhart Riegner** in August 1942, but withheld the information at the State Department's behest until late November 1942. On December 8, 1942, he met with President Roosevelt and presented him with a "Blue Print for Extermination," a twenty-page booklet that provided details of the **Holocaust**. Roosevelt issued a statement decrying Nazi atrocities; however, this was the first and last meeting between the president and Jewish leaders. Wise maintained that all rescue plans for Jews were meaningless without opening the doors to **Palestine**, a position that put him in conflict with **Peter Bergson**. The rabbi instigated the plan to collect funds to save 70,000 Romanian Jews in 1943, which was frustrated by the State Department despite approval by the Treasury Department. (See also **Emergency Rescue Committee, Judah Nadich, Pope Pius XII, Romania, Rabbi Abba Hillel Silver, Myron Taylor, Va'ad ha-Hatzala**, and **Sumner Welles**.)

SUGGESTED READINGS: Medoff, *The Deafening Silence*; Wise, *Challenging Years*.

Wisliceny, Dieter (1911–1948). **SS** officer in subsection of **RSHA (IVB4)**. As **Adolf Eichmann's** deputy, he coordinated the **deportation** of 55,000 Slovakian Jews to **Poland**. He also participated in the liquidation of Greek, Salonikan (March 1943), and Hungarian Jewry (March 1944). He surrendered to the Americans and gave invaluable affidavits to the **International Military Tribunal** at the initial **Nuremberg Trial**. Wisliceny implicated **Heinrich Himmler** and **Adolf Hitler** in planning the **Final Solution**. He wrote an affadavit on the role of **Amin Husseini**. Wisliceny's testimony was also used at the Eichmann trial. He was **extradited** to Bratislava and hanged in 1948. (See also **Greece, Salonika, Anton Vasek**, and **Working Group**.)

SUGGESTED READING: Finger, *American Jewry During the Holocaust*.

Witness to Liberation. American GIs who arrived in **concentration camps** forty eight hours or more after **liberation**. After visiting **Ohrdruf** on April 12, 1945, **General Dwight David Eisenhower** ordered soldiers stationed near concentration camps to visit the sites. (See also **Liberation**.)

SUGGESTED READING: United States Holocaust Memorial Museum, *1945: The Year of Liberation.*

Wittenberg, Yitzhak (1907–1943). Commander of the **United Partisan Organization (FPO)** in the **Vilna ghetto**. He was apprehended by the Germans and then freed by FPO fighters. The **Gestapo** demanded his surrender and threatened that the entire **ghetto** would be liquidated. Wittenberg surrendered and was executed; then the ghetto was liquidated. (See also **Abba Kovner**.)

SUGGESTED READING: Kowalski, *A Secret Press in Nazi Europe.*

Wolff, Karl (1900–1984). **SS** general. Head of **Heinrich Himmler's** personal staff, he lived in the **Fuehrer's** headquarters. Later, the general negotiated the surrender of German forces in **Italy** with American **OSS** officer Allen Dulles. Wolff was not tried at the **Nuremberg Trials**, but provided testimony. He was arrested by the German state prosecutor and charged with being complicit in the deaths of 300,000 Jews at **Treblinka**. He served six years of a fifteen-year sentence and was released in 1971.

SUGGESTED READINGS: Jones, *Hitler's Heralds*; Kurzman, *The Race for Rome*; Reitlinger, *The SS.*

Wolinski, Henryk "Waclaw" (1901–1986). Polish jurist. As a member of the **Armia Krajowa (AK)**, he prepared reports on the extermination of the Jews that were sent to the **Polish Government-in-Exile**. Wolinski was active in **Zegota** and advocated for Jewish rescue before the AK. He served as the liaison for the **Polish Home Army** with the **ZOB** during the April **Warsaw Ghetto Uprising**. He was awarded the title of **Righteous Gentile** in 1974.

SUGGESTED READING: Tomaszewski and Werbowski, *Zegota.*

Woortman, Joop (1905–1944). **Dutch** anti-Nazi resister and **Righteous Gentile**. He organized the rescue of Jews in Amsterdam in 1942. Woortman paid pickpockets to obtain **Aryan** papers, which were then given to Jews. His group found safe homes for both Jewish adults and children. In July 1944, the resister was arrested and taken to **Bergen-Belsen** where he died.

SUGGESTED READING: Paldiel, *The Path of the Righteous.*

"Work as a Means of Rescue." Concept utilized by **Siegfried Jagendorf, Moshe Merin, Mordechai Rumkowski, Jacob Gens**, and several other **Judenrat** leaders. This compromise entailed making their **ghettos** economically indispensable to the German war effort in the hope of saving some Jews. Several rabbis endorsed this survival technique. (See also **Ustredna Zidov**.)

SUGGESTED READING: Tushnet, *The Pavement of Hell.*

Working Group (Cz., Pracovna-Skupina). Underground Slovakian rescue organization established in Bratislava in March 1942 by Jewish Slovakian activists. The Group was led by **Gisi Fleischmann** and **Rabbi Michael Dov Weissmandel**. They smuggled the **Auschwitz Protocols** to the West. The Working Group successfully upheld a moratorium on **deportations** of Slovakian Jewry for almost two years by bribing Slovakian and **SS** officials, including a $50,000 bribe of **Dieter Wisliceny**. (See also **Budapest Rescue Committee, Europa Plan, Sano Mach, Dr. Josef Tiso, Vojtech Tuka, Ustredna Zidov**, and **Anton Vasek**.)

SUGGESTED READINGS: Campion, *In the Lion's Mouth*; Finger, *American Jewry During the Holocaust.*

World Jewish Congress (WJC). International Jewish advocacy organization created to replace Comite des Delegations Juives in August 1932. After 1933, it sought to protect German Jewry. WJC sent a representative to the **Evian Conference**, sponsored **Saly Mayer's** rescue efforts, employed **Gerhart Riegner**, established the **Relief Committee for the War Stricken Jewish Population**, called on the **Allies** to save the remaining Jews under Nazi control, and provided relief to those who were **liberated. Norbert Masur** negotiated with **Heinrich Himmler** late in the war to win the release of **concentration camp** inmates interned at **Ravensbrueck**. The WJC negotiated with West **Germany** regarding **reparations and restitution** after the war. (See also **American Jewish Conference, American Jewish Congress, Nahum Goldmann, Dr. Felix Kersten, Dr. Abraham Silberschein, Sidney Silverman, Kurt Waldheim, Wallenberg Bank**, and **Sumner Welles**.)

SUGGESTED READINGS: Bauer, *Jews for Sale?*; Finger, *American Jewry during the Holocaust.*

World Zionist Organization (WZO). Founded by the architect of modern **Zionism**, Theodor Herzl, in 1897 as an international federation of diverse Zionist groups. Under **Chaim Weizmann's** leadership, the organization was pro-British and played a pivotal role influencing the **Jewish Agency** in distributing **Palestine Certificates**. These permits meant life and death in the late 1930s and early 1940s. The WZO was roundly criticized for favoring young and healthy pioneers, leftist Zionists, and non-Orthodox **Jews**. (See also **Biltmore Programme, Jewish Cultural Reconstruction**, and **Ignacy Isaac Schwarzbart**.)

SUGGESTED READINGS: Rose, *Chaim Weizmann*; Segev, *The Seventh Million.*

WRB. (See **War Refugee Board**.)

WVHA (Wirschafts und Verwaltungshauptamt) (G., Economic and Administrative Main Office). The principal economic and administrative bureau of the **SS**. Founded on February 1, 1942 and based in **Berlin**, this organization was a huge corporate enterprise with extensive power. Headed by **Oswald Pohl**, the WVHA not only exploited **slave labor** (500,000 to 600,000), but arranged for inmate transfers with German corporations. German companies had to apply for slave labor and wait for approval before inmates were transferred. **Colonel Gerhard Maurer** headed the D II Department, which processed German corporate requests for **concentration camp** labor. There were twenty major **concentration camps** and 165 subcamps for slave and **forced labor** under its control. The WVHA was also responsible for all booty stolen from camp inmates and concentration camp construction. (See also **Bauleitung SS, DAW, German Earth and Stone Works, Rudolf Hess, Dr. Hans Kammler, Arthur Liebehenschel, Schein, Schmelt Organization**, and **Karl Sommer**.)

SUGGESTED READING: Lumsden, *The Black Corps*.

WZO. (See **World Zionist Organization**.)

Y

Yad Vashem, The Holocaust Martyrs and Heroes Remembrance Authority
(H., from Prophet Isaiah [56:5] "I will give them an everlasting name"). A
center for **Holocaust** archives, museums, and memorials in Jerusalem. Estab-
lished in Jerusalem in 1962 by the Israeli government, it includes markers in a
Garden of Remembrance honoring over 13,668 **Righteous Gentiles**. (See also
Yitzhak Arad, Hasidei umot ha-olam, and **Gideon Hausner**.)
    SUGGESTED READING: Young, *The Texture of Memory.*

Yalta Conference. Between February 4–12, 1945, **Josef Stalin, Winston Churchill**, and **Franklin Delano Roosevelt** met at Yalta in the Crimea. Among the
issues discussed were the **denazification** of **Germany** and procedures for setting
up an **International Military Tribunal** for **war criminals**. (See also **London
Charter Conference**.)
    SUGGESTED READING: Harris, *Tyranny on Trial.*

Yamaika, Zofia (1925–1943). Jewish **partisan**. She escaped from the **Warsaw
Ghetto** in 1942, joined the partisans, and edited *Gwardia Ludowa*. In the Jewish
underground, she worked with a special squad killing German spies and agents.
Entrapped by German police, Yamaika died fighting.
    SUGGESTED READING: Suhl, *They Fought Back.*

Yarnton Declaration (1990). Framework for agreeing on the memory of
Auschwitz. The accord developed by Jewish and Polish gentile scholars declared that 1.6 million people were killed at Auschwitz, of which 90% were

Jews and the rest of the victims were Polish Catholics, **Roma**, and **Soviet POWs**.

SUGGESTED READING: Young, *The Texture of Memory*.

Yekkes (Y., Germans). Derogatory term for German Jews. The word was mainly used by Eastern European Jews. (See also **Ostjuden**.)

Yelin, Hiam (1913–1944). Writer and **partisan** leader from **Kovno**. He was a communist officer in **Lithuania** and commanded the Anti-**Fascist** Struggle Organization in Kovno. He was based in the **Rudninkai Forest** and was joined by 350 Jews. Yelin coordinated attacks against German military installations with communist partisans in 1943. The **Gestapo** captured and executed him on April 6, 1944.

SUGGESTED READING: Tory, *Surviving the Holocaust*.

Yellow Badge-Triangle. Yellow Star of David that Jews were forced to wear in most parts of occupied Europe, **ghettos**, and **concentration camps**. The star was originally mandated by Pope Innocent III in 1215 to single out Jews by dress. In May 1937, Jewish concentration camp inmates in **Germany** were forced to wear a yellow triangle, vortex down, imposed over a red triangle to form the Star of David. This became the standard emblem for Jews in concentration camps. On September 1, 1941, all Jews six years of age or older, were forced to wear the star in public in Germany. (See also **Jewish Badge, Jood, Jude, Juif, Protectorate of Bohemia-Moravia, "Submarine," Tunis, Robert Weltsch**, and **Zid**.)

Yeshiva (H., academy). School for Jewish scholars specializing in **Talmudic** studies. Before, during (clandestinely), and after World War II, religious Jewish students studied in yeshivot. Some were relocated in Israel or America such as the **Mir Yeshiva**. In prewar **Poland**, there were 136 yeshivot with over 12,000 students. (See also **Yitzhak Halevi Herzog** and **Orthodox Judaism**.)

Yiddish. One thousand-year-old vernacular of **Ashkenazi** Jews developed in northern **France** and **Germany**. Based in large part on German and Hebrew, the language traveled east when many Jews were forced out of Western European countries. It was the *lingua franca* (common language) of Central and Eastern European Jewry with a standardized syntax. (See also **Jewish Anti-Fascist Organization, Itzkhak Katzenelson**, and **Ostjuden**.)

Yiddische Fareynitke Partisaner Organizatsye. (See **FPO**.)

Yiddish Scientific Institute (YIVO; IOW). Preeminent archival and cultural institution for Eastern and Central European Jewry. Located in **Vilna**, YIVO was completely destroyed by the Nazis. After the war, YIVO was rebuilt and rededicated in New York City. Its archives document the **Holocaust**. (See also **Philip Friedman**.)

Yishuv (H., settlement). Term given to the Jewish community of **Palestine** before Israel was a state. Its population grew from 337,000 in 1939 to 427,000 in 1944, despite the **White Paper**. Its underground organizations were active in arranging illegal immigration. Some 25,000 Palestinian Jews joined the British Army, including 4,000 women who joined the Auxiliary. In 1944, the **Jewish Brigade** was established mainly from the Yishuv. During the **Holocaust**, it had listening and rescue posts in Geneva and Istanbul. The Yishuv leadership did not think large-scale rescue operations were practical and used its limited funding for preparing the settlement for Holocaust survivors. (See also **Aliya Bet, David Ben-Gurion, Bergson Group, Bricha, Haavara Agreement, Haganah, Irgun, Jewish Agency, "Parachutists," Moshe Shertok, Enzo Sereni, Henrietta Szold, Stern Group, Chaim Weizmann, Youth Aliya**, and **Yitzhak Zuckerman**.)

SUGGESTED READINGS: Porat, *The Blue and the Yellow Stars of David*; Segev, *The Seventh Million.*

Yom Hashoah (H., Day of Destruction). Annual remembrance day for victims of the **Holocaust**. This commemoration grew out of the recognition of the **Warsaw Ghetto Uprising**. An official legal holiday in Israel, this observance takes place after Passover.

Yom Kippur (H., Day of Atonement). Holiest day in the Jewish calendar. Characterized by fasting and prayer, God seals each Jew's fate on this day. The Nazis always reserved extra cruelty for Jewish holidays. (See also **Aktion**.)

Youth Aliya (H., Youth Immigration). Founded by Recha Freir (who was eventually replaced by **Henrietta Szold**) in **Germany** in 1932. This organization brought young Jews, many without their parents or orphaned, to the **Yishuv**. The Youth Aliya operated legally between 1932–1939, and 5,000 youths made the trip successfully. During the war, an additional 10,000 escaped. From 1945–1948, 15,000 youngsters made the journey to **Palestine**. Youth Aliya also aided Jews in the **DP camps** and helped with absorption once Jews were in Palestine. (See also **Enzo Sereni**.)

SUGGESTED READINGS: Krantz, *Daughter of My People*; Offer, *Escaping the Holocaust.*

YRM. (See **Yugoslavian Resistance Movement**.)

Yugoslavia. Located in south central Europe with the Adriatic Sea washing its western shore. On December 1, 1918, a kingdom of south **Slavs** was formed of Serbs, Croats, and Slovenes. These people were members of the large Austro-

Hungarian Empire. The empire lost World War I and was broken up by the **Versailles Treaty**. In 1929, the new country adopted the name Yugoslavia. The country remained independent until the German invasion of 1941. **Croatia** became a German satellite and the rest of Yugoslavia was ruled by the German forces except along the coast from Croatia down through **Serbia**, which was occupied by the Italian Army. The Italians protected the Jews from murder. The **Ustashi** and the Germans instituted **genocide** against Serbs, Jews, and **Roma**. **Resistance** formed almost immediately by the Serbian Royalists, **Chetniks**, and the communists under **Marshal Tito**. The Chetniks eventually joined up with the Germans to attack Tito's **partisans**. Serbian **Macedonia** was ceded by the Germans to **Bulgaria**. **Backa** was annexed to **Hungary** with German blessings. There were 76,000 Jews in Yugoslavia, 25,000 of them **Sephardic**. Only 12,000 survived Croatian, Bosnian Moslem, and German killings. In October 1944 the partisans, with the aid of the **Red Army, liberated** Belgrade, the capital of Serbia. **Anton Pavelic** and the Croatian state lasted until May 1945. (See also **Andrija Artukovic, Austria, Bosnian-Herzogovinan Muslims, Italy, Grand Mufti of Jerusalem, Handzar, Jasenovac, Jewish National Committee, Rab,** and **Zagreb**.)

Yugoslavian Resistance Movement (YRM). The YRM was organized (summer 1941) and led by **Marshal Tito** and his native communist party. They freely admitted Jews into the ranks of the **partisans**. Over 75,000 Jews were in **Yugoslavia** before the war; 4,572 participated in the YRM, and 1,318 died fighting. Eighty percent of Yugoslavian Jews were murdered. The YRM boasted notable Jewish partisans. These included Mosha Pijade, Tito's advisor; Samuel Lerer, a division commander; Pavle Pap, leader of Dalmation uprising; and Dr. Roza Papo, physician and first woman general of the Yugoslavian army. Jewish physicians were the core of partisan medical corps. (See also **Rab** and **Zagreb**.)

   SUGGESTED READINGS: Romans, *The Jews of Yugoslavia*; Steinberg, *Jews Against Hitler*.

Z

"Z." (See **Zigeuner**.)

Zachor Institute (H. and Y., remember) An Orthodox organization concerned with recounting incidents of **Kiddush ha-Shem** that took place in **ghettos** and **concentration camps**. Zachor organization documents describe how religious Jews behaved throughout the war years. Its mentor, **Simon Zucker**, himself a Hasid, was a **Holocaust** survivor. (See also **Hasidism, Orthodox Judaism**, and **Zechor**.)

Zagreb. Capital of **Croatia** with a prewar Jewish population of 11,000. Despite the **Ustashi's** pro-**Nazi** stance, **Germany** invaded the country in April 1941. The Jewish population was subject to numerous **deportations** and **Aktionen**. The last deportations took place from May 5–10, 1943. In mid-1943, Aloysius Stepinac, the Archbishop of Zagreb, publicly denounced the murder of the Croatian Jews after most of the Jews had been murdered. After the massacre of Jews began, the Catholic Church aided Jews interned in Croatian **concentration camps**. The Italian legation reported atrocities committed by the **Nazis** and Ustashi. (See also **Anton Pavelic, Edmund Veesenmayer**, and **Yugoslavia**.)

   SUGGESTED READINGS: Lederer, *The Crimes of the Germans*; Morley, *Vatican Diplomacy*.

Zahlappell (G., roll call). (See **Appell**.)

ZAL (G., Zwangsarbeitslager). **Forced labor** camps.

Zalman, Friedrych. (See **Friedrych [Zalman] "Zygmunt."**)

Zamboni, Guelfo (1897–1994). Italian diplomat and **Righteous Gentile**. As counsel general in **Salonika** (1943), he saved 280 Greek Jews from **deportation** to **Auschwitz**. (See also **Greece**.)
   SUGGESTED READING: Poliakov and Sabille, *Jews Under the Italian Occupation.*

Zamosc. Province in eastern **Poland** containing a prewar Jewish population of 60,000. The **death camps, Belzec, Sobibor**, and **Treblinka**, were located in this area. **Odilo Globocnik** was determined to "Germanize" this region and make it **Judenrein**. In the spring of 1944, the Polish **resistance** battled Ukrainian insurgents. Numerous Polish Catholics from this locale were **deported** to **Auschwitz**. The **Red Army** liberated this province in July 1944.
   SUGGESTED READING: Arad, *Belzec, Sobibor, Treblink.*

Zbaszyn. Town on the Polish frontier. The Polish Ministry of Interior decreed on October 6, 1938, that Poles who had lived outside of the country for five years were no longer citizens. **Germany** responded by dumping 17,000 Jews at the Polish border in early November 1938. The Nazi treatment of the Jews was barbaric and thousands of Jews were stranded in Zbaszyn, including the parents of **Herschel Grynszpan**, who promptly wrote their son. (See also **Kristallnacht**.)
   SUGGESTED READINGS: American Jewish Committee, *American Jewish Yearbook, Vol. 41, 1939–1940*; Read and Fisher, *Kristallnacht.*

Zebra Uniforms (G., gestreifte kleider). Striped uniforms of harsh cloth, black and white or dark blue and white, which distinguished **concentration camp** prisoners.

Zechor (H., remember). A term associated with the memory of the **Holocaust**. (See also **Zachor Institute**.)

Zegota (name for the **Council for Aid to Jews**). Underground Polish Catholic organization founded in December 1942 and supported by the **Polish Government-in-Exile**, the **Jewish National Committee**, and the **Bund**. This group hid 2,500 Jewish children in Warsaw, forged papers, and provided material support to 3,000 to 4,000 Jews in Warsaw, **Lvov**, and **Krakow** from December 1942–January 1945. Two Jews, **Adolf Abraham Berman** and **Leon Feiner**, were on its Executive Board. (See also **Wladyslau Bartoszewski, Zofia Szczuska Kossack, Polish Workers Party, Irena Sendler**, and **Henryk "Waclaw" Wolinski**.)
   SUGGESTED READING: Tomaszewski and Werbowski, *Zegota.*

Zeitschel, Dr. Carltheo (b. 1893). **SS** major attached to the German Foreign Office. A virulent **anti-Semite**, he successfully lobbied Ambassador **Otto Abetz**

(September 1941) to persuade **Heinrich Himmler** and **Hitler** to **deport** Jews in **France** to the East. (See also **Theodor Dannecker**.)

SUGGESTED READING: Witte, "Two Decisions."

Zentralstelle fuer Juedische Auswanderung (G., Central Bureau for Jewish Emigration). Established in April 1938, this **Vienna** office was organized by **Adolf Eichmann**. Later offices were established in Prague and Amsterdam. The SS bureau was created to expedite the transfer of Jews from the **Greater Reich**. Unfortunately, most nations either closed their borders to Jews or admitted very few **refugees**. (See also **Alois Brunner** and **Evian Conference**.)

SUGGESTED READING: Arendt, *Eichmann in Jerusalem.*

Zhitomir. Ukrainian city bordering **Belorussia** and home to 30,000 Jews. Most Jews fled into the **Soviet Union** before German occupation. German and Ukrainian police rounded up the 10,000 Jews that remained from July–August 1941. The Jews were shot and buried in six mass graves. The **War Crimes** Investigating Committee discovered 9,263 bodies. The **Red Army liberated** this city on December 31, 1943. (See also **Tadeusz Borowski, Misha Gildenman, Siberia**, and **Ukraine**.)

SUGGESTED READING: Arad, Krakowski and Spector, *The Einsatzgruppen Reports.*

Zid; **Zyd**; **Zhid**. (Ru. or Slavic). Derogatory term for Jew.

Zidovsky Kodex (Sl., Jewish Code). Slovakian statute patterned after the **Nuremberg Laws**. (See also **Sano Mach, Josef Tiso**, and **Anton Vasek**.)

Ziemba, Rabbi Menachem (1883–1943). **Torah** sage and member of the Warsaw Council of Rabbis. He endorsed active **resistance** and raised funds for the **Warsaw Ghetto Uprising**. Ziemba refused an offer to escape the **ghetto** and was killed on the fifth day of the uprising.

SUGGESTED READINGS: Rosenbaum, *The Holocaust and Halakhah*; Zuker, *The Unconquerable Spirit.*

Ziereis, Franz (1905–1945). **SS** major and kommandant of **Mauthausen**. He was brutal, depraved, and unrepentant. Ziereis operated the gassing vans known as "auto cars." His young son enjoyed shooting prisoners from the administration building. He did not follow **Ernst Kaltenbrunner's** order to blow up inmates in nearby tunnels during the last days of the war. Ziereis was shot by the Americans when he tried to escape in May 1945. **Simon Wiesenthal** published the kommandant's deathbed confession. (See also "**Sonderwagon**.")

SUGGESTED READING: Sachar, *Redemption of the Unwanted.*

Zigeuner. (See **Roma**.)

Zigeunerlager. (G., "Gypsy" camp). **Concentration camp** for **Roma**.

Zill, Egon (1906–1974). Kommandant of **Natzweiler-Strutthof** and **Flossen-buerg**. Zill was tried and sentenced to life in prison in Munich in 1955, but he was released and died at his home in **Dachau** in 1974. (See also **Lothar Hart-jenstein**.)
   SUGGESTED READING: Segev, Soldiers of Evil.

Ziman, Henrik (1910–1987). Lithuanian Jewish **partisan** commander. A communist activist and important leader in Soviet-controlled **Lithuania**, Ziman tried to Sovietize the country and eliminate **Zionist** institutions. He retreated to the interior of **Russia** during the German invasion. Ziman was parachuted into Lithuania to assume control of the partisans in the **Rudninkai Forest. Vilna** and **Kovno** Jews joined the partisans until they were rescued by the **Red Army**. After the war, he held senior posts in the Lithuanian communist government.
   SUGGESTED READING: Kowalski, Anthology of Armed Jewish Resistance.

Zimetbaum, Mala (1922–1944). Jewish heroine. A Belgian, she served as an interpreter after **deportation** and helped many inmates at **Birkenau** due to her special position. She escaped on June 24, 1944, with a Polish Catholic, Edward Galinsky, from the plumbers' commando. They were captured trying to enter **Slovakia** two weeks later. In full view of female prisoners, Zimetbaum slit her wrists before the Nazis could execute her, and she slapped an **SS** officer. Zimetbaum became a symbol of **resistance**. (See also **Roza Robota**.)
   SUGGESTED READING: Czech, Auschwitz Chronicle.

Zionism/Zionist. The political and cultural movement among Jews to establish a Jewish homeland in **Palestine**. Zionists were on the cutting edge of political activism in Europe and America. There were **Socialist Zionists** called **Labor Zionists** and their youth groups. **Zionist Revisionists**, and its affiliates, were nonsocialist and procapitalist. General Zionists had no political agenda, but advocated the rebuilding of the Jewish settlement (**Yishuv**). They were the Hadassah, a health agency, and **ORT**, a vocational educational organization. **Mizrachi** (Religious Zionists) was a small stream in Orthodoxy that favored a **Torah**-type state in Palestine. Its youth group was called B'nai Akiva. Most Zionists in America were of Eastern European descent. Most of German descent saw the movement as unpatriotic. Orthodox Jews viewed the movement as antireligious. Communists, and others on the left, believed Zionism was a pipe dream that diverted Jews from seeking social justice in their home countries. (See also **Agudat Israel, Aliya, Beitar Revisionists, Biltmore Programme, Hachsharot, Haganah, Irgun, Orthodox Judaism**, and **Zionist Emergency Council**.)
   SUGGESTED READING: Wyman, The Abandonment of the Jews.

Zionist Emergency Council. Founded in 1939 as the Emergency Committee for Zionist Affairs. Headed by Rabbi **Abba Hillel Silver**, its principal mission was to convince the American public of the importance of a Jewish state in **Palestine**. The Council was criticized for not focusing on rescuing European Jewry during the **Holocaust**. (See also **Bergson Group** and **Rabbi Stephen S. Wise**.)

SUGGESTED READING: Finger, *American Jewry During the Holocaust.*

Zionist Revisionists. Party founded by **Ze'ev Jabotinsky** in the 1920s. It supported capitalism and opposed cooperation with the British. This party demanded a Jewish state outright on both sides of the Jordan. It's military wing, the **Irgun** (formed from the **Haganah** in 1931), pursued Arabs who terrorized the **Yishuv**. In January 1944, the Irgun declared war against the British for its policy of keeping Jews out of **Palestine** in the face of the **Holocaust. Beitar**, its youth group, was popular in the **Diaspora** and focused on self-defense. (See also **Peter Bergson, Josiah Clement Wedgwood, White Paper**, and **ZZW**.)

SUGGESTED READING: Bell, *Terror Out of Zion.*

Zissu, Abraham L. (1888–1956). Romanian **Zionist** activist. In 1944, he was able to obtain the release of imprisoned Zionists from the government. Fearful of the approaching **Red Army**, the Romanian government recognized Zissu as the **Jewish Agency** representative. In that position, the Zionist organized "illegal" immigration to **Palestine** and protected Polish Jewish **refugees** who found their way to **Romania**.

SUGGESTED READING: Butnaru, *Waiting for Jerusalem.*

Zivilarbeitslager (G., civilian work camp). Camps established for labor projects. Jews and **Slavs** were the primary **forced laborers**. When the tasks were completed, the Jews were killed or deported elsewhere. (See also **Deportation, "Impressing,"** and **Labor Camp**.)

ZKN. (See **Jewish National Committee**.)

Zloty. Polish currency.

ZOB (Zydowska Organizacja Bojowa) (P., **Jewish Fighting Organization; JFO**). Established during the summer of 1942 in Warsaw. The fighting group coalesced after **Friedrych (Zalman) Zygmunt** confirmed that **deportation** to **Treblinka** meant death. Based at **Mila 18**, the ZOB was the backbone of the **Warsaw Ghetto Uprising** and consisted of left-wing youth, pioneer, and **Zionist** organizations, which included **Bundists**, communists, and socialists. The **Zionist Revisionists** were also part of this fighting coalition. The ZOB forged alliances with Poles on the **Aryan** side of the **ghetto**. The **ZZW** fought separately during the uprising. (See also **Irena Adamowicz, Mordecai Anielewicz,**

Heshek "Zvi" Bauminger, Abraham Blum, Delagatura, Josef Glazman, Gwardia Ludowa, Zivia Lubetkin, Vladka Meed, Polish Workers Party, Mordechai Tenenbaum, Arie Wilner, Henryk "Waclaw" Wolinski, and Yitzhak Zuckerman.

SUGGESTED READINGS: Ainsztein, *The Warsaw Ghetto Revolt*; Steinberg, *Jewish Resistance.*

Zolli, Rabbi Israel (1881–1956). Chief Rabbi to Rome's 8,000 Jews. He unsuccessfully urged the Jewish community's leader, Uso Foa, not to supply the fascists with lists and addresses of Jews. (Foa has disputed Zolli's claims.) In 1943, he also claimed to negotiate with the Vatican's treasurer who agreed to supplement Gestapo Chief Herbert Kappler's demand for Jewish gold with 15 kilos from the Holy See. Zolli converted to Catholicism on February 13, 1945.

SUGGESTED READING: Hilberg, *Destruction of European Jews.*

Zolochev. Town located close to Lvov on the Polish Ukrainian border, with a prewar Jewish population of 7,000. Before Zolochev fell under German control in September 1941, most of the Jews were deported to the Russian interior by the Soviets. A three-day pogrom was immediately carried out by Ukrainians. The head of the Judenrat, Zigmund Mayblum, refused to cooperate with the Nazis and warned Jews of impending Aktionen; he was murdered by the Germans. On April 2, 1943, Germans and Ukrainians rounded up and murdered the remaining Jews and buried them in pits. (See also Deportation.)

SUGGESTED READING: Arad, Krakowski, and Spector, *The Einsatzgruppen Reports.*

Zorin, Shalom (Simon) (1902–1974). Jewish partisan commander. He formed Jewish Fighting Unit 106 in Minsk. He recruited Jews from the Minsk ghetto, including elderly women and children. Zorin's brigade battled Germans until the Red Army arrived in 1944. Over 700 Jews survived Nazi occupation in the surrounding forests. Zorin was wounded in July 1944. He immigrated to Israel after the war. (See Hersh Smolar.)

SUGGESTED READING: Gutman, *Resistance: The Warsaw Ghetto Uprising.*

ZOX. (See Zwiazek Organizaci Wojskowej.)

Zsido Tanacs (Hu., Jewish Council of Budapest). After the German occupation of Hungary, all Jewish organizations were disbanded and put under the jurisdiction of this body. This organization aided Raoul Wallenberg in rescuing Jews. It also helped Wallenberg foil the destruction of the Budapest ghetto. The Soviets arrived in Budapest on January 17, 1945.

SUGGESTED READING: Braham, *The Politics of Genocide.*

Zubinsdk, Jan (b. 1897). Polish agricultural engineer and member of the Armia Krajowa. A zoologist, he used the Warsaw zoo as a hiding ground for

Jews. He fought in the **Warsaw Polish Uprising** in 1944 and was recognized by **Yad Vashem** as a **Righteous Gentile**.

Zucker, Simon. Survivor of the **Lodz Ghetto** and **Auschwitz**. He was co-founder of **Zachor Institute** to perpetuate the memory of the **Holocaust** within the Orthodox tradition. (See also **Zechor**.)

Zuckerman, Yitzhak (**Yitzhak Cukierman** "Antek") (1915–1981). Leader of the **Dror** youth movement and a principal underground commander of the **ZOB**. He operated on the **Aryan** side of Warsaw and gained arms for the ZOB from the Polish **resistance**. Zuckerman escaped through the sewers with his wife, **Zivia Lubetkin**, and fought in the **Warsaw Polish Uprising** in August 1944. He was bitter regarding the **Yishuv's** lukewarm rescue efforts, but was active in the **Bricha** with his wife before they left for Israel. Zuckerman and Lubetkin founded the **Ghetto Fighters' Kibbutz** and Museum.

    SUGGESTED READING: Lubetkin, *In the Days of Destruction and Revolt.*

Zugang (G., newly admitted). A new prisoner arrival to the **concentration camp**.

Zur Vernichtung durch Arbeit (G., **Destruction Through Work**).

Zwangsarbeitslager (**ZAL**). (G., **forced labor** camp).

Zwartendijk, Jan (1896–1976). **Dutch** counsel in **Kovno**, also known as the "**Angel of Curaco**." Zwartendijk issued 2,200 **visas** in 1940 to Curaco to thousands of stranded Lithuanian Jews. Zwartendijk worked in concert with **Sempo Sugihara**. He ignored orders from the Dutch ambassador in **Riga** regarding the wording of the visas and risked his own life by staying in **Lithuania** after the consulates had closed. Zwartendijk saved 2,178 Jews. **Yad Vashem** is acting on a request to have him honored as a **Righteous Gentile**. (See also **Kobe** and **Mir Yeshiva**.)

    SUGGESTED READINGS: Levine, *In Search of Sugihara*; Lipman, "The Decent Thing."

Zwiazek Organizaci Wojskowej (**ZOX**). Military arm of the **Armia Krajowa**. This group provided explosives to Jewish **Sonderkommando** in **Birkenau** who revolted in October 1944. (See also **Roza Robota**.)

"Zydokomuna" (P., Jewish communist). Myth associating Jews with a Bolshevik conspiracy to take over **Poland**. The Nazis used this popular misconception for propaganda purposes.

Zydowska Organizacja Bojowa (**ZOB**). (P., **Jewish Fighting Organization**).

Zygielbojm, Shmuel Artur (1895–1943). Jewish diplomat. He fled to London and represented the Jewish **Bund** in the **Polish Government-in-Exile** (1940–1943). The diplomat advocated passively resisting the Nazi's order to ghettoize Warsaw. He met with **Jan Karski** in 1942. Zygielbojm tried to convince the **Allies** to intervene to stop the murder of Jews without success. After hearing from Arthur J. Goldberg, a member of the **OSS**, that the United States would not bomb **Auschwitz** nor areas near the **Warsaw Ghetto**, Zygielbojm committed suicide on May 12, 1943. He left a letter condemning Allied indifference. "By my death I wish to make my final protest against the passivity in which the world is looking on and permitting the extermination of the Jewish people."

SUGGESTED READINGS: Laqueur, *The Terrible Secret*; Ravel, *Faithful unto Death*.

"Zygmunt," (Zalman) Friedrych (1920–1943). Jewish activist and underground agent. He was smuggled out of the **Warsaw Ghetto** in July 1942 to confirm the existence of **Treblinka**. Zygmunt verified Treblinka's existence as a **death camp**, which in turn spurred the **JFO** to plan the **Warsaw Ghetto Uprising**. He accompanied a gentile railroad worker along the tracks leading to Treblinka. Zygmunt met an eyewitness escapee, Azriel Wallach, the nephew of **Maksim Maksimovich Litvinov**, who confirmed that **deportation** meant death. Moving through the sewers, he fought on both sides of the wall in the Warsaw Ghetto Uprising. During a rescue mission, he was captured by the Nazis and executed.

SUGGESTED READING: Bartoszewski and Lewin, *Righteous Among the Nations*.

Zyklon-B (Hydrogen cyanide). Pesticide and commercial name for **prussic acid**. These blue crystals turn into a deadly gas when oxidized. It was first tested in the **euthanasia** program. Kommandant **Rudolf Hoess** pioneered its application for mass murder after successfully testing it on **Soviet POWs** in September 1941. Zyklon-B was used in the **gas chambers** in many camps, although most camps (**Majdanek**, 1943) used carbon monoxide gas pumped into a chamber by an engine. Time of death was anywhere from thirty seconds to three minutes to twenty minutes, depending on the camp and the technology. **Heinrich Himmler** believed the use of gas as a means of mass murder was more "humane," efficient, and less taxing on the **SS**. Zyklon-B was also economical. The SS calculated that it cost 5 cents per victim to gas 2,000 people per application. (See also **Alex Zink Factory, Block 11, I. G. Farben, Walther Funk, Dr. Joachim Mrugrowsky, and Tesch and Stabenow, International Vermin Extermination Corporation Ltd.**)

SUGGESTED READINGS: Kogon, Langbein, and Ruckert, *Nazi Mass Murder*; Reitlinger, *The Final Solution*.

ZZW (Zydowski Zwiazek Wojskowy) (P., Jewish Military Union). Military wing of the **Beitar** Youth and part of the **Zionist Revisionist** movement organized by **Dr. David Wdowinski** in October 1942. The ZZW was actively involved in the **Warsaw Ghetto Uprising** (April 1943) in Muranowski Square, but not part of the **ZOB**.

SUGGESTED READINGS: Ainsztein, *The Warsaw Ghetto Revolt*; Mark, *The Uprising in the Warsaw Ghetto*.

BIBLIOGRAPHY

Aarons, Mark, and John Loftus. *Unholy Trinity: The Vatican, the Nazis, and Soviet Intelligence*. New York: St. Martin's Press, 1991.

Abitbol, Michel. *The Jews of North Africa During the Second World War*. Trans. Catherine Tehany Zentels. Detroit: Wayne State University Press, 1989.

Abrahamsen, Samuel. *Norway's Response to the Holocaust: A Historical Perspective*. New York: Holocaust Library, 1991.

Abrams, Alan. *Special Treatment*. Secaucus, NJ: Lyle Stewart, 1985.

Abzug, Robert H. *Inside the Vicious Heart: Americans and the Liberation of Nazi Concentration Camps*. New York: Oxford University Press, 1985.

Adler, Jacques. *The Jews of Paris and the Final Solution*. New York: Oxford University Press, 1987.

Ainsztein, Reuben. "The Enemy Within: Anti-Semitism Among Polish Soldiers in War-Time Britain." *Wiener Library Bulletin* 13, no. 596 (1959).

Ainsztein, Reuben. *The Warsaw Ghetto Revolt*. New York: Schocken Books, 1979.

Allied Control Authority for Germany. *Trial of Major War Criminals Before the International Military Tribunal, Nuremberg, I-XLII, 14 November 1945, 1 October 1946*. Nuremberg, Germany: 1947–1949.

American Jewish Committee. *American Jewish Yearbook, Vol. 41, 1939–1940; Vol. 42, 1940–1941; Vol. 43, 1941–1942; Vol. 44, 1942–1943; Vol. 45, 1943–1944; Vol. 46, 1944–1945; Vol. 47, 1945–1946*. Philadelphia: Jewish Publication Society of America, 1939–1946.

Andreyev, C. *Vlasov and the Russian Liberation Movement*. New York: Cambridge University Press, 1990.

Anger, Per. *With Raoul Wallenberg in Budapest*. Trans. David Mel Paul and Margareta Paul. New York: Holocaust Library, 1981. Holocaust Library, 1996.

Angress, R. "Who Really Was Bruno Bettelheim?" *Commentary* 90 (October 1990): 26–30.

Annas, George, and Michael A. Grodin, eds. *The Nazi Doctors and the Nuremberg Code.*
New York: Oxford University Press, 1992.

Arad, Yitzhak. *The Ghetto in Flames: The Struggle and the Destruction of the Jews in
Vilna in the Holocaust.* New York: Ktav, 1981.

Arad, Yitzhak. *Belzec, Sobibor, Treblinka: The Operation Reinhard Death Camps.* Bloomington: Indiana University Press, 1987.

Allied Control Authority for Germany. *Trial of Major War Criminals Before the International Military Tribunal, Nuremburg, I-XLII, 14 November 1945, 1 October
1946.* Nuremburg, Germany: 1947–1949.

Arad, Yitzhak, Shmuel Krakowski, and Shmuel Spector, eds. *The Einsatzgruppen Reports: Selections from the Dispatches of Nazi Death Squads in Occupied Territories of the Soviet Union, July 1941–January 1943.* New York: Holocaust
Library, 1989.

Arendt, Hannah. *Eichmann in Jerusalem: A Report on the Banality of Evil.* Rev. ed.
New York: Penguin Books, 1987.

Ausubel, Nathan. *Pictorial History of the Jewish People: From Bible Times to Our Own
Day Throughout the World.* New York: Crown Publishers, Inc., 1971.

Avni, Haim. *Spain, the Jews, and Franco.* Trans. Emanuel Shimoni. Philadelphia: Jewish
Publication Society of America, 1982.

Aziz, Philippe. *Doctors of Death.* 3 vols. Geneva: Ferni Publishing, 1976.

Bacque, James. *Just Raoul: The Private War Against the Nazis of Raoul Laporterie, Who
Saved Over 1,600 Lives in France.* Rocklin, CA: Prima Publishing, 1992.

Baker, Leonard. *Days of Sorrow and Pain: Leo Baeck and the Berlin Jews.* New York:
Macmillan, 1979.

Balabkins, Nicholas. *West German Reparations to Israel.* New Brunswick, NJ: Rutgers
University Press, 1971.

Barbash, Fred. ''Accounting for the Sins of Neutrality.'' *Washington Post Weekly*, February 17, 1997.

Bard, Mitchell G. *Forgotten Victims: The Abandonment of Americans in Hitler's Camps.*
Boulder, CO: Westview Press, 1994.

Bartoszewski, Wladyslaw T. *The Warsaw Ghetto: A Christian Testimony.* Boston: Beacon Press, 1987.

Bartoszewski, Wladyslaw T., and Zofia Lewin, eds. *Righteous Among Nations: How
Poles Helped Jews, 1939–1945.* London: Earliscourt Publishers, 1969.

Bartov, Omer. *Hitler's Army: Soldiers, Nazis and War in the Third Reich.* New York:
Oxford University Press, 1991.

Bassett, Richard. *Waldheim and Austria.* New York: Penguin Books, 1988.

Batty, Peter. *The House of Krupp.* New York: Stein & Day, 1967.

Bauer, Yehuda. *Flight and Rescue: Bricha.* New York: Random House, 1970.

Bauer, Yehuda. *From Diplomacy to Resistance.* New York: Atheneum, 1970.

Bauer, Yehuda. *My Brother's Keeper: A History of the American Joint Distribution Committee, 1929–1939.* Philadelphia: Jewish Publication Society of America, 1974.

Bauer, Yehuda. *American Jewry and the Holocaust: The American Jewish Joint Distribution Committee, 1939–1945.* Detroit: Wayne State University Press, 1981.

Bauer, Yehuda. *Jews for Sale? Nazi-Jewish Negotiations, 1939–1945.* New Haven, CT:
Yale University Press, 1994.

Begin, Menachem. *The Revolt: Story of the Irgun.* New York: Henry Schuman, 1951.

Bell, J. Bowyer. *Terror Out of Zion.* New York: St. Martin's Press, 1977.

Bellon, Bernard P. *Mercedes in Peace and War: German Automobile Workers, 1903–1945*. New York: Columbia University Press, 1990.

Ben-Ami, Yitshaq. *Years of Wrath, Days of Glory: Memoirs from the Irgun*. New York: R. Speiler, 1982.

Bendersky, Joseph. *A History of Nazi Germany*. Chicago: Nelson-Hall, 1985.

Benovet, John G. *SOE: Recollections and Reflections*. London: Bodley Head, 1981.

Ben-Zohar, Michael. *The Avengers*. New York: Hawthorn Books, 1967.

Ben-Zvi, Itzhak. *The Exiled and the Redeemed*. Trans. A. Abbady. Philadelphia: Jewish Publication Society of America, 1957.

Berenbaum, Michael. *A Mosaic of Victims: Non-Jews Persecuted and Murdered by Nazis*. New York: New York University Press, 1990.

Bergen, Doris L. *The German Christian Movement in the Third Reich*. Chapel Hill: The University of North Carolina Press, 1996.

Berhaim, Mark. *Father of Orphans: The Story of Janusz Korczak*. New York: Lodestar Books, 1989.

Berkley, George. *Vienna and Its Jews: The Tragedy of Success 1880s–1980s*. Cambridge, MA: Abt Books, 1988.

Berman, Morris. *Coming to Our Senses*. New York: Bantam, 1990.

Berndac, Christian. *The 186 Steps*. Geneva: Ferni Publishing, 1978.

Beschloss, Michael R. *Kennedy and Roosevelt: The Uneasy Alliance*. New York: Norton, 1980.

Bethell, Nicholas. *The War Hitler Won: The Fall of Poland, September 1939*. New York: Holt, Rinehart & Winston, 1972.

Bethge, Eberhard. *Dietrich Bonhoeffer: Man of Vision, Man of Courage*. Trans. Eric Mosbacher et al. New York: Harper & Row, 1970.

Beyel, Hans P. *Sex and Society in Nazi Germany*. Philadelphia: Lippincott Company, 1976.

Beyerchen, Alan D. *Scientists Under Hitler: Politics and the Physics Community in the Third Reich*. New Haven, CT: Yale University Press, 1977.

Bird, Kai. *The Chairman: John J. McCloy, The Making of the American Establishment*. New York: Simon & Schuster, 1992.

Black, Edwin. *The Transfer Agreement*. New York: Macmillan, 1984.

Black, Peter. *Ernst Kaltenbrunner: Ideological Soldier of the Third Reich*. Princeton, NJ: Princeton University Press, 1984.

Blayner, Michael S. "Herbert Pell, War Crimes and the Jews." *American Jewish Historical Quarterly* no. 6 (1976).

Block, Gay, and Malka Drucker. *Rescuers: Portraits of Moral Courage in the Holocaust*. New York: Holmes & Meier, 1992.

Blum, Howard. *Wanted! The Search for Nazi War Criminals in America*. Greenwich, CT: Fawcett Books, 1977.

Blumenfeld, Laura. "Fifty Years After the Lie: In Poland, a Ceremony of Peacemaking Finds Feelings Are Still Raw." *Washington Post*, July 15, 1996, B4.

Blumenson, Martin. *The Patton Papers*. Boston: Houghton Mifflin, 1974.

Boas, Jacob. *Boulevard des Miseres: The Story of Transit Camp Westerbork*. Hamden, CT: Archon Books, 1985.

Bondy, Ruth. *The Emissary: A Life of Enzo Sereni*. Trans. Shlomo Katz. Boston and Toronto: Little Brown & Company, 1977.

Bondy, Ruth. *"Elder of the Jews": Jakob Edelstein of Theresienstadt*. Trans. Evelyn Abel. New York: Grove Press, 1989.

Borkin, Joseph. *The Crime and Punishment of I. G. Farben*. New York: The Free Press, 1978.

Borzykowski, Tuvia. *Between Tumbling Walls*. Ghetto Fighters' House, Israel: Hakibbutz Ha-Meuchad Publishing House, 1976.

Bracher, Karl D. *The German Dictatorship*. New York: Praeger, 1970.

Braham, Randolph L. *The Destruction of Hungarian Jewry: A Documentary Account*. 2 vols. New York: Columbia University Press, 1963.

Braham, Randolph L. *The Hungarian Labor Service System, 1939–1945*. Boulder, CO: East European Quarterly, 1977.

Braham, Randolph L. *The Politics of Genocide: The Holocaust in Hungary*. 2d ed. New York: The Rosenthal Institute for Holocaust Studies of the City University of New York, 1994.

Braham, Randolph L. "Canada and the Perpetrators of the Holocaust: The Case of Regina v. Finta." *Holocaust and Genocide Studies* 9, no. 3 (Winter 1995): 293–318.

Braham, Randolph L., ed. *The Tragedy of Rumanian Jewry*. New York: The Rosenthal Institute for Holocaust Studies of the City University of New York, 1994.

Braybrooke, N. "Simone Wgol and Edith Stein, Modern Mystic Martyrs." *Christian Century* 81 (November 25, 1964).

Brecher, Elinor J. *Schindler's Legacy: True Stories of the List of Survivors*. New York: Plume, 1994.

Breitman, Richard. *The Architect of Genocide: Himmler and the Final Solution*. New York: Alfred A. Knopf, 1991.

Breitman, Richard, and Alan Kraut. *American Refugee Policy and European Jewry 1933–1945*. Bloomington: Indiana University Press, 1987.

Bridgman, Jon. *The End of the Holocaust: The Liberation of the Camps*. Portland, OR: Areopagtica Press, 1990.

Briggs, Asa. *The Channel Islands: Occupation and Liberation, 1940–1945*. London: B. T. Batsford, Ltd., (1995).

Brown, Daniel P. *The Beautiful Beast: The Life and Times of SS-Aufseherin Irma Grese*. Ventura, CA: Golden West Historical Publications, 1996.

Browning, Christopher R. *The Final Solution and the German Foreign Office*. New York: Holmes & Meier, 1978.

Browning, Christopher R. *Fateful Months: Essays on the Emergence of the Final Solution*. New York: Holmes & Meier, 1986.

Browning, Christopher R. *Ordinary Men: Reserve Police Battalion 101 and the Final Solution in Poland*. New York: HarperCollins, 1993.

Browning, Christopher R. "A Final Hitler Decision for the 'Final Solution.' The Riegner Telegram Reconsidered." *Holocaust and Genocide Studies* 10, no. 1 (Spring 1996): 3–11.

Bullock, Alan. *Hitler and Stalin, Parallel Lives*. New York: Knopf, 1992.

Burleigh, Michael, and Wolfgang Wipperman. *The Racial State: Germany 1933–1945*. Cambridge, England: Cambridge University Press, 1993.

Butler, Rupert. *An Illustrated History of the Gestapo*. Osceola, WI: Motorbooks International, 1993.

Butnaru, I. C. *The Silent Holocaust: Romania and Its Jews*. Westport, CT: Greenwood Press, 1992.

Butnaru, I. C. *Waiting for Jerusalem: Surviving the Holocaust in Romania*. Westport, CT: Greenwood Press, 1993.

Campion, Joan *In the Lion's Mouth: Gisi Fleischmann and the Jewish Fight for Survival*. Latham, MD: University Press of America, 1987.

Caracciolo, Nicola. *Uncertain Refuge: Italy and the Jews During the Holocaust*. Trans. Florette Rechnitz Koffler and Richard Koffler. Urbana and Chicago: University of Illinois Press, 1995.

Cargas, Harry James, ed. "The Unnecessary Problem of Edith Stein." *Studies in the Shoah*, Vol. 4. Lanham, MD: University Press of America, 1994.

Carlgren, W. M. *Swedish Foreign Policy During the Second World War*. New York: St. Martin's Press, 1977.

Carsten, F. L., ed. *The German Resistance to Hitler*. Berkeley: University of California Press, 1970.

Catholic League for Religious and Civil Rights. *Pius the XII and the Holocaust: A Reader*. Milwaukee, WI: Catholic League, 1986.

Chary, Frederick B. *The Bulgarian Jews and the Final Solution, 1940–1944*. Pittsburgh, PA: University of Pittsburgh Press, 1972.

Cicioni, Mirna. *Primo Levi, Bridges of Knowledge*. Herndon, VA: Bers Publishers, 1995.

Clay, Katrine, and Michael Leapman. *The Master Race: Lebensborn Experiment in Nazi Germany*. London: Hodder & Staughton, 1995.

Cohen, Asher. *The Halutz Resistance in Hungary, 1942–1944*. Leiden, Netherlands: E. J. Brill, 1986.

Cohen, Kate. *The Neppi Modena Diaries: Reading Jewish Survival Through My Italian Family*. Hanover, NH: University Press of New England, 1996.

Cohen, Michael J. *Churchill and the Jews*. London: Frank Cass Ltd., 1985.

Cohen, Naomi W. *Not Free to Desist: The American Jewish Committee 1906–1966*. Philadelphia: Jewish Publication Society of America, 1972.

Cohen, R. I. *The Burden of Conscience: French Jewish Leadership During the Holocaust*. Bloomington: Indiana University Press, 1987.

Cohen, William, and Juergen Svensson. "Finland and the Holocaust." *Holocaust and Genocide Studies* 9, no. 1 (Spring 1995): 70–94.

Cohn, Norman. *Warrant for Genocide*. New York: Harper & Row, 1967.

Conot, Robert. *Justice at Nuremberg*. New York: Carroll & Graf Publishers, 1983.

Conway, Martin. *Collaboration in Belgium: Leon Degrelle and the Rexist Movement, 1940–1944*. New Haven, CT: Yale University Press, 1993.

Cox, Geoffrey. *Psychotherapy and the Third Reich*. New York: Oxford University Press, 1988.

Crankshaw, Edward. *Gestapo: Instrument of Tyranny*. New York: Viking Press, 1956.

Crowe, David A. *History of the Gypsies of Eastern Europe and Russia*. New York: St. Martin's Press, 1994.

Crowe, David, and John Kolsti, eds. *The Gypsies of Eastern Europe*. Armonk, NY: Sharpe Publishers, 1991.

Czech, Danuta. *Auschwitz Chronicle, 1939–1945: From the Archives of the Auschwitz Memorial and the German Federal Archives*. New York: Henry Holt, 1990.

Dallin, Alexander. *German Rule in Russia, 1941–1945: A Study of Occupation Policies*. Boulder, CO: Westview Press, 1981.

Danner, Fred. "How Terrible was Ivan?" *Vanity Fair* (January 1992): 132ff.

Davidson, Eugene. *The Trial of the Germans*. New York: Macmillan, 1966.

Dawidowicz, Lucy S. *The War Against the Jews, 1933–1945*. New York: Holt, Rinehart & Winston, 1975; Reissue New York: Macmillan, 1986.

Dawidowicz, Lucy S. *The Holocaust and the Historians*. Cambridge, MA: Harvard University Press, 1981.

Dinnerstein, Leonard. *America and the Survivors of the Holocaust*. New York: Columbia University Press, 1982.

Dobroszycki, Lucjan. *The Chronicle of the Lodz Ghetto, 1941–1944*. New Haven, CT: Yale University Press, 1984.

Donat, Alexander, ed. *The Death Camp Treblinka: A Documentary*. New York: Holocaust Library, 1979.

Drexel, John, ed. *Encyclopedia of the 20th Century*. New York: Facts on File, 1991.

Drucker, Olga Levy. *Kindertransport*. New York: Henry Holt, 1992.

Dubnow-Erlich, Sophie. *Life and Work of S. M. Dubnow*. Ed. Jeffrey Shandler. Trans. Judith Vowles. Bloomington: Indiana University Press, 1991.

Dumbach, Annette E., and Jud Newborn. *Shattering the German Night: The Story of the White Rose*. Boston: Little Brown, 1986.

Dwork, Deborah. *Children with a Star: Jewish Youth in Nazi Europe*. New Haven, CT: Yale University Press, 1991.

Eck, N. "The Rescue of Jews with the Aid of Passports and Citizenship Papers of Latin American States." *Yad Vashem Studies* 21 (1957): 125–52.

Eckman, Lester, and Chaim Lazar. *The Jewish Resistance*. New York: Shengold Publishers, Inc., 1977.

Edelheit, Abraham J., and Hershel Edelheit. *History of the Holocaust: A Handbook and Dictionary*. Boulder, CO: Westview Press, 1994.

Ehrenburg, Ilya, and Vasily Grossman, eds. *The Black Book: The Ruthless Murder of Jews by German-Fascist Invaders throughout the Temporarily-Occupied Regions of the Soviet Union and the Death Camps of Poland During the War of 1941–1945*. Trans. John Glad and James S. Levine. New York: Holocaust Library, 1981.

Ehrmann, F., ed. *Terezin, 1941–1945*. Prague: Council of Jewish Committees in Czech Lands, 1965.

Eibeshitz, Jehoshua, and Anna Eibeshitz, comp. and trans. *Women in the Holocaust*. New York: Remember, 1993.

Einstein, Albert. *Out of My Later Years*. New York: Philosophical Library, 1950.

Elkins, Michael. *Forged in Fury*. New York: Ballantine, 1971.

Ernst, Edzard. "A Leading Medical School Seriously Damaged: Vienna 1938." *Annals of Internal Medicine* 120, no. 10 (May 15, 1995): 789–94.

Ezergailis, Andrew. *The Holocaust in Latvia, 1941–1944*. Riga, Latvia: The Historical Institute of Latvia, 1996.

Fackenheim, Emil. *The Jewish Return into History*. New York: Schocken Books, 1978.

Falk, Robert, Gabriel Kolko, and Robert Jay Lifton. *Crimes of War*. New York: Vintage, 1971.

Farago, Ladislas. *Aftermath*. New York: Avon, 1974.

Federber-Salz, Bertha. *And the Sun Kept Shining*. New York: Schocken Books, 1980.

Feig, Konnilyn. *Hitler's Death Camps: The Sanity of Madness*. New York: Holmes & Meier, 1983.

Feingold, Henry. *The Politics of Rescue: The Roosevelt Administration and the Holocaust*. Rev. ed. New York: Holocaust Library, 1980.

Fenyo, Mario D. *Hitler, Horthy, and Hungary*. New Haven, CT: Yale University Press, 1972.

Ferencz, Benjamin. *Less Than Slaves: Jewish Forced Labor and the Quest for Compensation*. Cambridge, MA: Harvard University Press, 1979.

Fest, Joachim C. *The Face of the Third Reich: Portraits of the Nazi Leadership*. Trans. Michael Bullock. New York: Pantheon Books, 1970.

Fest, Joachim C. *Plotting Hitler's Death: The Story of the German Resistance*. Trans. Bruce Little. New York: Metropolitan Books, 1996.

Figueiredo, Antonio de. *Portugal: Fifty Years of Dictatorship*. New York: Holmes & Meier, 1976.

Finger, Seymour Maxwell. *American Jewry During the Holocaust: A Report by the Research Director, His Staff and Independent Research Scholars Retained by the Director for the American Commission on the Holocaust*. New York: American Commission on the Holocaust, May 1984.

Fischel, Jack, and Sanford Pinsker. ''The Church's Response to the Holocaust.'' *Holocaust Studies Annual*. Vol. 2. Greenwood, FL: Penkeville Publishing Company, 1996.

Fischer, Julius. *Transnistria: The Forgotten Cemetery*. South Brunswick, NJ: Thomas Yoseloff, 1969.

Fischer, Klaus P. *Nazi Germany: A New History*. New York: Continuum, 1995.

Fleming, Gerald. *Hitler and the Final Solution*. Berkeley: University of California Press, 1984.

Flender, Harold. *Rescue in Denmark*. New York: Simon & Schuster, 1967.

Flood, Charles B. *Hitler, the Path to Power*. Boston: Houghton Mifflin, 1989.

Frankl, Viktor E. *Man's Search for Meaning: An Introduction to Logotherapy*. New York: Simon & Schuster, 1984.

Freidenreich, Harriet Pass. *The Jews of Yugoslavia: A Quest for Community*. Philadelphia: Jewish Publication Society of America, 1979.

Freidlander, Albert. *Out of the Whirlwind: A Reader of Holocaust Literature*. New York: Schocken Books, 1976.

Freiwald, Aaron, with Martin Mendelsohn. *The Last Nazi: Josef Schwammberger and the Nazi Past*. New York: W. W. Norton & Company, 1994.

Frieder, Emanuel. *To Deliver Their Souls*. New York: Holocaust Library, 1987.

Friedlander, Henry. *The Origins of Nazi Genocide: From Euthanasia to the Final Solution*. Chapel Hill: University of North Carolina Press, 1995.

Friedlander, Saul. *Pius XII and the Third Reich: A Documentation*. Trans. Charles Fullman. New York: Alfred A. Knopf, 1966.

Friedlander, Saul. *Kurt Gerstein: The Ambiguity of Good*. Trans. Charles Fullman. New York: Knopf, 1969.

Friedlander, Saul. *Nazi Germany and the Jews*. New York: HarperCollins, 1997.

Friedman, Maurice. *Martin Buber's Life and Work*. Detroit: Wayne State University Press, 1988.

Friedman, Philip. ''The Jews of Greece During the Second World War.'' *Jewish Social Studies* 5 (1953).

Friedman, Philip. *Their Brothers' Keepers: The Christian Heroes and Heroines Who Helped the Oppressed Escape the Nazi Terror*. New York: Holocaust Library, 1978.

Friedman, Philip. *Roads to Extinction: Essays on the Holocaust.* Philadelphia: Jewish Publication Society of America, 1980.

Friedman, Saul S. *Pogromchik: The Assassination of Simon Petliura.* New York: Hart Publishing Company, 1976.

Fuchs, Abraham. *The Unheeded Cry: The Life of Rabbi Michael Weissmandel.* New York: Torah Umesorah, 1984.

Galante, Pierre. *Operation Valkyrie.* New York: Dell, 1981.

Gallagher, Hugh Gregory. *By Trust Betrayed: Patients, Physicians and the License to Kill in the Third Reich.* Arlington, VA: Vandamere Press, 1990.

Gaon, Solomon, and Mitchell Serels. *Sephardim and the Holocaust.* New York: Yeshiva University Press, 1987.

Garlinski, Jozef. *The Enigma War.* New York: Scribner's, 1980.

Garlinski, Jozef. *Poland in the Second World War.* New York: Hippocrene Books, 1985.

Gellman, Irwin F. *Secret Affairs: Franklin Roosevelt, Cordell Hull and Sumner Welles.* Baltimore: The Johns Hopkins University Press, 1995.

Gies, Miep, with Alison Leslie Gold. *Anne Frank Remembered: The Story of the Woman Who Helped to Hide the Frank Family.* New York: Simon & Schuster, 1987.

Gilbert, G. M. *Nuremberg Diary.* 1947, Reprint New York: Da Capo Press, 1995.

Gilbert Martin. *Exile and Return: The Struggle for a Jewish Homeland.* Philadelphia: Lippincott, 1978.

Gilbert, Martin. *Final Journey: The Fate of the Jews in Nazi Europe.* New York: Mayflower Books, 1979.

Gilbert, Martin. *The Second World War: A Complete History.* New York: Henry Holt, 1989.

Gilbert, Martin. *Atlas of the Holocaust.* Toronto: Lester Publications, 1993.

Gilbert, Martin. *The Atlas of Jewish History.* New York: William Morrow & Company, 1993.

Gilbert, Martin. *The Day the War Ended.* New York: Henry Holt, 1995.

Gill, Anton. *An Honorable Defeat: A History of German Resistance to Hitler, 1933–1945.* New York: Henry Holt, 1994.

Gillingham, John R. *Industry and Politics in the Third Reich: Ruhr Coal, Hitler and Europe.* New York: Columbia University Press, 1985.

Goebbels, Joseph. *Final Entries 1945: The Diaries of Joseph Goebbels.* Ed. Hugh Trevor-Roper. Trans. Richard Barry. New York: G. P. Putnam's Sons, 1978.

Goldberger, Leo, ed. *The Rescue of Danish Jews: Moral Courage Under Stress.* New York: New York University Press, 1987.

Goldhagen, Daniel Jonah. *Hitler's Willing Executioners: Ordinary Germans and the Holocaust.* New York: Alfred A. Knopf, 1996.

Goldmann, Nahum. *The Jewish Paradox.* Trans. Steve Cox. New York: Fred Jordan Books/Grosset & Dunlap, 1978.

Golsan, Richard J. *Memory, the Holocaust and French Justice: The Bousquet and Touvier Affairs.* Trans. Lucy Golsan. Hanover, NH: University Press of New England, 1996.

Goralski, Robert. *World War II Almanac.* New York: Bonatiza Books, 1981.

Gordon, Thomas, and Max M. Witts. *The Voyage of the Damned.* New York: Stein & Day, 1974.

Gotz, Aly, Peter Chroust, and Christian Pross. *Cleansing the Fatherland: Nazi Medicine and Racial Hygiene*. Trans. Belinda Cooper. Baltimore: The Johns Hopkins University Press, 1994.

Graham, Robert. *Vatican Diplomacy*. Princeton, NJ: Princeton University Press, 1959.

Gribetz, Judah, Eduard Greenstein, and Regina S. Stein. *The Timetables of Jewish History*. New York: Touchstone/Simon & Schuster, 1993.

Gross, Leonard. *The Last Jews in Berlin*. New York: Simon & Schuster, 1982.

Grossman, Chaika. *The Underground Army: Fighters of the Bialystock Ghetto*. Ed. Sol Lewis. Trans. Shmuel Beeri. New York: Holocaust Library, 1987.

Grossman, Mendel, Zvi Szner, and Alexander Sened, eds. *With a Camera in the Ghetto*. New York: Schocken Books, 1977.

Gruber, Ruth. *Haven: The Unknown Story of 1,000 World War II Refugees*. Bergenfield, NJ: New American Library/Signet, 1984.

Grunberger, Richard. *Hitler's SS*. New York: Dorset Press, 1970.

Gutman, Yisrael. *The Jews of Warsaw, 1939–1943: Ghetto, Underground, Revolt*. Trans. Ina Friedman. Bloomington: Indiana University Press, 1982.

Gutman, Yisrael. *Resistance: The Warsaw Ghetto Uprising*. Boston: Houghton Mifflin, 1996.

Gutman, Yisrael, ed. *Encyclopedia of the Holocaust*. 4 vols. New York: Macmillan, 1990.

Gutman, Yisrael, and Michael Berenbaum, eds. *Anatomy of the Auschwitz Death Camp*. Bloomington: Indiana University Press, 1994.

Gutman, Yisrael, and Shmuel Krakowski. *Unequal Victims: Poles and Jews During World War II*. New York: Holocaust Library, 1986.

Gutman, Yisrael, and Avital Saf, eds. *The Nazi Concentration Camps: Structure and Aims: The Image of the Prisoner, the Jews in the Camps*. Jerusalem: Proceedings of the Fourth Yad Vashem International Historical Conference, 1984.

Gutman, Yisrael, and Avital Saf, eds. *She'erit Hapletah 1944–1948: Rehabilitation and Political Struggle*. Jerusalem: Yad Vashem, 1990.

Gutman, Yisrael, and Efraim Zuroff, eds. *Rescue Attempts During the Holocaust: Proceedings of the Second Yad Vashem International Historical Conference Jerusalem, April 8–11, 1974*. Jerusalem: Yad Vashem, 1977; New York: Ktav, 1979.

Gutteridge, Richard. *Open Thy Mouth for the Dumb: The German Evangelical Church and the Jews, 1879–1950*. Southampton, England: Camelot, 1976.

Habe, Hans. *The Mission*. New York: Signet, 1967.

Hackett, David A., ed. and trans. *The Buchenwald Report*. Boulder, CO: Westview Press, 1995.

Haesler, Alfred A. *The Lifeboat is Full: Switzerland and the Refugees, 1933–1945*. New York: Funk & Wagnalls, 1969.

Hale, Oron J. *The Captive Press in the Third Reich*. Princeton, NJ: Princeton University Press, 1973.

Hallie, Philip. *Lest Innocent Blood Be Shed: The Story of the Town of Le Chambon and How Goodness Happened There*. New York: Harper & Row, 1979.

Hancock, Ian. *The Pariah Syndrome: An Account of Gypsy Slavery and Persecution*. Ann Arbor, MI: Karoma Publishers, 1987.

Handler, Andrew. *A Man for all Connections: Raoul Wallenberg and the Hungarian State Apparatus, 1944–1945*. Westport, CT: Greenwood Press, 1996.

Harris, Whitney R. *Tyranny on Trial*. New York: Barnes & Noble, 1995.

Hartman, Geoffrey H., ed. *Bitburg in Moral and Political Perspective*. Bloomington: Indiana University Press, 1986.

Haveron, Tamara. *Eleanor Roosevelt: An American Conscience*. Chicago: Quadrangle Books, 1968.

Hecht, Ben. *Child of the Century*. New York: Signet Key, 1954.

Hehn, Paul N. *The German Struggle in World War II: German Counter-Insurgency in Yugoslavia, 1941–1943*. Boulder, CO: East European Quarterly, 1979.

Heilman, Uriel. "Chaim Herzog—Soldier and Statesman." *Jerusalem Post International Edition*, April 26, 1997.

Heller, Celia S. *On the Edge of Destruction: Jews of Poland between the Two World Wars*. Detroit: Wayne State University Press, 1994.

Heppner, Ernest G. *Shanghai Refuge: A Memoir of the World War II Ghetto*. Lincoln: University of Nebraska Press, 1994.

Herzer, Ivo, ed. *The Italian Refuge*. Washington, DC: The Catholic University Press, 1989.

Herzstein, Robert Edwin. *Waldheim: The Missing Years*. New York: Arbor House, 1988.

Herzstein, Robert Edwin. *Roosevelt and Hitler: Prelude to War*. New York: Paragon House, 1989.

Higham, Charles. *Trading with the Enemy: An Expose of the Nazi-American Money Plot, 1933–1949*. New York: Delacorte Press, 1983.

Hilberg, Raul. *The Destruction of European Jews*. 3 vols. Rev. ed. New York: Holmes & Meier, 1985.

Hillel, Marc, and Clarissa Henry. *Of Pure Blood*. New York: McGraw-Hill, 1976.

Hindley, Meredith. "Negotiating the Boundary of Unconditional Surrender: The War Refugee Board in Sweden and Nazi Proposal to Ransom Jews, 1944–1945." *Holocaust and Genocide Studies* 10, no. 1 (Spring 1996): 52–78.

Hirschmann, Ira. *Lifeline to a Promised Land*. New York: Vanguard, 1946.

Hirschmann, Ira. *Caution to the Winds*. New York: David McKay, 1962.

Hirshaut, Julien. *Jewish Martyrs of Pawiak*. New York: Holocaust Library, 1982.

Hitler, Adolf. *Mein Kampf*. Trans. Ralph Manheim. 1925. Reprint Boston: Houghton Mifflin, 1971.

Hoehne, Heinz. *The Order of the Death's Head*. New York: Ballantine, 1969.

Hoess, Rudolph. *Death Dealer: The Memoirs of the SS Kommandant at Auschwitz*. Ed., Steven Paskuly. Trans. Andrew Pollinger. Buffalo, NY: Prometheus Books, 1992.

Hoffman, Peter. "Roncalli in the Second World War: Peace Initiatives, the Greek Famine and the Persecution of the Jews." *Journal of Ecclesiastical History* 40, no. 1 (January 1989): 73–99.

Hoisington, William A. *The Casablanca Connection: French Colonial Policy, 1936–1943*. Chapel Hill: The University of North Carolina Press, 1984.

Horwitz, Gordon, J. *In the Shadow of Death: Living Outside the Gates of Mauthausen*. New York: The Free Press, 1990.

Hughes, H. Stuart. *The Sea Change: The Migration of Social Thought, 1930–1965*. New York: Harper & Row, 1975.

Huneke, Douglas. *The Moses of Rovno: The Story of Fritz Graebe, a German Christian*. New York: Dodd, Mead, 1985.

Hunt, Linda. *Secret Agenda: The United States Government, Nazi Scientists, and Project Paperclip, 1945–1990*. New York: St. Martin's Press, 1991.

Ioanid, Radu. *The Sword of the Archangel: Fascist Ideology in Romania*. Trans. Peter Heinezz. New York: East European Monographs, no. CCXCII, Columbia University Press, 1990.

Iranek-Osmecki, Kazimierz. *He Who Saves One Life*. New York: Crown Publishers, 1971.

Jackson, Robert. *The Case Against Nazi War Criminals*. New York: Alfred A. Knopf, 1946.

Jacobs, Louis. *The Jewish Religion: A Companion*. Oxford: Oxford University Press, 1995.

Jagendorf, Siegfried. *Jagendorf's Foundry: A Memoir of the Rumanian Holocaust, 1941–1944*. New York: HarperCollins, 1991.

Jelinek, Y. *The Parish Republic: Hlinka's Slovak People's Party, 1939–1945*. Boulder, CO: Westview Press, 1976.

Jens, Inge, ed. *At the Heart of the White Rose: Letters and Diaries of Hans and Sophie Scholl*. New York: Harper & Row, 1987.

Johnson, Paul. *Modern Times: The World from the Twenties to the Eighties*. New York: Harper & Row, 1983.

Johnson, Paul. *A History of the Jews*. New York: Harper & Row, 1987.

Johnson, Paul. *The Intellectuals*. London: Weidenfeld & Nicolson, 1988.

Jones, Nigel H. *Hitler's Heralds: The Story of the Freikorps, 1918–1923*. New York: Dorset Press, 1992.

Judge, Edward H. *Easter in Kishinev: Anatomy of a Pogrom*. New York: New York University Press, 1992.

Kahana, David. *Lvov Ghetto Diary*. Amherst: University of Massachusetts Press, 1990.

Karski, Jan. *The Great Powers and Poland, 1919–1945*. Lanham, MD: University Press of America, 1985.

Karski, Jan. *Story of a Secret State*. Boston: Houghton Mifflin Company, 1944.

Kater, Michael H. *Doctors Under Hitler*. Chapel Hill: University of North Carolina Press, 1989.

Kater, Michael H. *Different Drummers: Jazz in the Culture of Nazi Germany*. New York: Oxford University Press, 1992.

Katz, J. *Jews and Freemasons in Europe, 1723–1939*. Cambridge, MA: Harvard University Press, 1970.

Katz, Jacob. *From Prejudice to Destruction: 1700–1933*. Cambridge, MA: Harvard University Press, 1980.

Katz, Jacob. *The Darker Side of Genius: Richard Wagner's Anti-Semitism*. Hanover, NH: Dartmouth University Press, 1986.

Katz, Robert. *Death in Rome*. New York: Macmillan, 1967.

Katz, Samuel. *Lone Wolf: A Biography of Vladimir (Ze'ev) Jabotinsky*. 2 vols. New York: Barricade Books, 1996.

Katz, Steven T. *The Holocaust in Historical Context: The Holocaust and Mass Death Before the Modern Age*. Vol. 1. New York: Oxford University Press, 1994.

Katznelson, Yitzhak. *Vittel Diary*. Trans. Myer Cohen. Ghetto Fighters' House, Israel: Hakibbutz Ha-Meuchad Publishing House, 1964.

Katznelson, Yitzhak. *The Song of the Murdered Jewish People*. Trans. Noah H. Rosenblum. Tel Aviv: Ghetto Fighters' House Ltd., 1980.

Keegan, John. *Waffen SS: The Asphalt Soldiers*. New York: Ballantine Books, 1970.

Kendall, Harvey. *The Yugoslav Auschwitz and the Vatican*. Buffalo, NY: Prometheus Books, 1990.

Kendrick, Donald. *Gypsies Under the Swastika*. Hatfield, England: Hertfordshire Press, 1995.

Kersten, Felix. *The Kersten Memoirs, 1940–1945*. Trans. Constantine Fitzgibbon and James Oliver. New York: Macmillan, 1957.

Kitchen, Martin. *Nazi Germany at War*. New York: Longman House, 1995.

Klarsfeld, Beatte. *Wherever They May Be*. New York: Vanguard, 1970.

Koblik, S. T. *The Stones Cry Out: Sweden's Response to the Persecution of the Jews, 1933–1945*. New York: Holocaust Library, 1988.

Koch, H. W. *Hitler Youth: Origins and Development, 1922–1945*. New York: Barnes & Noble, 1996.

Kogon, Eugene. *The Theory and Practice of Hell: The German Concentration Camps and the System Behind Them*. Trans. Heinz Nordon. New York: Berkley Books, 1984.

Kohn, Moshe, and Aryel Tartakower, eds. *Jewish Resistance during the Holocaust. Proceedings of the First International Conference on the Manifestations of Jewish Resistance, April 7–11, 1968*. Jerusalem: Yad Vashem, 1971.

Korbonski, Stefan. *The Jews and the Poles in World War II*. New York: Hippocrene Books, 1989.

Korczak, Janus. *Ghetto Diary*. Trans. Jerzy Bachrach and Barbara Krzywicka. New York: Holocaust Library, 1978.

Korey, William. "Babi Yar Remembered." *Midstream* 15, no. 3 (1963): 24–39.

Kowalski, Isaac. *A Secret Press in Nazi Europe*. New York: Shengold Publishers, 1978.

Kowalski, Isaac N., ed. *Anthology of Armed Jewish Resistance, 1939–1945*. 3 vols. Brooklyn: Jewish Combatants Publishing House, 1986.

Krakowski, Shmuel. *The War of the Doomed: Jewish Armed Resistance in Poland, 1942–1944*. New York: Holmes & Meier, 1984.

Krall, Hanna. *Shielding the Flame: An Intimate Conversation with Dr. Marek Edelman, the Last Surviving Leader of the Warsaw Ghetto Uprising*. New York: Henry Holt, 1986.

Krantz, Hazel. *Daughter of My People: Henrietta Szold and Hadassah*. Northvale, NJ: Jason Aronson, 1995.

Kranzler, David, and Joseph Friedenson. *Heroine of Rescue: The Incredible Story of Rita Sternbuch*. Brooklyn: Mesorah Publications, 1984.

Kranzler, David. *Thy Brother's Blood: The Orthodox Jewish Response during the Holocaust*. New York: Mesorah Publications, 1987.

Kranzler, David, and Eliezer Gevirtz. *To Save a World: Profiles of Holocaust Rescue*. New York: CIS Publishers, 1991.

Krausnick, Herman, Hans Buchheim, Martin Brozat, and Hans-Adolf Jacobsen. *Anatomy of the SS State*. New York: Walker & Company, 1965.

Krier, Pierre. *Luxembourg Under German Occupation*. London and New York: October 1941. Privately printed.

Krizkova, Marie R., Kurt J. Kotouc, and Zdenek Ornest, eds. *We Are the Children Just the Same: Vedem, the Secret Magazine by the Boys of Terezin*. Philadelphia: Jewish Publication Society of America, 1995.

Kuehl, Stefan. *The Nazi Connection: Eugenics, American Racism and German National Socialism*. New York: Oxford University Press, 1994.

Kulka, O. D. "The Reaction of German Jewry to the National Socialist Regime." In *Living with Anti-Semitism: Modern Jewish Responses*, edited by Jehuda Reinnarz. Hanover, N.H.: University Press of New England, 1987.

Kurzman, Daniel. *The Race for Rome*. New York: Pinnacle Books, 1975.

Lacko, Miklos. *Arrow Cross Men, National Socialists, 1933–1944*. Budapest: Akademiaz Kiado, 1969.

La Couture, Jean. *De Gaulle, The Rebel, 1940–1945*. New York: Norton, 1990.

Lagnado, Lucette Matalon, and Sheila Cohn Dekel. *Children of the Flames: Dr. Josef Mengele and the Untold Story of the Twins*. New York: William Morrow, 1991.

von Lang, Jochen, ed. *Eichmann Interrogated: Transcripts from the Archives of the Israeli Police*. Trans. Ralph Manheim. New York: Vintage Books, 1984.

Langbein, Hermann. *Against All Hope: Resistance in the Nazi Concentration Camps, 1938–1948*. Trans. Harry Zohn. New York: Paragon House, 1994.

Lanzman, Claude. *Shoah: An Oral History of the Holocaust*. New York: Pantheon Books, 1985; New York: Da Capo, 1995.

Laqueur, Walter. *The Terrible Secret: Suppression of the Truth about Hitler's "Final Solution."* New York: Penguin Books, 1981.

Laqueur, Walter, and Richard Breitman. *Breaking the Silence*. Hanover, NH: University Press of New England, 1994.

Laska, Vera, ed. *Women in the Resistance and in the Holocaust: The Voices of Eyewitnesses*. Westport, CT: Greenwood Press, 1983.

Laskier, Michael M. "Between Vichy Anti-Semitism and German Harassment: The Jews of North Africa." *Modern Judaism* 11, no. 3 (October 1991): 343–69.

Latour, Anny. *The Jewish Resistance in France (1940–1944)*. Trans. Irene R. Ilton. New York: Holocaust Library, 1981.

Lazare, Lucien. *Rescue as Resistance: How Jewish Organizations Fought the Holocaust in France*. New York: Columbia University Press, 1996.

Leboucher, Fernande. *Incredible Mission: The Amazing Story of Pere Benoit, Rescuer of the Jews from the Nazis*. Trans. J. F. Bernard. Garden City, NY: Doubleday & Company, 1969.

Lederer, Zdneck, ed. *The Crimes of the Germans and Their Collaborators Against the Jews of Jugoslavia*. Belgrade: Zdneck, 1953.

"Lemkin, Raphael." *Current Biography 1950*.

Levenda, Peter. *Unholy Alliance: The History of Nazi Involvement with the Occult*. New York: Avon, 1995.

Levi, Primo. *Moments of Reprieve: A Memoir of Auschwitz*. New York: Collier Books, 1986.

Levin, Dov. *Fighting Back: Lithuanian Jewry's Armed Resistance to the Nazis, 1941–1944*. New York: Holmes & Meier, 1985.

Levin, Nora. *The Holocaust: The Destruction of European Jewry, 1933–1945*. New York: Schocken Books, 1973.

Levin, Nora. *While the Messiah Tarried: Jewish Socialist Movements*. New York: Schocken Books, 1977.

Levine, H. S. *Hitler's Free City: A History of the Nazi Party in Danzig, 1925–1939*. Chicago: University of Chicago Press, 1973.

Levine, Hillel. *In Search of Sugihara: The Banality of Good*. New York: The Free Press, 1996.

Levkov, Ilya, ed. *Bitburg and Beyond: Encounters in American, German and Jewish History*. New York: Shapolsky Publishers, 1987.

Levy, Alan. *The Wiesenthal File*. Grand Rapids, MI: William B. Eerdmans Publishing Company, 1993.

Lewin, Ronald. *Ultra Goes to War*. New York: McGraw-Hill, 1978.

Lewy, Guenter. *The Catholic Church and Nazi Germany*. New York: McGraw-Hill, 1964.

Lifton, Robert Jay. *The Nazi Doctors: Medical Killing and the Psychology of Genocide*. New York: Basic Books, 1986.

Lindwer, Willy. *The Last Seven Months of Anne Frank*. Trans. Alison Meersschaert. New York: Anchor, 1992.

Linklater, Magnus, Isabel Hilton, and Neil Ascherson. *The Nazi Legacy: Klaus Barbie and the International Fascist Connection*. New York: Holt, Rinehart & Winston, 1985.

Lipman, Steve. "The Decent Thing." *New York Jewish Week*, May 10, 1996.

Lipstadt, Deborah. *Denying the Holocaust: The Growing Assault on Truth and Memory*. New York: The Free Press, 1993.

Littell, Franklin H. *The Crucifixion of the Jews: The Failure of Christians to Understand the Jewish Experience*. Reprint ed. Macon, GA: Mercer University Press, 1986.

Lookstein, Haskel. *Were We Our Brothers' Keepers?* New York and Bridgeport, CT: Hartmore House, 1985.

Lovin, Robert. *Christian Faith and Public Choices: The Social Ethics of Barth, Brunner and Bonhoeffer*. Minneapolis, MI: Fortress Press, 1984.

Lowenstein, Sharon R. *Token Refuge: The Story of the Jewish Refugee Shelter at Oswego, 1944–1946*. Bloomington: Indiana University Press, 1986.

Lubetkin, Zivia. *In the Days of Destruction and Revolt*. Tel Aviv: Hakibbutz Hamevchad, 1981.

Lukas, Richard C. *Forgotten Holocaust: The Poles Under German Occupation, 1939–1944*. New York: Hippocrene Books, 1990.

Lumsden, Robin. *The Black Corps*. New York: Hippocrene Books, 1992.

Lutzer, Erwin W. *Hitler's Cross*. Chicago: Moody Press, 1995.

"Luxembourg." *Encyclopedia Judaica*, Vol. 11. Jerusalem: Keter/Macmillan, 1971.

Macintyre, Ben. *Forgotten Fatherland: The Search for Elisabeth Nietzsche*. New York: HarperPerennial, 1993.

MacDonald, Callum. *The Killing of SS-Obergruppenfuehrer Reinhard Heydrich*. New York: The Free Press, 1989.

Manchester, William. *The Arms of Krupp, 1587–1968*. New York: Bantam, 1970.

Mann, Charles C., and Mark L. Plummer. *The Aspirin Wars: Money, Medicine, and 100 Years of Rampant Competition*. New York: Alfred A. Knopf, 1991.

Manvell, Roger, and Heinrich Fraenkel. *The Canaris Conspiracy*. New York: McKay, 1969.

Mark, Ber. *The Uprising in the Warsaw Ghetto*. Trans. Gershon Freidlin. New York: Schocken Books, 1975.

Marrus, Michael R., and Robert O. Paxton. *Vichy France and the Jews*. New York: Schocken Books, 1983.

Marrus, Michael R. "Coming to Terms with Vichy." *Holocaust and Genocide Studies* 1, no. 1 (Spring 1995): 23–42.

Medoff, Rafael. *The Deafening Silence: American Jewish Leaders and the Holocaust*. New York: Shapolsky, 1987.

Meed, Vladka. *On Both Sides of the Wall: Memoirs from the Warsaw Ghetto*. Trans. Steven Meed. New York: Holocaust Library, 1979.

Merson, Allan. *Communist Resistance in Nazi Germany*. London: Lawrence and Wishart, 1986.

Miale, Florence R., and Michael Selzer. *The Nuremberg Mind: The Psychology of Nazi Leaders*. New York: Quadrangle Books, 1977.

Michaels, Meir. *Mussolini and the Jews: German-Italian Relations and the Jewish Question in Italy 1922–1945*. Oxford: Clarendon Press for the Institute of Jewish Affairs, London, 1978.

Michel, Jean with Louis Nucera. *Dora: The Nazi Concentration Camp Where Modern Space Technology Was Born and 30,000 Prisoners Died*. Trans. Jennifer Kidd. New York: Holt, Rinehart & Winston, 1980.

Modras, Ronald. "Of Saints and Antisemitism: Maximilian Kolbe Fifty Years Later." *SISCA Sassoon International Center for Study of Antisemitism at Hebrew University* (Fall 1991).

Morgan, Ted. *An Uncertain Hour: The French, the Germans, the Jews, the Klaus Barbie Trial, and the City of Lyon, 1940–1945*. New York: William Morrow, 1990.

Morganthau, Henry, III. *Mostly Morganthaus*. New York: Ticknor & Fields, 1991.

Morley, J. F. *Vatican Diplomacy and the Jews During the Holocaust, 1939–1943*. New York: Ktav, 1980.

Morrison, David. *Heroes, Anti-Heroes and the Holocaust: American Jewry and Historical Choice*. Jerusalem: Mila Press, 1995.

Morse, Arthur. *While Six Million Died: A Chronicle of American Apathy*. New York: Hart Publishing, 1967; Woodstock, NY: The Overlook Press, 1983.

Mosely, Leonard. *The Reich Marshal*. New York: Dell Publishers, 1975.

Mosse, George L. *Toward the Final Solution: A History of European Racism*. Madison: University of Wisconsin Press, 1985.

Mueller, Ingo. *Hitler's Justice: The Courts of the Third Reich*. Trans. Deborah Lucas Schneider. Cambridge, MA: Harvard University Press, 1991.

Nadich, Judah. *Eisenhower and the Jews*. New York: Twayne Publishers, 1953.

Nahon, Marco. *Birkenau: The Camp of Death*. Ed. Steve Bowman. Trans. Jacqueline Havaux. Tuscaloosa: University of Alabama Press, 1989.

National Catholic Register [Encino]. January 26, 1997.

Neske, Gunther, and Emil Kettering, eds. *Martin Heidegger and National Socialism*. New York: Paragon House, 1990.

Neufeld, Michael J. *The Rocket and the Reich: Peenemuende and the Coming of the Ballistic Missile Era*. New York: The Free Press, 1995.

New York Times: 1977; August 16–27, 1978; January 30, 1979; January 26, 1982; July 30, 1984; August 5, 1985; January 21, 1986; October 16, 20, 1996; April 15, 1997.

Nicholas, Lynn H. *The Rape of Europa: The Fate of Europe's Treasure in the Third Reich and Second World War*. New York: Alfred A. Knopf, 1994.

Nicholls, William. *Christian Anti-Semitism: A History of Hate*. Northvale, NJ: Jason Aronson, Inc., 1993.

Nicosia, Frances R., and Lawrence D. Stokes, eds. *Germans Against Nazism: Nonconformity, Opposition and Resistance in the Third Reich*. New York: Berg, 1991.

Nolte, Ernst. *Three Faces of Facism: Action Francaise, Italian Fascism and National Socialism*. New York: Holt, Rinehart & Winston, 1966.

Novitch, Miriam, ed. *Sobibor, Martyrdom and Revolt*. New York: Holocaust Library, 1980.

Novitch, Miriam. *Spiritual Resistance*. New York: Union of American Hebrew Congregations, 1981.

Novitch, Miriam, ed. *The Passage of the Barbarians: Contributions to the History of the Deportation and Resistance of Greek Jews*. Hull, England: The Glenvil Group, 1989.

Offer, Dalia. *Escaping the Holocaust: Illegal Immigration to the Land of Israel, 1939–1944*. New York: Oxford University Press, 1990.

Owings, Alison. *Frauen: German Women Recall the Third Reich*. New Brunswick, NJ: Rutgers University Press, 1993.

Paldiel, Mordecai. *The Path of the Righteous: Gentile Rescuers of Jews During the Holocaust*. Hoboken, NJ: Ktav, 1993.

Pankiewicz, Tadeusz. *The Crakow Ghetto Pharmacy*. Trans. Henry Tilles. New York: Holocaust Library, 1987.

Paris, Erna. *Unhealed Wounds: France and the Klaus Barbie Affair*. New York: Grove Press, 1985.

Penny, Frances. *I Was There*. Trans. Zofia Grifen. New York: Shengold, 1988.

Pentower, Monty. *The Jews Were Expendable: Free World Diplomacy and the Holocaust*. Urbana: University of Illinois Press, 1983.

Perechodnik, Calel, ed. *Am I a Murderer? Testament of a Jewish Ghetto Policeman*. Trans. Frank Fox. Boulder, CO: Westview Press, 1996.

Perl, William R. *The Four-Front War: From the Holocaust to the Promised Land*. New York: Crown, 1979.

Persico, Joseph. *Nuremberg: Infamy on Trial*. New York: Viking/Penguin Books, 1994.

Picleholz-Bernitsch, Olga. "Evaluation of Stuffhof Concentration Camp." *Yad Vashem Bulletin* 17 (1965): 34–49.

Plant, Richard. *The Pink Triangle: The Nazi War Against Homosexuals*. New York: Henry Holt, 1986.

Poliakov, Leon. *Harvest of Hate*. New York: Holocaust Library, 1979.

Poliakov, Leon, and Jacques Sabille. *Jews Under the Italian Occupation*. New York: Fertig, 1983.

Pool, James, and Suzanne Pool. *Who Financed Hitler? The Secret Funding of Hitler's Rise to Power*. New York: Dial Press, 1978.

Porat, Dina. *The Blue and the Yellow Stars of David: The Zionist Leadership in Palestine and the Holocaust, 1939–1945*. Cambridge, MA: Harvard University Press, 1990.

Posner, Gerald L., and John Ware. *Mengele: The Complete Story*. New York: McGraw-Hill, 1986; New York: Dell, 1987.

Posner, Gerald L. *Hitler's Children*. New York: Berkley, 1992.

Potichny, Peter, and Howard Astor, eds. *Ukrainian Jewish Relations in Historical Perspective*. Edmonton, Canada: CIUS, 1990.

Prager, Peter. "Love Prevailed on the Street of Roses." *The European Magazine* (March 7–13, 1996): 10–11.

Pressac, Jean-Claude. *Auschwitz: Technique and Operation of the Gas Chambers*. Trans. Peter Moss. New York: Beate Klarsfeld Foundation, 1989.

Presser, Jacob. *Ashes in the Wind: The Destruction of Dutch Jewry*. Trans. Arnold Pomerans. Detroit: Wayne State University Press, 1988.

Prittie, Terence. *Germans Against Hitler*. London: Hutchinson, 1964.

Proctor, Robert N. *Racial Hygiene: Medicine Under the Nazis*. Cambridge, MA: Harvard University Press, 1988.

Ramati, Alexander. *The Assisi Underground: The Priests Who Rescued Jews*. Trans. Padre Rufino Niccacci. New York: Stein & Day, 1978.

Rautkallio, Hannu. *Finland and the Holocaust: The Rescue of Finland's Jews*. New York: Holocaust Library, 1987.

Ravel, Aviva. *Faithful unto Death: The Story of Arthur Zygielbaum*. Montreal: Arthur Zygielbaum Branch of Workmen's Circle, 1980.

Read, Anthony, and David Fisher. *Kristallnacht: The Nazi Night of Terror*. New York: Random House, 1989.

Rector, Frank. *The Nazi Extermination of Homosexuals*. New York: Stein & Day, 1981.

Reimann, Viktor. *Goebbels*. Trans. S. Wendt. Garden City, NY: Doubleday, 1976.

Reitlinger, Gerald. *The Final Solution*. New York: Perpetua/Barnes & Noble, 1961.

Reitlinger, Gerald. *The SS: Alibi of a Nation, 1922–1945*. New York: Da Capo Press, 1989.

Rentschler, Eric. *The Ministry of Illusion: Nazi Cinema and its Afterlife*. Cambridge, MA: Harvard University Press, 1996.

Reutin, Rolf G. *Goebbels*. New York: Harcourt Brace, 1993.

Rhodes, Anthony. *The Vatican in the Age of Dictators, 1922–1945*. New York: Holt, Rinehart & Winston, 1973.

Rhodes, Richard. *The Making of the Atom Bomb*. New York: Touchstone Books, 1995.

Riefenstahl, Leni. *A Memoir*. New York: St. Martin's Press, 1995.

Rieff, P. "World of Wilhelm Reich." *Commentary* 38 (September 1966): 50–58.

Ringelblum, Emanuel. *Notes from the Warsaw Ghetto: The Journal of Emanuel Ringelblum*. Ed. and trans. Jacob Sloan. New York: Schocken Books, 1974.

Rittner, Carol, and John K. Roth, eds. *Different Voices: Women and the Holocaust*. New York: Paragon House, 1993.

Robertson, Edwin Hanton. *The Shame and the Sacrifice: The Life and Martyrdom of Dietrich Bonhoeffer*. New York: Macmillan, 1988.

Robinson, John L. *Born in Blood: The Lost Secrets of Freemasonry*. New York: M. Evans & Company, 1989.

Romans, J. *The Jews of Yugoslavia, 1941–1945: Victims of Genocide and Freedom Fighters*. Belgrade: Savez Jevrejskih Opstina Jugoslavje, 1982.

Rose, Norman. *Chaim Weizmann: A Biography*. New York: Viking, 1986.

Rosenbaum, Irving J. *The Holocaust and Halakhah*. New York: Ktav, 1976.

Ross, James R. *Escape to Shanghai: A Jewish Community in China*. New York: The Free Press, 1994.

Rothkirchen, Livia. "The Dual Role of the 'Jewish Center' in Slovakia." In *Patterns of Jewish Leadership in Nazi Europe, 1933–1945*, edited by Yisrael Gutman and C. J. Haft. Jerusalem, Israel: Proceedings of the Third Yad Vashem International Historical Conference (1979): 219–27.

Rousso, Henry. *The Vichy Syndrome: History and Memory in France Since 1944*. Trans. Arthur Goldhammer. Cambridge, MA: Harvard University Press, 1994.

Roy, Jules. *The Trial of Marshal Petain*. New York: Harper & Row, 1968.

Rudavsky, Joseph. *To Live with Hope, to Die with Dignity*. Lanham, MD: University Press of America, 1987.

Ruerup, Reinhard, ed. *Topography of Terror*. Trans. Werner T. Angress. Berlin: Verlag Willmuth Arenhovel, 1989.

Ryan, Allan. *Quiet Neighbors: Prosecution of Nazi War Criminals*. San Diego: Harcourt, Brace & Jovanovich, 1984.

Rymkiewicz, Jarostaw M. *The Final Station: Umschlagplatz*. Trans. Nina Taylor. New York: Farrar, Straus & Giroux, 1994.

Sabaliunas, Leonas. *Lithuania in Crisis: Nationalism to Communism, 1939–1940.* Bloomington: Indiana University Press, 1972.

Sabin, B. F., ed. *Alliance for Murder: The Nazi-Ukrainian Nationalist Partnership in Genocide.* New York: Sarpedon-Shapolsky, 1991.

Sachar, Abram L. *The Redemption of the Unwanted: From the Liberation of the Death Camps to the Founding of Israel.* New York: St. Martin's Press, 1983.

Safran, Alexandre. *Resisting the Storm: Romania, 1940–1947.* Jerusalem: Yad Vashem, 1987.

Saidel, Rochelle G. *The Outraged Conscience: Seekers of Justice for Nazi War Criminals in America.* Albany, NY: SUNY Press, 1984.

Sanders, Roland. *Shores of Refuge: A Hundred Years of Jewish Emigration.* New York: Henry Holt, 1988.

Schechtman, Joseph. *The Mufti and the Fuehrer.* New York: A. S. Barnes, 1965.

Schechtman, Joseph. *Rebel and Statesman: The Jabotinsky Story.* New York: Yoseloff, 1968.

Schleunes, Karl A. *The Twisted Road to Auschwitz: Nazi Policy Toward German Jews, 1933–1939.* Illini Books edition. Urbana: University of Illinois Press, 1990.

Schmidt, Matthias. *Albert Speer: The End of a Myth.* Trans. Joachim Neugroschel. New York: St. Martin's Press, 1984.

Schneider, Gertrude, ed. *The Unfinished Road: Jewish Survivors of Latvia Look Back.* Westport, CT: Praeger Publishers, 1991.

Schoenbrun, David. *Soldiers of the Night: The Story of the French Resistance.* New York: E. P. Dutton, 1980.

Schwarz, Ted. *Walking with the Damned: The Shocking Murder of the Man Who Freed 30,000 Prisoners from the Nazis.* New York: Paragon House, 1992.

Segev, Tom. *Soldiers of Evil: The Commandants of the Nazi Concentration Camps.* Trans. Haim Watzman. New York: McGraw-Hill, 1987.

Segev, Tom. *The Seventh Million: The Israelis and the Holocaust.* Trans. Haim Watzman. New York: Hill & Wang, 1993.

Seiden, Othniel J. *The Survivor of Babi Yar.* Denver, CO: Stonehenge Books, 1980.

Sereny, Gitta. *Into That Darkness.* New York: Vintage, 1983.

Sereny, Gitta. "John Demjanjuk and the Failure of Justice." *New York Review of Books,* October 8, 1992, 32ff.

Shamir, Iana, and Shlomo Shavit, eds. *Encyclopedia of Jewish History.* New York: Facts on File, 1986.

Shaw, Stanford J. *Turkey and the Holocaust: Turkey's Role in Rescuing Turkish and European Jewry from Nazi Persecution, 1933–1945.* New York: New York University Press, 1993.

Shirer, William. *The Rise and Fall of the Third Reich: A History of Nazi Germany.* New York: Simon & Schuster, 1960.

Shulman, Abraham. *The Case of Hotel Polski.* New York: Schocken Books, 1982.

Silver, Eric. *The Book of the Just.* New York: Grove Press, 1992.

Sime, Ruth Lewin. *Lise Meitner: A Life in Physics.* Berkeley: University of California Press, 1996.

Simpson, Christopher. *Blowback: America's Recruitment of Nazis and Its Effects on the Cold War.* London: Weidenfeld & Nicolson, 1988.

Simpson, Christopher. *The Splendid Blond Beast: Money, Law, and Genocide in the Twentieth Century.* New York: Grove Press, 1993.

Smith, Jean Edward. *Lucius D. Clay: An American Life*. New York: Henry Holt, 1990.

Smith, R. Harris. *OSS: The Secret History of America's First Central Intelligence Agency*. Berkeley: University of California Press, 1972.

Smolar, Hersh. *The Minsk Ghetto: Soviet-Jewish Partisans Against the Nazis*. Trans. Max Rosenfeld. New York: Holocaust Library, 1989.

Smolen, Kazimierz et al., eds. *KL Auschwitz Seen by the SS: Rudolf Hoess, Perry Broad, Johann Paul Kremer*. Warsaw: Interpress Publishers, 1991.

Snyder, Louis L. *Encyclopedia of the Third Reich*. New York: Paragon House, 1989.

Snyder, Louis L. *Hitler's Elite*. New York: Berkley Books, 1992.

Snyder, Louis L. *Hitler's German Enemies*. New York: Berkley Books, 1992.

Speer, Albert. *Inside the Third Reich: Memoirs by Albert Speer*. Trans. Richard Winston and Clara Winston. New York: Avon/Macmillan Company, 1971; New York: Galahad Books, 1995.

Staudinger, Hans, ed. *The Inner Nazi: A Critical Analysis of "Mein Kampf."* Baton Rouge, LA: Baton Rouge University Press, 1981.

Steinberg, Lucien. *Jews Against Hitler, (Not as a Lamb.)* Rev. ed. Trans. Marion Hunt. London: Gordon Cremonasi, 1978.

Steinberg, M. "The Trap of Legality: The Association of the Jews of Belgium." In *Patterns of Jewish Leadership in Nazi Europe, 1933–1945*, edited by Yisrael Gutman and C. J. Haft. Jerusalem, Israel: Proceedings of the Third Yad Vashem International Historical Conference (1979): 353–76.

Steiner, Erich Gershon. *The Story of the Patria*. Trans. Dinah Cohen. New York: Holocaust Library, 1982.

Stern, Ellen. *Elie Wiesel: Spokesman for Humanity*. Philadelphia: Jewish Publication Society of America, 1996.

Sternwell, Zeev, Mario Sznajder, and Maia Asheri. *The Birth of Fascist Ideology*. Trans. Davis Maisel. Princeton, NJ: Princeton University Press, 1994.

Stoltzfus, Nathan. *Operation Factory: Intermarriage and Rosenstrasse Protest in Nazi Germany*. New York: W. W. Norton Co., 1996.

Stroop, Juergen. *The Stroop Report: The Jewish Quarter of Warsaw Is No More!* Trans. Sybil Milton. New York: Pantheon Books, 1979.

Suhl, Yuri. *They Fought Back*. New York: Crown Publishing, 1967; Schocken Books, 1978.

Sydnor, Charles W., Jr. *Soldiers of Destruction: The SS Death's Head Division, 1933–1945*. Princeton, NJ: Princeton University Press, 1977.

Syrkin, Marie. *Blessed is the Match: The Story of Jewish Resistance*. Rev. ed. Philadelphia: Jewish Publication Society of America, 1976.

Szulc, Tad. *The Secret Alliance: The Extraordinary Story of the Rescue of the Jews Since World War II*. New York: Farrar, Straus & Giroux, 1991.

Szwajger, Adina Blady. *I Remember Nothing More: The Warsaw Children's Hospital and the Jewish Resistance*. New York: Pantheon Books, 1990.

Taylor, James, and Warren Shaw, comps. *The Third Reich Almanac*. New York: World Almanac, 1987.

Taylor, Telford. *The Anatomy of the Nuremberg Trials: A Personal Memoir*. Boston: Back Bay Books, 1992.

Tec, Nechama. *When Light Pierced the Darkness: Christian Rescue of Jews in Nazi-Occupied Poland*. New York: Oxford University Press, 1986.

Tec, Nechama. *Defiance: The Bielski Partisans.* New York: Oxford University Press, 1993.

ten Boom, Corrie. *Prison Letters.* Trans. J. B. Phillips. Old Tappan, NJ: Fleming H. Revell Company, 1972.

ten Boom, Corrie, and E. Sherrill. *The Hiding Place.* New York: Bantam Books, 1975.

Tenenbaum, Joseph. *Race and Reich: The Story of an Epoch.* New York: Twayne Publishers, 1956.

Teveth, Sabtai. *Ben Gurion and the Holocaust.* San Diego, CA: Harcourt Brace & Company, 1997.

Thalmann, Rita, and Emmanuel Feinermann. *Crystal Night.* New Trans. Gilles Cremonesi. New York: Holocaust Library, 1972.

Thomas, Gordon, and Max Morgan Witt. *Voyage of the Damned.* Greenwich, CT: Fawcett Books, 1975.

Tillion, Germaine. *Ravensbrueck.* Trans. Gerald Satterwhite. Garden City, NY: Anchor/Doubleday, 1975.

Tokayer, Marvin, and Mary Swartz. *The Fugu Plan: The Untold Story of the Japanese and the Jews During World War II.* London: Paddington Press Ltd., 1979.

Toland, John. *Adolf Hitler.* New York: Ballantine Books, 1976.

Tomaszewski, Irene, and Tecia Werbowski. *Zegota: The Rescue of Jews in Wartime Poland.* Montreal: Price Patterson, 1994.

Tory, Avraham. *Surviving the Holocaust: The Kovno Ghetto Diary.* Trans. Jerzy Michalowicz. Cambridge, MA: Harvard University Press, 1990.

Treece, Patricia. *A Man for Others: Maximilian Kolbe in the Words of Those Who Knew Him.* San Francisco: Harper & Row, 1982.

Trepper, Leopold. *Great Game.* New York: McGraw-Hill, 1977.

Troller, Norbert. *Theresienstadt: Hitler's Gift to the Jews.* Ed. Joel Shatzky. Trans. Susan E. Cernyak-Spatz. Chapel Hill: University of North Carolina Press, 1991.

Trunk, Isaiah. *Judenrat: The Jewish Councils in Eastern Europe Under Nazi Occupation.* New York: Stein & Day, 1977.

Trunk, Isaiah. *Jewish Responses to Nazi Persecution.* Trans. Gabriel Trunk. New York: Stein & Day, 1979.

Tushnet, Leonard. *The Pavement of Hell: 3 Leaders of the Judenrat.* New York: St. Martin's Press, 1972.

United States Government Printing Office. ''The Medical Case and the I. G. Farben Case.'' *Trials of War Criminals before the Nuremberg Military Tribunals.* 15 vols. Washington, DC: 1951–1952.

United States Holocaust Memorial Council. *Fifty Years After the Eve of Destruction, 1939, Days of Remembrance.* Washington, DC: 1989.

United States Holocaust Memorial Council. *Remembering the Voices That Were Silent, Days of Remembrance.* Washington, DC: 1990.

United States Holocaust Memorial Museum. *From Terror to Systematic Murder, 1941–1991, Days of Remembrance.* Washington, DC: 1991.

United States Holocaust Memorial Museum. *In the Depths of Darkness, 1942–1991, Days of Remembrance.* Washington, DC: 1992.

United States Holocaust Memorial Museum. *Assignment Rescue: The Story of Varian Fry and the Emergency Rescue Committee.* Washington, DC: 1993.

United States Holocaust Memorial Museum. *Revolt Amid the Darkness, 1942–1993, Days of Remembrance*. Washington, DC: 1993.

United States Holocaust Memorial Museum. *Darkness Before Dawn, 1944–1994, Days of Remembrance*. Washington, DC: 1994.

United States Holocaust Memorial Museum. *1945: The Year of Liberation*. Washington, DC: 1995.

United States Holocaust Memorial Museum. *Historical Atlas of the Holocaust*. New York: Macmillan, 1996.

United States Holocaust Memorial Museum. *Resistance during the Holocaust*. Washington, DC: 1997.

Urofsky, Melvin. *American Zionism from Herzl to the Holocaust*. Garden City, NY: Anchor/Doubleday Books, 1976.

Urofsky, Melvin. *A Voice that Spoke for Justice: The Life and Times of Stephen S. Wise*. Albany: State University of New York Press, 1982.

Vaksberg, Arkady. *Stalin Against the Jews*. Trans. Antonina W. Bouis. New York: Alfred A. Knopf, 1994.

Valentin, H. "Rescue and Relief Activities in Behalf of Jewish Victims of Nazism in Scandinavia." *YIVO Annual* 8 (1953): 224–51.

Vrba, Rudolf, and Alan Bastic. *I Cannot Forgive*. New York: Grove Press, 1964.

Warren, Donald. *Radio Priest: Charles Coughlin, the Father of Hate Radio*. New York: The Free Press, 1996.

Washington Post Weekly, February 17, 1997.

Wasserstein, Bernard. *Britain and the Jews of Europe, 1939–1945*. Oxford, England: Clarendon Press for the Institute of Jewish Affairs, 1979.

Watkins, T. H. *Righteous Pilgrim: The Life and Times of Harold Ickes, 1874–1952*. New York: Henry Holt, 1990.

Wdowinski, David. *And We Are Not Saved*. New York: Philosophical Library, 1985.

Webster, Paul. *Petain's Crime: The Full Story of French Collaboration in the Holocaust*. Chicago: Ivan R. Dee, 1991.

Webster's New Geographical Dictionary. Springfield, MA: G&C Merriam Company Publishers, 1972.

Wein, Berl. *Triumph of Survival*. Brooklyn: Mesorah, 1990.

Weissberg, Alexander. *Desperate Mission: Joel Brand's Story*. New York: Criterion, 1958.

Weitz, John. *Hitler's Diplomat: The Life and Times of Joachim von Ribbentrop*. New York: Ticknor & Fields, 1992.

Weitz, Margaret Collins. *Sisters in the Resistance: How Women Fought to Free France, 1940–1945*. New York: John Wiley & Sons, 1995.

Weizmann, Chaim. *Trial and Error*. New York: Harper & Row, 1949.

Wells, Leon W. *The Death Brigade (The Janowska Road)*. New York: Holocaust Library, 1978.

Wheal, Elizabeth-Anne, Stephen Pope, and James Taylor. *Encyclopedia of the Second World War*. Edison, NJ: Castle Books, 1989.

Whiting, Charles. *Otto Skorzeny*. New York: Ballantine Books, 1972.

Wiesenthal, Simon. *Every Day Remembrance Day: A Chronicle of Jewish Martyrdom*. New York: Henry Holt, 1986.

Wiesenthal, Simon. *Justice Not Vengeance*. New York: Grove Weidenfeld, 1989.

Wiesenthal, Simon, and Joseph Wechsberg, eds. *The Murderers Among Us: The Wiesenthal Memoirs*. New York: McGraw-Hill, 1967.

Wise, Stephen. *Challenging Years: The Autobiography of Stephen Wise*. New York: Putnam, 1949.

Wistrich, Robert S. *Who's Who in Nazi Germany*. London: Routledge, 1995.

Witte, Peter. "Two Decisions Concerning the 'Final Solution to the Jewish Question': Deportations to Lodz and Mass Murder in Chelmno." *Holocaust and Genocide Studies* 9, no. 3 (Winter 1995): 318–46.

Wood, Thomas E., and Stanislaw M. Jankowski. *Karski: How One Man Tried to Stop the Holocaust*. New York: Wiley & Sons, 1994.

World Jewish Congress. "Operation Safehaven." *United States National Archives* (April 14, 1945).

Wyden, Peter. *Stella: One Woman's True Tale of Evil, Betrayal, and Survival in Hitler's Germany*. New York: Simon & Schuster, 1992.

Wyman, David. *Paper Walls: America and the Refugee Crisis, 1938–1941*. Amherst: University of Massachusetts Press, 1968; New York: Pantheon Books, 1985.

Wyman, David. *The Abandonment of the Jews: America and the Holocaust 1941–1945*. New York: Pantheon Books, 1984.

Yahil, Leni. *The Rescue of Danish Jewry: Test of a Democracy*. Trans. Morris Gradel. Philadelphia: Jewish Publication Society of America, 1983.

Yahil, Leni. *The Holocaust: The Fate of European Jewry, 1932–1945*. Trans. Ina Friedman and Haya Galai. New York: Oxford University Press, 1990.

Young, James. *The Texture of Memory: Holocaust Memorials and Meaning*. New Haven, CT: Yale University Press, 1993.

Zarez, Ruth. "The Jews of Luxembourg During the Second World War." *Holocaust and Genocide Studies* 7, no. 1 (Spring 1993): 51–67.

Zawodny, Janusz K. *Nothing but Honour: The Story of the Warsaw Uprising, 1944*. Stanford: Hoover Institution Press, 1978.

Zentner, Christian, and Beduerftig Friedemann, eds. *The Encyclopedia of the Third Reich*. Trans. Amy Hackett. New York: Macmillan, 1991.

Zuccotti, Susan. *The Italians and the Holocaust: Persecution, Rescue and Survival*. New York: Basic Books, 1987.

Zuccotti, Susan. *The Holocaust, the French, and the Jews*. New York: Basic Books, 1993.

Zuckerman, Yitzhak. *A Surplus of Memory: Chronicle of the Warsaw Ghetto Uprising*. Trans. Barbara Harshaw. Berkeley: University of California Press, 1985.

Zuker, Simon. *The Unconquerable Spirit*. Ed. and trans. Gertrude Hirschler. New York: Zachor Institute & Mesorah Publications, 1980.

Periodicals

American Association for Polish-Jewish Studies. *Gazeta*. Cambridge, MA.

American Gathering of Jewish Holocaust Survivors. *Together*. New York.

American Society for Yad Vashem, Inc. *Martyrdom and Resistance*. New York.

Anti-Defamation League's Braun Center for Holocaust Studies. *Dimensions: A Journal of Holocaust Studies*. New York.

The Center for the Study of Ethnonationalism: The City College of the City University of New York. *The Genocide Forum: A Platform for Post-Holocaust Commentary*. New York.

Foreign Affairs. New York.

Forward. New York.

Holocaust and Genocide Studies. New York.

Institute for Labor and Mental Health. *Tikkun: A Bi-Monthly Jewish Critique of Politics, Culture and Society.* Oakland, CA.

Jerusalem Post. Jerusalem, Israel.

New York Times. New York.

Oxford University Press in association with the United States Holocaust Memorial Museum, *Holocaust and Genocide Studies.*

Patriot News. Harrisburg, PA.

Philadelphia Inquirer. Philadelphia, PA.

Proteus: A Journal of Ideas—Holocaust Studies. Shippensburg University, PA.

Simon Wiesenthal Center. *Response: The Wiesenthal Center World Report.* Los Angeles.

United States Holocaust Memorial Museum. *Update.* Washington, DC.

World Jewish Congress. *Dateline: World Jewry and the WJC Report* (October 1996). New York.

Yad Vashem: Jerusalem. Jerusalem.

Internet

Moss, Jim. Moderator. H-NET List for History of the Holocaust.

INDEX

Page numbers in boldface indicate a main entry.

About the Authors

ERIC JOSEPH EPSTEIN is Visiting Assistant Professor of Humanities at Pennsylvania State University in Harrisburg, where he teaches Holocaust Studies. He also coordinates the taping of Holocaust survivors in central Pennsylvania and has written numerous articles.

PHILIP ROSEN is Director of the Holocaust Awareness Museum at Gratz College. He has taught at both the secondary and college level and has instructed teachers in the areas of the Holocaust and Genocide Studies. He has written many articles on genocide and has interviewed many survivors and liberators.